ACTS

New Testament Series

NEW INTERNATIONAL BIBLICAL COMMENTARY

ACTS

DAVID J. WILLIAMS

Based on the New International Version

© 1985, 1990 by David John Williams
Hendrickson Publishers, Inc.
P. O. Box 3473
Peabody, Massachusetts 01961–3473
U.S.A.

Original Hendrickson Publishers edition 1990

First published jointly 1995, in the United States by Hendrickson Publishers, and in the United Kingdom by the Paternoster Press, P. O. Box 300, Carlisle, Cumbria CA3 0QS

Printed in the United States of America

Library of Congress Cataloging-in-Publication Data

Williams, David John.
    Acts /   David John Williams.
       p. cm. – (New International biblical commentary; 5)
    Includes bibliographical references and indexes.
    1. Bible. N.T. Acts — Commentaries. I. Bible. N.T.
    Acts English. New International. 1990. II. Title. III. Series.
BS2625.3.W55 1990
226.6'077—dc20   90–37331
                                                              CIP

ISBN 0–943575–20–6

British Library Cataloguing in Publication Data

Williams, David J.
    Acts. – (New International Biblical Commmentary Series; Vol. 5)
    I. Title II. Series
226.607

ISBN 0–85364–659–7

The pride of our labours is but toil and sorrow for it passes quickly away and we are gone . . .

Show your servants your work: and let their children see your glory.

Table of Contents

Foreword
New International Biblical Commentary

Although it does not appear on the standard best-seller lists, the Bible continues to outsell all other books. And in spite of growing secularism in the West, there are no signs that interest in its message is abating. Quite to the contrary, more and more men and women are turning to its pages for insight and guidance in the midst of the ever-increasing complexity of modern life.

This renewed interest in Scripture is found both outside and inside the church. It is found among people in Asia and Africa as well as in Europe and North America; indeed, as one moves outside of the traditionally Christian countries, interest in the Bible seems to quicken. Believers associated with the traditional Catholic and Protestant churches manifest the same eagerness for the Word that is found in the newer evangelical churches and fellowships.

We wish to encourage and, indeed, strengthen this worldwide movement of lay Bible study by offering this new commentary series. Although we hope that pastors and teachers will find these volumes helpful in both understanding and communicating the Word of God, we do not write primarily for them. Our aim is to provide for the benefit of every Bible reader reliable guides to the books of the Bible—representing the best of contemporary scholarship presented in a form that does not require formal theological education to understand.

The conviction of editor and authors alike is that the Bible belongs to the people and not merely to the academy. The message of the Bible is too important to be locked up in erudite and esoteric essays and monographs written only for the eyes of theological specialists. Although exact scholarship has its place in the service of Christ, those who share in the teaching office of the church have a responsibility to make the results of their research accessible to the Christian community at large. Thus, the Bible scholars who join in the presentation of this series write with these broader concerns in view.

A wide range of modern translations is available to the contemporary Bible student. Most of them are very good and much to be preferred—for understanding, if not always for beauty—to the older King James Version (the so-called Authorized Version of the Bible). The Revised Standard Version has become the standard English translation in many seminaries and colleges and represents the best of modern Protestant scholarship. It is also available in a slightly altered "common Bible" edition with the Catholic imprimatur, and a third revised edition is due out shortly. In addition, the New American Bible is a fresh translation that represents the best of post–Vatican II Roman Catholic biblical scholarship and is in a more contemporary idiom than that of the RSV.

The New Jerusalem Bible, based on the work of French Catholic scholars but vividly rendered into English by a team of British translators, is perhaps the most literary of the recent translations, while the New English Bible is a monument to modern British Protestant research. The Good News Bible is probably the most accessible translation for the person who has little exposure to the Christian tradition or who speaks and reads English as a second language. Each of these is, in its own way, excellent and will be consulted with profit by the serious student of Scripture. Perhaps most will wish to have several versions to read, both for variety and for clarity of understanding—though it should be pointed out that no one of them is by any means flawless or to be received as the last word on any given point. Otherwise, there would be no need for a commentary series like this one!

We have chosen to use the New International Version as the basis for this series, not because it is necessarily the best translation available but because it is becoming increasingly used by lay Bible students and pastors. It is the product of an international team of "evangelical" Bible scholars who have sought to translate the Hebrew and Greek documents of the original into "clear and natural English . . . idiomatic [and] . . . contemporary but not dated," suitable for "young and old, highly educated and less well educated, ministers and laymen [sic]." As the translators themselves confess in their preface, this version is not perfect. However, it is as good as any of the others mentioned above and more popular than most of them.

Each volume will contain an introductory chapter detailing the background of the book and its author, important themes, and other helpful information. Then, each section of the book will be expounded as a whole, accompanied by a series of notes on items in the text that need further clarification or more detailed explanation. Appended to the end of each volume will be a bibliographical guide for further study.

Our new series is offered with the prayer that it may be an instrument of authentic renewal and advancement in the worldwide Christian community and a means of commending the faith of the people who lived in biblical times and of those who seek to live by the Bible today.

W. WARD GASQUE

Abbreviations

AHG	*Apostolic History and the Gospel.* Edited by W. W. Gasque and R. P. Martin.
AV	Authorized or King James Version of 1611
BC	*The Beginnings of Christianity.* Edited by F. J. Foakes Jackson and K. Lake.
b.	Babylonian Talmud
CBQ	*Catholic Biblical Quarterly*
CD	Damascus Document
cf.	compare
chap(s).	chapter(s)
disc.	discussion
EQ	*Evangelical Quarterly*
ExpT	*Expository Times*
f (ff.)	and following verse or page (verses or pages)
Gk.	Greek
GNB	Good News Bible (Today's English Version). Old Testament, 1976; New Testament, 4th ed., 1976.
HDB	*Dictionary of the Bible.* Edited by J. Hastings. 5 vols. Edinburgh: T. & T. Clark, 1898.
HTR	*Harvard Theological Review*
IDB	*Interpreter's Dictionary of the Bible.* Edited by G. A. Buttrick, et al. 5 vols. Nashville: Abingdon Press, 1962.
j.	Jerusalem Talmud
JBL	*Journal of Biblical Literature*
JTS	*Journal of Theological Studies*
lit.	literally
LXX	Septuagint (pre–Christian Greek version of the Old Testament)
m.	Mishnah
mg.	margin

NEB	New English Bible. Old Testament, 1970; New Testament, 2d ed., 1970
NIDNTT	*New International Dictionary of New Testament Theology.* Edited by C. Brown. 3 vols. Exeter: Paternoster Press, 1975–78.
NIV	New International Version. Old Testament, 1979; New Testament 1973.
NTS	*New Testament Studies*
Perspectives	*Perspectives on Luke–Acts.* Edited by C. H. Talbert. T. & T. Clark, 1978.
4QFlor	Florilegium (Commentary on a selection of biblical passages)
1QS	Manual of Discipline
4QTLevi	Testament of Levi, Qumran Cave 4
RSV	Revised Standard Version. Old Testament, 1952; New Testament, 2d ed., 1971.
RV	Revised Version of 1881
Studies	*Studies in Luke–Acts.* Edited by L. E. Keck and J. L. Martyn.
TDNT	*Theological Dictionary of the New Testament.* A translation by G. W. Bromiley of *Theologisches Wörterbuch zum Neuen Testament.* 10 vols. Grand Rapids: Eerdmans, 1964–76.
v. (vv.)	verse (verses)

Introduction

J. B. Phillips writes in the preface to *The Young Church in Action*, his translation of Acts, that one cannot spend several months in close study of this book "without being profoundly stirred and, to be honest, disturbed. The reader is stirred," he says, "because he is seeing Christianity, the real thing, in action for the first time in human history. . . . Here we are seeing the Church in its first youth, valiant and unspoiled . . . a body of ordinary men and women joined in an unconquerable fellowship never before seen on this earth." But the reader is also disturbed, "for surely," he adds, this "is the Church as it was meant to be. It is vigorous and flexible, for these are the days before it ever became fat and short of breath through prosperity, or muscle bound by over-organization. These men did not make 'acts of faith,' they believed; they did not 'say their prayers,' they really prayed. They did not hold conferences on psychosomatic medicine, they simply healed the sick."[1] By modern standards they may have been naive, but perhaps because of their very simplicity, perhaps because of their readiness simply to believe, to obey, to give, to suffer, and, if necessary, to die, the Spirit of God found that he could work in them and through them, and so they turned the world upside down (see 17:6, RSV).

Acts is the only authentic record we have of the first years of the church's history. There are a few meager hints in Paul's letters of events that took place in these years. Josephus provides valuable background material and a number of corroborative details,[2] but if Acts had been lost there is nothing to take its place. Moreover, the rest of the New Testament would lie before us in two disjointed fragments, for Acts is the necessary link between the Gospels and the Epistles. The Gospels tell of the beginnings of Christianity, up to the point of our Lord's ascension. But if that were all we had, questions would abound. What was the sequel? What did the Lord do next? What became of his followers and his cause? The answers to these questions lie in Acts. Similarly with the Epistles: We find that they are apostolic letters addressed to churches in various parts of the Roman Empire. But if this were all we had, we would want to know when these churches came into existence, how they were formed, and by whom; and without Acts—incomplete and fragmentary though it is as a history—there would be no answer to many of these questions. "We would not only find it almost impossible to put Paul and his work in a chronological and geographical setting; we would still be largely in the dark about the development of Paul's great mission around the Aegean and the events that led up to it, and about his concern to go to Rome and to Spain (Rom. 15:22–29). We only realize the significance of Luke's Acts as a historical source if we make a conscious attempt to eliminate the information it contains from our knowledge of earliest Christianity."[3] As it is, Acts tells us enough to give most of the Epistles a historical setting and to attest to the apostolic character of most of their writers. We have only to consider how little we know of the spread of the gospel in the places not touched by its narrative to appreciate how much we owe to this book for what it does tell us.

What is more, we stand in the author's debt for presenting this information in such a readable form. Acts is arguably one of the most exciting books ever written. Where else would you find in so few pages "such a varied series of exciting events—trials, riots, persecutions, escapes, martyrdom, voyages, shipwrecks, rescues—set in that amazing panorama of the ancient world—Jerusalem, Antioch, Philippi, Corinth, Athens, Rome? And with such scenery and settings—temples, courts, prisons, deserts, ships, seas, barracks, theaters? Has any opera such variety? A bewildering range of scenes and actions passes before the eye of the historian. And in them all he sees the providential hand that has made and guided this great movement for the salvation of mankind."[4]

Authorship

It is almost an axiom of New Testament scholarship that whoever wrote the Third Gospel was also the author of Acts (see disc. on 1:1–5). Traditionally he has been identified with Luke, Paul's companion and physician. In the manuscripts of the Gospels, the heading "According to Luke" is always found for the Third Gospel. This Gospel has never been known by any other name.

The name *Loukas* (as it appears in the Greek) is probably an abbreviation of *Loukanos*, and it has been noticed that proper names contracted to an ending -*as* were common among slaves. This may have been Luke's background, since slaves were sometimes trained as physicians. But hard facts about him are scarce. He is named only three times in the New Testament (Col. 4:14; 2 Tim. 4:11; Philem. 24). From these references we gather that he was a Gentile and was with Paul in Rome when Colossians and Philemon were written and (probably) later when 2 Timothy was written, but at no time does he appear to have been a prisoner as Paul was on these occasions.

The evidence we have suggests that Antioch in Syria may have been his home. The earliest explicit statement to this effect comes in the anti-Marcionite prologue to the Third Gospel, which begins, "Luke, a physician by profession, belonged to Antioch." Eusebius and Jerome are also aware of this tradition, and two slender bits of evidence from Acts itself add some further support (assuming for the moment that Luke wrote the book). First, of the seven "helpers" whose names are given in 6:5, the only one whose place of origin is mentioned is Nicolaus, a Gentile from Antioch. This may reflect the author's particular interest in that city. Second, the Western text, which was taking shape in the second century, adds the words "when we were gathered together . . . " to 11:28. The setting is the church in Antioch, and the use of the first person would suggest that Luke himself was a member of that church at the time of the incident that he was describing. If we can accept this tradition, he may well have been one of those Greeks to whom the men from Cyprus and Cyrene preached in 11:20 (but see the disc. on that verse).

But the question still remains, Did Luke write Acts? Tradition is unanimous that he did. But what of the book itself? Does it throw any light on its own authorship? The internal evidence rests largely on the so called we-passages, in which the first person plural replaces the third person in the narrative—a total of ninety-seven verses in all. The first of these we-passages appears without warning in 16:10–17 (the voyage from Troas to Philippi), there is another in 20:5–15 and 21:1–8 (the voyage to Jerusalem), and yet another in 27:1–28:16 (the sea voyage from Caesarea to Rome). The suggestion has sometimes been made that the author has employed the first person in these passages simply as a literary device, the first person being found in other accounts of sea travel.[5] But if this were the case, why was he not consistent? He narrates a number of other voyages in the third person (9:30;

possibly 11:25f.; 13:4, 13; 14:26; 17:14; 18:18, 21). And in any case, most of the examples of first person plural narration on which this theory rests are drawn from Homer and other poets and are hardly comparable with Luke's historical prose. A. D. Nock goes so far as to say that a fictitious "we" of this kind would be virtually unparalleled and most improbable for a writer who makes as much claim as Luke does to historiography.[6]

If, then, the we-passages represent the genuine involvement of the narrator in the events, we can plausibly explain them only by assuming that the author of Acts was using either his own or someone else's diary. But the passages are written in a style indistinguishable from the rest of the book, so that if he was using someone else's work we must suppose that he rewrote it so thoroughly as to eliminate all trace of its original style, and yet so carelessly that he did not always remember to make the change from the first person to the third. The far simpler explanation is that he was using his own material and allowed the first person to stand to indicate at what points he himself had shared in the action. "From the beginning, this is the only way in which readers—and first of all Theophilus, to whom the two-volume work was dedicated and who must have known the author personally—could have understood the 'we' passages."[7] It follows that the author of Acts was a companion of Paul. And of a number of possible candidates, Luke is one of the very few who are not ruled out for a variety of reasons. We know that he was in Rome with Paul, as the diarist was, and though the evidence still falls short of proof, it at least points more certainly in Luke's direction than in any other.

But not everyone accepts this. The chief objection of those who do not is that no companion of Paul, whether Luke or anyone else, would have drawn the picture that this author draws of the apostle. No one who knew him, it is claimed, could have presented Paul as this book presents him. In the Epistles, almost to the end of his life, he was in conflict with those who resisted the free admission of the Gentiles into the church. In Acts, this problem is raised and settled largely within the space of one chapter (chap. 15), and nothing is heard of it again. In his epistles, Paul is passionate in the defense of his apostleship. Nothing is heard of this in Acts. In the whole book he is called an apostle twice, and that, again, within the space of one chapter (14:4, 14). The Paul of Acts, so it is said, has a Christology, a natural theology,

an eschatology, and an understanding of the law entirely incon-
sistent with the Paul of the Epistles.[8] He accepts the rules laid
down by the council; he circumcises Timothy; he undertakes a
rite of purification and helps others to do the same. Is this the
uncompromising controversialist of Galatians? I think it is.

It should be remembered that in Galatians Paul was dealing in white-hot urgency with a controversy that threatened the
very foundations of the faith. Naturally, in these circumstances,
he spoke vehemently against the imposition of the law on Gentiles. But elsewhere we find him taking the view that ritual acts
in themselves are neither good nor bad, except when the intention
makes them so. We are reminded of Emerson's quip about "foolish
consistency" being "the hobgoblin of little minds, adored by little
statesmen and philosophers and divines." For such consistency
we search the life of Paul in vain, for his was preeminently a great
mind. On the great fundamental principles of the faith he was
uncompromising; where these were not affected, he was the most
adaptable of people. Luke may not have fully understood him.
He may not have assimilated Paul's theology or felt as deeply the
issues that touched Paul profoundly. But all things considered,
"the objections to the view that he was acquainted with Paul are
not strong enough to outweigh the considerable evidence that he
was."[9] It must always be kept in mind that he would have seen
Paul from a perspective different from ours. We see him as a
theologian; Luke would have known him "as the missionary, the
charismatic and the founder of communities."[10]

Sources

Luke is the only New Testament writer who says anything
about his methods. Even so, he tells us very little. It amounts to
this: in writing the Gospel he used the best available sources
(Luke 1:1ff.). Moreover, in the case of the Gospel we are able to
see how he handled them, for two of his sources are known to
us—the Gospel according to Mark and a document now lost that
he shared with Matthew and that to some extent we are able to
reconstruct (the so-called Q). It is soon apparent to the reader
that, though Luke exercised his editorial prerogative of cutting
and polishing the material that came to him, he was nevertheless
remarkably faithful to his sources. In Acts, then, it is reasonable
to assume that he again drew on earlier material and that he was

no less faithful in transmitting it than he had been in transmitting his Gospel sources.

For the first half of the book (chaps. 1–12 and 15) he may have had an Aramaic source, or more than one. The clearest evidence of this appears in the first five chapters and in the chapters that tell of the "acts of Peter" (9:31–11:18; 12:1–17). The speeches of these chapters and parts of the narrative "have been shown to contain a large element of Semitism. Nor is this Hebraism of the kind which results from an imitation of the translation-Greek of the Septuagint, and which can be traced in other parts of the Lucan work. It can be shown to be Aramaism, of a kind similar to that which we recognize in the report of the sayings of Jesus in the Gospels."[11] The work of translating such sources (if, indeed, they did exist) may already have been done before they reached Luke. For the second half of the book, he had his own diary (as we suppose) on which to draw. This may have served as a source beyond the actual we-passages for the narrative in 16:18–20, 20:17–38, and part or all of 21:19–26:32.

A common approach to the question of sources is to consider the people and places from which Luke might have gathered his information. Much of the book is concerned with Paul, and we cannot doubt that Paul himself supplied much of what Luke did not already know of his hero, though the book is so completely stamped with Luke's own style that we cannot now tell how much of it might have come to him in this way. And then there were others—people like Timothy (see disc. on 13:13–52), Aquila and Priscilla, Aristarchus, Mark, Silas, and Sopater—with whom Luke was in touch at one time or another. They could have added—and in some cases almost certainly did—to his own knowledge of the story of Paul.

In piecing together the earlier (pre-Pauline) history, there were a number of avenues that Luke could have explored. If he was an Antiochene, for instance, there was Barnabas, who had come from Jerusalem and had become a leader in the Syrian church (4:36f.; 9:26f.; 11:22ff.). Another leader at Antioch was Manaen, who "had been brought up with . . . Herod" (13:1). It is striking that, of all the Evangelists, Luke tells us most about the family of Herod. Was Manaen the source of his "inside information"? As Paul's companion, Luke stayed with Philip in Caesarea and may have gathered the data of chapters 6 to 8 and chapter 10 from him (see disc. on 8:4–25 and 24:27). He also stayed with Mnason, whom he describes as a "believer since the early days" (21:16), meaning perhaps the Pentecost of chapter 2. What a fund of stories he must have had! Later Luke was with Mark in Rome (Col. 4:10; Philem. 24). Mark's home had once been a center of the church's life in Jerusalem, and much of Luke's information concerning the early church, especially as it touches Peter, must have come from this source (see disc. on 12:1–5). There were others also. Indeed, if the truth were known, it was probably a case of too much rather than too little information. Luke had no shortage of informants, and it must have been as great a problem to know what to leave out as what to put in. But he was writing for a purpose and so restricted himself to a careful selection from his sources to serve that purpose. What the purpose was, we shall come to in a moment.

Historical Accuracy

Can Acts be trusted as a reliable account of what happened? It was once the fashion to regard this book as a third-rate chronicle compiled in the middle of the second century, containing more legend than fact and brimful of historical blunders. Today there are few who would defend that view. Modern research has demonstrated that Acts is a remarkably accurate piece of writing. This will hardly surprise those who accept Lucan authorship. The weight of evidence now constrains us to find a setting for this book in the first century, not far removed from the events of which it tells, its author in close touch with the people concerned. Its historical accuracy is the more remarkable as we consider how wide a range of scene and circumstance the book covers, extending from Jerusalem to Rome and including all manner of populations, cultures, and administrations. And yet, in all this complex world through which his story takes him, and though he wrote without benefit of libraries and archives, in matters topographical, political, historical, and nautical, the author trips up not once.[12]

He is at home with the Sanhedrin and its parties in Jerusalem, the priests, the Pharisees, the temple guards, the princes of the house of Herod. He knows that Cyprus, Achaia, and Asia were governed by proconsuls (13:7; 18:12; 19:38), that Philippi was a Roman colony in which praetors had jurisdiction and were attended by lictors (16:20ff., 35ff.), that the magistrates of Thessalonica were called politarchs (17:8), that there were officers of the province of Asia known as "asiarchs" (19:31), that Ephesus reveled in the title of Temple Warden (19:35), that political power in that city was vested in the *dēmos*, the popular assembly, chaired by the "city clerk" (19:35ff.), and that the ruler of Malta was called "primus" (28:7). And not only does the author get such details right, but time and again he portrays the very atmosphere of the places in which his story is set: the excitable and intolerant crowds of eastern Jerusalem and the relative tolerance of cosmopolitan Antioch; the metropolis of Syria, where the first Gentile church was established by Jews; the Philippians' pride in their Roman status; the intellectual dilettantism of the Athenians; the superstition of the Ephesians—all this and more comes vividly to life in his pages. The really impressive thing about Acts is that the accuracy extends to the most trivial details—the sort of thing that a writer would not research in striving for verisimilitude. The very casualness of the accuracy is the guarantee that it is not contrived. And if we can trust the author for the details, then surely we can trust him for the broad sweep of his story (see further under Place and Date).

But he was no mere chronicler. "We must realize," warns Krodel, "that Luke the biblical historian approached his task like an artist who seeks to interpret reality, not like a chronicler who records one thing after another. He is not like a photographer whose product is to be an exact likeness, but like a painter whose canvas seeks to elicit a response to a message."[13] So he interpreted, selected, and arranged the events of his narrative to explicate a theme, and anything that did not bear on that theme he ruthlessly omitted. We hear nothing, for example, of the founding of the Christian communities of Egypt, Cyrenaica, northern and eastern Asia Minor, Armenia, eastern Syria, the Parthian kingdom, or Italy. So considerable are these omissions—Hengel speaks of Luke's "almost objectionable eclecticism" in the selection of his material[14]—that some scholars are inclined to view Acts more as a historical monograph than as a history of the church and to reserve the title "Father of Church History" for Eusebius (died ca. A.D. 339).

Luke was interested in only one strand of the church's history, namely, how it took the road from Jerusalem to Rome and how, at the same time, it passed from mission to the Jews to preaching God's message to the Gentiles (see further the disc. on Title and Purpose). Even then, there was much that Luke left out as not directly serving his purpose. But he should not be judged on his omissions. Only within the limits that he set himself should he be judged, and within those limits he has done remarkably well. Of course, there are problem areas (see e.g., the introduction to 15:1-21). Nor is Luke without his faults as a writer. "He abbreviates some events so much that they become almost incomprehensible, and hints at others quite briefly. At the same time he elaborates what he wants to stress, and makes use of multiple repetition as a means of writing. He can also combine separate historical traditions to serve his ends, and separate matters that belong together if as a result he can achieve a meaningful sequence of events."[15] For these reasons, he would not be regarded as a great historian by modern standards. But he was a competent writer and has succeeded in giving us a fresh, interesting, and accurate account of as much of the church's history as he chose to put on record.

But for some readers there is one insuperable objection to accepting Luke as a trustworthy historian, namely, his inclusion of miracles. His interest in the miraculous—and there is no denying that it was an interest—destroys, critics say, any credibility he might otherwise have had. But this criticism is valid only if there were no miracles. The evidence suggests that there were. Paul appealed as if to something beyond any doubt when he questioned the Galatians, "Does God give you the Spirit and work miracles among you because you do what the law requires?" (Gal. 3:5). Again, in Romans 15:18-19, with no thought or fear of contradiction, he makes a statement about God working miracles. Nor is it true to say, as some do, that Luke accepted uncritically or gullibly the miraculous. There are no miracles in Acts merely for miracles' sake. Dunn reminds us that "in Acts 8:18ff. Simon Magus is denounced for regarding the Spirit as a kind of magical power whose secret or technique one could buy; in 13:8-11 Christianity is represented in sharp contrast with magic; in 14:8-18 Luke strongly resists and rejects any temptation to portray Paul and Barnabas as 'divine men'; and in 19:13-16 he underlines the fact that the name of Jesus is no mere exorcistic formula capable of being used by any one learns it, but can be used only by those who call upon the name (cf. 2:21; 9:14, 21; 15:17; 22:16).[16] The charge of naiveté, Dunn says, has been unfairly leveled at Luke. "His uncritical attitude to miraculous power may simply be a faithful reflection of the undiscriminating attitude of the early Chris-

tian mission. He may simply be content for the most part to reproduce stories handed on to him without comment." So Dunn
concludes: "It is difficult to tell where Luke's role as a recorder
of traditions ends and where his own attitude emerges. . . . Perhaps the fairest way to evaluate Luke's treatment at this point is
to recognize him as one who, on looking back from the comparative calmness and sophistication of later years, was enamored and
thrilled by the enthusiasm and power of the early mission as he
heard of it from older witnesses and reports. If so, it is quite likely
that he wrote his account of Christian beginnings with the aim
of conveying something of the same impact and impression to
his readers; many of these past and present would testify to his
success."[17]

The Speeches

In a famous passage, Thucydides, the Greek historian, describes his dilemma concerning the speeches of his characters and
the policy that he adopted toward them. "It has been difficult,"
he said, "to recall the words actually spoken with strict accuracy,
both for me about what I myself heard and for those who from
various other sources have brought me reports. So the speeches
are given in the language in which, as it seemed to me, the several speakers would express, on the subject under consideration,
the sentiments most befitting the occasion, though at the same
time I have adhered as closely as possible to the general sense
of what was actually said."[18] But not all ancient historians were
as conscientious as Thucydides. Some of them composed speeches
quite freely and put them into the mouths of their characters with
little regard for historical probability, much less for historical fact.

This raises again in a special form the question of the historicity of Acts. Are the speeches that are found in this book genuine reports of what was said, or did Luke conform to common
practice and make them up? There are not wanting those who
hold the latter opinion, claiming that the speeches contain little
of the early preaching and much of Luke's own theology. This
assessment is based on an analysis of the speeches themselves,
a number of which show a common structure and all of which
give evidence of Luke's own language and style. But though it
is true that most of the early speeches do follow a similar pattern, it is also the case that that pattern is not confined to this

book. It is found, for example, in Mark 1:14–15 and in a number of passages in the Epistles (see further the disc. on 2:14–42). In short, the common structure is older than Acts and is found more widely than in Acts. It is reasonable to suppose, then, that it was the pattern of the church's preaching and not something imposed on the speeches by Luke himself.

In any case, within the broad similarity of the speeches there is a great deal of variety. First, they show a definite theological development, as one would expect if they were speeches made over a number of years—formative years at that. Moreover, at some points they reveal a theology quite distinctive from Luke's (see, e.g., the disc. on 4:24ff. and notes on the disc. on 7:1–53). Second, on occasion they reflect the distinctive traits of the original speaker. The Lucan accents are unmistakably there, but behind them we hear Peter speaking like the Peter of the First Epistle and Paul like the Paul we know from his writings (see, e.g., disc. on 5:30; 13:39; 15:13ff.; 20:17–38). Finally, two of the speeches (2:14–39 and 13:16–41) display the hermeneutical style of the rabbis, which one would hardly expect had Luke composed them himself. And if all of this points us back to the likelihood that Luke drew on sources, this is only confirmed by the telltale marks they have left on his Greek. "The style of the speeches is not as polished as one would expect if these were careful literary productions; there are in fact the kind of redundancies and minor incoherences which mark the incorporation of traditions into a redactional framework"[19] (see, e.g., notes on 3:16; 4:11; 4:25; 10:36ff., and the introduction to 10:34–43).

So we may assume that the speeches of Acts give us, in the Thucydidean "general sense," a reliable guide to what was actually said. They "are not Luke's invention," writes Bruce, "but summaries giving at least the gist of what was really said on the various occasions, and therefore valuable and independent sources for the life and thought of the primitive church."[20]

Place and Date

No one knows where Acts was written, though many have hazarded a guess. Suggestions include Rome, Caesarea, Antioch, Ephesus, and Corinth. Its language is said to point to some center in which Hellenistic influence prevailed, but this tells us little. Almost any sizable city east of Rome would fit that description.

Concerning its date, the cultural and political atmosphere of the book sets it firmly in the first century. But where in that century? A late date (A.D. 90–100) has been advocated on the grounds that it is not a mere chronicle of events but is clearly the product of reflection. It presents an interpretation of history, and this implies, it is argued, that the author stood at some distance from his subject. One wonders, however, whether thirty or forty years were necessary to give him that perspective. Again, in support of a late date, it has been claimed that the book displays the interests and outlook of the church of that time. The label of early catholicism has sometimes been attached to it. But where is the evidence in support of this claim? There is little interest in a strictly formulated rule of faith, in the establishment of "sound doctrine," in the doctrine of the church, in the development of the church's ministry, or in the sacraments of the church, all of which characterized the early catholicism of the late first and early second centuries.[21] On the contrary, for Luke the church as an institution was remarkably free, its communal life marked by a spontaneity that we do not find elsewhere in that period. "Neither the Apostles nor James exercise authoritarian direction of the church in Jerusalem, nor do Paul or others elsewhere. The church is led not by institutional authorities but by the Holy Spirit. By the Spirit the church is consolidated, but also disciplined and purified, and at the same time kept open to the mysterious and always new demands of God's will. And there is no trace of a high sacramentalism."[22] A comparison with writers who belong indisputably to the late first and early second centuries, such as Clement of Rome and Ignatius, shows just how far Luke might have gone in these directions. As it is, Acts breathes a different atmosphere. It belongs to another and earlier day.

Some put the writing of Acts between A.D. 60 and 70, and some specifically date it earlier than the death of Paul (it would appear that he died in the second half of Nero's reign, ca. A.D. 67) because Luke makes no mention of it. But this presupposes that his primary interest was to write a life of the apostle, whereas in fact he was mainly concerned to trace the progress of the gospel to Rome. Once the Good News had been preached in that city, what happened to Paul lay beyond the scope of his book (besides, it was probably known to Luke's readers) and is no guide to the date of its composition. Nevertheless, even if the book were written after Paul's death, a date not too much later is required because of Luke's ignorance of the contents of Paul's letters. It is also demanded by a number of small but significant points of historical detail that would have been almost impossible for a later writer to have achieved (see, e.g., the disc. on 18:1 and 21:38; also Hanson, pp. 8ff.). The casual recollection of names is another indicator that the book is early rather than late (e.g., 17:5; 19:33; 21:16; 28:11). The question is, How early?

The strongest objection to a date in the 60s for Acts is Luke's use of Mark's Gospel in the composition of his own. Assuming that the reference in 1:1 is to the Gospel in its present form and not to an earlier draft before he came across Mark (the supposed "Proto Luke"), we have a sequence of relative dates: First, Mark; second, the Gospel according to Luke; and third, Acts. But according to the earliest tradition, Mark was not written until after the deaths of Peter and Paul (Irenaeus, *Against Heresies* 3.1.1) and then some time (not much, perhaps) must be allowed for his work to have reached Luke and still more for Luke to have written his second volume. Indeed, some scholars think that a good number of years must have elapsed before Acts was begun. F. L. Cribbs argues this on the grounds that the second volume makes much greater use than the first of such concepts as "witness," "signs," and "believing";[23] S. G. Wilson argues the same case, but on different grounds. "It seems quite probable," he says, "purely on the basis of his eschatology, that Luke wrote Acts a considerable time after the Gospel, and that in the interim period his views developed and changed."[24] Even allowing that these writers have overstated their case, a date for Acts around A.D. 75 seems most likely, with Mark written perhaps in the late 60s or early 70s and Luke's Gospel soon after.

Title and Purpose

The title is not original. It was coined some time after the book's connection with the Gospel was severed and probably about the time that it gained recognition as canonical. It may owe its origin to the fact that the book stood before the Epistles in the canon, representing "acts" rather than "words." The earliest occurrence of the title is found in the anti-Marcionite prologue to Luke's Gospel (ca. A.D. 180), in the form "[the] Acts of [the] Apostles" (Gk. *Praxeis Apostolōn*). A little later, the Muratorian Canon entitled it "The Acts of *All* the Apostles." Subsequently, other variations appeared, but in whatever form, such a name for this book is neither adequate nor exact. Of the original twelve apostles, we read a good deal of Peter, a little of John, James, and Judas, and nothing at all of the others, except for an occasional mention of "the apostles" (the last of which is found in chap. 15) and a list of their names in 1:13. On the other hand, the book introduces us to a wide range of other characters who were not apostles. Sixteen of the twenty-eight chapters are devoted to Paul.

Neither does the title give any real indication of Luke's purpose. This is to be found in the opening verses. The book begins with a reference back to Luke's Gospel in which "all the things that Jesus began to do and to teach" (so the Greek) are recorded. This description of the first volume implies that the second contains all that Jesus continued to do and to teach. But how did Jesus continue his work? The purpose of Acts is to answer that question, and the key to it lies in 1:8. There the apostles were told that they would receive power when the Holy Spirit came upon them and in that power they would go out into all the world as Jesus' witnesses. They would continue his words and deeds. It would be as Jesus had said: "Whoever listens to you listens to me; whoever rejects you rejects me" (Luke 10:16). What Jesus had promised in Luke 6:40—that the disciple would be like his teacher— would be fulfilled. And so, once the Holy Spirit had come, Peter could either heal "in the name of Jesus" (3:6, 16, etc.) or simply declare, "Jesus Christ makes you well" (9:34). It was all one, for Jesus was active and present in the world—not as before, but in his witnesses inspired by his Spirit. It is worth noting that in this book the Holy Spirit is called the Spirit of Jesus (16:7).

It is in this context that we must understand Luke's concentration on Paul. It was not to defend Paul's memory, as is sometimes suggested, but to present him as the "paradigmatic witness."[25] To Luke's mind, this man's great significance lay in the fact that he was not an apostle—as least, not in the sense that Peter was—not one of the Twelve (though Luke knew that Paul had used the title). Unlike Peter, Paul had not been with Jesus in the days of his flesh (cf. 1:21f.), he had not been present at the outpouring of the Spirit. And yet, his achievement was no less than Peter's (Luke quite deliberately draws a series of parallels, between Peter in the first half of the book and Paul in the second, making precisely this point). So Paul exemplified the continuity of Jesus' work from the time of the apostles down to Luke's own day. Because Paul was a latter-day Christian, his life and work—more than that of the Twelve—was an attainable ideal to put before other Christians who had not been present in the exciting days of the church's beginning. Like him, they, too, could effectively witness for Christ. In them, no less than in the first generation, Jesus would continue his work.

Clearly, Luke was writing for Christians (represented by Theophilus), and this explains a number of other themes that run through the book. One is that of fulfillment. In a sense the whole of Acts can be seen as a kind of commentary on the text. "How fortunate you are to see the things you see! I tell you that many prophets and kings wanted to see what you see, but they could not, and to hear what you hear, but they did not" (Luke 10:23f.). Luke wanted his readers to understand that they were a privileged people and, in the light of that, to encourage them to get on with their task.

A second theme is that of the compatibility of church and state. There is in this book an "unmistakably and surprisingly irenic attitude towards Rome."[26] This has often been explained in terms of Luke's supposed interest in convincing Roman officialdom that Christianity was politically "safe." But C. K. Barrett makes the telling observation that "no Roman official would ever have filtered out so much of what to him would be theological and ecclesiastical rubbish in order to reach so tiny a grain of relevant apology."[27] It is better, then, to explain this motif as addressed to the needs of Christians. Maddox argues that in the church of Luke's day there was a growing resentment of the Roman state and, with it, an inclination to confront the state and to make martyrs of Christ's witnesses. But this was not Luke's way. Hence he was careful "to draw attention to the political innocence of the Christians, and to take on the whole an optimistic view of the imperial government." His view was that the proper business of Christians was "to live at peace with the sovereign power, so far as possible" and to adopt "a sober, inoffensive style of life and an attitude of respect towards the government."[28]

Another theme is that the Jews have excluded themselves from salvation by their persistent hostility toward the gospel. But why should Luke have to belabor this point with a Christian audience? Perhaps precisely because his readers were in danger of thinking otherwise. There may have been a real possibility that they could be made to think that they, not the Jews, were excluded. About this time the Jews introduced into their liturgy a prayer that apostates might be deprived of hope and that Nazarenes and all heretics might be damned. Attitudes were hardening on both sides, and it may have been an issue for Luke's church to know on which side were the heretics and on which the people of God. The Jews, because of their long tradition, were in a position of strength. Their attitude toward the Christians is well expressed in the words of John 9:28–29, "You are this fellow's disciple! We are disciples of Moses! We know that God spoke to Moses; but as for this fellow, we don't even know where he comes from!" Luke's response was to show that Jesus had fulfilled all that God had announced through the prophets, so that anyone who did not accept him would be separated from God's people and destroyed (3:23). It was the Jews, not the Christians—his readers—who were the apostates and heretics; it was they who were excluded, and this by their own choice, for the gospel had been preached to them from the first.

But if Acts was written to serve these didactic ends, are we not brought full circle back to the question of whether Luke's history can be trusted? This question is often posed as though he could only have been one thing or the other—a historian or a theologian, but not both. Yet there is no reason why he should not have been both, writing with a definite purpose but at the same time giving us a reliable account of what actually happened. After all, he expressly states that it was his theological purpose that led him to "carefully investigate everything from the beginning" (Luke 1:3). As Hengel remarks, "the radical 'redaction-critical' approach so popular today, which sees Luke above all as a freely inventive theologian, mistakes his real purpose, namely, that as a Christian 'historian' he sets out to report the events of the past that provide the foundation for the faith and its extension. He does not set out primarily to present his own 'theology.' "[29]

To sum up, then: If we were to look for one "umbrella" term by which to characterize this writer, we could do no better than to call him pastor. Luke "wanted to write history, but history that had a message for his contemporaries. Such an emphasis on the practical, pastoral motivation of Luke's writing leaves ample room for distinguishing various themes within this general description and, at the same time, shows where the center of gravity of Luke's interest lies. He was interested primarily in practical and not in 'theological' problems."[30] His concern was for the church of his own day, that it should understand where it stood and what it must do. But he writes as one who claims to have done his homework conscientiously and with integrity. We find no reason to doubt him. Though the story is incomplete, we may read it believing that what he wrote is true and that ordinary people filled with the Spirit really did do extraordinary things. They were done "in the name of Jesus," and so they turned the world upside down. Acts ends at 28:31, but the story of Jesus goes on wherever his Spirit finds men and women ready to believe, to obey, to give, to suffer, and, if need be, to die for him.

Notes

1. J. B. Phillips, *The Young Church in Action* (London: Geoffrey Bles, 1955), p. vii.

2. See, e.g., Hengel, *Acts*, p. 39.

3. Hengel, *Acts*, p. 38.

4. E. J. Goodspeed, *Introduction to the New Testament* (Chicago: University of Chicago Press, 1937), pp. 187f.

5. See, e.g., V. K. Robbins, *Perspectives*, pp. 215ff.

6. See "The Book of Acts" in A. D. Nock, *Essays on Religion and the Ancient World* (London: Oxford University Press, 1972), vol. 2, pp. 821ff.

7. Hengel, *Acts*, p. 66.

8. See, e.g., P. Vielhauer, *Studies*, pp. 33–50.

9. Hanson, p. 27.

10. Hengel, *Jesus*, p. 110.

11. C. H. Dodd, *The Apostolic Preaching and Its Development* (London: Hodder & Stoughton, 1944), pp. 19f.

12. See, e.g., Hengel, *Jesus*, p. 121: "[Luke's] knowledge of conditions in Judea during roughly the last fifteen years before the outbreak of the Judaean war and his special concern with the destruction of Jerusalem show how he was affected by these events and stood relatively close to them."

13. Krodel, p. 15.

14. Hengel, *Acts*, p. 35.

15. Hengel, *Acts*, p. 61.

16. Dunn, *Jesus*, pp. 168f.

17. Dunn, *Jesus*, p. 169.

18. Thucydides, *History of the Peloponnesian War* 1.22.

19. Marshall, p. 40.

20. Bruce, *Acts*, p. 21.

21. J. H. Elliott, "A Catholic Gospel: Reflections on 'Early Catholicism' in the New Testament," *CBQ* 31 (1969), pp. 213ff.

22. Maddox, p. 185.

23. F. L. Cribbs, *Perspectives*, p. 61.

24. S. G. Wilson, "Lukan Eschatology," *NTS* 16 (1969–70), p. 347. See also Hengel, *Jesus*, p. 107.

25. Hengel, *Acts*, p. 59.

26. Maddox, p. 21.

27. C. K. Barrett, *Luke the Historian in Recent Study* (London: Epworth Press, 1961), p. 63.

28. Maddox, pp. 96f.

29. Hengel, *Acts*, pp. 67f.

30. S. G. Wilson, *The Gentiles and the Gentile Mission in Luke–Acts* (Cambridge: Cambridge University Press, 1973), pp. 266f.

Note: A list of the abbreviations used in the commentary is found at the beginning of the book (see p. xv). See also "For Further Reading" (p. 457); full bibliographical references for works referred to in short-form notes within the commentary are supplied there.

§1 Jesus Taken Up into Heaven (Acts 1:1–11)

Acts and the Third Gospel clearly come from the same hand. Not only their common dedication, but their common interests and their unity of language and style leave this beyond doubt. Moreover, the way in which they are introduced—the Gospel with its relatively detailed preface, Acts with its shorter introduction echoing the other's language—points us to the fact that these are not simply two books by the same author, but two volumes of one book. This arrangement of a work into a number of "books" having a common preface, with the later books having their own brief introduction, was a not-uncommon feature of ancient writing (cf., e.g., Josephus, *Against Apion* 2.1–7; see *BC*, vol. 2, p. 491). Unlike the Gospel, there is no clear line of demarcation in Acts between the introduction and the narrative, for what begins as a reference back to the earlier preface becomes a brief résumé of the whole of the first book—a narrative that leads into the new material of the following section. The famous Greek satirist Lucian (b. ca. A.D. 120) gives it as a dictum that the transition from the preface of a book to its narrative should be gradual and smooth (*On Writing History* 55). Luke conforms to Lucian's requirements.

1:1 / The book is dedicated to **Theophilus**, a man of some standing, to judge by the address in the Gospel, "Your Excellency" (Luke 1:3, GNB). Luke explains that in his **former book**—clearly he means the Gospel—he had set out to give an account of "all that Jesus began to do and to teach until the day he was taken up to heaven." This reveals Luke's understanding of the scope of his first volume. It was concerned only with the beginning of Jesus' work, the implication being that that work went on beyond "the day he was taken up." Luke's thesis is this: Jesus remains active, though the manner of his working has changed. Now, no longer in the flesh, he continues "to do and to teach" through his "body," the church (see disc. on 9:5). This is the story of Acts.

1:2 / Before Luke takes up that story, he briefly recalls the events that brought the first book to a close. Prior to the ascension, Jesus had given **instructions . . . to the apostles he had chosen**. In the Gospel, the title "apostles" is limited to the Twelve (Luke 9:10; 17:5; 22:14; 24:10; cf. Matt. 10:2ff.; Mark 6:30), and it is said by Luke to have been conferred upon them by Jesus himself (Luke 6:13). In Acts also, the primary reference is to the Twelve, though verses 21 and 22 suggest that others may have been included and certainly that others shared the apostles' experience (see further the notes on v. 26). The title was later given a wider application (see 14:4, 14). As we see from verse 5, Jesus' instructions were concerned in part with the gift of the Spirit. But already the Holy Spirit was involved in what he was doing. For it was **through the Holy Spirit** that he was now teaching them. Some commentators prefer to attach this phrase to Jesus' choice of the Twelve, but the most natural reading of the Greek is to take it with the statement "he gave instructions" and to understand it to mean that, in his teaching, Jesus was invested with divine power and authority. At all events, we are here given notice that in the story that is about to unfold the Spirit plays a key role. The Spirit is mentioned four times in this chapter alone (vv. 2, 5, 8, 16).

1:3 / For **forty days** after his death, Jesus showed himself to his disciples. The Greek is literally, "through forty days," which appears to mean, not that he was with them continuously, but that he appeared from time to time during that period. **Forty** was often used as a round number, but in this instance it seems to refer to the actual number of days, the period being something less than the fifty days between Passover and Pentecost (see disc. on 2:1). The most comprehensive list that we have of Jesus' appearances begins in 1 Corinthians 15:5, though even this, as the Gospels show, is far from complete. The "many times" of GNB (not represented in the Greek) may be a fair assumption. And, of course, the more times they saw him, the less chance there was that they were mistaken. Notice how Luke underlines the reality of the experience by means of repetition: "he showed himself to them," "he was seen by them." Nor was this all, for he also talked with them and, as we learn from elsewhere, ate and drank with them, as he had done in earlier days (see 10:41; Luke 24:30, 42f.; cf. Luke 22:17–20). The outcome of all this was that they were left with an unshakable conviction that Jesus was alive and had been with them. It was "proven beyond doubt"—as strong an expression as Luke could have used. Had they not had these **convincing proofs**, the events described in this book would never have taken place.

His talking with them had been of **the kingdom of God**. This had been Jesus' theme from the beginning, as it would be theirs (see 8:12; 14:22; 19:8; 20:25; 28:23, 31), though they would preach it from a different perspective. For the kingdom had "come with power" only in the saving events of Jesus' death and its sequel (Mark 9:1). Even so, what they preached was not their own construction on those events, but was given to them now in Jesus' teaching about his death (see Luke 24:25f., 45ff.) and in the years to come by the Spirit of Jesus (see, e.g., 1 Cor. 2:10). In the phrase **after his suffering**, Luke uses a word that, more than most, reminds us of the cost at which our salvation was won (cf. 17:3; 26:23).

1:4 / Besides this, one other matter in particular found a place in Jesus' instructions: the apostles were not to leave Jerusalem, but were to wait there for **the gift** that he had told them about, that is, the gift of the Holy Spirit which the **Father** had **promised** (cf. Isa. 32:15; Joel 2:28–32; Acts 2:33, 39; Gal. 3:14; Eph. 1:13, and for Jesus' teaching, Matt. 10:20; John 14:16f., 25; 15:26; 16:7f., 13–15). In NIV, verses 4 and 5 appear to refer to something Jesus said on a specific occasion, as well they might. Perhaps we have in these verses a recollection of their last meeting with him (cf. vv. 6–8; Luke 24:48f.). But in the Greek, the use of the present participle suggests that the reference is, rather, to a number of occasions on which they came together and these instructions were given (cf. John 20:22). Clearly it was a matter of great importance to Jesus that his disciples should be ready for the gift that the Father had promised. The fact that they were ready and had expressed their readiness in expectant prayer may have been a condition of their receiving the gift. The location seems also to have been important. Their own inclination had been to go back to Galilee (see John 21), but Jesus stressed that they should remain in Jerusalem—**he gave them this command**; in the Greek the verb is one that Luke often uses for particular emphasis. But why Jerusalem, we cannot say, except that Isaiah had spoken of a new teaching issuing from the city and a new obedience that would follow (Isa. 2:3), and what had been spoken had to come true. In any case, there was something appropriate in the Father's gift being given in the very place where, not long before, a disobedient and rebellious people had put Jesus to death (cf. 7:51; Neh. 9:26). And here, of course, the greatest number of people would be found to receive the apostles' initial witness to Christ.

1:5 / Jesus promised that the power to witness would soon be theirs, when they were **baptized with the Holy Spirit** (cf. v. 8). This expression, used also by John the Baptist (see Matt. 3:11, etc.), is derived from baptism with water. As a metaphor of the gift of the Spirit it does not convey all that the gift entails, but it does give the required sense of an overwhelming experience. The promise was fulfilled within **a few days** (see disc. on 2:4; cf. 2:17; 11:15).

1:6 / So important did Luke regard the teaching of these few days before the ascension that he has left us three accounts of it: one in the Gospel (Luke 24:44–49), another in the preface of Acts, and a third in verses 6 to 8 of this section. Though the material may be based on the recollection of one particular occasion, perhaps Jesus' last meeting with the disciples, it may be regarded as typical of the instruction he gave throughout the post-resurrection period. The remaining verses of this section (9–11) give an account of the event that brought this period to a close. They are the fullest and perhaps the only account of the ascension in the New Testament, since the texts of Mark 16:19 and Luke 24:51 are probably not original. Because the passage stands alone, its historical value has been questioned and Luke accused of translating a purely spiritual event into an event in the material world. But even if the ascension is not actually described elsewhere, it is certainly implied in the frequent references to Christ at the right hand of God (e.g., 2:33f.; 3:21; John 6:62; Eph. 4:8–10; 1 Thess. 1:10; Heb. 4:14; 9:24; Rev. 5:6) and is twice clearly attested, once by Peter (1 Pet. 3:21f.), once by Paul (1 Tim. 3:16), the latter citing perhaps an earlier Christian hymn. It is difficult to imagine how Luke could have gotten away with such a story while the apostles or even their successors were alive if the event had not been much as he describes it. Certainly no other explanation is offered by the New Testament for the sudden end to Jesus' post-resurrection appearances. And yet, because Luke is describing in terms of this world an event that transcends it, a completely literal interpretation may not be possible. Nevertheless, we must not lose sight of the fact that something must have happened—something that convinced the apostles that Jesus had "ascended" and something (we may suppose) that could more nearly be described in these terms than in any other.

The question raised by the apostles in this verse could have been asked at any time during the forty days that Jesus was with them, since he spoke to them often about the kingdom of God (cf. v. 3). Indeed, the imperfect tense suggests that it was asked more than once. But if it was asked at their last meeting with Jesus, there is a certain poignancy in their failure right to the end to understand that the kingdom was not of this world (cf. John 18:36) but of the Spirit, to be entered only by repentance and faith. It would be unjust to suggest that the apostles had learned nothing from Jesus. In some respects they had come a long way (see disc. on v. 2; cf. Luke 24:45). But clearly they were wedded still to the popular notion of the kingdom of God as something political— that its coming would see the gathering of the tribes (see disc. on 3:21 and notes and the disc. on 26:7), the restoration of Israel's independence, and the triumph of Israel over its enemies. In this respect they had not progressed very far from their earlier hope of occupying the seats of power in such a kingdom (Mark 10:35ff.; Luke 22:24ff.). But given these hopes and against the background of Jesus' resurrection and his statements concerning the Spirit, their question, though mistaken, was a perfectly natural one. In Jewish thought, resurrection and the Spirit belonged to the new age. Indeed, the prophecy of Joel, to which Jesus had very likely referred them, may have given rise to the question they were now asking, for the prophet had spoken both of the pouring out of God's Spirit (Joel 2:28ff.) and of his restoring the kingdom to Israel (Joel 2:18ff.; 3:1ff.). Their sense of anticipation is expressed in the present tense of the Greek: not "will you?" but "Lord are you at this time going to restore the kingdom to Israel?"

1:7–8 / This was not the first time they had asked Jesus about what was to come, and as before, he gave them no answer. Instead, he drew their minds to their present duty (cf. John 21:21f.). The future was in God's hands, and it was not for them to know what it held, at least not in detail (cf. Mark 13:32). Their task was to be his **witnesses** (v. 8). This commission obviously had a special reference to the apostles, who would uniquely authenticate the gospel data—the life, the death, the resurrection, and the ascension of Jesus. In this sense they would be the foundation and pillars of the church (cf. Matt. 16:18; Gal. 2:9). But the church to be built upon that foundation would itself become "the pillar and foundation of the truth" (1 Tim. 3:15). Herein lies the secondary reference of Jesus' words. Not all are apostles, but all are commissioned to witness to the truth that they established. To all, therefore, the promise is given: **you will receive power when the Holy Spirit comes on you** (v. 8). The statements of this verse should be understood as cause and effect. Effective witness can only be borne where the Spirit is, and where the Spirit is, effective witness will always follow, in word, in deed (miracle), and in the quality of the lives of those who bear it (see disc. on 2:4).

The command had a universal scope. From Jerusalem they were to go out **to the ends of the earth** (v. 8). This supplies the corrective to the particularism of the apostles' question in verse 6, though it may be doubted whether at the time they understood it as such. At most, they probably took Jesus to mean that they should witness to the Jews of the Diaspora (see notes on 2:9ff.) and only in this sense preach "the forgiveness of sins . . . to all nations" (Luke 24:47; see disc. on Acts 10:10ff.). The thought of including the Gentiles would never have crossed their minds and was accepted later only with great difficulty. The Jewish nationalism of the early church died hard. But by the time Luke was writing that was largely a thing of the past, and the phrase **the ends of the earth** had taken on a wider meaning. It now embraced the Roman Empire, epitomized by Rome itself, and on that basis Luke adopted the program of this verse as a framework for his narrative.

1:9 / When these forty days of instruction were over, Jesus **was taken up**. They had taken the familiar path across the Kidron to the Mount of Olives (cf. v. 12), and somewhere in this vicinity the summit of Jesus' life was attained. Because the Jews thought of heaven as "above" and earth as "below," the movement of Jesus from the visible to the invisible world is expressed in terms of his going "up." The idiom may not seem appropriate to us, but it was to them and is found elsewhere in the New Testament, coupled with the thought of Jesus' exaltation (cf., e.g., Eph. 1:20;

Phil. 2:9; Heb. 1:3; 2:9). That thought is expressed here in the words **a cloud hid him from their sight**, for in biblical language the cloud was often a symbol of divine glory (cf., e.g., Exod. 16:10; Ps. 104:3). The language is pictorial and must be treated as such, and yet Luke is certain that something objective took place. Notice his emphasis on their seeing it: Jesus was taken up **before their very eyes**; "they were looking intently up into the sky as he was going" (v. 10). This was important, for they were to be witnesses of his ascension no less than of his life, death, and resurrection.

1:10–11 / In the long term, the apostles' appreciation of the ascension must have come from a combination of sight and (inspired) insight, the latter resting on Jesus' earlier teaching. But initially, there must have been enough given to their physical senses to convince them that this was their final parting with Jesus as they had known him. Luke expresses their experience in dramatic terms. He speaks of **two men dressed in white** appearing **beside them** (v. 10; cf. 10:30; 12:7; Luke 2:9; 24:4). They are introduced with the exclamation, "Look"—not apparent in NIV, but intended to convey a sense of surprise at the providential (cf. esp. 7:56; 8:27, 36; 10:30; 16:1), for Luke wants us to understand that the two "men" were angels (cf. Matt. 28:2f.; John 20:12). What he meant by an "angel" is not so clear. Perhaps all he wanted to say was that there was an overwhelming sense of the divine in what happened (see disc. on 5:19f.; 12:6ff.; cf. 7:30; 8:26; 10:3; 12:23, 27.23) such that the apostles were convinced that Jesus would come back as he had gone—visibly and manifesting the glory of God (this, of course, had been Jesus' teaching, cf., e.g., Mark 13:26; 14:62). But some time would elapse before his return. Hence the question, **why do you stand here looking into the sky?** (v. 11). Meanwhile, they had their instructions. For the present they were to remain in Jerusalem (v. 4), then they were to go out as his witnesses (v. 8). The emphasis here, as in the New Testament generally, is on the present duty of Christians rather than on speculation about Christ's return. However, in the knowledge that he would return, the apostles set about their present task "with great joy" (Luke 24:52f.). This passage is one of the few references in Acts to the Parousia (cf. 3:20f.; 10:42; 17:31; 23:6; 24:25; see also notes on 2:17ff. and disc. on 7:55f.).

Additional Notes §1

1:1 / Theophilus: The name means "friend of God" and has been taken to mean any friend of God, i.e., the Christian reader in general. Others have seen it as a pseudonym for someone who could not be named. But the name was not an uncommon one, and there is no good reason to think that Theophilus was not a real person of that name. The use of the title "Most Excellent" bears this out (Luke 1:3) and suggests, moreover, that he was a man of some importance. The title was appropriate to a man of the Roman equestrian order (an upper middle class social group) and is applied elsewhere in Acts to the procurators of Judea, since most procurators were of equestrian rank (see 23:26; 24:3; 26:25). Theophilus appears to have been a Christian.

Began: Some scholars regard this word as meaningless, the redundant auxiliary of Aramaic idiom. But in this context the sense I have suggested here seems the more likely. That Acts was simply the continuing story of Jesus tells against the theory proposed by H. Conzelmann, *The Theology of St. Luke*, that Luke divided history into three periods, of which the history of Jesus was "the middle time" and the events related in Acts the "period of the church." In reality, the whole two-volume work covers the one history of Jesus, which, to Luke's mind, belonged to the "last days."

1:3 / The kingdom of God: For a proper understanding of this term, it should be noted that both the Greek and the Hebrew or Aramaic words thus translated signify kingship rather than kingdom, rule rather than realm. Essentially, therefore, the kingdom of God "is not a community of Christians nor an inner life of the soul, nor yet an earthly paradise which mankind is bringing into being and which is in process of development" (G. Lundstrom, *The Kingdom of God in the Teaching of Jesus* [Edinburgh: Oliver & Boyd, 1963], p. 232), though it might embrace all these notions, but is, rather, God acting in his kingly power, exercising sovereignty and, in particular, asserting his rule for the overthrow of Satan and the restoration of humanity to a relationship with himself. But this was conceived of in various ways: sometimes in terms of God's eternal sovereignty and sometimes in terms of our present experience of him, but chiefly in terms of the kingdom's future manifestation, its onset marked by the "Day of the Lord," when God and/or his Messiah would appear, the dead would be raised, and the new age ushered in (see notes on 2:17ff.). Then all would know God, from the least to the greatest, and he would forgive them (Jer. 31:34) and pour out his Spirit upon them (Joel 2:28).

For Jesus' contemporaries, as for all generations before them, the kingdom conceived of in these terms was no more than a distant hope. With what astonishment, therefore, must they have heard Jesus' announcement that it had become a present reality (see, e.g., Mark 1:22,

27). "The right time has come," he said (i.e., the anticipated time of its manifestation), "and the kingdom of God has arrived" (Mark 1:15; cf., e.g., Luke 17:21). But, if Jesus was right (and the evidence of his life, his miracles, his resurrection, and the Pentecostal outpouring assure us that he was), then the kingdom clearly had not come in the manner expected. For the time being, it remained a personal and partial experience (though certainly a real one) for those who submitted to God's rule in Jesus Christ (cf. 1 Cor. 13:12). Only when Jesus returns will the kingdom be fully established and God's rule become all in all (see disc. on 3:19–21; 14:22; cf. 1 Cor. 15:24f.). Thus the Day of the Lord, which, in a sense, could be said to have come with the coming of Jesus, has been drawn out these many years until his coming again. Much of the language of the Old Testament describing the Day of the Lord is applied by the New Testament to "the Day of Christ," i.e., to the day of his return.

1:4 / **While he was eating with them**: The word thus translated (*synalizein*) is an unusual one, found in the New Testament only here and once (disputed) in the Old Testament (LXX Ps. 140:5). It is derived either from a word meaning "to meet" (GNB) or from a word meaning "salt," and from that, "to eat together." The latter is to be preferred, on the grounds that the author is recapitulating the events of Luke 24:42ff.

1:7 / **The times or dates**: The two Greek words represented by this translation have sometimes been regarded as synonymous. Certainly it is difficult always to maintain a clear distinction between them. But here **the times** (Gk. *chronous*) may be taken to mean space of time as such— the eras of the history of the world—and **dates** (Gk. *kairous*) the critical moments within those extended periods.

1:8 / **When the Holy Spirit comes on you**: Two different renderings of the Greek are possible here. The genitive case of **the Holy Spirit** could be governed by **power**, giving the sense "you will receive the power *of* the Holy Spirit who will come upon you" (cf. Luke 4:14; Rom. 15:13, 19), or it could be a genitive absolute with a temporal sense. The latter, adopted by NIV, is to be preferred.

You will be my witnesses: Here the genitive case of the personal pronoun presents us with two possibilities (some texts read the dative case, which gives us similar options). Either it is the objective genitive, expressing the thought that he is the one *about whom* they would testify, or the possessive genitive, indicating their personal relationship with him—they are *his* witnesses. Both of course are true, and the ambiguity may be quite intentional.

In Jerusalem, and in all Judea and Samaria, and to the ends of the earth: The fact that in the outworking of the history of the church the full import of Jesus' words was only slowly grasped and even then, for many of his followers, was like grasping a nettle, need not lead us to suppose that he never gave this instruction and that it came from a later hand. The history of Israel, as indeed of the church itself, is full of instances in which people did not attain the best ideals of their leaders.

The form of the saying shows a close acquaintance with the political and social context of that day. For a broader definition of **Judea**, see disc. on 10:37, but here **Judea** refers to that part of Palestine inhabited by Jews, apart from Samaria and Galilee (cf. 9:31; 11:29; 15:1; 26:20; 28:21) and sometimes even excluding Caesarea (cf. 12:19; see disc. on 10:1 and 21:10). But politically, under the procurators, this region and Samaria were governed from Caesarea as one province, as Luke's Greek clearly intimates, whereas Jerusalem was always regarded by the rabbis as separate from the rest of the province, as Luke also intimates, not only here but elsewhere in his writing (cf. 8:1; 10:39; Luke 5:17; 6:17; see notes on 2:9ff.).

The precise phrase, **to the ends of the earth** occurs in LXX Isa. 8:9; 48:20; 49:6 (cf. Acts 13:47, where Paul refers Isa. 49:6 to Barnabas and himself); 62:11; 1 Macc. 3:9, and if it seems somewhat strained to suggest that Luke saw Paul's preaching in Rome as its fulfillment, it is noteworthy that in the Psalms of Solomon 8:16; Pompey, a Roman, is said to have come from "the ends of the earth."

1:11 / **Men of Galilee**: It appears that most of the Twelve were Galileans, Judas Iscariot being perhaps the only exception.

§2 Matthias Chosen to Replace Judas (Acts 1:12–26)

The period between the ascension and Pentecost was one of waiting, but not of inactivity. Chiefly, for the disciples, it was a time of prayer, but it also saw them finding a replacement for Judas. In this connection, we have the first speech in Acts. Like most of the speeches in this book, it is probably only a summary of what Peter said. Nevertheless, behind Luke's report we can still catch the original tones of the apostle.

1:12–14 / As instructed, the apostles retraced their steps from the Mount of Olives to the city, there to await the Father's gift (cf. vv. 4, 5). They were quartered in an upper room. This would have given them a degree of privacy that suited their purpose well, for much of their time was spent in prayer (cf. Dan. 6:10). The notice of verse 14 may include their regular attendance at the temple (cf. Luke 24:53; Acts 2:46; 3:1), for in this regard there was no sense of distinction between them and their fellow Jews. The believers saw themselves simply as fulfilled Judaism, the beginning of eschatological Israel. Their practice continued to be that of Jews. But in view of the fact that men and women are said to have prayed together, the reference here will be chiefly to their private meetings. This being the case, the Greek throws an interesting light on their practice, for it speaks of them as meeting for "the prayers," as though a specific form of prayer was meant, though perhaps it means only a particular time of prayer (see disc. on 2:42).

It is characteristic of Luke that he should mention their meeting for prayer. Prayer was clearly something that he saw as most important. There are three things that we should notice in this connection: First, it was the practice of the early Christians to pray. As prayer had characterized the life of Jesus, so, too, it did the lives of his followers (cf. 2:42; 3:1; 4:24ff.; 6:4ff.; see further the disc. on 9:11). Luke is sure, moreover, that prayer always meets with a response (cf. vv. 24–26; 4:31; 9:40; 10:19f., 31; 12:5, 12; 22:10; 27:23–25; see further the disc. on 9:12). It therefore plays an integral, if undefined, part in the setting forward of God's purpose. Nowhere is this more evident than in the distinctly implied connection between the disciples' prayer before Pentecost and the pouring out of God's Spirit on that day. Second, in developing that point, Luke emphasized the disciples' persistence in prayer. They prayed **constantly** (v. 14), this word expressing the Greek imperfect, which points to repeated or habitual action. Third, their praying together was an expression of the unity that was a feature of the early church—**they all joined together** (v. 14). Their praying was probably also a factor in maintaining that unity (cf. 2:46; 4:24; 5:12; Rom. 15:6; Eph. 4:3).

It is also typical of Luke that he should draw attention to the part played by women in the church (cf. 5:14; 8:3, 12; 9:2; 12:12; 16:13; 17:4, 12; 22:4). Here he mentions their presence at these gatherings for prayer. The Greek is indefinite; it simply has "women," as though introducing them for the first time. However, they may have included the women already mentioned in the Gospel as Jesus' followers (Luke 8:2f.; 23:49, 55; 24:10). Others may have been the wives of the men. Mary, the mother of Jesus, is singled out as of special interest. This is the last mention of Mary in the New Testament, and significantly, our last glimpse of her is, as it were, on her knees. From the outset, women seem to have played a far greater part in the church than they ever did in the synagogue. But, for all that, they were not yet (if they have ever been) treated as equals (cf. Gal. 3:28), since they were evidently excluded from the meeting beginning at verse 15, which Peter addressed, "men, brothers" (so the Greek).

The reference to Mary leads to a mention also of Jesus' brothers. Earlier they had been skeptical of his claims (John 7:5; cf. Mark 6:4), but they are now included among the disciples. How this came about we are not told, but in the case of James (assuming he is the James of 1 Cor. 15:7), as with Paul, it may have been through an encounter with the risen Jesus (see disc. on 12:17 and notes). He may have influenced his brothers.

1:15 / One other matter claimed the disciples' attention, namely, finding a replacement for Judas. A meeting was held at which Peter presided (cf. Luke 22:32), and about one hundred and twenty "brothers" were present. The number is apparently a real one, so that no particular significance attaches to it (had that precise number been important Luke would not have said **about**). It is interesting, however, that in Jewish polity, one hundred twenty men was the minimum number required to constitute a proper community entitled to appoint a full panel of twenty-three judges to its local court. A community of less than that number could appoint only three. Peter's assumption of leadership is as we would expect from the Gospels, where he is clearly the dominant figure among the Twelve. The term "brothers" (NIV **believers**), used here for the first time in Acts, may have been the earliest Christian designation for church members.

1:16–17 / Peter's speech falls into two parts (vv. 16–20, 21–22), each introduced in the Greek by the same word (*dei*)—one that expresses a need, often a need that arises out of the will of God. The first necessity was that **the Scripture had to be fulfilled** (v. 16). The reference here is to Judas. He had been a member of the group, chosen to have a part in the work, and yet he had betrayed the Master (cf. John 13:18; 17:12). Peter's description of Judas as the **guide for those who arrested Jesus** (v. 16) vividly recalls the scene in the garden, which must have been imprinted on his mind forever (cf. Matt. 26:47ff.). And yet the facts concerning Judas are stated with great reserve. Perhaps Peter was only too conscious of his own shameful conduct that night. Perhaps, too, he now understood that, in a sense, we are all implicated in Jesus' death, so that no one person or group of persons was entirely to blame. The fact was that "Christ [had] died for *our* sins according to the Scriptures" (1 Cor. 15:3). Peter draws attention to the divine authorship of Scripture in his reference to the "Holy Spirit speaking through David" (v. 16; cf. 2:16; 3:18, 21, 25; 4:25; 15:7; 28:25).

1:18–19 / As verse 19 shows with its reference, in the third person, to the inhabitants of Jerusalem and their language, these verses are parenthetical, inserted by Luke to provide his readers with some background information. They give an account of Judas' death that, on the face of it, is quite different from Matthew's story. Matthew has it that Judas, overcome by remorse, threw down in the temple the money he had received for his act of betrayal and went out and hanged himself. The priests, unwilling to put "blood money" into the treasury, bought a potter's field with it—a worked-out clay pit—for use "as a cemetery for foreigners." This place came to be known as the "Field of Blood" (Matt. 27:3–9; cf. Zech. 11:12f.). Luke, on the other hand, asserts that Judas purchased the field himself, where **he fell headlong** (v. 18), literally, "became prone," bursting open and his insides spilling out (cf. 2 Sam. 17:23; 2 Macc. 9:7–18). The two accounts are difficult to reconcile. As long ago as Augustine it was suggested that, if Judas hanged himself in the field and the rope gave way, perhaps some time after his death, when his body was decomposing, Luke's account might be supplementary to Matthew's. But this explanation seems somewhat forced and we may simply have to accept that there were varying accounts of how Judas met his end. However, that Luke's account in Acts does go back to Peter may find some support in the fact that the expression, **the reward he got for his wickedness**, in almost identical form in the Greek, is found again in 2 Peter 2:13, 15 (cf. v. 24 and notes on v. 17). Two things at least are clear: Judas died a violent death, and in some way connected with him a plot of ground was bought that was called the **Field of Blood**. Tradition has located this field at the confluence of the Kidron, Tyropoean, and Hinnom valleys.

1:20 / In referring to the Scripture, Peter had in mind two verses in particular from the Psalms. The first, Psalm 69:25, is given here in a form adapted from the LXX to suit its present application. "Their" in the original has become **his** and "their tents," **his place** (that is, office or position). Such adaptation, whether it be Peter's or Luke's, may strike us as taking undue liberties with the text. But it was believed that all Scripture pointed to Christ or to the events attending his coming and that it was legitimate, therefore, to draw out the meaning in this way. Thus the psalmist's imprecation against his enemies became a prophecy of Judas' desertion. The second verse, in which the psalmist again utters an imprecation against his foes, became the warrant to appoint another in Judas' place. It is quoted almost verbatim from LXX Psalm 109:8 (108:8). The idea that they should make such an appointment was not suggested by the Scripture, but having formed the idea, they found confirmation in these verses for what they wanted to do.

1:21–22 / **Therefore**, said Peter, **it is necessary to choose one of the men who have been with us** (v. 21). This was the second "necessity" of Peter's speech (see disc. on v. 16). When Jesus had chosen the Twelve, it was obviously with the twelve tribes of Israel in mind. The apostles were to be a living parable of the new eschatological Israel that he was establishing. His intention must have been clear to his followers, and for the present, they saw it as important to maintain the number as a witness to the Jews. But once the church was firmly established and itself an effective witness, they seem no longer to have felt that need, and we hear of no further attempts to perpetuate the Twelve (cf. 12:2). Even now it may have been more the manner of Judas' loss than the loss itself that prompted them to seek a replacement.

But, having decided on this action, it was necessary now to state the qualifications that they would look for in his successor. Any candidate for the office would have to have been a close associate of the original Twelve from "the baptism of John" to the day when **Jesus was taken up** (v. 22). This requirement bears out the Johannine tradition that the first disciples had been drawn from among the followers of John the Baptist (cf. John 1:35, 43). In particular, the candidate would have to have been **a witness . . . of** (Jesus') **resurrection** (v. 21f., cf. 1 Cor. 9:1; 15:8; Gal. 1:15f.) Obviously this last point was of critical importance since the resurrection would be the linchpin of their proclamation of Jesus as "Lord and Messiah" (2:36). But it is equally clear from these requirements that the apostolic testimony was not to be confined to the final events of Jesus' life, but would include the whole of his ministry and, not least, his teaching (see disc. on 2:42; cf. Matt. 28:20). As for the candidate's personal qualities, he had to be a man of faith. Hence their prayer for guidance to him who knows "everyone's heart" (v. 24). The disciples themselves could tell whether he qualified in terms of verses 21 and 22, but they looked to God to judge his heart. For the candidate's witness would be both to the historical facts of Jesus' life and to the transforming effect of his grace in life of the believer. (For the title **the Lord Jesus** see notes on 11:20.)

1:23 / There were probably many who could have filled the vacancy on these terms, bearing in mind that the Twelve had been chosen from a much wider group, which itself, hardly less than the Twelve, had remained close to Jesus (cf. Mark 3:13f.; Luke 10:1; 1 Cor. 15:6). But most of them may have been in Galilee (see disc. on 9:31). This may be why only two names were considered: **Joseph called Barsabbas**, meaning either "son of the Sabbath" (he may have been born on that day) or "son of Sabba." Like many Jews, he also had a "secular" (in this case, Roman)

name, **Justus** (see notes on 12:12). He should not be identified
with Judas Barsabbas of 15:22, though they may have been related. The other nominee was **Matthias**.

1:24–25 / With the two candidates before them, the disciples joined in prayer that the *Lord*, who knew **everyone's heart**
(v. 24), would show them which of the two should be taken. It
is not clear to which person of the Godhead this prayer was addressed, but since the same verb "to choose" is used here as was
used in verse 2 of Jesus' choice of the apostles (also Luke 6:13;
John 6:70; 13:18; 15:16, 19) and since Peter had just called Jesus
"Lord" (v. 21), it is likely that the prayer was addressed to Jesus.
But the same title and the same description—he knows the thoughts
of the heart—is used elsewhere of the Father. This ambiguity,
where "Lord" can mean Father or Son, speaks volumes for the
estimate they had of Jesus. It is worth noticing also that as far
as Acts is concerned this concept of divine percipience only comes
to expression in Peter's words (cf. 15:17f.; see also 1 Sam. 16:7;
Jer. 17:10; John 2:25; 21:17). It is possible, then, that this is a genuine recollection of the apostle's own distinctive turn of phrase.
The office about which they were praying is described as a "service"
(Gk. *diakonia*), as all Christian ministry is intended to be (cf. Mark
10:43ff.). The terrible indictment of Judas was that he had left this
service **to go where he belongs** (v. 25)—a common euphemism
for one's final destruction. The apostle had become an apostate
and a warning to us all.

1:26 / They then set about discovering the Lord's answer
to their prayer by the time-honored means of "the lot" (cf. 1 Sam.
14:41). We should be clear that they did not conduct an election.
It was not a case of each disciple casting his vote, but of the choice
(humanly speaking) being made at random. The precise method
used is not known for certain, but it seems to have been the shaking of two stones together in a container, on each of which was
written one name (cf. Lev. 16:8), until one stone tumbled out.
The name on that stone was taken to be the Lord's choice. Luke's
expression is literally "the lot fell." Thus Matthias was chosen and
without further formality was numbered among the apostles.
Much is made of the fact that neither he nor the method by which
he was chosen is heard of again, as though the whole thing was
later seen as a mistake. But neither is anything heard of most of

the Twelve once their names had been listed in verse 13, and so
the silence of Acts is hardly grounds to condemn the man. As
for the method, the coming of the Spirit soon gave the church
a more certain guide to God's will, though at the time their use
of the lot was quite legitimate. Their desire was to discover the
man of God's choice.

Additional Notes §2

1:12 / **The Mount of Olives, a Sabbath day's walk from the city**,
mg.: "That is, about ¾ mile (about 1,100 meters)": This was the extent
to which a pious Jew was allowed to travel on the Sabbath, two thousand cubits, ingeniously reckoned by interpreting Exod. 16:29 in the light
of Num. 35:5. Luke's intention was simply to show that the ascension
took place near Jerusalem. But his use of this particular term "presupposes an amazingly intimate knowledge—for a Greek—of Jewish customs"
(Hengel, *Jesus*, p. 107). Some difficulty may be felt with the reference
of Luke 24:50 to Bethany, which is more than double a Sabbath day's
journey from Jerusalem, but if the words of the Gospel mean simply
"toward Bethany" (Gk. *pros Bethanian*), that difficulty is overcome. In any
case, it is hardly likely that Jesus would lead them into the village for
the ascension.

1:13 / **Upstairs to the room where they were staying**: The definite article (in the Greek) suggests that this was a place that should have
been known to Luke's readers. The reference may be, then, to the first
book, Luke 22:11f., to the room of the Last Supper, though a different
word is used in that passage. Traditionally this room has also been identified with that in which the church later met in the house of Mary, the
mother of John Mark, though this identification is not without problems
(see disc. on 12:12). It may also have been their place of meeting in 2:1
and the place where they met for prayer in 4:23–31.

Peter, John . . . and Judas son of James: The names of the apostles
are repeated, though they had already been given in the first volume
(Luke 6:14ff.). This may have been to show that, though all of them,
at the time of his arrest, had deserted the Master, only Judas had done
so through deliberate defection. At heart, the rest had remained loyal.
It may also have been to show that, though the separate works of each
would not be chronicled in this book, they nevertheless all took their
part in the work to which Jesus had called them. The two Lucan lists
agree, except for the omission here of Judas Iscariot, and differ only from
those of Matt. 10:2ff. and Mark 3:16ff. in having *Judas son of James* where
they have Thaddaeus (or Lebbaeus in some texts of Matthew). These

may be the same person and may be identified further with the "Judas" (not Judas Iscariot) of John 14:22.

Simon the Zealot ("the Canaanean," [which is Aramaic for "zealous"] RSV Matt. 10:4; Mark 3:18), so-called either because of his zealous temperament or because of some association with the party of the Zealots. NIV appears to have adopted the latter interpretation (cf. GNB), but we should note that precisely the same word is used by Paul of himself in 22:3 (cf. Gal. 1:14) and by James of members of the church in Jerusalem in 21:20. In neither of these cases can it be supposed that "Zealot" in the narrower sense of the party is implied.

1:14 / His brothers: Four men are described in the Gospels as the *brothers* of Jesus, namely, James, Joseph, Simon, and Judas (Matt. 13:55; Mark 6:3). Various views have been held as to the nature of their relationship with Jesus, but the most natural reading of the New Testament is that apart from the unique circumstances of Jesus' conception, they were his brothers in the usual sense of the word, i.e., the younger children of Joseph and Mary. This view is supported by the prima facie meaning of "firstborn" in Luke 2:7 and by the natural inference of Matt. 1:25 that after the birth of Jesus normal marital relations between Joseph and Mary ensued.

1:15 / A group numbering about a hundred and twenty: lit., "a crowd of names, about a hundred and twenty," where "names" may signify "persons" without distinction of sex (see H. Bietenhard, *"onoma,"* TDNT, vol. 5, p. 270), though some argue on the basis of the Syriac and Arabic versions that it means men as distinct from women. Peter's address implies that only men were present.

1:16 / Brothers: lit., "men, brothers," a rather formal mode of address indicating a sense both of the occasion and of the respect due to those present. Because this form of address recurs frequently throughout Acts (2:29, 37; 7:2; 13:15, 26, 38; 15:7, 13; 22:1; 23:1, 6; 28:17; cf. "men, Galileans," 1:11; "men, Judeans," 2:14; "men, Israelites," 2:22; 3:12; 5:35; 13:16; "men, Athenians " 17:22; "men, Ephesians," 19:35), it has been thought to reveal the hand of Luke. Even if this were so, it would be no objection to the essential historicity of any of the speeches in which it occurs.

1:17 / Shared in this ministry, lit., "received the portion of this ministry," or, perhaps, since the definite article is used, "his portion of this ministry." The word "portion" (Gk. *klēros*) means literally that which is obtained by lot. Here it is used figuratively, though it is interesting that Judas' successor was actually appointed by this means (cf. v. 26). It is also interesting that the same word is used in 1 Pet. 5:3, and in the same way, concerning an area of ministerial responsibility. Its use here, therefore, may be another echo of Peter's actual words (see disc. on v. 24).

1:22 / Beginning from John's baptism: This can be understood in a general sense (cf. GNB), and on this view, the candidate would have to have been a witness of John's ministry as well as of the ministry of Jesus. Such a requirement is consistent with the scope of the Christian message, which generally included the work of John the Baptist (cf., e.g., 10:37; 13:24f.). But some take the phrase as a reference only to John's baptism of Jesus, thus limiting the apostolic witness to the ministry of Jesus alone, which effectively began with that event. This is the less likely of the two possibilities. See disc. on 10:37.

1:26 / **He was added to the eleven apostles** to restore the number to twelve: Several writers have discussed the possibility of Essene influence in the role of the Twelve. They have been compared with 1QS 8.1: "In the council [?] of the community [where they are? or there shall be?] twelve men and three priests, perfect in all that is revealed in the Law." It has been suggested that the mention of "twelve men" is "an analogue to the college of the twelve apostles of Jesus" (B. Reicke, "The Constitution of the Church," in *The Scrolls and the New Testament*, ed. K. Stendahl, p. 151). But rather than a direct influence of Qumran on Jesus, the number in each case is better explained as derived independently from the number of Israel's tribes. See further J. A. Fitzmyer, *Studies*, p. 247, and Ehrhardt, pp. 13f., for the eschatological association of this number in both Christian and Essene circles.

At first, the term "apostle" appears to have been restricted to the Twelve (1:6, 12; 2:43; 4:35, 37; 5:2, 12, 18; 8:1), but soon it came to be applied to a wider group, of which Paul and Barnabas were the most notable members. Paul frequently refers to his apostleship in his letters (e.g., Rom. 11:13; 1 Cor. 15.9; Gal. 1:1), and 1 Cor. 9:1f. and 2 Cor. 12:12 should be noted especially for what they add to our understanding of the office. The primary qualifications of an apostle were that he had been an eyewitness of the post-resurrection appearance of Jesus (Acts 1:21; 1 Cor. 9:1) and had received a distinct call and commission from the risen Lord. The primary function of an apostle was to be a delegate of the risen Lord, going as his representative and in his authority. The idea of an authoritative representative may derive from the Jewish institution of the $\check{s}^e l\hat{u}h\hat{i}m$, the authorized messengers representing a person or group of persons (see K. H Rengstorf, "*apostolos*," *TDNT*, vol. 1, pp. 414ff.). So the apostles were the personal representatives of Christ, appointed and sent by him to preach the gospel and to found churches (Rom. 1:1; 1 Tim. 2:7; 2 Tim. 1:11). The new element here is the eschatological motive for the sending.

The authority of the apostles was confirmed by their "signs" (2 Cor. 12:12), but it was not something arbitrary or automatic that made them infallible. Paul was conscious of a distinction between his own opinion and the authoritative word of the Lord. The conflict between Peter and Paul (Gal. 2:11ff.) shows that even an apostle could act contrary to his convictions (Gal. 2:7–9; Acts 15:7ff.). The authority embodied in the apostles was one to which the apostles themselves were subject. Their authority was that of God (1 Thess. 2:13), and they themselves were subject to God (1 Cor. 4:1). It could be said that the authority of the apostles reposed in the gospel, so that even they could not with impunity preach another gospel (Gal. 1:16). In a sense, therefore, they were subject to the church, servants of Christ, administrators only of God's gifts to his people (1 Cor. 4:1; 7:23; 2 Cor. 4:5). But their role was a key one, and therefore, they are named first in the lists of ministries in 1 Cor. 12:28f. and Eph. 4:11. On the fluidity of ministries in the early church, see notes on 13:1.

§3   The Holy Spirit Comes at Pentecost (Acts 2:1–13)

The history of the early church was far more complex than Luke would have us believe. But we may still accept that it began with "a determinative Jerusalem Pentecost" that gave the church its impetus and character. The essential historicity of this event has been firmly established (see Dunn, *Jesus*, pp 135–56) To an outside observer, it might have appeared as an outburst of enthusiasm within the sect of the Nazarenes. To the believers, it was an episode of critical importance in the history of salvation (see Martin, p. 70), for it saw the fulfillment of the Father's promises in the prophecies of Isaiah 32:15 and Joel 2:28–32 (cf. 1:14f.), indicating thereby that a new age had dawned and that the kingdom of God had come (see disc. on 1:6).

2:1 / Pentecost was the second of the three great annual festivals of the Jews, Passover being the first and the Feast of Tabernacles the other (see Deut. 16:16). The greatest number of pilgrims attended the Feast of Pentecost, as that time of the year was best suited to travel (see disc. on 20:3b). This was no doubt a factor in the providential ordering of events. On this particular Pentecost—there is no certainty what year it was, though A.D. 30 is as likely a date as any—they (the believers) **were all together in one place**. By **all** we may assume that at least the hundred and twenty of 1:15 were included, but there may have been others from Galilee and elsewhere who had come up to Jerusalem for the festival (see disc. on 9:31). We are not told where the disciples were meeting. The number of people involved, especially if they now exceeded a hundred and twenty, makes it less likely that they met in a private house than in some open or public place, though it does not exclude the possibility (see notes on 1:13). On the other hand, the fact that the crowd was quickly aware of what was happening (cf. v. 6) may suggest that they were somewhere where they could be seen, such as the outer court of the temple (see disc. on 3:11; 21:27). The use of the word "house" in verse 2 does not rule this out (cf. LXX Isa. 6:1, 4; Luke 2:49), though we might have expected the temple to have been named if it were indeed their place of meeting.

2:2–3 / This much at least is certain: something happened that day to convince the disciples that the Spirit of God had come upon them—that they had been "baptized with the Holy Spirit" as Jesus had said they would be (1:5; cf. 2:17; 11:15ff.). As Luke describes it, there was **suddenly a sound like the blowing of a violent wind** (v. 2). Luke's comment that it **came from heaven** reflects his intention to describe not a natural but a supernatural event. Notice the word **like**. It was not the wind, but something for which the wind served as a symbol, namely, the divine presence and power (cf. 2 Sam. 5:24; 22:16; Job 37:10; Ps. 104:4; Ezek. 13:13; also Josephus, *Antiquities* 3.79–82; 7.71–77). Because **wind** suggests life and power, it became in both Hebrew and Greek the word for "spirit," and here the word signifies especially God's Spirit. And with the sound like wind there was also an appearance of **what seemed to be tongues of fire** (v. 3). Again, the expression **seemed to be** is important, for again the natural is used to express the supernatural. Here the Baptist's words in Matthew 3:11f. provide a clue to the meaning with their reference to Spirit, fire, and judgment. Once more God's Spirit is signified, now under the symbol of fire (cf. Exod. 3:2; 19:18; Ezek. 1:13), with the implication that he comes to purify his people (cf. Mal. 3:1ff.). One last piece of symbolism should be noticed: the appearance like fire rested upon **each of them** (v. 3). These disciples represented the whole church, and as such they all participated in the gift.

But to what extent were the sound and the appearance objective phenomena? In chapter 10, where Cornelius' experience is likened to that of the disciples in this chapter, no mention is made of sights or sounds. Because of this, there are those who argue that there was nothing seen or heard on this occasion and that Luke has presented as visible and audible what was purely an inner experience. But the fact remains that he has presented the two incidents quite differently, insisting here that there was something to be observed—**they saw** (v. 3). After a careful examination of the evidence, Dunn comes to the conclusion that "what came to them came not from the depths of their subconscious, individual or collective, but from beyond themselves, outside themselves. It was the experience of divine power unexpected in its givenness and in its accompanying features" *Jesus*, p. 148).

2:4 / But it was nonetheless also a subjective experience. Luke says as much with his expression **all of them were filled with the Holy Spirit**. To be "filled" (as distinct from being "full," see disc. on 6:3) expresses the conscious experience of the moment (see disc. on 4:8). They felt as well as saw and heard, and gave expression to their feelings by speaking **in other tongues as the Spirit enabled them**. This particular verb "to speak" (Gk. *apophthegesthai*) is peculiar to Acts in the New Testament (cf. v. 14; 26:25), but is used elsewhere in biblical Greek of the utterances of the prophets (e.g., LXX 1 Chron. 25:1; Ezek. 13:9; Mic. 5:12).

Their speaking **in other tongues** seems to mean something different from similar references elsewhere. Here, because "tongue" is used interchangeably with a word meaning "language" or "dialect" (Gk. *dialektos*, vv. 6, 8) and because what was said was apparently intelligible, we must suppose that recognized languages were spoken. But there is no reason to think that this was so on the other occasions in Acts when something like this happened (10:44ff.; 19:1ff.) and every reason to think otherwise in 1 Corinthians 12–14, where Paul's whole argument rests on the "tongues" not being understood and needing "interpretation" (not translation). It would appear, then, that in the Corinthian church and probably in Acts 10 and 19, the "tongues" were some kind of ecstatic utterance, what the NEB calls "the language of ecstasy" (1 Cor. 14:2) and Paul, on one occasion, "the language of angels" (1 Cor. 13:1), and on another, perhaps, "groans that words cannot express" (Rom. 8:26).

But is it likely that we should have two different phenomena? On the assumption that it is not, Luke has been accused of misunderstanding or reinterpreting an earlier tradition in which the "tongues" of Acts 2 were the ecstatic utterances of the other references. Either that, or the tradition came to him in a garbled form, and what really happened was that the disciples spoke in "tongues" (in the usual sense), but their hearers thought they heard the praise of God in their own languages. Dunn steers a middle course between these two explanations. He refers to the phenomena of modern Pentecostalism: "Perhaps the most strik-

ing feature of glossolalia in Pentecostalism for the present discussion is the number of claims of an 'unknown tongue' which
was actually a foreign language unknown to the speaker. . . . If
such claims can be made with such conviction in the twentieth
century, it is more readily conceivable that they were made at the
time of the first Christian Pentecost" (*Jesus*, p. 151). He then suggests that many of those present identified some of the sounds
uttered by the disciples with the languages of their homelands.
The impression that they were speaking in those languages was
heightened by the powerful spiritual impact of the disciples' ecstasy, and this is the story that came down to Luke. He, for his
part, gave it greater precision by clarifying the glossolalia into foreign languages proper and by introducing the note of universalism
(cf. v. 5). So Dunn cautiously sums up: "There is no reason to
doubt that the disciples experienced ecstatic speech on the day
of Pentecost. And there is good reason, both from the text itself
and from religious history parallels, to believe that the glossolalia
and disciples' behavior was such that many present thought they
recognized words of praise to God in other languages" (*Jesus*, p.
152).

2:5–11a / That something extraordinary had happened
soon became evident to the public at large. If the disciples had
been in their own quarters when the Spirit was given (see disc.
on v. 1), they must by now have moved into the street. They may
even have gone to the temple, "walking and jumping, and praising God" like the man in the next chapter. So, naturally, a crowd
gathered. Among them were Jews of the Diaspora (i.e., **from every
nation under heaven**, v. 5) who had made the city their home—
or at least that appears to be Luke's meaning by his choice of the
Greek verb *katoikein*. Many Jews, we know, did return from abroad
either to study (cf. 22:3) or simply to see out their days within
the walls of Jerusalem, among the latter, women especially, judging by the names found on Greek ossuaries (see disc. on 6:1).
At all events there were in the crowd people who could identify
in what language the believers were saying words of praise from
a wide range of languages. There were also some (Palestinian
Jews) who could point out to the others that the speakers were
Galileans. The condensed nature of Luke's narrative makes it
appear that the whole crowd made this observation, but it could
only have been those among them who knew the disciples or

could pick up their northern accent (cf. Matt. 26:73). That they should have commented on this is perhaps indicative of their surprise. Judeans tended to look down on Galileans.

2:11b-13 / Meanwhile, the disciples were telling in the "tongues" the great things that God had done (cf. Sir. 36:8), while those who heard them were **amazed and perplexed** (v. 12). The second, especially, of these two verbs expresses (in Greek) their utter confusion—they simply did not know what to make of such behavior (cf. 5:24; 10:17), though some did hazard the unkind suggestion that the disciples might be drunk (cf. Eph. 5:18). How true to life this all sounds and how candid Luke is in reporting it!

Additional Notes §3

2:1 / **When the day of Pentecost came**, lit. "was being filled up or fulfilled": This has been taken as a reference to the period between Passover and Pentecost, meaning that the latter was approaching but had not yet come when these events took place. The same verb is used of time elsewhere in Luke 9:51, where NIV renders, "as the time approached." However, all the circumstances point to its being the day of Pentecost itself, in which case we must understand the verb to mean that the day was already in progress ("being filled up"—the Jewish day was reckoned from the preceding sunset; see disc. on 20:7).

The name **Pentecost** is derived from the Greek word meaning "fifty," and was so called because the feast was kept on the fiftieth day (reckoning inclusively) after the day following the Passover Sabbath, i.e., on the fiftieth day from the first "Sunday" (as we would call it) after the Passover, when the first sheaf of the harvest was offered (Lev. 23:15f.). Because the time between the offering of the first sheaf and the formal completion of the harvest at Pentecost was seven weeks, Pentecost was sometimes called the Feast of Weeks (Exod. 34:22; Lev. 23:15; Deut. 16:9-12) and sometimes the Feast of the Harvest and the Day of First Fruits (Exod. 23; Num. 28:26). According to the Old Testament, Pentecost was to be proclaimed as a "holy convocation" at which every male Israelite was required to appear at the sanctuary (Lev. 23:21). Two baked loaves were to be offered, together with the sin and peace offerings (Lev. 23:17-20). Thus the people not only gave thanks to God for the harvest, but acknowledged their obligation to him under the covenant. In later years, Pentecost actually became the feast to mark the renewal of the covenant (Jubilees 6:17-22; see J. D. G. Dunn, "Pentecost," *NIDNTT*, vol. 2, p. 785) and by the second century was also a commemoration of the gift of the law at the time when the covenant was established (see notes on v. 6).

2:2-4 / What happened at this Pentecost marked the beginning of the church. There were, of course, many believers before this, but only now were they constituted as the "body of Christ." "In the full sense of the Church in vigorous life, redeemed by the cross of Christ, invigorated by the divine power, set forth on the path of work and worship, the Church certainly did not come into existence until the day of Pentecost" (L. L. Morris, *Spirit of the Living God* [London: Inter-Varsity, 1960], pp. 54f.). And what God gave that day he has never withdrawn. The Spirit that transformed the disciples and galvanized them into action remains with the church—he will "be with you forever," Jesus had promised (John 14:16; cf. Ps. 51:11). The baptism of the Spirit, therefore, has never been repeated and never needs to be. It is true that on two other occasions something similar happened (10:44-46; 19:1-6), but these are best understood, not as repetitions, but as extensions of the Pentecostal event, aimed at meeting special cases. But, though the event itself has not been repeated, it has been and still is appropriated by every believer. When we become members of the body that the Spirit brought into being at Pentecost, we take to ourselves the birthright of the body, which is the Spirit himself. When we become Christians, we participate in the baptism with the Spirit that uniquely took place on that day so long ago (cf. 2:38; 9:17; 11:17; 19:2; Rom. 8:9; 1 Cor. 12:13; Gal. 3:2; Eph. 1:13; Titus 3:5; Heb. 6:4; 1 John 3:24). Therefore, no one may ask whether the believer has been baptized with the Spirit, for the very fact of being in the body of Christ demonstrates that he or she has. There is no other way of entering the church. And since water baptism outwardly marks that entrance, it also becomes the outward sign of the believer's entry into the gift of the Spirit (see further the notes on v. 38). It may still remain, however, for the believer to become "full of the Spirit" (see disc. on 6:3), for we often "resist" the Spirit (cf. 5:3, 9; 7:51; Eph. 4:30; 1 Thess. 4:8; 5:19; Heb. 10:29) and must learn instead to trust and obey him (cf. 5:32; John 7:39; Gal. 3:1-5, 14).

All of them . . . began to speak in other tongues: For those to whom this gift is given—and it is not given to all, nor should all Christians expect to receive it (cf. 1 Cor. 12:6ff., 30; 14:5)—"tongues" are a means of "communication between the believer and God" (K. Stendahl, *Paul Among Jews and Gentiles* [London: S.C.M. Press, 1977], p. 113) and, especially, a means of giving praise, of responding emotionally to the mighty works of God. This was the case at Pentecost when, not the preaching (which was probably in Aramaic), but the praising beforehand, was expressed in "tongues." At the same time, "tongues" have an evidential value. "The purpose of the miracle [at Pentecost] . . . was not to lighten the labour of the Christian missionary, but to call attention at the first outset to the advent of the Paraclete" (H. B. Swete, *The Holy Spirit in the New Testament* [London: Macmillan, 1909], p. 74). It was, moreover, a sign of the Paraclete's work. As Kirsopp Lake observed, he would reverse the curse of Babel and let God's voice be heard again in every nation under heaven, as it had been when he gave the law (*BC*, vol. 5, pp. 114ff.). See notes on v. 6 below for the Jewish tradition to which he alludes. Later, "tongues" would provide evidence that God's Spirit was intended for Gentiles as well as for Jews (10:46; 11:15ff.) and later still would be a sign to the Ephesian "disciples" that the Holy Spirit had indeed come (see disc. on 19:2; cf. 1 Cor. 14:22 where they are thought of as a sign to unbelievers).

2:6 / **Each one heard them:** Cf. vv. 8, 11. Some light may be thrown on Luke's understanding of Pentecost by the custom, dating from at least the second century A.D., of regarding this festival as a commemoration of the giving of the law. Exodus 20:18 has it that "all the people perceived the voices" (though "voices" means "thunderings" in this context), and the rabbis interpreted this to mean that all the nations of the world heard the promulgation of the law. If this notion were current also in the first century, then Luke may have intended his readers to see the allusion. At this Pentecost, the "new law"—the proclamation of the messianic age and of the Messiah—was promulgated to the nations as the old law had been, thus breaking down "the barrier, the dividing wall of hostility" (Eph. 2:14).

2:9–11 / **Parthians, Medes and Elamites . . . Cretans and Arabs:** For many Jews, distance was no bar to their paying the half-shekel temple tax every year or even to their going themselves to the temple for one or more of the great annual festivals. Over a hundred thousand are estimated to have attended Passover in Jesus' day (see Jeremias, *Jerusalem*, p. 83).

That the Jews were widely dispersed is attested by a number of ancient writers (Josephus, *Wars* 2.345–401; Strabo, quoted by Josephus, *Antiquities* 14.110–118; Philo, *On the Embassy to Gaius* 36; cf. also Esther 3:8; 1 Macc. 15:15f.; John 7:35). It was almost literally true Jews could be found in "every nation under heaven" (v. 5), so that although Luke's list was probably intended as an actual catalog of the nationalities present that year (see B. M. Metzger, *AHG*, pp. 123ff.), it could also be regarded as representative of a great many more.

Broadly speaking, the list carries the reader from east to west, with a change of construction in the Greek sentence to mark, perhaps, the transition from the Parthian Empire to that of Rome. Thus **Parthia** itself, as the farthest east, is mentioned first, a district southeast of the Caspian Sea, then **Media**, a district west of the Caspian and south of the Zagros Mountains, and then **Elam**, the ancient name for the Plain of Khuzistan, watered by the Kerkheh River, which joins the Tigris just north of the Persian Gulf. **Mesopotamia**, the first name in the changed construction of the sentence, was a general term used to describe the whole of the Tigris-Euphrates Valley, where the spheres of influence of the two empires met. These were the lands to which first the Israelites and then the Judeans had been deported in the eighth and sixth centuries B.C. and in which many of them had chosen to stay. This was the earliest and most populated area of the Diaspora.

The inclusion of **Judea** next in the list has struck many people as odd. So much so, that several alternative readings have been proposed, though with little textual support (see Bruce, *Book*, p. 62). A number of scholars, including Bruce, believe that "we should probably think of Judea in its widest possible sense, denoting the extent of the land controlled directly and indirectly by the Judean kings David and Solomon, from the Egyptian frontier to the Euphrates" (*Book*, p. 62). This suggestion has the attraction of accounting for those countries of the eastern Mediterranean that otherwise would be unrepresented. But we should not exaggerate the difficulty of interpreting **Judea** in the ordinary sense. A distinction was made between Jerusalem and the rest of the province (see notes on 1:8), and to the original compilers it may not have seemed as incongruous as it does to us to include the neighboring Judeans among the visitors.

Mention is then made of the visitors from Asia Minor—**Pontus** in the northeast (see disc. on 18:2); **Cappadocia**, south of Pontus; **Phrygia**, west of Cappadocia, separated from it by Lycaonia (the Roman province of Galatia now cut across these lands; see notes on 13:14); and **Pamphylia** on the south coast between Cilicia (see notes on 6:9) and Lycia (see disc. on 13:13). By **Asia** is meant, as elsewhere in Acts (6:9; 16:6; 19:1, 10, 22, 26, 27; 20:4, 16, 18; 21:27; 24:18; 27:2), the Roman province of that name. It comprised the western coast of Asia Minor, including the regions of Mysia, Lydia, and Caria and many of the offshore islands (see disc. on 19:1a). There were Jews to be found in these lands by the third century B.C. (Josephus, *Antiquities* 12.119–124). A century later their number was increased (in addition, that is, to voluntary migrations) by the resettlement of two thousand Jewish families from Mesopotamia in Lydia and Phrygia (Josephus, *Antiquities* 12.145–153; see disc. on 13:14). The middle chapters of Acts (13–19) are themselves a witness to the continuing presence and importance of the Jews in Asia Minor.

They are followed in Luke's list by the Jews of **Egypt**. Both the Old Testament (e.g., Jer. 44:1) and the Elephantine Papyri of the fifth century B.C. and other archaeological materials give evidence of their early and well-established settlements in Egypt, and by the first century A.D. they are said to have numbered in that country one million (Philo, *Flaccus* 6; cf. Josephus, *Antiquities* 14.110–118; for the Jews of Alexandria see notes on 6:9). From Egypt they had penetrated westward into **Libya** (a broad term for North Africa west of Egypt), and these Jews are represented in the catalog by those who came from "the parts of Libya near Cyrene," i.e., from the district known as Cyrenaica, which lay to the east of the Syrtis Major (the Gulf of Sidra; see disc. on 27:17) and of which **Cyrene** was the chief city. Strabo mentions the presence of Jews in this city in particular (Josephus, *Antiquities* 14.110–118).

From farthest west were the Roman Jews (cf. 1:8; see disc. on 28:16). How long Jews had been there we do not know, but they are named in an expulsion order of 139 B.C. No doubt they soon returned and were joined by others. Their numbers were further increased by the many families Pompey brought to **Rome** in 62 B.C. and who received their freedom and settled down, for the most part beyond the Tiber. Though unpopular, they prospered, and estimates of their number in the first century A.D. have been put as high as seventy thousand. The Roman Jews are mentioned in Luke's list in company with other Romans who had been converted to their faith (see notes on 6:5). It is unlikely that the latter were the only Gentile converts in Jerusalem at the time, but it may have been Luke's purpose to draw special attention to their presence at the founding of the church.

Finally, in what appears to be an afterthought, he notes the presence also of Cretan and Arabian Jews. To the Greco-Roman mind, **Arabia** meant, not the whole of the Arabian peninsula, but only that part of it immediately to the east and south of Palestine where lay the kingdom of Nabatea (see disc. on 9:23–25). Their mention at the end of the list may mean that they were not present in Jerusalem in great numbers and were only remembered later when the list was checked over. On the other hand, the special mention of Cretan Jews is strikingly in accord with the statement of Philo that all the more notable islands of the Mediterranean—and he cites Crete especially—were "full of Jews" (*Embassy to Gaius*, 36).

2:13 / **They have had too much wine:** The word **wine** (*oinos*) can mean either "new wine" or "sweet wine." If the former is accepted, there is the difficulty that at Pentecost there was no new wine, strictly speaking, the earliest vintage being in August. It may be best, therefore, to accept the meaning "sweet wine." The ancients had ways of keeping wine sweet all the year round.

§4   Peter Addresses the Crowd (Acts 2:14–41)

Though not the first speech in Acts (cf. 1:16–22), this is the first to proclaim the Christ event, that is, it is the first instance of the *kerygma*. It touches on the ministry and death of Jesus, but its chief concern is to show that Jesus is the Messiah, and to this end it lays greatest emphasis on his resurrection and ascension.

As we shall see, this speech sets the pattern for much of the other preaching in Acts. From a survey of all the instances of *kerygma* in Acts, C. H. Dodd has identified six basic elements: the age of fulfillment has dawned; the fulfillment is in the person and work of Jesus, especially his death and resurrection, the latter demonstrating him to be the Christ; Christ has been exalted; the Holy Spirit in the church is the sign of Christ's present power; Christ will return; and listeners need to repent and believe. Not all these elements are present each time Christ is proclaimed, but they appear often enough to produce a definite pattern. However, the fact that this pattern can also be traced beyond Acts, for example, in Mark 1:14f. and in a number of Paul's epistles (cf., e.g., Rom. 10:8f.; 14:9f.; 1 Cor. 15:1ff.), draws the sting of the criticism that these speeches, because of their overall similarity, are the product of Luke's own inventiveness (see Dodd, *Preaching*, pp. 7ff.). And when we further observe that "most of the forms of the *kerygma* in Acts show in their language a strong Aramaic coloring, we may recognize the high probability that in these passages we are in fairly direct touch with the primitive tradition of the Jesus of history" (Dodd, *History*, p. 73).

There is no question, however, that Luke has left his own stamp on the speeches. This is only to be expected when we consider that they are merely indications of what was said, not verbatim reports (cf. v. 40). Nevertheless, we have every reason for confidence that Luke has done no more than play the part of an editor, not inventing, but faithfully retaining the gist of what was said and sometimes even the actual words of the original speakers. As for this present speech in particular, we should note the following: first, it fits very well the occasion to which it purports to belong; second, in its exposition of Scripture there survives a very primitive argument for the messiahship of Jesus in which is displayed the hermeneutical style of the rabbis (see B. Lindars, pp. 38-45, esp. p. 42; and E. E. Ellis, p. 198-208); and third, in general it "reflects an earlier stage in the development of Christian theology than the thought of the New Testament as a whole" (Neil, p. 74). On this evidence we are entitled not only to regard the speech as typical of the preaching of the church in its first years but also to credit Luke with having a reliable account of what was actually said on this occasion.

2:14 / Faced with the situation described in the previous section, **Peter stood up**—the sense is "stepped forward," indicating, perhaps, a newfound confidence—and backed by the other apostles, **addressed the crowd**. There is no need to suppose that he spoke in any other than his own mother tongue (Aramaic, cf. 21:40), though what he said was no less inspired than when he had spoken in "tongues." Luke uses the same verb as before (cf. v. 4), with its sense of a prophetic utterance. Despite their gibes, Peter addressed the crowd courteously, "Men, Judeans, and all of you who live in Jerusalem" (see notes on 1:16).

2:15-21 / The explanation of their behavior was not that they were drunk, but that the prophecy of Joel had been fulfilled. The particular passage he had in mind was Joel 2:28-32, which is given in full according to the text of the LXX, with some modifications. Thus we have **in the last days** (cf. 1 Tim. 4:1; 2 Tim. 3:1) instead of "after these things" and the insertion of **they will prophesy** in verse 18 and of **signs** in verse 19. These changes help fit the text to the context, the "signs" being intended perhaps as a reference to their speaking in tongues and the "prophesying" to what Peter was doing right then, for prophecy was as much proclamation as it was prediction (see disc. on 11:28). Dunn (*Jesus*, p. 160) sees in the eschatological thrust of these changes further evidence that Luke was using a primitive source (cf. Dodd, *Scriptures*, p. 48). B. J. Hubbard (*Perspectives*, p. 195) sees much of what follows in Acts as an exposition of this passage from Joel.

When Joel first spoke these words the land had been devastated by locusts. This was seen by the prophet as a warning, in the light of which he called on the people to repent. Repentance, he said, would be met by forgiveness; rain would fall on the land; wheat and oil would abound; and "after these things," God would pour out his Spirit, not on a few as hitherto, but on **all people** (vv. 17f.; cf. Joel 2:28f.; also Num. 11:29). This would precede **the great and glorious day of the Lord** (v. 20; cf. Joel 2:31). To Peter's mind, that day—the day of salvation—had come; hence the change in the first line to **in the last days**. Consequently, **everyone who** now called on the **name of the Lord** (Jesus, cf. v. 36; 4:12; see disc. on 1:24) would be saved. For the limitation of this promise to Israel, see the discussion on verse 39.

2:22 / With the renewed address **Men of Israel** (see disc. on 3:12 and notes on 1:16), Peter drew their attention from the signs of the last days to the Savior. He wanted them to hear about **Jesus of Nazareth** (cf. 3:6; 4:10; 6:14; 22:8; 24:5; 26:9). This was the name by which Jesus was known to them, if they knew him at all (bearing in mind that there were visitors in the crowd); and it was under this name that he had died (John 19:19). But the Jews' estimate of Jesus, evident in their hounding him to the cross, was in striking contrast with his true status, for he was demonstrably a man **accredited by God**. No one could have done the **miracles, wonders and signs** that he had unless God were with him (cf. John 3:2). Peter did not yet ascribe divine power to Jesus. He was content to speak of him as God's agent, God working **through him**. Even so, this was a bold claim to make before such an audience. Not that the miracles themselves were likely to be disputed, for they were a matter of public record—**as you yourselves know** (cf. 26:26). But there was likely to be some dispute about the source of the power. Jesus had once been accused of working miracles by the power of Satan (Mark 3:22).

2:23 / But there was more to God's purpose for Jesus than the working of miracles. It was his **set purpose** that Jesus should die. When Jesus himself had first broached this subject with the disciples, they met it with revulsion (Mark 8:31f.). To them it was unthinkable that the Messiah should die. But with new insight (see disc. on 1:2; cf. John 16:13; 1 Pet. 1:10–12) Peter now understood that Jesus had to be handed over to the Jewish authorities and by them to the Romans (the **wicked men** of this verse, that is "lawless men," Gentiles as seen through Jewish eyes). Jews and Romans alike were serving God's purpose, though they were no less answerable for what they had done—the paradox of free will and predestination that confronts us constantly in this book (cf., e.g., 3:18; 4:28; 13:27). Peter's reference to their **nailing him to the cross** may be compared with other vivid descriptions by him of the crucifixion (5:30 and 10:39), surely the language of one who had witnessed Jesus' sufferings and on whose mind they had left a lasting impression (cf. 1 Pet. 5:1).

2:24 / Thus was Jesus treated by men, **but God raised him from the dead** (see note on 4:10). The antithesis is stated with dramatic force (cf. 3:15; 4:10; 10:39). The resurrection, no less than his death, was God's plan for Jesus, for the Scripture had foretold it. **It was impossible**, therefore, **for death to keep its hold on him**. What was foretold must be fulfilled. So God freed him from **the agony of death**, the resurrection being likened here to a birth out of death—a remarkable metaphor, if indeed that is what Peter meant. The phrase "pains of death" is found in LXX Psalms 17:5 (18:5) and 114:3 (116:3), but it is possible that the Greek version has misread the Hebrew and that, instead of "pains," we should have "bonds." The unvocalized Hebrew could be read either way, though in Psalm 18:5 the parallelism clearly favors "bonds," with death and the grave personified as hunters lying in wait for their prey with nets and nooses. Similarly here, the reference to Jesus being "set free" and to death not being able to **keep its hold on him**, seem to settle the matter in favor of "bonds." It is tempting, then, to accept C. C. Torrey's suggestion that Luke (or an earlier translator) had before him an Aramaic source containing Peter's speech and that, influenced by his knowledge of LXX Psalm 17:5, he translated as "pains" what had been intended as "bonds" (pp. 28f.).

2:25–28 / With the declaration of verse 24, the speech had reached its climax. It only remained now to show that a resurrection had been foretold in Scripture, that its reference was to the Messiah, and that by fulfilling the prophecy, Jesus "was declared with power" to be the Messiah (cf. Rom. 1:4). Peter did this by reference to Psalm 16:8–11. It seems likely that these verses were an ancient testimonium used by the first Christians in support of their belief that God had raised Jesus. It is true that the text is taken from the LXX and not the Hebrew (not unnaturally, since the LXX permits a resurrection interpretation more readily than the Hebrew), but this does not necessarily mean that its use belonged only to a later, Greek-speaking church. The rabbis also interpreted Psalm 16:9 (in its Hebrew form) as a reference to resurrection. When first written, the psalm was the prayer of a godly man expressing his confidence that God would not abandon him to **the grave** (v. 27; cf. Ps. 16:10). Now whether this meant that he hoped to be spared an untimely death or, in the event of death, to be shown **the paths of life** after it, is unclear (v. 28; cf. Ps. 16:11). But Peter, following the rabbis, took the psalm in the latter sense and applied it to the preservation or restoration of the body after the grave.

2:29–31 / His exposition of the psalm is based on two assumptions: first, that David wrote it. Once this is allowed, it then becomes obvious that David did not write the psalm about himself, but about another, since his own tomb was proof positive that his body was still in the ground. (Cf. 13:36 for the same argument from Paul. On David's tomb, see Neh. 3:16, Josephus, *Antiquities* 7.392–394; 13.284–287; 16.179–187; *War* 1.61; Jerome, *Epistles* 46). But if David wrote of another, he did so as a prophet, and in the same prophetic vein (as Peter again supposes) he wrote Psalm 132:11, with its promise that God would make one of his sons king (v. 30; cf. 2 Sam. 7:12–16; 22:51; Pss. 89:3, 4, 29, 35ff.; 132:17). David, in fact, may not have written the psalm. And in any case, the singular is used in a collective sense. It was of a line of kings that the psalmist wrote and not of any one king in particular, as verse 12 clearly shows. But Peter understood it of one king, the Messiah (Gk. *christos*, v. 31; see note on 11:20 and disc. on 13:23). But if Psalm 132 spoke of the Messiah, why not others? Thus the messianic interpretation of Psalm 132:11 was carried back to Psalm 16:10, now slightly altered to meet the case (see disc. on 1:16) by reading **his body** (picked up from v. 9 of the psalm) in place of "your faithful servant" (v. 27, lit. "holy one"). The messianic reference of Psalm 16 was Peter's second assumption: it was the Christ who **was not abandoned to the grave** and whose body did not **see decay** (v. 31; cf. 13:35). Notice that the tense of the verbs has also been changed. They are now in the past (the Gk. aorist), because from Peter's standpoint they spoke of something that had already happened. There is no evidence that Psalm 16:10 (unlike 16:9) ever received a messianic interpretation in Judaism in the first century A.D. or earlier.

2:32–33 / The prophecy of Psalm 16 had been fulfilled; God had raised **this Jesus** from the dead (v. 32), as Peter and the others could affirm (lit. "Jesus, of whom we are witnesses"; see note on 4:10). Jesus was therefore shown to be the Messiah. But the story did not end there. Resurrection was followed by ascension. This is the reference of verse 33, though the dative case of the Greek should perhaps be rendered "with the right hand of God" (as NEB), not **to the right hand**, in a possible allusion (Luke's, not Peter's) to LXX Psalm 117:16 (118:16), "the right hand of the Lord has exalted me," the same verb as in this verse. But the point remains that Jesus had been exalted to a place of power and authority, marked by his receiving **from the Father the promised Holy Spirit** to give to human beings (v. 33). There may be yet another allusion to the Psalms in these words, this time to the version of Psalm 68:18 quoted by Paul (Eph. 4:8): "When he ascended on high, he . . . gave gifts to men." For Peter declared that what they now saw and heard was Jesus' gift **poured out** on his people (v. 33). Significantly, in the quotation from Joel it was God who would pour out his Spirit (v. 17), but now Jesus acted on God's behalf. He had become the divine executor.

2:34-36 / Thus Peter's proclamation was of Jesus as Lord. Confirmation of this was found in Psalm 110:1, which Jesus himself had cited (Luke 20:41-44). This psalm was first addressed to a king on his accession, expressing the importance of his role in the theocracy. But, as Jesus' use of it shows, it was by his time widely accepted as written by David of the Messiah—the **Lord** (Gk. *kyrios*) to whom the **Lord** (i.e., God; Gk. *kyrios*) addressed the invitation: **Sit at my right hand** (v. 34). And since Jesus (whom they had crucified! see note on 4:10) was the Messiah, it was he who now sat with God in the heavenly world (cf. Eph. 1:20) as both **Lord and Christ** (v. 36; see note on 11:20). In terms of the quotation, the **Lord** must be interpreted only as a title of honor, not yet as an ascription of deity, though it may not have been far from Peter's thought that this "Lord" was indeed "*the* Lord."

2:37-38 / On hearing this, **the people . . . were cut to the heart** (v. 37). Some of them may have been implicated in Jesus' death, if only by giving their tacit approval to the action taken by others; and now the sting of Peter's words took effect—"this Jesus, whom you crucified" (v. 36). They had crucified the Lord! They begged, therefore, **Brothers, what shall we do?** and were told, **Repent . . . every one of you**—literally, "Change your mind," but in biblical usage this implies a change in one's whole style of life (see disc. on 3:19; cf. 8:22; 17:30; 20:21; 26:20)—and **be baptized . . . in the name of Jesus Christ** (v. 38). Baptism was the sign of repentance and (on God's part) of the forgiveness of sins (cf. 5:31; 10:43; 13:38f.; 26:18; see disc. on 3:19) and the gift of his Spirit (see notes on 2:2ff. and disc. on 18:25 and 19:4 for the baptism of John, which only anticipated these things). The distinctions of number in the Greek verbs are significant in this connection. The call to repentance and baptism—the individual's response to God's grace—is in the singular, but the promise, **you will receive the gift of the Holy Spirit** (v. 38), is in the plural, for the Spirit is given to the community of which the individual becomes a part (see notes on v. 4). The rite of baptism was administered **in the name** of Jesus Christ (v. 38), where **in** represents the Greek preposition *epi*, "upon," and **the name** means "the person." That is to say, Jesus Christ and faith in him were the basis upon which this baptism was offered and the promise attached to it was made. This ties in with the evidence that at baptism it was the custom to make a confession of Jesus as Lord (see disc. on 11:17; 16:31; cf. 8:37; Rom. 10:9; 1 Cor. 12:3; Phil. 2:11).

2:39 / What a wonder of grace is evident here, in that the promise of the previous verse was made to the very people who not long before had invoked the blood of Jesus upon themselves and their children (Matt. 27:25). But it was also made to those whom Peter described as **far off**. It is unlikely, however, that the apostle intended to include the Gentiles in this statement. More likely it was a reference to the Jews of the Diaspora. Had he meant otherwise, we might have expected a specific mention of the Gentiles, as in 22:21. It is true there is an analogous phrase in Ephesians 2:13, 17 (cf. Isa. 57:19; also Isa. 2:2; 5:26; Zech. 6:15), where the reference is to the Gentiles, but we must not look in Peter's first public address for the wider vision that Paul later had. For Peter it was still a matter of **our God** in the narrow sense of Jewish nationalism, and even the reference in 3:26 to Jesus being sent "first" to the Jews does not necessarily imply "then to the Gentiles also" in the Pauline sense, but only the long-cherished hope that in the new age the Gentiles would flock to Mount Zion to join in the worship of God (see, e.g., Ps. 22:27; Isa. 2:2f.; 56:6–8; Zeph. 3:9f.; Zech. 14:16; Psalms of Solomon 17:33–35; Sibylline Oracles 3.702–28, 772–76). That Peter had not yet grasped the full scope of the good news is evident from chapter 10 (see esp. the disc. on 10:9ff.; cf. 5:31). The last line of verse 39 is an allusion to Joel 2:32, thus completing and complementing the earlier quotation, for none can call on the name of the Lord (as v. 21) except the Lord calls first. The initiative in salvation is always with God. Even repentance and faith are his gifts (5:31; 11:18).

2:40 / Much more was said by Peter, of which Luke has given us only the general thrust: **Save yourselves from this corrupt generation**. The **corrupt generation** were the Jews, in consequence of their rejection of Jesus. The sense of the verb in he **warned them** is to testify to the truth while protesting against false views that stood in the way of accepting it (cf. 8:25; 10:42; 18:5; 20:21, 24; 23:11; 28:23). The second verb, **he pleaded**, is in a tense (the imperfect) that implies that Peter made repeated appeals.

2:41 / The outcome was that many **accepted his message** and **were baptized**. When and where these baptisms took place Luke does not say. There may well have been some lapse of time in which further instruction was given. But effectively about three thousand people were added that day to the church. The full truth behind this statement, namely, that it was the Lord who added them, is expressed in verse 47 (cf. v. 39; 5:14; 11:24). The number is only an approximation (**about**; see disc. on 1:15), but we need not doubt that it was something of that order. Many of these people must have been familiar with Jesus, and it may only have needed what they had now seen and heard to persuade them that he was indeed the Christ (cf. John 4:35–38). Among the converts there were, no doubt, Jews of the Diaspora, some of whom may subsequently have formed the nuclei of churches in their own lands. Others may have stayed in Jerusalem to swell the ranks and strain the resources of the infant church (see disc. on vv. 44f.).

Additional Notes §4

2:15 / **These men are not drunk. . . . It's only nine in the morning!** lit., "the third hour." Wine was generally drunk by the Jews only with meat, and if they ate meat at all, it was only at the end of the day (cf. Exod. 16:8). Normally, then, they took no wine until evening. This, of course, may not have held good in every case (cf. Eccles. 10:16f.), but in this case Peter denied that they had broken with custom. His argument probably rests on nothing more than that the hour of the day was too early for drinking, though some have suggested that he may have had in mind more specifically the hour of prayer, before which pious Jews would not eat, much less drink; on festivals such as this they would avoid both food and drink until midday. The weight of evidence suggests, however, that the morning sacrifice, and consequently the morning prayer, was at sunrise (the first hour), so that Peter can hardly have been referring to it (see disc. on 3:1).

2:17–20 / **In the last days . . . before the coming of the great and glorious day of the Lord**: Time, for the Jews, was characteristically divided into two ages, this age and the age to come, and the reference in Joel is to the point of transition between them. The age to come was the age of God's kingdom (see notes on 1:3), and Peter says (as Jesus had taught) that it had indeed come. The gift of God's Spirit, like the resurrection of Jesus and much else besides in his life and work, was a sign of its coming—a token that salvation, which to the Jew had always belonged to the future, was now to be had in the present (see disc. on 5:32). But the distinction between the two ages proved not to be as clearcut as the Jews had envisioned. This age was still a present reality, and the new age was not fully come. Neither, then, was the work of salvation finished; nor could it be until the transition from this age to the next was completed at Jesus' return (cf. 3:19ff.). By citing the whole passage from Joel, Peter may in fact have been moving from Pentecost to the Parousia, with the suggestion that just as the Spirit was a sign of the new age, so was he also a pledge of its consummation (cf. 2 Cor. 1:22; 5:5; Eph. 1:14; see disc. on 1:10f.).

I will pour out my Spirit (v. 17), lit., as in the LXX, "I will pour out *of* my Spirit" (the Hebrew is simply, "I will pour out my Spirit"): The thought of the Greek may be that God's Spirit remains with him and we can only receive a part, not the whole. Or the intention may be to direct our attention to the diversity of the Spirit's gifts and operations, the whole of which we can never see (cf., e.g., 1 Cor. 12:14ff.; 1 Pet. 4:10).

Wonders in the heaven above . . . blood and fire and billows of smoke. The sun will be turned to darkness and the moon to blood (vv. 19, 20): Nature is often represented in Scripture as expressing sympathy with the acts of God (e.g., Isa. 13:10, 13; 34:4, 5), and it is difficult to know in every case how literally such statements should be taken, though for the most part they are simply a means of drawing attention to God's dealings with human beings. It is a kind of metaphor that is found in the poets of many nations.

2:22 / **Miracles, wonders and signs, which God did among you through him**: Though all three terms refer to miracles, they are by no means synonymous. The first is lit., "powers" (Gk. *dynamis*). Luke is fond of using this word of the inherent power of Jesus (10:38; cf. Luke 1:35; 4:14, 36; 5:17; 6:19; 8:46), so the plural is aptly applied to the outward manifestation of this power, whether in Christ himself, as in this reference (cf. Luke 10:13), or through his disciples (cf. 8:13; 19:11; see disc. on 1:8). The second word, **wonders** (Gk. *teras*), was that most commonly used of miracles by nonbiblical writers, meaning an abnormal occurrence portending the approach of some event of special importance. It is noteworthy that it is always found in the New Testament in conjunction with the third word in our text, **signs** (e.g., 2:43; 4:30; 5:12; 6:8; 7:36; 14:3; 15:12), as indicating that only significant portents are meant— those that point to God's presence (see Dunn, *Jesus*, p. 163). On three occasions (4:16, 22; 8:6) the term "sign" (Gk. *sēmeion*) occurs without any other accompanying word for miracle, very like the usage in John (see F. L. Cribbs, *Perspectives*, pp. 50ff.).

As you yourselves know: The criticism has sometimes been leveled at the speeches of Acts that they contain little factual material about the life of Jesus. But one would hardly expect it—in the early speeches at least. Many of the people addressed would have been familiar with the facts of Jesus' life, as evidenced by this statement. This criticism could be made with greatest effect of the later speeches, but in any case it must be kept in mind that Luke aimed to give no more than an outline of what was said on any occasion, and he could always assume that his readers had read the first volume (the Gospel) and were familiar with the details of Jesus' life. The statement of this verse, taken literally as a reference to miracles done by Jesus in Jerusalem and Judea, supports the tradition preserved in John's Gospel of such a ministry (cf. John 2:23; 3:2; 5:1–9; 7:31; 9:1–12; 11:38–47).

2:34–35 / **Psalm 110:1** is quoted several times elsewhere (Matt. 22:43ff. and parallels; 1 Cor. 15:25; Heb. 1:13; 10:13) and is often alluded to (7:55, where Jesus stands rather than sits; Mark 14:62; Rom. 8:34; Eph. 1:20, 22; Col. 3:1; Heb. 1:3; 8:1; 10:12; 12:2; 1 Pet. 3:22). C. H. Dodd's conclusion is undoubtedly justified, therefore, that "this particular verse was one of the fundamental texts of the *kerygma*, underlying almost all the various developments of it" (*According to the Scriptures*, p. 35). The argument in Acts 2:34f. is strictly parallel to the earlier argument involving the use of Psalm 16:8–11. It was assumed that the psalm was messianic. It could not have applied to David, for it said, **sit at my right hand**, and David had not ascended to heaven. But Jesus had, and so the psalm was fulfilled in him. He could properly be styled "Lord."

2:38 / **Be baptized, . . . in the name of Jesus Christ**: The name of Jesus signifies his person, his power, and in a sense, his presence. When the believers spoke the name of Jesus, they believed that he was personally involved in what was happening, working through them as his agents. Thus in his name the sick were healed (3:6, 16; 4:7, 10), miracles took place (4:30), demons were exorcised (19:13), sins forgiven (10:43). Salvation was dependent on his name (4:12); the disciples taught and preached in his name (4:17f.; 5:28, 40; 8:12; 9:15, 27, 29). People called upon his name (2:21; 9:14; 22:16), gave praise to his name (19:17), suffered for his name (5:41; 9:16; 15:26; 21:13), and were baptized in his name (2:38; 8:16; 10:48; 19:5).

That baptism was administered in the name of Jesus does not necessarily call into question the trinitarian formula of Matt. 28:19. It only means that as the church was called to be Christ's, so in mentioning the rite by which its members gained entrance his name was especially prominent. It was belief in him as the Christ that constituted the ground of their admission (cf. Matt. 16:16).

You will receive the gift of the Holy Spirit: The demands and promises of this verse may be implied, even when not expressed, in all the preaching of Acts. This is, for example, the only speech that ends with the offer of God's gift, the Holy Spirit, but it can hardly be doubted that this gift was intended for all who at any time turned away from their sins and believed.

§5 The Fellowship of the Believers (Acts 2:42–47)

It is a feature of Luke's method in these early chapters to intersperse his narrative with little cameos of life in the early church, intended, no doubt, as models for the church of his own day (see R. J. Karris, *Perspectives*, p. 117). This section contains the first of these sketches. It touches on a number of matters: the teaching, the miracles, the fellowship, and the prayers. Other such summaries are found in 4:32–35; 5:12–16; 9:31; 12:24. Compare also 5:42; 6:7, and 28:30f., which are similar in effect but tied more closely to the preceding narratives. Of the lifestyle depicted in the passage before us, C. F. D. Moule writes: "Whenever the Acts account may have been written, there is nothing here that seems incompatible with the very earliest days of the Christian Church in Jerusalem" (p. 16); Dunn remarks of the miracles in particular, "We need not doubt that it is a sound historical fact that many healings of a miraculous sort did occur in the early days of the first Christian communities and of the early Christian mission. . . . Periods of religious excitement have always produced healers and a crop of healings hailed as miraculous by those present at the time" (*Jesus*, pp. 163f.).

2:42 / Luke mentions four things that may have characterized the church's meetings especially but were not all confined to their meetings. First, they took part in **the apostles' teaching**. The Greek indicates that they gave the apostolic teaching their constant attention (the meaning of the verb itself heightened by the imperfect tense). From the use of the definite article, "the teaching," it seems that a specific body of instruction is indicated. Second, they took part in **the fellowship**. The word thus translated (Gk. *koinōnia*) means "sharing in" or "causing to share in" something or someone, and in this context we should understand the implied object to be God. God was present, and the whole community shared in his Spirit (see disc. on vv. 3, 4, 38; cf. 2 Cor. 13:13). Despite their differences and difficulties (cf. 5:1–11; 6:1–7; 11:1–18; 15:1–21), this common bond held them together. But in addition to this broader meaning of the word, *koinōnia* is employed in the New Testament in the sense of the collection and distribution of gifts, in which the fellowship of the believers found particular expression (cf. Rom. 15:26; 2 Cor. 8:4; 9:13; Heb. 13:16). In the light of the verses that follow (44, 45), we should almost certainly include this sense in the meaning of this verse. Third, they shared in **the breaking of bread**. This phrase does not compel us to understand anything more than an ordinary meal. But in view of the definite article, "the bread," a particular meal may be indicated, and what more likely than the Lord's Supper? Fourth, they prayed. The one verb governs each of the activities mentioned in this verse, so that they gave their "constant attention" to them all, and not least to "the prayers." Again, the use of the definite article suggests a particular reference (see disc. on 1:14), either to specific prayers or to times of prayer, corresponding, perhaps, to the regular Jewish prayers (see disc. on 3:1). But in any case, prayer, whether formal (cf. 3:1; 22:17; Luke 24:53) or informal (cf. 4:24), whether at fixed times or as occasion demanded, was of the very warp and woof of their lives. It was integral to the whole forward thrust of the church, and in Luke's eyes at least, the vitality of the church was a measure of the reality of their prayers (cf. v. 47; see disc. on 1:14).

2:43 / Paul's letters provide early evidence that believers possessed "gifts of healing and miraculous powers" (cf. 1 Cor. 12:9f.; Gal. 3:5), though he implies that such gifts and powers belonged especially to the apostles (cf. Rom. 15:19; 2 Cor. 12:12). The same is implied here in Luke's statement that **many wonders and miraculous signs were done by the apostles** (see notes on 2:22). They were, of course, no more than God's agents (the word "by" is literally "through"; see notes on 1:26). The power was God's (cf. 1:8), and whether by deed or by word—for the preaching was itself a kind of miracle—they were channels of his grace (see further the disc. on 5:12). Luke often draws attention to the awe engendered by the miracles (cf. 3:10; 5:5, 11, 13; 19:17). This was probably his intention here, but in the Greek there are simply two statements (albeit, closely linked): "awe came to everyone"—the reference is probably to non-believers—and "many signs and wonders came about through the apostles."

2:44–45 / **All the believers were together** (v. 44; see disc. on v. 42). One result of this was their readiness to share their belongings with one another. They made this their practice. The verb is in the imperfect and could be rendered "they kept on having all things (in) common." Spirituality for these Christians was inseparable from social responsibility (see Deut. 15:4f.; cf. Acts 6:1–6; 11:28; 20:33–35; 24:17; Luke 19:8). The whole thing appears to have been an ad hoc arrangement, but a necessary one for all that. The poverty prevailing in Palestine in the first century is almost unimaginable, but the already desperate case of most Palestinians must have been exacerbated for the church by the fact that many of its early members had abandoned their source of livelihood in Galilee and many of its subsequent converts from elsewhere had stayed on in the city, held there by the intimacy and intensity of the fellowship and the hope of the Lord's return.

2:46 / Every day the believers met in the temple. We are not told what they did there, but we may assume that they participated as fully as anyone could in the temple rites (see disc. on 3:1; cf. 21:16). They had not ceased to think of themselves as Jews, though unlike most Jews, they recognized that the Messiah had come. Beyond this, **they ate together.** The Greek could mean either "at home" or "from house to house." The latter is to be preferred and implies that a number of homes were available to them for their Christian meetings (see notes on 14:27). On these occasions they **broke bread,** which raises the question of whether we should give to this phrase the same meaning as in verse 42 or regard it now as simply a reference to ordinary meals. The additional words, "eating the food," and the absence of the definite article (cf. v. 42, "the bread") suggest the latter, though the argument is by no means conclusive. Their fellowship was marked by joy (see disc. on 3:8) and a "simplicity of heart" (NIV **sincere hearts**). This expression is found in the New Testament only here, though kindred ideas occur. It suggests both sincerity (cf., e.g., 1 Cor. 5:8; Phil. 1:10) and single-mindedness (cf. Rom. 12:8)—a condition in which deeds and thoughts alike are controlled by one motive, namely, a desire to please God. Like joy (cf. 13:52), "simplicity of heart" is a gift of the Spirit, but like much of the Spirit's work, it is grounded in the recipient's wholehearted obedience (see notes on 2:2ff.).

2:47 / Their fellowship was further characterized by their **praising God.** Such a manner of life could not help but impress others, and consequently the church enjoyed **the favor of all the**

people. There was no hint as yet of any separation of church and synagogue. In this atmosphere of acceptance and good will, the number of **those who were being saved** grew daily. The present participle, "were being saved," gives the sense that they were being maintained in a state to which they had already come. They had been saved (cf., e.g., Rom. 8:24) and were now being "shielded," as Peter puts it, "by God's power until the coming of the salvation that is ready to be revealed in the last time" (1 Pet. 1:5; cf., e.g., Rom. 8:23). The steady growth of the church was due ultimately to **the Lord** (Jesus; cf. v. 21; see notes on 11:20). There was much (essential) human activity, but it was he who **added to their number**.

Additional Notes §5

2:44 / **All the believers were together**: The phrase that Luke uses here (Gk. *epi to auto*) has a primarily local sense (it occurs again in 1:15; 2:1, 47; 4:26; 1 Cor. 11:20; 14:23)—"they all met together." But in view of the stress that Luke lays in these early chapters on the oneness of the believers, it is almost certain that he intended the deeper secondary meaning that GNB expresses in its rendering: they "continued together in close fellowship."

2:45 / **Selling their possessions and goods, they gave to anyone as he had need**: This practice is comparable with that of the Essenes, who practiced communal ownership of property (Philo, *Every Good Man is Free* 12.86; *Hypothetica* 11.10–13; 1QS 6) and maintained a communal purse administered by "stewards" (Josephus, *Antiquities* 18.18–22; cf. 1QS 6.19–20; see disc. on Acts 4:34). But whereas this was a rule with the Essenes, with the Christians it remained an individual and voluntary matter. Thus in 12:12ff. we find Mary still with her house and servants, while Barnabas' gift of the price of a field in 4:37 may have been mentioned as especially noteworthy.

2:47 / **Enjoying the favor of all the people** (cf. Luke 2:52): The word translated **favor** is that commonly rendered "grace." It is often used of finding favor in God's sight (cf. Luke 1:30; Acts 7:46), and that sense would be possible here, "having (God's) favor before all the people." But the word is also used of human goodwill, and NIV is probably right to adopt that meaning in this verse (cf. 7:10). Yet another possibility would be "giving (God) thanks before all the people."

§6 Peter Heals the Crippled Beggar (Acts 3:1–10)

Of the Roman historian Livy it has been said that though "the conflicts and issues and struggles in the story of Rome are, of course apparent to him . . . they are described in terms of individuals; there are not 'movements' or 'tendencies' or 'forces' at work unattached to men. History," for Livy, "is the record of 'doings of men' " (R. H. Barrow, p. 87). So also for Luke. He tells his story by means of paradigmatic people and events. The events of this chapter illustrate the opposition that the church soon encountered from the Jewish authorities, and the man on whom the spotlight is focused is Peter.

The narrative that begins here and runs through to 4:22 bears some similarity to the events described in 5:17–42, with their sequence of arrest, threat, defense, release, and rejoicing. This has led to speculation that these are simply different versions of the same incident, with yet another appearing later, in 12:1–9, that shares with chapter 5 a story of an escape. But in assessing a theory like this it must be remembered that the author (assuming that he was who we think he was) was not far removed from the people about whom he was writing. In other words, there were living checks and controls on all that he wrote, sufficient to give us confidence that the story was much as he has told it and that the many differences between the present narrative and those of the later chapters exist because they were, in fact, different incidents.

In these early chapters of Acts the time and sometimes the sequence of events is uncertain. This particular incident, for example, could have happened at any time up to some years after the events of the previous chapter. The assurance with which Peter acts here may well have grown out of some considerable experience of what Jesus' power could do, while his statements in the speech that follows (3:11–26) concerning the person of Jesus may well have been the fruit of long reflection (illuminated by the Holy Spirit). Again, it may well have been the case that the apostles were now under much closer scrutiny by the authorities than they had been at first, due to growing official resentment of their preaching, both concerning its subject (see disc. on 4:2) and its success. The authorities were certainly quick to step in on this occasion.

3:1 / The principal feature of the daily routine of the temple was the offering of the morning and evening sacrifices, the former soon after dawn, the latter at the ninth hour, that is, around midafternoon (Josephus, *Antiquities* 14.64–68). At these times the devout would gather in the temple for prayer and to await the priestly blessing (cf. Luke 1:8–10, 21f.; see notes on 10:9). This was the intention of the two apostles on this occasion.

3:2–3 / As they approached the temple, they were accosted and asked for a handout by **a man crippled from birth** (v. 2)—Luke may be careful to note the length of time to highlight the miracle (cf. 4:22), though such details are frequently found in his writing (cf. 9:33; 14:8; Luke 13:11). The man was regularly stationed at the **gate called Beautiful**, which is probably to be identified with the Shushan Gate in the eastern wall of the temple (see note). He may already have been at his post when the story opened, though the Greek allows the possibility that he intercepted Peter and John as he was being carried to the gate by his friends. They had performed this service every day for a long time, it would seem, so that the lame man must have begged from many people over the years. In the light of this long experience, he may have begged from the apostles, as he had many others, hoping for something, but expecting nothing, and perhaps not even noticing from whom he asked.

3:4 / The apostles did have something they could give him, but first Peter had to gain his attention. No mention is made here of the beggar's faith (but cf. v. 16), but Peter **looked straight at him** (the Greek has the sense of a fixed gaze; cf. 1:10; 3:12; 6:15; 7:55; 10:4; 11:6; 13:9; 14:9; 23:1) and commanded, **Look at us!** perhaps to see if there was faith. At Lystra a lame man was similarly healed when Paul "saw" that he believed (14:9). That man had probably heard Paul preaching, as this man may have heard Peter and the others or even Jesus himself preaching in the temple. He may have known Peter and John by sight, so that when he looked at them and knew who they were he recalled what they had said and done in this place on other occasions or what others had told him about them. So faith in Jesus may have been aroused, if not already present.

3:5–6 / The beggar had expected money, and in this he was disappointed. Peter and John had none (by chance or by choice? cf. Matt. 10:9). But they gave him hope of something better, for Peter's second word of command was this: **in the name of Jesus Christ of Nazareth, walk** (v. 6; cf. 1 Pet. 1:18, where silver and gold are contrasted with the far more precious gift of salvation, that is, healing). The premise upon which all healing in Jesus' name is sought is that the name not only expresses his person (see disc. on 2:38 and notes), but that the power implied in his being the Christ is available to all who call upon him. This is what the man must have done, and Jesus did not disappoint him. Krodel remarks that "the name of Jesus" runs "like a red thread through these two chapters" (p. 26). The phrase is found in 3:6, 16; 4:10, 18, 30.

3:7–8 / As Peter took him by the hand and helped him to his feet, his feet and ankles became strong, **he jumped to his feet, and began to walk** (v. 8). The change from the aorist, "he stood," to the imperfect, "he started walking around," illustrates the vivid detail of this narrative, which may well have come from Peter himself. Such vividness is also a characteristic of Mark's Gospel, with which Peter is traditionally linked (see disc. on 10:14; 10:34–43; 12:1–5). The picture is completed with the description of the man as **walking and jumping, and praising God**. Every word expresses joy—a note commonly heard in Luke's writing (cf. 2:43; 4:21, 24; 5:41; 8:39; 11:23; 12:14; 13:48, 52; 15:3; 16:25, 34; 19:17). There is much in this story that would have excited a doctor's interest (cf. 9:18; 13:11; see Col. 4:14).

3:9–10 / With the man prancing and praising God as he accompanied them into the temple, it is hardly surprising that the apostles soon found themselves at the center of a crowd. The people recognized the man as the beggar, so that later there was no shortage of witnesses to the genuineness of the cure. This was to prove useful (4:16). The crowd's own response to what had happened was one of surprise and amazement (cf. 8:13), touched perhaps with fear (so the Greek hints; cf. 2:43). Fear is not necessarily the same as faith, but in this case faith seems to have grown out of fear (cf. 4:4). Perhaps they remembered the words of Isaiah, "Then will the lame leap like a deer, and the mute tongue shout for joy" (Isa. 35:6; cf. Matt. 11:5).

Additional Notes §6

3:1 / **Peter and John**: Because he seems to play such a minor part in the story (cf. also 8:14ff.), it has been suggested that John's name was simply added to comply with the biblical rule that at least two witnesses are required to establish a matter (Num. 35:30; Deut. 17:6; 19:15; cf. Matt. 18:15ff.; 1 Tim. 5:19). But Luke might just as well have played down John's role, preferring to carry the history forward by focusing on Peter alone.

3:2 / **The temple gate called Beautiful** (also v. 10): The temple had numerous gates (cf. the plural in 21:30), but neither the Mishnah nor Josephus speak of a "Beautiful Gate." The discussion about which gate it was generally ranges among three possibilities: first, the Shushan Gate in the eastern wall of the temple, leading from the outside into the Court of the Gentiles. Not only was this gate close to Solomon's Colonnade but also to the market for the sale of doves and other offerings, and so a fitting site for the beggar to choose. Notice that after the healing they "went into the temple" (v. 8), where they spoke to the crowd in Solomon's Colonnade (v. 11) (see J. Finegan, *The Archaeology of the New Testament*, pp. 129f.). The second possibility is the Nicanor Gate, which led from the Court of the Gentiles into the Court of the Women. The description given of this gate by Josephus, *War* 5.201–206, marks it as especially magnificent, with doors of Corinthian bronze work (it was also called the Corinthian Gate). Since the Court of the Women was the place of assembly for the services, the beggar might well have chosen to make his stand at this point (see J. Jeremias, *"thyra,"* *TDNT*, vol. 3, p. 173, n. 5; G. Schrenk, *"hieron,"* *TDNT*, vol. 3, p. 236). From the Court of the Women a further gate led to the Court of Israel, where only Jewish men were permitted to enter. This is sometimes said to have been the Nicanor Gate rather than the other. This identification rests largely on rabbinic sources, which may be less reliable in this matter than Josephus. On balance, the Shushan Gate is the most likely, but see Hengel, *Jesus*, pp. 102ff. (cf. 3:11; 21:27).

3:6 / **Jesus Christ of Nazareth**: Luke, much more frequently than the other Evangelists, names Jesus from his hometown. In a post-resurrection setting, this reflects "an awareness of [Christ's] continuity with the Jesus of history" (C. F. D. Moule, *Studies*, p. 166).

§7 Peter Speaks to the Onlookers (Acts 3:11–26)

Luke's report of Peter's speech in Solomon's Colonnade very likely contains a genuine recollection of what was actually said on this occasion. But in any case we may regard it as typical of what was generally said at this time by Christians in their approach to Jews. The speech exhibits a more developed Christology than that of the Pentecost address—or at least the Christology is expressed in far richer terms, though these are still distinctively Jewish and of the earliest period of the church. Here Peter stresses the role of Jesus as the Suffering Servant of God and as the Prophet-like-Moses who must be obeyed. "The chosen people with whom God covenanted are challenged to acknowledge Jesus as the fulfillment of ancient prophecy and promises, and are given this chance to return to God before Messiah comes again to bring God's purposes to fruition" (Neil, p. 84).

3:11 / The outer court of the temple, the Court of the Gentiles (see note on v. 2), was surrounded by porticoes, of which the one known as **Solomon's Colonnade** lay along the eastern wall (see Josephus, *Antiquities* 15.391–420; cf. 20.219–223). In its colonnades the scribes held their schools and debates (cf. Luke 2:46; 19:47; John 10:23), and the merchants and money changers conducted their business (Luke 19:45f.; John 2:14–16). It was also a favorite meeting place of the Christians (5:12; cf. 2:46; 5:20f., 42; Luke 24:53; John 10:23), and it was here that Peter now spoke to the crowd, the beggar still clinging to him and John.

3:12–13 / Peter's first concern was to deny that the miracle had been done by any **power or godliness** in either John or himself (v. 12). There was no need, therefore, for the people to stare at them (see disc. on v. 4) as though they had done something great. What had been done was due entirely to God, whom he identified as **the God of Abraham, Isaac and Jacob, the God of our fathers** (v. 13). This description is first found in the Exodus narrative (Exod. 3:6, 15f.; 4:5; cf. Acts 7:32) but recurs from time

to time in the Old Testament on other important occasions (e.g.,
1 Kings 18:36; 1 Chron. 29:18) and may have been intended here
to underscore God's covenant faithfulness. Peter's address, **Men
of Israel** (v. 12; see note on 1:16), may have had the same purpose. The theme of God's faithfulness becomes an important one
in the latter part of the speech (vv. 25f.), but is hardly less important here, where it is the premise behind Peter's statement in
verse 13. God had **glorified his servant Jesus** precisely because
the promise of the covenants had been fulfilled in him.

Both the description of Jesus as the Servant and the reference to his being glorified are drawn from the prophecy of Isaiah
52:13–53:12, which begins: "My servant . . . will be . . . highly
exalted" (see notes 8:32f. and 11:20). Almost certainly Peter had
in mind the resurrection and ascension of Jesus and was in effect
claiming that this prophecy had been fulfilled in those events,
in which God had not only manifested his divine presence and
power, but invested Jesus with divine glory. In turn, the glorified Jesus had endowed his apostles with power to act in his
name. Thus had Jesus manifested his own presence in the healing that had just taken place (see v. 16)—all of which demonstrated
God's very different estimate of his servant than the nation had
had of him. For their part, they had **handed him over to be killed**
(lit., "Jesus, whom you handed over"; see note on 4:10), and even
when the Roman governor, Pontius Pilate, had decided to set him
free (the Greek suggests that he had given judgment to that
effect), they had still **disowned him** and brought such pressure
to bear on the governor that in the end he had acceded to their
demand (cf. John 19:15; also Acts 28:18f.).

3:14 / Thus they had sent to his death an innocent man,
one indeed who was **holy and righteous**. Taking **holy** to mean
"one devoted to the service of God," it is possible that Peter was
still thinking in terms of the Servant of Isaiah 52–53, though the
reference is generally thought to be wider than that (cf., e.g.,
2 Kings 4:9; Ps. 106:16). Its use here may even owe something
to Peter's already having employed it in quoting from Psalm 16:10
(2:27, "your Holy One"). At all events, whatever its derivation,
it was by now a recognized description of Jesus by the church
(cf. 4:27; John 6:69; 1 John 2:20; Rev. 3:7; also Mark 1:24; Luke 4:34).

As for the second epithet, "righteous," it can hardly be
doubted that it was inspired by the prophecy of Isaiah, for there

the Servant is called God's righteous Servant (Isa. 53:11; cf. Isa. 11:5; 42:6; Jer. 23:5; 33:15; Zech. 9:9; Enoch 38:2; 46:3; 53:6). The title is found again on Stephen's lips in Acts 7:52, and in 22:14 is used by Ananias. Here was another recognized description of Jesus (cf. 1 Pet. 3:18; 1 John 2:1; see note on 11:20, also R. F. Zehnle, p. 52, who thinks that the title "holy and righteous" was "a messianic epithet of the prophet like Moses").

But for all Jesus' evident qualities as expressed in these titles, the fact remained that the nation as a whole had **disowned** him—the same word as in verse 13 but now more highly charged. Against all the evidence that Jesus was "holy and righteous" they had deemed Pilate to have done them a favor by having him killed and a murderer set free in his place.

3:15 / The enormity of what they had done was driven home: **You killed the author of life**. The word **author** represents a Greek word whose range of meaning includes "leader," "founder," and "author" (cf. 5:31; Heb. 2:10; 12:2), the latter especially in the sense of one from whom anything good or bad in which others share first proceeds. This may have been the meaning intended by Peter, for in this very place Jesus had proclaimed himself as the giver of life (John 10:28; cf. John 1:4). On the other hand, it could be as well argued that the sense intended by Peter was "leader." With the resurrection in mind, his thought may have been of Jesus as the first of many who would follow in being raised from the dead (see disc. on 4:2; cf. 1 Cor. 15:20). It was certainly of the resurrection that Peter went on to speak. For over against the sorry story of the nation's rejection of Jesus, God had **raised him from the dead**. The apostles were **witnesses of this**. The Greek runs, "[Jesus] whom God raised, of whom we are witnesses" (see notes on 4:10), making it clear that their brief included more than the resurrection—they were his witnesses in the broadest sense of the term (cf. 1:8, 22; 10:39)—though, of course, the resurrection was the theme to which they constantly returned.

3:16 / Here then was the explanation of what had happened to the lame man. God had glorified his Servant by raising him to the place of ultimate power, and by the exercise of that power he had healed the man. Peter asserted this with considerable emphasis. Twice the "name" is mentioned with reference

to Jesus (see disc. on v. 6), and once Jesus is actually named, so
that three times in this verse it is stated that he was the source
of the healing. Emphasis is also given to the means whereby it
was brought home to the man. **By faith** (the Greek has the sense,
"on the grounds of faith") **in the name of Jesus, this man . . .
was made strong**. Here Jesus is said to have been the object of
saving faith. But the faith itself was awakened "through Jesus"
(so the Greek; cf. 1 Pet. 1:21), that is, through his being preached
by the apostles. From first to last, then, Jesus was truly the author
of life for this man.

3:17 / The mood of the speech changes in the second half
from reproof to conciliation, marked by the change of address.
Peter now spoke to the crowd as his **brothers**. What they had done
to Jesus, he said, they had done in ignorance. This could even
be said of their leaders (cf. Matt. 22:29; John 5:39). Behind this
concession there probably lies the ancient distinction between sins
done "with a high hand" and sins done unwittingly (cf. Num.
15:27–31). In the latter event, as in the present case, though guilt
remained, there was room for mercy (cf. 13:27; Luke 23:24; John
8:19; 1 Cor. 2:8; 1 Tim. 1:13).

3:18 / There was the added factor that Jesus' death had
been determined by God—the paradox once again of human responsibility for predetermined events (see disc. on 2:23). That it
had been predetermined was reflected in the Scriptures, the whole
thrust of which, according to Peter, was that the **Christ would
suffer** (see note on 11:20). A difficulty arises here in that the
theme of a suffering Messiah, far from being found in **all the
prophets**, is discernible in very few. In view of this, we should
probably understand **the prophets** collectively, so that what any
one of them said is attributed to them all. And in any case, in
a broad sense, they did all anticipate the messianic redemption,
though they may not have known it or the means whereby it
would be accomplished (cf. 1 Pet. 1:11). And now, what God had
foretold through the prophets, he had **fulfilled** in the events outlined in this speech.

3:19-20 / These things, therefore, constituted Good News.
Peter did not explicitly make the connection, but he clearly implied that because of what Jesus had done God would "wipe
away" sins—not only those relating directly to the death of Jesus,

but all sins—if only the sinners would repent and **turn to God**. This phrase throws into relief what is meant by repentance (see disc. on 2:38): it is not simply a change of heart, but such a change as enthrones God in the heart. Thus repentance and faith become almost synonymous (cf. 9:35; 11:21; 14:15; 15:19; 26:18, 20; 28:27). The promise that God will forgive sins is expressed by means of a striking figure: "to wipe out"—all trace of sin is removed. When God forgives, he forgets. Moreover, repentance opens the way to all the blessings of the kingdom of God, whether present or future (see notes on 1:3 and 2:17). Most commentators agree that the **times of refreshing** refer to the future and to Jesus' return (but cf. Matt. 11:28; see disc. on 1:10f.). In this connection, however, the verse has sometimes been understood in the sense that the time of Jesus' return is determined by the response that people make to the gospel ("Repent, so that he may send . . . "). But this cannot be. The time of his return is already fixed, and nothing can change it. **Times . . . from the Lord** is literally "from the face of the Lord" (cf. 5:41; 7:45). They are represented as present before God in the sense that he has unalterably decreed and determined them (cf. 1:7; see also the disc. on v. 21). That we do not know the time is our reason for preaching the gospel, not that by preaching it we can hasten the time. But this aside, the point remains that to share the blessings of his coming again we must first turn to God. The description of Jesus in this verse as the **Christ who has been appointed for you** should not be taken to mean that this appointment had only been made subsequent to the ascension and that he had not been recognized as the Messiah at his first coming. All the evidence suggests that he had been and that he was conscious himself of being called to that role from as early as his baptism. On the verb "to appoint" or "to choose," see discussion on 22:14.

3:21 / It was true that Jesus' messiahship was not yet acclaimed outside the church and would not be until he came again. Meanwhile, **he must remain in heaven** (on **must**, see disc. on 1:16), not in retirement, but ruling the church and the world **until the time comes** (lit., "times"; the plural may be intended to convey the idea that it is still a long way off; cf. v. 20) **for God to restore all things**. There is an important sense in which the renewal of all things has already begun with the coming of Jesus— or even earlier, with the coming of John the Baptist (cf. Mal. 4:5f.;

Matt. 11:14; 17:11). But the thought here is of the consummation of the kingdom on Jesus' return (see note on 1:3). This had been announced by God long ago **through his holy prophets** (cf. v. 18; Isa. 34:4; 51:6; 65:17; etc.).

3:22 / The fulfillment of Scripture remained Peter's theme, with a reference now to Deuteronomy 18:15–19. The quotation from the LXX is not an exact one (Bruce, *Acts*, p. 113, thinks it is a conflation of several verses), but nothing hangs on the differences. For Luke, as for Peter himself, a general reference to the passage was probably all that was intended. The text comes from a context in which Moses was warning against the use of divination as a means of ascertaining God's will. "God has not permitted you to do so," he said, but "will raise up for you a prophet." The original sense was that he would send them a prophet from time to time as occasion demanded, but the use of the singular, **a prophet**, led to the view that one prophet in particular was intended, a second Moses, who would appear at the end of the age, either as the Messiah or as some other eschatological figure (see, e.g., John 1:21, 25; 6:14; 7:52 mg.; 1QS 9.10f.; 4QTLevi 5–7; and M. Black, *Scrolls*, p. 61; see also notes on 11:20). The Samaritans, among a number of other groups, had inherited this tradition, and the Prophet-like-Moses, under the name of Taheb, "the Returning One," was the dominant figure of their eschatology, where, significantly, he was seen as the "Restorer," who would bring people back to true religion (cf. John 4:25; see J. MacDonald, p. 443). Precisely this association of ideas seems to have taken Peter from talking about the time "for God to restore everything" (v. 21) to quoting from Deuteronomy 18:15–19 (cf. 7:37).

3:23 / The reference to Deuteronomy served a dual purpose. First, it helped to set forward the messiahship of Jesus under another title (Peter evidently interpreted the Prophet as the Messiah). Second, it helped to bring the speech to its point of appeal, for the prophecy embodies a warning (expressed here, it appears, with the help of language borrowed from Lev. 23:29, though similar language is found in a number of passages; cf. Gen. 17:14; Exod. 12:15, 19; Lev. 17:4, 9; Num. 15:30): **Anyone who does not listen to him will be completely cut off from among his people**. The warning is probably against willful disobedience. Such a warning is never out of place in Christian preaching, but always it belongs, as here, in a context of tender concern (cf. "Now, brothers" v. 17).

3:24 / In the Greek, this verse is closely linked with verses 22–24: "For Moses said, 'The Lord your God will raise up for you a prophet like me. . . . Indeed, all the prophets from Samuel on, . . . have foretold these days.' " The theme of punishment, however, has been left behind, and Peter has returned to the thought of the renewal of all things, speaking now of its beginning—**these** [present] **days**—rather than of its completion at Jesus' return. Samuel may have been singled out for either of two possible reasons. There is found in the book bearing his name the fundamental prophecy concerning the offspring of David (2 Sam. 7:12), and Peter may have wished by implication to include "Son of David" in his description of Jesus. But Samuel was also regarded as the founder of the prophetic schools and the pattern of all later prophecy (cf. Heb. 11:32) so that **all the prophets from Samuel on** may mean nothing more than "all prophecy" (cf. "all the prophets" vv. 18, 21). At all events, what had been prophesied had now taken place (cf. Matt. 13:16f.; Eph. 3:9f.).

3:25 / As Peter saw it, the ultimate concern of all prophecy was well expressed by God's promise to Abraham: **Through your offspring all peoples on earth will be blessed** (Gen. 22:18; cf. Gen. 12:3; 18:18; 26:4). Our text differs from the LXX in that the latter has "nations," the word often translated "Gentiles," whereas the Greek reads "families" (*patriai*; NIV **peoples**). The change may be deliberate, either by Luke or his source, to avoid the impression that Peter was already open to the thought of receiving Gentiles freely into the church. But in LXX Psalm 21:28 (22:27) and 1 Chronicles 16:28 we find the phrase "families of nations," which suggests that the two words could be used of the same people and that the one has been loosely used of the other in the passage before us. In any case, it is difficult to avoid the conclusion that Peter did mean to include the Gentiles, though certainly only in a qualified sense, by his reference in the following verse. NIV's translation of the present verse probably gives the sense of the original, that it would be through Abraham's descendants, that is, through the nation, that "all the people on earth would be blessed." But the Hebrew, followed by the LXX, has only the singular, "descendant" (lit., "seed"), and this (as in the case of Deut.

18:15-19, see disc. v. 22) led to its being understood as one descendant in particular, the Messiah. In this case, however, the interpretation was peculiarly Christian. There is no evidence that either Genesis 22:18 or any of the other similar passages ever received a messianic interpretation in pre-Christian Judaism. Paul applied the passage in this sense in Galatians 3:8, and almost certainly it was in this sense that Peter used it here. To the beneficiaries of the covenant, therefore, he could announce that its promise had been fulfilled to them in Jesus. The Greek lays some stress on the pronoun **you**, as though he is saying, "You of all people, considering your privileged position, ought to welcome him."

3:26 / This emphasis on their privilege under the covenant brings the speech to a close: **When God raised up his servant, he sent him first to you**. "Raised up" accurately translates the Greek, only the reference here is not to the resurrection but to the incarnation, in the sense of bringing someone onto the stage of history (cf. GNB's "chose"). The same expression is used of the Prophet in verse 22. The point here is that God chose and sent him to the Jews first. Again, the **you** is emphatic: "To you, of all people." This statement is in line with Jesus' own insistence on restricting his ministry to the Jews (Matt. 15:24), since it was only right that the promise should be fulfilled to them first (cf. 13:46; Rom. 1:16; 2:10). But this did not mean that he cared any less for the Gentiles (cf., e.g., Matt. 28:19; John 10:16; 17:20; Acts 1:8). We may suppose, therefore, that when Peter spoke of his being sent to the Jews first, it was with something at least of the spirit of Jesus, so that he might have added, "and to the Gentiles also," if only in the sense that they must become Jews in order to share in the blessing (see disc. on 2:39; 10:10ff.). What this blessing was has already been stated (vv. 20, 21, 24), but by his use of the present participle, "blessing you," Luke may have included to express the additional truth that that blessing continues to be offered. The participle is qualified by the phrase "in turning away each of you from your wicked ways," which NIV has correctly taken as instrumental. The turning away (effected by God, see disc. on 5:31) is the means by which the blessing is entered into. We should notice further that the appeal is to the individual— **each of you**—and is expressed in terms of "turning away" from wickedness, whereas earlier (v. 19) it was seen as a "turning to"

God. True repentance entails both and is the only appropriate response on the part of those favored by hearing the gospel.

Additional Notes §7

3:13 / **His servant Jesus**: No other Old Testament passage has influenced the New Testament more than the so-called Servant Songs of Isaiah (42:1ff.; 49:1-3, 5, 8; 50:4-9; and esp. 52:13-53:12). Apart from the formal quotations (Matt. 8:17; 12:18-21; Luke 22:37; John 12:38; Acts 8:32f.; Rom. 10:16; 15:21), there is a clear allusion to Isa. 53:10-12 in Mark 10:45 and 14:24. Mark 9:12 probably echoes Isa. 53:3, and other possible allusions have been found in Matt. 3:15 (cf. Isa. 53:11) and Luke 11:22 (cf. Isa. 53:12) and in the use of "to be delivered up" in Mark 9:31; 10:33; 14:21; etc., including Acts 3:13 (cf. Isa. 53:12). The voice at Jesus' baptism outlined his ministry in terms of Isa. 42:1. The actual title "Servant" is confined to this speech in Acts (3:13, 26) and to the prayer of the church in Acts 4:27, 30, but the influence of the Servant figure is clear in Rom. 4:25; 5:19; 8:3f., 32-34; 1 Cor. 15:3; 2 Cor. 5:21; Heb. 9:28; and 1 Pet. 2:21-25; 3:18. J. Jeremias concludes that "there is no area of the primitive Christian life of faith which was not touched and stamped by the *Ebed* (servant) Christology" ("*pais theou*," *TDNT*, vol. 5, p. 712). It belongs, he says, "to the most primitive age of the Christian community" (p. 709) and indeed must be traced back to Jesus himself (pp. 712ff.). See further the notes on 8:32f.

Before Pilate: The Greek (lit. "at Pilate's face") can mean simply "before," "in the presence of," someone. But sometimes it has a more hostile sense, denoting a face-to-face confrontation (cf. 25:16; Gal. 2:11). So perhaps here. The Jews met Pilate's proposal to set Jesus free with a point-blank refusal.

3:14 / **A murderer**: i.e., Barabbas, a bandit (John 18:40) who had committed murder in a political uprising (Mark 15:7; Luke 23:18f.). The Greek has "a man, a murderer," in accordance with the idiom in which "a man" is joined with another noun signifying a discreditable occupation. The expression is stronger than if the word **murderer** were simply used on its own. Thus the contrast between Barabbas and the author of life is more starkly drawn.

3:16 / NIV has made good sense out of the contorted Greek of this verse. The following is a literal translation by Hanson, p 74: "And at the faith of his name this man, whom you see and know, his name has made strong, and the faith which is through him has given him this wholeness in the presence of you all." A number of suggestions have been made to account for the difficulty of this sentence: first, that an Aramaic phrase has been misunderstood; second, that the second mention of "his name" is a later addition—without it, God would naturally be understood as the subject of the sentence and this makes good sense—third, that Luke made several attempts at drafting the sentence and forgot to tidy it up in the final editing, so that his various attempts are all muddled up in the present text.

3:18 / **His Christ:** the phrase is found in Psalm 2:2, and that verse is quoted in Acts 4:26. Peter may have had the psalm in mind here. The phrase "the Christ of God" indicates the relationship of "belongingness" that Christ has toward God, which is perhaps a mark of the early Christology of these chapters.

3:21 / **Until the time** (Gk. "times"; see earlier disc.) **comes for God to restore everything:** This restoration was thought of by most Jews in political terms—the restoration of national independence and the gathering of the tribes (see disc. on 1:6; 26:7). Jesus, on the other hand, had spoken of it in moral and spiritual terms. As for Peter, he probably stood somewhere between, sharing Jesus' spiritual emphasis but restricting the hope to Israel alone (see disc. on 2:39; 3:26), thus confirming "the impression that we are faced here with an address of a very early origin" (Ehrhardt, p. 19; cf. Dunn, *Jesus*, p. 160).

§8   Peter and John Before the Sanhedrin (Acts 4:1–22)

4:1 / It would appear that John as well as Peter spoke to the crowd—the Greek has simply, "as they were speaking"—and that they were still speaking when the authorities intervened, though they had evidently said enough for an effective presentation of the gospel (cf. v. 4). **The captain of temple guard**, that is, "the chief officer" (cf. 5:24, 26; RSV Neh. 11:11; Jer. 20:1; 2 Macc. 3:3; Josephus, *Antiquities* 20.125–133; *War* 6.288–309), was not only a priest, but second only in dignity to the high priest himself. To him belonged the general supervision of the temple worship and personnel. Under him were other officers (cf. Luke 22:4, 52), each in charge of a corps of temple police and charged with the responsibility of patrolling the temple, guarding its gates and its treasures. With the chief officer were **the priests**, probably those on duty for the evening sacrifice, whose service may have been disturbed by the throng that had gathered about the apostles, and some **Sadducees**, representing the temple hierarchy, perhaps no less angry at the disturbance than were the ordinary priests but angry for other reasons as well. The verb used to describe their "coming up to" the apostles is commonly used of coming suddenly and sometimes of coming with hostile intent (Gk. *ephistanai*). Both senses probably apply in this case.

The Sadducees were one of several sects within the Judaism of that day. Their number was small. For the most part they comprised the high priestly families (see disc. on v. 6) and the "elders," heads of ancient families whose tradition of leadership went back a long way in Israelite history. The Sadducees represented an aristocracy that seems to have been haughty and exclusive. Their power was declining, but as long as the office of high priest was in their hands (as it was throughout this period) and with it the administration of the temple, they were still a force to be reckoned with. The party died out after the destruction of the temple in A.D. 70. In politics they were pragmatic conservatives. They

found it expedient to keep on good terms with the Romans. Thus
when Jesus appeared to them as a revolutionary figure whose
movement would bring reprisals from Rome, their hostility toward
him was aroused (John 11:48). It was further inflamed by his inter-
ference in the temple (Luke 19:45–48), so that in the end it was
the Sadducees who brought about his death. And when his movement survived his death, it was they who remained its most persistent opponents (see disc. on 23:9), political considerations being
still to the fore—they wanted nothing to disturb the status quo.

4:2–3 / But though this may have been the chief factor
in their opposition to Jesus' followers, it was not the only one.
Their enmity stemmed also from their religious conservatism.
Unlike the Pharisees, who gave considerable weight to the "oral
law"—the large body of tradition and interpretation that had
grown up around the Scriptures—the Sadducees held that only
the written law had permanent validity, and even then their interest was largely confined to the precepts relating to the cultus
and the priesthood. In applying the law they held strictly to the
literal interpretation, and on this basis repudiated many of the
doctrines held by the Pharisees, including the expectation of a
general resurrection of the dead (cf. 23:8; Luke 20:27; Josephus
Antiquities 18.16–17). But the difference between the Sadducees
and the Pharisees went deeper than matters of interpretation.
Theirs was, in a sense, a class warfare, waged over the very right
to teach and interpret the Scriptures. The Pharisaic scribes, who,
for the most part, were not priests, were contending for what had
always been a priestly prerogative, whereas the Sadducees, for
their part, saw themselves as the guardians of this ancient right.
It was vexing for the Sadducees, therefore, to find the followers
of Jesus—"unschooled, ordinary men" (v. 13)—also claiming the
right to interpret the Scriptures and doing so both in the temple
and in support of a doctrine that the temple hierarchy denied.
For Peter and John were teaching **in Jesus the resurrection of the
dead** (v. 2).

Like the Pharisees, the Christians looked for a general resurrection (of the good; see disc. on 24:15), but unlike them they
grounded their expectation "in Jesus," because his resurrection
was the pledge that others would also rise (cf. 1 Cor. 15:21f.). This
particular teaching is not found explicitly in the speech of 3:12–
26, though we need not doubt for that reason that it was included

in what they said. Luke's intention was only to provide us with
the main thrust of the speech, which had to do with Jesus' messiahship. At all events, it was plain to the Sadducees that the doctrine of the general resurrection was being taught on the basis
of the (alleged, they would say) resurrection of Jesus, and they
were determined to nip this teaching in the bud. On the pretext
of a breach of the peace they had the apostles arrested, and **because it was evening** (v. 3), held them over for trial the next day.
It is not clear whether the beggar was also arrested, though he
was certainly present in court when the case was heard.

4:4 / Two results had followed from the apostles' preaching: the hostility of the authorities was aroused, and **many who
heard the message believed**. To this Luke adds the comment **and
the number of men grew to** (lit., "became") **about five thousand**.
In saying this, he uses a word that usually denotes **men** as distinct from women, and presumably this is his meaning here.
However, probably he means not that five thousand males were
added that day but that the converts on this occasion, who may
also have included women, brought the total number of men
among the believers to about five thousand. Again, the figure is
not an exact one (cf. 1:15; 2:41).

4:5 / Something of the strength of the forces gathered
against them can be gauged from this verse and the following
one. The three orders mentioned here are apparently those of the
Sanhedrin. Under the Romans, this supreme council of the Jews
possessed considerable independence of jurisdiction, both civil
and criminal. It could order arrests by its own officers, as in this
case (cf. 9:1f.; Matt. 26:47), and was empowered to dispose of
cases that did not involve capital punishment. Capital cases required the confirmation of the Roman procurator (cf. John 18:31),
which was generally given. The Sanhedrin comprised, first, the
chief priests, probably indicated here as **the rulers** (cf. v. 23), including the ruling high priest, other high priests who had lost
office, and other members of the families from which they were
drawn; second, the **elders**, tribal and family heads (see disc. on
v. 1); and third, the **teachers of the law**, that is, the scribes or legal
experts (cf. 23:6; Josephus, *War* 2.411–416; *Life* 189–198; *Against
Apion* 2.184–187). The Sanhedrin numbered seventy-one in all,
including the high priest who presided, with both Sadducees and

Pharisees represented, the latter among the scribes, the former by the priests and the elders. The Sadducees were in the majority, but were often compelled for fear of the people to accede to Pharisaic opinion (Josephus, *Antiquities* 18.16–17; cf. Acts 5:34ff.), for the Pharisees, despite their own exclusiveness, were remarkably popular (see Jeremias, *Jerusalem*, p. 266).

If this verse does not describe a full meeting of the Sanhedrin, which may have been difficult to arrange at short notice, it implies at least that a representative body of council members met the next day **in Jerusalem**. The city was always their meeting place, but Luke has probably added this note for the benefit of his Gentile readers. But where in the city did they meet? According to Josephus, the council chamber was at the eastern end of the first, that is, the oldest, wall, immediately to the west of the temple area and between it and the Xystus, a large paved area farther still to the west (*War* 5.142–155). But the Mishnah has it that the council met in a room within the temple itself known as the Gazith, "the Chamber of Hewn Stones" (m. *Middoth* 5.4). Josephus is the better authority, though the Mishnah may still be right in calling the hall the Gazith, a possible reference to Xystus.

4:6 / This particular meeting included **Annas the high priest**, who had been high priest in the years A.D. 6–14 but had been removed from office by the Roman procurator. Like other "retired" high priests, he retained not only the title but also many of the rights and obligations of the office. The difficulty here is that the title is given to Annas alone, and this seems to suggest that he was also regarded as the president of the Sanhedrin, whereas it was usually the ruling high priest who presided (cf. 5:17; 7:1; 9:1; 22:5; 23:2, 4; 24:1). But as the head of **the high priest's family**, Annas may have retained the presidency though he had lost the office of high priest. Caiaphas, the present high priest, was his son-in-law. The **John** of this verse may be "Jonathan" (the reading of the Western text), one of Annas' five sons who succeeded Caiaphas in A.D. 36; **Alexander** is otherwise unknown to us. Present also were **the other men of the high priest's family**. This could refer simply to the family of Annas or, more generally, to all who belonged to the small group of families from which the high priests were chosen. Among them would be those who held permanent office in the temple administration, including "the captain of the temple guard" (v. 1), the temple overseer, and the treasurers (see Jeremias, *Jerusalem*, p. 179). It is evident, then, that whoever else was present, the Sadducees were out in force. This was only to be expected. It was, after all, their quarrel with the apostles. The apostle John, who was an acquaintance of the high priest (John 18:15), would later have been able to furnish these names to an interested church.

4:7-10 / According to the Mishnah, the Sanhedrin was arranged in a semicircle so that the members might see one another (m. *Sanhedrin* 4.3). This arrangement may be reflected in this passage, where it is said that they made Peter and John "stand in the middle" (v. 7, so the Greek), though the expression can be used in the more general sense of "standing in front" (cf. 14:6; Mark 3:3; John 8:3). During the investigation the councilors would sit (cf. 6:15; 23:3), while the accused, the witnesses, and those speaking stood (cf. 5:27, 34; 6:13; 23:9; Mark 14:57, 60). For most prisoners it was a daunting experience to stand before the council (see Josephus, *Antiquities* 14.168-176), but not for these two apparently. Nuances of speech are not easy to catch in the written word, but in verse 9, for example, in Peter's words **if we are being called to account today for an act of kindness shown to a cripple** we seem to hear the tones of indignation, perhaps even of sarcasm, but certainly not of a man overawed by the dignity of the council. Luke attributes this confidence (explicitly in Peter's case, by implication in John's) to their being filled with the Holy Spirit. They had become "different people" (cf. 1 Sam. 10:6). To say that they were "filled" does not call into question the permanence of the gift of the Spirit at Pentecost. The Spirit remains with his people, as Luke well understood. But there are moments when they are more aware of his presence (cf. 2:4; 4:31; 13:9; Luke 12:11f.; 21:14f.), and such a moment was this, as the apostles prepared to make an answer for the hope that was in them (cf. 1 Pet. 3:15). Strangely, they were not questioned about their preaching of the resurrection, for which they had been arrested, but about the healing that had preceded it (see further the disc. on v. 14). The two things were connected, of course, and it could, on the one hand, be said that the Sanhedrin was simply starting at the beginning. On the other hand, they may not have wished to discuss the resurrection of Jesus, having found already that they could not disprove it.

The address **rulers and elders of the people** (v. 8) again suggests that the apostles especially had to deal with the Sadducees (see disc. on v. 5). Peter began by pointing out that they had done **an act of kindness . . . to a cripple** (v. 9). Surely this was no ground for complaint. Twice in these verses the demonstrative pronoun **this** is used of the man, as though Peter were actually pointing to him as he spoke. Behind the phrase **he was healed** is the same Greek word that is used in verse 12 with the wider meaning "to save." The line between physical and spiritual well-being is always a fine one in biblical thought (cf. Mark 10:52; Luke 7:50). As for the source of the healing, it was by **the name of Jesus Christ of Nazareth** (see note on 2:38). This Jesus, these very council members (**you**) had sent to his death, but God has **raised** him **from the dead** (v. 10).

4:11 / Already the speech had become another declaration of Jesus' messiahship—he is the Christ (v. 10)—and this theme was maintained as Peter quoted Psalm 118:22. Originally **the stone** was intended to represent Israel or Israel's king and **the builders** who rejected the stone equalled the heathen, the builders of the empires of this world. Or perhaps "the builders" was used initially of those in Israel who despised some small beginnings of a new era. At all events, the reference came to be understood of the Messiah, perhaps by the Jews (cf. Luke 19:38 to Ps. 118:26, though rabbinic literature offers no instance of a messianic interpretation of v. 22), certainly by the Christians, who saw in "the stone" a reference to Jesus and in "the builders" these council members and their kind (see E. E. Ellis, pp. 205ff.). Among a number of changes from the LXX in the text as cited here, the addition of **you** drives home the application, whereas the substitution of "despised" for a word that means simply "to reject" (GNB; NIV **rejected** [Gk. *ho exouthenētheis*; LXX *exoudenōsin*]) underscores the accusation. The **stone** on which these **builders** had poured their contempt had turned out to be the **capstone** of the building, literally, the "head of the corner"—perhaps not so much the stone at the top, as NIV suggests, but the stone at the base of the corner, uniting the two walls that met at that point and took their line from it (cf. Eph. 2:20).

4:12 / The Christian use of Psalm 118:22 had been suggested by Jesus himself, who had quoted it in answer to much the same question as that put to the apostles on this occasion (v. 7; cf. Luke 20: 1–18). In Jesus' case, he had gone on to speak

in terms of Isaiah 8:14f. and Daniel 2:35, of the stone as destroy-
ing those who rejected it. Here Peter points to the other side of
that coin by presenting the stone as the source of salvation. It
is worth noticing that in 1 Peter 2:6f. he mentions both sides (cf.
also Rom. 9:33; Eph. 2:20) and the connecting link in his thought
there, as perhaps here between verses 11 and 12, is Isaiah 28:16,
which appears to have been interpreted of the Messiah in the Aramaic versions of the Old Testament, or targums. Peter was thinking now, not simply of the miracle of the lame man, but of what
that miracle signified—generally, the whole salvation of humanity, to which "the name" was as essential as it had been in this
particular case of healing (see note on 2:38 for "the name"). In
Jewish thought the Messiah was never essential to the kingdom,
which could be spoken of as coming either with or without him.
But the Christians had learned that their Messiah was indispensable. One preposition is used twice in this verse (Gk. *en*, translated variously "through" and "by" but most characteristically
meaning "in"). It gives the sense that Christ is both the agent and,
as it were, the location of our salvation; he brought it about and
only in him can we find it (cf. John 14:6; 1 Tim. 2:5f.). The use
of the word "must" (see disc. on 1:16), together with the statement
that God has **given** this name, reminds us that this is his appointed way of salvation. There is no other way. For the Christian
message as the announcement of salvation (see 13:26, 47; 16:17).

4:13 / Again it would appear that John spoke as well as
Peter and with the same confidence. The word translated **courage** means to speak holding nothing back. It was a gift for which
they prayed ("boldness," vv. 29, 31) and a feature of their preaching (cf. 9:27f.; 13:46; 14:3; 18:26; 19:8; 26:26; 28:31; also Eph. 6:20;
1 Thess. 2:2). On this occasion the council members were aston-
ished at their boldness, the more so since the apostles were obviously **unschooled, ordinary men**. Probably their dress and their
way of speaking gave them away. This is not to say that the council necessarily regarded Peter and John as completely ignorant and
unlettered (taking the Greek at its face value), but only that they
were lacking in the formal training of the scribes—they were laymen! The same complaint had been made of Jesus (John 7:15),
who had also surprised his hearers with his boldness of bearing
and speech. Indeed, it may have been the council's recollection
of Jesus that lay behind the comment: **They took note that these**

men had been with Jesus. We cannot think that they only now discovered that Peter and John were Jesus' disciples. They must have known this much, at least, about them. But now it was borne in upon them how like Jesus they were. When Pilate had condemned Jesus, they had thought that they had heard the last of him (Why else put him to death?). But they had reckoned without the power of the Spirit (cf. Luke 21:15), and in these Spirit-filled men Jesus in a sense stood before them again. Would they never be rid of him?

4:14 / As for the healing, there were two grounds only on which Peter and John could justly be punished: The first was if it were a hoax—but not even the council thought this. The evidence of the cure was incontrovertible, **since they could see the man who had been healed standing there with them**. Notice the word **standing**. He was a cripple no longer. The second was if they had worked the miracle by some unlawful means (cf. Deut. 13:1–5; Mark 3:20ff.). The council's opening question, "By what power or what name did you do this?" (v. 7) suggests that they had been investigating this possibility. "The name" in this connection has reference to magical formulae (see disc. on 19:13 and Marshall, p. 99). But from the first, Peter had ascribed the miracle to "the God of Abraham, Isaac and Jacob" (3:13). Ultimately, it was God's power that had healed the man, and no charge could be laid for making that claim.

4:15–18 / In some embarrassment, perhaps, the council chamber was cleared while the members argued the case. Their chief concern was to keep **this thing from spreading** (v. 17); the reference can hardly be to the miracle, news of which had already spread throughout the city, but to the teaching about Jesus and the resurrection. Since they had condemned Jesus, their credibility was at stake. But though they had been able to make some sort of case against Jesus, it was difficult to formulate a charge on which to condemn his disciples—the more so since the miracle had obviously caught the public imagination. The form in which their question is asked in the Greek, **What are we going to do with these men?** (v. 16) expresses their utter perplexity. In the end, the best they could do was to issue a warning that under no circumstances were the apostles to speak or to teach in (Gk. "upon") Jesus' name, that is, to make Jesus the basis of their teaching (see disc. on v. 2) or to claim him as their authority.

4:19-20 / For their part, Peter and John declared that they had no option but to speak of what they had **seen and heard** of Jesus (cf. John 1:14; 2 Pet. 1:16–18; 1 John 1:1.; but also John 20:29; 1 Pet. 1:8). Their first obedience was to God (cf. Luke 20:25), and they asked their judges to judge for themselves what was right in the matter—to obey them, or God. The fact that both apostles are mentioned may mean that each was appealed to by the council and that each answered to this effect.

4:21-22 / The council "added threats to their warning" (the sense of the Greek), but in view of the popular interest in the miracle could do little more. Characteristically, Luke draws attention to the praise of God that flowed from this incident (see disc. on 3:8) and also to the age of the man (cf. 9:33; 14:8; Luke 2:52; 3:23; 8:42; 13:11). Luke's own comment on the incident is expressed in his use of the word "sign" (so the Greek). A "sign" could be simply a miracle (see note on 2:22), but to Luke it was clearly a miracle that signified that the day of salvation had come.

Additional Notes §8

4:3 / **Because it was evening, they put them in jail**: In the Mishnah, *Sanhedrin* 4.1, it is said, "Judgments about money may be commenced in the day and concluded in the night, but judgments about life must be begun in the day and concluded in the day." This prohibition, based on Jer. 21:12, may explain why the apostles' trial was held over until the next day. The Jews only used imprisonment for such precautionary purposes. It was never in itself a mode of punishment.

4:4 / **The number of men grew to about five thousand**: Difficulty has been found with this figure, which is said to be out of all proportion to the population of Jerusalem. It is especially difficult if this was only the number of men; the figure would have to be at least doubled to give the total number of believers. But what was the population of Jerusalem at this time? Hecataeus of Abdera, in about 300 B.C., put the figure at 120,000 (Josephus, *Against Apion* 1.161–212). According to Josephus, it had reached 2.7 million by A.D. 65 (*War* 6.420–427; cf 2.280–283), but this figure is far too high. Modern estimates of the population of Jerusalem at the time of Jesus vary between 25,000 (Jeremias) and 250,000 (Hanson). The latter figure may still be too high, but improvements to the water supply effected by Herod the Great would allow for at least 70,000. It may still be thought that a figure of even 10,000 Christians is disproportionately high, but the possibility should be kept in mind that they did not all live in Jerusalem. Luke may have been giving an estimate of the number of believers in the country districts as well, including Galilee (cf. 2:41, 47; 6:7; and see disc. on 9:31).

4:10 / **Whom you crucified but whom God raised from the dead**: This construction with relative clauses is characteristic of Luke's style in the early speeches of Acts (2:24, 32, 36; 3:13, 15; 4:27; 5:30; 10:38, 39; 13:31, 37), where reference is made to the activity of God in and through Jesus. Hanson, p. 78, thinks "it is possible that Luke is in these expressions reproducing early doctrinal formulae."

4:11 / The sentence that incorporates the quotation is very clumsily formed. The Greek has simply, "this is" (NIV **he is**). The reference is clearly to Jesus, but in the previous verse "this" (Gk. *houtos*) refers to the man who was healed. The awkwardness of the Greek may point to Luke's use of a source.

4:15 / **They ordered them to withdraw from the Sanhedrin**: How did Luke get his information about what went on in the council? His narrative could have been based on deduction, but there may have been those in the council who were sympathetic to the new sect and from whom the story was gleaned. Or it may have come from Paul. It is highly unlikely that Paul was himself a member (see disc. on 7:60; 26:10), but he was close to one who was (see disc. on 5:34). Or again, Luke appears to have had access to Herodian sources, and the story may have come indirectly through them (see disc. on 13:1; cf. Luke 8:3).

§9 The Believers' Prayer (Acts 4:23–31)

4:23 / On their release, Peter and John immediately **went back to their own people**, that is, the believers, and told them what had happened. For their place of meeting, see notes on 1:13 and the discussion on 12:12. Their specific mention of **the chief priests and elders** again points to the Sadducees as their chief opponents (see disc. on vv. 6, 8).

4:24 / The seriousness of what they had to tell and their sense of dependence upon God were such that the whole group fell to prayer. The expression **they raised their voices together** has been taken to mean that they were all inspired to say exactly the same words, but that implies too mechanical a view of inspiration. They may all have prayed in turn (as others suggest), but in that case Luke has given us only the general thrust of their various prayers. Some have gone further, to suggest that he simply composed what he thought to be an appropriate prayer for the occasion, but that runs into the snag that it reflects a very different view to Luke's own of the part played by Herod and Pilate in Jesus' death. In the Gospel he shows Pilate, especially, to have been a reluctant participant, whereas here both he and Herod are cast in leading roles among those who brought it about (see also notes on v. 27). Perhaps the best explanation is that one person prayed and all assented, either by repeating the prayer phrase by phrase or by adding their Amen at the end. At all events, it was an occasion that showed them all to be "one in heart and mind" (v. 32; see disc. on 1:14).

The prayer itself may have been based on the prayer of Hezekiah (Isa. 37:16–20), and like that prayer, its dominant theme is God's sovereignty. This is declared at the outset in their address to God (cf. Rev. 6:10 and the description of Christ in 2 Pet. 2:1; Jude 4). The Greek word *despotēs* denotes "absolute ownership and uncontrolled power," especially that of a master over a slave. Compare Luke 2:29 where "your slave" (so the Greek) answers to it, as here "your slaves" (so again the Greek) in verse 29. It also expresses here, as often in the LXX (cf. Job. 5:8; Wisdom 6:7), the sovereignty of God in creation. The same word is used of the gods in classical Greek, but the creator of **the heaven and the earth and the sea** is no "despot" as they often were. His rule is absolute, but never exercised in the absence of wisdom and love. Nor is it restricted to the act of creation. He is the Sovereign no less in human affairs: "He does as he pleases with the powers of heaven and the peoples of the earth. No one can hold back his hand or say to him: 'What have you done?' " (Dan. 4:35).

4:25-27 / The thought of God as the God of history, implied in verse 24, becomes explicit in the verses that follow by reference to Psalm 2:2f., which God spoke **by the Holy Spirit through . . . David** (v. 25; see disc. on 1:16). In the first instance, this psalm was addressed to a king, reminding him that at his coronation he had been acclaimed "the Lord's anointed" (i.e., "messiah"). Understandably, with its use of such terms as "his anointed," "my king," and "my son," the psalm had come to be understood of the eschatological Messiah (though not exclusively so), at least by the middle of the first century B.C. (see disc. on 13:23; cf. Psalms of Solomon 17:24ff.; 4QFlor. 1.10-13). In applying it to Jesus, therefore, the Christians were drawing on an established tradition. But for them uniquely the Messiah was at the same time the Servant of God (v. 27)—a juxtaposition of ideas that owed its origin to Jesus' own messianic consciousness (see notes on 3:13; 8:32f.; 11:20). For as early as his baptism, Jesus had seen himself in terms of both Psalm 2:7 (cf. 13:33; Heb. 1:5; 5:5) and Isaiah 42:1, part of the first "Servant Song" (Luke 3:22), aware that his role as king depicted in the psalm would only be fulfilled in his serving and giving his life "to redeem many people" (Mark 10:45). His further description as God's **holy** servant (v. 27) reminds us of his devotion to God and to the task to which God had called him (cf. 3:14), whereas the reference to his being made Messiah probably means the same as in 10:38, where his baptism seems to be indicated.

Since the Christians understood the psalm to speak of Jesus, it followed that the details of the psalm were those of Jesus' life, especially the events that led to his death. Thus **the kings of the earth** (v. 26) were identified as Herod the Tetrarch, that is, Herod Antipas, who was loosely referred to as "king" (cf. Mark 6:14), **the rulers** as Pontius Pilate, **the nations** as the Romans who had carried out the crucifixion, and **the peoples** as "the peoples of Israel," where the Greek has the plural, assimilating the wording of verse 27 to the quotation. The inclusion of Israel among those who **met together . . . against . . . Jesus** (v. 27) expresses the insight that the sole criterion for the people of God is their recognition of Jesus as the Messiah. Old Israel, having failed to meet that requirement, was replaced by the new. Like the old, however, the new Israel of God, the church, was chosen by God's grace, not for privilege but for service (cf. Rom. 2:28, 29; Gal. 6:16; Eph. 1:11,14; Phil. 3:2, 3; Titus 2:14; 1 Pet. 2:9,10). For the title Christ (Anointed One, Messiah), see notes on 11:20.

4:28 / Those who "met together . . . against . . . Jesus" (v. 27) represented in human terms a considerable force. Nevertheless, they were under God's sovereign control. He turned their anger to his own ends (cf. Ps. 76:10), for they only did what he **had decided beforehand should happen** (cf. 2:23; 3:18). The phrase **your power** is literally "your hand," a common expression in Scripture for "the divine power when actively manifested, as in the deliverance of his people or the working of signs" (Rackham, p. 61; cf. v. 30 for the Hebraic expression "to stretch out the hand," also Exod. 3:20; 13:3; 15:6; etc.) and one that in this book is closely associated with the Spirit of God. In sum, the message of this verse is a "comfortable word" to all Christians. There may be incidents in the Christian life hard to bear, but there are no accidents, for "in all things God works for the good of those who love him" (Rom. 8:28).

4:29–30 / In recognition of this, the believers brought their plight to "God's throne, where there is grace" (Heb. 4:16, GNB). Notice that their supplication was left to the last and that even then they did not ask to be spared hardship, but only for courage to face it and to keep on speaking the message **with great boldness** (v. 29; see disc. on v. 13). Such a prayer involves a curious paradox, in that boldness of speech was regarded as the privilege of free men, not of slaves, and yet in the same breath they called themselves "slaves" (so the Greek). This was tantamount to their saying, "Thy will be done." Courage it would seem came no more easily to these people than to us. Peter and John had indeed shown boldness before the Sanhedrin, but to maintain their courage they were dependent upon the Holy Spirit whose

gift it was (cf. 9:17, 27). They would certainly need it, for the
servant is not greater than his Lord (John 15:20), and if the Lord
is the Suffering Servant, they could expect nothing less than to
suffer with him (cf. Col. 1:24; Heb. 13:12f.).

As for their enemies, they simply prayed: **Lord, consider
their threats** (v. 29). Interpreted according to strict grammar, this
would have to be referred to those who had threatened Jesus, but
according to sense, it must be related to the apostles' recent experience (v. 18). Psalm 2 had spoken of the destruction of God's
enemies, but there was no petition for destruction in this prayer.
These things could (and should) be left with God (cf. Rom. 12:19).
Instead, they asked that God would **stretch out** [his] **hand** (see
disc. on v. 28) and would **perform miraculous signs and wonders** (see notes on 2:22) **through the name of** [his] **holy servant
Jesus** (v. 30; for the title, see disc. and notes on 3:13 and notes
on 8:32f. and 11:20; for "the name," see notes on 2:38). The
Greek is literally "while you reach out," qualifying the main
clause, "enable us . . . to speak." This construction makes it clear
that though the miracles met real needs they were also seen to
have a corroborative value, for people would know that none
could do these works unless God were with them (cf. John 3:2;
Heb. 2:3f.).

4:31 / They had prayed for power, and with power they
were answered, in both the short term and the long (though, of
course, they must often have prayed along these lines). Immediately **the place where they were meeting was shaken**, as though
by an earthquake—a not uncommon sign of God's presence (cf.
16:26; Exod. 19:18; Ps. 114:7; Isa. 6:4; Ezek. 38:19; Joel 3:16; Amos
9:5; Hag. 2:6)—and **they were all filled with the Holy Spirit**. In
that power they **spoke the word of God boldly**. We need not suppose that the preaching took place there and then. The force of
the Greek is that they made it their practice to preach (in this,
in part, lay the long-term answer to their prayer). The view that
this is a variant account of the Pentecost narrative and that they
were speaking in tongues has no warrant at all. On the momentary experience of being **filled with the Holy Spirit**, see notes
on 2:4 and the discussion on 4:8.

Additional Notes §9

4:25 / **You spoke by the Holy Spirit through the mouth of your servant, our father David**: This probably represents the meaning intended by Luke, though the Greek is decidedly awkward, if not "absolutely ungrammatical" (*BC*, vol. 4, p. 46). The difficulty may be due to its being translation Greek. C. C. Torrey, on his theory of a written Aramaic source, reconstructed the text to mean "that which our father, your servant, David said by command of the Holy Spirit" (pp. 16f.). Bruce believes that the only way to translate the text as it stands is to take David as the mouth (i.e., mouthpiece) of the Holy Spirit (*Book*, p. 105), and this in effect is what NIV has done. Leaving aside the difficulties, the general effect of the words is to stress that God was in control of the medium as well as the message.

4:27 / **Your holy Servant**: The Greek (*pais*) can mean "child," and the suggestion has been made that this is a reference to the "son" of Ps. 2:7 (where, however, the LXX uses a different word). But this is far less likely than that this is the familiar description of Jesus in terms of the Servant of Isaiah.

Whom you anointed: On the use of the relative clause, see note on 4:10. If we are right in supposing that this refers to Jesus' baptism, it again reflects a different viewpoint to Luke's own (see disc. on v. 24). As the birth narratives show, Luke regarded Jesus as the Messiah from his birth.

§10   The Believers Share Their Possessions (Acts 4:32–37)

Here we have the second in Luke's series of cameos of the inner life of the church (see disc. on 2:42–47). In this, he takes up again the theme of their fellowship. Of the other matters dealt with in the earlier sketch, he has already had something more to say about prayer (4:23–31) and will shortly add something on the subject of miracles.

4:32 / For the expression **all** (Gk. *plethos*) **the believers**, see note on 6:2. One of the most remarkable features of life among the early believers was their unity. This is expressed here in the words they were **one in heart and mind**, a typically Hebraic turn of phrase indicating their complete accord (cf. 1 Chron. 12:38). It is a general statement to which there were exceptions (see disc. on 5:1–11), but the exceptions only proved the rule, which was the more remarkable in view of the steady growth of the church. This unity, based on the recognition that "there is one Lord, one faith, one baptism . . . one God and Father of all" (Eph. 4:4f., GNB)—in short, on their mutual love of God—was demonstrated, as it had been from the first, in their readiness to meet one another's needs, their love of neighbor (cf. 2:44f.). Thus **no one claimed that any of his possessions was his own** (again, a general rule to which there were exceptions). From Luke's expression, however, it is clear that the believer still "owned" his belongings until such time as he saw fit to dispose of them, that is, they were not practicing a thoroughgoing communalism but were simply a caring community responding to the needs of others as they arose. The response was a purely voluntary one, in contrast to the Qumran community, where the sharing of goods was a rule imposed upon all of its members (see note on 2:45).

It is probably true that their willingness to sell their belongings owed much to their expectation that Jesus would soon return (see disc. on 2:44). It may also be true that it contributed to their later state of acute need (cf. 11:27–30; 24:17; Rom. 15:26;

Gal. 2:10). But this does not entitle us to condemn what they did. Discipleship is always costly in one way or another (cf., e.g., Luke 9:23–26; 14:25–33), and who is to say that this was not the right price for them to pay? After all (though they may not have known it) the city was soon to be destroyed, and God in his infinite wisdom may well have guided them to use what they had while they had it. Subsequently, their poverty became an occasion of blessing both to them and to those who ministered to them (cf. 2 Cor. 9:11f.).

4:33 / The strong sense of social responsibility just noted was matched by no less a care for people's spiritual well-being. Despite the ban imposed upon them by the Sanhedrin, the apostles continued to give their testimony (the Greek is that specific) **to the resurrection of the Lord Jesus**. The tense of the verb (imperfect) indicates that this was their practice, whereas the verb itself, a compound form (Gk. *apodidoun*), is more expressive than the simple verb "to give." It belongs especially to the language of commerce and means "to pay a debt." Perhaps Luke was suggesting that they "owed it" to others to preach Jesus and to Jesus himself because he had called them to this task (1:8, 22; 4:20). The addition of the title **Lord** to Jesus' name may mean that they preached him as Lord by virtue of his resurrection (cf. 2:36). Moreover, they preached **with great power**. This refers primarily to the effectiveness of their preaching—words backed by behavior and character and infused by the Spirit—but may also point to the occurrence of miracles (cf. 2:43; see disc. on 4:30). Finally, we are told that **much grace was upon them all**. Though the apostles are mentioned specifically, we should probably take **them all** as meaning the church generally. This statement can be understood, as in 2:47, of the favor (the Greek word *charis* can mean "favor" or "grace") in which they were held by the people. It is better, however, following NIV, to understand it of God's grace (cf. 6:8; Luke 2:40). This gives better sense to the connection expressed in the Greek (not shown in NIV) between this and the following verse, namely, that the absence of need among the believers (v. 34) was evidence of the constraint of God's grace upon them (cf. 2 Cor. 5:14).

4:34–35 / The language of these verses, with the Greek imperfect being used throughout, makes it clear that the believers did not dispose of their property all at once. Rather, they sold it off bit by bit as needed. The statement of verse 35 takes us beyond that of 2:44 in a way that is entirely consistent with the increase in the number of believers. The earlier reference appears to have been to individuals meeting the needs of others on a purely ad hoc basis. Now the whole system of relief was properly organized, as it was in the synagogues. Here for the first time we read of a common fund administered by the apostles. Distribution from the fund was made to the needy (cf. 6:1), so that the apostles themselves may have been beneficiaries (cf. 3:6). As trustees also, they would have been in a ticklish position, but clearly the church had confidence in them. Among others to have benefited from the fund may have been those who had suffered deprivation for no other reason then that they were believers (cf. John 9:22; 12:42; 16:2).

4:36-37 / Over the years, many must have participated in the fund as both recipients and donors, but one contributor is now singled out for particular mention—**Joseph, a Levite from Cyprus, whom the apostles called Barnabas** (v. 36). Barnabas was soon to play a leading role in the church's missionary outreach. His introduction here, therefore, serves the dual purpose of providing a fitting example of the way in which possessions were shared, while alerting us to his importance in the story that is yet to be told. A third purpose may have been to set off the contrast between the picture of the church given here and the conduct of two of its members in the following narrative (5:1-11). In the Greek these two paragraphs (4:32-37 and 5:1-11) are joined by the adversative conjunction "but." The ancient law forbidding the Levites to own land (Num. 18:24; Deut. 10:9) appears to have long since been disregarded (cf. Jer. 32:7ff.; Josephus, a priest, had land near Jerusalem, *Life* 422-430). It is not clear whether the land that Barnabas sold was in Cyprus or in Palestine, but the fact that his kinswoman, John Mark's mother, had property in Jerusalem may point to the latter. It is said only that he was born in Cyprus.

Additional Notes   §10

4:35 / **And put it** (the money) **at the apostles feet**: Haenchen argues that behind this expression is an old custom whereby one setting his foot on a person or object acquired rights of property and free disposal over the same (p. 231). But even if Haenchen is right in deriving the term from this custom, as used here it probably did not imply any legal right to the property. Alternatively, the expression may derive from the usual attitude of the teacher and the taught, the former sitting on a raised seat and the latter on the ground at his feet (see disc. on 22:3). The thought is that the gifts were given to the care and authority of the apostles.

4:36 / **Joseph . . . whom the apostles called Barnabas**: lit., "Joseph who was called Barnabas from the apostles." The preposition "from" used in the sense of "by" is odd but not without precedent. Luke employs it in this sense in 2:22. Ehrhardt's suggestion that he was called "Barnabas of the apostles," having purchased from them his right to this office, is hardly convincing (p. 21). Luke adds that the name means **Son of Encouragement**, "nabas" reflecting either the Aramaic $n^e waha$, "pacification," "consolation" (the abnormal Greek transcription being eased by the contemporary soft pronunciation of *b*) or some form of the root *nb*, "to prophesy." In the latter event, the name would be strictly "son of a prophet" or "of prophecy," but exhortation was supremely a prophetic function (15:32; 1 Cor. 14:3), and in any case, Luke is less concerned with the derivation of the name than with indicating the man's character.

A Levite from Cyprus: Soon after the time of Alexander the Great, and possibly before that time, there were Jews in Cyprus, and 1 Macc. 15:23 indicates that they were there in considerable numbers. Josephus reports that they were flourishing on the island at the beginning of the first century B.C. (*Antiquities* 14.199), and Philo says that a large and presumably prosperous community spread throughout the island in the first century A.D. (*Embassy to Gaius* 28).

§11 Ananias and Sapphira (Acts 5:1–11)

The idyllic picture of the church presented in 4:32–37 had to be qualified. The church must soon have made the painful discovery that sin could enter into its fellowship, and because it suited his theme, and was a matter of particular interest to him, Luke chose to mention what was probably an early and notorious instance of sin in connection with the common fund. Ehrhardt sees the story of Ananias and Sapphira as a test case for the question whether a rich man could be saved—important for the church of Luke's day—and Luke's reply to that question (v. 4), that riches are not in themselves bad but constitute a sore temptation to the Christian (p. 22). Thus the story illustrates the "mortal danger present in the attachment to the world effected through possessions and riches" (S. Brown, p. 107).

5:1–2 / Two members of the community, **a man named Ananias** and his wife, Sapphira (v. 1), conspired to deceive their fellow believers. Like Barnabas (4:36f.), they sold some land, but unlike him they kept back part of the proceeds before handing over the rest to the apostles (see notes on 4:35). The verb "to keep" (Gk. *nosphizein*) that occurs here and in verse 3 and again in the New Testament only in Titus 2:10 is used in the LXX of Achan's keeping back some of the booty of Jericho that had been devoted to God (Josh. 7:1). The rarity of the word in the New Testament suggests that Luke deliberately drew on the language of the Old Testament passage to point his readers to the comparison.

5:3–4 / How Peter became aware of what they had done we are not told. There may have been an informer, or Peter may have had the gift of percipience. At all events, Peter charged Ananias with the deceit. The question **How is it that . . . ?** (v. 3) implies that it need not have happened—that Ananias had it in his own power to avoid sin. As it was, the expression in verse 4 (lit., "to lay in the heart," a Hebraistic phrase) shows that it was the result of long and careful deliberation. Indeed, the reference to

Satan's having taken control of his heart (lit., Satan had "filled his heart") may even suggest that it had become something of an obsession with him. Like all sin, that of Ananias and Sapphira touched God more than anyone else: their lie was essentially to the Holy Spirit (v. 3), that is, to God himself (v. 4). The negative of verse 4 does not mean that they had not also lied to other people, but is intended to stress the most serious aspect of what they had done.

Part of the tragedy of their sin was its senselessness. **Didn't it belong to you before it was sold?** Peter asked. **And after it was sold, wasn't the money at your disposal?** (v. 4). There was no constraint on them to sell. No one was obliged to give to the fund, much less to give all that they had. It was not what they gave that mattered, but the spirit in which they made the gift, and in this Ananias and Sapphira had erred. They had wanted to appear more generous than they were while remaining better off than they seemed to be (were they hoping now to draw on the fund themselves?), though they could not have held back much, else the disparity between what they offered and what they were known to have sold would have been too apparent. All things considered, they paid dearly for the little they had expected to gain.

5:5 / At Peter's exposure of his guilt, Ananias **fell down and died.** There seems little doubt that Luke saw this as a miracle. But it is as a miracle that it presents the greatest difficulty to the modern mind. For it suggests an almost magical manipulation of God's Spirit by the apostle. The incident belongs, of course, to an age that had no doctrine of secondary causes and that sought a supernatural explanation for any event that baffled the understanding. On that basis, it has been suggested that Ananias' death was simply a chance occurrence and this story a legend that grew out of the attempt to explain it. Nearer the truth, perhaps, is the suggestion that Ananias died of shock caused by the disclosure of his deception, bearing in mind that this was a society in which it was consciously felt to be "a dreadful thing to fall into the hands of the living God" (Heb. 10:31) and that, until Peter had spoken, Ananias may not have seen the full import of what he had done. But as the narrative stands—and it bears all the marks of an early tradition, a story simply told, a bare recital of facts with no reasons given for what happened—no such explanation will account

for Sapphira's death, which Peter announced beforehand. Moreover, though they may have been the first, they can hardly have
been the only sinners to have come to the public notice, yet what
happened to them appears to have been quite exceptional. Perhaps, then, Luke was right to see (as we suppose he did) the
supernatural in these events—a miracle of judgment that, no less
than the miracles of healing, was a sign that the kingdom of God
had come (see disc. on 4:22; cf. 13:11; Matt. 16:16–19; 18:18; John
20:23). For the God of this kingdom intends to judge sin. He did
it on the cross; he will do it at the last day; and he does it now
among his own people. **Great fear seized all who heard what had
happened** (see disc. on 2:43). The Greek would be better rendered "all who were listening to these things," for the reference
here appears to be to those present, as distinct from verse 11. The
setting may have been a church "service."

    5:6 / No sooner had Ananias died than **the young men
came forward, wrapped up his body, and carried him out and
buried him**. Whether any attempt was made to contact Sapphira
we are not told. Their home may have been in the country and
impossible to reach quickly. Even so, it seems somewhat precipi-
tate to have buried the husband without telling the wife. It was
customary to bury the dead quickly—but not that quickly, and
generally not until sufficient time had elapsed to ensure that death
had taken place (cf. 9:37). However, there were exceptions to the
rule of allowing the dead to lie for a time, and in this case, if the
church believed that the death was an act of divine judgment,
they may have felt that the usual formalities should be dispensed
with. Or the explanation may be that it was a rule at that time
that the dead should not lie overnight in Jerusalem. This could
explain the statement that they **carried him out**. And if the body
had to be moved, a tomb would have been as good a place as
any to put it. Ananias would not have been **buried** as we understand it, with earth covering the body, but laid in a rock-cut tomb,
many of which from this period may be found outside the walls
of Jerusalem (but not on the west, from where the prevailing
winds blow!). Little preparation would have been required for
such a burial, assuming that a tomb was available. It was simply
opened and closed by a stone. There is no need to see in **the
young men** an official order within the church, though the natural distinction between them and the elders may have formed

the basis of later ministries (cf. 1 Tim. 5:1; Titus 2:1–6; 1 Pet. 5:5; 1 Clement 1.3; 3.3; 21.6; Polycarp, *Philippians* 5.3). They were simply "the younger men" (RV mg.). The word translated **wrapped up** is not the usual expression for dressing a corpse in its laying-out robes, perhaps because no such clothes were available and there was no time to obtain them. Alternatively, this word could be translated "placed him together," that is, they composed his limbs so that he could be carried more conveniently to the grave.

5:7–10 / About three hours later—it is not clear whether this is reckoned from the death or from the burial, but it may indicate the approach of the next hour of prayer (see disc. on 3:1 and note on 10:9)—Sapphira **came in** (v. 7). Where this took place is unclear. What is clear is that the horror of the offense, underlined by what had already happened, was uppermost in Peter's mind. Not from any unkindness, then, but out of a deep sense of its seriousness, he went straight to the heart of the matter, with no mention yet of Ananias' death. He gave Sapphira every chance to retract their lie, but when she persisted in it (or did he name the actual amount of the sale and was this her confession of guilt?), he announced that they had sinned against **the Spirit of the Lord** by testing whether indeed he did know all things (cf. 1:24; 15:10; Exod. 17:2, 7; Deut. 6:16; Ps. 78:41, 56; etc.)—the rhetorical question amounts to a statement. They stood condemned, and Peter announced Sapphira's doom. By now he could confidently predict what it would be. In effect, this was a sentence of death, and when she heard it she too **fell down at his feet and died** (v. 10). Again, we may look for a secondary cause in the shock of finding herself discovered and under a curse. But the hand of God in all this cannot be ruled out. He had interposed to deal with a danger that had threatened the church. Sapphira was carried out by the same young men who had buried her husband and was laid beside him. The name Sapphira, in Greek and Aramaic, was found on an ossuary in Jerusalem in 1923. There is, of course, no proof that it held the remains of this woman.

The question remains, Why them? Why did they in particular have to suffer this fate? It may be useful to draw an analogy between what happened to them and the penalty inflicted on Nadab and Abihu in the early days of the Israelite priesthood. They had approached God in a wrong spirit and for this reason had died, for God has warned that those who would serve him must give heed to his holiness (Lev. 10:3). And in the same way, Ananias and Sapphira had suffered the consequences of taking God's holiness lightly (cf. Jude 11). Notice that, in the story of Nadab and Abihu, Aaron and his family were forbidden to mourn those whom God had punished. This may have some bearing on the passage before us. In the early days of the church, the lesson had to be learned that sin among the saints is no trifling matter. And this was a sin that Jesus had often condemned, for theirs was hypocrisy of the worst kind. They had sought by deception to gain a name for godliness and good works. Once such a spirit gains a toehold in any community, there is an end to real fellowship. For how can people speak the truth each with his neighbor except there be the sincerity of love (Rom. 12:9)?

5:11 / The deaths of Ananias and Sapphira made a deep impression on both the church and the wider community—we should give to the words **great fear** their full force, no matter that a reference to fear was a regular feature of miracle stories (cf. v. 5; see disc. on 2:43). In bringing the narrative to a close, Luke uses the word **church** for the first time in Acts. Whether or not the Christians themselves were using this word at the time, Luke may have meant us to understand by it that there was a growing consciousness among them of their role as the people of God. *Ekklēsia*, "church," is one of two words used in the LXX for the congregation of Israel. Since the other, *synagōgē*, had come to be used more and more by the Jews both of their meetings and of the place in which they met, the Christians chose to describe themselves as the *ekklēsia*.

Additional Notes §11

5:1 / **A man named Ananias . . . with his wife Sapphira**: Were they Christians? No certain answer can be given, but the following points should be noted: first, Acts 4:32 indicates that all who were engaged in the community of goods were believers; second, most New Testament references to Satan's activities relate to Christians rather than to unbelievers (e.g., Matt. 16:21–23; Luke 22:3; John 13:2, 27; 1 Cor. 7:5; Eph. 4:27; 1 Pet. 5:8f.; also 1 Chron. 21:1); and third, Christians are quite capable of lying (Col. 3:9), of "grieving the Holy Spirit of God" and of "putting out the Spirit's fire" in their lives (Eph. 4:30; 1 Thess. 5:19; see note on 2:4). If Ananias and Sapphira were numbered among the believers, what happened to them may be compared with what took place in 1 Cor. 5:5 and 11:30. In each of these instances it may be right to think that Christians were disciplined but not finally damned. Paul's description in 1 Cor. 3:12–15 of those whose works will fail to pass muster in the judgment but who will themselves be saved, though only as if they had "escaped through the flames," is perhaps apposite to each of these cases and to that of Ananias and Sapphira in particular.

5:3 / The premeditated nature of Ananias and Sapphira's deceit in a situation where they should have known better (cf. Rom. 2:17ff.) may sufficiently account for the very different treatment meted out to them as compared with Simon Magus in 8:20–23. Simon was given opportunity to repent and to pray for forgiveness.

5:6 / On the removal of the dead from Jerusalem, see A. Guttmann, *Hebrew Union College Annual*, 1969–70, pp. 251–75.

§12   The Apostles Heal Many (Acts 5:12–16)

In this further description of the inner life of the church, the emphasis is now on the power that was at work among them, especially through the apostles. The effectiveness of their witness in both word and deed explains the attack made upon them, which is the subject of the section following this one.

5:12 / **The apostles performed many miraculous signs and wonders** (see notes on 1:26 and 2:22). It would appear from this, as from the earlier passage (see disc. on 2:43), that the gift of miracles was confined to the apostles. With the appointment of the Seven, however, it was soon extended at least to Stephen (6:8) and Philip (8:6, 13). Later Paul and Barnabas exercised the gift (14:3; 15:12; 19:11ff.; Rom. 15:19; 2 Cor. 12:12), and from Paul's writings, we know that others also possessed "gifts of healing and miraculous powers" (1 Cor. 12:9f.; Gal. 3:5). How widespread this was, we do not know. But on the evidence available to us, it might be fair to say that the gift of miracles was generally vested in the leaders of the church, partly perhaps to accredit them in the eyes of outsiders as Christ's representatives. But it is not to this that Luke refers here when he speaks of miracles done **among the people**, but to the church. In the singular, the word *laos*, "people," nearly always means the people of God. Luke adds that their favorite meeting place at this time was in Solomon's Colonnade (see disc. on 3:11 and Ehrhardt, p. 19, for the contrast with the Essenes), and it was probably here (as the juxtaposition of ideas would suggest) that many of the miracles were performed (cf. 3:1–10).

5:13–14 / Being often in the temple, the believers would have come under the notice of the many others who frequented its courts, and the scene thus suggested may have been the context of Luke's remark in verse 13. Whenever the Christians were met together **no one else dared join them, even though they were highly regarded by the people** (cf. v. 26). This reluctance to intrude was no doubt due to a healthy respect for the divine power evident in these meetings. But there is no contradiction with verse 14. A hesitation to join a church meeting need not have held any back from joining at other, more convenient, times. And many did, both men and women who **believed in the Lord**, literally, "who believed the Lord," the sense being that they took the Lord at his word (for the title, see note on 11:20). The mention of women is another reminder of their role in the life of the church (see disc. on 1:14). The tense of the Greek verb, **were added** (imperfect), gives the sense that men and women kept on being added, whereas the passive voice carries the implication that it was God who did the adding (cf. 2:41, 47).

5:15–16 / The association of ideas might lead us to conclude that it was the men and women of verse 14 who now gave play to their new faith by bringing others to the apostles for healing. But surely they would have known that the power to heal was not inherent in any person, much less in a shadow, though it might please God to use both as "means of grace." It is better, then, not to look for a link between verses 14 and 15, but to see verse 15 as a reference to the response of the nonbelievers to the growing fame of the apostles, Peter especially (cf. 19:12; Mark 6:56). That they should have sought Peter's shadow was in line with the popular idea of the time that "to be touched by a man's shadow means to be in contact with his soul or his essence and to be influenced by that, whether it be for better or for worse" (P. W. Van Der Horst, "Peter's Shadow," *NTS* 23 (1977), p. 207). It was downright superstition, yet out of it some may have come to a true faith. "The lesson is taught that spiritual influence can be conveyed through material things. The instances however are few and the appeal has the least permanent effect. The people throng the street, but do not come into the church" (Rackham, p. 69). Meanwhile, news of these things spread beyond the city **and crowds gathered . . . from the towns around Jerusalem, bringing their sick and those tormented by evil spirits** (v. 16; cf. Matt. 4:24). **All of them were healed**, we are told, but blanket statements like this must often be read in the sense of "many" or "some" rather than **all** (see disc. on 9:35). At all events, by these contacts the way was being prepared for the advance of the gospel from Jerusalem into Judea.

Additional Notes §12

5:12 / **The apostles performed many miraculous signs:** lit., they were done "through the hands of the apostles," though NIV is probably right to adopt the simpler translation. The laying on of hands was often the mode of Jesus' healings (Mark 6:5; etc.), and because he commanded it (Mark 16:18), it would often have been the mode of the apostles' healings also (cf. 9:12, 17; 14:3; 19:11; 28:8; also 3:7; 9:41). But the Greek need not be pressed to imply that they were always done in this way. On the practice of laying on hands for healing, see Dunn, *Jesus*, p. 165.

5:13 / **No one else,** lit., "no one of the rest": It is not completely clear who "the rest" were. Were they the rest of the believers, in contrast to the apostles? But nowhere else are the apostles regarded as objects of fear to their fellow believers. Or were they the nonbelievers in contrast to "all the believers" (v. 12)? This is the view adopted by NIV and is probably correct. Passages such as 1 Thess. 4:13 and 5:6 suggest that "the rest" had become almost a technical term for nonbelievers.

5:16 / **Their sick and those tormented by evil spirits:** The New Testament maintains a clear distinction between ordinary illness and demon possession, even when the symptoms are the same. People who were sick were healed by the laying on of hands or by anointing; people possessed by demons by commanding the demons to depart (e.g. Matt. 10:8; Mark 6:13; Acts 8:7; 19:12). Though often called **evil** (e.g., 19:12, 13, 15, 16; Luke 7:21; 8:2), in this verse the spirits are described as "unclean" (so the Greek; cf. 8:7; Matt. 10:1; Mark 1:27; 3:11; 5:13), because an unclean life was thought to have led to the possession; because possession led to an unclean life—the demoniac wandering, for example, into places where ceremonial defilement could be incurred (cf. Mark 5:3)—or because the demoniac was excluded from fellowship with God. The heathen were called unclean for the same reason.

§13 The Apostles Persecuted (Acts 5:17–42)

Such was the impact of the Christians on the city (they were not necessarily numerous, but they were in the public eye; see note on 4:4), that the city fathers, chiefly the Sadducees, decided again on overt action against them, or at least against their leaders. The broad similarity between the arrest and trial of the apostles described here and the earlier arraignment of Peter and John has already been noted, as has the parallel between their escape and Peter's escape in 12:6–19 (see disc. on 3:1–11). Other critical questions relating to this passage will be discussed in the exposition and notes to follow. Mention need be made here only of the further parallel that has sometimes been found between the passion of Christ and the treatment meted out to the Christians in this and the following chapters (see also the disc. on 19:21–41). Thus Gamaliel's speech and its outcome (5:35–40) have been likened to Pilate's verdict in Luke 23:15f., and the stoning of Stephen and the subsequent persecution of the church to the intransigence of the Jewish people displayed in the trial and death of Jesus. With regard to the latter, a convincing case can be made that Luke has modeled the narrative of Acts on the Gospel story (see disc. on 7:54–8:1a). Whether the same can be said of the larger section beginning here and running through to the story of Stephen is another question, though it certainly shows in more general terms how Christ continued to suffer—as well as to act and to teach— in his body, the church (see disc. on 1:1; cf. 9:4f.; Col. 1:24).

5:17–18 / Though the people in general continued to regard the believers with favor (cf. 2:47; 5:13, 26), the animosity of **the high priest and all his associates**, who were members of the party of the Sadducees, continued to grow. This reference will include those mentioned in 4:6, but may indicate further that the high priest now had the general support of all the Sadducees, who, of all Jews, most resented the Christian emphasis on the resurrection. Their **jealousy** (Gk. *zēlos*) was an outbreak of partisanship (a common meaning of the word) against those of a con-

trary view. Undoubtedly, the spread of teaching related to the resurrection of Jesus was the underlying cause of their hatred, mingled still with their dread of any movement that was likely to
disturb the delicate balance of society and therefore their own position of power within it. The context, however, implies that the
apostles were arrested because of the miracles. If this was so, it
was probably only the pretext. In any case, the apostles found
themselves in **the public jail** awaiting trial before the Sanhedrin
the next day (v. 18; see note on 4:3).

5:19–20 / But before the day came, they were set free by
an angel, with the command that they should **go, stand in the
temple courts, . . . and tell the people the full message of this
new life** (v. 20). "To stand" is expressive of the boldness with
which they were to preach (cf. 2:14), and the temple was the most
public place in which to do it. It was also the most appropriate
place, as the "house of God." Their theme was to be the life to
which the whole apostolic preaching referred (hence, "this life"),
the life that is given by him who is himself the resurrection and
the life (cf. 3:15; 4:12; John 11:25). Ehrhardt connects this instruction with Jesus' lament over Jerusalem (Luke 13:34) and suggests
that here, for the last time, Jesus is heard (through the apostles)
making his appeal to its people (p. 26).

The story of the apostles' release has received a variety of
explanations. Some say that it was due to a natural phenomenon,
such as an earthquake or lightning, others, that someone well-
disposed toward the believers let them out—the jailer perhaps,
or someone else with the jailer's connivance. The Greek word
translated **angel** can mean simply "a messenger" (cf. Luke 7:24;
9:52; James 2:25) and so could mean here a human agent, though
in biblical Greek the word is used more often of a divine agent—
an "angel" in the generally accepted sense of the word. But even
supposing that this is the sense in which Luke used the word,
it is still argued that the "angel" was in fact human, either mistaken for an angel by the apostles in the excitement of the night
or transformed into one in the telling or retelling of the story in
subsequent years. Dunn is among those who allow "the hand
of legend a role in shaping the miracles of liberation" (5:19–24;
12:6–11; 16:26; 28:3–6). "The stories," he says, "were probably in
a developed state when they reached Luke, having gained somewhat in the telling" (*Jesus*, p. 166). Along similar lines, Bruce points

out that "in classical literature we can trace a special 'form' in which it had become customary to describe unaccountable escapes from prison, and elements of this 'form' have been detected here," though he hastens to add that " 'form criticism' of this kind tells us little about the real facts of the matter which is being narrated" (*Book*, pp. 119f.; see also J. Jeremias, "*thyra*," *TDNT*, vol. 3, pp. 175f.). Certainly, for Luke, an "angel" meant more than simply a synonym for the unknown. Angels are often linked in his writing with prayer, but even apart from that, they represent the presence of God, often the response of God to the needs of his people (see disc. on 1:10f.; 12:6ff.). Thus, although Luke may not have known exactly how their escape was achieved, he was at least certain that God's sovereign power lay behind it and that "the course of the gospel cannot be hindered by prisons or bonds, since God's arm is strong enough to burst the locks of prison doors" (J. Jeremias, *TDNT*, vol. 3, p. 176). More than this we cannot say, except to add that the objection to any theory of divine intervention on the grounds that nothing was achieved by it is entirely unwarranted. To the apostles it must have brought great encouragement at a time when they needed it most. And had the Sadducees eyes to see it, it might also have shown them how useless it was to try to stem the tide of the new movement. Strange to say, when later they had the opportunity, they appear never to have questioned the apostles' means of escape. One wonders whether they feared to have further evidence of the supernatural made public (cf. Matt. 28:11–15). But of course Luke does not give all the details, and questions may have been asked.

5:21 / Obedient to the angelic command, the apostles were in the temple at dawn, preaching to those who had come for the morning sacrifice (see disc. on 3:1). Meanwhile, ignorant of their escape, the council had assembled. This was now the full Sanhedrin; it seems to have been a smaller group that interrogated Peter and John earlier (4:5ff.). On that occasion it seems to have been largely a Sadducean attempt to silence the preachers, but now the Pharisees could bring their minds to the matter.

5:22–26 / Officials were sent—apparently some of the temple police—to bring the prisoners into the council (for the location of the council chamber, see disc. on 4:5), but to the astonishment of all, the police reported that the prisoners could not be found. No sign of their escape had been uncovered (doors locked, etc.), and the prison guards were seemingly unaware of what had happened. Those council members most nearly affected by the news are mentioned specifically: **the captain of the temple guard** (v. 24), whose responsibility it was to keep the prisoners safely in custody (see disc. on 4:1), and **the chief priests** (4:24), that is, the Sadducees, at whose instigation the apostles had been arrested (v. 17). They were at a loss either to account for their disappearance or to know what to do next (see disc. on 2:12). In this state of utter bewilderment, they received the news that their erstwhile prisoners were back **in the temple courts teaching the people** (v. 25). The chief officer now went with his men; the apostles were again taken into custody and brought at last to the council, but without harassment, for the guards were afraid of the crowd. For their part, the apostles offered no resistance. The lesson of Matthew 5:38ff. had been learned (cf. Luke 22:50f.). That the people were quite capable of becoming violent and hurling stones at anyone who met with their displeasure is well attested, and the guards were wise to tread cautiously (cf. 21:27ff.; John 8:59; 10:31; see also disc. on Acts 7:58).

5:27–28 / The setting in the Sanhedrin was as before, only now there were twelve where before two prisoners had stood (see disc. on 4:7). The high priest, as president of the council (see disc. on 4:5), opened the proceedings by going straight to the heart of the matter. Contrary to their instructions, he said, the apostles had taught **in this name** (lit., "upon his name," see disc. on 4:18). As Luke reports it, it would seem that the high priest could not bring himself to speak the name of Jesus but instead referred to him indirectly and contemptuously as **this man**. The instructions to which he alluded had, of course, been given only to Peter and John, but were clearly intended for all and were assumed to have been made known to all. The result of their disobedience, he said, was that the city was full of their teaching and that the blame for Jesus' death was likely to be laid at the Sanhedrin's door. Indeed, the high priest accused the apostles of having this as their objective. Now it was true that the apostles were quite prepared to lay blame where blame was due, but this was always merely incidental to their preaching. Far from being concerned with apportioning blame for this one sin, their great objective was to preach the forgiveness of all sins. But obviously the council was very sensitive on this point, as they had good reason to be (see Matt. 27:25).

5:29 / All the apostles spoke in defense of their action, but beyond noting that Luke makes no attempt, even if he could, to reproduce what they said. Instead, Peter is again the focus of attention (see note on 3:1). Even then, we probably only have an outline of his defense. The speech as we have it has exactly the same import as the statement of 4:19 but, if anything, is more decisive in tone, as was only to be expected in view of recent events (vv. 19, 20). There was no denying that they had disobeyed the Sanhedrin's instructions, but they had had no alternative but to obey God—a priority that all Christians are bound to accept (cf. Luke 12:8ff.; 14:25–33).

5:30 / In speaking of **the God of our fathers**, Peter was using a phrase that immediately pointed to the great acts of God in the past. To these, God had now added this, that he had "raised up Jesus." There is nothing in the Greek text that corresponds to NIV's **from the dead**, so that it is at least possible, perhaps probable, that this is not a reference to the resurrection but to the raising up of Jesus as the Messiah, as God had raised up other deliverers throughout the history of Israel (cf. Judg. 2:18; 3:9, 15; etc.). This sense certainly gives a better sequence to this verse and the next. First, God gave them a messiah, then they killed him, then God raised him (a different word) from the dead to the place of dignity and power that was now his (v. 31). These verses express the familiar contrast between the human rejection of Jesus and his divine vindication (cf. 2:23f.; 3:14f.; 4:10), here rendered the more striking by the reference to Jesus' being hanged on a tree. The expression is characteristically (though not exclusively) Petrine (cf. 10:39; 1 Pet. 2:24; but see Acts 13:29) and is perhaps deliberately aimed at associating the crucifixion with the curse of Deuteronomy 21:22f. (which, however, spoke of the hanging of an already dead body on a tree; cf. Josh. 10:26; see note on 9:4 for Paul's use of Deut. 21:22f.). The effect of this would have been to highlight the guilt of those who had subjected Jesus to such a death and at the same time to set the act in sharper contrast with the action of God in glorifying his Servant. To this contrast Luke has made his own contribution by choosing a verb that pictures the leaders' part as though they had done him to death with their own hands. On the construction "whom you had killed," see note on 4:10.

5:31 / But God had raised the crucified Jesus **to his own right side**, or better, "by means of his right hand" (see disc. on 2:33), as **Prince** (translated "Author" in 3:15; see note on 11:20) **and Savior** of humanity. The verb can mean both "to raise," in the literal sense, and "to exalt." In that latter sense, it is used in the LXX of the exaltation of the Servant of God in Isaiah 52:13, and almost certainly Luke (whose language this is), but perhaps Peter also, intended to make this allusion. The title **Savior** occurs here for the first time in Acts and again only at 13:23. It is little used in the Gospels (Luke 2:11; John 4:42) and, for the most part, belongs to the later books of the New Testament. But this is perhaps more accidental than significant. Jesus himself was fully aware of his saving mission (Luke 19:10), as were the apostles (cf. 2:21; 4:9, 12), so that though the title itself may not have been widely used, what it signified lay at the very heart of the faith from the outset. Its use here may owe something to the Moses/Christ typology of the early church, this reference being virtually equivalent to the manner in which Moses is described in 7:35.

As Savior, Jesus had come to **give repentance and forgiveness of sins to Israel**. Peter's statement does not necessarily exclude other peoples, but again, it would appear that he had not yet grasped the universal implications of the gospel (see disc. on 2:39 and 3:26). But even without that wider vision these were bold words to address to the Sanhedrin. The Jews had a saying that God keeps salvation in his own power (b. *Sanhedrin* 113a), and here was Peter ascribing salvation to Jesus. How precisely Jesus was able to save or the people to receive his salvation is not explained. Peter may have said more than Luke tells us, or he may have left such questions unanswered, contenting himself simply with this bald statement of his belief (cf. 4:12).

5:32 / He ended by adding that the apostles were **witnesses of these things**, that is, to the facts on which this faith rested—the life, death, resurrection, and ascension of Jesus (cf. 1:3, 9). But there was another witness also, **the Holy Spirit**. This reference can be understood in two senses. First, the very fact that the Holy Spirit had been given at Pentecost was evidence that the day of salvation had come (see notes on 2:17ff.). But now the Holy Spirit himself bore witness with the apostles that this was indeed the day of salvation. With this, we may compare the words of Jesus in John 15:26f., where the same twofold witness is mentioned, with the further thought that the Spirit brings this witness home to the people's hearts, convincing them that the apostolic testimony is true (cf. 15:28; Rom. 8:16). Notice, too, the connection in the verse before us between obedience and the gift of the Spirit, which would "seem to be in substantial conceptual agreement with John 14:15–16, which teaches that if a man keeps Christ's commandments, the Father will give him 'another Counselor' who will remain with him forever" (F. L. Cribbs, *Perspectives*, p. 50; cf. v. 29, and see notes on 2:4).

5:33 / Peter's rejoinder did nothing to appease the council. Already sensitive to blame for their part in Jesus' death and suspecting that the apostles were deliberately attempting to bring them into public disrepute, they heard this blunt accusation (v. 30) only as confirmation of their suspicions, and it inflamed them all the more against the apostles. Luke graphically describes them as "being sawn asunder (in heart)." Their immediate reaction was to pass sentence of death upon the apostles, perhaps on the pretext of blasphemy, but really on no better grounds than that they had dared to defy the Sanhedrin by teaching a doctrine to which it (or some of its members at least) took great exception.

5:34–35 / However, wiser counsel prevailed. The Sanhedrin was restrained by one of its number, a Pharisee named Gamaliel (cf. 22:3). Asking that the apostles be removed from the chamber, he urged his colleagues to be careful in what they did with these men, for God might be with them (cf. v. 39). It may seem strange that a Pharisee, a member of the sect that had many times been at loggerheads with Jesus (e.g., Luke 5:21, 30; 7:30; 11:53; 15:2; 16:14; see also Luke 11:39–52; 12:1; 16:15; 18:9–14), should now come to the defense of Jesus' followers. There is ample evidence, however, that it had not been all antipathy between Jesus and the Pharisees (cf. Luke 7:36; 11:37; 14:1; John 3:1ff.; 7:50; 19:39), and in any case, the issue was now very different from the one that had divided them. Then, it had been a question of due regard for the law. The Pharisees had a clear understanding of how the law should be kept, and when they saw that Jesus did not conform to their view, some went so far as to speak of contriving his death (Mark 3:6, though in the end it was the Sadducees rather than the Pharisees who were chiefly

responsible; see disc. on 4:1f.). In this regard, nothing had
changed. The Pharisees were as quick to condemn Stephen as
they had been to condemn Jesus when the law was at stake (see
disc. on 6:12–14; 8:1). But for all that, Christians and Pharisees
had much in common, not least their belief in the general resurrection of the dead, though few Pharisees accepted the grounds
on which the Christian belief rested (see disc. on 4:2; cf. 15:5;
23:6ff.; 26:4ff.). And it was this issue that now brought Gamaliel
to their defense. The Sadducees repudiated the doctrine, and the
Pharisees were glad of any excuse to take cause against them (cf.
23:6–9). Because they were a political force to be reckoned with,
when a Pharisee spoke in the council, the Sadducees were bound
to take notice.

5:36–39 / Gamaliel argued, on the one hand, that if it
were no more than a human movement, it would soon disap-
pear (v. 38, Gk. "be overthrown," as of a rebellion) with the loss
of its leader, as other movements had. In the recent past, he reminded them, there had been **Theudas** (v. 36) and **Judas the Galilean** (v. 37), each of whom had been killed and their followers
scattered. On the other hand, if the Christian movement had its
origin in God, how could they hope to withstand it? Such advice
was typically Pharisaic in both temper and content. It picked up
the leading point in their theology, namely, that God rules the
world by a wise providence that is over all. Everything, they said,
was in God's hand except the fear of God, by which they meant
that God is sovereign and the human part is simply to obey and
to leave the issue with him. The Sadducees, in contrast with this,
held a doctrine of human self-determination. Nevertheless, for
the reason mentioned earlier (see on vv. 34–35), the council followed Gamaliel's advice (v. 38f.).

5:40 / The apostles were recalled and sentenced to be
whipped. The charge of blasphemy (if indeed that had been the
charge) was apparently dropped, leaving only the lesser charge
of disobedience. It was within the competence of the Sanhedrin,
and also of the lower synagogal courts, both to sentence and to
carry out punishment without deference to the Roman authorities in any case other than a capital offense (cf. 22:19; Mark 13:9;
2 Cor. 11:24). The maximum penalty prescribed by the law for
a minor offense was forty blows (Deut. 25:2f.), though in practice this was reduced to thirty-nine for fear of exceeding the

number. The punishment was generally carried out with a three-thonged scourge, and in some cases in which the maximum penalty was applied the victims are known to have died from its effects (b. *Makkoth* 3.14; cf. also b. *Sanhedrin* 9.5). Thus, though a "minor" penalty, it was a severe one and in this case we may suppose that the apostles felt the full severity of the law. They were then ordered (with as much effect as before, cf. v. 42) **not to speak in the name of Jesus** ("upon the name . . . "; see disc. on 4:18) and so were released.

5:41 / If one prophecy of their Lord had been fulfilled in all this (John 16:2), another was fulfilled in its sequel (Matt. 5:11f.). Despite the scourging, the apostles left the council **rejoicing because they had been counted worthy of suffering disgrace for the Name** (cf. 21:13). Luke's description provides us with a striking oxymoron—*"worthy* to suffer *disgrace"*—though the event itself was to become a commonplace in the church (cf. 16:23ff.; Rom. 5:3f.; 2 Cor. 6:8–10; Phil. 1:29; 1 Pet. 1:6; 4:12–16). What they endured brings to mind Paul's remark in 2 Corinthians 4:17: "For our light and momentary troubles are achieving for us an eternal glory that far outweighs them all."

5:42 / The narrative is brought to a close with another sketch of church life (see disc. on 2:42–47). **They**—chiefly the apostles, but possibly others also—**never stopped teaching and proclaiming the good news**, both in public (in the temple) and in private, in their believers' meetings in the house churches (see note on 14:27). Their message was essentially this: "The Messiah has come in the person of Jesus." This must have rankled with the Sadducees especially, since this claim for Jesus was always based on the fact of his resurrection, but there was little they could do about it while the Christians remained popular and the Pharisees unwilling to take the Sadducees' side against them (see disc. on 6:12ff.).

Additional Notes §13

5:21 / **They called together the Sanhedrin—the full assembly of the elders of Israel**: lit., they called together "the council and all the senate of the children of Israel." But was the senate, as some have suggested, a body other than the Sanhedrin—perhaps men of age and experience, who were asked to join the council as assessors or who constituted some other assembly, larger perhaps than the Sanhedrin and only summoned on special occasions? The term is found nowhere else in the New Testament, but in the LXX is used in several places of the Sanhedrin itself (1 Macc. 12:6; 2 Macc. 1:10; 4:44; 11:27), and for that reason and because in vv. 27 and 34 "Sanhedrin" is used alone, it is probably best to regard the "and" in the literal translation of this verse simply as explanatory of the whole phrase and intended to emphasize that this was a full meeting of the council.

5:31 / **Savior**: It is sometimes suggested that this title came into use only after the church entered a Hellenistic environment. Here there were many "saviors" already, not least the Roman emperor himself. But no Christian could affirm "Caesar is Savior." What would have been more natural, then, than for them to transfer his title to Jesus, who was, after all, "another king" to believers (17:7)? The idea, however, is not peculiarly Hellenistic, and the soil from which the Christian use sprang is much more likely to have been the Old Testament, though the prevailing atmosphere of Caesar worship may well have hastened its growth. In the Old Testament, God is Savior, and when the salvation of which he is the author was found to be in Christ, the title Savior was easily given to him.

5:34 / **A Pharisee named Gamaliel**: the son of Simon and perhaps the grandson of Hillel (according to a late and doubtful tradition) and certainly the father of the first Jewish patriarch after the fall of Jerusalem, whom we call Gamaliel II. He represented the liberal wing of his party, the school of Hillel, as opposed to that of Shammai. The influence Gamaliel was able to exert on the Sanhedrin is readily explainable. We have already observed that the Pharisees, though a minority in the council, had the political power to impose their will on the majority (see disc. on 4:5). Besides this, Gamaliel was himself highly respected. He was the first to whom the title Rabban ("our teacher") was given, a title higher than Rab ("teacher") or Rabbi ("my teacher"). Later, it was said of him, "Since Rabban Gamaliel died there has been no more reverence for the Law, and purity and abstinence died out at the same time" (m. *Sota* 9.15).

5:36–37 / **Theudas appeared . . . After him, Judas the Galilean appeared**: Gamaliel is represented as citing two cases in which revolutionary movements came to nothing. The first was under a certain Theudas. Josephus also mentions a Theudas who gave himself out to be a prophet and gathered around him "a great part of the people." This uprising was put down by the procurator Crispius Fadus. Some of Theudas' followers were killed, others were captured. He himself was beheaded (*Antiquities* 20.97–99). But a serious chronological discrepancy must be faced if the Theudas of Josephus is the Theudas of Luke. The latter is said to have arisen before **the time of the census**, i.e., before about A.D. 6–7, whereas Josephus places him in the reign of Claudius, about A.D.

44–45. But are they the same? Because Josephus goes on to speak of Judas, there are many who say that they are and that Luke has drawn his information from Josephus, making an error in so doing by failing to notice that the Jewish historian's reference to Judas is parenthetical and that Judas had, in fact, preceded Theudas. But comparing the two accounts there is little to suggest that Luke made use of Josephus and much that points to an earlier date for Luke than would be possible if he had borrowed from the other (the *Antiquities* appeared about A.D. 94). However, Josephus may provide us with a solution. In describing the events that preceded the rebellion of Judas he remarks: "At this time [i.e., in the days when Varus was governor of Syria] there were ten thousand other disorders in Judea, which were like tumults" (*Antiquities* 17.269–270). Of these innumerable disturbances, he gives an account of no more than four, though in the same chapter he adds: "Judea was full of robberies, and whenever the several companies of the rebels could light upon anyone to head them, he was created a king immediately." Now amid so many outbreaks, spoken of but not described, it is not difficult to suppose that one may have been led by another Theudas. The name, contracted from Theodorus or Theodotus ("God's gift"), was not uncommon and was one that would appeal to Jews as the Greek equivalent of a number of Hebrew names. On this basis, Luke's Theudas has been identified with Matthias ("a gift"), son of Margalothus, an insurgent at the time of Herod the Great who features prominently in Josephus' narrative (*Antiquities* 18.147–150). This identification, of course, cannot be proved.

If Luke's accuracy has been called into question over Theudas, it is remarkably confirmed by his reference to Judas. For Gamaliel speaks of his insurrection as coming to nothing—as he could only have done at this time (say about A.D. 34–35), but not some ten years later, when the followers of Judas again gathered to form what Josephus calls the "fourth philosophy of the Jews" (*War* 2.117–118; *Antiquities* 18.1–10). They were later known as the Zealots (see *BC*, vol. 1, pp. 421ff.). Luke alone (reporting Gamaliel) mentions that Judas was put to death. The census to which Luke refers in connection with Judas was taken in A.D. 6–7 after Archelaus had been deposed and Judea brought under direct Roman rule. The census was related to the introduction of a tax, and it was against this tax that Judas had rebelled (*Antiquities* 18.1–10).

5:38–39 / If their purpose or activity is of human origin . . . But if it is from God . . . : Their purpose may refer specifically to the apostles' intention to defy the Sanhedrin by preaching (v. 19; cf. 4:20) and their . . . activity to their preaching generally. The change in the Greek from the subjunctive in the first of the two conditional clauses to the indicative in the second may indicate that the second is more likely. But, of course, the language was Luke's, not Gamaliel's.

§14   The Choosing of the Seven (Acts 6:1–7)

This chapter and the next, which are largely an account of the "acts of Stephen," serve a twofold purpose. First, they complete Luke's picture of the early church while it was still for the most part confined to Jerusalem, noting certain problems that arose in connection with the common fund and how they were resolved. Second, they set the scene for the later chapters that tell of the church's expansion beyond Jerusalem. This they do in two ways: first, by tracing the course of events that forced many believers to flee the city, taking the gospel with them into Judea and Samaria and ultimately "to the ends of the earth" (1:8), and second, by exemplifying what was to be the pattern of that later expansion. Jewish resistance comes to a head in these chapters. There is a progression from warning (4:21) to flogging (5:40) to death (7:58), with Stephen's death marking "the final failure of the mission to the capital" (J. C. O'Neill, p. 85). For now "the people," who are portrayed positively in the earlier chapters, become the mob aligned with their leaders. They reject the gospel, not considering themselves worthy of eternal life (as Paul would put it), and the church turns to the Gentiles (cf. 13:46). This did not happen at once, nor did it happen deliberately to begin with (humanly speaking); but happen it did, and here in the "acts of Stephen" is where the story begins (see further the disc. on 7:54–8:1a). Hengel finds a number of distinctive and even "un-Lukan" expressions in this chapter that betray the "bedrock of a source" (*Jesus*, p. 3).

6:1 / Luke has no precise references to time in this part of the book, and the notice of time which introduces this narrative simply places it in the early days of the church. Throughout this period **the number of disciples was increasing**, and here the word **disciple** makes its first appearance in Acts as a title for Christians (cf. vv. 2, 7; 9:36; 11:26; 19:1–4). That the term **disciple** was still used makes it clear that the disciples of Jesus formed the nucleus of the church and that the relationship that Jesus had

had with them remained the pattern of his relationship with the church. A feature of the life of the early church was their readiness to meet the needs of their poor (cf. 2:44f.; 4:32ff.). Whether what was given was in service or material goods is not known, but we see here that it was given **daily**. We notice, too, that it is described as a "ministry"—the same word as that used in verse 4 of the ministry of preaching. "There are different kinds of service, but the same Lord" (1 Cor. 12:5). But such were the demands on this service as the church continued to grow that it ceased to be carried out as well as it might have been, a problem made the more acute by their being now (perhaps there always had been) disparate groups within the church that met separately. In addition to all the difficulty of maintaining communications that that entailed, there was still but one fund to serve them all. Under these circumstances it was inevitable that someone would be overlooked—and someone was.

A group called by Luke the "Hellenists" (NIV **Grecian Jews**) complained that their widows were being neglected. From the tense of the verb (imperfect) it would appear that this neglect had been going on for some time, and for this the Hellenists blamed the "Hebrews" (NIV **Hebraic Jews**). But who were these Hellenists and Hebrews? The terms are most commonly understood in a linguistic sense, the Hellenists as Greek-speaking Jews (who had little incentive to learn Aramaic and so, for the most part, did not) and the Hebrews who spoke Aramaic in addition to Greek. By this definition Paul was a Hebrew, and so he calls himself in Philippians 3:5 (cf. 2 Cor. 11:22). In more recent discussions, these definitions have been further refined by making the language in which they worshiped the criterion for Hellenists and Hebrews, rather than the language of their everyday life. Others, not satisfied that the distinction was simply one of language, have suggested that these Hellenists may also have been "Hellenized Jews"—that they belonged to a "liberal" synagogue, not holding as fast to the law and the temple as some. This suggestion rests on the cognate verb sometimes having the sense "to imitate Greek manners and customs." But in most cases it means only "to speak Greek," and in any case, it must be remembered that the Hellenists had returned to Jerusalem for no other reason than their devotion to the law and the temple. "As a rule they were certainly not 'liberal' and were probably closer to the attitude which Paul says he had when he was a Pharisee. . . . Otherwise they would not

have returned to Judea, the culture and economy of which was
hardly attractive, and would have chosen somewhere other than
Jerusalem to live" (Hengel, *Jesus*, p. 18). It is difficult, then, to go
beyond the linguistic definition of the term—a conclusion confirmed by the fact that the term is limited to Jerusalem, the majority of whose population spoke Aramaic. In the Greek-speaking
Diaspora, the name Hellenist would have been meaningless.

So, then, the Hellenists of this passage were Christians
drawn from the Greek-speaking synagogues of Jerusalem (presumably by the preaching of bilingual Hebrews) and forming their
own Greek-speaking Christian community. They were a minority
within a predominantly Hebrew church. The apostles themselves
were, of course, Hebrews. And if anyone in particular was at fault
over the neglect of the Hellenists' widows it was they, for they
administered the common fund. It is hard to believe that this neglect was deliberate (as Dunn suggests, *Unity*, p. 272). More likely,
they were simply unaware of the problem, largely because they
had too much to do.

6:2–4 / No sooner was the complaint made by the Hellenists (and it was never denied) than the matter was taken in
hand. **The Twelve**—the only place in Acts where the apostles are
given this title—**gathered all the disciples together** and, in effect,
made confession that they had not run the fund properly; nor
were they able to do so. Time was the problem, for they had to
give first priority to **the ministry of the word of God** (v. 2; cf. v.
4) and to **prayer** (v. 4). Again, the definite article, "the prayer"
(so the Greek), implies that a particular form or time of prayer
was in view (the church "services"? cf. 1:14 and 2:42 for "the
prayers" and 3:1 and 10:9 for the times of prayer). They suggested,
therefore, that seven others should be appointed to administer
the fund in their place. They should be men **known to be full
of the Spirit and wisdom** (v. 3; cf. v. 5; 7:55; 11:24; 13:52; Luke
4:1). A distinction needs to be made between being "filled with
the Spirit" and being "full of the Spirit." Being filled has reference to a momentary inspiration (see disc. on 4:8), being full, to
the believer's possession of the Spirit, or better, the Spirit's possession of the believer (see notes on 2:2ff.; cf. Gal. 5:25) and his
endowment of the believer with spiritual gifts. In this case the
church was to look for men with the gift of practical wisdom that
would enable them to manage the fund.

6:5–6 / **This proposal pleased the whole group** (see note on v. 2), and they chose the seven men listed in verse 5. The first thing that one notices about them is that they all have Greek names. This in itself does not mean that they were all Hellenists, though it very well may. Many Palestinian Jews bore Greek names, such as Philip, Didymas, and Andrew among the Twelve. But with the exception of Philip, the Seven does not contain any of the more familiar Jewish-Greek names that are attested for this region (see Hengel, *Jesus*, pp. 144f.). If, then, the Seven were Hellenists, their selection by a meeting of the whole church says much for the grace of the Hebrew majority and for the sense of unity that they all had in Christ. The things that held them together were greater far than their differences.

We cannot say that we know anything of the Seven except for Stephen and Philip. According to a late tradition, these two had been of the Seventy (Epiphanius, *Panarion* 20.4; cf. Luke 10:1ff.), and if Jesus had sent the Seventy into Samaria (cf. Luke 9:52; 17:11), this might explain Philip's subsequent work in that area. But this is sheer speculation. What we do know of the two will be discussed in the following sections. Here, we need only notice that Stephen is said to have been **a man full of faith and of the Holy Spirit** (v. 5). His was a faith not different in kind from the faith that all Christians have, but exceptional in the extent to which he was willing to trust Christ, to take him at his word and to risk all for Christ's sake. Of the rest, **Nicolas from Antioch** is noteworthy in that he was a Gentile by birth, having been first **a convert to Judaism** and then to the Christian faith (v. 5). Josephus reports that the Jews of Antioch were particularly active in proselytizing (*War* 7.43–53), and Nicolas' conversion may be a case in point. Ramsay sees his inclusion in the Seven as most significant. "The Church was wider than the pure Jewish race; and the non-Jewish element was raised to official rank," though as Ramsay himself concedes, there was nothing in this out of harmony with the viewpoint of those more conservative Jewish Christians who (later) wished to keep the church within the ambit of the Jewish rebellion (*Paul*, p. 375; cf. p. 157). The reference to Nicolas introduces for the first time in Acts the name of the city that would soon become the springboard for the Gentile mission. Luke's own name has sometimes been associated with Antioch (see Introduction and the disc. on 11:19–30), and for this reason also he may have been interested in mentioning the city.

The seven men whom the church had selected were presented to the apostles, who in turn **prayed and laid their hands on them** (v. 6). This is the first mention in Acts of the laying on of hands (other than for healing; see note on 5:12) as the rite by which church members were designated for specific tasks (cf. 13:3). In the Old Testament it signified sometimes a blessing (cf. Gen. 48:14), sometimes a commissioning (cf. Num. 27:18, 23), and so was a fitting mark of the church's recognition of God's gifts in these men and of their dedication to the service of God and the church. Moreover, that it was the apostles who laid hands on them (but see notes) indicates that the Seven had apostolic authorization for what they would do: they would act, with regard to the fund, as the apostles' representatives (cf. 13:3; 1 Tim. 4:14; 5:22; 2 Tim. 1:6).

6:7 / Thus, in a context of prayer and a spirit of good will, the church put its house in order. Unity was maintained. The impression is given that the resolution of this matter brought renewed blessing—**the word of God spread**; that is, the apostolic preaching of Christ (see disc. on 5:20) was heard by more and more people, and consequently **the number of disciples in Jerusalem increased rapidly.** The imperfect tense of the verb in each of these statements emphasizes that this was an ongoing process (cf. 2:41; 4:4; 5:14; 6:1). Among those won to the new faith were many **priests** who had come up to the city to serve their turn in the temple and had, perhaps, heard the gospel as it was preached in the temple. We are told that they were **obedient to the faith.** This verb is found in Acts only here and may have been chosen deliberately to suggest that they were especially under pressure, perhaps from the Sadducean hierarchy, to renounce the faith (understood in an objective sense as a body of belief; see disc. on 14:22) and yet had remained true. It seems unlikely that these priests held any special position within the church. The reference of this verse may be to the work of the Twelve now that they could give themselves to preaching unimpeded by other cares. One supposes that it was chiefly among people whose language and culture they shared, namely, the Hebrews. The next section may speak of a parallel work of Stephen among the Hellenists. In each case, Jerusalem remained the scene of their labors.

Additional Notes §14

6:1 / **Their widows:** There is reason to think that among the Hellenists generally women predominated (see disc. on 2:5), and of all people, these single, older women from the Diaspora would have been most vulnerable. Often they would have relied entirely on the support of the community. On the care of widows in the early church, see James 1:27 (cf. Deut. 14:29; 24:19; 26:12; Isa. 1:17; Zech. 7:10). In time, an order of widows developed (1 Tim. 5:3-16; Ignatius, *Smyrnaeans* 13.1; Polycarp, *Philippians* 4.3), but neither here nor in 9:39 is there any reason to think that it had already made a nascent appearance.

6:2 / **All the disciples** (see disc. on v. 1): The word *plethos*, which occurs in this phrase, is found with two meanings in Acts; first, "a crowd, a large number of persons" (so 2:6; etc.) and, second, "the full assembly or congregation." The latter is intended here and in v. 5, in 4:32 and 15:12. In each of these verses the reference is to the full assembly of Jerusalem Christians. With the spread of the gospel the same term is applied later to the Christians in Antioch (15:30). It is striking that a similar expression, "the many," is used in the Dead Sea Scrolls of the Essenes as they met in session to decide common matters (see 1QS 6.1, 7-9, 11-18, 21, 25; 7.16; 8.19, 26; CD 13.7; 14.7, 12; 15.8).

To wait on tables: This could mean to serve food at tables (cf. Luke 16:21; 22:21, 30), but "tables" was also a figure of speech for financial transactions, because money lenders sat at tables to do their business. The word is used in this sense in Matt. 21:12; 25:27; Luke 19:23; John 2:15, and probably here, with the apostles asserting that they should not leave their primary ministry to serve as bankers and money distributors.

6:3 / **Choose seven men:** There are a number of parallels in rabbinic literature to the appointment of a board of seven men as delegates or representatives of others. Ehrhardt suggests that the authority for appointing the Seven and the means whereby they were set apart for their work are found in Num. 11:16f.—the story of the appointment of the seventy to assist Moses. "We know from the Talmud that the rabbis maintained that these seventy men were ordained with laying on of hands. We have therefore good reason to believe that this was the precedent for St. Peter and the Apostles' ordaining the Seven—instead of seventy—in the way in which they were ordained, with laying on of hands" (p. 30).

Though their task was "to serve" (Gk. *diakonein*) and their work was referred to as a "service" (Gk. *diakonia*), the Seven were never called "deacons" (Gk. *diakonoi*). The first mention of deacons in the New Testament is not found until Phil. 1:1. In Rom. 16:1 a deaconess is mentioned. Tradition has it that the appointment of the Seven marked the beginning of this order (see Irenaeus, *Against Heresies* 1.26; 3.12; 4.15; Cyprian, *Epistles* 3.3; Eusebius, *Ecclesiastical History* 6.43), but the New

Testament offers tradition little support. It is noteworthy, for example, that when the early church wished to distinguish Philip from his namesake, the apostle, it did not call him "Philip the deacon," but "Philip the evangelist" (21:8). With the scattering of the Hellenists (see disc. on 8:1b), the role of the Seven with regard to the fund seems to have passed to "the elders" (see note on 11:30).

Full of the Spirit and wisdom: cf. v. 5, "full of faith and of the Holy Spirit." In each case it seems best to take "wisdom" and "faith" as a particular manifestation of the Spirit's work in their lives, though the order of the words in the second makes this more difficult. The sense, then, is probably that they were "full" of the Holy Spirit (see disc. on 6:2-4), and this showed especially in their faith and wisdom. The alternatives are to see each phrase as expressing only one idea. "Full of the wisdom that the Spirit gives," and "Full of the faith that the Spirit gives," or to interpret each as meaning that they had two separate gifts: "Full of faith or wisdom and full of the Holy Spirit," i.e., of the divine enthusiasm. Neither is as satisfactory as the first suggestion.

6:5 / Nicolas from Antioch, a convert to Judaism, lit., "Nicolas, a proselyte": "Wherever the Jews went in the Gentile world, their presence gave rise to two conflicting tendencies. On the one hand the Jew possessed the knowledge of the one true God; and amidst the universal corruption, idolatry, and superstition of the ancient world, this saving knowledge exercised a powerful attraction." On the other hand, this knowledge was enshrined in a law that in many respects proved much less attractive (Rackham, p. 240; see also J. Murphy-O'Connor, *St. Paul's Corinth*, p. 80). Consequently, among those who were drawn to Judaism there were varying degrees of commitment. Some went the whole way, submitting themselves to instruction, circumcision, and baptism and thereafter offering sacrifice in the temple, though in practice this latter requirement may often have been waived. More women than men accepted Judaism, because of the requirement of circumcision in the case of men. Others, while not prepared to go so far, still worshiped and studied in the synagogues. It is commonly held that in Acts the latter are indicated by the terms "those worshiping God" (Gk. *sebomenoi*; cf. 13:43; 16:14; 17:4, 17; 18:7), "those fearing God" (Gk. *phoboumenoi*; cf. 10:2, 22; 13:16, 26), and those who are "religious" (Gk. *eusebēs*; cf. 10:2, 7 and the verb in 17:23), whereas the former, the full converts, are alone called "proselytes" (Gk. *prosēlytos*; cf. 2:10; 6:5). An exception to this rule, however, is found in 13:43 with the expression "the worshiping proselytes" (Gk. *tōn sebomenōn prosēlytōn*). It would appear that these are the same people as those called "God-fearers" in 13:16, 26, and on that basis we may assume that the word "proselytes" is used here, not of full converts to Judaism, but simply of those Gentiles who attended the synagogue in Pisidian Antioch. But see Marshall, p. 229, for a different interpretation.

6:6 / They presented these men to the apostles, who prayed and laid their hands on them: Though the church was certainly instructed to choose the Seven, it is not quite as clear as NIV makes out who **prayed and laid their hands on them**. If the grammatical agreements of the Greek are any guide, then it was done by the whole church acting "in the presence of the apostles." This view is supported by D. Daube, who believes that by this act the people made them their representatives, as the Israelites had once made Levites their representatives by laying hands on them (Num. 27:18; Deut. 34:9) (*The New Testament and Rabbinic Judaism*, pp. 237ff.). But allowing that there may be an agreement, not of grammar, but of sense, the flow of the Greek sentence suggests, rather, that it was the apostles who laid hands on them (appointed them) with prayer. This interpretation is made explicit in the Western text. In the light of v. 3, "we will turn this responsibility over to them" (unless we take the "we" to mean the whole church), the latter interpretation appears to be the most likely, the more so as it follows broadly the pattern of Matthias' appointment (1:15ff.)—the apostles initiate the process, the people play their part in choosing the person, but the apostles make the appointment. See note on 6:3.

§15 Stephen Seized (Acts 6:8–15)

6:8 / Although the Seven were appointed to an administrative role within the church as a whole, they may already have had a wider ministry within their own Hellenistic circles (still assuming that they were Hellenists), so that the picture we now have of Stephen as a preacher need come as no surprise (see Hengel, *Acts*, p. 74; Dunn, *Unity*, p. 270). He is described as **a man full of God's grace**—a phrase capable of bearing the double sense of enjoying God's favor (cf. 18:27) and of being gracious himself toward others (cf. Luke 4:22). Stephen appears to have been a man of great personal charm. He was also an effective preacher (cf. v. 10), whose ministry was accompanied by signs of divine power in the **great wonders and miraculous signs** (see notes on 2:22) that he did **among the people**. This little pen-sketch establishes Stephen at once as a true (if unofficial) member of the apostolic college (cf. 4:33; 5:12; 8:13; Luke 24:19).

6:9 / Naturally, the Christian Hellenists were drawn to their own kind, and so it was that Stephen found himself in debate with **members of the Synagogue of the Freedmen (as it was called)**—clearly a Hellenist synagogue (or more than one; see note) to which Stephen himself may once have belonged (as an Alexandrian? see note). And because it had links also with Cilicia, it is tempting to suppose that Paul was even then a member (see disc. on 9:11). This would help to explain his involvement in Stephen's death (7:58; 8:1). It may also explain why he singled out these Hellenists in 9:29 (assuming that it was they) to hear the gospel for which Stephen had died. On the other hand, if "The Freedmen" was indeed a Hellenist synagogue and if Paul's description of himself as a Hebrew meant what Luke meant by that term, then the suggestion that he and Stephen had once belonged to the same congregation must be ruled out. In any case, Paul appears to have lived in Jerusalem from an early age and may have had no strong personal links with the land of his birth, though obviously some ties with Cilicia did still remain (cf. 9:30; see disc. on 22:3).

6:10–11 / Inspired by the Spirit (cf. v. 3), Stephen spoke with such cogency that his opponents were unable to get the better of him in arguments (cf. Luke 12:12; 21:15; 1 Cor. 1:17; 2:6; 12:8f.). So they resorted to other means. They hired informers to accuse him of **blasphemy against Moses and against God** (v. 11; cf. 17:5). Spirit-filled preaching will often have the effect of hardening opposition. Strictly speaking, **blasphemy** means to offer an insult to God, but in this case it probably meant that he had "blasphemed" God in his representative, by speaking against Moses (see further disc.).

6:12–14 / Whether intended or not, this charge had repercussions wider than Stephen himself. The whole church would be affected in some degree, and the Christian Hellenist community in Jerusalem virtually wiped out (see disc. on 8:1b). From the Sanhedrin to "the man in the street," it turned into enemies those who had until now at least tolerated the believers. This in turn removed the one thing that had restrained the Sanhedrin from a thoroughgoing persecution of the believers, namely, their popularity (cf. 2:47; 5:13, 26). At the same time—and for the first time—the Sanhedrin was itself united in its resolve to do something about them (see disc. on 5:34f.). Stephen was the first victim of this new resolve. He was brought before the council, where the accusations against him became more specific (and more exaggerated). **This fellow**, they said, **never stops speaking against this holy place and against the law** (v. 13). Abundant evidence from the first century shows how sensitive the Jews were on these issues (see, e.g., Josephus, *War* 2.145–149 and 12.223–227; *Antiquities* 18.29–35). Undoubtedly the charge was false in the form in which it was made. But false witnesses do sometimes hint at the truth, and Stephen did hold opinions on the law and the temple that must have been as disturbing for many Christians as they were for Jews.

The key to Stephen's thought lies, perhaps, in the vision of Christ that he had at the end of his trial. He saw Jesus as "the Son of Man standing at the right hand of God" (7:56) and from this may have understood that, like the celestial Son of Man of Daniel 7:13ff., Jesus of Nazareth had received authority and honor

and power and would be served by all nations. Here, then, was
one greater than Moses (cf. Luke 11:31f.). The implication of this
Christology was that "the traditional Jewish 'saving event' of the
exodus and the revelation of Sinai were basically devalued in the
light of the time of salvation which had now dawned with Jesus"
(Hengel, *Jesus*, p. 23). Not that Jesus in Stephen's teaching stood
apart from Moses. On the contrary, he was, for Stephen, the
Prophet-like-Moses (see disc. on 7:35ff., also 3:22). Hence his estimate of him as the law-giver. Notice the charge in verse 14.
Stephen did not teach that Christ "is the end of the law" (Rom.
10:4), only that he had changed the law (lit. "the customs," both
the written law and the oral traditions; see disc. on 4:2f.; cf. 15:1;
21:21; 26:3; 28:17). This was broadly true. Christ had reinterpre-
ted the law in terms of its spirit—God's will is fulfilled in the com-
mandment to love. But in certain specific instances he had actually
set the law of Moses aside. The regulations concerning purity were
a case in point. The important thing now was not ritual purity
but a clean heart (Mark 7:15). Thus, in the saying about destroy-
ing the temple and in three days raising another (John 2:19; cf.
Gospel of Thomas 71), he had declared the temple obsolete as
the place of expiation. Cleansing would now come through his
own death and resurrection (cf. Mark 15:38; John 4:21ff.; Eph.
2:20ff.; Heb. 10:20; 1 Pet. 2:5; note that in the Gospels the Son
of Man terminology is often connected with the idea of the Suffering Servant who would give his life for the many; see disc.
on 7:55f.). Clearly Stephen had understood Jesus' teaching and
had made it his own. But he had gone further than Jesus. Not
simply had the temple lost its expiatory function, but it had had
no legitimate function ever. From the outset, it had been a mistake (see disc. on 7:47ff.). Even so, we cannot think that he, any
more than Jesus, ever threatened to tear it down as the witnesses
claimed (v. 14).

    6:15 / When the witnesses against Stephen had finished,
all who were sitting in the Sanhedrin looked intently at him (see
disc. on 3:4). What they saw was a man whose **face was like the
face of an angel**. This is the description of one whose communion
with God was such that something of the divine glory was reflected in him. Oddly, the same had been said of Moses (Exod.
34:29ff.; cf. 2 Cor. 3:12–18). He and Stephen had this in common, then, that they bore the mark of having been with God.

And yet Stephen was accused of "speaking against Moses and against God" (v. 11). Plainly the accusation was false, and this was his vindication by a higher court (see disc. on 7:55f.). Meanwhile, for the members of the Sanhedrin, it must have been a disquieting experience, for Judges 13:6 describes the face of an angel as "frightening." So God's messengers will sometimes be to those who are bent on resisting his will.

Additional Notes §15

6:9 / **The synagogue of the Freedmen**: There appear to have been many synagogues in Jerusalem (cf. 24:12), though we may dismiss the talmudic tradition that assigns to the city no less than four hundred and eighty. This number was probably fixed upon as the numerical equivalent of the Hebrew word "full" in Isa. 1:21, a city "full of Justice." For a brief but useful discussion of the synagogues of Jerusalem, see Hengel, *Jesus*, pp. 16ff. The question here is how many synagogues are indicated in this verse—one, or more than one? Bruce, *Book*, p. 133, holds that there was only one "attended by freedmen and their descendants from the four areas mentioned." This is also the opinion of Jeremias, *Jerusalem*, pp. 65f., who identifies it with a synagogue discovered in 1913–14 in excavations on Ophel (see also H. Strathmann, *"Libertinoi," TDNT*, vol. 4, p. 265). The construction of Luke's sentence, however, favors the view that two synagogues are indicated, one for Freedmen, Cyrenians, and Alexandrians, the other for Cilicians and Asians. Others hold that there are three: that of the Libertines, another of the men of Alexandria and Cyrene, and another of the men of Cilicia and Asia. Others make it five. Some scholars have suggested the emendation of the Greek *Libertinon*, "of freedmen," to *Libystinon*, making them Jews "of Libya" and the synagogue that of a group of African Jews from Libya, Cyrene, and Alexandria (listed from west to east). This suggestion is an attractive one, but lacks textual support. In any case, the Libyans are usually *Libystikoi* in Greek. More commonly, the **Freedmen** have been regarded as the descendants of the Jews who were taken to Rome by Pompey about 60 B.C. and afterwards liberated by their Roman masters. These people and their descendants would have enjoyed the rights of Roman citizenship (Suetonius, *Tiberius* 36; Tacitus, *Annals* 2.85; Philo, *Embassy to Gaius* 23). But Sherwin-White doubts whether after such a long interval their descendants would still be called "Freedmen" (p. 152). There is some evidence for a "synagogue of the Libertines" (the same word as in our text) at Pompeii.

Jews of Cyrene . . . and Asia: see notes on 2:9ff.

Alexandria: a great seaport on the northwestern coast of the Egyptian delta, on the narrow isthmus between the sea and Lake Mareotis.

The city was founded in 322 B.C. by Alexander the Great and named after himself. Probably there was no city, next to Jerusalem, in which the Jewish population was so numerous as in Alexandria. Two of the five districts of the city (the eastern sector) were called the Jewish, from the number of Jews dwelling in them. Alexandria was the intellectual and literary center of the Diaspora. It was here that the Greek Old Testament, the Septuagint (LXX), and other works, such as the Book of Wisdom, were produced. Here lived the famous teacher Philo (20 B.C.—A.D. 50); here Apollos was trained (18:24); and here, too, Stephen may have belonged by birth and education (see disc. on 7:9ff.). The literary remains of the Alexandrian Jews testify to intellectual energy, missionary concern, and a profound seriousness about the Scriptures. These traits are evident in both Stephen and Apollos. Points of contact can also be established between Stephen and Philo (see, e.g., disc. on 7:22; see further L. W. Barnard "St. Stephen and Early Alexandria Christianity," *NTS* 7 [1960–61], pp. 31–45, esp. pp. 44f.).

Cilicia: The area to which the classical name of Cilicia applied is geographically bipartite. The western part, known as Tracheia, is a wild plateau of the Taurus range, reaching to the coast in steep and rocky terrain. Promontories form small harbors that sheltered pirates from prehistoric to Roman times. The second part of Cilicia, the region east of the Lamus River known as Cilicia Pedeias, is a fertile plain between Mount Amanus in the south and the Taurus Mountains in the north, with the sea to the west. The vital trade route between Syria and Asia Minor lay through its twin majestic passes, the Syrian Gates and the Cilician Gates (see disc. on 14:21; 15:41). For the political divisions of the region, see notes on 15:23. Not much is known of the Jewish population of Cilicia, except that there was a considerable community settled in Tarsus, the most significant city of Cilicia Pedeias, from the time of the Seleucids (see disc. on 9:11). The Babylonian Talmud, *Megillah* 26a, refers to a synagogue of the *tarsiyim* in Jerusalem, which Strathmann identifies with the Cilician synagogue of this verse (see earlier references).

§16 Stephen's Speech to the Sanhedrin (Acts 7:1-53)

More than most, this speech of Stephen has been subject to that skepticism that is inclined to regard all the speeches of Acts as Luke's own composition. There is no denying that Luke's hand may be seen in them all in their literary style and vocabulary. But there is about each of them a distinctiveness that not only fits each to its context, but in some cases, at least, to the speaker's own writings elsewhere (see, e.g., disc. on 5:30, 13.39; 15:13ff.; 20:17-38). To attribute this entirely to Luke's art is to give him greater credit than he deserves. In short, there is every reason for confidence that the speeches are genuine reflections of what was actually said, and Stephen's no less than the others. In this case, of course, there are no external criteria on which to base such a judgment. But there is an aptness about the speech and features that certainly mark it off from the others. "The speech is so distinctive within Acts and chapters 6-8 contain such distinctive features that the most plausible view is that Luke is here drawing on a source which has preserved quite accurately the views of the Hellenists or of Stephen in particular . . . Certainly the whole narrative explains the subsequent persecution of the Hellenists so well that there is no real reason to doubt its essential historicity" (Dunn, *Unity*, pp. 270f; see also L. W. Barnard, "St. Stephen and Early Alexandrian Christianity," *NTS* 7 [1960-61], pp. 31ff.).

A striking feature of the speech is its emphasis on Moses. He looms larger here than in any other speech in Acts, larger indeed than Christ himself, to whom there are only two references in all of the fifty-two verses—and even then not by his own name, but allusively, once in a reference to the Prophet-like-Moses (v. 37) and once in connection with the prophets in general "who predicted the coming of the Righteous One" (v. 52; cf. the same phenomenon in Paul's speech in 17:22-31). It is possible, of course, that Stephen was not allowed to complete what he wanted to say and that, had he been, he would have gone on in the usual way to declare that the Servant, whom men had killed, had been raised by God from the dead (for as it stands there is no mention, either, of the resurrection, which is central to most other speeches). It is possible, too, that Moses was especially important to Stephen as prefiguring Christ (this was certainly the case with a number of Jewish sects; cf. esp. vv. 35–38) and that the story of Moses was always an integral part of his proclamation. However, without entirely dismissing this last possibility, the overriding reason for the dominance of Moses in this speech lies nearer to hand.

Stephen had been charged on two counts: that he had spoken against the temple, and against the law and, therefore, against Moses (6:11, 14). In meeting these charges, he set about showing how the nation itself had spoken against Moses. And this rebellious spirit had not only manifested itself during the lawgiver's lifetime but had characterized the whole history of the nation (vv. 9, 35, 39, 51, 52). Stephen's defense (it was not defense at all in the technical sense) was not to deny their accusations (his own safety appears not to have been a consideration) but to counterattack with charges of his own. His weapon was Israel's history, and his strategy to recite that history at length, explicating two themes. (This use of the Old Testament follows a familiar literary pattern; see, e.g., Josh. 24:2–13; Neh. 9:7–13; Pss. 78; 105:12–43; 106:6–42; Ezek. 20; Judith 5:6–18.) The first of these themes we have already indicated, namely, that the Jews themselves, who had received God's law, had not obeyed it and were guilty, in that sense, of "speaking against Moses." The second, in response to their charge concerning the temple, was that "the Most High does not live in houses made by men" (v. 48). In developing this point, Stephen adopted a position unlike that of any other writer in the New Testament. Where others saw the temple as having once had a place in the divine economy, though now no longer, Stephen saw it as a mistake from the first. In his view, the temple was never intended by God.

The extraordinary amount of space that Luke has allocated to the speech may be due in some part to its very distinctiveness. To this day, people have been fascinated by it, and Luke himself may have been no exception. Moreover, he saw Stephen as a significant figure in the history that he was narrating—a pioneer and in some sense an exemplar of the new direction that the church was to take. He was, so to speak, the connecting link between Peter and Paul—a link indispensable to the chain of salvation history that God was forging. Luke's information concerning Stephen, and the speech in particular, could have come from any one of a number of possible sources, including Philip and Paul.

7:1–3 / As president of the Sanhedrin (see disc. on 4:5), the high priest, probably Caiaphas, opened the proceedings with a formal question (v. 1), to which Stephen gave him the courtesy of an equally formal reply: **Brothers and Fathers** (v. 2; cf. 22:1; see note on 1:16). He then launched into one of his two major themes. His first objective was to show that "the Most High does not live in houses made by men," and this accounts for his reference to **the God of glory** appearing to Abraham (v. 2). The phrase is suggestive of that particular manifestation of God's glory that came to be known as the "Shekinah"—God's glory dwelling with men. The Shekinah was associated especially with "the tabernacle of the Testimony" (cf. v. 44; Exod. 25:8; 40:34–38) and at a later date with the temple (Ezek. 43:2, 4). But Stephen established at the outset that God needs neither temple nor tent, for he appeared to Abraham while he was living in **Mesopotamia**.

This was, strictly speaking, the fertile region east of the river Orontes, covering the upper and middle Euphrates and the lands watered by the rivers Habur and Tigris, that is, modern eastern Syria and northern Iraq. It included Haran. But Greek and Roman writers from the fourth century B.C. extended the use of the term to describe the whole Tigris-Euphrates Valley, that is, the modern state of Iraq. Thus Stephen speaks of Abraham's original home of Ur in Babylonia as being in Mesopotamia, before he had gone to live in Haran (v. 2). Moreover, he cites God's call of Abraham as coming to him in Ur rather than in Haran, as Genesis 11:31 has it. None of this presents any difficulty. It was simply a matter of conflating the biblical evidence, for both Genesis 15:7 and Nehemiah 9:7 (cf. Josh. 24:3) make it clear that Abraham's call was from Ur no less than from Haran. With this, Jewish tradition also agreed (cf. Philo, *On Abraham* 70–72; Josephus, *Antiquities* 1.154–157). It is not inappropriate, therefore, that Stephen should adapt the account of Abraham's call from Haran to give expression to the earlier call and germane, of course, to his purpose. For by this means the point was made even made forcefully that God's call came to Abraham far from this land (v. 4) and from "this holy place" (6:13; cf. v. 7).

7:4–5 / Maintaining this theme, Stephen went on to show how God was present with Abraham in all of his wanderings. These took him first from Ur to Haran. Genesis 11:31 tells us that this migration was led by Abraham's father, Terah. Stephen assumes this when he recalls that it was after Terah's death in Haran that God's call came to Abraham again, and again he moved on. However, the details of his narration are here at odds with the Genesis story. He speaks of Abraham as leaving only after Terah died, whereas the evidence of Genesis is that Terah lived for many years after the departure of Abraham (cf. Gen. 11:26, 32; 12:4). Either, then, Stephen was mistaken (and Genesis at this point is susceptible to misunderstanding; Terah's death is anticipated in Gen. 11:32) or he was drawing on a different tradition. The Samaritan version of Genesis 11:32, for example, has Terah dying at one hundred forty-five years instead of two hundred five. Either way, nothing hangs on the point as far as the speech is concerned, though if the detail does reflect a different tradition, it makes it more likely that the speech came to Luke from a source and not out of his own head, since the LXX, Luke's own preferred version, bears no trace of this tradition (see note on v. 46).

From Haran, **God sent him** (i.e., Abraham) **to this land where you are now living** (v. 4)—Canaan, as it was then. Stephen's use of the pronoun **you** may mean that he was not himself a Palestinian. Otherwise, apart from this instance, he appears to oscillate between the first and second person depending on whether he wishes to associate himself or not with the events he is describing (e.g., vv. 15, 52). As for Abraham, he still had no place in this country to call his own (cf. Heb. 11:13–16)—not so much as **a foot of ground** (v. 5; this may have been a proverbial saying; cf. Deut. 2:5). The reference is probably to Abraham's earlier years in Canaan. Later, he did at least have a burial ground (see v. 16), though even this was his only by right of purchase, not as God's gift. God did promise, however, that one day **he and his descendants . . . would possess the land** (v. 5; cf. Gen. 12:7; 13:15; 15:18; 17:8; 24:7). Canaan, of course, was only ever possessed by Abraham "in" his descendants, never in his own right. But in the context of the Hebrews' corporate view of society, the promise was a valid one, though, for a long time, because he had no children, it must have sorely tried Abraham's faith (v. 5; cf. Gen. 15:1–6; Rom. 4:16–22).

7:6–7 / To this promise was added the rider that when Abraham did have descendants, before the land would be theirs, they would live **in a country not their own** where they would be slaves and maltreated for four hundred years (v. 6). In Exodus 12:40 the number of years is given as four hundred thirty for the same period, but the difference is simply that of a round figure as against a more precise calculation (cf. Gal. 3:17). The quotation contained in these verses is from LXX Genesis 15:13f., with some alteration (nothing of any consequence) and the addition, as it would seem, of some words from Exodus 3:12. The latter served to make explicit what is only implied in the Genesis passage, namely, that Abraham's posterity would return to Canaan once they were released from their bondage, there to worship God. The phrase **in this place** (v. 7) probably means nothing more than the land, though there is a similarity in the Greek to the phrase used by Stephen's accusers in 6:13.

7:8 / It was at this time that God gave to Abraham the rite of **circumcision** as a sign of the covenant (cf. Gen. 17: Rom. 4:11). From Abraham it passed to his descendants, and thus the history is carried forward to the story of Joseph. Stephen's only reason for mentioning circumcision may have been to effect transition in his narrative from Canaan to Egypt. On the other hand, he may have seen it as providing further support for his thesis. For the covenant of which circumcision was the sign embraced the Jews' whole relationship with God, and yet it had been established by God without reference to either the temple or the law.

7:9–14 / It would appear that much of the detail of these verses is here simply for its own sake. It was part of a story that they all loved to hear. Nevertheless, the speaker did not lose sight of his theme and employed the familiar detail in some part, at least, to further his objective. So, for example, there is a constant reiteration of the word **Egypt** (vv. 9, 10, 11, 12, 15) to remind his hearers that God is not bound to any one place (and because of Stephen's Alexandrian background? see note on 6:9). He was with Joseph in Egypt **and rescued him from all his troubles** (vv. 9, 10; cf. Gen. 39:2, 21). He gave him "grace " or "favor" (Gk. *charis*) and **wisdom** to interpret Pharaoh's dreams and to propose sensible measures against the famine of which the dreams were a warning (v. 10; cf. Gen. 41:37ff.; Ps. 105:16–22). It was of God, therefore, that Pharaoh **made him ruler over Egypt** (v. 10) and that Joseph was able to succor his family (vv. 11–14). All this God did in Egypt, working salvation for his people in spite of, and indeed through, the evil done by them to Joseph (cf. 2:23f.; 3:15f.; 4:10–12). In giving their number as **seventy-five in all** (v. 14), Stephen was following the text of LXX Genesis 46:27 and Exodus 1:5. The Hebrew text numbers them only as seventy. But compare LXX Deuteronomy 10:22, which has only seventy. Josephus (*Antiquities* 2.176–183) follows the Hebrew seventy, and Philo gives the two numbers.

   7:15–16 / When Jacob and his sons died, **their bodies were brought back to Shechem** (the modern Nablus, between Mount Gerizim and Mount Ebal), **and placed in the tomb that Abraham had bought** (v. 16). According to Genesis 50:13, however, Jacob was laid to rest, not in Shechem, but in the cave of Machpelah at Hebron. Some have sought to overcome this difficulty by suggesting that only his sons are the subject of the verbs in this sentence, or that the **he** of verse 15 is Joseph, not Jacob. But a further difficulty must still be met. Joseph is the only son of Jacob who is expressly said to have been buried in Shechem (Josh. 24:32). The burial place of the others is not mentioned, or even that their bodies were taken from Egypt. According to Josephus they were, but he says that they were buried at Hebron (*Antiquities* 2.198–200). Only Samaritan tradition, as far as we know, agrees with Stephen that it was at Shechem, which by now had become the center of Samaritan life (Sir. 50:26; Josephus, *Antiquities* 11.340–345). When we consider the prominence of Shechem as compared with Hebron at the time of the conquest, there is certainly no difficulty in accepting that it might have been chosen instead of Machpelah as the resting place of all of the sons. What is striking, however, is that Stephen must have been aware of the tradition that Jacob at least was buried in Hebron, yet he chose not to mention it (see note on v. 46).
   Another problem is presented by Stephen's description of the burial place. Abraham did buy a grave site, but it was the cave of Machpelah from Ephron the Hittite (Gen. 23:16). The tribe of Hamor did sell land to Shechem, but it was to Jacob (Gen. 33:19; Josh. 24:32). How, then, can we explain the statement of

the passage before us? Perhaps the two stories were confused in popular tradition. Or Stephen may have interpreted the second in the light of Abraham's having earlier set up an altar at Shechem. Putting it another way, it was Abraham's earlier hallowing of the spot that led ultimately to its purchase by Jacob, and so in a short-hand sort of way it could be said that Abraham had bought the field (cf. disc. on 1:18f.). But perhaps the simplest explanation is that of Bruce, who suggests that Stephen has telescoped the two accounts, as he did in the story of Abraham's call in verse 2 (*Book*, p. 149, n. 39). That this has produced difficulties may point to an author other than Luke, and that he has allowed these difficulties to remain may tell us something about Luke's editorial policy.

7:17-19 / During the years that the Israelites spent in Egypt two things were happening that, in human terms, paved the way for the Exodus and the fulfillment of God's promise (cf. v. 7): first, the number of Abraham's descendants was increasing (v. 17; cf. Exod. 1:7), and second, the Egyptian attitude toward them was hardening (Exod. 1:9, 12). Stephen repeats the words of Exodus 1:8 when he tells how a **king, who knew nothing about Joseph, became ruler of Egypt** (v. 18). This statement could be understood literally, especially if the notice marks the return to a native dynasty (the eighteenth or, more likely, the nineteenth) after the rule of the Hyksos kings, but more likely it meant that the kings chose not to recognize Joseph's service (cf. Matt. 25:12 for this use of "to know"), either because of his association with the Hyksos or because the number of his people posed a threat. The Egyptian answer to the "Hebrew problem" was to use them as forced labor and to compel them to practice infanticide (v. 19; confined to male children, according to Exod. 1:15f.; cf. Matt. 2:16ff.).

7:20-22 / It was at this time that Moses was born (v. 20; cf. Gal. 4:4 and see note on 22:3 on the frequent occurrence of the verbs "born . . . cared for . . . taught" in ancient writers). Stephen recounts the story of Moses in three parts, corresponding to the three periods of forty years that made up his life (cf. vv. 23, 30). First was his providential upbringing. At birth **he was no ordinary child** (v. 20; cf. Exod. 2:2; Heb. 11:23), literally, "beautiful to God." This may be a Hebrew idiom with the sense almost of a superlative, "a very beautiful child" (GNB, cf. Jonah 3:3, "a very important city," i.e., "a very large city"). Or it may mean that in God's judgment he was beautiful, that is, that he found favor with God (cf. 23:1). If the latter, it was a conclusion drawn from the story that follows. After three months, when they were no longer able to hide him, Moses' parents exposed him, but Pharaoh's daughter found him and brought him up as her own son (v. 21; cf. Exod. 2:1–10; Josephus, *Antiquities* 2.232–237). Stephen was indebted more to tradition than to the Old Testament when he declared that Moses **was educated in all the wisdom of the Egyptians** (v. 22; cf. Philo, *Life of Moses* 1.5; 2.83; Josephus, *Antiquities* 2.232–237; this notion subsequently played a considerable part in Jewish legends about Moses; cf. also Luke 2:52). Stephen may again have drawn on tradition in describing him as a **powerful in speech and action** (v. 22; cf. Josephus, *Antiquities* 2.238–242; 3.13–21). This is very like the description of Jesus in Luke 24:19 and may have been made so by Luke, though it may also have been part of Stephen's purpose to show how alike Jesus and Moses were (see disc. on vv. 33–39).

7:23–25 / In the second part, with the story of the middle years of Moses' life, the other of Stephen's two themes appears, namely, that Israel had shown a rebellious spirit throughout its history. Joseph had experienced it when his brothers turned against him (v. 9; cf. Gen. 37:11; John 1:10f.), but it now became even more apparent in the people's refusal to accept Moses' efforts on their behalf. In the main, Stephen was following the narrative of Exodus 2:11 when he told how Moses **decided to visit his fellow Israelites** (v. 23). But he added to the biblical narrative the reference to Moses' decision (cf. Heb. 11:24f.), expressing it in such a way as to imply that the idea was not his own, but that it was "laid upon his heart" (so the Greek) by God. Stephen wanted to show that Moses was living out God's will and that the people's resistance was, therefore, nothing other than their resistance to God (cf. 6:11). The dating of this incident to the time **when Moses was forty years old** (v. 23) has no authority in the Old Testament, which tells us only that he was eighty years old when he went to Pharaoh to ask for the people's release (Exod. 7:7) and one hundred twenty years old when he died (Deut. 34:7). However, *Midrash Tanhuma* on Exodus 2:6 says that "Moses was in the palace of Pharaoh twenty years, but some say forty years, and forty years in Midian, and forty years in the wilderness." Stephen's words echo this tradition.

On the occasion about which Stephen was speaking, Moses saw an Israelite **being mistreated by an Egyptian** (v. 24). He intervened on behalf of the Israelite, killing his oppressor. As the Old Testament tells the story, it would appear that the thing was done in secret and that Moses intended it so (Exod. 2:12). But as Stephen told it, it was done with the Hebrews' full knowledge and in the hope that it would establish him as their leader—**Moses thought that his own people would realize that God was using him to rescue them** (v. 25; cf. Josephus, *Antiquities* 2.205–216). He did not reckon, however, with their unresponsiveness, and in fact, they did not understand (v. 25; cf. vv. 35, 39).

7:26–29 / This was borne out the next day when he would have acted again as their leader. Two Israelites were fighting, and when Moses attempted to reconcile them by appealing to them as brothers, **the man who was mistreating the other pushed Moses aside** (v. 27; cf. v. 39; Exod. 2:14). This detail is not found in Exodus, but again it underlines the contumaciousness of Israel. It was this, according to Stephen, rather than his fear of Pharaoh (as in Exodus), that caused Moses to flee (cf. Josephus, *Antiquities* 2.254–257, where the cause is the jealousy of the Egyptians). So **Moses fled to Midian, where he settled as a foreigner** (v. 29; cf. Exod. 2:16)—a region that is generally thought to have lain in northwestern Arabia on the eastern shore of the Gulf of Aqaba (Ptolemy, *Geography* 6.7.27; Josephus, *Antiquities* 2.254–257). Since, however, Midianites are known to have penetrated westward (Num. 10:29), the land of **Midian** in this reference may be taken to include the Sinai peninsula. Moses married a Midianite woman, Zipporah (Exod. 2:21), and by her had two sons, Gershom and Eliezer (v. 29; cf. Exod. 2:22; 4:20; 18:3; 1 Chron. 23:14f.).

7:30–34 / The third part of the story covers the years of the Exodus. Verse 30 is literally "when forty years were fulfilled," suggesting that all was proceeding according to divine plan (see disc. on v. 23). It was now that God appeared to Moses **in the flames of a burning bush** (v. 30; cf. Exod. 3:2ff.). The **angel** of Stephen's narrative is plainly none other than God (cf. vv. 31, 33; Exod. 3:2, 7; 1 Cor. 10:1–4; 2 Cor. 3:15–18). And so, for a moment (whether intentionally or not), we are back with the earlier motif of God revealing himself in whatever place seemed good, not in any one place. And wherever God appeared, that place was **holy**

ground. So Moses was told to take off his sandals (v. 33), as later the priests would do in the temple in their daily service. In Exodus 3:1 these events are located at Horeb, but elsewhere the Old Testament uses that name interchangeably with Sinai, and there is no difficulty, therefore, in Stephen's naming that mountain. On approaching the theophany **to look more closely** (v. 31, the word implies careful observation), Moses was shown that this was indeed the God of his ancestors. The description of God in verse 32 immediately calls to mind the covenant promise to Abraham and his descendants (vv. 6, 7; cf. 3:13), with the implication that God would now save his people as he had promised and that in doing so would use Moses as his agent (cf. Exod. 3:7-10). The sequence of events in Exodus 3:5-10 is reversed by Stephen for no apparent reason. The quotation of Exodus 3:6 in verse 32 is not an accurate reproduction of the LXX. It has affinities with the Samaritan recension (but see note on v. 46).

7:35-38 / And now Stephen leaves the narrative style of his discourse to make instead four statements concerning Moses, each marked in the Greek by the repeated demonstrative "this (man)." At the same time, a subsidiary theme, the parallel between Moses and Christ, makes its appearance (see disc. on v. 22). The first statement concerns the rejection of the one whom God sent (v. 35). In this connection Stephen cites Exodus 2:14, **Who made you ruler and judge?** (v. 35; cf. v. 27), but notice how he himself describes Moses, not merely as judge, but as "ruler and redeemer" (so the Greek). The allusion to Christ is unmistakable, for though he is never called "redeemer" in the New Testament, he is called "a ransom," a related word in the Greek, and the work of redemption is clearly his (Luke 1:68; 2:38; 24:21; Titus 2:14; Heb. 9:12; 1 Pet. 1:18f.; see note on 8:32f.). Significantly, the title "redeemer" belongs to God in the Old Testament, but Stephen saw Moses both as the type of Christ and as acting for God and therefore able to bear such a name. That this was indeed an act of divine redemption is expressed in the words he was sent **through** (lit. "with the hand"; see disc. on 4:28) **the angel** (v. 35), that is, with the help of God himself (see disc. on v. 30).

By the hand of God, Moses was able to do **wonders and miraculous signs** (see note on 2:22) **in Egypt, at the Red Sea and for forty years in the desert** (v. 36). There is nothing in this second statement that cannot be borne out by the Old Testament, but again the allusion to Christ is unmistakable, the more so as Luke brings Stephen's expression into line with descriptions elsewhere of the work of Christ and of his followers (cf. 2:22, 43; 6:8). It could be said of both Christ and Moses that their ministry was confirmed by miracles. The third statement could also be said of both—that they were prophets. Moses had declared, **God will send you a prophet like me** (v. 37; cf. Deut. 18:15ff.), and Luke's readers (if not Stephen's hearers) would yet again have picked up the allusion to Christ, for he was deemed to be the eschatological Prophet-like-Moses (see disc. on 3:22 and note on 7:46).

Stephen's fourth statement concerns Moses' role with **the assembly in the desert** (v. 38). It could not have been lost on the Christian reader that the people of Israel are here called in the Greek text "the church" (*ekklēsia*). This word is generally reserved in the New Testament for Christian use (see disc. on 5:11), and in its use in this verse we may see Luke's hand underlining what he saw to be Stephen's point and inviting us to see in Moses the type of Christ, the mediator of the new covenant (cf. Heb. 8:16; 9:15; 12:24). Moses was both "with (lit. 'in' or 'among') the people" and **with the angel who spoke to him on Mount Sinai**, that is, with God (v. 38; cf. Exod. 20:1)—he stood between God and the people. The Sanhedrin, of course, would not have accepted, or even seen, the typology, but they would have readily agreed that Moses was the mediator of **the living words**, that is, the law, seen as the way to life (v. 38; cf. Exod. 19:1–6; 20:1–17). As far as the Sanhedrin was concerned, this was Stephen's most telling point. Herein lay Moses' greatness.

7:39–41 / And yet, for all his greatness, neither Moses himself nor the law that he had mediated was obeyed (v. 39; cf. v. 53; Exod. 16:3; Num. 11:4f.). The details of the exodus story were well known, and Stephen had no need to rehearse them. It was sufficient for his purpose simply to highlight those features of the story that showed that the Israelites were a contentious people. Thus in the desert to which God had brought them, they turned against him (cf. Exod. 6:11). **In their hearts** they **turned back to Egypt** (v. 39; cf. Exod. 16:3; Num. 11:4f.), for they were hankering after the worship of idols. Indeed, no sooner had Moses gone up on the mountain than they lapsed into idolatry. They asked Aaron to make them other gods at the very time that Moses was on the mountain receiving the law. The people complained that they did not know what had happened to Moses, and in his place they wanted gods that they could see. Notice that there was no recognition of the true God. As far as they were concerned, it was simply Moses who had brought them out of Egypt (v. 40), and in his absence and their own blindness, **they made an idol in the form of a calf** and **brought sacrifices to it** (v. 41; cf. Exod. 32:2–6; 1 Kings 12:28). The Scripture speaks of the handiwork of God, in which people should rejoice; these people had a feast in honor of their own (v. 41).

7:42–43 / From that first act of idolatry it was but a short step to the wholesale adoption of other religions, a sin that in one sense was of their own doing (cf. Eph. 4:19, "they have given themselves over to sensuality"), but in another sense it was an act of divine retribution: **God turned away** (or possibly, "God turned them back") **and gave them over to the worship of the heavenly bodies** (lit. "to the army," i.e., the sun, moon and stars; v. 42). They turned away from the creator, "the Lord of hosts," and were doomed to worship the creature, "the host of heaven"— a picture of spiritual decline found also in Romans 1:18ff. (cf. Josh. 24:20; Isa. 63:10). The sun and the moon and the stars were believed to be either gods or their habitation. The Old Testament has many references to the worship of the stellar deities (cf. Deut. 4:19; 17:3; 2 Kings 17:16; 21:3; etc.).

In support of this view of Israel's history, Stephen cited Amos 5:25–27 from **the book of the prophets** (apparently a single scroll containing the Twelve Minor Prophets). As we have it, the quotation follows the text of the LXX with little variation, retaining the question of verse 25, "Did you bring me sacrifices and offerings . . . ?" (v. 42), which in the Greek expects a negative reply. The Hebrew text of Amos is less specific, but is usually understood in the same way. But the prophet cannot have meant that no sacrifices were offered for **forty years in the desert** (v. 42). This would have been in direct contradiction with such passages as Exodus 24:4f. and Numbers 7:10ff. What he probably meant was that not merely were sacrifices offered but the worship of the people was then from the heart. He saw those years in the desert as a golden age from which the empty ritual of his own day was a far cry. But Stephen, with his very different presuppositions, found another meaning in Amos' words. As he understood it, the prophet was complaining that though much was done in those desert years that passed for worship, it was not of the heart, and so not what it purported to be. For Stephen, the question of verse 42 was answered by the following verse. It was not God whom they worshiped, but Molech and Rephan (so the LXX). Historically, of course, this may not have been so (though the possibility of such worship was recognized; cf. Lev. 18:21; 20:2–5), but what Stephen meant was that, having already turned away from God in their hearts, in effect they had turned "the tabernacle of the Testimony" (v. 44) into **the shrine of Molech** (v. 43). Ultimately, Israel's persistence in this rebellion had brought upon them God's judgment, and they were driven **into exile beyond Babylon** (v. 45; cf. 2 Kings 24:10–17). At this point Stephen left behind him both the LXX and the Hebrew texts. They speak of "Damascus," for Amos had the Assyrians in view. But the Babylonian exile meant more to Stephen's hearers than the Assyrian deportation, and so he made the change.

7:44–46 / From describing their worship, Stephen came by a natural progression to speak of their place of worship, but here again Israel's propensity for rebellion was shown. The first sanctuary had been **the tabernacle of the Testimony** (v. 44), which is how the LXX (incorrectly) translates the Hebrew "Tent of Meeting" (Exod. 27:21), though the name was not inappropriate. This tent had been sanctioned by God, **made as God directed Moses, according to the pattern he had seen** (v. 44; cf. Exod. 25:9, 40; 26:30; 27:8), and in all the years that had followed, through the conquest of Canaan, **until the time of David** (v. 45), it had proved adequate to the needs of Israel's worship. But David, uneasy that he lived in a house made of cedar while the ark of God was kept in a tent (2 Sam. 7:2), asked that he might be allowed to **provide a dwelling place for the God of Jacob** (v. 46)—this language echoes Psalm 132:4f. This was not to be, but the prophet who brought him this message brought him also another: God would establish David's "house," that is, he would give him descendants, and his son would build God a house (2 Sam. 7:11–13, RSV). It would appear that for Stephen this promise was fulfilled, not in the building of the temple, but in the coming of Christ.

7:47–50 / Nevertheless, the temple was built (v. 47). The clue to Stephen's understanding of this development lies in the conjunctions of these verses (NIV *but*). The first (Gk. *de*), taken alone, is ambiguous. It could be adversative, setting the state-

ment of verse 47 over against that of the previous verse, or it could
be simply transitional, marking the change of subject from David
to Solomon. The second, however, is strongly adversative (Gk.
alla), clearly opposing verses 47 and 48. But verse 48 appears to
furnish the reason why David did not build "a dwelling place for
the God of Jacob," in which case we must understand the conjunction of verse 47 to be also adversative. In short, as far as
Stephen was concerned, the temple was built contrary to God's
purpose. Solomon had "built him a house" (v. 47), but **the Most
High God does not live in houses made by men** (v. 48), literally,
"made with hands." This was a word commonly used by Greek
philosophers and Jews alike in their condemnation of idolatry (see,
e.g., Lev. 26:1; Isa. 46:6; Sibylline Oracles 3:650f.; 4.8–12; Philo,
Life of Moses 1.303; 2. 165 and 168; cf. v. 41; 17:24; Heb. 9:11, 24).
Was Stephen calling the temple an idol? The Old Testament gives
a far different picture than this of the temple and the circumstances in which it was built.

The operative word in this verse is "live." Stephen may well
have agreed that God could be found in the temple, but this word
would suggest that he was confined there, and as Stephen had
maintained throughout, that was simply not so. Had not God
been found in Mesopotamia, in Egypt, in the desert? The Alexandrian philosophers had been developing the doctrine of the
divine nature, and from them, perhaps, Stephen had learned how
absurd it was to suppose that the creator could be confined with
walls. But this truth had already been revealed in Scripture. Solomon himself had recognized it in his dedicatory prayer (1 Kings
8:27; 2 Chron. 6:18; cf. also 2 Chron. 29:10–19), so too had **the
prophet**, with reference perhaps to the building of the second
temple after the exile (v. 48; Isa. 66:1f.; cf. John 4:21; Acts 17:22ff.).
The passage cited is one of the few in the Old Testament that
seems to denounce the temple root and branch. The text of the
LXX is used with only a few minor changes.

The position to which Stephen had come in these verses
went far beyond any other that we find in the New Testament.
Elsewhere we meet with the idea of the temple's role being now
fulfilled by Christ and, therefore, of the temple's redundancy, but
nowhere such an outright condemnation of the temple as such.
M. Simon has suggested that to Stephen the temple meant from
the beginning "a falling away from the authentic tradition of Israel" as God had inspired and directed it, so that Israel's was "a

debased and corrupt form of religion" (p. 45), especially now that One greater than the temple had come (Matt. 12:6). Not only was the temple unnecessary, but it had become another instance of the people's perversity. The two themes of Stephen's counterattack thus met and mingled. Some have seen in Stephen's opposition to the temple evidence of "Samaritanism," but this is not a necessary conclusion. He could have been influenced by a number of other sects (see note on v. 46) or have arrived quite independently at this position.

7:51–53 / These verses have sometimes been explained as Stephen's response to the increasing impatience of his audience, as if he felt that the angry murmurs of the council would allow him no more time for speaking. There may be something in this, though it could be maintained equally as well that the whole speech had been leading up to this conclusion and that these verses, far from being an interruption to the steady development of his argument, are its most fitting conclusion. At all events, the speech ends with a bitter and abrupt declaration of Israel's rebellion, expressed in a collection of Old Testament phrases. They were a **stiff-necked people, with uncircumcised hearts and ears** (they had not cut away their sin, i.e., repented and believed) words that had often been spoken before in reference to Israel (cf. Exod. 33:3, 5; 34:9; Lev. 26:41; Deut. 9:6; 10:16; Jer. 4:4; 6:10; also Rom. 2:25, 29)—who in the past had resisted **the Holy Spirit** (cf. Num. 27:14, Isa. 63:10) and were still deaf to God's message (v. 51). Their fathers had killed God's messengers, the prophets (cf. 1 Kings 19:10, 14; Neh. 9:26; Jer. 26:20) who had spoken beforehand of the Righteous One who would come, and when he had come, they had completed their fathers' work by killing him too (v. 52). The reference is, of course, to Jesus and apparently to his role as the Suffering Servant (cf. esp. Isa. 53:11, RSV; see disc. on 3:13 and notes on 8:32f.).

This spirit of rebellion, which had reached its nadir in their treatment of Jesus, was evident also in their response to the law. There was a tradition, to which Stephen referred, that the angels had been involved in the transmission of the law (cf. LXX Deut. 33:2; Jubilees 1:27ff.; Gal. 3:19; Heb. 2:2), though precisely what Stephen meant by this reference is not clear. The Greek could be taken in the sense either that the Israelites had received the law "as the angels had appointed that they should," or that they had received it "as the ordinance of the angels." In any case, Stephen's intention was to enhance the dignity of the law. The law had come with notable sanctions, yet they had not obeyed it. No proof of this statement is given. Stephen had passed the point where he could carefully argue the case. But at the back of his mind there may have been their specific breach of the law in their treatment of Jesus (cf. Exod. 20:13). Hence his use of the word "murderer" (v. 52; in the Greek it is a noun, not a verb). It was they who were the lawbreakers, not he.

Additional Notes §16

7:43 / **You have lifted up the shrine of Molech and the star of your god Rephan**: so LXX Amos 5:26, which differs from the Hebrew in having "tent" for "Sikkuth" and "of Moloch" for "your king" (Heb. *mal*^{e}*kk*^{e}*kem*). The translators of the LXX may have had another reading, *mil*^{e}*kkōm* (cf. 2 Kings 23:13) or believed that they were interpreting the Hebrew. Sikkuth was a Babylonian deity, Molech, an Ammonite (1 Kings 11:7), whose worship seems to have been associated with the sacrifice of children in the fire (Lev. 18:21; 20:2–5; 2 Kings 23:10; Jer. 32:35; cf. 2 Kings 17:31). In addition, the LXX has "the star of your god Raiphan" for "Chiun your images, the star of your god." Probably the LXX read, not the word "Chiun" but "Kewan," of which Raiphan is a corruption through Kaiphan. Kewan was an Assyrian name for the planet Saturn, which explains "the star of your god."

7:45 / **Joshua**: In Greek, the name is identical with "Jesus." From the *Epistle of Barnabas* (12.8) onwards, many early Christian writers regarded Joshua as a type of Jesus (cf. Heb. 4:8). Hanson wonders whether Stephen intended to link the two, giving to the words **they took the land from the nations** the sense he "gained possession of the Gentiles," with a double reference to both Joshua and Jesus (p. 101).

7:46 / It has sometimes been suggested that Stephen was a Samaritan (see, e.g., J. Munck, p. 285; and C. H. H. Scobie, "The Origin and Development of Samaritan Christianity," *NTS* 19 (1972–73), pp. 391–400), and certainly there are points of contact in this speech with the Samaritans (see disc. on vv. 4, 16, 32, 37, 47–50). But in the light of that people's bitter opposition to Judah and to the house of David, the tone of Stephen's comment in this verse must rule out any suggestion that he was himself a Samaritan (see M. H. Scharlemann, *Stephen: A Singular Saint*). There were a number of other Jewish sects having affinities with the Samaritans that could equally as well have influenced Stephen, whether directly or indirectly (see M. Black, *The Scrolls and Christian Origins*, pp. 48ff.).

§17 The Stoning of Stephen (Acts 7:54–8:1a)

It is difficult to avoid the conclusion that, in part, Luke has modeled the life and death of Stephen on the Gospel story. Elements include Stephen's ministry of miracle and the spoken word, the inability of his adversaries to match him in debate, the trial before the Sanhedrin, the false witnesses, the high priest's question, the reference to the Son of Man, Stephen's dying prayer, and the petition for the forgiveness of his murderers. To some extent this may have been a purely literary device—Luke's desire for consistency of style. There may also have been a theological motive, namely, to show how Christ continued to suffer in his body, the church (see disc. on 1:1 and the introduction to 5:17–42). But the differences between the two narratives are as important as the similarities (see, e.g., Hengel, *Jesus*, pp. 21f.) and are such that we must allow the essential historicity of this story. In any case, Stephen's real significance for Luke was not so much in his likeness to Jesus as in what he exemplified of the church's history at this point—a wind of change that would set the church on a new course from Jerusalem to "the ends of the earth" (1:8) and from Judaism to a Christianity that had Good News for all people. The suggestion that the martyrdom of Stephen has been influenced by the trial of Paul (cf., e.g., 21:28; see disc. on 19:21–41) has little to commend it.

7:54 / By the time Stephen had finished speaking, the roles of those involved in this trial had effectively been reversed. It was as though the Sanhedrin were on trial and Stephen's speech for the prosecution. With Stephen thundering against them, it is highly unlikely that they would have allowed him to continue, even had he intended to do so. No charge was more hateful to the Jew than that he had broken the law (cf. John 7:19), and no such charge could have been made with greater force than Stephen had made it against the Sanhedrin. Their reaction was a violent one, expressed in the same terms as in 5:33, but with the additional comment that they **gnashed their teeth at him** (cf. Luke 13:28).

7:55–56 / But Stephen seems no longer to have been aware of those who sat in judgment of him. Looking up into heaven (see 1:11 for the direction and 3:4 for the look) he **saw the glory of God, and Jesus standing at the right hand of God** (v. 55). Luke says that Stephen was **full of the Holy Spirit** (v. 55), meaning that this vision was not simply the result of a momentary inspiration, but the climax of a life lived in the Spirit (see note on 2:4 and disc. on 4:8 and 6:3). He was characteristically a man "full of the Holy Spirit." It was to the Spirit, therefore, that he owed his theological insights (see disc. on 6:12–14), and now by the same Spirit—for this is the implication of the passage before us—those insights took on definite shape in his mind's eye. **Look!** he cried, **I see . . .** [Jesus as] **the Son of Man**—the celestial figure of Daniel 7:13ff. (see disc. on 6:12ff.)—**standing at the right hand of God** (v. 56). But why standing? Elsewhere Jesus is represented as sitting (cf., e.g., 2:34; Mark 16:19; Heb. 1:3, 13). The thought may be that he had risen to receive Stephen into heaven or to plead his case in the heavenly court, as though two trials were in progress: this one, conducted by the Sanhedrin, and another, which alone would determine Stephen's fate (cf. Matt. 10:28). Jesus had promised, "Whoever acknowledges me before men, the Son of Man will also acknowledge him before the angels of God" (Luke 12:8). But Jesus' reference had been to the final judgment, and in line with this, C. K. Barrett has suggested that this was for Stephen a glimpse of the Parousia (see disc. on 1:10f.). "Only dying Stephen was in a position to see the coming Son of Man. It was at the 'last day,' in the hour of death, that the Son of Man would be seen" ("Stephen," p. 36). There is a difficulty with this in that Christian death is usually thought of in terms of going to Jesus, not of Jesus coming to meet the Christian. On the other hand, the Son of Man terminology is frequently found in the Gospels in connection with teaching about the Parousia. Barrett, therefore, may well be right. Apart from the Gospels, and indeed, apart from the word of Jesus himself, this is the only place in the New Testament where he is called Son of Man, though there may be a hint of the title in 17:31 (Rev. 1:13 has an allusion to Dan. 7:13). It was certainly not part of Luke's vocabulary.

7:57–8:1a / On hearing what must have seemed to them an outrageous claim that Jesus, whom they had put to death, was at the right hand of God, the Sanhedrin determined to put Stephen to death too. No mention is made of any formal condemnation and sentence. Instead, the story moves quickly to its climax. Stephen was bundled out of the city, as the law required for what they were about to do (Lev. 24:14)—perhaps to the traditional site beyond Saint Stephen's Gate—and there he was stoned to death. Luke tells the story with economy of detail and yet with great dramatic force. As Stephen called again and again on the Lord Jesus to receive his spirit (cf. Luke 23:46), he was pelted again and again with stones (v. 59, the force of the Greek tense), until he fell to his knees and then to the ground dead. Or perhaps he deliberately knelt (v. 60). The usual posture for a Jew at prayer was to stand (cf. Matt. 6:5), though kneeling was not unknown (cf. 1 Kings 8:54; Ezra 9:5). But kneeling became the distinctive Christian attitude, adopted perhaps from Jesus' own practice (cf. 9:40; 20:36; 21:5; Luke 22:41; Eph. 3:14; Phil. 2:10). And like Jesus, Stephen's last prayer was one of committal and of forgiveness for others (v. 60; cf. Luke 23:34). The latter, like Stephen's vision, may have had reference to the Last Judgment.

Meanwhile, the witnesses, whose part it was to throw the first stones (Lev. 24:14; Deut. 17.7; cf. John 8:7), the better to perform their task **laid their clothes at the feet of a young man named Saul** (v. 58). Thus we are introduced for the first time to the man who will become the central figure of the book. Of his life to this point, more will be said later (see disc. on 22:3). Here we need only ask why he was present at Stephen's death. We have already noticed the difficulty of having him a member of the synagogue of the Freedmen (see disc. on 6:9). Similarly, the proposal that he was a member of the Sanhedrin is not without its problems (see disc. on 26:10). Perhaps the most satisfactory solution is that he was there simply as an interested spectator, though already a man of some importance. There was a custom that permitted outsiders, especially students, to stand at the rear of the council chamber (see B. Reicke, p. 145), and on an occasion such as this, one who was more devoted to the traditions than most of his contemporaries (Gal. 1:14), and who in any case wanted to be noticed by his superiors, may well have availed himself of this opportunity and then followed from the chamber to the place of execution. At the time, he approved wholeheartedly of the execution of Stephen (the force of the Greek). But the memory of this event was to haunt him for the rest of his life (cf. 22:20; 1 Tim. 1:13). For the sake of convenience we will hereafter refer to Saul by his Roman name Paul, though this is not used in Acts until chapter 13.

Additional Notes §17

7:58 / **A young man named Saul**: The application of the term **young man** was fairly broad. It could denote a man of up to about forty years old. Josephus applied it to Herod Agrippa I when he was at least forty (*Antiquities* 18.195–204).

7:60 / **When he had said this, he fell asleep**: The characteristic expression for Christian death (e.g., 1 Thess. 4:15), though never applied to Christ. Because he died, we need only "fall asleep." But was Stephen's death a legal execution or murder? The talmudic rule is that "the blasphemer is not culpable unless he pronounces the Name (of God)." But even supposing that that rule applied in Stephen's day, there is nothing in the speech as we have it, or even in v. 56, to show conclusively that Stephen was guilty in those terms. J. Klausner, *From Jesus to Paul* (London: Macmillan, 1944), p. 292, takes the view that Stephen was not technically guilty and attributes his death to certain "fanatical persons" among the bystanders "who decided the case for themselves." They "did not trouble themselves about the judicial rule," he says, but simply "took Stephen outside the city and stoned him." But the text makes no mention of these people, and Luke gives the impression that at least some of the proper forms were adhered to. It seems best, therefore, to regard Stephen's death as a legal execution.

The real difficulty (and the reason most often given for regarding his death as a lynching and not a judicial sentence) lies in the relationship that this incident presupposed between the Roman government and the Sanhedrin. There seems to be no doubt that under both Herodian and Roman rule the Sanhedrin had no authority to execute the death sentence but had to refer all such cases to the governor (but see disc. on 21:27ff.). On this occasion, however, the Sanhedrin may have found itself in circumstances where the Roman authority was unusually relaxed, such as the interim between Pontius Pilate's recall in A.D. 36 and the arrival of his successor, Marcellus. But even if A.D. 36 is thought to be too late for Stephen's death, at least it must have taken place in Pilate's last years as governor. This was a time when the imperial policy of placating the Jews had been reaffirmed following the removal of Sejanus. Pilate had been an appointee of Sejanus, and now his own position was at risk and he had to tread softly. The Sanhedrin would have known this and may have expected to be able to put matters right with the governor even though they were acting unlawfully. In any case, with the governor two days away in Caesarea, they were in no mood to await his approval. The situation that had made Stephen's death possible may also have abetted the persecution that followed in which other Christians appear to have died (see 26:10).

§18   The Church Persecuted and Scattered
(Acts 8:1b–3)

Though it would be foolish to suppose that the believers were anything other than a minority in Jerusalem, they had by this time made their presence felt at every level of the city's life and, on the whole, had been well received. But the storm that broke over Stephen brought in its wake a decline in their popularity (cf. 6:12), which in turn enabled the Sanhedrin to take much stronger action against them. The word "persecution" occurs here for the first time in Acts (v. 1), and for the first time ordinary believers were directly affected. But again we are reminded that "in all things God works for the good of those who love him" (Rom. 8:28; see disc. on 4:28). Because of the persecution many believers fled the city, and by this means the gospel began to spread (cf. 8:4–40; 11:19–30).

8:1b / Until now the Sadducees had been the chief antagonists of the Christians (cf. 4:1, 5f.; 5:17), whereas the Pharisees, if Gamaliel is any criterion, had adopted a more neutral position (5:34ff.). But Paul, a Pharisee (23:6; Phil. 3:5), now abandoned the milder stance of his teacher and took the lead in a concerted attempt to root out the new teaching. His prominence is indicated by the mention of his name three times within the space of a few verses (7:58–8:3) and by the fact that the persecution seems to have faded away after his conversion. The reason for the Pharisees' change of policy is not hard to find. They were devoted to the law and its institutions, which Stephen had attacked. In some respects, they felt affinity with the Christians (cf. 15:5; 23:6ff.; 26:4f.; see disc. on 5:34), but once the Christians questioned the validity of the law as the Pharisees understood and interpreted it, they felt the full weight of Pharisaic opposition. It is reasonable to suppose, however, that their fury was not directed equally against all the believers, but especially against those who were most closely associated with Stephen and who probably shared his views. In short, the Hellenists were probably the main target of their attack, so that it was they for the most part who were compelled to leave Jerusalem. No doubt the Hebrew Christians were also affected. Some may have fled with the Hellenists. But we need not understand by the word **all** that every member of the church left the city; verse 3 shows that they did not. Luke is prone to use "all" in the sense of "many" (see disc. on 9:35). But even of those who left, many may soon have returned; and of those who remained or returned, the greatest number were Hebrews (see discussion on 15:1).

Meanwhile, whoever else fled the city, the apostles did not (on the tradition of Christ's command that they stay, see Eusebius, *Ecclesiastical History* 5.18.14; Clement of Alexandria, *Stromateis* 6.5). Their known association with the temple would have spared them the charges that were leveled against Stephen. They would therefore have been relatively safe, though safety was never a consideration with them (see disc. on 4:19ff.; 5:40). Rather, they remained, we may suppose, from a sense of duty. Of the Christians who did leave the city, Luke gives us a vivid picture of their being "scattered like seed" throughout the regions of Judea and Samaria—a dispersion (or Diaspora, from the same Greek root as "scattering") of the new Israel corresponding to that of the old and a "sowing" that would bear much fruit (cf. v. 4). They were the real founders of the Gentile mission.

8:2 / **Some godly men buried Stephen**. Elsewhere this expression is usually used of pious Jews (e.g., 2:5), and such these men may have been. But on the whole, it seems more likely that they were Christians whose piety, like that of their Jewish counterparts, was expressed in terms of the law (cf. 22:12). Thus, they may have had little sympathy with Stephen's views, but he was still their brother in Christ. It was a mark of the devout that they paid great attention to the proper burial of the dead, and of those who had died by execution no less than others. But though criminals should be properly buried, it was forbidden that they should be publicly mourned (m. *Sanhedrin* 6.6). The fact, then, that these devout men buried Stephen **and mourned deeply for him** might furnish an argument in support of the view that he was not legally put to death but lynched by the mob. On the other hand, it might speak of their courage.

8:3 / If verse 2 shed a little light on these dark days, verse 3 plunges us back into the darkness. Here was a very different expression of zeal for the law. The word used of Paul's activities (he **began to destroy the church**) can describe the devastation caused by an army or a wild beast tearing its meat. It conjures up a terrible picture of the persecutor as he went from **house to house**—perhaps every known Christian home and at least every known place of Christian assembly (see note on 14:27). The relentlessness of the pogrom is underlined by the reference to women being **dragged off** as well as men, though Luke is interested in any case to draw attention to the presence and role of Christian women (see disc. on 1:14). Paul himself gives a more detailed account of this persecution in 26:9–11 and refers to it several times in his letters (1 Cor. 15:9; Gal. 1:13, 22f.; Phil. 3:6; 1 Tim. 1:13).

Additional Notes §18

8:1 / **The church at Jerusalem**: Here for the first time in Acts the church is so described. Hitherto the church has been thought of as one, and no information has yet been given of any effort by the Christians to reach out into the countryside of Judea. But now Luke drops a hint that there would soon be new "churches"—local expressions of the one church—as the gospel was carried elsewhere by fleeing Christians.

Throughout Judea and Samaria: These two regions (Luke's word) formed one province under the procurator of Judea (see note on 1:8). That Christians found acceptance among the Samaritans has been seen as further proof of Stephen's "Samaritanism." That case, however, remains to be proved (see note on 7:46). The Christian Hellenists may have been accepted for no other reason than that they were fleeing from the Jewish hierarchy.

§19 Philip in Samaria (Acts 8:4–8)

Luke's history is anecdotal and is carried along by reference to just a handful of people and what they said and did. With his subject now the history of the church's early expansion, Luke turns for an exemplar to Philip. One of the Seven and influenced no doubt by Stephen, Philip took the church two important steps forward. First, he preached to the Samaritans. O. Cullmann attaches great importance to this episode as marking "the actual beginnings of the Christian mission" to a non-Jewish community (pp. 185–94; but cf. Luke 9:52ff.; 10:30ff.; 17:16; John 4:5–42). Second, he baptized a Gentile. By the nature of the case, this made little impact on the church, but it illustrated Luke's theme, and the more so since in the Ethiopian the gospel reached "the ends of the earth" (1:8; cf. Irenaeus, *Against Heresies* 3.12.8; 4.22.2). In ancient geography, Ethiopia was regarded as the far boundary in the south of the inhabited world.

The suggestion has sometimes been made that the story of the Ethiopian eunuch was either made up on the basis of certain Old Testament passages or at least modified in the light of those passages. Critics point to Zephaniah in particular, which in the LXX mentions "Gaza" and "Azotus at noonday" (or "of the south"), prophets borne by the Spirit, and the welcoming of men from the south (Zeph. 2:4, 11f.; 3:4, 10; cf. also Ps. 68:31). And indeed it seems likely that Luke's language was colored by the language of Zephaniah. But that is as much as we can say. It is just as likely that the coincidences of the story brought the prophecy to Luke's mind as that the prophecy supplied him with the details. Philip may have been Luke's informant for both of the stories in chapter 8, though in the case of the work among the Samaritans, there were others, like Paul, who could have supplied him with details (cf. 15:3).

8:4 / This verse picks up the reference in verse 1 to believers leaving the city. Wherever they went they preached the message. This statement embodies two words characteristic of

Luke: "to preach the Good News," which is found only once in the other Gospels but ten times in Luke and fifteen times in Acts—a truly missionary word—and "to go through" (NIV **wherever they went**), which Luke uses constantly (though not exclusively) of missionary journeys. With the advantage of hindsight, he saw that the scattering of the believers did constitute a series of missionary journeys, though of course at the time they were not thought of as this.

8:5-8 / The general statement of verse 4 is immediately followed by a particular instance: **Philip went down to a city in Samaria** (v. 5). The best manuscripts have "the city of Samaria," but even if we accept the definite article, there is still some uncertainty about which city was meant. Sebaste was "the principal city" of the area, but was predominantly Gentile (cf. Caesarea, 10:1) and neither the religious nor the ethnic center of the Samaritans. Sychar is a possibility (cf. John 4:5ff.), and Gitta (location disputed, but the traditional birthplace of Simon Magus) has been suggested. Philip's ministry is briefly described. First, it centered on the proclamation of Jesus as **the Christ** (v. 5). One wonders whether this was made in terms of the Prophet-like-Moses, for it was in these terms that the Samaritans conceived of their own Messiah, the Taheb (see disc. on 3:22 and 7:37). At all events, the situation must have been similar to that described in John 4:25ff., with Philip giving a name to the one whom they were expecting. Second, his ministry was marked by exorcisms and healings. In this it followed the pattern of the apostles (cf. 3:1ff; 5:16; also 6:8) and indeed of Jesus himself. Luke more often than the other Evangelists maintains a clear distinction between ordinary illness and demon possession (see note on 5:16), as instanced in this passage. Of the various healings that he notes, those of the lame and the paralyzed are especially frequent in this book, no doubt because they were seen to be signs that the messianic hope was being fulfilled (cf. Isa. 35:3, 6). And third, Philip's ministry resulted in joy (see disc. on 3:8).

§20   Simon the Sorcerer (Acts 8:9–25)

8:9–11 / Among the crowds that "paid close attention to what Philip said" (v. 6) was one Simon, a Magus (see notes). He practiced the charms and incantations of the East and by these means had held the Samaritans in his thrall for **a long time** (v. 11). They called him **the Great Power** (v. 10), apparently at his own suggestion (v. 9). From the New Testament, as indeed from later sources relating to the Samaritans in particular, we learn that "power" was a name given to any angelic or divine being (cf., e.g., Rom. 8:38; Eph. 1:21; 3:10) and sometimes even to God himself (Mark 14:62). In the light of this, it would appear that the Samaritans believed Simon to be the incarnation of some such being. Little wonder then that they **gave him their attention** (v. 10), though with gentle irony Luke uses the same expression here as in verse 6 to describe the attention that they now gave to Philip.

8:12–13 / Philip's preaching here is described as being about **the good news of the kingdom of God**, which now, of course, revolved about the person and work of **Jesus Christ** (v. 12; see disc. on 1:3 and notes and the disc. on 19:8). The result of this preaching was that many Samaritans **believed Philip**, that is, they gave credence to what he said and so believed in Jesus as the Messiah. On this basis **they were baptized, both men and women** (v. 12; see disc. on 1:14). For reasons of his own, which soon become clear, Simon Magus also professed faith and was baptized, after which **he followed Philip everywhere** ("he paid close attention," see disc. on 2:42), being astounded at the **great signs and miracles** (lit. "powers") that he saw being done (v. 13; see note on 2:22). This is perhaps another touch of Lukan irony, for Simon was supposed to be "the Great Power" and for a long time had astounded others (vv 9–11). It was the power, not the holiness, of the new faith that impressed him (v. 23).

8:14–17 / When news reached Jerusalem that the people of Samaria **had accepted the word of God** (v. 14; the reference is a general one to the region), the apostles sent Peter and John to them. The fact that they were sent by the whole group acting as a collegiate body shows that no one leader had as yet emerged (see disc. on 9:27 and notes on 11:30 and 12:17). But why were Peter and John sent at all? Before attempting to answer this question, we should first observe the expressions that are used of these Samaritans: they "paid close attention to what (Philip) said" (v. 6); "they believed Philip as he preached the good news" (v. 12); they **accepted the word of God** (v. 14); they were **baptized into the name of the Lord Jesus** (v. 17), where the Greek preposition *eis* expresses the thought of commitment to the one in whose name the rite was administered (see note on 2:38 and the disc. on 14:23 and 19:5); and finally, as a result of all this, "there was great joy in that city" (v. 8). There is no hint of any deficiency in their faith. Certainly Philip recognized none, else he would not have baptized them. Nor did Peter and John find anything lacking, for as far as we know, they preached nothing more to them before laying hands upon them (but cf. v. 25). It is hard to believe, then, that the Spirit's work of regeneration had not been done in their lives. And yet the apostles prayed that these Samaritans **might receive the Holy Spirit, because the Holy Spirit had not yet come upon any of them** (vv. 15, 16). How does this fit with the teaching elsewhere that Christians are, without exception, both born of the Spirit and endowed with the Spirit at new birth (see notes on 2:4 and 38)? A clue may be found in Luke's use of the phrase **Holy Spirit** without the definite article (so the Greek in vv. 15, 17, 19). The anarthrous (without the article) form often seems to place greater emphasis on the Spirit's activity than on his person; what may have been lacking in Samaria was the outward manifestation of that activity in the more evident gifts of the Spirit (cf. 10:46; 19:6). The reference in verse 18 to Simon's seeing something when the Spirit was given may bear this out, as also the verb "to come (lit., fall) upon" (v. 16), which in 10:44 and 11:15 is used of the Spirit's coming in a way that was marked by outward signs. We hasten to add, however, that this is not always the way of his coming, as 1 Corinthians 12:29f. makes abundantly clear.

But still the question remains, Why were the apostles sent? There is no indication that the laying on of hands, much less of apostolic hands, was a necessary or even normal part of Christian initiation. Nor was it unusual for a period of time to elapse between baptism and the reception (experience) of the Spirit (cf. 9:17f.; 10:44; 1 Cor. 12:13). Nor have we any reason to think that the gift of the Spirit was administered exclusively by the apostles— or anyone else, for that matter. In fact, a careful examination of Acts shows that the pattern of conversion and initiation varies in every case for which we have details, the only common element being the presence of faith in Jesus marked by the outward sign of that faith, namely, baptism into / in / upon his name. Arising out of this, two observations must be made: First, no satisfactory answer to the question can be given that ignores the peculiar social and historical factors that obtained in this situation. The Samaritans needed to be shown that they were fully incorporated into the Christian community. Without a clear connecting link between the church in Samaria and that in Jerusalem, the schism that had for so long plagued Jewish-Samaritan relations might well have been carried over into the church. There could easily have been Jewish Christians who would "not associate with" Samaritan Christians (cf. John 4:9) had not something like this united the work of Philip with that of the Jerusalem apostles. Second, whatever explanation is given, it would be a mistake to treat this incident as establishing the normal pattern for all admissions into the church.

8:18–19 / When Simon saw what had happened, he betrayed the motive for his own apparent conversion. He, too, wanted the power that he had first seen in Philip and now saw at work in the ministry of the apostles. Thinking that it could be bought, **he offered . . . money** to Peter and John (v. 18; cf. 2 Kings 5:20ff.). In the manner of the time Simon had probably bought other secrets from masters of magic (cf. 19:19) and no doubt thought that he was about to do so again and by this means restore and even enhance his former reputation.

8:20–23 / But Peter soon put him right, and in unmistakable terms (cf. 5:3, 4, 9). He declared in effect that Simon was an unregenerate reprobate and wished that his money and he might go to hell. Was he thinking of Judas when he said this? That Simon had thought to obtain God's gift in this way and to administer it to all and sundry without reference to faith or repentance shows how little he understood either of God or of his gifts. The thought had come from a heart **not right before God** (v. 21; the phrase is taken from Ps. 78:37; cf. 13:10). Despite his baptism and profession of faith, Simon had "no part or share in the message" (v. 21, so the Greek), that is, he had not entered into the meaning of baptism and had neither truly confessed Jesus as Lord nor received his salvation. Moreover, when Peter told him to repent and to pray for forgiveness, the form of the Greek expresses doubt that he would, so far did he seem to be from God. Verse 23 reads literally, "For I see that you are for a gall of bitterness and a chain of sin." The second half of this statement is reminiscent of Isaiah 58:6; the first half is derived from Deuteronomy 29:18. In the latter, any turning away from God is described as "a root . . . that produces . . . bitter poison." The precise sense in which Peter applied this to Simon depends on our interpretation of the Greek preposition *eis*. It is generally taken as equivalent to *en*, "in," meaning that Simon was in this condition, that he was "a bitter and poisonous plant" and a **captive to sin**. But the preposition has been understood as equivalent to *hōs* "as," denoting the evil function that Simon would fulfill in the church if he continued as he was. This is the sense of the similar expression in Hebrews 12:15.

8:24 / The intention of Simon's final request to Peter and John is not certain. It may express genuine repentance. Certainly there is no further condemnation of him, and the request for prayer on his behalf does not rule out the possibility that he also prayed for himself. Nor must we allow the later stories of Simon as the arch-heretic to color our interpretation. But for all that, the suspicion remains that he was more concerned to escape punishment than he was to turn to the Lord (cf. 1 Sam. 24:16; 26:21).

8:25 / The story ends with a summary statement from which we learn that the apostles gave further instruction to the believers (for the verb "to give testimony " see disc. on 2:40) after which they started out on their return journey, preaching as they entered a number of Samaritan villages. Philip may have accompanied them, since this gives better sense to verse 26. Thus, the work among the Samaritans ends as a joint venture between Hellenists and Hebrews. Philip's return to Jerusalem (if that is what it was) may have been after the Pauline persecution had abated (9:31). There is no strict chronology in this part of Acts.

Additional Notes §20

8:9 / **A man named Simon had practiced sorcery in the city and amazed all the people of Samaria**: There is no need to doubt that Simon was a historical figure, though we must dismiss much of the legend that has attached itself to his name. Luke describes him as a *magus*, or rather as practicing the lore of the magi. Strictly speaking, the magi were the priestly caste of Persia, and since the religion of Persia was Zoroastrianism, they were therefore Zoroastrian priests. Strabo (*Geography* 15.727 and 733) and Plutarch (*On Isis and Osiris* 46) were familiar with them in the Mediterranean area, and they appear in the New Testament in Matt. 2:1–12; Acts 8:9–24; 13:6–11. Josephus, *Antiquities* 20.141–144, tells of a magus of Cyprus named Atomos, who was attached to the court of Felix at Caesarea. The magi of Acts and Josephus were Jews or Samaritans. This makes it clear that the term was by no means confined to Persians but had come to indicate a "profession." In this sense Philo speaks highly of the magi for their research into the facts of nature (the "true magic," he calls it; see *Every Good Man Is Free* 74 and *On the Special Laws* 100). A similar appreciation of the magi is found in Cicero (*De Divinatione* 1.91). But not all magi enjoyed (or deserved) this good reputation. The term "magus" was also applied to adepts of magic of various kinds. Philo refers to these as "charlatan mendicants and parasites" (*Special Laws* 3.101; cf. also Juvenal *Satires* 6.562; 14.248; Horace *Satires* 1.2.1). Simon seems to have belonged to this second category. Ramsay describes the magi (esp. the lower sort who appealed to the widespread superstition of the ancient world) as the strongest influence that existed in that world and one that must either destroy or be destroyed by Christianity (*Paul*, p. 79).

8:10 / **The divine power** (lit., "the power of God") **known as the Great Power**: The qualification, "of God," was probably added by Luke for the benefit of his readers. As far as the Samaritans were concerned, the word **power** on its own would have suggested the supernatural, if not the divine. In the second phrase the word **great** seems superfluous unless *megalē* is not the Greek adjective but the transliteration of a Samaritan expression meaning "revealing." Simon may have given himself out to be "the Revealing Power."

§21 Philip and the Ethiopian (Acts 8:26–40)

8:26 / If these stories of Philip belong in the sequence and close connection in which we now have them, then either he returned with the apostles to Jerusalem and from there set out for Gaza, or Peter and John returned without him and he traveled directly from Samaria. The Greek favors the first, in that Philip's instruction was to go "on" the road, not **to** the road as in NIV; and the road to Gaza ran from Jerusalem. There were, in fact, two roads—the more northerly, which went first to Ashkelon and then by the coast, and the other, which went by way of Hebron and then westward through the desert. It may have been to this that Luke was referring when he added, "This is a desert," rather than to its disuse. Or it may have been to Gaza itself (the Greek is ambiguous), for the old city had been destroyed and its site remained largely "a desert" (so Strabo described it, *Geography* 16.2.30; cf. Zeph. 2:4). The new city had been built nearer the sea (it, too, was destroyed, in A.D. 66). Verse 36 perhaps decides that Luke's note refers to the country through which the road ran.

More important than where he was is how Philip came to be there. It was through **an angel of the Lord**, and in view of the later references to the part played by the Spirit (vv. 29, 39; see disc. on 5:19), we have no hesitation in identifying the angel with "the Spirit of the Lord," as was common in Jewish thought (cf. 23:9). In short, Philip was on this road by divine guidance— an inner compulsion, perhaps, to which Luke has given this vivid description.

8:27–28 / No sooner had Philip felt this constraint than he "got up and went" (v. 27; cf. 16:10). The Greek gives the sense of an immediate response. Philip's behavior in all of this narrative is reminiscent of the stories of Elijah in the way in which he obeyed divine guidance and came and went unexpectedly (cf. 1 Kings 17:2, 9f.; 2 Kings 1:3, 15). God's guidance is always most evident where there is a willingness to obey (cf. John 7:17).

The inland, desert road to Gaza was not, apparently, the most frequented route. Philip was therefore surprised to find another traveling the same way. This is expressed in the exclamation, "[Look!] an Ethiopian" (v. 27; see disc. on 1:10f.). In the biblical context, Ethiopia corresponds to Nubia (modern Sudan) and means here in particular the Nilotic kingdom ruled by queens from Meroe, south of modern Khartoum. The man himself was **an important official**. Indeed, he was the treasurer and, in that capacity, may have come into contact with Egyptian Jews and been attracted to their faith. He was also a **eunuch** (v. 27). In some contexts this might mean only that he was "an official" (see LXX Gen. 39:1), but here he is called an official and a eunuch, and from this it would appear that **eunuch** is intended in the literal sense. This being so, the Ethiopian was barred by Jewish law from full participation in their religion, even had he wished to convert (Deut. 23:1; but cf. Isa. 56:3–8), though he may have preferred, like so many others, to remain a God-fearer (see note on 6:5). There was certainly nothing unusual in such a person visiting Jerusalem to worship (v. 27), and we meet him as he was returning home, beguiling the time by reading what may have been a memento of his visit, a scroll containing part of the Old Testament.

8:29–31 / The Ethiopian was traveling only slowly. His **chariot** was probably not the light war chariot but a covered wagon drawn by oxen and made even slower by the retinue that a man of his dignity must have had. And now for the second time Philip came under the divine constraint. The Spirit said, **Go to that chariot and stay near it** (v. 29). Obedient, he ran to catch up with the group. This in itself would have occasioned no surprise. What may have surprised, however, was that he spoke to the official, whose importance should have put him beyond Philip's reach. But as God had put him there, so he gave him the opportunity. It was customary in the ancient world to read aloud, and when Philip heard the official reading (or a slave reading to him), he asked him whether he understood the passage. The man said that he did not; nor could he without some explanation. Then perceiving (by his dress or his speech) that Philip was a Jew, he invited him **to come up and sit with him** (v. 31) and explain the passage to him. By his choice of words Luke gives to the Ethiopian's invitation a sense both of urgency and of good manners.

8:32-35 / The Ethiopian had been reading Isaiah 53:7, 8. The text of the LXX that Luke has accurately reproduced (with only one minor addition) differs in these verses from the Hebrew at a number of points but is sufficiently close to express the prophet's intention. Luke regularly uses the LXX regardless of whether the original speaker used it or not. But on this occasion, the Ethiopian was most likely reading that version, and it would probably have been the version with which Philip was most familiar. These particular verses speak of the Servant suffering for others but in the end reaping his reward (a hint of the resurrection? see disc. on 26:23). It was ready-made as a starting point for the evangelist, and the Ethiopian's question, **Who is the prophet talking about?** gave him his opening.

Jewish scholars had already answered this question in a number of ways. Some held that the Servant was the nation (cf. Isa. 44:1; LXX 42:1). Others maintained that the Servant was Isaiah himself; others again that he was the Messiah, but interpreted in such a way as to avoid any suggestion that the Messiah would suffer. Both concepts—suffering and messiahship—appear in the Jewish treatment of Isaiah 53, but always separately. It was only in the teaching of Jesus that these ideas were first brought together and Isaiah 53 interpreted of a suffering Messiah. From Jesus (cf. Luke 22:37; 24:25-27, 44-47) the disciples learned to use this passage as the key to finding his death and resurrection elsewhere in the Scriptures, and so Philip, starting from this passage, **told him the good news about Jesus** (v. 35; see disc. on 10:34 for the expression, he **began to speak**).

8:36 / To this he must have added instruction about the proper response to the gospel (cf., e.g., 2:38, 41; 3:26; 8:12), for when they came to a convenient place (its discovery seemed almost providential; see disc. on 1:10f. for "Look! . . ."), the Ethiopian asked, **Why shouldn't I be baptized?** Again, there is a note of polite but urgent appeal (cf. v. 31; Ps. 68:31), though the form of words is almost certainly Luke's. The question echoes what is thought to have been an early baptismal formula in the use of the verb "What is to prevent . . . ?" which occurs again in 10:47 and 11:17 in a baptismal context. To this question a strict Jew would have alleged two impediments: the man was a Gentile; and the man was a eunuch. But Philip looked only for repentance and faith and was evidently assured of both in this case.

But because the original text makes no mention of the Ethiopian's response, verse 37 was added. It is not original, but is not without interest, for it reflects what was probably another feature of the early baptismal liturgy, namely, a formal interrogation leading to the credal statement "I believe that Jesus Christ is the Son of God" (cf. 11:17; 16:31).

8:38 / Assuming that they were on the road that went by way of Hebron, the identification of the spot they had reached as Bethzur is not improbable (Jerome, *Epistles* 103). At all events, the carriage was stopped and **both Philip and the eunuch went down into the water**. This may only mean "to the water," but it was baptism by immersion (notice "they came up out of the water," v. 39) according to the common (though hardly universal) practice of the early church (cf. Rom. 6:4 and Col. 2:12, which imply as much, as also 1 Cor. 10:2 and 1 Pet. 3:20ff.; the *Didache* 7.3 regards immersion as not essential).

8:39 / Afterwards the two men parted company. The Western text adds the words shown in brackets: "the Spirit [Holy fell upon the eunuch, but the angel] of the Lord" (note that in Greek the adjective—in this case "holy"—often follows the noun). This reading is not well supported, but in this case it is easier to imagine that these words were accidentally left out than that they were deliberately added later. In other words, the longer reading may be original. But in any case, from the fact that the official **went on his way rejoicing**, we can fairly assume that the Spirit had "fallen upon him" in accordance with the promise of 2:38 (see disc. on 3:8). Nor does the longer reading make any difference to our understanding of what happened to Philip. Whether "angel" or **Spirit**, it is all one (see disc. on v. 26). There is no need to read a miracle into the manner of Philip's departure, though Luke's expression is undoubtedly a striking one (cf. 1 Kings 18:12; 2 Kings 2:16; Ezek. 3:14). The same verb is used by Paul in 1 Thessalonians 4:17 of believers being "caught up" to meet the Lord, in 2 Corinthians 12:2, 4, of being "caught up" himself into heaven, and by Luke in Acts 23:10 of Paul being "carried away" by the soldiers. Here it probably means that Philip was again under a strong inner compulsion to go where he did.

8:40 / So then, led by the Spirit, Philip **appeared at Azotus** (Ashdod), on the coastal plain some eighteen miles northeast of

Gaza. Like Gaza, it had been one of the five cities of the Phil-
istine shore. More recently, both cities had been restored by Ga-
binius and Herod the Great and had mixed Jewish and Greek
populations (as did the whole area, with bitter rivalry between
them; see disc. on 9:30; 10:1; 21:10; 24:7). Philip may have stayed
for some time in Azotus, as indeed in all of the towns that he
visited, so that this verse may cover what was actually a protracted
journey. Because of the nature of the area, this gives a hint of
the Gentile mission to come, though Philip probably confined
himself to the Jewish communities in which he may have established a number of Christian groups (or strengthened them; see
disc. on 9:32ff.). The two verbs in the discussion in verse 4, used
of Philip in this verse, reinforce the impression that this was a
"missionary journey" (see Hengel, *Acts*, p. 79, for the suggestion
that an eschatological motive lay behind Philip's mission). From
their position between Azotus and Caesarea, Lydda and Joppa
may have been on his itinerary, as also Jamnia and Antipatris.
In time he reached Caesarea, the seat of Roman power in the province (see disc. on 10:1), and here made his home (21:8). Whether
Philip was already settled in Caesarea at the time of the events
of chapter 10, or whether they preceded his coming, we cannot
tell.

Additional Notes §21

8:26 / **Go south**: The Greek word means "middle of the day,"
but from the position of the sun at noon, it acquired the sense adopted
here. But if the command was to travel at noon, Philip's ready obedience is even more striking—temperatures in this region can be very high—
to say nothing of his running to catch up (v. 30).

8:27 / **Candace, queen of the Ethiopians**: Candace was not a per-
sonal name, but the title of the female rulers of the kingdom (cf.
"Pharaoh"). The title is attested in Strabo, *Geography* 17.820; Pliny *Natural
History* 6.186 and Pseudo Callisthenes, *History* 3.18.

8:32–33 / The importance of the Servant Songs of Isaiah, esp.
the fourth (Isa. 52:13–53:12), has already been stressed (see note on 3:13).
The fourth song was fundamental to the Christian demonstration of the
necessity of Christ's death. But did Luke himself see that necessity? Because the verses quoted here speak only of the Servant's humiliation,

not of his death, it has been said that Luke lacked interest in what was achieved by Christ's suffering (the atonement). But his writing is not without reference to Christ's suffering for others (e.g., 20:28; Luke 22:19f.), and the mention of the **lamb** even in these verses would surely have connoted sacrifice to anyone of that day. But in any case, is it fair to assume that the choice of verses was Luke's? Or if it was, that they were chosen without reference to the context? The quotation may have been intended simply to identify the passage and to indicate that the whole was to be referred to Jesus as the Messiah.

The Greek of v. 33 (Isa. 53:8) presents some difficulties of translation. It begins, "In (by?) humility his judgment was taken away." Does this mean (as some say) that by humbling himself his judgment was canceled, or that in his humiliation, i.e., in the violence done to him, the fair trial that was his due was withheld? The latter conforms more closely to the Hebrew and is adapted by NIV. The passage continues, "Who will describe his generation?" This probably means, "Who will declare the wickedness of his generation?" though it could mean that his posterity (i.e., those who have life through him) are beyond number. NIV appears to adopt yet another possible interpretation, namely, that he will have no posterity to describe because of his untimely death. The Hebrew at this point asks the question, "As for his generation, who considered that he was sent off from the land of the living (stricken for the transgression of my people)?" in the sense that it passed without notice,

§22 Saul's Conversion (Acts 9:1–19a)

As far as Luke was concerned, the conversion of Paul was the single most important result of the "Stephen affair." Its importance is borne out by his threefold repetition of the story here, in 22:5–16, and in 26:12–18. Luke's authority must have been Paul himself. The three accounts differ in detail, and it is not easy to say to what extent this was due to Paul—or to Luke—though we may be reasonably certain that some, at least, of the variations were Paul's as he adapted the later accounts to his different audiences (see further the disc. on 21:37–22:5). In any case, the central fact of a climactic experience is established beyond any doubt in Paul's own writings (1 Cor. 9:1; 15:8f.; 2 Cor. 4:6; Gal. 1:12–17; Phil. 3:4–10; 1 Tim. 1:12–16).

The story is told as though what happened had objective reality. Some modern scholars have questioned this. Instead, a psychological reason has sometimes been suggested. It was "the final outcome," says Weiss, "of an inner crisis" caused by Paul's sense of failure to keep the law (J. Weiss, vol. 1, p. 190). If Romans 7:14–25 reflects his preconversion experience, this theory has something to commend it, though it is far from an adequate explanation. Others attribute Paul's experience to an attack of epilepsy or to his falling into an ecstatic trance. Some have argued that the whole thing has been fabricated from a legendary tale. Paul's own explanation, however, was that he had had an encounter with the living Christ in a way that differed from his subsequent "visions and revelations" (2 Cor. 12:1), so that he could only describe it as the last of Christ's post–resurrection appearances (1 Cor. 15:8). Paul was no stranger to the experience of Christ as a power within (Rom. 8:10; Gal. 2:20), "but at Damascus he not only experienced power within but more than that, he perceived a person without—not only the gift of grace but the appearance of the risen Jesus. His claim that his seeing of Jesus was something distinctive therefore was not lightly made and cannot be lightly dismissed" (Dunn, *Jesus*, p. 109). Only his utter conviction of the reality of what happened will sufficiently explain the outcome—"a radical change from a self-centered to a Christ-centered life, a complete submission to Jesus Christ in which he becomes a disciple of the Master and a servant of the Lord, and his entrance into the kingdom of God on earth into that apostolic service which is the task of the Christian community" (T. W. Manson, pp. 13f.).

9:1–2 / The persecution of the church in Jerusalem continued, with Paul **still breathing out murderous threats against the Lord's disciples** (v. 1)—threats that may not have been entirely hollow (see disc. on 22:4 and 26:10). Not content with this, he wished also to extend his efforts beyond the city (see disc. on 26:11). From 26:10 it is evident that he was already acting under a commission from the high priest, but now **he went to the high priest** (probably Caiaphas) and asked that his mandate be extended to allow him to look for those **who belonged to the Way in Damascus**, men and women, and to bring them back to Jerusalem (v. 2; see disc. on 1:14). The expression "the Way" is peculiar to Acts (cf. 19:9, 23; 22:4; 24:14, 22) and may have originated with the Jews who saw the Christians as those who had adopted a distinctive way of life. But it must have soon come into use among the Christians as an apt way of describing themselves as the followers of him who is the way (John 14:6f.; the sectarians at Qumran also spoke of themselves as "the way," e.g., 1 QS 9.17f.; CD 1.13). That there were followers of "the Way" in Damascus, whose presence is otherwise unaccounted for, reminds us of how selective Luke has been in telling his story. The expression **if he found** (v. 2) does not throw doubt on their presence but on Paul's ability to apprehend them, for these were not simply the recent refugees (8:1), but Christians who had their homes in Damascus and had evidently been able to combine their Christian faith with their Jewish practice in a manner acceptable to their fellow Jews. It was a question, then, of whether the numerous synagogues of Damascus would cooperate with Paul in acting against those of their fellow members who chose to acknowledge Jesus as the Christ. The **letters to the synagogues** (v. 2) would be a help, for though the Sanhedrin had no legal authority outside Judea, its reputation did give it some moral authority over the Jews of the Diaspora (see Sherwin-White, p. 100). Paul would also have had to seek the cooperation of the local magistrates, but the name of the Jewish Sanhedrin may have carried sufficient weight even with them for him to be confident of their acquiescence, if not their active assistance. At all events, he appears to have set out with high hopes of success. He was accompanied by a number of men, detached perhaps from the temple guard, to help with the arrests.

9:3-5 / Damascus, if not the oldest city in the world, is at least deserving of the title of most enduring. It lies northwest of the Ghuta Plain, west of the Syrian-Arabian Desert and east of the Anti-Lebanon Mountains. Its region was an oasis, watered by a system of rivers and canals and famous for its orchards and gardens. From time immemorial, Damascus had played an important role as a center of religion and commerce. It was a natural communications center, linking the countries of the Mediterranean with the East. From Damascus the tracks ran across the desert to Assyria and Babylon, south to Arabia, north to Aleppo. From Jerusalem there were two ways that Paul could go to Damascus. One was the road that led from Egypt and kept near the coast until it struck inland across the Jordan north of the Sea of Galilee. To join this road, he must first have traveled westward to the sea. The other led through Neapolis and Shechem, across the Jordan south of the Sea of Galilee and northeastward to Damascus. Being the shorter of the two ways, this was his most likely route.

As Paul drew near to Damascus, **suddenly a light from heaven flashed around him** (v. 3). The Greek word is one often used of lightning, and in this way Luke has attempted to give us some idea of its intensity, though the circumstances are such that clearly no natural phenomenon was intended by the description. In 22:6 the time is fixed at "about noon," and in 26:13 the light is said to have been "brighter than the sun" and to have enveloped Paul's companions as well as himself. Light is often associated in Scripture with the revelation of God (cf. 12:7), and this was clearly the case here. It was the glory of which Stephen had spoken (7:2) appearing to Paul, according to Stephen's theme, in a land not his own. More precisely, it was the glory of God shining "in the face of Christ" (2 Cor. 4:6), for though the narrative itself does not say so in so many words, elsewhere we are told that Paul saw Jesus (cf. vv. 17, 27; 22:14; 26:16): Not Jesus as others had seen him, but the ascended Son, resplendent in the glory of the Father, blinding to the human eye, for no one can look upon the face of God (cf. Exod. 33:20).

Paul and those who were with him (so 26:14) fell to the ground. A sound was heard that came to Paul as the voice of Christ: **Saul, Saul, Why do you persecute me?** (v. 4). The Semitic form of his name (Shaul) is used in each of the three accounts—a reminiscence, surely, of his actual experience. For the solemn repetition of the name, compare Genesis 22:11, Matthew 23:37, and Luke 10:41; 22:31. At first he must have been utterly confused, sensing only that he was in the divine presence. Hence the address **Lord** in his question. The reply came, **I am Jesus, whom you are persecuting** (v. 5; cf. 22:8, "I am Jesus of Nazareth"), and with it the first lesson that Paul had to learn, namely, that Christ had a "body," a tangible presence on earth, the church (see disc. on 1:1; cf. Rom. 12:4, 5; 1 Cor. 6:15; 8:12; 10:16f.; 12:12ff.; Eph. 1:23; 4:4, 12, 16; 5:23; Col. 1:18, 24; 2:19), so that it was he whom Paul had hurt in persecuting his people (cf. Matt. 25:40, 45; Luke 10:16). And he made two further discoveries. First, the Christians had been right in proclaiming the resurrection of Jesus. The use of his name here expresses Paul's realization that the Jesus of history was the Christ of this appearance. Second, Gamaliel had also been right, for Paul had indeed been found to be fighting against God (cf. 5:39).

9:6-8 / In due course Paul would be told what to do, but from this moment on he was a new man (cf. 2 Cor. 5:17; Phil. 3:4ff.). He could never completely forget the past, but it had been forgiven (see disc. on 3:19), and God had a new task for him. It will be noticed that in 26:16-18 a brief account is given, as though it happened at this juncture, of what that task would be. But the narrative in that chapter has been condensed by omitting all reference to Ananias, from whom Paul would learn only later for what purpose Christ had laid hold of him (see disc. on vv. 15f.; 22:12-16, also 22:17-21). Meanwhile, his companions were much less affected than he was by what had happened. They had seen the light, they had heard the sound (v. 7; cf. 22:9; 26:14), and like Paul they had dropped to the ground (26:14, though here they are described as now standing); but only he had understood the voice, and he alone was blinded by the sight (22:11 explicitly links his blindness with the light). Jesus had once called his kind blind guides to the blind (Matt. 15:14; 23:16), and blind now, Paul was led by others into Damascus (v. 8), where he was lodged in the house of one Judas in Straight Street (cf. v. 11). Details such

as the name of his host and of the street where he lived indicate
a source close to the events (cf. 16:15; 17:6f.; 18:2f.; 21:8, 16;
also 10:6).

9:9–12 / Here Paul remained for three days, neither eating nor drinking—a sign, perhaps, of his contrition or done, perhaps, in anticipation of further revelations (cf. v. 6, and see disc.
on 13:2) or perhaps simply because of his state of shock. As he
fasted he prayed. As a devout Pharisee Paul must often have
prayed. But perhaps for the first time he was learning the difference between "saying prayers" and praying (the believer's response to God's grace to him in Christ). The proud Pharisee of
Jesus' parable had taken the other man's place (Luke 18:9–14). This
passage brings home the importance of prayer both for Paul himself and in the mission of the church. At every critical point in
the story, we find people praying (10:2, 9; 13:2, 3; 14:23; 16:13,
16, 25; 20:36; 21:5; 22:17–21; 27:35; 28:8; see also the disc. on 1:14).
It is also the first of several passages in which visions are associated with prayer (cf. 10:2–6, 9–17; 22:17–21; 23:11; cf. also 16:9,
10; 18:9, 10; 26:13–19). Whatever else we make of this phenomenon,
we must allow that it expresses the conviction that in each case
the prayer was answered (see disc. on 1:14). In this particular case,
one vision was matched by another (cf. 10:1–23). In one, Paul saw
a man coming to him; in the other, that man himself, Ananias,
was directed to go to Paul and to lay hands on him for healing
(cf. 1 Sam. 3:4ff.; see note on 5:12).

Verse 11 is the first of five references in Acts to the city of
Paul's birth. Perhaps as old as Damascus, Tarsus was the chief
city of Cilicia Pedeias (see notes on 6:9 and 15:23). To judge from
the extent of its remains, its population in Roman times must have
been close to half a million. The city had all the elements needed
to make it the great commercial center that it was: a good harbor,
a rich hinterland, and a commanding position at the southern
end of the trade route across the Taurus Mountains, through the
Cilician Gates, to Cappadocia, Lycaonia, and inner Asia Minor
generally. The city passed into Roman hands from the crumbling
Seleucid Empire before 100 B.C., though effective rule was not
achieved until after 66 B.C. Under the later Seleucids, it had become one of the three great university cities of the Mediterranean world. Strabo speaks of the Tarsian university as even
surpassing, in some respects, those of Athens and Alexandria

(*Geography* 14.5.13). It was especially important as a center of Stoic philosophy, and to Tarsus, therefore, Paul may have been indebted for his familiarity with the tenets of that school of thought (see disc. on 17:18), though not from his early life in Tarsus (see disc. on 22:3), but from the years that he spent there later (see disc. on 9:30). His own trade of tent making was an important Cilician industry (cf. 18:3).

9:13–14 / Ananias is introduced into the narrative simply as a "disciple." He was a Jewish Christian with a strong attachment to the law and held in high regard by the Jews of Damascus (see disc. on 22:12). He may have been the Christian leader. News had reached him of **all the harm** done by Paul in Jerusalem, and now that Paul had arrived in Damascus he had no wish to meet him (cf. v. 26). Luke presents Ananias' torment in dramatic form as a dialogue with the **Lord** (Jesus), and here are found two further names for Christians (cf. "the Way," v. 2). They are called **saints** (v. 13, lit., "holy or separated ones," cf. vv. 32, 41; 26:10, and for the verb, 20:32; 26:18). The Old Testament had applied this term both to individuals and to Israel as a whole, but Ananias had no hesitation in using it now of Christians, the new "Israel of God" (Gal. 6:16). Noticeably, in 26:10, Paul used the same term himself, perhaps in conscious repetition of Ananias, unless, of course, the language was Paul's all along. At least six of his letters are addressed to those who are "called (to be) saints." Secondly, Christians are also "those who call on your [Jesus'] name." This phrase echoes 2:21 (a quote of Joel 2:32) and is used again in verse 21 and in 22:16. This description means that they believe in Christ, and significantly, it is closely linked in 1 Corinthians 1:2 with the address to Christians as "the saints." Another distinctive feature of the passage is the frequent use of the title **Lord** of Jesus. This was common at the time when Paul was writing his letters and may, again, reflect his own language in recounting the story to Luke.

9:15–16 / The Lord's command to Ananias to go to Paul was repeated, and at the same time it was shown him what Paul's destiny would be. He was "a vessel of [God's] choice," a metaphor drawn from the work of the potter. As the potter made vessels for various uses, so God made human beings for his own purposes (cf. Jer. 18:1–11; 22:28; Hos. 8:8; 2 Cor. 4:7; 2 Tim. 2:20, 21). In Paul's case, it was to take up the mantle of the Suffering

Servant (cf. Col. 1:24), for he would be "a light to the nations," that Paul might "carry God's name" (continuing the metaphor of the vessel) **before the Gentiles and their kings and before the people of Israel** (v. 15; cf. 26:22; Isa. 49:6. see disc. on 13:47). Notice that this service would include the Jews, but the order of words emphasizes the Gentiles. This was a striking turnabout for Paul the Pharisee (see disc. on 10:9ff. and note on 10:28). To carry out this service would entail much suffering for Paul, as for the Servant himself (but not as a punishment for the past, simply "for the Lord's sake"). How much he would suffer would be shown him from time to time (e.g., 20:23), and we see something of this in the epistles (e.g., 1 Cor. 4:9ff.; 2 Cor. 6:4, 5; 11:23–28; Phil. 3:4ff.; Col. 1:24; 2 Tim. 4:6). All this Ananias communicated to Paul when they met (22:14f.).

9:17–19a / Ananias overcame his reluctance to go, if not his fear, and went to the house in Straight Street. Here he laid his hands on Paul, announcing that he had been sent by Jesus that Paul might **see again and be filled with the Holy Spirit** (v. 17). A nice touch is found in his opening words, **Brother Saul** (v. 17). No word of reproach, but a warm welcome into the fellowship of the church (cf. v. 27). The laying on of hands should be seen as a token of his healing, not of his being filled with the Spirit—much less as the means whereby that gift was bestowed. Paul's filling with the Spirit is better linked with his baptism, but again, not as the means but as the outward sign of an inward and spiritual grace (see disc. on 2:38). His sight was restored (Luke's description of the process employs medical language), he was baptized (at the hands of Ananias?), took some food, and was "strengthened"—possibly another medical term—and so was ready for what lay ahead.

Additional Notes §22

9:4 / Why do you persecute me? The answer to this question has been found in Gal. 3:13. Before his conversion Paul regarded Jesus as accursed in terms of Deut. 21:22f. (see disc. on 5:20). For this reason, he blasphemed him (1 Tim. 1:13) and tried to make others blaspheme him (Acts 26:11), i.e., to say, "Jesus be cursed" (1 Cor. 12:3). After his conversion, Paul still went on saying, "God made Christ a curse," but now added two words, "for us" or "for me" (cf. also Gal. 2:20). See J. Jeremias, *The Central Message of the New Testament* (London: SCM Press, 1965), pp. 35f.

9:17 / The Lord . . . has sent me so that you may . . . be filled with the Holy Spirit (cf. 22:12ff.): In view of Paul's later insistence in Gal. 1:1, 11f. that he received his apostolic commission, not from human hands, but directly from Christ, it is worth noting with Bruce that, first, Paul in Galatians is defending himself against the charge that he received his commission from the original apostles. The part played by Ananias would not have affected his argument, even if he was the Christian leader in Damascus. Second, in any case, Ananias played the part of a prophet, so that his words were the words of the risen Christ (*Book,* pp. 200f.).

§23 Saul in Damascus and Jerusalem (Acts 9:19b–31)

Here we see how seriously Paul took his new vocation as a man "saved to serve." But the pattern for the Twelve had been first to be with Jesus then to be sent out (Mark 3:14), and Paul soon found the need to be alone for a while with the Lord (cf. Mark 6:31). His own writings add a number of details to Luke's narrative at this point.

9:19b–22 / As the bearer of the Sanhedrin's commission, Paul would have been expected to preach in the synagogues of Damascus, and so he did, using them as he would the synagogues of his later travels as a platform for preaching the gospel (cf. 13:5; 14ff.; 14:1; 16:13; 17:1f., 10; 18:4, 19; 19:8; 28:17, see note on 13:14). His message took his hearers by surprise (v. 21), for he preached about Jesus, not against him, declaring him to be **the Son of God** (v. 20). To Jewish ears, this phrase could mean a number of things, but most importantly in this connection, it was an official title of the king (e.g., 2 Sam. 7:14; Pss. 2:2 and 89:27, 29) and, by extension, of the eschatological king, the Messiah (Enoch 105:2; 4 Ezra 7:28, 29; 13:32, 37, 52; 14:9). It was at least in this sense that Paul called Jesus **Son of God** (see v. 22 and note on 11:20), but in view of his recent experience, he may not have been far from the distinctively Christian use of the term of the divine nature of Jesus. Paul alone uses this title in Acts (13:33), and it is no accident that it is also of central importance in his epistles (e.g., Rom. 8:3; Gal. 4:4; Col. 1:15–20) and figures in his own account of his calling to be an apostle (Rom. 1:1–4; Gal. 1:16). In regard to this it is also worth noticing that the verb **raised havoc** (v. 21, Gk. *porthein*) is found nowhere else in the New Testament, except in Galatians 1:13 and 23 in reference to the very matter mentioned here in this verse. Notice again the description of Christians as "those who call on his name" (see disc. on v. 14).

The reference in verse 22 is not to Paul's preaching (as GNB), but to Paul himself becoming **more and more powerful**. He was going from strength to strength in his new life (the imperfect tense; cf. Ps. 84:7). His preaching and its effect on his hearers are described in the latter half of the verse. The Greek verb (lit., "to bring together," hence "to compare") suggests that his preaching consisted largely of comparing the Old Testament with the events of Jesus' life to demonstrate that he was the Messiah (for another note on Paul's preaching technique, see disc. on 17:3). This suggests that he was familiar with Jesus' life. This is hardly surprising. Even as a persecutor, through controversies and legal hearings he would have picked up a great deal, if he did not already have firsthand information. And since his conversion he had probably been under instruction from Ananias and others.

9:23–25 / In Galatians 1:17 Paul says that following his conversion he spent some time in Arabia, and in 2 Corinthians 11:32f. he gives further details of his time in Damascus. Putting all this together, it seems likely that after his initial stay in Damascus Paul went to Arabia, which probably means Nabatea (see notes on 2:9ff.). He may have remained there for anything up to two or three years (the Jews reckoned inclusively, so that the "three years" of Galatians need refer to little more than one complete year), preaching possibly, but thinking through what he believed in the light of his conversion experience. Ultimately, he returned to Damascus, the point marked in Luke's narrative perhaps by the words, **after many days had gone by** (v. 23). By now the Jews of the city would have recovered from the surprise of his conversion and would no longer have been prepared to tolerate his preaching of Jesus. So they planned to kill him (cf. v. 29; 20:3, 19; 23:21; 25:3; 2 Cor. 11:26) and according to 2 Corinthians, were able to enlist the aid of the Nabatean ethnarch (NIV "governor") in the attempt.

It appears that by now Damascus had come under the rule of the Nabateans. Their king, Aretas IV, had been at war with his son-in-law, Herod Antipas. With the death of Tiberius in A.D. 37 and the consequent withdrawal of Vitellius, the Roman governor of Syria, whose aid had been promised to Herod, Aretas may have pushed as far north as Damascus. This supposition, based in part on Paul's reference, is borne out by there being no imperial coins of Damascus from the late 30s until 62. In A.D. 62–

63 the image of Nero begins to appear, which suggests that the city had passed again to the Romans. Meanwhile, at the instigation of the Jews, the Nabatean ethnarch posted guards at the gates of the city, keeping watch for Paul day and night. We can only guess why they were involved. Perhaps Paul's preaching in Nabatea had stirred up trouble in the Jewish communities. Or perhaps the Nabateans felt that it was to their advantage to cooperate with the Jews. Aretas may have wished to make an ally of the Sanhedrin. At all events, they were involved, and Paul's life was at risk. But he was not without help. One night "his disciples" lowered him through an opening in the wall, and he made his escape (v. 30; cf. Josh. 2:15; 1 Sam. 19:12). He seems to have felt that this was a low point in a career marked by suffering (2 Cor. 11:30ff.).

9:26 / When eventually Paul returned to Jerusalem (according to Gal. 1:18, three years after his conversion), he found it difficult to gain acceptance by the church. He particularly wanted to see Peter (Gal. 1:18), but neither Peter nor anyone else wanted to see him (cf. v. 13). They must have heard of his conversion, but since then may have heard little or nothing about him. They were unsure of him. Indeed, they did not believe **that he really was a disciple** and were naturally afraid of him. He brought no letters of recommendation (cf. 18:27).

9:27 / In the end it was Barnabas who **brought him to the apostles**. How he and Paul made contact or why Barnabas should now have come to Paul's aid we do not know. There are no grounds for supposing, as commentators sometimes do, that they were students together in Tarsus (see disc. on 22:3). The explanation probably lies simply in the kind of person Barnabas was. Notice his explanation of Paul's conversion. It makes explicit what is only assumed in the earlier narrative, namely, that Paul **had seen the Lord** [Jesus] (cf. also v. 17). Notice also the stress on how boldly **he had preached . . . in the name of Jesus** in Damascus, making the point, perhaps, that he had been filled with the Spirit no less than they (see disc. 4:13, 29, 31). This account of Paul's meeting with the apostles may seem at odds with his own account in Galatians 1:18f., but the differences are more apparent than real and arise from the different objectives of the two writers. It was important for Luke to show that Paul was accepted by the apostles, whereas for Paul in Galatians it was important to assert his independence of them. He is at pains, therefore, to point out that of the Twelve he met only with Peter. James, the Lord's brother, was also present (see note on 12:17). From Galatians we learn that his visit was only a brief one, two weeks in all.

9:28–30 / Having won the confidence of Peter and James, Paul spent much of these two weeks "going in and out with them" (so the Greek), which probably means that he had a number of private meetings with them, not the public ministry implied by NIV. He did preach in public, but not to the extent that he became personally known to "the churches of Judea" (Gal. 1:22). Those public appearances he did make were confined to his "disputes" with the (Jewish) Hellenists. Luke uses the same word concerning the debates of "the Freedmen" with Stephen (6:9), only now the roles are reversed. In the earlier passage it was the men of the synagogue who disputed with Stephen, here it is Paul who disputed with them. But was it the same synagogue? There is, of course, no way of telling, but it is at least likely that he did single them out because of their part in Stephen's death. At all events, he spoke boldly to whomever it was **in the name of the Lord** (v. 28); that is, his message centered on Jesus whom God had made both "Lord and Christ" (cf. 2:36). The result was that the Hellenists made an attempt on Paul's life. When **the brothers** got wind of this, they took Paul **down to Caesarea and sent him off to Tarsus** (v. 30). That the others are called **the brothers** underlines the unity of the church of which Paul was now a member. The **Caesarea** of this narrative is the harbor city of that name, hence the expression "to take down (to the sea)." Paul's own account of this incident in 22:17–21 includes a vision that he had in the temple in which the Lord told him to flee from Jerusalem, for he would send him away. And now a veil is drawn over Paul's life until he reappears some ten years later (11:25ff.). We only know that he spent these years preaching in "Syria and Cilicia" (Gal. 1:21). They were probably also years of study (see W. C. van Unnik, pp. 56ff., who suggests that his studies centered on the Greek language and culture; but see disc. on 22:2).

9:31 / Luke brings the section to a close (and in a broader sense, the whole narrative that had its beginning in the story of Stephen) with a brief statement concerning the state of the church (see disc. on 2:43–47). It now **enjoyed a time of peace**. This is directly linked with the conversion of Paul, but there were other factors not mentioned by Luke. The Sanhedrin was now faced with more pressing matters. First, there had been a change of high priest. In A.D. 37 Caiaphas had been deposed, and in his place Vitellius had installed first Jonathan (see disc. on 4:6), then his brother Theophilus (A.D. 37–41). Second, there had been a change of emperor in the same year, with Caligula succeeding Tiberius. The new emperor was far less sympathetic to the Jews than Tiberius had been (see B. Reicke, p. 193), and this soon become evident. In the summer of A.D. 38 Herod Agrippa I, on his way to the kingdom granted him by Caligula (see disc. on 12:1), made a parade in Alexandria that incited riots between the Jews and the Greeks of that city. This interracial strife spread to other cities. The Greeks of Jamnia raised an altar to the emperor, only to have the Jews tear it down. Caligula intervened by ordering that his image be set up in the temple (A.D. 39; see Josephus, *Antiquities* 18.261–268). This profanation was only averted by Herod Agrippa's pleas, but the threat hung over the heads of the Jews as long as Caligula ruled. He was assassinated in A.D. 41.

Meanwhile, the church was "built up." This term generally refers to spiritual growth, but may include the development of the church's organization (see disc. on 11:30). At the same time it **grew in numbers** because of two things: **the fear of the Lord** [Jesus] and the encouragement of **the Holy Spirit**. The word translated **encouraged** (in Gk. the noun *paraklēsis*) can mean variously "invocation," "consolation," or "exhortation." Here it probably means the latter, in the sense that the church's preaching (exhortation) was made effective by the Holy Spirit. It should be noticed that the word **church** is in the singular, though the reference is to a number of Christian communities. There is but one "body" of Christ, no matter how distant or different the parts. Here we have the first reference in Acts to the presence of believers in Galilee. That they have not been mentioned before this is due in part to Luke's schema. But in any case, "Galilee played no important part in the further development of earliest Christianity" (Hengel, *Acts*, p. 76).

Additional Notes §23

9:25 / **His followers**, lit., "his disciples": If we accept the text at its face value, these were apparently Jews converted by Paul or Jewish

Christians attracted to his teaching (evidence of his considerable powers of leadership?). The possessive pronoun **his**, however, has been questioned by a number of scholars, not on textual grounds (it is well attested) but because in vv. 19 and 25 "disciples" is used absolutely. Alford claims that the pronoun is an unusual use of the genitive as the direct object (otherwise unexpressed) of the verb **took**, giving the sense "the disciples took *him*" (vol. 2, pp. 104f.). B. M. Metzger suggests that the normal accusative of the direct object was corrupted to a genitive in the earliest manuscripts (*A Textual Commentary on the Greek New Testament*, p. 366).

9:31 / **Judea, Galilee and Samaria:** It has been said that this verse betrays Luke's ignorance of the geography of the Holy Land, in that he seems to think that Galilee and Judea shared a common frontier. Acts 15:3 is Luke's answer to that.

§24   Aeneas and Dorcas (Acts 9:32–43)

With Paul waiting in the wings, Peter now returns to the limelight. We last heard of him in 8:25, and this section picks up the thread of that narrative. No doubt the apostles made frequent journeys "throughout Judea, Galilee and Samaria" visiting the Christian communities. The next two chapters tell of one journey in particular, which had far-reaching consequences. There is no way of telling when this happened in relation to the events of 9:1–31.

9:32–35 / The story opens with Peter visiting **the saints** (see disc. on v. 13) **in Lydda**. This was the Lod of the Old Testament (1 Chron. 8:12). It lay some twenty-five miles from Jerusalem on the way to the coast, where the Plain of Sharon begins to rise (the Shephelah) to the central ranges. Lydda was a predominantly Jewish town in a region of otherwise mixed population (see disc. on 8:40), which accounts for the presence also of Christians. This was still the time when Christians were drawn entirely from among the Jews. Philip may have evangelized Lydda, but its proximity to Jerusalem makes it likely that there were believers there from an earlier date, even from the time of Jesus himself. In Lydda Peter met a paralytic named Aeneas. He is not expressly called a disciple (cf. v. 36), but from the nature of Peter's visit and since he apparently knew Jesus' name, it seems that he was one. That Aeneas bore a Greek name does not rule against his being a Jewish Christian (see note on 12:12). In responding to his need, Peter made it quite clear that he was only the intermediary. The healer was Jesus (cf. 3:6; 10:38). **Jesus Christ heals you**, Peter told him, adding, **Get up and take care of your mat** (v. 34; cf. Luke 5:17–26; Acts 14:8–12). These last words are an interpretation of Luke's ambiguous Greek, which simply says that Peter told him to "spread for himself." This may well refer to his bedclothes, but it could just as well mean, "Get yourself something to eat." Either way, it was something he had been unable to do for eight years (see disc. on 3:2). As a result of this miracle, many (the sense in which **all** is used) in both Lydda and Sharon **turned to the Lord** [Jesus]. The Plain of Sharon stretched from Carmel to the south of Joppa, but the reference here will only be to that part of the plain in the vicinity of Lydda.

9:36–38 / Meanwhile, in Joppa, **a disciple named Tabitha . . . became sick and died** (vv. 36, 37). Like Aeneas, she had a Greek name too (cf. v. 33; see disc. on 12:12), Dorcas, meaning, like Tabitha, "a deer." Luke describes her as "full of good works and acts of mercy" (v. 36), where the sense is that her life had been devoted to these things. Her loss was deeply felt by the Christian community. Among the Jews three days were allowed to elapse between death and burial to ensure that death had taken place (see disc. on 5:6), but more than this seems to have kept the disciples from burying Tabitha. Her body was washed, but not anointed, and was **placed in an upstairs room** (v. 37) in anticipation, perhaps, of a miracle. After all, Jesus had raised the dead and had himself been raised, and his servant Peter was now in the neighboring town (cf. 5:12ff.). Two men were sent to Lydda to bring him.

9:39–42 / Like Lydda, Joppa was a predominantly Jewish town. It was built on a rocky outcrop that projects from the coastline. A natural breakwater of rocks formed its harbor, which Josephus describes as dangerous for shipping (*War* 3.522–531). But it was the only natural anchorage on all that coast from Accho to Egypt. Peter responded at once to the message from Joppa ("he got up and went," see disc. on 8:27). On arrival he was made aware of how great a loss the church had sustained. The widows were there showing him the garments **that Dorcas had made** (imperfect tense—it had been her practice) **while she was still with them** (v. 39). The participle in the middle voice implies that the widows were actually exhibiting the clothes on themselves (for widows, see note on 6:1).

Peter cleared the room as Jesus had done at the raising of Jairus' daughter (Mark 5:40; but cf. Luke 8:54). But unlike Jesus, he first knelt in prayer before speaking the word of command (see disc. on 1:14 and 7:60; cf. e.g., John 14:12–14) The use of the name Tabitha in that command suggests that Luke was following a source close to the Aramaic in which Peter had spoken. He would in fact have said in Aramaic, "*Tabitha, cumi*," which is only a little different from Jesus' words to Jairus' daughter, "*Talitha, cumi*"

(Mark 5:41). But such a coincidence, even when other similarities between the two miracles are taken into consideration, is no proof that the one is derived from the other (see notes). The raising of the dead was included in Jesus' commission (Matt. 10:8), and we need not doubt that Peter exercised in this way the power and authority given to the apostles by Jesus. In any case, there are a number of dissimilarities between the two stories, such as Dorcas' gradual restoration (v. 40; cf. Luke 8:54) and Peter's care not to touch her (for fear of becoming unclean? cf. Num. 19:11) until she was fully restored (v. 41; cf. Luke 8:54). When Dorcas was on her feet, he called **the believers** ("the saints," see disc. on v. 13), including **the widows**—those most nearly affected by her death—and presented her to them alive (v. 41). As in Lydda, the miracle led to further conversions (there is nothing wrong with a faith engendered by miracles as long as it leads to a faith that rests upon Jesus). No distinction is intended between these people "believing in the Lord" and those at Lydda "turning to the Lord" (in each case *epi* with the accusative). The expressions mean the same—a commitment of themselves to the Lord (cf. esp. 11:21).

9:43 / **Peter stayed** on in **Joppa**, perhaps to instruct the new believers (cf. 2:42). It is noteworthy, however, that he stayed **with a tanner** named Simon. Leather workers were considered to be unclean (m. *Ketuboth* 7.10), and if Peter had had to overcome personal scruples to stay with Simon (the attention that Luke draws to his trade suggests that he did; see disc. on v. 41 and 10:9ff.), this notice serves as an interesting preface to the story that follows.

Additional Notes §24

9:36–41 / R. T. Fortna has observed an "astonishing number of lexical parallels" between the Johannine account of the raising of Lazarus and this story in Acts (*The Gospel of Signs* [London: Cambridge University Press, 1970], p. 84). Parallels have also been found in the Old Testament (cf. 1 Kings 17:17–24; 2 Kings 4:32–37). But none of these account for the origin of the story. Dunn, *Jesus*, p. 165, thinks it quite likely that the tradition goes back to a genuine episode in the ministry of Peter, though he does wonder whether Tabitha was simply in a coma.

§25   Cornelius Calls for Peter (Acts 10:1–8)

The importance that Luke ascribed to the story of Peter and Cornelius can be measured by the space that he gave to it. The story is told in detail in chapter 10, retold in chapter 11, and touched on again in chapter 15. The issue it raised was a critical one. To date the gospel had been well established in Jerusalem and was extending throughout the Jewish territory (9:31). It was only a matter of time, therefore, before the limits of that territory would be reached (both geographically and demographically), and the problem of Gentile eligibility would have to be faced. What was needed was a test case something to show clearly what God's will was in the matter—and the case of Cornelius met that need. Of course, Luke had the advantage of hindsight. He saw a far greater significance in the admission of Cornelius and his friends into the church than anyone could have at the time. At first, it was probably seen as something exceptional, certainly not a precedent by which to establish a rule, much less an incentive to actively seek other Gentiles to bring into the church. And Luke himself understood this. His history shows that he was well aware that the question of Gentile eligibility remained a disputed one for many more years to come (see disc. on 15:1, 5 and 21:20ff.). Nevertheless, by the time of the Jerusalem council, the case of Cornelius (if we can accept Luke's own account) was recognized as a precedent by the church leaders, so that Luke's estimate of its importance was not without grounds.

10:1 / The setting for the opening scene (vv. 1–8) is Caesarea. This site had once been a Phoenician outpost called Straton or Strato's Tower, but Herod the Great had rebuilt it and made of it a city suited to his own taste: Roman in obedience, Greek in culture. He provided it with a magnificent man-made harbor that, according to Josephus, was larger than the Piraeus, the port of Athens (*Antiquities*, 15.331–341). But otherwise it was a typical Greco-Roman city of that day, with its theater, amphitheater, hippodrome, and temple dedicated to Caesar. As one would expect, there were more Gentiles than Jews in Caesarea, though the Jews were a substantial minority. Friction between them and the Gentiles was endemic (see Josephus, *Antiquities* 20.173–184; *War* 2.266–270; 284f. and the disc. on 8:40; 9:30; 24:27). Among the Jews generally, because of the character of the city and because it was also the center of the Roman administration of the province, Caesarea was hated. They called it "the daughter of Edom" and would often speak of it as though it were no part of Judea (see disc. on 21:10). As the capital, it was also the main garrison of the troops of the province, and at the time of Luke's narrative these included **the Italian Regiment** ("cohort" in Roman terms), of which Cornelius was a centurion.

10:2 / He was a **devout and God-fearing** man, that is, he was attracted to the Jewish religion, but not to the extent that he had fully accepted it (see note on 6:5), as Peter's remark in verse 28 and the comments of others in 11:2ff. show. Nevertheless, as far as it went, there was nothing half-hearted about his religion. His religious practice included almsgiving and prayer. Where NIV has **to those in need**, the Greek has "to the people" (*laos*). In Luke's writing this expression usually indicates Israel (whether old or new; see disc. on 5:12), so that we may assume that "the people" to whom he gave alms were Jews. It was believed by the Jews that almsgiving effected atonement for sin (cf. Sir. 3:14, 30; 16:14; cf. also Tobit 14:10f.; Sir. 29:12; 40:24), but we cannot believe that Cornelius saw what he did in this light (see vv. 3–6 for his prayer). Naturally (in that society), **all his family**, that is, his household, including his servants, adopted his religion (see note on 10:48). This reference to Cornelius' household and to the reputation that he had for good works (v. 22) implies that he had settled down in Caesarea and had been there for some time. It was probably here that he had been drawn to the worship of God.

10:3–6 / The story begins on a note of worship. It was "the ninth hour," a regular time of prayer for the Jews (see disc. on 3:1 and note on 10:9) and no doubt for Cornelius also. We have already been told that it was his practice to pray (v. 2), and all of his prayers may have focused on one thing (notice how the **prayers** of v. 4 become the "prayer"; cf. v. 31), namely, that he and his household might be saved (cf. 11:14). The first step toward the answer to that prayer came in **a vision** in which **he distinctly**

saw an angel of God (v. 3; see disc. on 9:10). The Greek has that he saw an angel "in a vision openly," that is, he was not in a trance, as we read later that Peter was (v. 10), but in a waking state. But for all that, we may still suppose that it was an inner—albeit real—experience of God speaking to him (when we read of angels in this book we are never far from the thought of the Holy Spirit; see disc. on 8:26). As Luke tells the story (giving it a dramatic form), the angel spoke Cornelius' name much as the Lord had called to Paul on the road to Damascus, and Cornelius answered in much the same manner: **What is it, Lord?** (v. 4; cf. 9:4f.). The language may be Luke's, but he wants us to understand that Cornelius felt himself to be in the divine presence (the word **fear**, v. 4, is a particularly strong one). He was assured, however, that his **prayers and gifts to the poor** had gone up **as a memorial offering before God** (v. 4; cf. Isa. 43:1). This is the language of sacrifice, and its intent is expressed by GNB when it says that God was pleased with him and would lead him to salvation (cf. Rom. 2:6). This is a story of God's grace. But Peter, too, had a part to play.

10:7–8 / Step-by-step obedience to divine guidance is the key to this story. Cornelius immediately **called two of his servants and a . . . soldier and sent them to Joppa** (vv. 7, 8). Clearly, Peter was not known to him personally, but he may have known him by name and reputation; and he may have known that he was in Joppa and felt constrained to send for him. The mutual trust between the centurion and his servants and the soldier, who was also **a devout man**, is revealed in verse 8: **He told them everything that had happened.** The distance they had to travel was about thirty miles. They must have been mounted, since they appear to have arrived in Joppa soon after noon the next day.

Additional Notes §25

10:1 / **A man named Cornelius**: The name of a great Roman family to which belonged the Scipios and Sulla, though the centurion may have been of much humbler origin. Sulla had manumitted ten thousand slaves in 82 B.C., all of whom would have taken the name Cornelius. By now it must have been widespread. The name is the second of the three that a Roman normally bore (see note on 13:9). This brief form of naming a Roman without the cognomen was an old-fashioned practice not found outside the army by the middle of the first century A.D. It is surely no coincidence that the only two people who have this type of name in Acts are both soldiers (cf. 27:1) at precisely the period when only soldiers were likely to be using it (see Sherwin-White, p. 161). Hanson asks, "Is this the sort of detail which somebody writing in the second century, or at the very end of the first, when the custom must have for some considerable time lapsed, is likely to have invented, imagined, or guessed?" (p. 11).

The Italian Regiment: or as the Greek runs, "the cohort called 'the Italian.'" There is inscriptional evidence for the presence of an Italian cohort in Syria in the second half of the first century A.D. (also in the second century); see *BC*, vol. 5, p. 441ff.), and it is consonant with this that such a cohort should have been in Caesarea at this earlier date. It was almost certainly an auxiliary unit, since the legions were not stationed in the smaller provinces such as Judea. It could be argued, of course, that the cohort, or Cornelius alone, had been detached from a legion for service at Caesarea or even that Cornelius had retired and was simply living there. Tacitus does mention an "Italian legion" (*History* 1.59). But an inscription found in Austria at the end of the last century mentions an officer of the second Italian cohort. It describes the cohort as belonging to "the archery division of the Syrian army," and as the legionnaires were not archers, it implies that the Italian cohorts were in fact auxiliary units (see further Sherwin-White, p. 160).

§26 Peter's Vision (Acts 10:9–23a)

10:9–16 / Now the scene shifts to Joppa and to the events immediately prior to the arrival of Cornelius' men. **About noon,** Peter went to the housetop to pray (see notes)—a convenient place away from the activity of the house and often used in this way (cf. 2 Kings 23:12; Neh. 8:16; Jer. 19:13; 32:29; Zeph. 1:5). These roofs were flat and accessible by an exterior stairway. Normally Peter would have eaten before this. Jews did not start the day with a meal, but ate later in the morning (see b. *Shabbath* 10a). By noon, therefore, Peter had become **hungry** (the Greek is probably intensive—"very hungry") **and wanted something to eat** (v. 10). He was praying as the meal was being prepared, and as he prayed **he fell into a trance** (Gk. *ekstasis,* v. 10; cf. 11:5; 22:7). The different vocabulary points to a different experience from that of Cornelius (cf. v. 3). Luke probably means that Peter was dreaming. And without denying that God spoke to him in this way, we can see how the dream was conditioned by his immediate circumstances. Rackham suggests that he may have already been pondering the question of Jewish-Gentile relations, pressed upon him by his visit to Joppa, with its shipping and its hint of faraway places (p. 150). Add to this his hunger and the image of the awning over his head, or perhaps of sails glimpsed in the harbor below, and all the ingredients were there for the imagery of the dream. For **he saw** (lit., "he sees," a rare use of the historic present by Luke for greater vividness) **heaven opened and something like a large sheet being let down to earth by its four corners** (v. 11). Within it were **all kinds of four-footed animals, as well as reptiles of the earth and birds of the air** (v. 12)—the three categories of living creatures recognized in the Old Testament (Gen. 6:20, RSV; cf. Rom. 1:23). When Peter told this story later, he added to the menagerie "wild beasts" (11:6), but the **all** of this verse had already included them.

The point to notice is that the contents of the sheet encompassed creatures both clean and unclean according to the law (Lev.

11). Then came the command, **Get up, Peter; kill** (sacrificially, Gk. *thyein*) **and eat,** making no distinction between the two categories. Peter was horrified, and something of the old Peter appears in the vehemence of his reply: **Surely not, Lord!** (cf. Matt. 16:22; 26:33; John 13:8), to which he added a protest like Ezekiel's, **I have never eaten anything impure or unclean** (v. 14; cf. Ezek. 4:14; also Lev. 10:10; 20:25; Dan. 1:8–12; 2 Macc. 6:18ff.). These words take us back to the teaching of Jesus in Mark 7:15 and to the inference drawn by the Evangelist (who is traditionally associated with Peter): "In saying this, Jesus declared all foods 'clean' " (Mark 7:19)—an inference that may owe its origin to this housetop experience, for the voice that had said, "Kill and eat" added, **Do not call anything impure that God has made clean** (v. 15; cf. 6:12ff.; for the Petrine tradition, see disc. on 3:7f; 10:34–43; 12:1–5). Twice the vision was repeated—Peter saw it three times in all—then he awoke (cf. Jonah 3:1).

But what did it mean? Clearly, it had to do with the cancellation of the Jewish dietary laws. Not that it mattered in itself if Jewish Christians continued to live by these laws, as long as Christ was all in all. But it did matter that adherence to the dietary laws profoundly affected Jewish-Gentile relations. In the house of a Gentile, a Jew could never be certain that the food had been prepared as required by the law (cf. Gen. 9:4; Lev. 17:10, 11, 14). To eat the food, therefore, was to run the risk of defilement—a risk that many Jews (and Jewish Christians) were not willing to take. It was in this connection that the revelation to Peter had its immediate application. There was, of course, more to the Jewish antipathy toward the Gentiles than simply a concern over food. The Gentiles themselves were considered unclean (cf. Gal. 2:15; see note on v. 28). But if Peter could be freed from his scruples over the dietary laws to the extent that he would enter a Gentile home, he was not far from accepting the Gentiles themselves as "clean."

10:17–20 / Peter was "completely at a loss" to know what the dream meant (see disc. on 2:12), but just then the men sent by Cornelius arrived at the house. The exclamation "Look!" (not represented in NIV) signals that Luke saw this as providential (v. 17; see disc. on 1:10). Being aware of the sensibilities of the Jews, they remained outside the gate that led from the road through the front part of the house to the inner court, and from here they inquired after Peter (v. 18). With this, the vision began to be explained. The Spirit brought it home to Peter that his dream and these visitors were somehow connected and that he should do as they wished without hesitation, that is, without questioning the lawfulness of the matter (see disc. on 11:12).

10:21–23a / Peter obeyed the divine guidance, as Cornelius had (v. 7). He made himself known to the men, and they told him their mission (cf. Luke 7:4f.). They described their master as a **righteous and God-fearing man**, who was **respected by all the Jewish people**, that is, by the Jewish community in Caesarea, adding that the angel had told him to hear what Peter had to say. This detail was not mentioned earlier (11:14 adds a further detail that shows why it was so important for Cornelius to hear him). Though a guest himself, Peter was apparently at liberty to offer the visitors hospitality for the night. It was easier for a Jew to have Gentiles stay with him than for a Jew to stay with Gentiles. Nevertheless, this kindly act was probably a great step forward for Peter.

Additional Notes §26

10:9 / **About noon . . . Peter went up on the roof to pray**: When they had access to the temple, devout Jews would gather there for prayer at the time of the morning and evening sacrifices, that is, at dawn and midafternoon (see disc. on 3:1), with perhaps a further gathering for prayer at sunset. Away from the temple, the practice seems to have been adopted of observing the third, the sixth, and the ninth hours for prayer (cf. Ps. 55:17; Dan. 6:10). The custom of prayer three times a day passed very early into the church (*Didache* 8.3).

§27 Peter at Cornelius' House (Acts 10:23b–48)

10:23b–29 / The setting for the third scene of this story is again Caesarea. The journey to the capital seems to have taken the best part of two days (v. 30), probably because the Christians were not mounted. Peter took with him six companions—Jewish Christians like himself (v. 45, lit., "men of the circumcision"; see disc. on 11:2)—who, according to a variant reading of 11:11, had been staying with him in Simon's house. Their road lay along the coast, and since Apollonia was situated about halfway between Joppa and Caesarea, they very likely stayed there overnight. They arrived in Caesarea about midafternoon the next day (v. 30). Meanwhile, so certain was Cornelius that Peter would come, and knowing approximately how long it would take him, he was ready and waiting for him with his **relatives and close friends** (v. 24). Presumably he had told them also "everything that had happened" (v. 8) and had invited them to be present to witness its outcome.

Cornelius met Peter in the spirit of that other centurion (Luke 7:6) by humbly kneeling before him. With equal humility Peter would not accept a reverence that belonged only to God (cf. 14:14f.; Luke 4:8; 8:41; Rev. 19:10; 22:8f.). They seem to have talked for a while before entering the house. In this way, perhaps, Peter learned how much they knew of the story of Jesus, for he was able to assume a certain knowledge of the events of Jesus' life when he addressed the whole group. Moreover, what Cornelius had to tell him, coupled with his own recent experience, must have helped Peter to see what was the last step required by his dream, namely, that he should cast aside his scruples concerning the Gentiles. His opening words, therefore, when he spoke to them all were to announce that God had shown him not to think of any person as **impure or unclean** (v. 28). How well Peter had learned this lesson is seen in 1 Peter 2:17. Then he asked the question that, oddly, had not been asked before, Why did you send for me? (v. 29).

10:30–33 / Cornelius replied by outlining the events of three days past that he saw as an answer to prayer (v. 31). The details differ slightly from the earlier verses, but only for the sake of variety. Essentially the two accounts are the same. He remarked on Peter's kindness in coming (lit., "you have done well . . . ," an expression of thanks, cf. Phil. 4:14; 2 Pet. 1:19; 3 John 6) and ended these preliminaries by declaring that they were all ready to hear **everything the Lord** had **commanded** Peter to say (v. 33). Cornelius assumed that Peter, like himself, was a man under authority, so that what he said would come to him as God's command. He had already been told that Peter's words would lead to salvation (11:14). His salvation, therefore, lay in his obedience. And notice the reference to their being gathered **in the presence of God** (v. 33). In a sense, this is true of every situation in life, but never more so than when the gospel is being preached. Those who meet in such circumstances do well to remember the company they keep (cf. Matt. 18:20).

10:34 35 / This speech is the first recorded preaching of the Good News to the Gentile world. It must be assumed, of course, that these were almost entirely "devout" people like Cornelius himself and that they were familiar, therefore, with the Jewish Scriptures. It must also be assumed that they knew something of the story of Jesus. Thus they were more or less prepared for what they heard and to that extent hardly typical of the Gentile world as a whole. Peter was able to preach to them much as he had to the Jews; it is not until we come to Paul's speeches in Lystra and Athens that we find a distinctive approach to the Gentiles. Nevertheless, these people were Gentiles, and that fact marks a new and important departure for the church.

In other respects also this speech holds a peculiar interest. It has often been remarked that verses 37 to 40, with their attention to the earthly life of Jesus and being unique among the speeches of this book, could well have formed the ground plan of Mark's Gospel. In view of the traditional association of Peter with Mark, this can hardly be accidental (see also disc. on 3:7f.; 10:14; 12:1–5). There is, moreover, a clear theological development in comparison with Peter's earlier speeches (2:14–39; 3:12–26), and this, together with the fact that it sits so well with his experience at Joppa and Caesarea, gives us every confidence that we have in these verses a fair indication of what he said on this

occasion. How Luke came by the speech we can only guess, but
the evidence points strongly to his use of a source. "It is one of
the most ungrammatical pieces of Greek that Luke ever wrote.
One cannot avoid the impression that though, as usual, Luke has fixed
its final form, older elements are included in it" (Hanson, p. 124).

Peter's sense of the occasion is expressed by Luke's use of
the formula "he opened his mouth" (v. 34, NIV **began to speak**),
which often marked a particularly solemn occasion. He began by
commenting on the change in his own thinking: **I now realize
. . . that God does not show favoritism** (v. 34). The phrase "upon
the truth" expresses both his surprise at this discovery and his
grasp of what had now been revealed. It was not something new
(cf. Deut. 10:17; 2 Chron. 19:7; Job 34:19; Mal. 2:9), but it was
a truth that the Jews had largely lost sight of. And for Peter, it
did come as a new discovery that God was impartial. From this
it followed that a person's acceptance with God rested, not on
nationality, but on a proper disposition of the heart: he **accepts
men from every nation who fear him and do what is right** (v.
35). This is not to say that nothing else is needed. The emphasis
on Jesus in this speech gives the lie to that. Jesus is integral to
our salvation. Rather, what Peter meant is that if the attitude is
right, then given the Good News, there is no one who cannot
be saved. And so, without further ado, he spoke the saving word
that they had gathered to hear.

10:36–38 / The Good News started with God. It was his
message, and he sent it **to the people of Israel**. It concerned **peace
through Jesus Christ** (v. 36), that is, he was God's agent in bringing about peace between God and humanity (cf. 2 Cor. 5:18ff.).
Peace is here synonymous with salvation. The last phrase of verse
36 stands apart from the syntax of the sentence as a parenthesis,
almost as though the speaker realized that he may have conveyed
a false impression of Jesus. He was indeed God's agent, but not
as others had been. For unlike any other, he was **Lord of all** (cf.
Rom. 14:9). For a long time now Peter had regarded Jesus as "Lord
and Christ," as in 2:36, and for all intents and purposes had
ascribed to him a place in the Godhead (see disc. on 1:24). But
always his horizons had been those of a Jew, and he had never
thought of Jesus as any other than the Lord and Christ of the
Jews (see disc. on 2:39). For these many years his God had been
too small. He now saw his mistake.

This was new ground for Peter, but in verse 37 he returned to more familiar territory (and in some part familiar also to Cornelius and his friends), namely, to what had happened **throughout Judea**, where **Judea** is used in the broadest sense to include the whole Jewish homeland (cf. Luke 1:5; 7:17; 23:5). This note of the geographical extension of Jesus' ministry may well be a Lukan touch, so too the care with which his ministry is separated from that of John the Baptist (by comparison with Mark). This ensures that Jesus should not be thought of as John's successor. But broadly speaking, Peter's outline of "the great event" is as we find it in Mark, with its **beginning in Galilee after the baptism that John preached** (v. 37; cf. "beginning from John's baptism," 1:22; cf. also Mark 1:4, 14ff.). Jesus' ministry is spoken of chiefly in terms of his healing **all who were under the power of the devil**—a prominent theme in Mark's Gospel (cf., e.g., Mark 1:23, 32, 39; for the construction with the relative clause "who went about healing," see notes on 4:10). Peter may have regarded these as greater than other healings, so that Jesus' ability to deal with the lesser could be assumed. He had only to say, then, that Jesus had gone about **doing good** (v. 38, Gk. *euergetein*; the corresponding noun, *euergetes*, "benefactor," was commonly applied by the ancient world to its rulers). His good works are attributed to **the Holy Spirit and power** with which God had **anointed him** (v. 38). Some interpret this of the incarnation (cf. Luke 1:35), but because it follows the reference to John the Baptist, it is better to understand it of Jesus' baptism. Jesus himself affirmed that he had been "anointed" with the Spirit, without pin-pointing when it happened (Luke 4:18). But that he had been anointed was proof that **God was with him** (v. 38). This last statement might seem to draw too hard a line between Jesus the man and the divine source of his power. Certainly there was no question of Jesus' humanity (cf. v. 38, "Jesus of Nazareth"). But neither was there any question that he was more than a man, for he received as of right the divine titles **Lord of all** (v. 36) and "judge of the living and the dead" (v. 42). Confirmation that he is rightly called by these names had come with the resurrection.

10:39–41 / As in the Gospel, Peter traced Jesus' ministry from Galilee to **the country of the Jews**, that is, to Judea in the narrow sense of the Roman province (cf. v. 36), and finally to **Jerusalem**, where Jesus met his death (v. 39). The role of the apostles (the **we** of our text) as witnesses is mentioned especially in this connection, not because the earlier ministry had no place in their testimony, but because Jesus' death and resurrection was the crux of the matter, without which there was no Good News (see disc. on 1:21f.; cf. 2:32; 3:15; 5:32). We find again in verse 39 the expression that we noticed earlier in 5:30: they put Jesus to death **by hanging him on a tree** (see disc. on that verse and also 2:23). Earlier Peter may have used the expression to drive home to Jews the horror of what they had done. This was not, of course, his intention here, but it had become his accustomed way of stating what happened (cf. 1 Pet. 2:24). One wonders, however, what these Romans, to whom crucifixion was the most shameful of deaths, made of the "Good News" that the Lord of all had been nailed to a cross by their own troops. Peter's claims for Jesus were only believable in that God had **raised him from the dead on the third day** (v. 40). This is one of only two references outside the Gospels to the resurrection taking place "on the third day." The other is found in 1 Corinthians 15:4. The phrase is especially characteristic of Luke's Gospel, where it occurs six times. Verse 40 adds the striking comment, showing that nothing was left to accident, that God **caused him to be seen**—admittedly by only a handful of people, but those best qualified to be his witnesses. To this end **God had already chosen** them (v. 41; cf. John 17:6ff.), and they would convince others. In their own minds, there was no doubt that Jesus had risen, for they had eaten and drunk with him. This note of their drinking with Jesus adds to the information in the Gospels (Luke 24:30; 43; John 21:12, 15; but see Luke 22:18).

10:42–43 / Finally, Jesus commissioned his witnesses (the apostles). This is the occasion referred to in 1:4, and Luke repeats the verb that he used there to express again the urgency of the command to **preach to the people** (v. 42). **The people** (Gk. *laos*) usually means Jews (see disc. on 5:12), but it was Jesus' intention that they should go also to Gentiles (cf., e.g., 1:8; Matt. 28:19), and in this context (cf. v. 34) the word must be given that wider meaning. The message they were to **preach . . . and to testify** (see disc. on 2:40) was in part that Jesus had now been **appointed as judge** (v. 42). Paul was to witness to the same truth in Athens (17:31; cf. also 24:25; for the return of Jesus, see disc. on 1:10f.). The commission to proclaim Jesus as judge is not found in the other accounts of his final charge, but given the highly condensed nature of all of these reports, this comes as no surprise. The idea certainly had a place in Jesus' own teaching (cf. Luke 12:8f.; 19:11–27; John 5:22, 27), and we cannot doubt that it was included in his "instructions" (1:2). His description as the judge **of the living and the dead** (v. 42) picks up the thought of verse 36 that he is the "Lord of all" and anticipates a general resurrection when "there will be a resurrection of both the righteous and the wicked" (24:15). The criterion both of judgment and of salvation is indicated in verse 43: **everyone who believes in him** ("into him" the idea is of commitment to Christ, cf. 14:23; 19:4; 24:24; 26:18) **receives forgiveness of sins**; those who do not— this is clearly implied—will remain in their sins and will face Christ as judge (cf. John 8:21, 24). The use of the singular, "everyone," should be noted. To the thought of Christ's universal lordship it adds the warning that we are individually accountable to him. The importance of faith in Christ is underlined by Luke's placing these words at the end of the verse (in Greek, a position of emphasis). The phrase, **through his name** (v. 43) reminds us again of Christ's indispensable role in our salvation—a salvation that **all the prophets** (spoken of collectively as in 3:18) had seen beforehand (v. 43). They, of course, had thought of God as the one who would save, but the right to have mercy and to freely pardon (Isa. 55:7) had passed to Jesus when God made him "Lord and Christ" (2:36). On this high note, though unintentionally, the speech came to an end.

10:44 / **While Peter was still speaking** (his "began" in 11:15 may simply mean that he had not finished), **the Holy Spirit came on all who heard the message**. A comparison of this with other passages in Acts in which the coming of the Spirit is described reveals a number of differences (2:1ff.; 8:14ff.; 9:17; 19:1ff.; see also note on 18:25). His coming was not dependent on public confession or on the lapse of time. It was not prayed for; nor did it follow baptism with water or the laying on of hands. The Spirit simply came as they listened with receptive hearts to what Peter was saying. When he spoke of the forgiveness of sins for everyone who believes in Jesus (v. 43), they must have believed. This agrees with Peter's own account of the matter (11:17) and with the implied answer to Paul's question in Galatians 3:2: "Did you receive the Spirit by observing the law, or by believing what you heard?" In short, faith in Christ is the one essential to receiving God's Spirit. Anything mentioned in this book over and above that one requirement must be explained by reference to the particular circumstances of the people concerned (see notes on 2:4 and 38 and disc. on 8:14ff.).

10:45–46a / Peter's Jewish-Christian companions (and perhaps even Peter himself) were amazed at what had happened (v. 45). The Jews had a dictum that the Holy Spirit never fell on a Gentile, and yet God had unquestionably poured out **the gift of the Holy Spirit** on these Gentiles (v. 45). The genitive (**of**) in the phrase "the gift of the Spirit" must be understood as a genitive of apposition—the gift was the Spirit himself, whose presence was evidenced by their **speaking in tongues** (v. 46), probably in the sense of ecstatic utterance, as in 1 Corinthians 12–14 and elsewhere (see disc. and notes on 2:4).

10:46b–48 / No one could now say that these Gentiles were "impure or unclean" or withhold from them the rite of admission into the church, for they had received the Spirit just as the Jewish believers had received him (at Pentecost, cf. 11:15). The words **just as** need not mean that the two events were identical in every respect, but only that they were like enough to suggest the comparison. So Peter put the question: **Can anyone keep** (Gk. *kōlyein*, "prevent") **these people from being baptized with water?** (v. 47; see disc. on 8:36 for the possibility that the form of this question was determined by the baptismal liturgy). In the Greek text, the word **water** has the definite article, meaning "the water of baptism." No objection was raised, and Peter directed that Cornelius and his friends be baptized **in the name of Jesus Christ** (v. 48). The preposition is instrumental (Gk. *en*). They were to be baptized by means of the formula that employed that name (cf. *epi*, "upon," in 2:38 and *eis*, "into," in 8:16). We are not told who actually administered the rite, but it appears not to have been Peter himself, who may have been conscious of the same danger of partisanship that Paul sought to avoid by not himself baptizing his converts, at least as a general rule (cf. 1 Cor. 1:14–17). No mention is made of circumcision (cf. 11:3) or of anything additional to their baptism. Peter was invited to stay with Cornelius, and from 11:3 it is clear that he did (the Greek has "certain days," not necessarily the **few days** of NIV). His acceptance of Gentile hospitality gave practical expression to the theological truth he had preached (vv. 34ff.).

Additional Notes §27

10:25–27 / **As Peter entered the house . . . Peter went inside**: The Western text removes the awkwardness of this double entry by making the first his entry into the city and the second that into Cornelius' house: "And as Peter was approaching Caesarea one of the slaves ran ahead and announced his arrival. And Cornelius leapt up and met him. . . ." This is undoubtedly a gloss, based on the custom of sending a slave to meet a notable person.

10:28 / **It is against our law for a Jew to associate with a Gentile**: The word rendered Gentile is not the usual word thus translated, but another (Gk. *allophylos*) meaning "one of a different race," which is found only here in the New Testament. For a Jew, it would represent a much gentler way of speaking of Gentiles. The word, of course, is Luke's but he may have wanted to show with what delicacy Peter handled this situation. No such delicacy is evident in 11:3. The attitude of postbiblical Judaism toward non-Jews was, for the most part, harsh in the extreme. To the Jews, Gentiles were godless, rejected by God, and given over to every form of uncleanness. And to have dealings with them was to contract their uncleanness (see, e.g., *Midrash Rabbah* on Lev. 20; also Juvenal, *Satires* 14.103; Tacitus, *History* 5.5). Some Jews allowed that the Gentiles might have a limited participation in the kingdom of God, but most regarded them as beyond hope and destined for hell. Against this background we see how startling Jesus' teaching must have been that reversed the popular expectation to include the Gentiles in the kingdom to the exclusion of the (unbelieving) Jews (cf. Matt. 8:11f.; Luke 13:29). As with much of his teaching, his followers were slow to accept it.

10:36–38 / The grammatical looseness of the speech reaches its apogee in these verses. Literally, 36 runs: "The word (accusative) that he sent to the sons of Israel giving good news of peace through Jesus Christ, he is Lord of all." There is no main verb to govern "the word." In v. 37, "beginning" is wholly ungrammatical. It is a participle in the nominative masculine singular and can apply to no noun in the sentence, but must assume Jesus as its subject.

10:48 / **He ordered that they be baptized**: The subjects of this baptism were Cornelius and the "large gathering" assembled by him to hear Peter (v. 27), including, we may suppose, "all his family" (v. 2), which may have included children. That the whole family and even the whole household (servants, etc.) should be baptized with the head of the house would have been a natural assumption in that society and as much a mark of family solidarity as of their own faith (cf. 16:15, 33; 18:8; 1 Cor. 1:16; 16:15; the solidarity of the family could also have adverse effects, see Titus 1:11). That the children of believers were regarded as part of the "household of faith" can be readily maintained (see, e.g., 1 Cor. 7:14; Eph. 6:1–3; Col. 3:20), but it must be equally emphasized that membership in Christ does not derive from physical descent or ritual act (cf., e.g., Gal. 3:11, 26).

§28   Peter Explains His Actions (Acts 11:1–18)

11:1–3 / The final scene in this story of Gentile conversion is played out in Jerusalem, with Peter having to defend what he had done. Apart from the fundamental question of whether Gentiles should be included or not, there were practical issues. How could Jewish Christians who regarded themselves as still bound by the law have fellowship with those who did not? Surely any Gentile who became a believer must also submit to the law? These are the sorts of questions that must have been thrown up to Peter by **the circumcised believers** (v. 2), literally, "those of the circumcision," meaning simply Jewish Christians. Strictly speaking, of course, the whole church at this time could be described in this way, since there were no Christians who were not also Jews. But Luke's narrative was compiled at a time when "those of the circumcision" had become a more or less distinct group who wished to maintain the Jewish traditions exemplified by this rite (cf. Gal. 2:12; Titus 1:10). So Luke used the expression as significant to his readers, though it only had its origin in the events that he was narrating. It was true, nevertheless, that even then there were those in the church who were especially sensitive to the issues that Peter had raised, and the term is appropriately applied to these people (cf. 15:5; see further note on 15:1). Their criticism focused on Peter's having been a guest in the home of a Gentile. This was a serious breach of church polity, and something of the bitterness of their feelings comes out in the phrase **uncircumcised men** (v. 3). This description was the greatest reproach that Jews had of Gentiles, for it emphasized their exclusion from the covenant.

11:4–17 / Peter's defense was simply to explain **everything to them precisely as it had happened** (v. 4). Probably all that the church had heard was the outcome and nothing of what had led up to his preaching to Cornelius. The story as retold is basically the same as in the previous chapter. Such minor differences as there are have already been noticed, for the most part, in the ear-

lier discussion. This account is briefer than the other, but, if anything, more vivid, as, for example, in the description of the sheet
as coming **down to where** [he] **was** (v. 5), and his looking intently
into it (v. 6; see disc. on 3:4). These two details explain how Peter
had known that the sheet had contained animals of all kinds, including some that were not lawful to eat. The story is told in the
first person and from Peter's own point of view. Thus, it begins
with his vision (vv. 5–10). In the Spirit's instruction that Peter
should go with the men who were **right then** at the gate (v. 11,
a notice of time that is absent in chap. 10), NIV effectively retains
the expression of 10:20 that he should go without **hesitation** (v.
12). But the best text has the word here in a different form and
with a different meaning (the active instead of the middle voice
of the participle), reflecting Peter's changed perspective. Originally the Spirit had prompted him to go "without hesitation"; now
he understood that the Spirit had meant that he should go
"without making distinctions" between Jew and Gentile.

He had taken with him **six brothers** (v. 12; see disc. on
10:23b), and on their arrival in Caesarea they had all gone into
the house of "the man," as the Greek, followed by NIV, has it (v.
12). By now everyone (including Luke's readers) knew who was
meant. Cornelius had told them **how he had seen an angel** (lit.,
"the angel"—the one that we are now familiar with) who instructed him to send for Peter, by whose words he and his household would be saved (v. 14; see disc. on 10:32). Peter had spoken,
and as he had done so (see disc. on 10:44), the Holy Spirit had
come down on them, as he had on the Jewish believers **at the
beginning** (v. 16), that is, on the day of Pentecost when they had
been baptized with the Spirit (v. 16; see disc. on 1:4f.; 2:2f.). Jesus'
promise concerning this, cited again in this verse, must be taken
to mean that Spirit baptism would be given in addition to baptism with water, not to replace it, so Peter had ordered that rite
once he had seen that God had given the other. **Who was I**, he
asked, **that I could oppose God** (v. 17, Gk. *kōlyein*, "prevent").
This language may again echo the baptismal liturgy (see disc. on
8:36 and 10:47). It was also customary in that liturgy (or so we
suppose) for the candidate to make a confession of Jesus as Lord
(see disc. on 2:38 and 8:36), and there may be a hint of this in
the almost credal statement of verse 17: **us, who believed in** (*epi*)
the Lord Jesus Christ (see disc. on 9:42)—words that Cornelius
and the others may themselves have uttered.

11:18 / In the face of this evidence (and there were six witnesses to support it, v. 12), Peter's critics had nothing more they could say. They accepted what had happened, concluding with Peter that God had **granted even the Gentiles repentance unto life**. Repentance no less than forgiveness (cf. 10:43; also 3:26; 5:31) is God's gift, and in giving it he "does not show favoritism" (10:34; cf. 20:21; 26:20). The story ends characteristically on a note of praise. A well-supported reading of this verse has the verb to praise in the imperfect, allowing us to suppose that not only on this occasion, but as a common feature of their life, the Jewish church ascribed glory to God. Thus the writer, about to pass to other things, depicts the state of things that he leaves behind

---

Additional Notes §28

11:2 / **When Peter went up to Jerusalem**: It is not said that he was summoned to Jerusalem to give account of his actions. However, the fact that he had his six companions with him, who could have supported his story (v. 12), may suggest that he went expecting to have to defend himself. Perhaps to avoid the impression that he was summoned by the others, the Western text has "so Peter after some time wished to go to Jerusalem."

11:17 / **Us, who believed**: The construction of the Greek is such that it seems best to take the participle "having believed" as referring to both the Gentiles and the first Jewish believers, emphasizing still further the similarity of their experience. Exercising the same faith in Jesus Christ, they received the same gift of God through him.

§29 The Church in Antioch (Acts 11:19–30)

Luke now leaves the "acts of Peter" for the time being. He will return to them again in chapter 12, after which, except for a brief reappearance in chapter 15, Peter passes out of the narrative and Paul becomes the focus of attention. The author's purpose in these present chapters (8 to 12) is both to tell the story of the church's early expansion (exemplified by certain carefully selected events) and at the same time to prepare the ground for the story of the Pauline mission. Thus he has given an account of the conversion of Paul and of the preaching to Cornelius that demonstrated the legitimacy of Paul's later work. And now he tells of the founding of the church in Antioch, which became the springboard of that great missionary thrust into the Roman Empire.

Again we must acknowledge that we do not know how the incidents in this part of the book relate to one another in time. Luke has arranged his material to show the westward march of the gospel, and so the story of the church in Antioch has been left until now in preparation for chapter 13 and those that follow, which will take us from Antioch to Asia Minor and beyond. But in fact, the preaching of the gospel in that city may have been contemporaneous with, or even earlier than, some of the events narrated in chapters 8 to 10.

11:19 / Luke returns again to Stephen's death and its aftermath of the scattering of believers (8:4) and now follows them northward through Phoenicia. Twenty years later there were Christian communities in Ptolemais, Tyre, and Sidon that no doubt dated from this time (21:3, 7; 27:3; see disc. on 8:4 for the verb "they went through"). From these ports some sailed to Cyprus. Others went on to Antioch in Syria. This city, situated on the Orontes some fifteen miles from its mouth, had been founded ca. 300 B.C. as his capital by Seleucus I Nicator (312–281 B.C.) and was one of sixteen cities similarly named by him in honor of his father Antiochus. With the collapse of the Seleucid dynasty and the Roman occupation of Syria, Antioch became the capital and military headquarters of the new province. Under Augustus and Tiberius, aided by Herod the Great, it was enlarged and beautified in the Roman manner, the road systems extending from it were improved, and its seaport of Seleucia Pieria further developed. Thus the communications of Antioch with the Levant and, indeed, with the whole of the empire, were made far more rapid and secure than they had been before. This was to prove useful to the church.

From the first, the city had had a mixed population, which by this time numbered about eight-hundred thousand. The number of Jews has been put at about twenty-five thousand (see Josephus, *Antiquities* 12 119–124; 2 Macc. 4). Josephus called it the third city of the empire after Rome and Alexandria; others are not so sure that it was not the second. It has been described as "a bastion of Hellenism in the Syriac lands . . . the inevitable meeting point of the two worlds" (G. Dix, p. 33). This mix of cultures had good and bad results. It gave rise, on the one hand, to the literature and art that won Antioch the praise of Cicero (see *Pro Archia* 4) but, on the other, to the luxury and immorality that made it as infamous as it was famous. Juvenal blamed Antioch for the disintegration of Roman morality, when, as he put it, "the waters of Syrian Orontes flowed into the Tiber" (*Satires* 3.62). And yet, for all that, this city had its part to play in the history of salvation. For with its mix of race and culture, it was ready-made for breaking down "the dividing wall of hostility" between Jews and Gentiles and forming them both into the "one body of Christ" (Eph. 2:14ff.).

11:20–21 / At first, the believers confined their preaching to the Jews (v. 19). But in Antioch, where the prevailing moral climate drove many to seek for something better, the Jews had attracted large numbers of Gentiles to their synagogues. Many became proselytes, but many more (as we suppose) remained "God-fearers" (see disc. on 6:5f. and notes), and before long some believers, **men from Cyprus and Cyrene**, found themselves preaching to these people (for so we take the **Greeks** of v. 20 to have been). Notice the word **also** (v. 20). They had not abandoned their preaching to Jews, but were preaching to Jews and Gentiles in mixed congregations. Their message concerned the lordship of Jesus, which would have been more appropriate to these people of various backgrounds than the announcement that he was the

Messiah (cf. 8:12; 9:20, 22; 18:5), and they had good results. The juxtaposition of verses implies that the **great number of people who believed and turned to the Lord** in verse 21 were largely the God-fearing Gentiles of the previous verse. That this happened with such apparent ease compared with the difficulties experienced in the case of Cornelius could be attributed to the Antiochene Jews being more accustomed than the Judeans to the presence of Gentiles in their synagogues. But in any case, from the freedom with which the Christians were able to order their affairs, it would appear that they had soon separated from the synagogues, so that they were not under the same external pressure as were the Judean Christians to have Gentile converts submit to the law. Thus the church's polity could soon be described as "doing as the Gentiles did" as far as circumcision and the dietary laws were concerned (cf. 15:1; Gal. 2:11–14). The rightness of this new direction seemed to be confirmed, moreover, by **the Lord's hand** being **with them** (v. 21, lit., "the hand of the Lord"; see disc. on 4:28).

11:22–24 / When the church in Jerusalem heard of these developments, **they** (apostles and elders? see note on v. 30) **sent Barnabas to Antioch** to investigate (v. 22). This was not necessarily a hostile reaction. There were those, of course, who held that Gentile converts should accept the "yoke of the law" (see disc. on 15:10; cf. 11.2f.; 15:1), but not all shared that opinion or held it as strongly as they did. It is better, perhaps, to see their sending of Barnabas as an attempt to establish a relationship with the Christians of Antioch, in the same way that Peter and John had been sent to the Samaritans (8:14ff.). Being a Cypriot, Barnabas was a wise choice (cf. v. 20).

On arriving in Antioch, Barnabas rejoiced **when he saw the evidence of the grace of God** (v. 23; see disc. on 3:8). That he **saw** may mean that there were visible tokens of the blessing—perhaps a change in lifestyle, perhaps the more manifest of the Spirit's gifts (see disc. on 8:14ff. and 10:46). Barnabas found nothing defective in their faith or wanting in their instruction, for he added nothing to them. He only urged **them all to remain true to the Lord with all their hearts** (v. 23; cf. 15:32), that is, that they continue as they had begun, allowing nothing to shake them in their attachment to Jesus. The imperfect tense of the verb "to urge" (or encourage) implies that he remained in Antioch and that this was his theme for as long as he was there. Ever the encourager (4:36), he showed himself to be also **a good man** (a description unique in Acts) and **full of the Holy Spirit and faith** (v. 24). These were the qualities that had made Stephen so effective a minister (6:5), and under God Barnabas proved no less able. It appears to have been through him as much as anyone that **a great number of people were brought** ("added"; cf. 2:47) **to the Lord** (v. 24; note the implied link between the first and second halves of this verse). Barnabas seems to have become a leader in the church in Antioch, as was only to be expected from his long association with the apostles. No doubt he made a report in due course to Jerusalem

11:25-26a / Such was the growth of the church that before long Barnabas felt the need of an assistant, and his thoughts turned to Paul (cf. 9:27), who for some years now had been going from place to place in Syria and Cilicia "preaching the faith he once tried to destroy" (Gal. 1:21ff.). Barnabas may have heard something of this by report, enough to convince him that Paul was the right man for Antioch. Tarsus lay northwest of the Syrian capital and could be reached by either land or sea. His quarry was not easy to find. It was only after a thorough search (the force of the Greek) that Barnabas found Paul and they returned together to Antioch. Here **for a whole year** they worked together (v. 26), instructing the church after the example of the apostles (2:42; cf. Matt. 28:20), until such time as the church, having come to a measure of maturity, sent them out to the wider work of the "first missionary journey" (13:3ff.). It may have been that in these months at Antioch Paul first glimpsed the real scope of his calling to be "an apostle to the Gentiles" (Gal. 2:8). The Greek text of verse 26 is not completely clear, though NIV gives what is probably the best sense: **Barnabas and Saul met with the church**. However, a number of alternatives have been suggested, of which we mention one that is particularly attractive: "they were brought together in the church," drawing attention to the fact that the association formed in Antioch between Barnabas and Paul was of inestimable value to the church's mission.

11:26b-30 / Two other matters of interest are noted by Luke in this section: First, **the disciples were called Christians first at Antioch** (v. 26). In the New Testament, Christians never call themselves by this name; nor is it likely that the name was given to them by the Jews. It must be attributed, therefore, to others in the city and is testimony to the church's having forced its presence on their attention as a group of people with their own identity. It may be no accident that the two statements of verse 26, the one referring to their numbers, the other to their name, are closely linked in the Greek. The word "Christian" is a Latin formation by which plural nouns ending in *-iani* denote the partisans of the person named; for example, the Herodians were the supporters of Herod Antipas. H. B. Mattingley has suggested that the term *Christiani* was modeled, as an Antiochene joke, on the *Augustiani*, the organized brigade of chanting devotees who led the public adulation of Nero—both the enthusiasm of the believers and the ludicrous homage of the imperial cheerleaders being lampooned by the comparison ("The Origin of the Name Christian," *JTS* 9 (1958), pp. 26ff.). But the name "Christian" may well be older than the institution of the *Augustiani*, and certainly so if we think that by this note Luke meant that the name originated at this time. However, the possibility remains that it was coined as a joke, and it may have been in that sense that Agrippa II used it in 26:28 (cf. 1 Pet. 4:16).

The second matter is the provision made by the church in Antioch, as famine threatened, for the relief of **the brothers living in Judea** (v. 29). Luke's language is designed to show the unity between these two groups of believers. The prophet Agabus, who had come with a group of others from Jerusalem, warned the Antiochene Christians that **a severe famine would spread over the entire Roman world** (v. 28; cf. 24:5; Luke 2:1). And so it did, broadly speaking. The reign of Claudius (A.D. 41–54) was remarkable for the famines that afflicted various parts of the empire. The first, second, fourth, ninth, and eleventh years of his reign are recorded as years of famine in one district or another (see Suetonius, *Claudius* 18; Tacitus, *Annals* 12.43; Dio Cassius, *Roman History* 60.11; Eusebius, *Ecclesiastical History* 2.8). According to Josephus, Judea was affected between A.D. 44 and 48 (*Antiquities*, 20.49–53). But, for the church in Antioch, forewarned was forearmed. The believers decided that **each according to his ability** would send help to Judea (v. 29; cf. 1 Cor. 16:2). Their desire was **to provide help for the brothers**, where the Greek could mean that they would send as much as they could "for ministry," recalling the similar expression in 6:1 and making the point that this was simply on a larger scale what had been the church's practice from the beginning (cf. 2:44; 4:32–35; see also the disc. on 20:1–6). The plight of the Judean Christians would have been especially desperate in these famine years, for among those most likely to have fled Judea during the persecution would have been those best able to support themselves elsewhere. The church may have been deprived of its more wealthy members at the very time when their help was needed most. How welcome these gifts from Antioch must have been! The monies raised by the church in Antioch were carried by Barnabas and Paul and put into the hands of **the elders**, who appear to have become the leaders in Jerusalem with James perhaps already at their head (v. 30; see disc. on 12:17 and notes; for the aptness of this whole enterprise, cf. Paul's dictum in Gal. 6:6 with vv. 22, 27). This visit of Paul to Jerusalem has sometimes been identified with that of Galatians 2:1–10, but on the whole this seems unlikely (see disc. on 15:1–21). When Barnabas and Paul had completed their task, they returned north, taking with them John Mark (12:25).

Additional Notes §29

11:20 / **Greeks**: The manuscripts vary between "Hellenes," i.e., "Greeks," and "Hellenists," the word used in 6:1 and 9:29—the latter having the better textual support, the former making better sense. It would hardly have been remarkable if they had preached to the Hellenists, if by that was meant Jewish Hellenists, since both the preachers and the congregations must have been of that ilk. Luke wants us to understand that this was a new departure, and if "Hellenists" is still to be accepted as the reading, it must be as practically synonymous with "Hellenes," meaning "Greek-speaking Gentiles."

Telling them the good news about the Lord Jesus: "There is a certain intrinsic parallelism between the development of the earliest Christian conception of mission and the development of Christology. This parallel development, too, is hinted at in Luke's account. In Luke, as in Paul, the absolute *ho kyrios* or *ho kyrios Iēsous* (*Christos*), 'the Lord' or 'the Lord Jesus Christ,' is by far the most frequent title. This corresponds to the terminology of the Greek-speaking community outside Palestine" (Hengel, *Acts*, pp. 103f.). This is not to say that the title **Lord** for Jesus was unknown in the Palestinian church. On the contrary, it is very old. Echoes of its early use are found in the Aramaic phrase *Marana tha*, "our Lord come," in 1 Cor. 16:22 and Rev. 22:20. And yet it may not have been as much used by the Palestinian church as by the Greek. This is accurately reflected in Luke's writing by the relatively infrequent occurrence of the absolute *ho kyrios* of Jesus in the first five chapters of Acts as compared with its general use at a later date (2:36, 47; 5:14; cf. 1:21 "the Lord Jesus"; in 4:33 the reading is uncertain, and in one or two places it is not certain which person of the Godhead is meant, e.g., 1:24). In these early chapters the title more often belongs to the Father (2:20f., 25, 30; 3:19, 22; 4:26). Taking this further, it is only in these chapters that we find Jesus called by the archaic titles "Servant" (3:13, 26; 4:27, 30) and "Prophet-like-Moses" (3:22). Common also is the titular use of *"Christos,"* "Messiah" (2:31, 36; 3:18, 20; 4:26; 5:42; 8:5; 9:22; 17:3; 18:5, 28; 26:23). Another relic from the early days of the church is the name "Son of Man" (7:56, and see disc. on 17:31). Mention should also be made of the "Righteous One" (3:14; 7:52; 22:14). Though this name is found also in the later literature of the church, it may be regarded as another primitive title of Jesus—similarly, "Leader" or "Author" (3:15; 5:31). Hengel comments: "Even if all these christological allusions were to be 'redactional,' this terminology is quite certainly not fortuitous; rather, the titles have been chosen deliberately. In other words, here too Luke works with the 'historical-theological' understanding which is his hallmark. In reality, however, it is extraordinarily difficult to distinguish between 'redaction' and 'tradition' in Acts: to deny in principle the presence of earlier traditions in the speeches composed by Luke makes them incomprehensible and is no more than an interpreter's whim" (*Acts*, p. 104).

11:26 / **The disciples were called Christians first at Antioch**: The infinitive, *chrēmatisai*, could be translated "called themselves" and the passage understood to mean that the name "Christian" was coined by the church to give expression to a new self-consciousness. On this understanding of the term, B. J. Bickerman has come to the view that "Christian" meant "a slave of Christ" ("The Name of Christians," *HTR* 42 (1949), pp. 109–24). But the evidence of the New Testament is that this was not a name by which Christians called themselves at that time, though by Luke's time it probably was, hence his antiquarian interest in its place of origin.

11:27 / **Some prophets**: If 1 Corinthians is any guide, it may not have been unusual to find a number of men and women in a local congregation exercising the gift of prophecy (see 1 Cor. 11:4f.; 14:29; cf. also Acts 13:1). But besides these, there were others who exercised this gift more widely. These are the "prophets" referred to in the lists of charismata (1 Cor. 12:28f.; Eph. 4:11; cf. Eph. 2:20; 3:5), and to this group belonged Agabus and the others. The role of the prophet was both to proclaim (cf. 2:18; 19:6; 21:9) and to predict. Agabus was noted for his predictions (cf. 21:10f.). In their capacity as preachers, the prophets' work is described as exhortation (15:32), edification, and consolation (1 Cor. 14:3). The reaction of unbelievers to their ministry shows that they were preachers of the whole message of God (1 Cor. 14:24f.). In the context of the church meeting, their ministry is described as a "revelation" (1 Cor. 14:26ff.), which appears to mean that it was usually a spontaneous utterance in response to a distinct moving of the Spirit—Agabus is twice said to have uttered his prediction "through the Spirit" (11:28; 21:11; see disc. on 13:1–3). Unlike the gift of tongues, prophecy communicated intelligibly to the church. Two tests were to be applied to what the prophet said: first, the opinion of other prophets (1 Cor. 14:29) and, second, the apostolic *kerygma* (1 Cor. 14:37f.) Prophets, therefore, were not sources of new truth, insofar as they were preachers, but expositors of the truth otherwise revealed. G. B. Caird suggests that it may have been to them that we owe the beginning of our hymnody (*The Apostolic Age*, p. 64). On the fluidity of ministries in the early church, see note on 13:1.

11:28 / The Western text adds at this point: "And there was much gladness. And when we were gathered together, . . . " including the author in what he was describing (cf. the so-called we-passages, 16:10–17; 20:5–15; 27:1–28:16). This reading reflects the tradition that Luke was a native of Syrian Antioch; however, it must be regarded as dubious.

11:30 / **The elders** (cf. 14:23; 15:2, 4, 6, 22, 23; 16:4; 20:17; 21:18): To understand the emergence of this order, we must remember that the church had been wracked by two persecutions (assuming that the embassy from Antioch was later than A.D. 44; 8:1ff.; 9:1ff.; 12:1ff.). These had driven away significant numbers of Christians, including, we may suppose, others of the Seven besides Philip and, perhaps more recently, those who remained of the Twelve (cf. 12:1, 2, 17). And in any case, the Twelve did not want to be involved in the day-to-day administration of the church. Thus the early leadership of the church in Jerusalem had been lost (though for a time the apostles may have returned to the city when important decisions had to be taken; cf. 15:2ff., perhaps also 11:1 and 22) and this, together with the natural inclination of the church to accept the precedent of the synagogue, probably led to the appointment of elders. This in turn became a precedent for other churches to follow (14:23; 20:17). The elders were sometimes called "overseers" (Gk. *episkopoi*; see note on 20:28; cf. Phil. 1:1; 1 Tim. 3:1f. Titus 1:7) or simply "those . . . who are over you" (1 Thess. 5:12). Unlike their Jewish counterparts, they seem to have had a spiritual role as pastors and teachers as well as an administrative function (cf. 20:17; 1 Tim. 5:17; James 5:14; 1 Pet. 5:1–4), and from 1 Tim. 4:14; 5:22 and 2 Tim. 1:6 we may infer that their appointment was marked by the laying on of hands. See further the note on 14:23 for the manner of their appointment.

§30 Peter's Miraculous Escape from Prison (Acts 12:1–19a)

This chapter illustrates both the suffering entailed in the service of Christ (12:1–19) and God's judgment on those who inflict it (12:20–25). It also exemplifies the power of prayer. However, not for these reasons chiefly has Luke told the story of Peter's rescue from prison, but for its own intrinsic interest and for the explanation it gives of Peter's disappearance from the narrative after dominating the first half of the book. This has probably determined the placing of this material here and not earlier, as a concern for strict chronology might have suggested; Peter's leaving to go to "another place" (v. 17) makes way for the emergence of Paul and the story of his missionary work. In short, this chapter is transitional, standing in a similar relation to the two halves of this book as chapter 1 does to the Gospel and the first half of Acts. There is much in this chapter that brings to mind the vivid style of Mark's Gospel and adds strength to the supposition that the same authority (Peter) stands behind both. On the general similarity of this story to the stories of imprisonment and escape in the earlier part of the book, see the discussion on 3:1–11.

12:1 / The church had enjoyed a brief respite after the "Pauline persecution" (see disc. on 9:31), but soon it was again being harassed, this time by **King Herod**, that is, Herod Agrippa I, son of Aristobulus and grandson of Herod the Great. Born in 10 B.C. and educated in Rome, he rose from being a rash adventurer to good fortune and high position, first through his friendship with Caligula, then by the favor of Claudius. In A.D. 37 he was granted the realm of his uncle Philip, the tetrarch of Iturea, who had died in A.D. 34 (cf. Luke 3:1). With this he was also granted the title of king. Subsequently, the district of Abilene was added to Herod's territory (formerly governed by Lysanias) and later still (A.D. 39), the domain of Herod Antipas, another uncle, which gave him Galilee and Perea. In A.D. 41 he received from Claudius the control of Judea and Samaria, thus interrupting for a while Rome's direct rule of that region through the procurators. With this final addition to his realm, Herod Agrippa I held an area roughly equal in extent to his grandfather's. But unlike Herod the Great he also enjoyed the good will of the Jews. This he was careful to cultivate, and no doubt it was in pursuit of their favor, especially that of the Sadducees, that he launched this attack on **some who belonged to the church**—the church leaders, apparently.

12:2 / Thus **he had James, the brother of John** (the sons of Zebedee), **put to death with the sword**. Although Luke has said nothing of the other apostles, this notice suggests that they were no less active than Peter (and John) and perhaps James' nature as a "son of thunder" (Mark 3:17) marked him out in particular as a victim. Death **with the sword** (beheading) was not a punishment sanctioned by the Jewish law, though apparently practiced from time to time by the Jews. Its use in this instance suggests that the charge against James was something of a political nature. He may have spoken out on some matter against Herod himself (were Jewish hopes for a Messiah beginning to center on Herod Agrippa?) A late account of James' martyrdom is given by Clement of Alexandria in Eusebius' *Ecclesiastical History* 2.9. Another late, but unreliable, tradition has it that John was put to death at the same time.

12:3–5 / When Herod saw that his action pleased the Jews (chiefly the Jewish hierarchy, we suppose), he had Peter arrested (the same word is used of Jesus' arrest in Gethsemane, Luke 22:54) with the intention of doing to him as he had to James. The expression in the Greek, "to lead up" (v. 4), means to bring the prisoner before the tribunal (a similar word is used of Jesus in Luke 22:66). This was to have been done in public (cf. John 19:13), and since it was Passover and many Jews were present, it would have been a great public relations exercise on the part of Herod, demonstrating his loyalty to the Jewish religion. But it could not be done during the festival. That would be counterproductive (cf. Mark 14:1f.). So Peter was held in prison until the actual days of the festival were over. The feast of Unleavened Bread, incorporating Passover, ran from Nisan 14 (the day of the Passover) to Nisan 21 (see Deut. 16:1–8). Every precaution was taken to ensure that Peter stayed put (in the light of earlier happenings? 5:18–25).

It was Roman practice (presumably retained under Herod's rule) to divide the night into four watches, with each watch of three hours being kept by four soldiers. The usual procedure would require that two should guard the prisoner within the cell, chained to him one on each side (cf. v. 6, also Josephus, *Antiquities* 18.195–204), and that two should be outside guarding the doors (cf. v. 10). Peter's situation looked hopeless. Notice the emphasis on **prison, soldiers, chains, sentries** in verses 4 to 6. But while Peter lay in chains behind iron doors, **the church was . . . praying . . . for him** (v. 5). The imperfect tense in the Greek indicates that they made repeated prayer, to which Luke adds that they also made it **earnestly** (v. 5), the same word (though in a slightly different form) as that used in Luke 22:44 of Jesus' prayer in the garden. It speaks of a prayer that issues from the very heart of the petitioner (cf. 26:7). But the prayer, as indeed all prayer, was not answered simply because of their fervor or the frequency with which they made it, but because God chose to do so. Prayer is always a matter of "not my will but yours be done" (Luke 22:42; see disc. on 1:14; 4:29).

12:6–10 / On the eve of his trial (and certain execution), as Peter slept, **suddenly** [lit., "Look!" see disc. on 1:10f.] **an angel of the Lord appeared and a light shone in the cell** (v. 7; cf. Ps. 127:2; 1 Pet. 5:7; on the association of light with divine manifestations, see 9:3; Luke 2:9). Peter was awakened by the angel striking him on the side. The Greek could almost be rendered, "he kicked him in the ribs." As he got up, the chains fell from his hands. He dressed and was led by the angel out of the prison. All the while Peter thought he was dreaming (v. 9, the same word as for his vision at Joppa, 10:17). There were three gates to pass. The first two may have been left open while the soldiers were sleeping, or else Peter and the angel were allowed to pass as servants. But no servant would have been expected to pass beyond the outermost gate at this time of night, and a different course was needed. Here **the iron gate leading to the city . . . opened for them by itself** (Rackham likened this to the rolling away of the stone on the first Easter morning), **and they went through it** (v. 10). It was Easter again, and Peter was like one returned from the dead. Josephus describes in similar terms (Gk. *automatōs*) the opening of the eastern gate of the inner court of the temple "of its own accord about the sixth hour of the night" (*War* 6.288–309).

It is commonly assumed that Peter was held in the Antonia at the northwestern corner of the temple area (the Western text mentions his going down steps; cf. 21:35, 40). At all events, it appears to have been somewhere in the city. As for the manner of his escape, it must be admitted that "there are indeed some features of the narrative which would lead a police detective to conclude that it was a skillfully planned 'inside job' " (Bruce, *Book*, p. 249). And we are certainly not obliged to look for the miraculous in every biblical narrative that could be explained otherwise. But the fact remains that Luke himself believed that something of this kind happened. He may not have known all the details, but his conviction that God had sovereignly intervened is expressed by his reference to the angel (see disc. on 1:10f.; 5:19f.). It is instructive to compare this story with the account of Paul and Silas' release from the Philippian jail (16:26). In both instances, prayer is specifically mentioned, and if we question the possibility of an escape by miraculous means, are we not doubting God's willingness and ability to act where there are people at prayer? But why Peter should be delivered (at the cost of the lives of the soldiers) and not James is a mystery of the divine will that has been repeated countless times from that day to this (cf. John 21:18ff.).

12:11-17 / According to Luke, Peter was quick to recognize the hand of the Lord in all this (v. 11). But having been handed his freedom, he had enough sense to get away quickly and made off at once **to the house of Mary the mother of John, also called Mark** (v. 12; see note on 14:27). A late tradition names this as the house of the Last Supper, but this identification is rendered uncertain by the fact that that house belonged to a male "householder" (Mark 14:14f.) and that Papias cites a tradition that Mark "had neither heard the Lord nor been his personal follower" (Eusebius, *Ecclesiastical History* 3.39.15). Because John Mark was soon to figure in the narrative, his mother is identified by reference to him. No mention is made of his father. Mary may have been a widow and was evidently a woman of some means. The mention of **the outer entrance** (v. 13) implies that hers was a house with a courtyard (cf. 10:17). Rhoda was evidently the portress at this door (cf. John 18:16), and if the establishment could run to this, there were probably other servants inside.

The story that follows is full of true-to-life detail: the recognition of Peter's Galilean accent (cf. Matt. 26:73) as he called

to the servant who answered his knocking (and her name is remembered); her leaving him there for sheer joy, the door still un-
opened, as she ran to tell the others the news; the disbelief with
which her announcement was greeted; the attempt to find some
other explanation—**You're out of your mind, they told her. . . .
It must be his angel** (v. 15), that is, his guardian angel who had
assumed his form and voice, Peter himself, to their mind, being
dead—and at length, as **Peter kept on knocking** (v. 16), the decision to find out who it was by the simple expedient of opening
the door, which they all went to do together. When at last Peter
could make himself heard over the hubbub of their excitement
(see disc. on 13:16 for the motion with the hand), he told them
how the Lord had delivered him and asked that this news be
passed on to **James and the brothers** (v. 17). This James is the
brother of Jesus, who had risen or was rising to the position of
head of the church in Jerusalem (cf. 15:13; 21:18). He was well
enough known at the time of Luke's writing to need no further
identification. **The brothers** are simply the other members of the
church, who were perhaps meeting for prayer even then elsewhere in the city.

His message delivered, Peter **left for another place** (v. 17),
though where exactly we do not know. One suggestion has been
that this incident preceded the missionary tour of 9:32ff., in which
case **another place** was Lydda, Joppa, and Caesarea. More likely
he withdrew altogether from the territories of Herod Agrippa. On
this assumption, some suppose that he went to Antioch and that
the incident of Galatians 2:11–14 took place at this time. But Peter's
flight from Jerusalem took place no later than A.D. 44, the likely
year of Herod's death, whereas the episode in Antioch is best
dated after about A.D. 49–50 (see disc. on 15:1–21). Others suppose that he went to Rome, but Paul's letter to the Romans, written about A.D. 56, implies that no other apostle had visited the
city, and this appears to have remained the case until he arrived
there himself in about A.D. 60 (cf. 28:22). There remains a slender
possibility that Peter worked for a while in Asia Minor (see disc.
on 16:7). At all events, he was back in Jerusalem for the council
described in chapter 15.

12:18–19a / The discovery that Peter had escaped was not
made until the next morning, by which time he was well away.
Herod evidently suspected that the guards had connived at his

escape. They were **cross-examined**, where the sense is that they were tried (v. 19; cf. 4:9; 24:8; 28:18), and were put to death for their dereliction of duty (cf. 16:27; 27:42). After this, though he was wont to make his residence in Jerusalem (Josephus, *Antiquities* 19.328–331), Herod "went from Judea to Caesarea and stayed there a while" (v. 19b; see note on 1:8 and the disc. on 21:10), which remained, as under the Romans, the administrative capital of his realm.

Additional Notes §30

12:2 / With the sword (cf. Mark 6:27): According to Mishnah, *Sanhedrin* 7.1ff., the Sanhedrin had power to inflict four kinds of penalty: stoning, burning, beheading, and strangling. This passage is of particular interest, for it refers to the manner in which beheading used to be carried out "by royal command," a reference to the Romans, whose practice we may assume Herod followed.

12:12 / John, also called Mark: As with Paul, his Roman name (Mark) is most often used (15:39; Col. 4:10; 2 Tim. 4:11; Philem. 24; 1 Pet. 5:13), though in 13:5, 13, he is simply called John. It was not uncommon for first-century Jews to bear a Greek or Roman name in addition to their Hebrew name (cf. 1:23; 4:36; 9:33; 13:1, 9), the similarity of sound appearing to have sometimes guided the choice, for example, Joses / Jason, Joshua / Justus. From Col. 4:10 we learn that Mark was a kinsman of Barnabas, and this relationship explains why he accompanied Barnabas and Paul on their return to Antioch in 12:25 and became their companion in their missionary work. For his somewhat checkered association with Paul, see disc. on 13:5, 13; 15:36–40. At a later date he was associated also with Peter (see disc. on 3:7f.; 10:14, 34–43; 12:1–5).

12:15 / It must be his angel: The notion of a guardian angel capable of assuming the bodily appearance of the person protected is found in the Scriptures. We see it at both the corporate and the individual level: the angels of the churches (Rev. 2 and 3) and the angels of "these little ones" (Matt. 18:10). Compare also Gen. 48:16; Dan. 3:28; 6:22; Tobit 5:4; Heb. 1:14; and *Midrash Rabbah* on Eccles. 4:4. J. H. Moulton believes that the idea derives from Zoroastrianism ("Zoroastrianism," *HDB* vol. 4, p. 991).

12:17 / James: See disc. on 1:14 and note and the disc. on 9:27. Tradition has it that he was made first bishop of Jerusalem by the risen Jesus and the apostles (Eusebius, *Ecclesiastical History* 7.19). This cannot be accepted, though his relationship with Jesus was no doubt a factor in his rise to leadership. He appears to have presided over the council of Jerusalem (15:1-35), and it was to him that Paul made his reports when he visited the city (21:18). Under James the church became, if anything, more firmly attached to its Jewish matrix (see note on 15:1), and the earlier rapport between the Christians and the Pharisees was re-established (see disc. on 5:34f.). Therefore, when the Sadducees put James to death during the interim between the procurators Festus and Albinus, the Pharisees protested on behalf of the Christians to Herod Agrippa II (Josephus, *Antiquities* 20.197-203; see disc. on 25:13).

§31   Herod's Death (Acts 12:19b–25)

Verses 19b to 23 are a kind of footnote to the previous section, adding nothing to the main thrust of the narrative, but giving a point of reference to secular history (cf. Luke 3:1f.). They do, however, contain the salutary warning that God is on the throne to judge as well as to save. The section ends with a note on the progress of the gospel and the return of Barnabas and Paul to Antioch.

12:19b–23 / The death of Herod Agrippa I is recorded also by Josephus (*Antiquities* 19.343–352). The two accounts are complementary. According to Josephus, Herod died after three years as king of Judea and in the seventh year of his total reign (see disc. on v. 1). On this evidence we should unhesitatingly place his death in the early months of A.D. 44 (which makes Peter's imprisonment during the Passover no later than A.D. 43). However, listed among the coinage of Herod Agrippa I are two that purport to come from the eighth and ninth years of his reign. If these are genuine, the evidence of Josephus would have to be set aside. But the doubt raised by the coins is offset by the likelihood that the festival during which he died was the quadrennial games instituted by Herod the Great in honor of the emperor and to commemorate the founding of Caesarea, and these games must have been held in A.D. 44. On the whole, we are inclined to stick with Josephus and to accept this as the year of the king's death.

During the festival, Herod made an oration from his seat in the theater to mark the settlement of a dispute between himself and the cities of Tyre and Sidon. These were free, self-governing cities within the province of Syria and important centers of trade (see disc. on 21:3 and 27:3). Josephus says nothing of this dispute, or of the Phoenician embassy, only that the king made an oration. What the trouble had been between him and the Phoenicians we do not know, though it was probably something to do with trade. The extent of Herod's rule was considerable, and if he chose to encourage another port, such as Berytus (Beirut), for which he had a "peculiar regard" (Josephus, *Antiqui-*

ties 19.335–337), and made regulations by which traffic was diverted from Tyre and Sidon, it was in his power to cut off at least half their commerce. This, in fact, may have been what happened, for Luke tells us that the people of the two cities sued for peace because **they depended on the king's country for their food supply** (v. 20; they depended heavily on Galilean wheat). The embassy had been sent to Caesarea and had succeeded in winning over the king's chamberlain, Blastus, and through him a reconciliation had been effected. They had not, of course, been at war in any other than a commercial sense, for both Herod and the Phoenician cities were subject to Rome.

With the matter settled, Herod (dressed, as Josephus tells us, in a silver robe that caught the rays of the rising sun in a dazzling display) announced his good intentions toward the two cities. Their representatives (as we suppose) greeted this as the utterance of a god. Indeed, they may have kept this up as a chant (note the imperfect), on which Josephus comments: "He did not rebuke them, nor did he repudiate their impious flattery" (see disc. on 9:31). Josephus adds that Herod then saw an owl (Eusebius, *Ecclesiastical History* 2.10 has an "angel"), which he took to be an omen of evil. In any case, he was struck down by a disease. Luke saw this as an act of divine retribution (v. 23; cf. vv. 7–11). His gruesome phrase **he was eaten by worms and died** (v. 23) corresponds to Josephus' description of violent abdominal pains that led to the king's death five days later (Luke's **immediately** need only mean that the symptoms appeared then, not that he died right away). The description of the disease should probably be taken as a real account of Herod's affliction in the medical terms of the day rather than as a stereotyped description of the death of a tyrant (cf. 2 Macc. 9:5–12). Marshall suggests that "appendicitis leading to peritonitis would fit the symptoms" (p. 213), Neil that he died of "a cyst produced by tapeworm" (p. 152).

12:24 / So died the church's persecutor. Meanwhile the church itself continued to prosper—another of Luke's summary statements (see disc. on 2:42–47). "The seed is the word," said Jesus (Mark 4:14), and Luke tells us now that the seed **continued to increase and spread**. In the Greek text, this verse is identical with the first part of 6:7 (cf. also 19:20).

12:25 / The last verse of the section completes the earlier narrative of Barnabas and Paul's mission of mercy in bring-

ing famine relief to Jerusalem (11:27–30). The reference to John
Mark comes here at the end to explain his presence in Antioch
for the story that follows.

Additional Notes §31

12:25 / **From Jerusalem**: By far the best-supported reading for
this verse in the Greek manuscripts is "to Jerusalem," and on the grounds
that it is also the most difficult reading, it should perhaps be accepted.
Either way there is a primitive error in the text (corrected in later manu
scripts) or we have an odd use of the Greek—the preposition *eis*, "into"
or "to," having to be read as equivalent to *en*, "in," and the phrase "in
Jerusalem" qualifying, not the verb "returned," as the word order would
suggest, but the participle "having fulfilled" (NIV **finished**).

§32 Barnabas and Saul Sent Off (Acts 13:1–3)

Chapter 13 marks a most significant point in the history. Hitherto, Jerusalem and Judea have been the scene of the believers' activities and Peter the most prominent figure. But now the base of operation moves (at least for Luke's purposes, ignoring, perhaps, other spheres of activity) to Antioch in Syria, and Paul becomes the center of attention. The very phrase by which Luke refers to the church in Antioch—a quasitechnical term in the Greek—seems to indicate its new status. The Christians are no longer merely "a great number of people" (11:21), but are now "the church" in that place (cf. 11:22 where the same form of expression is used of the church in Jerusalem) and ready as such to carry the gospel another step farther toward "the ends of the earth" (1:8). We have in this chapter the first piece of planned missionary work that we know of, though the church's decision to embark on this venture was not exactly its own but made in response to the Spirit, whose initiative it was and in whose power the mission was carried out. The NEB heads this section, "The Church Breaks Barriers," but Luke is careful to stress that these changes were no human expedient but the onward course of salvation history.

13:1 / The church in Antioch included a number of **prophets and teachers** (see note on 11:27). It is not clear whether this notice means that there were two groups of ministers or whether the twofold description applied to them all. In any case, they all appear to have enjoyed a certain status, such that they might fairly be called the "elders of the church in Antioch," whose official position was enhanced by their special gifts—elders like those in 1 Timothy 5:17 who worked hard "at preaching and teaching." Their role was perhaps analogous to that of the Twelve in the early days of the church. We could call them "the Five."

Their names are full of interest, embracing a wide range of social and possibly racial backgrounds. **Barnabas** is mentioned first, as being perhaps the senior in status or in faith (see disc.)

on 4:36 and 11:24). Then there is **Simeon** (Simon). His name is Jewish, but he bore the Latin nickname **Niger,** "the Black." Because he is named in association with a Cyrenean, it has been thought that he too may have come from North Africa and may have been the Simon of Cyrene who bore Jesus' cross (Luke 23:26). But if Luke had intended that identification, it is odd that he has spelled the name differently. It may be, then, that **Niger** was added precisely to distinguish this Simon from the Cyrenean, as indeed from all the other Simons known to the church (e.g., 10:5f.). The third, **Lucius,** has a Latin name. This may mean that he was of Gentile extraction, but not necessarily (see note on 12:12). The mention of his birthplace suggests that he may have been one of those "men from . . . Cyrene" who first preached the Good News to Gentiles in Antioch (11:20). There is little reason to think that he is the author. Again, the names are spelled differently, and if Luke refrained from divulging his own identity elsewhere, except for the occasional use of "we," it is unlikely that he would have given it away in this fashion. Nor is there any reason to identify him with the Lucius of Romans 16:21. The fourth, **Manaen,** that is, Menahem, is of special interest because of his association with the court of Herod Antipas. The evidence of the Greek inscriptions suggests that he bore a court title as the companion and confidant of the tetrarch. Thus Manaen may have been Luke's source of information on Herod Antipas (Luke says more about Herod than any other Evangelist). Manaen's name is Jewish. It means "comforter" and is found in Josephus (*Antiquities* 15.373–379) as the name of an Essene who foretold (for he too was a prophet) that Herod the Great would become king. The association of the name with these Idumean rulers may be no more than coincidental. On the other hand, once the prophecy had been fulfilled, Manaen may have become a favorite name among the Herodians. Manaen was probably from the upper classes. The last name is Paul's, still in its Jewish form, **Saul,** as has been Luke's practice to this point (see disc. on v. 9).

13:2 / Having been introduced to its leaders, we are now shown the church in Antioch at worship. The word translated **worshipping** is that usually employed in the LXX for the service of priests and Levites in the temple (Gk. *leitourgein;* cf. our "liturgy"). The subject **they** will have particular reference to the prophets and teachers, but should not be confined to them, for the whole church will have been involved in both the worship and the decision that was taken at this time (cf. 1:15; 6:2, 5; 14:22; 15:22). Because they were fasting we may conclude that the church was in a state of high expectation. Not much later than this, fasting often preceded a "high day" (cf. *Didache* 7.4), and they may have believed that such a day was at hand. This sense of expectancy was linked with their recognition (and the reality in their lives) of the lordship of Jesus—**they were worshipping the Lord**. It is possible, moreover, that they had already been praying about a missionary venture, had asked the Lord who should lead it, and were expecting his answer to that prayer. This possibility rests on a Greek particle that is almost impossible to translate but lends to the sentence a certain emphasis, as though the Spirit was affirming what they had already proposed—"Yes indeed," **set apart for me Barnabas and Saul** (Paul uses the same word, "to set apart," of himself in Rom. 1:1 and Gal. 1:15). This message may have come through one of the prophets, but the church was convinced that it was the Spirit who had called the two men and that it was to the Spirit's own work that he had called them: **Set apart for me . . . I have called them**. And this verb is in the middle voice—"I have called them *for myself.*" They accepted the call, and so Paul became, in Ramsay's words, "Saint Paul the Traveler."

13:3 / The church responded as readily as their leaders had done and commissioned them for the work. Again, the context was one of prayer and fasting, and their calling was given formal expression by the laying on of hands, presumably by the elders on behalf of the people. This was not so much an "ordination" as an act of identification by which the church went, in a sense, with those who would go in their name. It was also a token of the church's prayer for blessing upon them (see disc. on 6:6). It is not actually said that this would be a missionary work, but that is clearly implied. Nor is anything said of any provision for the support of the workers. We do know, however, that both Barnabas and Paul were later committed to the principle of self-support (cf. 1 Cor. 9:6; see disc. on 18:3), and it may have been on this basis that they began.

Additional Notes §32

13:1 / Barnabas, Simeon, . . . Lucius, . . . Manaen, . . . and Saul: The Greek gives the impression that there may have been two groups, Barnabas, Simeon, and Lucius in the one, Manaen and Paul in the other. Should we then regard the first group as prophets and the second as teachers? It would certainly agree with 11:26 to restrict Paul to the role of teacher (though it does not preclude his being a prophet). Luke never describes Paul as "prophesying," whereas he is regularly said to have "taught" (15:35; 18:11; 20:20; 28:31). If teachers did not have quite the same status as prophets (cf. 1 Cor. 12:28; Eph. 4:11), and if Paul was a teacher, this might help to explain Mark's behavior when Paul later assumed the leadership of the missionary expedition over Barnabas.

Teachers: Prophets gave spontaneous utterance; teachers apparently had a more sustained ministry (not necessarily any less inspired than the prophets'). Unlike the Christian prophet, the teacher had a contemporary model in the synagogue and from the synagogue inherited a position of honor in the church. His task was to instruct the church, making use of the Old Testament and the traditions of the life and teaching of Jesus. There appears to have been a certain fluidity and overlap in the ministries and offices of the early church. Thus, in the case of Barnabas and Paul, those who were prophets and teachers might function also as elders and, with the change of circumstance, as apostles. (See 14:4. Cf. 15:22 where Judas and Silas are called "leaders" with 15:32, where they are "prophets." Later, Silas is effectively an apostle, though he is never called by that name.)

13:2–3 / While they were . . . fasting . . . they fasted and prayed: In early Christian practice fasting was not uncommonly linked with prayer (cf. 14:23 and variants of Matt. 17:21; Mark 9:29; Acts 10:30). The Jews had extended the practice of fasting far beyond the one fast prescribed by the law (the Day of Atonement; cf. 27:9), and Jesus assumed that his disciples would continue the practice (Matt. 6:16–18; but cf. Matt. 9:14f.). It is a denial of self-satisfaction as the ideal of life.

§33 On Cyprus (Acts 13:4–12)

The end result of the "first missionary journey" was a giant step forward for the church, though in terms of the actual distance covered it was a more modest achievement. It took Barnabas and Paul to Cyprus and then through parts of Asia Minor. Luke has sometimes been accused of inventing the itinerary set out in this narrative, but this seems highly unlikely. First, it is hard to believe that he would have included the story of Mark's defection if he had been giving free rein to his fancy. Second, most of the places visited were quite insignificant. If Luke had been inventing, he would surely have taken his heroes to more exciting locations. And third, some places are named where Luke mentions nothing happening—Seleucia, Perga, Attalia. One wonders why if they were not already part of the story as it had come to him.

This present section seems to have held a twofold interest for Luke. The first lay in the incident involving Elymas. Here again Luke has been accused of inventing or at least elaborating an earlier story. But this narrative does not fit the mold of other similar stories (see *BC* vol. 5, pp. 186ff.) and gives no other hint of fabrication. Luke probably saw it as a parallel to Peter's confrontation with Simon Magus (8:9ff.). His other interest was in the emergence of Paul as a missionary leader.

13:4–5 / It was natural that the missionaries should go first to Cyprus, though from Luke's comment that they were **sent by the Holy Spirit** (v. 4; cf. v. 3 where the church "sent them off"), we may assume that conviction was added to the dictates of common sense. Cyprus was Barnabas' homeland, it was easily accessible, and almost certainly there were Christians already there (11:19f.; 21:16). John Mark accompanied them (v. 5). His family connection with Barnabas (see note on 12:12) and so, perhaps, with the island, may have been the determining factors in his being chosen. Because he is not named in the commissioning, his role was perhaps a subordinate one. He may have attended to their day-to-day needs, though the term used to describe him (Gk. *hypēretēs*, "servant," "attendant," "minister") is sometimes used of Christian ministers in an official sense (26:16; 1 Cor. 4:1), and on that basis it has been suggested that Mark served as a catechist and may also have baptized the converts. On the other hand, the use of the corresponding verb (*hypēretein*) in 20:34 and 24:23 favors the sense that he was simply their general factotum.

When the Romans annexed Cyprus in 58 B.C. they transferred the seat of government from Salamis to new Paphos (see disc. on v. 6). Salamis, however, remained an important center of trade. Being only about 130 miles southwest of Seleucia, their port of departure (v. 4), it naturally presented itself to the missionaries as their first port of call. The Jewish settlement in the city was large enough to support a number of synagogues, and it was on these that Barnabas and Paul concentrated their efforts (see disc. on 9:20). The details of their work have gone unrecorded, except for the brief statement that **they proclaimed the word of God in the Jewish synagogues** (v. 5). Nothing is said of any response or of how long they remained in Salamis before **they traveled through the whole island . . . to Paphos** (v. 6). There is no reason to think that they extended their ministry beyond those in touch with the synagogues.

13:6–12 / In this sketchiest of accounts, something may be gleaned from the expression "they traveled through" (v. 6), which Luke constantly uses of missionary journeys (see disc. on 8:4). Thus, in crossing the island (about ninety miles from Salamis to Paphos) they may have preached in a number of synagogues. Their destination was Paphos, a new city that had developed under the Romans (to be distinguished from the old town of that name about eleven miles to the southeast of the new). Here they may well have preached for some time, gaining some notoriety, before they were summoned by the governor, Sergius Paulus, to preach before him. Luke correctly styles him a proconsul, for the island had been a senatorial province since 22 B.C.

In the governor's retinue was a Jew named Elymas Bar-Jesus (vv. 6, 8; cf. Josephus, *Antiquities* 20.141–144; Tacitus, *History* 1.22). The name Elymas is apparently based on the Arabic *alim*, meaning "wise," or on an Aramaic derivation from it. Luke calls him a magus. Strictly speaking, the magi were the priests and wise men of Persia, but this magus was no more than a charlatan, whom Luke also calls a **false prophet** (v. 6; see note on 8:9). However, his description of the governor as **an intelligent man** (v. 7) implies that Sergius Paulus had not been taken in by Bar-Jesus, who, for his part, had wit enough to see that if the governor were won over by the Christians his own chance of bringing him under his power would be lost. He therefore set himself **to turn the proconsul from the faith** (v. 8; "faith" here means primarily the body of Christian belief, though the subjective idea of faith as trust cannot be ruled out altogether; see disc. on 14:22). Paul's response was to look Bar-Jesus in the eye (see disc. on 3:4) and say, **You are a child of the devil** (perhaps in indignant contrast to his name, "son of Jesus," that is, "son of a savior") and **enemy of everything that is right**, "making crooked the ways of the Lord which are straight" (v. 10, so the Greek; cf. Isa. 40:3; Hos. 14:9); that is, instead of pointing the way to God, he was obstructing the way. **The hand of the Lord** (perhaps "the Spirit of the Lord"; see disc. on 4:28) **is against you. You are going to be blind** (v. 11). And so he was. The blindness may have overtaken him gradually— Luke speaks of **mist and darkness** coming over him (v. 11)—but in the end it was total. Later he had difficulty finding (Gk. "was seeking for") anyone to act as his guide.

The immediate purpose of the miracle (for Luke clearly implies this) was to punish Bar-Jesus for resisting the gospel (see disc. on 5:5; spiritual blindness is spoken of as a punishment for a similar offense in 28:26f.). However the reference in verse 11 to **a time** may mean that he would only remain blind until he repented. In other words, the judgment may have been conditional and the punishment in the nature of a warning. Meanwhile, the miracle served the further purpose of demonstrating the power of the gospel. **When the proconsul saw what had happened, he believed** (v. 12), though what he believed we are not told. It may have been in Jesus as Lord in the Christian sense, or it may only have been in the reality of the divine power that had now been displayed (cf. 8:18ff.). Luke says nothing of his being baptized, which is surprising in such a case.

The reference to Paul's name in verse 9 should be noted. A great deal has been made of Luke's having mentioned the change of name in the context of Paul's meeting with Sergius Paulus, as though Paul had taken the governor's name. But that they shared the name may be only coincidental. For Luke gives the impression that Paul already had the two names—one Jewish, the other Roman (see note on 12:12)—but now chose to use the latter, feeling perhaps that it was more appropriate now that he had moved away from a predominantly Jewish sphere into the Roman world. His preaching to Sergius Paul may have brought it home to him that he had moved into a different world, and the change of name may have expressed his growing perception of what God would have him do in it (see disc. on 9:15f., i.e., it had a theological as well as a sociological import). His Jewish name, Saul, is only found again in Acts in the two accounts of his conversion (22:7; 26:14) and not at all in his epistles.

It is noteworthy also that from this time Paul is usually named first before Barnabas (hitherto the reverse has been the case; cf. 11:30; 12:25; 13:2; but see 14:14; 15:12). This may mean that Paul had become the dominant partner in the missionary team. In verse 13 it even becomes "Paul and his companions," literally, "those around Paul," a classical expression depicting Paul as a leader.

Additional Notes §33

13:7 / The proconsul (Gk. *anthypatos*): All Roman provinces were divided into two classes, those that required troops and those that did not. The latter were administered by the Senate and ruled by proconsuls; the former were under the administration of the emperor. The larger of the imperial provinces were ruled by legates or propaetors of senatorial rank, with one or more legions at their command, the smaller by procurators of equestrian rank, as was the case with Judea. Cyprus had once been included in the imperial province of Cilicia, but was declared a senatorial province in 22 B.C. Under Hadrian it appears to have again become an imperial province, but by the time of Severus it was again being ruled by a proconsul.

Attempts to identify Sergius Paulus in nonbiblical sources center on three inscriptions: a Greek inscription found at Soli refers to the proconsul Paulus; a Latin inscription names Lucius Sergius Paullus as one of the curators of the Tiber under Claudius, and another Greek inscription found at Kytheria may also bear the name Sergius Paulus. In addition, W. Ramsay and J. G. C. Anderson discovered in 1912 an inscription near Pisidian Antioch that mentions a "Lucius Sergius Paullus, the younger son of Lucius." In 1913 Ramsay discovered the woman's name Sergia Paulla on an inscription in the same region. These discoveries played an important part in his theory that the family of Sergius Paulus were Christians (see *The Bearing of Recent Discovery on the Trustworthiness of the*

New Testament [London: Hodder & Stoughton, 1915], pp. 150–72). B. Van Elderen, however, has seriously questioned Ramsay's theory and is also skeptical of the value of the first two inscriptions for the identification of Sergius Paulus and uncertain of the value of the third, though it offers the "most attractive possibility of the three" (*AHG*, p. 156; see pp. 151–56 for his full discussion).

13:9 / **Saul—who was also called Paul**: As a Roman citizen Paul would have borne three names: a praenomen (like our Christian or given name), a nomen, i.e., the name of his clan (*gens*), this name ending in *-ius*, and a cognomen, the surname or family name, showing the branch of the clan to which he belonged. Paul (Latin Paullus) is his cognomen (see disc. on 22:26ff.). Marshall points out that "a Roman citizen could have a fourth name (his signum or supernomen) given at birth and used as a family name; in Paul's case this could have been his Jewish name 'Saul,' which he would use in a Jewish environment" (p. 220).

§34   In Pisidian Antioch (Acts 13:13-52)

The missionaries cross to Asia Minor, where Paul's first recorded sermon is preached in Antioch. The speech is given at length, so that on other occasions Luke needed only to say that Paul "proclaimed the word of God in the Jewish synagogues" (13:5; 14:1; etc.) without feeling obliged to give the content of the preaching each time. And like the speech, the response was also a paradigm, with some Jews believing but many rejecting the gospel. It is possible to see in the pattern of ministry outlined in this passage a parallel between Jesus and Paul. Simeon had announced that Jesus would be "a light for revelation to the Gentiles" (Luke 2:32), and in Antioch Paul defined his task in precisely these terms (13:47). Notice too "the similarity of the setting between Jesus' inaugural address and Paul's (Luke 4:16f.; Acts 13:14f.); the division created by the sermon, the reference to Gentiles and the opposition. These parallels show that Jesus' ministry is continued in Paul's, even as Jesus' ministry stands in continuity with the salvation history of the past (13:17-23)" (Krodel, p. 54; see also the disc. on 19:21-41).

It has often been remarked that this sermon bears a striking resemblance to the speeches of Peter in both outline and content and to a lesser extent to the speech of Stephen (both contain a résumé of Israel's history). Because of this broad similarity, the authenticity of one or the other or of them all has been questioned and their similarity attributed entirely to Luke. Certainly they all bear the stamp of his language and literary style, but it must be doubted that he freely composed them. It is now widely accepted that all of the early preaching followed a common pattern that to some extent was based on rabbinic models (see disc. on 2:14-42). These models, no less than the form of preaching based on them, were familiar to Paul, and naturally he adopted this pattern himself. But for all that, the speech has its own character, with hints of Paul's own ideas and vocabulary. Luke's source may have been Paul himself (the speech was probably like most of his synagogue sermons) or possibly Timothy (cf. 16:1), who was later a colleague of Luke.

13:13–14a / From Cyprus the missionary party sailed for Pamphylia on the central south coast of Asia Minor (cf. 2:10). This was for the most part a low, marshy, fever-ridden region, though at some points the Taurus Mountains, which made travel to the north so difficult, reach to the sea. Politically, Pamphylia was never of great importance and was usually combined for administrative purposes with one or the other of its neighboring provinces (Lycia and Galatia). After a journey of about one hundred sixty miles, they reached the Bay of Attalia. From there (apparently, since no mention is made of Attalia itself as an intermediate port), they went up the Cestrus to a port within easy reach of the capital, Perga (see further the disc. on 14:25). Here Mark called it quits and went home. No reason is given, though many have been proposed: resentment at Paul's taking precedence over Barnabas, disagreement over policy concerning the Gentiles or the extent to which the Gentile lands should be penetrated, or simply homesickness. Whatever it was (and Luke's later friendship with Mark may have sealed his lips), Paul did not take it kindly (see further the disc. on 15:38).

Acts gives no indication of any preaching in Perga at this time. We must always keep in mind, of course, the summary nature of the narrative. But if in fact they did not stay there, it has sometimes been supposed that this was due to Paul's falling sick and needing to hasten inland to a better climate. Ramsay infers from Galatians 4:13 that Paul was struck down by malaria (these coastal lands were notoriously subject to that disease) and that this was also the "thorn in my flesh" of 2 Corinthians 12:7 (*Paul*, pp. 94ff.). It must be questioned, however, whether a sick man could have faced the rigors of crossing the Taurus Mountains. There may have been a better reason for their leaving Perga behind them: no evidence exists (either literary or archaeological) of any synagogue in that city, and they still had no thought of making a direct approach to the Gentiles.

It may have been their intention, by traveling northward, to reach the road from Ephesus that passed through Antioch of Pisidia and to return by this way to Syria. At all events, they made their way up into the Pisidian mountains to Antioch. When Paul later wrote of dangers from floods and from robbers (2 Cor. 11:26), no other journey is more likely to have been in his thoughts than the one they made now. The floods of the Pisidian highlands are mentioned by Strabo, who wrote of the Cestrus and Eurymedon rivers tumbling down the heights and precipices to the Pamphylian Sea, and the Romans were still far from suppressing the wild clans of Pisidian robbers who made these mountains their home.

Antioch lay on the lower slopes of the mountain now known as Sultan Dagh and on the banks of the river Anthius—a commanding position well protected by natural defenses, as it needed to be, for in earlier days this had been the borderland of Pisidia and Phrygia, with Antioch a Phrygian city (Strabo, *Geography* 12.557). Later, when these had no political significance, the Roman province of Galatia now cutting across the ancient divisions, the expression "Antioch of Pisidia" (or "Pisidian Antioch," as some manuscripts have it) came into vogue. This distinguished the city from another Phrygian Antioch on the river Maeander. It is clear from 14:24 that Luke was aware that "Pisidian Antioch" was not, strictly speaking, in Pisidia, but in Phrygia. It was one of a number of cities of that name founded by Seleucus I Nicator (see disc. on 11:19). After the defeat of Antiochus III by the Romans in 188 B.C., it was declared a free city and in 36 B.C. was given by Antony to Amyntas of Galatia. On the latter's death in 25 B.C. the city was incorporated into the Roman province of Galatia and at the same time was made a colony (Colonia Caesarea, though the old name was retained in popular usage; for colonies, see note on 16:12). For the next hundred years it was the center of the Roman efforts against the mountain robbers.

During the reign of Claudius (A.D. 41–54), which saw Paul and Barnabas come to the city, Antioch reached its greatest height of importance. Throughout this period the romanization of both the city and the region was proceeding. New roads were built radiating out from the city to the southwest and the southeast. The latter became a link in a southern loop of the road from Ephesus to the East. These roads were primarily for military purposes, but before long they would serve to carry "the word of the Lord . . . through the whole region" (v. 49). Antioch had a mixed population of mostly Romans, Greeks, and Phrygians. But the Seleucid kings had settled many Jews throughout this area, and like most of the larger towns of Asia Minor, it too had its Jewish community.

13:14b–20a / On the Sabbath, Paul and Barnabas **entered the synagogue and sat down** (v. 14). This need not have been their first Sabbath in Antioch, so they could have been known by now to the officials, though it is not impossible that strangers should be invited to speak (generally a synagogue had only one "official," but to have more than one was not unknown). At all events, they were now invited to speak to the people (v. 15; cf. Luke 4:16–30). As soon as the Scriptures had been read, Paul rose to accept the invitation (the practice in Palestine was to sit, cf. Luke 4:20; but here, apparently, it was to stand). The motion with the hand was a customary gesture by which speakers gained their hearers' attention (v. 16; cf. 12:17; 19:33; 21:40; 26:1). The audience on this occasion included both Jews and God-fearers, that is, interested Gentiles (see note on 6:5). Addressing them separately, Paul called the Jews "Israelites" (see note on 1:16), as befitting the outline of Israel's history he was about to give. His purpose was in part to appeal to national pride, and so he spoke of their election— God chose "this people of Israel" (v. 17)—and of how God had made them **prosper** (lit., "had exalted" them, i.e., raised them out of nothing to become great in numbers and strength; cf. Exod. 1:7, 9) **during their stay in Egypt**. From Egypt he had brought them out with **mighty power** (v. 17, lit., "with his arm"; cf. "with his hand," 4:28) and, if we accept the variant reading of verse 18, had "carried them in the desert as a father his children," which better suits the tone of this speech than the reading adopted by NIV (the variant texts differ by only one letter). So God had brought them into Canaan where he had destroyed ("brought down"; cf. Luke 1:52) the seven nations that were in the land (Deut. 7:1) and had given the land to his people. **All this took about 450 years** (v. 20). This figure is apparently reckoned from the end of the patriarchal age—four hundred years in Egypt (cf. 7:6), forty years in the desert, and ten years in conquering Canaan. It will be noticed that Paul regarded the land as effectively theirs long before they had actually gained possession, for "he who promised is faithful" (Heb. 10:23).

13:20b–23 / God had met the continuing needs of his people by giving them judges and, in Samuel's day when they had asked for a king, by giving them **Saul . . . who ruled forty years** (v. 21). This period of Saul's rule is not mentioned in the Old Testament, but Josephus expressly states that it was forty years

(*Antiquities* 6.378, but cf. 10.143), and this is not unreasonable, since Ishbosheth was forty years old when he succeeded his father (2 Sam. 2:10). Saul does not usually figure in these historical surveys. His mention, then, may reflect the preacher's personal interest in a king whose name he bore and whose tribe was his own (cf. Phil. 3:5). But Paul falls back into line by culminating his history with David. David's importance was that he prefigured the Messiah, and Paul made this point (in effect) by a composite quotation of Psalm 89:20, **I have found David**; 1 Samuel 13:14, **a man after my own heart**; and possibly Isaiah 44:28, **he will do everything I want him to do** (a description in the first instance of Cyrus, who is there called "messiah"). This last ascription, how ever, has been questioned by M. Wilcox, who argues that the words are not from Isaiah at all, but from the Targum of 1 Samuel 13:14, which replaces the phrase "a man after his own heart," found in both the MT and the LXX, with words that could be rendered "a man who does [or will do] his will" (pp. 21ff.). If Wilcox is right, it would appear that the quotation was made by someone familiar with the Aramaic version, though the sermon itself was probably delivered in Greek.

Not only was David a type of the Messiah, he was the Messiah's progenitor, as God had said he would be. The promise had been that a line of kings of his own house would succeed him (2 Sam. 7:12–16; etc.; see disc. on 2:30). But Paul, like Peter, interpreted the singular as one king in particular, Jesus, whom he called **the Savior** (v. 23). Here too, Paul followed Peter in his use of this title (see disc. on 5:31), though in this case it may have been suggested by Psalm 89, which speaks of God as "the Rock my Savior" (Ps. 89:26). In any case, that psalm reminds us that though human deliverers are sometimes called saviors (cf., e.g., Judg. 3:9, 15), that title belongs especially to God. It was almost certainly in that divine sense that Paul used it of Jesus.

13:24–25 / But before Jesus there was John the Baptist (cf. 1:22; 10:37). Doubtless something of John's ministry was known in Antioch, but the preacher recalled its salient points, mentioning his call to Israel to turn from their sins and his "baptism of repentance" that had accompanied that call (see disc. on 19:4). But chiefly he spoke of John as a witness. The Baptist had firmly denied that he was the Coming One (cf. John 1:20, 26f.; 3:27ff.) and instead had pointed the people to Jesus. Paul would now do the same.

13:26-31 / The second half of the speech is prefaced by a more personal form of address. Paul calls the Antiochenes his **brothers**. As before, he distinguished between Jews and Gentiles, though both may be included in the address "men, brothers" (v. 26; see note on 1:16). Certainly the announcement was made to both that "the message of this salvation" (i.e., the salvation intimated by John) had been sent to them (v. 26). The Greek has, "sent out," referring perhaps to its issuing from Jerusalem, the place of its first proclamation, though it could mean its coming out from God as its author (cf. Gal. 4:4, 6). One catches a note of wonder that this should have happened in their own generation (cf. 2:29; 3:25). But there was a dark side to the story. The Savior had been put to death in Jerusalem. Again like Peter (3:17), Paul, on the one hand, seems to offer some palliation of guilt for this crime on the grounds that the people who lived in Jerusalem, and even their leaders, **did not recognize Jesus** as the Savior, nor did they understand **the words of the prophets** (v. 27; cf. 14:16; 17:30; John 8:19; 1 Cor. 2:8; 1 Tim. 1:13). On the other hand, verse 28 makes it clear that he did not excuse them altogether, and his words carry a note of warning. The Antiochenes should not do (in effect) as those others had done who, **though they found no proper ground for a death sentence,** had still contrived to put Jesus to death (v. 28; cf. the similar wording of Pilate's declaration, Luke 23:22). Notice how little mention is made of the part played by the Romans in all this. (Remember, Antioch was a Roman colony! But see also the Introduction for Luke's purpose in writing.) Such blame as Paul apportioned was laid to the Jews.

The last clause of verse 29 appears to have the same Jewish leaders who put Jesus to death taking him **down** again **from the tree** (see disc. on 5:30; cf. Gal. 3:13) and laying him in the grave. Taken literally, this agrees with the apocryphal Gospel of Peter 6:21-24, though from the canonical Gospels we know that it was his friends, not his enemies, who performed this last service. And yet two of his friends were members of the Sanhedrin (Luke 23:50f.; John 7:50ff.; 19:38ff.). Was this what Paul meant? He was certainly acquainted with more than the bare facts of the passion narrative (cf., e.g., 1 Cor. 11:23) and may have been aware of all of these details. Or was he here simply speaking in general terms? In any case, the important point is that in putting Jesus to death these people had unwittingly **carried out all that was written about him** (v. 29; cf. 2:23; for particular scriptures, see 4:11 and

8:32f.). But God had **raised him from the dead**—the familiar contrast between the human antipathy toward Jesus and his divine vindication (v. 30; cf. 2:24, 32; 3:15; 4:10; 5:30f.; 10:40). And his resurrection could be verified, for Jesus had appeared ("who had appeared"; see note on 4:10) to his followers over a span of **many days** (v. 31). These were the same people who **had traveled with him from Galilee to Jerusalem** and were therefore well qualified to be his witnesses, as they were to that day (v. 31; cf. 10:39–42). Paul did not mention the ascension, but it is implied in Jesus' being no longer present for people to see for themselves.

13:32–37 / Neither did Paul say anything of Jesus' appearance to him, perhaps because the circumstances were different and he had not followed Jesus as the others had done or seen him die. So instead of including himself among the witnesses, he presented himself as an evangelist (v. 32; cf. 1 Cor. 15:11). The Good News concerned the Messiah whom God had promised to their fathers and had now sent (cf. 26:6; Rom. 15:8). It was addressed especially to Jews—**us, their** (i.e., the ancestors') **children**—though Paul may have intended to include with them those Gentiles who worshiped God, looking on them as the "spiritual descendants" of Abraham (cf. Rom. 4:11). The focal point of the Good News was the resurrection of Jesus, and in this connection Paul cited the words of the Second Psalm. For the use of this psalm as a testimonium, see the discussion on 4:26. By way of commentary on the psalm, two further passages are adduced: Isaiah 55:3 (slightly modified) and Psalm 16:10, introduced by Paul declaring that in raising Jesus it was God's intention that he should **not . . . decay** (v. 34). This language anticipates that of the psalm in the next verse. The preacher's purpose in quoting these passages was to show that blessing had flowed to others from the resurrection of Jesus (**I will give you** [plural], v. 34; see disc. on 4:2). All the quotations are from the LXX (in any case Paul was presumably preaching in Greek), and this explains the connection between Isaiah 55:3 and Psalm 16:10. The word rendered **holy** in the Isaiah citation (v. 34, lit., "the holy things") reappears in the Psalms quote as the **Holy One** (v. 35). Thus, the two verses are linked by a piece of common vocabulary. But this coincidence is then made to express a relationship of cause and effect between the two. Verse 35 is introduced by a causal conjunction (Gk. *dioti*) from which the reader is expected to understand that the blessings that God had promised to David have been given to others "because" of the resurrection. That is, the resurrection of Jesus is an assurance that the kingdom of God has arrived, bringing forgiveness and the restoration of all things in its train. As a lesser miracle was once said by Jesus to be a sign of forgiveness (Mark 2:10), the greater miracle of the resurrection was even more a sign of that blessing. For the Christian use of Psalm 16, see the discussion on 2:29–31. Paul's exegesis and the presuppositions on which it is based are exactly the same as Peter's. But Paul adds something of his own. In verses 36 and 37 he contrasts David's achievement, which was limited to his own generation, with the achievement of Jesus, which remains effective forever, for the **one whom God raised from the dead** did not suffer decay (v. 37, another echo of Ps. 16:10; for the construction "whom God raised," see note on 4:10).

13:38–39 / Again addressing his audience as his **brothers** (cf. v. 26), Paul now states unequivocally that forgiveness of sins is through Jesus (v. 38; cf. 2:38; 3:19; 5:31; 10:43; 26:18) and that this forgiveness is available to **everyone who believes** in him (v. 39). The Greek preposition *en* with the verb "to believe" gives the sense of "resting in," that is, of trusting the one concerned—in this case Jesus. (See also the disc. on 9:42 and 10:43.) At this point, we meet with another Pauline distinctive in the verb "to justify" (v. 39), his preferred way of expressing the idea of forgiveness. But there is a difficulty in its use in this passage. On the face of it, this verse seems to imply that within certain limits, that is, insofar as it is obeyed, the law of Moses can provide the basis of justification, as though Christ's work were simply to make up the shortfall between humanity's obedience and God's expectation. This is a very different understanding both of the law and of the work of Christ to that found in Paul's epistles (cf., e.g., 2 Cor. 3:9; Gal. 2:16, 20). But the difference between this passage and the epistles is more apparent than real. The "everyone" of verse 39 includes the Gentiles (or so it seems) without any reference to their keeping the law, and so, we conclude, this verse does affirm, with the epistles, the all-sufficiency of Christ's work.

Another difficulty, again in view of Paul's later writing (cf. Rom. 3:23–26; 5:5ff.; but cf. also Rom. 4:25; 8:34; 2 Cor. 5:15), is that justification is not specifically linked in this verse with Jesus' death, but with his whole messianic character (of which, however, death was a part; cf. vv. 26–29). But with a Jewish audience it had first to be established that Jesus was the Messiah. The resurrection was the key to that, hence the emphasis not only of this sermon but of all the early preaching in Acts. Only with their acceptance of his messiahship could the Jews be expected to come to grips with the fact and the manner of Jesus' death. For most, however, his crucifixion remained an insuperable obstacle to accepting him as Messiah (cf. 1 Cor. 1:23; Gal. 6:12, 14).

13:40–41 / The sermon ended with an appeal to awaken every conscience (cf. 2:40; 3:23; 17:31). Paul had spoken of "everyone who believes" (v. 39). He now issued a warning to everyone who did not. It is expressed in the words of Habakkuk 1:5, where the prophet speaks of the people's failure to recognize what was happening in their day (the rise of Babylon) as God's doing. Similarly God was involved in the Jesus event, and it was inviting disaster not to recognize this. Again the quotation is from the LXX, which, with its reading **Look, you scoffers!** (v. 41) for the Hebrew "keep watching the nations," lent itself particularly well to Paul's purpose, as did the additional words **and perish,** which may be inferred from the Hebrew but are not expressed in the Hebrew text.

13:42–43 / Interest was aroused, and as Paul and Barnabas were leaving the synagogue **the people invited them to speak further about these things on the next Sabbath** (v. 42). It is not clear in the Greek who did the inviting. It may have been either the people or the officials; no subject is expressed. Nor is it certain that the invitation was for the following Sabbath, though this is the most likely meaning. The Greek has a phrase that could mean that they were invited to speak "between Sabbaths," that is, during the week. At a later time it was customary to read a portion of the law in the synagogue on "Mondays" and "Thursdays." If this was already the custom in Antioch of Pisidia, the invitation may have been to one of these meetings (cf. 17:11). Verse 44 does not necessarily rule this out. But some were not prepared to wait and followed the two missionaries from this meeting to hear more at once. These included Jews and Gentiles (see note on 6:5 on their description as **devout converts**). Paul and Barnabas urged these people **to continue in the grace of God** (v. 43; cf. 11:23). Does this mean that they were already persuaded that Jesus was the Messiah? That gives the best sense, though it could mean that having known something of God's grace (say, through the history of their people) they were now to believe in Jesus as its latest and greatest expression. Grace was a theme on which Paul loved to dwell (cf. 14:3; 20:24, 32).

13:44–48 / News of the new teaching spread throughout the city, thanks, no doubt, to the Gentiles who had heard Paul in the synagogue, and **the next Sabbath almost the whole city gathered to hear the word of the Lord** (v. 44). This influx filled the Jews with **jealousy** (v. 45). This could mean that they resented the success of the missionaries. A more likely meaning, however, is that they were jealous of their own privileged position (cf. v. 17). All the old ingrained animosities were aroused. They simply could not accept a teaching that opened such floodgates. For themselves and their adherents they could accept a message as God-sent and tolerate some change in their teaching and practice, but they could not endure that the Gentiles should be made equal with God's ancient people. Thus "they spoke against what Paul was saying and insulted . . . " (v. 45, so the Greek; cf. 18:6). Whom they insulted is left unexpressed. It may have been Paul or it may have been the subject of Paul's preaching; they may, perhaps, have denied that Jesus was the Christ (see disc. on vv. 38f.).

On the other hand, the Gentiles were clearly enthusiastic about what they had heard (v. 48), which seemed to put beyond any question in the minds of the two missionaries that the Gentiles were intended by God for "the light of the gospel of the glory of Christ" (2 Cor. 4:4). It had been Israel's calling to bring that light to such people, but Israel, as represented by the synagogue in Pisidian Antioch, had declined that role (the same verb "to reject" is found both here and in Rom. 11:1, 2), and it had passed instead to the church. This perception is expressed in terms of Isaiah 49:6 (slightly shortened), from the second of the Servant Songs. The original meaning of the Servant is uncertain, but that he denotes Israel is at least the oldest interpretation for which literary evidence can be found (see disc. on 8:32–35, also the note on 3:13). This is the interpretation adopted by Paul, except that he applies it to the church. They were to be **a light for the Gentiles** (v. 47). That one Servant Song should be interpreted thus and another, the last, of the Messiah (see disc. on 8:32–35 and notes) may seem odd, but the Jewish (and Christian) exegete felt no obligation to be consistent in the interpretation of Scripture.

It had been necessary, Paul and Barnabas declared, that the word of God should be spoken first to the Jews (v. 46), for the promise had been to them; and in any case, this had been the pattern laid down by Jesus himself (Matt. 10:5; Acts 1:8; cf. Rom. 1:16; 2:9f; 11:11). But the Jews had forfeited their privileged position (cf. Matt. 22:8). They had, in fact, passed judgment upon themselves, putting themselves out of the way of eternal life (the life of the age to come, i.e., the kingdom of God; see note on 1:3 and 2:17). The word of God would henceforth be preached to the Gentiles. This point is repeated with great emphasis at the end of the book in 28:25–28 (cf. Eph. 2:11–22). Barnabas agreed with Paul and both spoke of the matter, **boldly** (v. 46), in view of the evident hostility of their audience (see disc. on 4:13).

This was a decisive step in the new direction in which God was taking his church, and for Paul it was perhaps his "coming of age" as an apostle to the Gentiles. He had been told at the beginning that he would make God known to the Gentiles (9:15), and events at Antioch had finally established him in that role. However, his commission had also included preaching to the people of Israel, and it remained his heart's desire that all Israel should be saved (Rom. 9:1–3, 10.1). Never did he cease to identify himself with them. Always in every place that he went he would go first to the Jews, and when one synagogue turned him out he would go to another (cf. 18:6; 19:9). But there was no longer now any question that he would also go to the Gentiles. There was a good response from the Gentiles on this occasion (probably God-fearers for the most part), **and all who were appointed for eternal life believed** (v. 48). The idea of appointment in this verse is not meant in a restrictive sense. The thought is not of God limiting salvation to the few, but of extending it to the many, in contrast to the exclusiveness of the Jews. And of course this divine choice did not obviate the need for personal faith. Indeed, some take the verb to be in the middle voice, not the passive, and render, "as many as had set themselves [by their response to the Spirit's prompting] for eternal life became believers."

13:49–52 / As a Roman colony, Antioch would have been the natural administrative center of the *regio* called the Phrygian (cf. 14:6; 16:6; 18:23 for other regions within the province; see Ramsay, *Paul*, pp. 102–4, 109–12, and the disc. on 16:12 for the *regiones* of Macedonia), and the strategy (if such it was) of planting the church in such a center clearly paid off, for **the word of the Lord spread through the whole region**, that is, the number of believers increased. Seeing this, the Jews set about inciting a more general opposition by enlisting the aid of **the God-fearing women of high standing and the leading men of the city** (v. 50). In Phrygia women enjoyed considerable prestige and sometimes even occupied official positions. But these particular women were also adherents of the synagogue, and it may have been through them that the leading men, possibly their husbands, were drawn into the matter. (For the similar status and influence of Macedonian women, see note on 16:13. For the attraction of Judaism to women in general, see Josephus, *War* 2.559–561; Strabo, *Geography* 7.2, and Juvenal, *Satires* 6.542.) The upshot was that **they stirred up persecution against Paul and Barnabas, and expelled them from their region** (v. 50). "The world does not remain passive when God makes his assault upon it, but it fights back in its own way" (Krodel, p. 53). From the decisiveness of the action, it is not unlikely that the **leading men of the city** included the magistrates, the *duumviri*. We may take it for granted that Roman legal practice prevailed in Antioch (as indeed in Lystra and possibly Iconium; see disc. on 14:1-7 and 8–20). In accordance with this practice, and in the interests of peace and good order, the magistrates could impose a temporary exile (though not summarily in the case of a Roman citizen, but Paul does not appear to have asserted his rights). Magistrates were usually appointed annually, and it would be unwise to return from such an exile at least until the magistrate concerned had completed his year.

The missionaries responded to this treatment by performing an action that would have been meaningful, at least to the Jews—**they shook the dust from their feet in protest against them** (v. 51). Strict Jews performed this symbolic action on entering the Holy Land from abroad, lest the land be contaminated with the dust of profane places. By doing it now against the Jews of Pisidian Antioch, they declared them in effect to be no better than the pagans among whom they lived; these Jews were profane and no longer part of true Israel (cf. 18:6; 22:22f.; Neh. 5:13; Luke 9:5; 10:11). With this, Paul and Barnabas set out along the road to the southeast that would bring them to Iconium, about one hundred miles distant. Meanwhile their fate did not dampen the enthusiasm of the disciples whom they left behind. As often, Luke brings his account to a close on a note of joy (see disc. on 3:8), but in verse 52, as nowhere else, he explicitly associates this joy with its author, **the Holy Spirit**. He mentions also its grounds. These were twofold: the inclusion of the Gentiles in the blessing of eternal life (v. 48) and the spread of this Good News throughout the region. It was only right, after all, that what brought joy to God in heaven should bring joy to his people on earth (cf. Luke 15:7, 10, 23).

Additional Notes §34

13:14 / **From Perga they went on to Pisidian Antioch**: In terms of the current political divisions, this journey took them from Pamphylia into the province of Galatia. The name Galatia derives from the Gauls, who not only invaded central and western Europe in the fourth and third centuries B.C., but also moved into and dominated Asia Minor. In the latter part of the third century, they were driven out of the rich cities of the western coast by Attalus I of Pergamum into the high plateaus of the interior where, though never a majority, they gained the upper hand and ruled over the more numerous tribes of the Phrygians and Cappadocians. Their chief cities were Tavium, Pessinus, and Ancyra (Ankara). During the Roman civil wars of the first century B.C., the Galatian prince Amyntas acquired a large domain that, by favor of Augustus, he was allowed to retain. This "kingdom of Galatia" comprised, besides Galatia proper, parts of Phrygia, Lycaonia, Isauria, Pisidia, Pamphylia, and western Cilicia. In 25 B.C., Amyntas' kingdom passed into the hands of the Romans. The administration of some of the territories he had acquired was subject to fluctuation (by the mid 40s western Cilicia, with part of Lycaonia, belonged to the kingdom of Antiochus of Commagene), but by and large the area of Amyntas' dominion comprised the Roman province of Galatia (see also note on 2:9f.).

They entered the synagogue: The synagogue in the Diaspora necessarily played a far more important part in Jewish life than did the synagogue in Judea. It was the general meetinghouse and community hub, the schoolhouse, the courthouse, and the archive, as well as the locus of religious education and worship. It was to the synagogue that Paul and his colleagues went whenever they came to a new town (see disc. on 9:20). And the synagogue provided not only a convenient point of contact for the Christian missionary but an audience prepared for the message. There were three more or less distinct groups of people to be found there: Jews by birth, proselytes, and God-fearers (see note on 6:5). The latter have been described as a "providentially prepared bridgehead into the Gentile world," for they were an informed audience, familiar with the Scriptures and the messianic hope of the Jews, but at the same time profoundly aware that they were themselves excluded from that hope as long as they remained as they were. These God-fearers "always remained second-class citizens. Proselytes were buried in Jewish cemeteries in Jerusalem and Rome and elsewhere . . . but not 'God-fearers.' From an official point of view, despite their visits to synagogue worship and their partial observance of the law, the 'God-fearers' continued to be regarded as Gentiles, unless they went over to Judaism completely through circumcision and ritual baptism" (Hengel, *Acts*, p. 89). It is hardly surprising, then, that when they were told that "the messianic hope had come alive in Jesus, that in him the old distinction between Jew and Gentile had been abolished, that the fullest blessings of God's saving grace were as readily available to Gentiles as to Jews," many of this class gladly embraced that Good News (Bruce, *History*, pp. 276f.). They formed the nucleus of many of the early Christian congregations (along with a scattering of Jews), and through them the church had entry into the Gentile world that lay beyond the ambit of the synagogue.

13:15 / After the reading from the Law and the Prophets: Luke's writings are our only authority for the manner in which the services of the synagogue were conducted at this time (cf. Luke 4:16). But if later custom is any guide, we can add to the little he tells us that the service began with the Shema (covering Deut. 6:4–9; 11:13–21; Num. 15:37–41), which was followed by prayers (m. *Megillah* 4.3) and two readings: one from the Law, the other from the Prophets. The second reading was expounded and an exhortation drawn from it (cf. Luke 4:17ff.). The service ended with a blessing. For attempts to deduce from Paul's allusions what readings were set for that day in the synagogue, see Ramsay, *Paul*, p. 100; J. W. Bowker, "Speeches in Acts; A Study in Proem and Yelammedenu Form," *NTS* 14 (1967–68), pp. 96–111; and E. E. Ellis, p. 200.

13:33 / You are my Son: In the exposition, we have adopted the view that Psalm 2:7 is quoted with reference to the resurrection of Jesus. It is not certain, however, that this is the case. The text says nothing of Jesus being raised to life; it speaks only of his being "raised up," and it is possible that the reference is simply to his coming as the Messiah (the same verb, *anistanai*, is used in this general sense in 3:22; 7:37; cf. Deut. 18:15). Paul, however, does refer this verse to the resurrection in Romans 1:4 (cf. also Heb. 1:5), and this has determined our interpretation of the present passage, together with the resurrection's being always central to the case that Paul was arguing, namely, that Jesus is the Messiah. B. Lindars holds that Psalm 2:7 was first used by the Christians as a testimonium of the resurrection, and that its application to the earlier events of Jesus' life was a secondary development (pp. 138–44). It is sometimes argued that this verse gave rise to the belief that Jesus was adopted by God as his Son at the resurrection and that only later did Christians believe that he was God's Son during his earthly life. It is more likely, however, that their prior conviction that he was divine sent the first Christians searching for texts such as this and not that the texts shaped their belief.

13:39 / Justified from everything you could not be justified from by the law of Moses: It is noteworthy that the interpretation of this verse outlined in the exposition of verse 39 above, which on balance we have rejected, corresponds broadly to the Jewish doctrine of salvation, except for the role of Christ. Basic to that doctrine was the belief that righteousness was determined by obedience to the law. Conformity to the law was righteousness; disobedience was sin. But perfect obedience was not expected. The Jews had no conception of sinless perfection. They recognized that within the heart were two impulses, one good, the other evil. The righteous person was the one who nurtured the good impulse and restrained the evil so that in the end his or her good deeds outweighed the bad. But because of the impulse to evil, there was always the possibility that a person might "fall short of the glory of God," and in this eventuality repentance and God's mercy came into play. The relationship between mercy and justice was never clearly defined in Judaism, but for all that, repentance played a large part in Jewish thought; so much so that G. F. Moore calls it "the Jewish doctrine of salvation" (*Judaism*, vol. 1, pp. 114, 117, 500). Repentance and forgiveness bridged the gap created by any shortfall in the Jew's good works, but insofar as he or she was able to keep the law, there was no need of grace. There are those who say that this was essentially the doctrine that Paul was preaching, except that for him Jesus was now the focus of God's grace and the means whereby it was extended to sinners. But even if Paul was still working within this frame of reference, he had come far enough toward his later understanding to perceive that the demands of the law were simply beyond the capabilities of sinners, for he speaks of those things from which the law was "unable" to justify. The work of Jesus was not merely a safeguard against possible failure, but a gracious provision for human beings who had failed.

§35 In Iconium (Acts 14:1–7)

The pattern of ministry exemplified in the previous section is repeated in this. The story is told only briefly, since the course of events in Iconium was much as it had been in Pisidian Antioch, the one significant difference being that, despite persecution, Paul and Barnabas remained in the city until their very lives were in danger. Luke has expressed this somewhat awkwardly (see vv. 2 and 3)—a sign perhaps of "a clumsily retained page from a logbook" (Haenchen, p. 423, who, however, rejects this view).

14:1 / Iconium was built on the edge of a high plateau overlooking plains made productive by streams from the Pisidian mountains. It was a center for agriculture, and the prosperity it drew from this was enhanced by its position at the junction of several roads (see disc. on 16:6). Iconium had been a Phrygian settlement, and it would appear that the people still regarded themselves as Phrygian, though the city was apparently grouped with the Lycaonian cities of Lystra and Derbe in one of the administrative regions of the province. In verse 6 Luke shows that he is aware of a distinction between Iconium and the others. Under the Romans its fame and prestige grew. It was honored by the emperor, who conferred on it the title Claudiconium. In the late empire, when the province of Galatia was divided, Iconium became the capital of Lycaonia.

The hostility of the Jews that had forced Paul and Barnabas to leave Antioch did not deter them from following the same procedure here as they had in that city. They **went as usual into the Jewish synagogue**, first, because the pattern "first the Jews and also the Gentiles" was a divine necessity (see disc. on 13:46) and, second, because in practical terms it made good sense (see disc. on 9:20 and note on 13:14). As a result of their preaching many believed, both of the Jews and of the Gentiles (lit. "Greeks") who (as we suppose) frequented the synagogue.

14:2–4 / Luke characterizes their ministry as **speaking boldly for the Lord** (v. 3; see disc. on 4:13). The Greek preposition in this phrase (*epi*) implies two things: that the lordship of Jesus was their theme and that he (as the Lord) was their strength and stay. Hence their boldness and his confirmation of what they said **by enabling them to do miraculous signs and wonders** (v. 3, lit. "by granting signs and wonders to happen through their hands"; see notes on 2:22 and 5:12). This notice provides a context for the particular miracle around which the events in Lystra revolved (14:8-20) and is corroborated by Paul's own reference in Galatians (3:5). The phrase **the message of his grace** (v. 3) occurs again in 20:32 as a description of the gospel (cf. also 13:43). But again there were **Jews who refused to believe** (v. 2). Indeed, the expression may be stronger than this, including the thought of "rebellion." They stirred up opposition, and eventually the whole city became aware of the hostility of the Jews toward the Christians and became divided in its support of the protagonists. The very difficulty of this situation may have kept Paul and Barnabas in Iconium longer than they would otherwise have stayed. In verse 4, for the first time, Paul and Barnabas are called **apostles**, and only again in verse 14.

14:5-7 / A critical point was reached in an already tense situation when it was learned that the Jews and their leaders were planning, in concert with **the Gentiles**, to resort to physical violence (v. 5). So far, it seems, nothing more than abuse had been thrown at the apostles, and only the Jews had been involved (but see notes on vv. 2f.). Some commentators take the phrase **with their leaders** to mean that the magistrates had been drawn into the affair; but **their** is more likely to refer to their own Jewish leaders, and the reference to stoning (intended perhaps as a punishment for blasphemy) bears this out. In short, the Jews had apparently resorted not to the courts (cf. 18:13), but the expedient of inciting mob violence against the Christians (cf. 17:5). The situation was now dangerous in the extreme, and nothing was to be gained by the two missionaries staying there any longer. They fled, therefore, to Lystra and Derbe (v. 6; cf. Matt. 10:23). Once there, they did not confine their work to the two towns, but **continued to preach the good news** throughout the Lycaonian region of the province (vv. 6, 7).

Additional Notes §35

14:1 / **As usual**: NIV is probably right to interpret this as their doing the same as they had in Antioch by going first to the synagogue, though for this meaning a different expression is used in 17:2. The alternative is to understand it as indicating that Paul and Barnabas entered the synagogue "at the same time," making the point that their ministry was a joint one.

14:2-3 / The awkwardness of these verses is smoothed out in the Western text: "But the chiefs of the synagogue and the ruler [of Iconium] raised persecution and made the minds of the Gentiles hostile to the brothers. But the Lord soon gave peace" (v. 2). The last clause prepares the way for v. 3. The Western text agrees with other texts in having a persecution in v. 5; thus there are two persecutions in the Western text. The text of Codex Vaticanus and its allies, reflected in NIV, has the more difficult reading, with only one attack of fairly long duration and mounting intensity.

§36   In Lystra and Derbe (Acts 14:8–20)

It would appear that there was no synagogue in Lystra. The fact, then, that Paul and Barnabas preached in this city, even if they had not gone there expressly for this purpose, marks yet another important departure for the church. Moreover, since there was no audience prepared for their message (see note on 13:14), a new approach in its presentation was called for. Something of what this was is evident in these verses, which include a brief impromptu speech addressed to a pagan audience. The speech is incomplete as a statement of the gospel, for it lacks any mention of the cross and the resurrection of Jesus. It is more a pre-amble to the gospel, laying a foundation in a precise statement of natural theology.

In contrast with the previous section, these verses present a narrative rich in detail, and it is tempting to think that this was due to Timothy's eyewitness account, for he was probably a native of Lystra (see disc. on 16:1). That part of the story that concerns the healing of a lame man has some features in common with the miracle in 3:1–10. This need not concern us. In describing similar miracles, the same author is likely to use some of the same expressions. There is sufficient difference of detail to leave us in no doubt that the stories are different, though the inclusion of the one may have been determined by the other, Luke wanting to demonstrate that Paul was no less effective an apostle than Peter (cf. also 8:9ff. and 13:6ff.). As for its sequel, the story of the apostles' identification with the gods, this is far too striking for Luke to have invented, whereas the reference to Paul's being stoned appears to be corroborated by Paul himself.

14:8–10 / Lystra lay in a fertile valley some twenty miles southwest of Iconium. Not long before this it had formed part of a small principality ruled from Derbe by a chieftain named An-tipater, who was on good terms with Cicero (*Ad Familiares* 13.73), though others spoke of him as "the robber." Antipater was ousted from his territory by Amyntas, after whose death Lystra and Derbe were incorporated in the Roman province of Galatia. Lystra was singled out by Augustus as the site for a Roman colony to be, like Antioch, a bulwark against the robber clans of the Pisidian mountains. The town therefore received some Roman settlers. There were also the usual Greeks. But for the most part its population was Lycaonian (as was Derbe's also), and despite its colonial status, it seems to have remained a somewhat rustic outpost.

A handful of Jews may also have been found in the town (see disc. on 16:1), but no mention is made of a synagogue; nor have the remains of one ever been found. Determined, nevertheless, to preach the gospel, the missionaries had to try something new. What they needed was a place of public concourse, and the forum was the obvious place. And for the same reason— that it was the meeting and market place of the town—a beggar would also have chosen the forum as his regular pitch. So it was that the lame man of this story was "sitting in his customary place" (the force of the Greek) when Paul noticed him. He may have already heard the missionaries on several occasions, but now he caught the apostle's eye. Paul saw evidence of faith—"the man's heart shone in his face"—and he spoke the healing word (cf. 3:4, 6). Immediately **the man jumped up** (aorist tense) **and began to walk** (imperfect tense; v. 10; see disc. on 3:8). Luke comments that the man **was lame from birth and had never walked** (v. 8; cf. 3:2).

14:11–14 / It was not something done in a corner. In fact, Paul seems to have shouted his command to the lame man at the top of his voice (v. 10). A large number of the townsfolk were therefore witnesses to the miracle. Their reaction was immediate and dramatic (cf. 3:9f.). They were at least a bilingual people, understanding and speaking Greek (the language in which Paul and Barnabas must have preached) in addition to their native tongue, with perhaps some knowledge of Latin. But in their excitement they now **shouted in the Lycaonian language**, acclaiming Paul and Barnabas as gods. Verses 11 and 12 have a change of tense similar to that noted in verse 10, only not so clearly shown in the English. Literally, "they lifted up their voice" with a sudden outburst (aorist) and then went on to devise names for the two, which they used of them repeatedly (imperfect). Barnabas they identified with **Zeus**, the head of the Greek pantheon, Paul with **Hermes**, his messenger, **because he was the chief speaker** (v. 12;

cf. Gal. 4:14; see Hanson, p. 148, for other instances of this kind of thing). The Lycaonians had probably long since syncretized their own gods with those of Greece. It has been objected that Hermes was the messenger of Zeus, not his spokesman. But this is mere quibbling. If the two gods were thought of together, Hermes would naturally be thought of as spokesman. He was, after all, the patron of orators. That the people reacted as they did is entirely consonant with what we know of their beliefs, bearing in mind that Lystra was no sophisticated metropolis. Ovid tells how Jupiter and Mercury (the Latin counterparts of Zeus and Hermes) once visited an aged couple, Philemon and Baucis, in the neighboring district of Phrygia (*Metamorphoses* 8.611ff.). On the basis of this legend, the people of Phrygia and Lycaonia were wont to make pilgrimages to the place of this supposed visit, and archaeological evidence shows that the cults of the two gods flourished side by side throughout this region until as late as the third century A.D. The apostles, of course, would have understood nothing of what the Lycaonians were saying and would have learned only later of the names they had given them.

We can only guess at some of the locations in this story and must assume certain lapses of time. Perhaps, then, Paul and Barnabas had returned to their lodging when news reached them that the priest of Zeus, **whose temple was just outside the city** as the protecting deity (v. 13), was about to offer bulls to them in sacrifice (cf. Ovid, *Metamorphoses* 4.755; Persius, *Satires* 2.44). The **wreaths** were those used to garland the victims and perhaps also to adorn the priest, the altar, and the attendants (cf. Virgil, *Aeneid* 5.366; Euripides, *Heracles* 529). It is not clear in the Greek to which gate the sacrificial procession was heading. Some see here a reference to the gate of the town, others to the atrium of the house in which the apostles were staying (cf. 10:17; 12:13). The latter is argued on the grounds that when Barnabas and Paul (the order of their names is dictated by the reference to Zeus and Hermes; see disc. on 13:9) realized what was happening they **rushed out** [of the house] **into the crowd**. But the expression could mean equally as well that they ran out of the city, and we prefer this sense, understanding **the gate** to have been that of the temple. So then, it was to the temple they ran, tearing their clothes in token of their distress (cf. Gen. 37:29, 34; Josh. 7:6; Judith 14:16f.; Matt. 26:65) and shouting to the people as they forced their way through the crowd.

14:15–18 / Both Paul and Barnabas spoke (cf. v. 18), but what we have here is probably the gist of what Paul said. His theme was that to worship the creature (**We too are only men, human like you,** v. 15) was inexcusable, for the creature was only evidence of the creator, who alone deserved to be honored. They had come, he said, **bringing you good news** concerning **the living God** who manifests his life in creation (v. 15; cf. 4:24; 17:24 citing Exod. 20:11)—a manifestation to which Paul would naturally appeal before such an audience. With Jews (or God-fearers) the message began with the Scriptures (revealed theology) and was the announcement that the Scriptures had been fulfilled. But with these Gentiles, it began with natural theology and was concerned with the basic proposition that there is but one God. This God is also the God of history, who, until now, had **let all nations go their own way** (v. 16), that is, without summoning them as he did now to turn from **these worthless things** to himself (v. 15). The reference may have been to idols in general (cf. Jer. 2:5), or Paul may have been pointing as he spoke to the preparations being made even then for the sacrifice. The implication seems to be that their ignorance of God in the past was not culpable (see disc. on 3:17; 13:26; cf. 17:30f.), though this would no longer be so now that the Good News had been announced. Paul takes a much harder line in Romans 1:18ff., but his purpose there was a different one (in any case, cf. Rom. 3:25f.).

To turn . . . to . . . God is to believe in God (v. 15; see disc. on 9:42). The language here is remarkably like that of 1 Thessalonians 1:9, which describes how the Macedonians had "turned to God from idols to serve the living and true God." This was probably a common way of expressing Gentile conversion, but what is missing here and is found in Thessalonians is the essentially Christian component of that description: "and to wait for his Son from heaven, whom he raised from the dead—Jesus, who rescues us from the coming wrath." Paul must have included this in his preaching at Lystra at some time or other (though perhaps not on this occasion), for disciples were made (cf. vv. 20, 21), but Luke has seen fit not to report it. His readers had already heard the gospel in the earlier speeches. Instead he reports what is distinctive to this speech, namely, Paul's argument for the existence of God.

Three "proofs" are given, in each case the tense (present participle) indicating the ongoing nature of God's activity. Each proof expands upon the other. The witness is not, as at Athens (17:27) and in Romans 2:15, to human consciousness and conscience, but simply to God's presence in nature, demonstrated, first, by showing **kindness** (v. 17). More specifically, he is shown to be present, second, by giving **rain from heaven and crops in their seasons** (v. 17). This point is seen to be the more telling, as we realize that Zeus was spoken of in precisely these terms. It has even been suggested that Paul was citing a hymn to Zeus that may have been sung on this very occasion (the words of this verse do appear to be rhythmical). Rain was regarded as a sign of divine favor, and in this speech, as in the Old Testament, God's goodness and power in giving rain and making the crops is asserted against the impotence of the gods of the heathen (see esp. Jer. 14:22; cf. also 1 Sam. 12:17; 1 Kings 18:1). As a consequence of the rain, God demonstrates his presence, third, by giving food and filling hearts with **joy** (v. 17). Joy translates the ordinary Greek word for "good cheer," often associated with wine in particular. But even if the gospel is not included in this outline, this word may have been intended to point beyond its ordinary meaning to a deeper happiness brought by a richer gift than "grain and wine" (cf. Ps. 4:7), namely, the joy that springs from knowing Jesus as Lord (cf. 2:28 where the same word is used). By these arguments, and only then with great difficulty, did Paul and Barnabas restrain the people **from sacrificing to them** (v. 18).

14:19-20 / Their work in Lystra resulted in a little band of believers being gathered. But the missionaries were not left to go about their business in peace. The antagonism of the Jews of Antioch and Iconium pursued them even to this remote spot (for some, a journey of over a hundred miles), where they again stirred up trouble (see 13:50; 14:2, 5; also 17:13). It may have been easy to win the crowd to their side because the apostles had spurned their divine honors (cf. 28:6; Gal. 1:6). Nevertheless, some persuasion was needed, and this may well have been along the lines that the two men were imposters, perhaps even that their power stemmed from some malevolent force. So, with the crowd behind them, the Jews stoned Paul, executing at last the punishment on which they had set their hearts in Iconium (v. 5). Then as a final indignity, **thinking he was dead** (v. 19), they dragged him out of the town as they might a piece of garbage, to dump him outside the gate. However, when the believers came (to bury him?), they found him alive and able to go back to the town with them. Luke has no intention of presenting this as a miracle of restoration to life (note his comment, **thinking he was dead**). Nevertheless, we may see the hand of God in his survival. Paul showed great courage in going back to the town, though it is unlikely that the magistrates had been involved, so he had nothing to fear at that level. Indeed, as a Roman citizen he had a strong case to put before them against his assailants had he wished to do so. As it was, he chose not to prosecute, but simply to leave. The next day he and Barnabas set out for Derbe (see disc. on v. 21). These experiences must have brought vividly to Paul's mind what had happened to Stephen (7:58). They certainly left an indelible impression on Paul himself (cf. 2 Tim. 3:11)—literally, if Galatians 6:17 is a reference to the scars that still remained from his time in Galatia. He mentions stoning in Second Corinthians as part of his apostolic experience.

§37 The Return to Antioch in Syria
(Acts 14:21-28)

14:21-23 / Derbe has only recently been located, some sixty miles southeast of Lystra (see B. Van Elderen, *AHG*, pp. 156ff.). The importance of this town (such as it was, but see disc. on v. 8) lay in its proximity to the border of Roman Galatia and the client kingdom of Antiochus IV of Commagene. Here the apostles **preached the good news . . . and won a large number of disciples** (v. 21, lit., "discipled many"; cf. Matt. 28:19). One of these later accompanied Paul to Jerusalem as a delegate of his church (20:4). Derbe is the only town of those we know they visited in Galatia in which they met with no persecution (cf. 2 Tim. 3:11). Perhaps winter was coming on, making conditions too difficult for the Jews to pursue them. From here it would have been possible for Paul and Barnabas to have continued eastward and to have reached Syrian Antioch by way of the Cilician Gates, though if it were late in the year the prospect of the Gates would have been daunting. But in any case, they needed to go back the way they had come for the sake of the converts. There was some risk in doing so, but by now the magistrates may have completed their office, and as long as they maintained a low profile the risk would have been minimal.

Thus Paul and Barnabas returned to Lystra, Iconium, and Antioch, strengthening the believers and encouraging them **to remain true to the faith** (v. 22; cf. 11:23). This encouragement was necessary, for these people were easily moved, and they were soon in danger of accepting "another gospel" (Gal. 1:6; 3:2; 5:1). Continuing persecution by the Jews appears to have been a factor in this (cf. Gal. 6:12). It is a question whether **the faith** means the believers' trust in the Lord or the doctrine that they held. The definite article points to the latter (cf. 6:7; 13:8; 16:5), though we cannot doubt that the missionaries spoke of the other also, teaching, moreover, that faith in Christ necessarily entails suffering (notice the **must** of verse 22; see disc. on 1:16). The **kingdom of**

God is referred to in its future sense as the ultimate goal of salvation (see note on 1:3). NIV shows this teaching about suffering and entering the kingdom as the very words of the apostles, as indeed they may have been, if they had struck a deep root in the heart of one of their hearers (why not Timothy?).

This ministry of confirmation was accompanied by a work of organization, for in each church they **appointed elders** to take care of the spiritual and temporal needs of their people (v. 23; see note on 11:30). These elders were commissioned **with prayer and fasting**, as the missionaries themselves had been (13:2, 3), and were thus commended **to the Lord** [Jesus], **in whom they had put their trust** (v. 23; cf. 20:32). For the expression "to believe into," see disc. on 10:43. The perfect tense of the verb indicates that they had sometime past come to this faith and were continuing in it (cf. 15:5; 16:34; 19:18).

14:24-28 / In verse 24 we find again that expression that suggests that Paul and Barnabas "made a missionary journey" through Pisidia (see disc. on 8:4 and 13:13 for the region)—preaching peace where the Romans were still at war. So they retraced their steps to Perga. It is impossible to say how long it had been since they had set out from the Pamphylian capital, but the time should be reckoned in years (suggestions ranging from one year to four have been made). The distances covered were not great, but much had been achieved and presumably much time spent in the process (cf. 13:49, 52; 14:1, 3, 6, 21). Little is known of the history of Perga in the Roman period. It was extensively rebuilt in the second century A.D., but the town that was visited by the apostles was much as it had been in Seleucid times. Its setting was one of great beauty, lying as it did between and upon the sides of two hills, with before it a wide valley watered by the Cestrus and behind it the Taurus Mountains. What results the missionaries had of their preaching in Perga we do not know, though Luke's silence on the matter has been taken to mean that they were not very encouraging. They appear not to have stayed long in the city before making their way across the Pamphylian plain to the port of Attalia, where they were much more likely to find a ship than in the river port (see disc. on 13:13). From here they returned to Syria.

Back in Antioch, they gathered the church and gave a full report of their doings, acknowledging that their achievement was

God's—the phrase "with them" (v. 27, so the Greek; cf. 7:9; 11:21; 15:4) means much the same as **through them**, only it expresses more their own awareness of God's presence. Their motto could have been, "Immanuel, God with us" (Matt. 1:23), for it was he who **had opened the door of faith to the Gentiles** (v. 27)—a striking coincidence with Paul's use of the same metaphor elsewhere (1 Cor. 16:9; 2 Cor. 2:12; Col. 4:3). Thus God confirmed that it was not through circumcision and the like that people would enter in and be called by his name, but simply through the door of faith in Jesus as Lord (cf. 11:18 and 20:21). In saying that the missionaries **reported** these things, Luke has used the verb in the imperfect. This may mean that the report was repeated as the two met with different groups scattered throughout the city. But the word **church** is in the singular. There may have been a number of groups meeting separately, but there was only one church. The final note is quite indefinite, but it probably does mean that they remained in Antioch for **a long time** (v. 28).

Additional Notes §37

14:22 / **We must go through many hardships**: This has sometimes been classed as a we-passage, as though Luke were including himself (see disc. on 16:10). It is better treated, however, as simply a general use of the first person—"we Christians."

14:23 / **Paul and Barnabas appointed elders**: Though the verb meant originally "to elect by show of hands," it appears as though the choice, humanly speaking, was with the apostles. But cf. Titus 1:5ff. where perhaps the same procedure is used but at least the opinion of the congregation seems to be taken into account (cf. also 1:23ff.; 6:13).

14:27 / **They gathered the church together**: For a discussion of the physical limitations imposed upon the Christians because they had to use private homes (cf. 8:3; 12:12; 16:15; 17:5; 18:7; 20:8) and for the possible social and theological results, see J. Murphy-O'Connor, *St. Paul's Corinth*, pp. 153ff.; also R. Banks, *Paul's Idea of Community*, pp. 45ff., for the makeup of these house meetings.

§38 The Council at Jerusalem (Acts 15:1–21)

The acceptance of the Gentiles into the church without the necessity of circumcision (with the implication of submission to the whole law) might seem to have been assured after the conversion of Cornelius and his friends. At that time, even in Jerusalem, the bastion of Jewish tradition, those Christians who had met to consider the matter had agreed that God had "granted even the Gentiles repentance unto life" (11:18), though they probably never dreamed that this would be anything more than an exceptional case. Since then, things had changed dramatically, and the rapid influx of Gentiles into the church in both Antioch and the cities of southern Galatia had raised again the whole question of Gentile admission or, more precisely, the terms on which they should be admitted. It was one thing to accept the occasional God-fearer into the church, someone already in sympathy with Jewish ways; it was quite another to welcome larger numbers of Gentiles who had no regard for the law and no intention of keeping it.

The point of view of the Jewish Christians deserves our understanding. As far as most of them could tell, the law remained determinative for their lives. They had no clear teaching of the Lord to the contrary (cf., e.g., Matt. 5:18; Luke 2:21; Gal. 4:4). We know now that the church (by and large) came to see that Jesus had in fact opened for us "a new and living way . . . through the curtain," that is, by his sacrifice of himself for our sins that we might "draw near to God" (Heb. 10:20ff.), but this was not seen at once or by all, and there were many at this time who continued to live by the law and saw no reason to change (cf. 21:20). It must have been with growing alarm, therefore, perhaps even with anger, fanned by the rising winds of Jewish nationalism, that some of them (Christians of Jerusalem for the most part) heard reports of what was happening in the north. The burning question for them was how those who still felt themselves bound by the law could have any dealing with those who did not. The only answer they could give was that the Gentiles must accept the "yoke" of the law (v. 10), that is, they must become Jews before they could be granted full Christian status. The matter came to a head when a number of Jewish Christians came to Antioch advocating this policy. The ensuing controversy led to the convening of a council in Jerusalem that marked the end of the matter as far as Acts was concerned, though in fact it remained a vexing question for many more years to come. The council had to weigh the two principles of liberty and obedience. The outcome was a triumph of love.

Along with others, Paul was sent by the church in Antioch to represent them at this council. This raises the question whether this was one of the two visits to Jerusalem mentioned in Galatians 1:18f. and 2:1–10. It is generally agreed that the first of these is the visit of Acts 9:26–30, but opinion is divided as to whether the second, Galatians 2:1–10, is the one described in this chapter or the famine visit of Acts 11:30. In support of the latter, it is pointed out that this is the second visit following Paul's conversion, as Galatians 2:1–10 appears to be also. It is further pointed out that Paul made the journey "by revelation" (Gal. 2:1f.) and that this could be a reference to the prophecy of Agabus in Acts 11:27f. And once this identification is made, we are then able to link the visit of "some men . . . from Judea" in Acts 15:1 with those who had come "from James" in Galatians 2:12. It is certainly easier to think of the incident described in Galatians 2:11–14 as happening before rather than after the council, since it reflects a spirit so contrary to that which marked the end of that meeting. But "from James" need only mean "from Jerusalem," and these people could have been recalcitrants who did not abide by the council's decisions. Nor was Paul in Galatians necessarily recounting all of his visits, and the kind of revelation that he had in mind was not the kind that comes by human beings but directly from God (cf. Gal. 1:1, 12).

Besides these things, there are a number of serious difficulties in identifying Galatians 2:1–10 with Acts 11:30. First, the apostles are not mentioned in the passage in Acts, whereas in Galatians Paul says that he and Barnabas met with Peter and John and James the Lord's brother. Nor can it be supposed, in light of those passages in which the elders are clearly distinguished from the apostles (e.g., 15:4, 6; 16:4), that the term "elder" is used in Acts 11:30 in a sense that includes both. Second, it is not easy to fit Titus into the visit of Acts 11:30, since Barnabas and Paul are alone mentioned as the delegates of the church in Antioch. But Titus *is* included in Galatians 2:1. Third, if the incident of Galatians 2:11–14 took place before the council, as might be supposed on this identification, we should have expected the point at issue to have been circumcision, not the dietary laws. Fourth, it is easier to think of Paul and Barnabas being confirmed in their work among the Gentiles, as they are in Galatians 2:1–10, after rather than before the "first missionary journey." As far us we know, before that journey their work in Cilicia and Syria had extended no further among the Gentiles than the synagogues of the region had already done. There is another side to this, too. If the "first missionary journey" followed instead of preceded Galatians 2:1–10, the history of Acts 13 and 14, with its narrative of the apostles' decisive turning to the Gentiles, would seem to be entirely without point. Fifth and finally, there is the chronological problem. The visit of Acts 11:30 cannot be put any later than A.D. 46, when the famine was at its height. But if Stephen met his death in the last years of Pilate's term as governor, say the mid 30s, which also fits with the evidence relating to Paul's stay in Damascus (see notes on 7:60 and 9:23ff.), even if we allow for some inclusive reckoning in Galatians, it is impossible to fit the "three years" and the "fourteen years" of that letter into the time required (Gal. 1:18; 2:1). Related to this is that in Acts 11:30 Paul was still subordinate to Barnabas, whereas this does not appear to be so in Galatians 2:1–10.

We are led, then, to the view that the visit of Galatians 2:1–10 is that of Acts 15:1–29. There is much to commend it. Both accounts have to do with the same question of circumcision and the law, involving Paul and Barnabas and the leaders of the church in Jerusalem. In both accounts they come to a common mind and adopt a common policy. Acts, it is true, describes a large gathering, and Galatians a private meeting. But in Galatians there are clearly others in the background, including the advocates of Gentile circumcision (cf. Gal. 2:4f. and Acts 15:5). The differences between the two accounts may be explained by reference to the aims of each writer. Luke was writing for the whole church and wanted simply to inform his readers of the results of the meeting. Paul was writing to a particular group about particular matters (see further disc.). There is certainly nothing contradictory in the two accounts.

Nevertheless, it may fairly be asked, If Paul wrote Galatians after the council, why were there still Christians demanding circumcision of the Gentiles (the reason for Paul's writing), contrary to the council's decision? Why did he not cite that decision in resisting that demand? But if we allow that Galatians was written at least later than the beginning of the "second missionary journey," there was no need for him to actually quote the "decrees." He could assume that his readers were already familiar with them, for he himself had delivered them to the Galatians (16:4) and needed only to remind them in broad terms of the dispute (Gal. 2:1–10) and add his own theological arguments against the necessity for anything more than faith in taking hold of salvation. That some Jewish Christians did not adhere to the agreement and had stirred up trouble in the Galatian churches is neither surprising nor grounds for supposing that the council had not yet taken place when Paul wrote.

It is also said that Peter's vacillation in Galatians 2:11–14 is incomprehensible if the council had met shortly beforehand. But the point at issue (as we have noticed already) was not circumcision, as it was at the council, but the dietary laws. And if the situation described in Galatians suggests that Peter did not draw from the council's decision the implications he should have, we can only assume that this was an instance—by no means out of character—in which he simply acted without thinking. Barnabas did the same (Gal. 2:13), and it only goes to show how strong a hold the old ways still had on these people and how hard it was for them to adopt a new way of life.

Another argument brought against the identification of Acts 15:1–29 with Galatians 2:1–10 is that the Galatians passage is only the second visit mentioned by Paul in the letter, whereas Acts 15:1–29 is Paul's third. This is a problem only if we accept the premise that Paul was enumerating his visits. But nothing compels us to do so. We should understand here why he wrote the letter. It was to show, first, that he was independent of the other apostles and, second, that they were in agreement with him regarding the gospel. And because the famine visit of Acts 11:30 had no bearing on either of these matters, he might well have omitted it. Galatians 1:20 is often appealed to in support of the proposition that Paul was recounting all his visits, but in that verse he only affirms that what he does say is the truth. Galatians 2:1–

10 may have been only the second visit of any significance for the argument of the epistle.

The question of which visit this was is not the only one raised by this chapter. Another concerns the historicity of the speeches of Peter (vv. 7–11) and James (vv. 13–21), the former because some of its language could have been Paul's (esp. v. 11; cf. 13:38ff.; Gal. 2:15f.; Eph. 2:8), the latter because the argument seems to turn on the Greek version of Amos 9:11f. and it is assumed that James would have quoted in Hebrew and spoken in Aramaic. But there is no reason why the council should not have been conducted in Greek and no reason, therefore, why James should not have quoted from the LXX. A native of Galilee would almost certainly have been bilingual from childhood. The several points of contact between his speech and the letter that bears his name is, moreover, some proof of the historicity of both. There are also points of likeness between Peter's speech and his earlier utterances, including some quite distinctive expressions, which gives us confidence that this is a genuine reminiscence of what he said. And if at times it does sound like something Paul might have said, perhaps that is how it was. Peter may have spent long hours in Paul's company before making this speech (Gal. 2:1–10) and may have picked up some of Paul's language. Of course it is always possible that Luke has allowed his own familiarity with Paul's turn of phrase to color his report of Peter's speech.

Again, there is the question of Paul's attitude to the so-called apostolic decrees. It is a fact that he makes no reference to them in his own writings, even when it would seem to have been most appropriate to have done so, as in Romans 14 and 1 Corinthians 8–10. This has led to the suggestion that the recommendations of Acts 15:20 were totally unacceptable to him, but that Luke has told it quite differently on the basis of meager evidence and in the interests of his own point of view. But against his not mentioning the decrees must be set the equally important fact that there is nothing in all of his writing to suggest that he disapproved of them. It may well have been that he simply preferred to argue his own case rather than cite the decision reached by the council. In any case, the decrees were addressed only to the church in Antioch and the province of Syria-Cilicia (see disc. on 15:32). Paul delivered them also to the churches of southern Galatia (16:4), since these were "daughter churches" of

Antioch but he may have felt it inappropriate to publish them farther afield. Nevertheless, the principle that underlay them, of consideration for the "weaker brother," is one that he taught in all the churches (cf., e.g., Rom. 14:21; 15:1–3; 1 Cor. 8:9–13), and so he could say of the council's decision: "Those men added nothing to my message" (Gal. 2:6). Nor was Paul opposed in principle to the idea of life being regulated by rules. He believed that his own teaching upheld the law (Rom. 3:31), and his epistles are full of exhortations to live by the letter no less than by the spirit of the law (cf., e.g., Rom. 13:8–10; Eph. 5:1, 3ff., 31; 6:2f.). His own practice, where it was appropriate (and probably by personal preference; see note on 26:5), was that of a Jew (cf. 16:3; 18:18; 20:6, 16; 21:26; 27:9; 1 Cor. 9:19; 11:2–16). Of course, he knew now that obedience to the law could no longer be regarded as the basis of salvation (cf. Gal. 2:15f; see disc. on Acts 13:39), but for Paul the law remained the authoritative guide to Christian living (see further the disc. on 21:24). Broadly speaking, this was the conclusion reached by the Jerusalem council, so that Luke's picture of Paul's concurrence is entirely consistent with the picture we have of Paul from his own writings.

15:1–2 / The question of Gentile admission seems to have become an issue for the church in Antioch only when **some men came down from Judea . . . and were teaching** that circumcision was necessary for salvation (see further the disc. on v. 5). Paul saw at once that a fundamental issue was at stake and, together with Barnabas, engaged in **a sharp dispute and debate with the Judeans** (v. 2, in the light of 14:27). The unity of the church was under threat, and the only solution seemed to be to **go up to Jerusalem to see the apostles and elders about this question** (v. 2), the apostles returning, perhaps, from elsewhere for this purpose (see disc. on 12:17). A number of delegates were appointed, including Paul and Barnabas **with some other believers**, a reference, perhaps, to the prophets and teachers of 13:1 and Titus, if Galatians 2:1–10 is any guide. Strict grammar would require that it was the Judeans who made the decision to send the delegates to Jerusalem. It is far more likely, however, that the local church took the decision.

15:3–5 / The delegates were **sent . . . on their way** by a party of church members (v. 3) who traveled some of the way with them, for so the expression means. This was a sign of their respect and affection for them (cf. 20:38; 21:5, 16; also Paul's being met in 28:15). Their road took them along the coast through Berytus (Beirut), Sidon, Tyre, and Ptolemais, probably to Caesarea, and thence to Jerusalem (see note on 9:31). Phoenicia had been evangelized at the same time as the church had been established in Antioch (11:19; cf. also 21:3ff., 7), so that in all of these centers, as in Samaria also (cf. 8:25), there were Christian communities to be visited and **told how the Gentiles had been converted** (v. 3). The Greek verb implies that the telling was done in some detail (it only occurs here and in 13:41), and without exception, their report brought joy to all who heard it (v. 3; see disc. on 3:8). Thus they came to Jerusalem with all the weight, as it were, of the northern churches behind them.

The Antiochenes were welcomed by the assembled church and its leaders (some commentators have the impression that this reception was more restrained) and again told the story of all that **God had done through them** (v. 4, lit., "with them"; cf. 14:27; it is "through them" in 15:12). Notice the emphasis in these reports on God's hand in the matter, with the implication that if God had blessed the work it was clearly his intention that the Gentiles should be freely admitted. Not everyone present accepted this proposition, and those who did not were quick to express their own view. Basing their teaching, perhaps, on passages such as Exodus 12:48f. and Isaiah 56:6, they declared that it was necessary (Gk. *dei*; see disc. on 1:16) to circumcise Gentiles and to charge them to keep the law. The covenant mentioned in Isaiah 56:6 was held to be that of circumcision. These advocates of circumcision **belonged to the party of the Pharisees**—the first mention of any converts from that sect other than Paul (v. 5). They were **believers**, where the perfect participle is intended perhaps to emphasize the reality of their faith (see disc. on 14:23), that is, they were fully convinced that Jesus was the Messiah, though they thought of him still as the king of Israel from whose kingdom the Gentiles would be excluded unless they accepted its law (cf. 1:6).

15:6–7a / The initial meeting described in verse 4 may have been intended as no more than an official reception, and none of the leaders may have wished to debate the central issue on this occasion. Instead, the gathering may have been dismissed to allow the leaders to discuss the matter in private (v. 6). Galatians

2:1–10 may be Paul's own account of this private meeting, and in that event, the discussion evidently centered on the particular case of Titus. The Pauline passage indicates that the apostle John was present in addition to the others mentioned by Luke. Luke's account of the episode is somewhat sketchy, and we are obliged to speculate about some of the details. We have already suggested that a private meeting may be indicated in verse 6. The opening words of the next verse (**much discussion**) may also refer to that meeting. But then the passage goes on to speak of "the whole assembly" (v. 12) and "the whole church" (v. 22). We assume, then, that when Peter stood up to speak (v. 7b), the whole church had been reassembled and that these were the final speeches according to an agreed agenda.

15:7b–11 / Peter began with a reminiscence of the events that had culminated in the conversion of Cornelius, his family, and his friends (see 9:32–11:18). It had all happened, he said, **some time ago** perhaps ten or twelve years before (v. 7). At that time it had seemed clear that it was God's will that the Gentiles be saved. The Greek runs, "that they should hear the message . . . from my lips believe" (v. 7), and it is noteworthy that the phrase "through the mouth of" occurs only in Peter's speeches (1:16; 3:18, 21; 4:25; but cf. 22:14). Another Petrine idiom appears in the next verse: God **knows the heart** (v. 8; cf. 1:24), in this context with particular reference to sin and to the need of all for salvation. And God has offered salvation to all, making **no distinction between . . . them** (v. 9; cf. 10:20, 34; 11:12). That this was so had been borne out by his gift of the Holy Spirit to the Gentiles, made in "exactly the same way" (the force of the Greek, v. 8) as it had been to Jewish believers (cf. 10:47; 11:17). Thus the Gentiles, deemed by the Jews to be unclean, had been "cleansed" of their sins (NIV **he purified their hearts**) by faith in Jesus (v. 9; cf. 10:15, 28; 11:9). This, indeed, was the only way of cleansing for Gentiles and Jews alike. If either were to be saved, it would be **through the grace of our Lord Jesus** alone as they believed in him (v. 11; Pauline language? but for the idea cf. 3:16; 4:10–12; 10:43). Why then, Peter asked, should anyone be encumbered with a **yoke** (that is, of the law; see Sir. 51:26; Ps. Sol. 7:8; 17:32) **that neither we nor our fathers have been able to bear?** (v. 10)— Peter, no less than Paul, endorsed the charge laid by Stephen (7:53; cf 13:39; Gal. 6:13; see also Matt. 11:28ff.). He warned that any attempt to revert to a religion of law was to **try to test God** (v. 10), for it called into question his power to cleanse the hearts of the uncircumcised by his Spirit. With this speech Peter bowed out of the history of Acts.

15:12 / The meeting was hushed as **Barnabas and Paul** spoke (the order of the names perhaps reflects the way in which the Jerusalem people saw them; see disc. on 13:6ff.). Between them they described the events of their recent work among the Gentiles, with particular emphasis on **the miraculous signs and wonders God had done among the Gentiles through them** (v. 12; cf. v. 4) in clear demonstration of his blessing upon the work (cf. John 3:2; Heb. 2:4). Beyond this recital of facts they apparently made no attempt to justify what they had done. Peter had already argued its rightness in the light of his own experience, and James would show that the Scripture also furnished a defense.

15:13–18 / James was the last to speak. Literally, "he answered saying," as though responding, not to a spoken question but to the expectation of the council that he would have something to say, for he appears by now to have been at the head of the church in Jerusalem (see disc. on 12:17 and notes). His reputed attachment to the Jewish law must have made his defense of the position already adopted by the previous speakers the more impressive. He began with the familiar address "men, brothers" (v. 13; see disc. on 1:15), a significant one in this context. He then referred back to Peter's speech, calling him by the old Hebrew form of his name, "Simeon" (cf. 2 Pet. 1:1). Simeon, he said, had spoken of a "visitation" by God (so the Greek, v. 14)—a reference to the events involving Cornelius, made in the familiar language of Scripture (but in the epistles, the verb is found only in James 1:27). On this occasion God had taken **from the Gentiles a people for himself** (v. 14, lit., "for his name"; see note on 2:38). This was a paradox; for the word **people** (*laos*) is that usually applied to Israel in distinction to the Gentiles, but here the Gentiles are included in the people of God.

To this summary of Peter's speech James then added **the words of the prophets** (v. 15)—plural, though he cites only one prophet, either as including others who spoke along the same lines, or as referring to the Book of the Twelve Prophets. The quotation is from Amos 9:11f. in what appears to be a rather free reproduction of the Greek version, including perhaps a phrase from Isaiah 45:21, "who foretold this long ago" (cf. 3:21). The passage speaks of two things: first, the restoration of the nation, both as God's people and as an undivided people, with the north and south again under one king, as in former days— the rebuilding of "David's fallen tent" (v. 16; cf. Amos 9:11)— and second, the restoration of the kingdom to its former greatness, once again incorporating the neighboring countries. It is the second point that makes the passage relevant to this speech, especially in the form in which it appears in the LXX. The difference between the Greek version and the Hebrew revolved around a confusion over two Hebrew words. First, the Hebrew text of Amos 9:12 has the house of David "possessing" (Heb. *yîrešû*) what is left of the land of Edom and all the nations that were once God's—a reference to the countries that once made up David's kingdom. But the LXX has the rest of mankind (i.e., the Gentiles) "seeking" (Heb. *yidᵉrešû*) the Lord who calls them his own (lit., "upon whom my name is pronounced," an expression found elsewhere in the New Testament only in James 2:7). Second, the Masoretes (Jewish scribes) read the unvocalized Hebrew word '-d-m as "Edom" and made it the object of the sentence; the translators of the LXX read the same word as "man" and made it the subject (either result can be achieved by a different vocalization of the same Hebrew consonants). As a consequence, in the LXX Israel does not possess the lands, but the nations are converted.

Broadly speaking, however, the result in both the Hebrew and the Greek texts is the same, namely, the inclusion of other peoples in the future kingdom of Israel. It is possible, then, that the use of the LXX is due to Luke, but that James was known to have quoted this passage in support of the admission of Gentiles. On the other hand, there is no a priori reason why he should not have quoted the LXX himself, since the council may well have been conducted in Greek. Most Palestinians, and especially Galileans, would have been familiar with that language, whereas some of the Antiochenes may not have spoken Aramaic. That the prophecy was used in a sense very different from the original intention was in accordance with the exegetical methods of the day. A belief that Christ could be found in all the Scriptures enabled James to interpret the house of David of his church and the prophecy as a whole of the church gathering to itself all the nations (see disc. on 1:20).

15:19-21 / On the basis of this interpretation, James recommended that the Gentiles who were turning to God (i.e., believing in God; see disc. on 9:42) should not be troubled, that is, nothing more than faith should be asked of them as necessary for salvation. The reasoning by which James came to this position is not clear, but it may have been that because the prophecy mentioned no demands made of the Gentiles on entering the kingdom, none were required. But once in the kingdom certain things could fairly be asked of them. These things (the so-called apostolic decrees) should be set out, he said, in a letter. The authoritative tone in which he said this (the Greek uses the emphatic personal pronoun) leaves little doubt that James was in the chair, summing up and putting forward a practical resolution.

As they stand (but see note on v. 20), the decrees touch on both the ethical and the ceremonial aspects of the law. The Gentile converts were asked, one, **to abstain from food polluted by idols**; two to keep themselves **from sexual immorality**—there may have been an intended connection between these two, for idolatry often involved immorality; but "immorality" is sometimes taken to mean marriage within the forbidden degrees (cf. Lev. 18:6-18)—three, not to eat **the meat of strangled animals** (which therefore still retains its blood, cf. Lev. 17:10, 13); and four, not to eat any **blood** itself (v. 20; cf. Lev. 3:17; 7:26; 17:10; 19:26; Deut. 12:16, 23; 15:23). It has long since been observed that these decrees could well be a summary of the law of Leviticus 17-28 that bound, not only Israel, but foreigners living among them. But was their introduction now a denial of the freedom that had just been won for the Gentiles? Some have thought so, but in proposing the decrees James had had in mind a very different objective from that of the circumcision party. They had said that obedience to the law was necessary for salvation (v. 1), whereas for James the decrees were aimed simply at enabling those who were saved to live in harmony with one another. As far as anyone knew there would always be Jewish Christians who would remain true to the law (cf. 21:20f.), and it would have been impossible for them to have any dealing with the Gentile believers unless the latter observed these basic requirements. James' final remark seems to mean that since the Jewish Christians were prepared to lay aside their long-standing prejudice against Gentiles, Gentile Christians should be ready to make some concessions to Jewish scruples. For the law had been read **from the earliest times**

. . . **in the synagogues** (v. 21). That is to say, it had been part of Jewish life for so long that they could not lightly lay it aside. There is some precedent for the council's decision in what were called the "Noachian laws," which (in rabbinic opinion) had been given to Noah and were binding on all Gentiles (cf. Gen. 9:4; see G. F. Moore, *Judaism*, vol. 1, pp. 274f., 339).

Additional Notes §38

15:1 / **Some men came down from Judea**: Although the church in Judea remained closer to its Jewish matrix than the church elsewhere, it was far from being a "monolithic block," particularly in the early period. There were those who remained intransigent on the question of obedience to the law (see disc. on 11:1f. and 21:20). But there were others—Hengel thinks a large proportion of Palestinian Christians—who "will have been openly sympathetic to developments outside Palestine, while at the same time mistrusting the heightened emphasis on obedience to the Law" among their own people (*Acts*, pp. 101f.). But they were swimming against the stream. A number of factors were at work throughout this period to force them back into the mold of their earlier faith. Hengel writes of the "increasing pressure from the Jewish milieu in Palestine and the constant danger of new persecutions (1 Thess. 2.14f.), the increasing influence of James the brother of the Lord and the 'elders' (cf. Acts 11:30; 12:17), the decline of the influence of the former disciples of Jesus, the 'Twelve,' and with it the decline in the direct tradition about Jesus in Palestine" (*Acts*, p. 113).

15:20 / **To abstain from food polluted by idols**, lit., "to abstain from the pollution of idols": In the light of v. 29, where the noun does refer to what was "sacrificed to idols," NIV has probably understood this verse correctly. It is possible, however, that **idols** has a wider connotation and that the prohibition here is not simply against eating food but against participating in anything associated with idols. That it was easy for Christians to run these risks is evident from 1 Cor. 8:10.

From sexual immorality: The most ancient manuscript we possess, the so-called Chester Beatty papyrus (P^{45}), has no reference to immorality, but only to idolatry, things strangled, and blood. Nevertheless, the reading is sufficiently well supported for us to accept it with confidence.

From the meat of strangled animals: The Western text omits the reference to things strangled both here and in v. 29. In 21:25 the "decrees" are again referred to, and again D (representing the Western text) omits this particular reference. The omission allows the prohibitions to be interpreted as touching simply on ethical matters, namely, idolatry, immorality, and "blood," i.e., murder. In addition the Western text has a warning not to do to others what one would not have done to oneself (the Golden

Rule in negative form; cf. Tobit 4:15; *Didache* 1.2; b. *Shabbath* 31a). This text appears as an attractive alternative to those who argue that Paul could not have endorsed the decrees as they appear in the accepted text (see introduction to this section). But neither the scribe who produced the Western text nor those who prefer his reading show any appreciation of the situation in the church of the first century or of Paul's own attitude toward the law. This text reflects a later period of the church, when the legalistic controversy of the first century was a thing of the past and a new moralism had crept into Christian circles. There is considerable evidence that the decrees as we have them were not only issued but observed in the Gentile churches for many years after their promulgation (cf. Rev. 2:14, 22; Justin Martyr, *Dialogue* 34.8; Minucius Felix, *Octavius* 30.6; Eusebius, *Ecclesiastical History* 5.1.26; Tertullian, *Apology* 9.13; Pseudo-Clementine *Homilies* 7.4.2; 8.1, and 19—perhaps also Lucian, *On the Death of Peregrinus* 16, who tells us that the Christians broke with Peregrinus because "he was discovered . . . eating one of the things which are forbidden to them").

§39   The Council's Letter to Gentile Believers (Acts 15:22-35)

15:22-29 / James' recommendation met with the approval of **the whole church** (v. 22), that is, of all who were present. Outside the council, however, there remained a significant number of Jewish Christians who wished to take a much harder line with the Gentiles. They continued to disturb the Pauline churches for some years to come. Nevertheless, the council did represent a broad consensus of the church and was an expression of the real unity that was still felt by all Christians (cf., e.g., 4:32). In addition to the letter that James had proposed (v. 20), it was **decided to choose some of their own men**, meaning from among the Jerusalem representatives, to join with the delegates from the north in conveying the council's decision to the church in Antioch (v. 22). The present participle, *hegoumenous*, signifies that they were leaders of some sort, probably elders. Later, in verse 32, they are called prophets. Silas was apparently the Silvanus of the epistles (2 Cor. 1:19; 1 Thess. 1:1; 2 Thess. 1:1; 1 Pet. 5:12), but of Judas Barsabbas we know nothing, though it has been conjectured that he was the brother of Joseph Barsabbas (1:23), in which case, like his brother, he may have been a follower of Jesus "beginning from John's baptism" (1:21f.).

So the letter was sent, not as from the council, but from the church in Jerusalem (**the apostles and the elders**, v. 23), which still regarded itself as having the authoritative voice in the affairs of the whole people of God. There is some uncertainty as to how the word **brothers** relates to the rest of the phrase in verse 23, but NIV is probably right to take it as standing in apposition to **the apostles and elders**, so that whatever their authority, they wrote to the church in Antioch as brothers to brothers. The letter was not an encyclical, but was addressed specifically to the Gentile Christians **in Antioch, Syria and Cilicia** (v. 23). At this time Syria and (eastern) Cilicia were administered from Antioch as one province (this ceased to be the case after A.D. 72). Evidently the church in this province was predominantly Gentile. See 23:26 for the form of address.

The church leaders had several objectives in writing this letter: First, they acknowledged that although those who had disturbed ("shaken") and troubled the church in Antioch had come **from us** (v. 24; cf. Gal. 2:12 for the same expression and Gal. 1:7; 5:10 for the same problem), they had not represented the church in Jerusalem, but had acted on their own authority. Second, they vindicated Paul and Barnabas, who had withstood the troublemakers, and honored them for risking **their lives** (lit., "handing over their lives") **for the name of our Lord Jesus Christ** (v. 26; but they had also been "handed over" to the care of God's grace, 14:26; cf. 2 Tim. 1:12. For "the name," see note on 2:38). The sufferings of the two missionaries in the course of their recent journey were evidently well known. Notice the warmth of the expression **our dear friends Barnabas and Paul** (v. 25; cf. the shaking of hands in Gal. 2:9; see disc. on v. 12 for the order of the names). Third, they authorized Judas and Silas, as representing the church in Jerusalem, to speak in support of what the letter contained. And fourth, they set out those things that the council had agreed they should ask of the Gentiles.

The "decrees" are the same as in verse 20, except for a slight change in order. The text is subject to the same variants as those discussed in the notes on that verse, with the further addition here (v. 29) in the Western text of the words "going on in the Spirit." The letter emphasized that the council had kept its demands to a minimum (v. 28) and that what was asked of them was necessary only in the interests of harmony, not of salvation. The final comment, **you will do well to avoid these things** (v. 29), that is, the things prohibited, cannot be interpreted to mean "you will be saved." It does, however, reflect the conviction that the council's decision had been reached under the guidance of the Holy Spirit (cf. 10:19f.; 13:2f.). This belief is made explicit in verse 28, where the form of expression does not mean that they put themselves on a par with the Spirit, but only that they were willing to submit to his guidance (cf. Josephus, *Antiquities* 16.162–166 for the letter of Augustus: "It seemed good to me and to my council . . ."). Because of a number of resemblances between this letter, First Peter, and First and Second Thessalonians, with all of which Silas' name is associated, it is tempting to think that he wrote it on behalf of **the apostles and elders**. Copies of the letter were probably kept in Antioch and Jerusalem, to which Luke would have had access.

15:30–35 / The letter was read to the assembled church in Antioch to their great joy, since it reassured them of their status (vv. 30, 31; for **the church**, Gk. *plethos*, see note on 6:2). Its demands were apparently accepted without demur (they may already have been doing these things under instruction from their own leaders). Judas and Silas added their own words of encouragement to what had been written. The Greek verb in verse 32 can mean that they either "encouraged," "comforted," or "exhorted," and perhaps they did all three. Thus they "strengthened" the church in Antioch (v. 32, lit., "made firm"; cf. "shaken," v. 24). This was the work of prophets, and so they are called in this verse (see note on 11:27). After a time they returned to Jerusalem, the Antiochenes sending them off with prayers for their peace and safety (v. 33). Verse 34 is not original and thus is relegated to the margin by NIV. It was an attempt to explain Silas' presence in Antioch at a later date for the "second missionary journey." But verse 33 presents no real difficulty as long as we allow for the elapse of some time between it and verse 40—time enough for Paul to have sent for Silas, asking him to go with him. Meanwhile, Paul and Barnabas and **many others** [strictly, "others of another kind"—perhaps lesser lights in the church] **taught and preached the word of the Lord** in Antioch—the preaching directed perhaps to winning outsiders, the teaching to establishing them in the Lord.

Additional Notes §39

15:23 / **Syria and Cilicia**: At this time eastern Cilicia (Cilicia Pedeias; see note on 6:9) was administered by Syria. Western Cilicia (Tracheia) had a more checkered history. It was given by Antony to Cleopatra (36 B.C.), later by Augustus to Amyntas. It passed to Archelaus of Cappadocia, then to Antiochus IV of Commagene, and was finally united with eastern Cilicia as one province in A.D. 72 (see also disc. on 23:35).

§40 Disagreement Between Paul and Barnabas (Acts 15:36–41)

The outcome of the council naturally gave added impetus to the spread of the gospel. Paul and Barnabas would have had no doubts that their earlier decision to go to the Gentiles had been the right one, but to have the approval now of the other apostles and the elders of the church in Jerusalem must have been as encouraging for them as for their converts. A "second missionary journey" was therefore proposed. But they were destined not to make it together. A difference of opinion between them led to each going his separate way. Barnabas went to Cyprus, and we hear no more of him in Acts. Paul remains the focus of attention as he returns to Galatia and then embarks on a new enterprise.

15:36 / **Some time later,** probably as spring approached and it again became possible to travel, Paul suggested to Barnabas that they should revisit the **brothers in all the towns** of their previous journey. Nothing more than this is suggested, but it may already have been Paul's intention to start a new work once this visitation was done.

15:37–39 / But when it came to planning the journey, they could not see eye to eye on whether Mark should go with them again. Barnabas wanted **to take** him (aorist tense), Paul did not want **to take him** [present tense, i.e., as a continuing member of the missionary team, liable at any time to desert them], **because he had deserted them in Pamphylia and had not continued with them in the work** (v. 38). In the original account of Mark's defection (13:13), a different word is used—a neutral term that means simply "to go away." The expression here (from the Greek word, we get "apostate") has more the sense of "disloyalty." **A sharp disagreement** ensued (v. 39, Gk. *paroxysmos*) that resulted in the two friends parting company. It is possible that there was more to the quarrel than Luke has told us. The incident of Galatians

2:11–14 may have occurred at this time, in which Barnabas as well as Peter vacillated on the question of eating with Gentile believers. The matter seems to have been quickly settled (but see Dunn, *Unity*, p. 254), but the memory of it may have remained to exacerbate this present dispute.

So it was that two missionary expeditions instead of one set out from Antioch (cf. Ps. 76:10). The work of visitation was divided between them, with Barnabas going to Cyprus and taking Mark with him. His concern in this incident was probably for Mark's welfare; whereas Paul's concern was for the work, and he was afraid that Mark might be a hindrance. Happily the breach between them was healed in time. Paul refers to Barnabas in friendly terms in 1 Corinthians 9:6 and Colossians 4:10 and in a way that implies that Barnabas was known to those churches. Perhaps the two worked together again, though Acts makes no mention of it. Similarly with Mark: Paul later speaks of him with approval as one of the few who had helped him (Col. 4:10f.; Philem. 24), and it was Mark (together with Timothy) that he wanted close to him at the end of his life (2 Tim. 4:11).

15:40–41 / In place of Barnabas Paul took with him Silas, and with the church's blessing (cf. v. 40 with 14:26), they set out by land for the cities of southern Galatia. Silas now assumed the role of "supporting cast" that Barnabas had played, though he would never attain the stature of Barnabas. He is never called an apostle (cf. 14:14). He may have commended himself to Paul for two reasons: his readiness to deal sympathetically with the Gentile believers and his possession (implied in 16:37) of Roman citizenship. That no mention is made of Barnabas and Mark being similarly sent out with a blessing means nothing except that Paul is now the center of Luke's attention.

As they journeyed to Galatia, Paul and Silas had the opportunity to visit as many churches of Syria-Cilicia as lay on their route, some of which Paul himself may have had a hand in establishing (see disc. on 9:30; 11:25). Luke again uses the word that suggests that this was a "preaching tour" (v. 41; see disc. on 8:4), and in this way (together with the reading of the letter from the council) these churches were strengthened (cf. v. 32; 14:22). Thus, by way of Tarsus and the Cilician Gates the missionaries made their way westward.

§41 Timothy Joins Paul and Silas (Acts 16:1–5)

Paul's return trip to southern Galatia appears to have been much less eventful than his first visit. The only incident of any significance on which Luke comments is the addition of Timothy to the missionary team. Other than that, he remarks only that the decision of the council was delivered to the churches of this region and that they were growing in maturity and numbers. This section can be viewed as closing off Luke's account of the council and, indeed, his whole narrative of the opening of the door of faith to the Gentiles that began in 13:1 (see also the disc. on 9:31).

16:1–3 / Since the missionaries came from the east, the towns are named in reverse order from the previous visit: **Derbe and Lystra** (v. 1). The verb used in this connection (Gk. *katantan*) implies that they stayed for a time in each. Here they met up (again?) with a young man named Timothy. He is introduced as a believer ("Look! a disciple named Timothy was there," v. 1), and from verse 2, it would appear that he was one of relatively long standing. To find someone like this, ready and eager for service, must have seemed providential (see disc. on 1:10 for this sense of the exclamation "Look!"). But Paul's decision to add Timothy to the missionary team was also guided by the good report that he had had of him from **the brothers at Lystra and Iconium** (v. 2; cf. 6:3; 1 Tim. 3:7; cf. also 1 Tim. 1:18; 4:14; 2 Tim. 1:6). Thus began an association between the two that ended only with Paul's death, and that was characterized by such an affection that Paul would call him his son (1 Cor. 4:17; 1 Tim. 1:2).

From the repeated preposition, **to Derbe and then to Lystra**, it would appear that the meeting with Timothy took place in the latter and that Lystra was his hometown (this is supported by the reference in 20:4, where it is evident that Derbe was not). Paul may even have lodged with Timothy's family on the occasions when he was in Lystra. He certainly writes of the faith of his mother and grandmother as though from personal knowledge (2 Tim. 1:5). Luke agrees with Paul in describing Timothy's mother as "faithful," adding that she was a **Jewess**, but his father **was a Greek** (v. 1). Because nothing is said to the contrary, it would appear that his father was a pagan and, from the tense of the verb in verse 3, that he was now dead. Marriages of this kind were forbidden by Jewish law (Ezra 10:2), but when they happened and there were children, the children were regarded as Jews (j. *Yebamoth* 2.6). Clearly, in Timothy's case the Jewish influence was predominant (2 Tim. 3:15). But for some reason—his pagan father may have prevented it—he had never been circumcised. This placed Timothy in an anomalous situation. For all intents and purposes he was a Jew and yet was barred from any effective work among Jews because he was known not to be circumcised (v. 3). So Paul circumcised him (the rite could be performed by any Israelite). This may seem odd in the light of what has gone just before, but no principle was at stake as it had been in 15:1 and Galatians 2:3. It was a matter of expediency, nothing more (cf. 1 Cor. 7:19; Gal. 5:6; 6:15).

16:4 / Though **the decision reached by the apostles and elders** had been intended only for the Gentile Christians of Syria-Cilicia, the missionaries passed them on to the churches of southern Galatia. The proximity of these churches to Syria and that they had been established from Syrian Antioch were sufficient reasons for doing so (on Paul's practice elsewhere, see introduction to 15:1–21).

16:5 / The promulgation of the council's decision concerning the status of Gentile believers, supported no doubt by further teaching, resulted in the Galatian churches being **strengthened in the faith** (see disc. on 14:22 for "the faith"). The verb in this statement is found elsewhere in Acts only in the story of the healing of the lame man in the temple (3:7, 16; but cf. 15:32, 41, for the same thought). Perhaps Luke was suggesting that the churches of southern Galatia were now ready "to stand on their own feet" and to accept responsibility for the task of evangelism. So they **grew daily in numbers** (see disc. on 2:47). As in 6:7 and 9:31, there was a correlation between the inner life of these believers and the outward growth in their numbers.

§42 Paul's Vision of the Man of Macedonia (Acts 16:6–10)

Nothing is said of any plans Paul might have had for what they would do once they had seen how the Galatians were getting on (though we might guess that he had set his sights on Ephesus, the capital of the province of Asia; cf. v. 6). Instead, the emphasis is entirely on the divine guidance that took them to Macedonia. The story is told with a minimum of detail, which only heightens the impression that they were carried along, as it were, by the irresistible wind of the Spirit, much as Paul and Barnabas had been on the earlier journey (cf. 13:1–3).

16:6 / The reference in verse 2 to Iconium suggests that it too was visited by the missionaries. It would have made an ideal headquarters from which to visit all the other towns, and there is some reason for thinking that this was their arrangement and that Iconium was their base. The inference of verse 6 is that it was from this town that they set out when the work of visitation was done (notice the reference to Phrygia and recall Iconium's background; see disc. on 14:1). Many roads lay before them. By traveling westward they would soon have crossed into Asia (cf. 19:1). Or they could have taken one of the roads to the south to Perga and Attalia and the other cities of the Pamphylian coast. But neither of these directions was chosen; the Spirit seemed to be holding them back. So they set out instead for the north.

Luke describes this journey as taking them **through the region of Phrygia and Galatia** (see disc. on 8:4 for the verb). The precise meaning of the phrase **Phrygia and Galatia** is a matter of some debate. The Greek can be rendered either "Phrygia and the Galatian region" or "the Phrygian and Galatian region." In the former, Phrygia is treated as a noun referring to a region that lay partly in the province of Asia and partly in Galatia, embracing in the latter the cities of Iconium and Antioch. "The Galatian region" is then seen to be a separate area, that part of the Roman province that lay to the north of the Phrygian lands and had been the old kingdom of Galatia (see note on 13:14). On this understanding, it is possible that they visited Ancyra, the capital of the province and the meeting place of all great roads to the north. The alternative rendering, in which Phrygia is treated as an adjective, does not rule out the possibility that they visited Ancyra or other cities of northern Galatia. It simply tells us even less than the other about the route that they took. On this understanding, the only information we have is that the missionaries passed through the one region that was traditionally part of Phrygia but, in terms of Roman political divisions, was now part of Galatia— "the Phrygo-Galatian region." Although certainty is impossible, several considerations weigh in favor of the latter, not least the similar reference in 18:23, where again Paul is said to have gone "through the region of Galatia and Phrygia." On this occasion, his destination was Ephesus, and it is hard to believe that he would first have traveled northward through the old kingdom and then back through Phrygia, adding three hundred miles to his journey, rather than stick to the one region and follow in a direct line to Ephesus. If we accept that only one region is meant, the reverse order of the words in 18:23 ("Galatia and Phrygia" instead of "Phrygia and Galatia") must be due to the fact that the phrase has now to cover all the cities of the first journey, not simply the Phrygian towns of Iconium and Antioch. Strictly speaking, of course, Derbe and Lystra were Lycaonian cities, but one could hardly expect the phrase "the Lycaono-Galatian and Phrygo-Galatian region." Instead, Luke has used the simpler expression "the Galatian region" to cover Derbe and Lystra and "Phrygia" to cover Iconium and Antioch.

16:7 / At all events, they came eventually to **the border of Mysia**. This was a rather indefinite region in the northwest of Asia Minor, by this time incorporated into the province of Asia. Having come, perhaps, to Dorylaeum, where the roads parted, Paul and his companions may at first have intended to continue northward into the province of Bithynia, where many cities must have beckoned. But again they felt constrained by the Spirit not to take that direction. (Was there another apostle at work in this area? cf. 1 Pet. 1:1.) So they turned westward to Troas instead. The unique description of the Spirit in this verse should be noticed. The change from "the Holy Spirit" (v. 6) to **the Spirit of**

Jesus has no significance other than to remind us that the Spirit is as closely associated with the Son as with the Father (cf. John 14:16, 26; 16:7) and may be variously called "the Spirit of God" (Matt. 10:20), "the Spirit of Christ," or "the Spirit of Jesus" (cf. Rom. 8:9; Gal. 4:6; Phil. 1:19; 1 Pet. 1:11).

16:8 / On the face of it, the expression **they passed by** (Gk. *parerchesthai*) **Mysia** would suggest that they skirted Mysia to the south. But they must have entered the region at some point to reach Troas. Perhaps, then, in this instance it means "to pass through without preaching." So they came directly to Troas—Colonia Augusta Alexandria Troas, as it was now called. It had been founded near the site of ancient Troy by Antigonus, one of Alexander's successors, and named in honor of Alexander. Under the Romans it had developed into a large and important city. The prohibition on preaching in Asia (v. 6) may have kept the missionaries from preaching in Troas, but Paul was to return here on other occasions (20:6; 2 Cor. 2:12; 2 Tim. 4:13), and whether by him or some other, a church was soon established.

16:9 / Troas was the main port for travelers between Asia and Macedonia, and it may not be unrelated to this that Paul had a vision in Troas of a Macedonian **standing and begging him, "Come over to Macedonia and help us."** (For dreams as a means of divine guidance, cf. 2:17; 10:9ff.; 18:9; 23:11.) The presence of Macedonians in the city may have shaped the dream, though the message nonetheless came from God. It was a cry for help of a spiritual nature.

16:10 / The missionaries recognized Paul's dream as divine guidance (the verb means "to put together" like our "putting two and two together") and immediately "sought" for the means to obey (so the Greek)—inquiring about shipping and so on (on their ready response, cf. 8:26f.). We have in this verse the first of the so-called we-passages (16:10–17; 20:5–15; 21:1–18; 27:1–28:16) in which it is commonly thought that the author of Acts had now become a participant in the events he was describing. He may have kept a diary on which he later drew.

§43 Lydia's Conversion in Philippi
(Acts 16:11–15)

The story that begins here and runs through to 21:16 covers
the greatest years of Paul's life—years that saw the foundation of
the churches of Macedonia, Achaia (Greece), and Asia and the
writing of some of his most important epistles. The story is told
by means of a few typical pictures (see disc. on 3:1–10) by which
Luke is able to show both the power of the gospel and the effect
of its meeting with the other powers of that day: philosophy, religion, and the Roman state. At a number of points the story is
corroborated and filled out by Paul's letters. However, some of
the details of Luke's narrative have been questioned, especially
his account of Paul and Silas' imprisonment and the earthquake
that interrupted it. Parallels have been adduced from other literature in proof that the story is a fabrication or at least a highly em
bellished account of what really happened (cf., e.g., 5:17ff.; 12:7ff.;
the Testament of Joseph 8:4; the Acts of Thomas 154ff.; Euripides,
Bacchae 443ff., 586ff.; Epictetus, *Lectures* 2.6.26). Haenchen complains that Luke has told the story "with the full array of Hellenistic narrative art, so that the glory of Paul beams brightly"
(p. 504). And there may be something in this as far as its telling
is concerned—Luke was an artist. But again we must insist that
the form of the story is no guide to its essential historicity (see
disc. on 5:19f.). A charge has also been brought against Luke that
the rest of the town seems not to have been affected by the earthquake that set the two missionaries free. But we do not know that
this was the case, and to argue from Luke's silence on the matter
is a hazardous proceeding. Indeed, their release the next day may
have been due precisely to a fear inspired in the magistrates by
the earthquake. It is certainly hard to imagine why Luke should
have invented the story if nothing happened at all, whereas there
is much in the topographical and political details of the narrative
to suggest that in fact he had access to firsthand information. The
whole account has a ring of truth about it.

Luke seems to have been struck by the strangely representative nature of what happened at Philippi. There were other conversions, we know, but three are made to stand out in particular:
Lydia's, the slave girl's (by implication), and the jailer's. Together
these three epitomized all whom the Jews held in contempt—
women, slaves, and Gentiles—and if anything marked the diver-
gence of the new faith from the old it was these conversions at
Philippi. Not only had the gospel crossed the Aegean, but it had
bridged the far more difficult gulf of sexual, social, and racial distinction (cf. Gal. 3:28; Col. 3:11). The suggestiveness of these details may account for the space that Luke has devoted to the
mission in Philippi. But it is also possible that this place had a
special interest for Luke, in that it may well have been his home
for a number of years until he rejoined Paul at the close of the
"third missionary journey."

16:11 / From Troas, Paul and his companions (Silas, Timothy, and now, apparently, Luke) sailed to Samothrace, an island
off the coast of Thrace about halfway between Troas and Neapolis.
They made Samothrace in one day and the mainland the next
(cf. 20:6). Luke may have seen this good crossing as a sign of
God's approval. Neapolis was their port of disembarkation. They
were now in Macedonia.

16:12 / When the last of the Macedonian kings fell to the
Romans at Pydna in 168 B.C., the country was annexed by Rome,
but in the settlement made the following year was declared free.
Nevertheless, to curb the free spirit of the Macedonians, the
country was divided into four republics, each under a separate
jurisdiction. This arrangement lasted until 148 B.C. In that year
a Macedonian uprising was crushed, and the country was made
a province of Rome. From A.D. 15 to 44 it was combined with
Achaia and Moesia into one large imperial province, but from A.D.
44 was again a separate senatorial province (see note on 13:7).
Through all of this, the old fourfold division of the country appears to have been retained, and Luke demonstrates his local
knowledge by referring to it in this verse (see Sherwin-White, p.
93; cf. also 13:49ff.). The Greek of this verse is confused, but the
reading adopted by GNB probably represents what Luke intended, namely, that Philippi was "a city of the first district of
Macedonia." It was certainly not "the leading city of the district

of Macedonia" (RSV) nor even of this particular subdivision (NIV). That distinction belonged to Amphipolis, and Thessalonica was the capital of the whole province.

The missionaries appear not to have lingered in Neapolis, but to have gone straight to Philippi, about ten miles to the west. Originally a small mining town founded to exploit the gold deposits of the nearby Pangaeus Mountains, Philippi had survived the failure of the lodes because of the commercial importance of its position astride the Via Egnatia, the chief route between Asia and the West. Its name derived from Philip II of Macedon (359-336 B.C.), who took the town from the Thasian Greeks. Following the battle of Philippi (42 B.C.), the town was enlarged by the settlement of a number of veterans. It was in Antony's mind to make it a colony, but it was only after his defeat by Octavius in the battle of Actium (31 B.C.) that Philippi was granted that status. With it came more Italian settlers. The most cherished possession of such a colony was its "Italian right" (the *ius Italicum*) "by which the whole legal position of the colonists in respect of ownership, transfer of land, payment of taxes, local administration, and law, became the same as if they were upon Italian soil; as, in fact, by a legal fiction, they were" (*BC*. vol. 4, p. 190). The colonists themselves have been fairly described as "a miniature likeness of the great Roman people" (J. B. Lightfoot, *St Paul's Epistle to the Philippians* [London: Macmillan, 1868], p. 51), and in both Luke's account of Paul's visit to Philippi and Paul's own letter to the Philippians, we are constantly brought face to face with the political life of Rome, in particular, with the power and pride of Roman citizenship (vv. 21, 37; Phil. 1:27; 3:20). This is not the first colony to have appeared in the narrative, nor will it be the last, but Luke makes a point of noting its status—**Philippi, a Roman colony**—partly, perhaps, because of his own interest in Philippi, but also because it helps to shed light on the narrative.

16:13 / On the Sabbath the party **went outside the city gate to the river** in search of any Jews who might have met there for worship. The Greek text has them simply going "out of the gate," and as long as we understand "the gate" to be that of the city, NIV has given the sense of it. But another identification is possible. A little over a mile to the west of the city, on the Via Egnatia, stood a Roman arch, now in ruins; and a little beyond this ran the river Gangites, a tributary of the Strymon. The erec-

tion of an arch of this sort often accompanied the founding of
a colony and was intended to symbolize the dignity and privileges
of the city. It could also mark the *pomerium*, a line encircling an
empty space outside the city within which no buildings or burials
were permitted or strange cults allowed to be introduced. The Jews
may therefore have been obliged to hold their meetings at this
distance, beyond this gate. Here the missionaries expected to find
their **place of prayer**. The Greek has only the one word, *proseuchē*,
which can mean either the act of praying or the place in which
it is done, in the latter sense sometimes denoting a building (e.g.,
a synagogue). But Luke's use of the word here probably means
that there was no building, just a regular meeting spot in the
open. When Jews were obliged to meet in this way, as far as possible they would do so near a river or the sea to facilitate their
ceremonial washings, and so at Philippi, it would seem. Here Paul
and his companions found some women—the absence of men
may explain the lack of a synagogue, since at least ten men were
needed before a synagogue could be established. They **sat down**
[the usual posture for teaching among Jews, though in this case
it may simply indicate informality] **and began to speak to the
women who had gathered there**. Considering the small regard
ancient Jews had for women as people to be taught, we are again
reminded of how important a part women play in the story of
Acts by comparison (see disc. on 1:14).

16:14–15 / At least one of these women was converted,
though not necessarily at their first meeting. The imperfect tense
of the verb "to hear" in verse 14 suggests that she heard the missionaries on more than one occasion. Her name was Lydia, and
that was also the name of her country—though it no longer existed independently, but had long since been absorbed into the
province of Asia—for she was from Thyatira, a city of Lydia.
Dyeing was one of the stable industries of that city, and it was
probably from there that Lydia bought her **purple cloth** (v. 14).
It was a luxury trade, and Lydia must have been a relatively
wealthy woman to be engaged in it. She may have been a contributor, therefore, to the several gifts that Paul later received from
this church (Phil. 4:10ff.; 2 Cor. 11:18f.). She is described as **a
worshiper of God** (v. 14, i.e., a God-fearer; see note on 6:5), and
it may have been in Thyatira that she was introduced to the Jewish faith, for there is evidence that the Jews of Thyatira were espe-

cially involved in the dyeing trade. Thus the way had been prepared in her for the gospel. But Luke attributes her readiness **to respond** (v. 14) to something more than her background. **The Lord opened her heart** (v. 14; cf. Luke 24:45; see disc. on 2:47). This must always be the case. Without in any way diminishing the importance of repentance and faith and of preaching the faith of Christ, there can be no life in Christ unless the gospel comes "not simply with words, but also with power, with the Holy Spirit" (1 Thess. 1:5; cf. Eph. 1:18). But Luke mentions it now perhaps to show that just as God had called them to this work, so he confirmed that calling by working with them (cf. 14:27). They had all "spoken to the women" (v. 13), but Luke attributes Lydia's conversion, insofar as it lay in human hands, to Paul, who was no doubt the chief speaker. So Lydia became **a believer in the Lord** (v. 15), and in that faith **she and the members of her household**, that is, of her whole establishment, home and business, were baptized. Possibly Euodia and Syntyche and the other women of Philippians 4:2f. were among them (see note on 2:38 for baptism and note on 10:48 for the inclusion of the household). Lydia gave expression to faith with good works (cf., e.g., 10:46; 19:6), persuading the visitors to accept her hospitality for as long as they remained in the city (see disc. on 9.6ff. for Luke's habit of naming Paul's hosts). No doubt her home became the first "church" in Philippi (tradition places it in the village that has taken her name, not far from the ruins of Philippi; see disc. on 14:27 and notes). Some have identified her as Paul's "loyal yokefellow" of Philippians 4:3.

Additional Notes §43

16:12 / **A Roman colony**: The word "colony" occurs in the New Testament only here, though other cities named in Acts are known to have been colonies, e.g., Antioch of Pisidia (13:14), Iconium (14:1), Lystra (14:6), Troas (16:8), Corinth (18:1), Ptolemais (21:7), Syracuse (28:12), and Puteoli (28:13). Roman colonies were of three kinds and of three periods: those of the earlier republic, before 100 B.C., established in conquered towns as guardians of the frontier and centers of Roman influence; those of the Gracchan period—the agrarian colonies—established to provide land for the poorer citizens; and those of the civil wars and the empire, intended for the resettlement of soldiers at the end of their service. Unlike the earlier colonies that were established by a formal law and carried out by a commission, these "military colonies" were simply set up by the emperor, who would nominate a legate to give effect to his will. To this class, Philippi belonged. The community thus constituted possessed the *ius Italicum*, which carried the right of freedom (*libertas*), that is, they were self-governing, independent of the provincial government; the right of exemption from tax (*immunitas*); and the right of holding land in full ownership, as under Roman law, and of using Italian legal procedures and precedents. In 16:16–40 we have a clear picture of this procedure and one, moreover, that belongs precisely to this time (see Sherwin-White, p. 76).

16:13 / **We expected**: There are a number of textual variants here. The reading adopted by NIV implies that the missionaries did not know for certain where the Jews met or even *if* they met. The fact that the word "river" lacks the definite article in the Greek may support this—"we went out to a riverside." On the other hand, it may be right to accept the reading "where prayer was accustomed to be made." This suggests that they had prior information and knew where to look.

The women who had gathered there: It is noticeable that in the three Macedonian towns, Philippi, Thessalonica, and Berea, women are mentioned especially as influenced by the gospel. This corresponds to the considerable freedom and social influence enjoyed by Macedonian women, who were hardly less active than the men in public affairs (cf. 17:4, 12; see W. W. Tarn and G. T. Griffith, *Hellenistic Civilization*, pp. 98f.; W. D. Thomas, "The Place of Women in the Church at Philippi," *ExpT* 83 (1971–72), pp. 117–20).

§44   Paul and Silas In Prison (Acts 16:16–40)

See introduction to the previous section.

16:16–17 / The missionaries appear to have gone week by week to the place of prayer for a number of weeks, and as they did so, they were followed on several occasions by a demented slave girl whose shouting made them the center of public attention. The force of the Greek of verse 17 is that she "kept on following" and "kept on shouting" about them. Luke describes her in a curious way (not apparent in NIV): She had "a spirit," he says, "a python" (v. 16). The word "python" originally meant a snake, but by way of various associations, it had come to be used sometimes of ventriloquists, and ventriloquism was a trick often employed by fortune tellers and other charlatans. Something of this may be implied in Luke's phrase "the python spirit." But more than mere ventriloquism is implied, for it would seem from the narrative that some prophetic power was claimed for the girl, so that the phrase may reflect the popular estimate of such power, namely, that she was inspired by Apollo, the god of prophecy, called by the Greeks Pythian Apollo because he was supposed to have killed the snake that guarded the Delphic Oracle. Luke accepts this estimate, insofar as it attributed her prophetic gift to some source other than herself, but put his own Christian construction on it. Like Paul, he saw the gods of Greece and Rome as "fronts" for the power of Satan (1 Cor. 10:18–22) and the girl's condition, therefore, as something distinctly unwholesome. He uses a verb (translated by NIV as **fortune-telling** , v. 16) that occurs in the New Testament only here, but is found several times in the LXX concerning false prophets who practiced the heathen arts of divination contrary to the law of Moses (e.g., Deut. 18:10ff.; 1 Sam. 28:8[9]; Ezek. 13:6; 21:29[34]; Mic. 3:11; etc.). Thus GNB, for example, probably conveys the sense, if not the actual words, of Luke's text, when it describes the girl as having "an evil spirit" (v. 16).

In this spirit she kept shouting in public that the missionaries were **servants** [lit., "slaves"] **of the Most High God** and that
they had come announcing the way of salvation. To the pagans
of Philippi, this would have meant deliverance from the powers
governing their fate; to Luke's Christian readers much more (see
disc. on 4:12; 5:31). Her cries bear a striking resemblance to those
of the demoniacs encountered by Jesus, even to the use of the title
the Most High God (cf. Luke 4:34, 41, where the same verb "to
shout" is employed; and esp. 8:28; see disc. on 19:15). The title
was commonly used among the Jews of the Diaspora and by Gentiles in reference to the Jewish God (though not exclusively so;
see BC, vol. 5, pp. 94f.), and the girl may have picked it up in
this way. But Luke himself had no doubt that she was possessed
by a demon (cf. v. 18) and that she spoke with demoniacal insight.

16:18 / The day came, however, when Paul became **so
troubled** by the girl's behavior (the word combines the ideas of
grief, pain, and anger; it is used of the Sadducees in 4:2) that
he turned on her and **in the name of Jesus Christ** ordered the
spirit to come out of her (see note on 2:38 for "the name," and
cf. 3:6 for the command). The same strong word of command is
found in Luke's narrative of the Gerasene demoniac (Luke 8:29),
and in a way, the situation here was similar to that faced by Jesus
at Gerasa. The outcome was also the same. **At that moment the
spirit left her** and with it went a valuable asset that had brought
the girl's owners "a great deal of money" (v. 16), for we must suppose that she also lost her powers of ventriloquism, or whatever
else it was that she did. With a nice touch of humor Luke uses
the same verb "to go out" of both the spirit and the assets.

16:19 / When the girl's owners saw (or later discovered)
what had happened, they were quick to react (Paul had touched
the highly sensitive "hip-pocket" nerve; cf. 19:23–41). **They seized
Paul and Silas and dragged them into the marketplace to face
the authorities**. The more general word for **authorities** is used
here; their correct title is found in the next verse. Timothy and
Luke do not appear to have been involved, either as generally
less conspicuous, less "Jewish," or simply not there at the time.
The we-passages cease at verse 17 (see disc. on vv. 10 and 40).

16:20–21 / The chief governing power of a colony was
vested in the duumvirs, two annual magistrates, who, in the past,

though the practice may by that time have died out, had styled themselves "praetors." A duumvir of Philippi is a title borne out by inscriptions. The duumvirs would normally be found in the forum, as they were on this occasion (v. 19). This site has been excavated, and we can now see its regular outlines, with the city jail and public buildings bordering it. On the northern side of the forum stood a rectangular podium from which politicians probably made their orations and magistrates dispensed justice. These ruins date from only the second century A.D., but the plan of the forum had probably changed little since the time of Paul, and we may assume that it was to this place with similar facilities that he and Silas were taken and charged with **throwing** [the] **city into an uproar** (v. 20)—what this means can be seen from 17:6f.—and, as Jews, with introducing their own customs among the Romans (v. 21). Their accusers maintain a clear distinction between themselves and the accused: **These men** [a contemptuous phrase] **are Jews,** we are **Romans**. As inhabitants of a Roman *colonia* they could lay claim to that proud title (but cf. v. 37).

There is no certain evidence that proselytizing, whether by Jews or anyone else, was forbidden by Roman law, as is sometimes supposed. There was a law, however, forbidding Roman citizens to practice any foreign cult not sanctioned by the state (i.e., not a *religio licita*). This law was rarely enforced, and many Romans did in fact practice illicit cults (cf. 18:12ff.). The authorities were generally content to apply three tests as a rule of thumb to any new religion: Would it upset the dominant position of Roman cults? Was it politically safe? Was it morally desirable? If these tests were satisfied, toleration was complete, and the law was let lie. But there were cases on record where it had been invoked to restrain the excesses of some sect or other (the Druids, the Magians, the devotees of Isis), and it may have been the hope of these Philippians that the law would now be enforced to curb the activities of Paul and Silas. But on the whole it seems less likely that their appeal was to legal precedent than to racial prejudice. Notice the emphasis on the two men being Jews. Though imperial policy generally favored the Jews, at the grass roots level they were generally disliked (cf. Cicero, *Pro Flacco* 28; Juvenal, *Satires* 14.96-106), perhaps never more than at this time when feeling against them was running particularly high in Rome itself (see disc. on 18:2). The girl's owners were probably playing on this. Their objective was to harass the Christians, and by presenting them as Jews who were a threat to their Roman traditions, they succeeded very well in their aim.

16:22–24 / All semblance of legal procedure was lost as emotion took over. Normally the magistrates should have formally arrested the prisoners either for immediate trial or to be held over pending a later hearing. Instead, with the enraged crowd milling about them, the duumvirs themselves (so apparently the Greek) stripped them and (arbitrarily) **ordered them to be beaten** (v. 22; cf. 2 Cor. 11:25; 1 Thess. 2:2), a characteristically Roman method of punishment administered by the lictors (Gk. "rod-bearers"), the "officers" of verse 35. This punishment, even had they been found guilty, was illegal in the case of a citizen, but the duumvirs did not yet know that Paul and Silas were Roman citizens, and they, for their part, may not have been able to make themselves heard or understood in order to tell them. The instance cited by Cicero of a prisoner remorselessly flogged while shouting that he was a Roman shows how easily they might have protested in vain (*In Verrem* 5.62; cf. also Acts 22:25). There may also have been a difficulty with language. Roman citizens were supposed to have a knowledge of Latin, but there were no proficiency tests, and Paul and Silas may simply not have understood what was going on until the matter had already gotten out of hand. At all events, they were **severely flogged** (lit., "many blows were laid upon them"), after which **they were thrown into prison** (v. 23) and indeed into the innermost cell (this throws the subsequent miracle into sharper perspective). As an additional torture, they were chained to the wall with their feet held in stocks. Sleep under these conditions would have been out of the question.

16:25 / Paul and Silas were not crushed by these events. On the contrary, midnight found them **praying and singing hymns to God** (cf. 5:41). In this way, perhaps with no intention of doing so, they witnessed effectively to their fellow prisoners, some of whom may have been under sentence of death (see disc. on v. 27). The Greek verb implies that the prisoners gave them their closest attention, and the tense (imperfect) shows that the missionaries held it throughout (cf. Rom. 8:28; 2 Cor. 2:14; Phil. 4:6, 7). There is no suggestion that Paul and Silas prayed for their own release. Probably their prayers were of praise.

16:26 / To the miracle of grace being demonstrated in the missionaries' lives God added another, a miracle of nature: **suddenly there was . . . a violent earthquake** (cf. 4:31 and 12:6ff., both associated with prayer). The neighborhood of Philippi was prone to these tremors (Luke's "violent earthquake" may be an exaggeration), but the timing and scale of this one were certainly providential (see Ehrhardt, p. 94). The jail was shaken to the extent that the doors were sprung and the moorings of the prisoners' fetters were loosened, but no lives were lost (at least not in the jail). It is not even clear that the prisoners could have escaped. They would still have been in chains, though the chains themselves were now free from the walls, and in Paul and Silas' case their feet were probably still in the stocks. In any case they may have had no time to collect their thoughts before the jailer was on the spot.

16:27 / This man's first thought when he saw through the dust and darkness that the doors were ajar was that the prisoners had escaped. In this circumstance, it seemed to him that his only recourse was to take his own life. By Roman law, if a jailer lost a prisoner for whom he was responsible, even, it would seem, if by a natural disaster, he was liable to the same punishment that his prisoner should have suffered (cf. 12:19; 27:42). The jailer's intention was probably to avoid the disgrace of a far worse death than by his own sword. One would expect him to have looked into the cells before he took this extreme course, but the shock of the earthquake may have temporarily robbed him of his senses.

16:28–29 / The light by which the jailer saw that the doors were open was enough for Paul to see what he was about to do (or else he guessed it by what he heard) and also, perhaps, to assess the situation inside the jail. So he called out that all the prisoners (not only himself and Silas) were still there. At this, and in view of all that had happened—the earthquake, the Christians' singing and praying, their present calm, and what the slave girl had said about them (v. 17)—it must now have been borne in upon the jailer that these were indeed the "servants of the Most High God." He immediately judged them to be more than ordinary men, and taking a light, he **rushed in and fell trembling before Paul and Silas** (v. 29; cf. 10:25; 14:11).

16:30–31 / But the girl had also said something about salvation. He asked, therefore, what he must do to be saved. This
question had nothing to do with the punishment he had feared,
seeing that the prisoners were safe. Rather, the events of the night
had put the fear of the Most High God into him, and it was salvation in this sense that he sought. The answer that Paul and Silas
returned makes this clear. They told him that he must **believe
in** [*epi*, "towards"] **the Lord Jesus**. Only in this way would he be
saved. Behind this statement lies the early Christian confession
"Jesus is Lord" (see disc. on 9:42). The missionaries assured him,
moreover, that not only he but his whole family could be saved,
though this should not be taken to mean that his faith was sufficient for their salvation also. They too would have to believe (see
note on 10:48).

16:32–34 / By this time the jailer had already brought
them out of their cell (cf. v. 30). But now, as the guards (whose
presence is implied in v. 29) made the jail secure (the Western
text of v. 30 adds this comment, but this too may be implied),
he had probably taken them into his house (but see disc. on v.
34; in all likelihood the house was next to the jail) where both
he and his family could receive fuller instruction. The theme of
this further teaching was still the lordship of Jesus (v. 32, taking
the genitive "of the Lord" to be objective), and so they were
brought to confess Jesus as Lord. The perfect participle (v. 34)
is perhaps intended to make the point that they had come to a
full profession of this faith (see disc. on 14:23). Their new life was
demonstrated at once in two ways: the jailer himself tended the
prisoners' wounds from their beating, and **he and all his family
were baptized** (v. 33; see notes on 2:4, 38, and disc. on 10:44).
Notice his priorities: care for others before himself. These were
also the prisoners' priorities, for they first spoke about Jesus to
the jailer and his family before allowing him to minister to their
needs. After the baptism (had they gone outside to the prison
well?), the jailer **brought them into his house and set a meal
before them** (v. 34). Any hesitation at eating with Gentiles had
long since passed for these two (see disc. on 10:9ff.). As for their
host, **he was filled with joy . . .** —**he and his whole family** (v.
34; cf. 1 Pet. 1:8f.), a characteristically Lukan observation (see disc.
on 3:8). In making it, Luke uses the cognate verb of the noun
in 2:46 that describes the joy of the early believers in the meals

they shared. Whatever the intention, therefore, of this little group as they sat down to eat, the meal was an "Agape," a love feast. It may also have included a celebration of the Lord's Supper. Later the prisoners were returned to their cell.

16:35 / We do not know what the original intention of the magistrates was in jailing Paul and Silas—whether for one night or for longer. If for longer, they now changed their minds. The Romans were highly susceptible to omens, and in their own way the duumvirs may have been as deeply affected by the earthquake as the jailer had been. At all events, they sent their lictors (**officers**) the next morning with orders to let them go.

16:36–37 / The jailer brought them news of their release with the instruction that they were to **go in peace** (v. 36), not in the sense of the familiar Jewish greeting, but that they were to go quietly. This they refused to do. They staged a "sit-in," refusing to leave the jail until the duumvirs in person brought them out. It was not simply that as Roman citizens they had been beaten, but that they had been beaten without trial. The ancient Lex Valeria (500 B.C.) and Lex Porcia (248 B.C.), subsequently confirmed by the Lex Julia, had prohibited the beating of citizens. But Sherwin-White points out that by this time the middle of the first century A.D.—these laws had been modified. There were now circumstances "in which . . . a Roman citizen might properly be chained or beaten at the orders of a Roman magistrate" (p. 73), but in no circumstances without first being heard. It was only right, therefore, that the magistrates should make an admission of their fault. Nor was it simply a question of satisfying the demands of outraged justice; it was important that they should take this stand for the sake of the church. Had they left the city under the cloud of a public disgrace, the church might also have suffered from public prejudice and the spread of the gospel been impeded.

16:38–40 / At the news that their prisoners were Roman citizens, the magistrates became alarmed, for should their actions be exposed they would be degraded from their social rank and barred from holding any office in the future. On the other hand, it was their duty as magistrates to maintain peace, and the prospect of further disturbances like that of the previous day was hardly less alarming, especially as the teaching of the two men

could be construed as contrary to Roman customs (cf. v. 21). The
duumvirs were in a quandary. They did go to the prison **to appease them** (v. 39) but then made their own demand on the two
men that they leave the city. As citizens they could not be summarily expelled (see disc. on 13:49). Nevertheless, Paul and Silas
acceded to this demand, but they were not to be hurried. First
they went to Lydia's house, where they spoke to the assembled
brothers (v. 40). Evidently the work had gone ahead in Philippi,
and there were now a number of Christians. Nothing is said of
the appointment of the "overseers and deacons" of Philippians
1:1. We may be meant to assume that the procedure of 14:23 was
followed here as elsewhere, unless Luke himself made the ap-
pointments at a later date as Paul's proxy, for he apparently stayed
behind as Paul and Silas and Timothy took their leave. The we-
passages only resume when Paul comes this way again in 20:5.
Their unhurried departure must be attributed in large part to their
physical condition. Both Paul and Silas had been badly knocked
about and showed remarkable courage in traveling at all.

Additional Notes §44

16:37 / **We are Roman citizens**: The very boast made by the
owners of the girl (v. 21). It may be asked how Paul and Silas (apparently)
could prove that they were citizens. The same question arises in 22:25.
Given time, the provincial records in their hometowns could have been
consulted, but as itinerants (by far the exception in the ancient world;
the general mass of the population stayed put), they may each have carried a copy of his *professio* or registration of birth, in which his Roman
status would have been recorded. These were convenient in size, being
small wooden diptychs (see Sherwin-White, pp. 144ff., esp. 148f.). To
claim Roman citizenship falsely was punishable by death (cf. Suetonius,
Claudius 25).

§45　In Thessalonica (Acts 17:1–9)

From Philippi, Paul and his companions traveled to Thessalonica. Here they followed their usual pattern of ministry wherever a synagogue could be found. They would preach there, and from the synagogue would come their first converts. But from the synagogue also came their fiercest opponents, and in Thessalonica the Jews again succeeded in having the missionaries effectively banished (cf. 13:50). The story is told briefly, the lack of detail making us feel the loss of Luke's company. By telling us only the story of their relationship with the synagogue, Luke gives the impression that the missionaries were only in Thessalonica for three Sabbaths, but it is clear from Paul's letters that they were there for much longer—long enough for a church to be established with its own leaders (1 Thess. 5:12) and for outlying areas to be reached with the gospel (1 Thess. 1:7); long enough to warrant Paul's working "day and night" so as not to be a burden on the church (1 Thess. 2:9; 2 Thess. 3:8); and long enough for the church at Philippi to send him gifts (Phil. 4:16).

17:1 / By following the Egnatian Way to the west and the south, they passed through Amphipolis and Apollonia, apparently without making a long stay in either. The comment that in Thessalonica **there was a synagogue** implies that there was none in these towns (no evidence of any has ever been found). The two towns may only be mentioned, therefore, as their overnight stopping places, and if we make the further assumption that each of these stages of about thirty miles was completed in one day, then we must conclude that they made the journey on horseback, perhaps thanks to Lydia's generosity.

Thessalonica (formerly called Therma) had been refounded by Cassander and named after his wife, the daughter of Philip II of Macedon and the half-sister of Alexander the Great. It became the capital of one of the four republics into which Macedonia was divided in 167 B.C., and when these were later combined to form one province (148 B.C.), it became the capital of the whole (see

disc. on 16:12). Because the city had sided with the eventual vic-
tors of the battle of Philippi, it was rewarded by being made a
"free city," governed on Greek rather than Roman lines by its own
elected magistrates and by its citizen assembly (*dēmos*; see disc.
on vv. 5f.). Luke refers to each of these institutions, giving the
magistrates their correct title of "politarchs," attested by a number of inscriptions found in this area. The provincial governor had
his residence in Thessalonica, and important military and naval
bases were located there also. In Paul's day it was one of the great
seaports of southeastern Europe, with an estimated population
of about two-hundred thousand. Its Jewish community appears
to have been correspondingly large, certainly so by comparison
with Philippi, which is only as one would expect. There would
be little to attract Jews to a military colony and much that would
draw them to a cosmopolitan and commercial city such as this.

17:2-3 / The missionaries began their work in the synagogue **as** was Paul's **custom** (v. 2; cf. Luke 4:16 for the same
expression). There for three Sabbaths **he reasoned with them
from the Scriptures, explaining and proving** his message (vv. 2,
3). Since Luke has already furnished us with an example of Paul's
synagogal preaching (13:16-41), he is here content merely to hint
at his message (the direct speech is probably due to Luke's familiarity with Paul's preaching—he did not have to be there to
know what he said) and instead gives us an insight into his
method. He began with the Scriptures (lit., "from the Scriptures"),
but instead of straight teaching, as in the synagogues of the East,
he seems to have proceeded by means of "discussion" (Gk. *dia-
legesthai*; cf. our "dialectic")—an expression that appears here for
the first time in Acts (cf. v. 17; 18:4, 19; 19:8, 9; 20:7, 9) and may
indicate a change of style in response to a different environment.
"True, it was proclamation, but it was not take-it-or-leave-it proclamation. It was proclamation plus explanation and defence"
(W. Barclay, *AHG*, p. 166; but see G. Schrenk, *"dialegomai," TDNT*,
vol. 2, p. 94). Out of this discussion he was able to "explain" the
Scriptures (lit., to "open" them; cf. Luke 24:32) from his own
Christian perspective and so to "prove," first, that Jesus was the
Christ (see note on 11:20); second, that the Christ **had to suffer**,
that is, to die (see disc. on 1:16); and third, that he had to **rise
from the dead** (v. 3). If there were any doubts earlier about the
centrality of the death of Jesus in Paul's preaching (see disc. on

13:39), they are here dispelled. The outline resembles 1 Corinthians 15:3f., and as that passage makes clear, it was the gospel preached not only by Paul, but the message preached by them all.

17:4 / The result of this preaching (as so often elsewhere) was that some Jews were **persuaded**, including perhaps Aristarchus (see disc. on 20:4) and Jason (cf. vv. 5, 7); but by far the best response was from the **God-fearing Greeks** (see notes on 6:5 and 13:14), of whom Secundus may have been one (see disc. on 20:4). Among the God-fearers were **not a few prominent women**, though the Greek could equally mean "wives of the leading men." In Macedonia either was possible (see note on 16:13; see also disc. on 1:14; 13:50). That the converts are said to have **joined Paul and Silas** implies that the missionaries had by now withdrawn from the synagogue and were conducting separate meetings (see disc. on 14:27 and notes). The verb "to join" is literally "to assign by lot" and occurs here in the passive—these people "were allotted to Paul and Silas [by God]" (see disc. on 2:47). But some take the passive as equivalent to the middle voice, "they threw in their lot" with the missionaries. From the outset this church was predominantly Gentile, and before long the great majority of its members appears to have come straight from a pagan background with no previous contact with the synagogue (cf. v. 5).

17:5 / Though Paul was permitted to speak in the synagogue for only three Sabbaths, his letters indicate that he and the others stayed in Thessalonica much longer than this (see introduction to this section). Indeed, they seem to have had no thought of leaving. But the jealousy of the Jews would not leave them in peace (cf. 13:45). They determined to be rid of Paul and Silas and formulated a plan to bring them before the assembly on a charge of sedition. And to give some grounds for this charge, they **rounded up some bad characters from the marketplace** and organized them into staging a riot (cf. 14:4f., 19; 1 Thess. 2:14–16). No charge was better calculated than that of treason to start **a riot in the city**, and with the stage thus set for the successful prosecution of the missionaries, the rioters, presumably led by the Jews, **rushed to Jason's house in search of Paul and Silas in order to bring them out to the** *dēmos*, that is, to "the assembly of the people" (NIV mg).

17:6–7 / But their plans went awry. Paul and Silas could not be found, and without them they could hardly appear before the assembly. In frustration, therefore, they seized **Jason and some other brothers** (v. 6) and dragged them, not to the assembly as originally planned, but to the politarchs, accusing them of offering hospitality to the seditionists. The charge had to be shouted because of the melee. Concerning Paul and Silas they alleged that they had **caused trouble all over the world** (lit., "have turned the world upside down," i.e., the Roman Empire)—an exaggeration, of course, but an indication of how close communications were between the Jews of the Diaspora. The "first missionary journey" had evidently left a deep impression on the Jews of Asia Minor, and this was known to their co-religionists in Macedonia. In detail the charge was two-pronged. Paul and Silas were accused of **defying Caesar's decrees**—an assertion difficult to understand, if it had any basis, unless Paul's preaching had been construed as a prediction of a change of ruler; there were imperial decrees against such forecasts—and of saying that there was another king (v. 7). This was the same charge that had been brought by the Jews against Jesus (cf. Luke 23:2; John 19:12, 15). In neither case was it deserved, for the kingdom they preached was not of this world. But to the Jews "Christ" meant "king," and since the latter was the title generally applied to the emperors in the lands east of Rome, they could maliciously accuse the Christians of proclaiming a rival to Claudius. That Christians so often called Jesus "Lord" would have lent further color to this accusation.

17:8–9 / These charges were made in public with disturbing effect on both **the crowd and the city officials** (v. 8). The accusations were serious and had to be taken seriously. But on investigation, the politarchs seem not to have found the evidence as convincing as the accusers had hoped (cf. v. 9, they **let them go**), though they did impose certain penalties on the Christians. They "took security" from Jason and the others that Paul and Silas would not preach any more in Thessalonica. This explains the missionaries' sudden departure. In 1 Thessalonians 2:15, 18, we have Paul's own reflection on this turn of events, which he attributes to Satan through the instrumentality of the Jews. He might not have taken his dismissal so tamely had Jason not given his word. As it was, he and Silas had no option but to abide by it. Paul's removal did not put an end to the harassment of the

Thessalonian Christians. Those who were left behind were subjected to a persecution that to Paul (who of course would know) seemed as severe as that which the Jewish Christians had endured (1 Thess. 2:14; 3:1–5; 2 Thess. 1:6). Nor did his absence lessen the calumnies of the Jews against him in particular (1 Thess. 2:13–16).

Additional Notes §45

17:3 / **The Christ had to . . . rise from the dead**: In the earlier preaching it was always said that God raised Jesus (cf. 2:24, 32; 3:15; 4:10; 5:30; 10:40; 13:30). Now for the first time Paul declares that Jesus rose as though of his own volition (but cf. 17:31). This may be evidence of a developing Christology. Compare the possible use of the middle voice in 2 Tim. 2:8: "Remember Jesus Christ who raised himself from the dead."

§46 In Berea (Acts 17:10–15)

17:10 / Under cover of darkness, perhaps for fear of further violence should they be seen, the missionaries were sent off by "the brothers" to Berea, some forty-five miles southwest of Thessalonica. There is no mention of Timothy; he may have stayed in Thessalonica only to catch up with Paul again in Athens (see disc. on v. 16). Berea, which lay at the eastern slopes of Mount Vermion, had been founded in the fifth century B.C. In 168 B.C. it became the capital of one of the republics into which Macedonia was then divided (see disc. on 16:12). Livy described the city of Paul's day as still a "noble town" (*History of Rome* 45.30; cf. the description of the Berean Jews in v. 11). Beyond Mount Vermion lay Illyricum, and when Paul wrote in Romans 15:19 of having "fully proclaimed the gospel of Christ" from Jerusalem to Illyricum, he may have had in mind this present episode (but see disc. on 20:2). In the present circumstances the attraction of Berea may have been that it was not at the Egnatian Way and was, according to Cicero, "a town difficult of access" (*In Pisonem* 36.89). They must have hoped to avoid pursuit, and to a degree that hope was fulfilled. At least they had a respite from their persecutors, during which they were able to follow Paul's "usual habit" of proclaiming the Good News in the synagogue in this city also.

17:11–12 / Luke describes the Berean Jews as **of more noble character than the Thessalonians**. This might mean "more generous" in their support of the missionaries, but NIV is probably right to refer the expression to their attitude to Paul's preaching. They readily accepted the possibility that what he said was true (Luke's use of the optative seems intended to give this sense), then tested it against their own study of Scripture (the verb "to examine" is used elsewhere by Luke of judicial inquiry; cf. Luke 23:14; Acts 4:9; 12:19; 24:8; 28:18). This they did **with great eagerness**, meeting with Paul, not only on the Sabbath, but **every day** (v. 11; cf. v. 17; 19:9; see disc. on 13:42). Thus the intellect and the will (but also the heart and, of course, the Holy Spirit; see disc. on 16:14) were involved in the response of those who came to faith. This point is made clearly in the Greek by the conjunction between verses 11 and 12 (not shown in NIV). These converts included Jews and Greeks (initially God-fearers from the synagogue) and, among the latter, **a number of prominent . . . women** (see note on 16:13; see also disc. on 1:14; 13:50). The way the sentence runs: "Many of them believed, both of the women . . . and not a few men" (v. 12, so the Greek) probably indicates that women were especially prominent in this church. Of the men, "Sopater son of Pyrrhus" may have been an early convert (20:4).

17:13 / Even the Jews who did not believe were "more noble" than most, in that they did not interfere with Paul and the others—unless, of course, it was they who reported their activities to the Thessalonians. At all events, it was only when some Jews from Thessalonica arrived that there was any overt opposition. The use of Paul's name alone in this notice probably means that he was their main target. But how were they to strike at him? The earlier prohibition of the politarchs had no force beyond their own city, and no evidence exists "that the police forces of different cities ever acted in concert" (Sherwin-White, p. 98). If, then, the law was to be invoked against him, fresh charges would have to be laid. So the Thessalonian Jews set about **agitating the crowds and stirring them up**, doubtless alleging as before that the Christians were traitors to Rome (cf. vv. 5–7).

17:14–15 / These allegations put all the Christians at risk, but since Paul was the focus of the Jews' attack, **the brothers** thought it best for him to leave (v. 14). A number of them traveled with him to the coast, where it may have been his intention to wait for Silas and Timothy. But here he may have found a ship bound for Athens and so, with the Bereans still for company, he went to that city, sending instructions back that the others should join him there **as soon as possible** (v. 15). Assuming that he went to Attica by sea (see note), his port of embarkation was probably Dion (Colonia Julia Diensis), near the foot of Olympus. This town was connected directly by road with Berea.

Additional Notes   §46

17:14 / **To the coast**, lit., "as far as to the sea": A variant read-ing, not well attested, has "as to the coast," as though this was a feint to deceive the Jews (cf. AV "as it were"), implying that Paul actually went by land to Athens. This should be compared with the Western text, which explicitly states that Paul went by road, though "he neglected Thessaly, for he was prevented from preaching the word to them" (cf. 16:6–10). Rackham points out that "between Macedonia and Thessaly lay a great barrier in the huge mass of Mt. Olympus; and that the mountain forced the road from the one country into the other to run along the coast. Hence, even if St. Paul had intended to go to Greece on foot, he would have been obliged to go as far *as to-the-sea*, i.e., the sea-coast, before he could join the road" (p. 300).

§47 In Athens (Acts 17:16–34)

The great interest of this section lies in Paul's speech to the council of Areopagus. It provides us with a paradigm of his preaching to pagans, where, rather than "beginning with Moses and all the prophets" (Luke 24:27), that is, with the "revealed theology," his approach was by way of "natural theology." An earlier example of this method was seen in 14:15–17. But Paul was here facing a very different audience from the Lystrans. With them he had spoken of God as the one who gave the seasons and the crops, but with the Areopagites a philosophical approach was demanded and an appeal not so much to the evidence of nature as to the inner witness of God to human consciousness and conscience. But the question remains, Could (or would) Paul have made such a speech? The closest we can come to it is in Romans 1–3, but that letter has a different purpose and therefore a different emphasis (a much harder line against idolatry) to that found in this speech. And yet, when these verses are compared with Romans, no essential difference comes to light, and we find nothing that the writer of Romans could not have said. Moreover, the speech fits comfortably "into the category of a widespread type of religious propaganda literature found in both Jewish and pagan writings" (H. Conzelmann, *Studies*, p. 225). In short, there is nothing here that is not in keeping with Paul's having made such a speech, whereas if it were Luke's own invention (as some people allege) we might have expected two things that are lacking: a more explicitly Christian content (but see W. Barclay, *AHG*, p. 166, for its implicitly Christian character) and a far better result from it. It does come to us now in Lukan accents, but we may accept it as essentially Paul's.

17:16 / Paul's journey to Athens took him from Macedonia into the province of Achaia. After the defeat of the Achaean League by the Romans in 147 B.C., this area was administered from Macedonia, until 27 B.C. when it became a separate senatorial province. From A.D. 15 to 44 it was again combined with

Macedonia, together with Moesia under the rule of the Moesian legate (see disc. on 16:12), but was again a separate province when Paul knew it. Its capital was at Corinth, but Athens was undoubtedly its most prestigious city. By now the greatest days of Athens were behind it, but it still could be fairly described as the intellectual capital of the Greco-Roman world and, at the same time, the religious capital of Greece. It was also the repository of some of the finest treasures of art and architecture. The Roman general Sulla had sacked the city in 86 B.C., but damage had been largely confined to the private quarters. Subsequently, under Augustus and to a lesser extent his successors, the Romans had added to the many public buildings that adorned the city.

Assuming that Paul came from Berea by ship (see note on v. 14) and that he landed at the Piraeus, he would have made his way to the city by the Hamaxitos Road. Five miles of walking would have brought him to the Dipylon Gate and eastward from here to the agora (NIV "marketplace," v. 17) and the Acropolis. As Paul walked this and the other streets of Athens, on every side, in niches and on pedestals, in temples and on street corners, his eye would have fallen on the works of great artists. But he saw their representations of gods and demigods, not as objects of beauty, but as examples of senseless idolatry (cf. Philostratus, *Life of Apollonius of Tyana* 4.19). At first his intention may have been not to preach until Silas and Timothy had arrived. But he was so **greatly distressed** by what he saw that he could not rest (the verb corresponds to the noun in 15:39—he suffered a paroxysm). We learn from 1 Thessalonians 3:1–2 that Timothy did rejoin Paul in Athens, but was sent back "to strengthen . . . and encourage" the Thessalonians. Silas, it appears from 18:5, did not arrive from Berea until Paul had gone to Corinth. He and Timothy arrived together, Timothy returning from this second visit to Macedonia.

17:17 / Meanwhile, Paul's first recourse was to the synagogue, where at least he would find some sympathy for the horror that he felt at the idolatry of these people and at the same time could share the gospel with his countrymen. The Jews were probably not numerous in Athens, but as usual their community provided him with a base from which to work (see disc. on 9:20 and note on 13:14). His method of presenting the gospel was the same as in Thessalonica (see disc. on v. 2), but here he also carried this method into the agora, where **he reasoned . . . with those**

who happened to be there, much as Socrates had done in this very place 450 years earlier.

17:18 / Athens was a cosmopolitan city, and Paul would have found himself with a motley crowd in the agora. But it was not only with *hoi polloi* that he came into contact, but with some of the philosophers who also frequented that place, Epicureans and Stoics. He met with them more than once (so the Greek imperfect), but still they did not really grasp what he was saying. They heard him speak of **Jesus and the resurrection**, but to their ears it sounded as though he was **advocating foreign gods** (lit., "demons," but in the neutral Greek sense). Apparently they misconstrued his message to be about two deities, Jesus and his consort, Anastasis (the Greek word for resurrection), understanding them perhaps as Healing (Jesus sounds something like this in Greek) and Restoration. It is not surprising that they should think this, for the Athenians themselves had raised altars to Modesty, Pity, Piety, and the like (cf. Pausanias, *Description of Greece* 1.17). The philosophers' interest in Paul's teaching was probably no more than academic, but there may have been just a hint of threat in it, because in Athens the introduction of strange gods, though common enough, was a capital offense if for this reason the local deities were rejected and the state religion was disturbed (cf. Xenophon, *Memorabilia* 1.1; Josephus, *Against Apion* 2.262–275). Some philosophers saw nothing in Paul's teaching and dismissed him out of hand as **this babbler** (the word has the sense of a "retailer of secondhand ideas"). Others felt, however, that his teaching warranted closer investigation, and to this end they brought him before the council of Areopagus (v. 19). There is nothing to suggest that Paul was on trial. Rather, it seems to have been a kind of preliminary hearing to ascertain whether charges should be laid. In the end nothing came of it, and Paul was allowed to walk away unhindered (v. 33).

17:19–21 / The Areopagus was the most venerable institution in Athens, its history reaching back into legendary times. Despite the curtailment of much of its ancient power, it retained great prestige. Its function had varied from time to time. At some periods its jurisdiction was limited to cases of capital crime; at others it had to do with a wide range of legal, political, educational, and religious matters, as indeed at this time (so it seems), since the Athenian *dēmos* was more or less defunct (Athens was a free city with the right to govern its own affairs). The council took its name from a little hill overlooking the agora—the Hill of Ares—where a flight of steps cut into the southeastern side and the remains of rock-hewn benches may show where it used to meet. But in time it became customary for the council to meet elsewhere, probably in a roped-off section of the Stoa Basileios at the northwestern corner of the agora (see J. Finegan, "Areopagus," *IDB*, vol. 1, p. 217).

The opening question is literally, "Is it possible to know this new teaching . . . ? (v. 19), and without hearing the tone of voice, it is impossible to know whether this was asked courteously or sarcastically, but since some weight is put in the Greek text on the phrase **this new teaching,** it may have been sarcastically. Perhaps because of this attitude and their poor response later to what he regarded as a most significant speech, Luke was not impressed with the Athenians. In an aside he makes the comment that they were a shallow lot, who **spent their time** [the imperfect indicates that this was their habit] **doing nothing but talking about and listening to the latest ideas** (v. 21) and never (by implication) coming to grips with what they heard. Nor did Luke hold this opinion on his own. It was shared by some of their own countrymen (Thucydides, *History of the Peloponnesian War* 3.38; Demosthenes, *First Philippic* 43; *The Letter of Philip* 156f.).

17:22–23 / Whatever the spirit in which it was asked, Paul took their question seriously and set about answering it. Standing and addressing them in the style of their own public speakers ("men, Athenians"; but see note on 1:16), he remarked: **I see that in every way you are very religious** (v. 22). Now the word translated "religious" (*deisidaimonesteros*) can have either a good sense or a bad (the corresponding noun appears to be used in a derogatory sense in 25:19). It is a comparative and can mean either that they were more devout than most in the practice of their religion or more superstitious. Perhaps Paul deliberately chose the word with kindly ambiguity so as not to offend his hearers while, at the same time, expressing to his own satisfaction what he thought of their religion. They would learn soon enough what his opinion really was. Meanwhile, evidence that they were indeed "very religious" abounded on every side. But one inscription in particular had caught Paul's eye. He had noticed an altar with the dedication: TO AN UNKNOWN GOD (v. 23). He took this now as his "text." Of course there was no connection between this god and the God whom he would proclaim. He was not suggesting for one moment that they were unconscious worshipers of the true God but was simply looking for a way of raising with them the basic question of all theology: Who is God?

17:24 / Paul's answer to that question is that God is the creator. He has **made the world and everything in it**. The proposition comes straight from the Old Testament (e.g., Gen. 1:1; Exod. 20:11; Neh. 9:6; Ps. 74:17; Isa. 42:5; 45:7); the language, however, does not, for there is no corresponding word in Hebrew for "the world." The Hebrew Bible speaks of "the heaven and the earth" or "the all" (Jer. 10:16). "The world" (Gk. *kosmos*) is found in Greek-speaking Judaism (Wisd. 9:9; 11:17; 2 Macc. 7:23), but Paul's choice of it here may have been influenced less by that than by the use made of it by Plato and Aristotle. In any case, his point was that the world was not a thing of chance, but the work of God. A number of things follow from this: First, God is not detached from the creation, as the Epicureans thought, and second, God is greater than the creation. Therefore he cannot be confined to **temples built by hands** (the Stoics would have heartily agreed, though from a different premise). Again, Paul's words had an edge to them, and this time it may have been noticed, for "made with hands" was an expression commonly used by Greek philosophers and Jews alike in their attacks on idolatry (see disc. on 7:48). The second half of this verse may be a deliberate echo of the sentiment expressed in Solomon's prayer (1 Kings 8:27).

17:25 / Moreover, third, God does not need anything that we can supply. The verb means "to need in addition," as though necessary to make God complete. The Roman Epicurean Lucretius (d. 55 B.C.) had borne witness to the notion that God "needs nothing from us" (*On the Nature of Things* 2.650), and his Greek counterparts must have nodded their approval of Paul at this point. But Paul's teacher was again the Old Testament. Psalm 50:7–15 makes this very point (cf. also 2 Macc. 14:35; 3 Macc. 2:9; Philo, *Special Laws* 1.291). It is evident from the fact that God is himself the source of human life. What, then, can we give to God? This thought is expressed emphatically in the Greek, "Not by human hands is he served," and then underlined by the present parti-

ciple, "he [God] keeps on giving" life. This description of God
is drawn from Isaiah 42:5 (cf. Gen. 2:7; Wisd. 1:7, 14), but Paul
may have intended a double meaning, for life (Gk. *zōē*) was popularly linked with Zeus, and he would have them know that God,
not Zeus, was the source of life (see disc. on 14:17). The best commentary on this verse is found in 1 Chronicles 29:14. David prays:
**Who am I, and who are my people, that we should be able to
give** [anything to you, i.e., to God]? **Everything comes from you,
and we have given you only what comes from your hand.**

17:26 / If God is the creator, then he is the creator of
human beings in particular. Concerning this Paul has two things
to say. First, **from one . . . he made every nation of men**. The
Greek does not say who or what the one is. From "the one
nature," "the one Father," "the one man" have all been suggested,
and in the end they all come to much the same thing. But Paul
probably meant "the one man," Adam. There is also uncertainty
as to how **every** should be understood. Was Paul contemplating
"the whole human race," or should we translate *pan ethnos*, "every
nation," as though he would draw attention to their distinctiveness while at the same time asserting their common origin? Either
could be argued from the Scripture, but the latter is probably the
better rendering of the Greek (many Athenians would have cared
for neither, for it was popularly held that they had "sprung from
the soil," i.e., that they were indigenous and therefore different—
superior—to others). The result was that the nations now inhabited the whole earth. But this, too, came within the ambit of
God's sovereign control. For he **determined** beforehand **the times
set for them and the exact places where they should live**. Here
again we are faced with more than one possible interpretation,
depending on how we have understood the first half of the verse.
If the whole human race is in view, then **the times** means the
cycle of seasons of which Paul had spoken at Lystra (14:17), or
perhaps the life span of each person, and **the exact places where
they should live** the natural boundaries between the land and
the sea (see esp. Ps. 74:17; cf. Job 38:8–11; Ps. 105:5–11). But if
the reference is, as we suppose, to every nation, then the thought
is of the eras that belong to particular nations—their rise and fall,
much as Jesus had spoken of "the times of the Gentiles" (Luke
21:24)—and of the places where these nations are found. In this
way Paul moved from speaking of God as creator to God as the

Lord of history, perhaps deliberately setting his own belief in divine providence over against the fatalism of his Stoic auditors.

17:27 / Not only is God the creator of life, he is also both the source and the goal of human aspirations, for he made human beings that they might **seek him and perhaps . . . find him**. This has been understood of the philosophical search for truth, but Paul's thought is still firmly rooted in the Old Testament, with its references to seeking and finding God (e.g., Ps. 14:2; Prov. 8:17; Isa. 55:6; 65:1; Jer. 29:13). He does, however, use an expression that had a philosophical association—"to reach out for him." Plato had used it of vague guesses at the truth. In a similar, though more concrete, sense, it occurs several times in the LXX of groping about in the dark (Deut. 28:29; Job 5:14; 12:25; Isa. 59:10). But the word itself simply means "to touch," as in Luke 24:39 and 1 John 1:1, and this may have been Paul's sense, that is, of some palpable assurance of God's presence that is everywhere and always possible in a world that he has made (cf. Rom. 1:20). It is God's purpose that we should seek him, but the verbs "to reach out" and "to find" are expressed in such a way (the optative mood) as to show that his intention has not been realized. This was due to sin, but Paul does not say so here. His aim here was to focus, not on the problem of sin, but on the possibility of knowing God. He asserts, therefore, that God **is not far from each one of us**. This could have been said by a Stoic, but not in the sense that Paul intended. They saw God (the Soul of the Universe) as immanent in all things and in that sense "not far from any one of us." But the God of whom Paul spoke, though close, was neither identical with his creation nor impersonal, as in the Stoic philosophy, but the living, personal God of the Old Testament (cf., e.g., Ps. 145:18; Jer. 23:23f.). And notice his use of the singular, **each one of us**. It reminds us again that this God seeks to establish personal relationships (cf., e.g., 3:26). How different from the Stoic's union with Universal Reason!

17:28 / To drive home his point, Paul cites some lines of Greek poetry. NIV renders this verse on the assumption that there are two quotations. But the first is not introduced as such; nor has the diction or meter of poetry. It is better to treat it as an allusion than as a direct quotation. There is some difficulty also in identifying its source. A ninth-century A.D. Syriac writer,

Isho'dad, attributes the poem to Minos of Crete and identifies
Paul's words in Titus 1:12 as a quotation from the same source.
But Clement of Alexandria is sure that the quotation in Titus is
from Epimenides, also a Cretan (*Stromateis* 1.14.59). Clement is
generally assumed to be right and Isho'dad to have been confused
by the fact that Epimenides wrote about Minos (see *BC*, vol. 5,
pp. 246–51). At all events, the line makes the point, as does the
other, that God is near since we depend upon him at every turn.
Paul was, of course, reading his own ideas into the poems. Neither
spoke of his God, and when the second asserted that **we . . .
are his offspring** (Gk. *genos*), the thought was of humanity as
a "spark of the divine" in Stoic terms, whereas Paul's thought was
of humanity as made in the "image" of God (the only legitimate
image in a world of idolatry). The second line is a quotation from
a work by the Cilician poet Aratus (d. ca. 315 B.C.) entitled "Phae-
nomena." However, a similar line has been found in Cleanthes
(ca. 330–231 B.C.). Paul's reference to your **poets** (plural) may be
a recognition of this, unless the reference is backwards as well
as forwards to include the words of Epimenides.

17:29 / Because human beings are both like God and dependent upon God, it is absurd to think that **the divine being**
can be portrayed by human art. The work of art is dependent on
the artist's imagination; it is also inanimate. On both counts it
is inferior to the person who made it. How much more, then,
to the God who made human beings! Paul's thought is best expressed by the phrase "God is Spirit" (John 4:24), for what is spiritual cannot be represented by an image of **gold or silver or stone**
(cf. Ps. 115:4ff.; Isa. 37:19; 40:19; 46:7ff.). But even as he con-
demns idolatry, he is concerned to conciliate his hearers. Notice
his use of the first person—not "you," but **we** should not think
along these lines.

17:30–31 / The speech ends with the announcement that
everyone should turn from evil ways (v. 30), that is, from idolatry,
in view of the fact that their creator is also their judge. Hitherto
he had **overlooked** their **ignorance**, but no longer (cf. 14:16; Rom.
3:25). (Note: Paul did not say that there had been no divine retribution for sin in the past. Romans 1:18 is decided proof to the
contrary. But the past had been relatively excusable because of
ignorance.) Behind the **but now** of verse 30 lies the familiar con-

cept of the new age inaugurated by Christ (see notes on 1:3 and
2:17ff.). Through him God had dealt definitively with the problem of sin. But for that very reason, he had now laid humanity
under a new accountability. The offer of salvation in Christ carried with it the threat of judgment if that offer was refused. Judgment and salvation go hand in hand; both are vested in Christ;
both give expression to the righteousness of God. This brought
Paul to declare that God has fixed a day **when he will judge the
world with justice** (v. 31; see disc. on 1:10)—a reference to Psalm
96:13—and has appointed a **man** to carry it out. How else could
a God who is Spirit reveal himself as the judge and appear on
the tribunal? Moreover, **he has given proof** [Gk. *pistis*, "faith," so
"plighted faith, a pledge"] **of this** [appointment] . . . **by raising
him from the dead** (v. 31). By **man** it seems unlikely that Paul
meant to stress the humanity of Jesus. Rather, he may have had
in mind the Son of Man whose resurrection had declared his
divine sonship (cf. Rom. 1:4; see disc. on 6:12 and 7:56). He could
not, of course, use that phrase here. "Son of Man" would have
been meaningless to the Athenians.

17:32–34 / Until now Paul had probably carried most of
his audience with him. But as soon as he started talking about
repentance (which implies sin) and judgment (which implies
moral responsibility) and the resurrection and return of Jesus
(which ran counter to all their ideas of death and immortality;
see note on v. 18 and Bruce, *Book*, pp. 363f.), he had lost them—
or at least most of them. Some derided, some deferred judgment (v. 32), and only a handful made a positive response to the
gospel, among them **Dionysius, a member of the Areopagus** (v.
34). Tradition has it that he became the first bishop of Athens
(Eusebius, *Ecclesiastical History* 3.4.10 and 4.23.3). Another convert was **a woman named Damaris**. It has been conjectured that
she was either a foreigner or a woman of the lower classes, for
no respectable Athenian woman would have been in the agora
to hear Paul speak. But her conversion could have come through
the synagogue or under some other circumstance; verse 34 does
not necessarily express the result of this meeting.

Besides the two who are named there were **a number of
others** (v. 34), but the impression is given that there were not
many, and no mention is made in the New Testament of any
church in this city. Indeed, when Paul was later reflecting on his

work in these parts, he wrote of "the household of Stephanas" as the first converts in Achaia, and they were apparently Corinthians (1 Cor. 16:15). He was, of course, writing to the Corinthians and may only have meant that Stephanas was the first in their part of Achaia, but still it remains that we have no evidence of a church in Athens. This has led some writers to suggest that Paul's determination "to know nothing" when he came to Corinth "except Jesus Christ and him crucified" (1 Cor. 2:1f.) was a reaction to his preaching in Athens "with eloquence" and "superior wisdom" that had failed to produce corresponding results. It must be doubted, however, that overall his preaching in Athens was any different from that in Corinth or elsewhere, though the response in Corinth was undoubtedly better. What Paul learned from Athens above all was that "the world through its wisdom" could not know God (1 Cor. 1:21).

Additional Notes §47

17:18 / Epicurean and Stoic philosophers: The founder of the Stoic school of philosophy was Zeno of Citium in Cyprus (335–263 B.C.). They took their name from the Stoa Poikile in the agora at Athens, where Zeno was wont to teach. His teaching was systematized and extended by Chrysippus (ca. 280–207 B.C.), the "second founder" of Stoicism. Subsequently, elements of Platonism were incorporated into it. The first lesson of Zeno's teaching was that the philosopher should practice virtue. But for virtue he needed knowledge, and the only true knowledge was that gained from the senses. And since the senses only respond to what is material, the Stoics held that reality belonged only to material things. They were materialists. They owned the existence of God, but he too was in some sense material. Sometimes they thought of him as a personal and loving deity. More commonly they equated him with nature, teaching that all things are produced from him and will at last be absorbed into him again. This included human beings, who were a "spark of the divine," whose souls were immortal, but who would survive death only in the sense that they returned to the Soul of the Universe to be reabsorbed into the fire of the divine spirit. So the Stoics were pantheists and held that the gods of popular mythology were simply expressions of the Universal Reason. They taught that the universe was governed by unchanging laws. They were therefore fatalists and held that the only way to happiness was to be in harmony with the inevitable course of events. They were conscious of both physical and moral evil in the world. They taught that, though the virtuous might have to suffer, no real evil happens to them, nor real good to the vicious. As a Stoic one trained oneself to rise superior to all the circumstances of life and to human passion, to be "self-sufficient"—"a king," or rather, "a god" in oneself. The Epicureans were named from Epicurus, born in 341 B.C. on the island of Samos. Their human ideal was a state in which the body was free from pain and the mind from disturbance—detachment was their ideal, not indulgence, as "epicure " suggests today. Thus human beings became the measure of all good for themselves and human senses the medium whereby that good was assessed. They too were materialists, but the Epicureans were different from the Stoics in teaching that the world was formed merely by the chance agglomeration of atoms (a theory derived from Democritus and learned by Epicurus from his disciple Nausiphanes). The gods had no involvement, therefore, in creation. Indeed, they cared for neither the world nor its inhabitants, but themselves followed to perfection the life of detachment that was the Epicurean ideal. Thus the Epicureans were practical atheists, though they did not deny the existence of the gods—we have an idea of them, therefore they must be real (the atoms of which the gods are also formed throw off "husks" that strike the senses of the human mind). The Epicureans sought happiness in a simple life—by restraining the senses, not crushing them as the Stoics attempted to do. Death, they believed, brought a dispersion of one's constituent atoms, and so one ceased to exist.

17:19 / They . . . brought him to a meeting of the Areopagus: NIV interprets the Greek as meaning that they brought Paul before the council, not simply to the place called Areopagus. The construction of the Greek (*epi* with the accusative) is what we should expect for taking someone before an official body such as this (cf. 16:19; 17:6; 18:12), and the mention of Dionysius the Areopagite in v. 34 seems to confirm this view. In any case, the reference in v. 22 to Paul's standing "in the middle of the Areopagus" (so the Greek) would be awkward if the hill, not the council, were intended.

17:23 / An altar with this inscription: TO AN UNKNOWN GOD: The Greek traveler Pausanias (second century A.D.) tells how along the Hamaxitos Road there were raised at intervals "altars of gods both named and unknown" (*Description of Greece* 1.1.4). About the same time, Philostratus noticed the same thing (*Life of Apollonius of Tyana* 6.3.5). Jerome probably had such statements in mind when he suggested that Paul replaced the plural "gods" by the singular as better suiting his purpose (*Commentary on Titus* 1:12). This may indeed be what happened, and there may be no difficulty in allowing the preacher this license. But we should not dismiss the possibility that the inscription did occur in the singular. There were evidently a number of these altars, and if more than one was dedicated to only one deity, they could be referred to comprehensively as "altars to unknown gods" (see Bruce, *Book*, p. 356).

§48 In Corinth (Acts 18:1–17)

Corinth was the most important city to which Paul had come since leaving Syrian Antioch, and he stayed there longer than in any other city (as far as we know). Luke tells us of the establishment of the church in Corinth, but nothing of its life. For this we must turn to Paul's letters. So little does Luke say of this church that he has opened himself to the charge of being less interested in Corinth than in Macedonia and Ephesus (Rackham, p. 322). There may be something in this, but the reason lies more in Luke's method and purpose in writing. He is not concerned to give a detailed account of the work in every place, but only a broad view of how the Christian mission developed. This he does by means of exemplars, and having already shown how Paul preached and worked wherever he went, he has no need to repeat himself here. Thus eighteen months of work in Corinth are summed up in one verse (v. 11). Something else now claimed Luke's attention. On one occasion during these eighteen months Paul was brought before the proconsul Gallio on the charge of disseminating an illicit religion. The charge was dismissed, and for Luke this was an important demonstration of the compatibility of the Christian faith with the Roman state (see also disc. on 19:23–41 and 26:31).

18:1 / Timothy appears to have rejoined Paul at Athens, but then to have returned to Macedonia, and Silas had not yet come from Berea (see disc. on 17:16). So Paul was alone again as he journeyed the fifty miles from Athens to Corinth (i.e., by land, but he may have taken ship to Cenchrea). Corinth lay at the western end of the isthmus that joins the Peloponnesus with the mainland, and through it passed all the traffic between the peninsula and the north; its two harbors, one on either side of the isthmus, made it a focal point of the sea trade between East and West. The history of Corinth had been a long one. Its greatest fame had been under Periander (ca. 625–583 B.C.), but having survived many earlier wars, it fell victim at last to the Romans. Because of the leading role it had played against them as a member

of the Achaean League, the consul Mummius burned and razed
the city, slaying its men and selling its women and children into
captivity (146 B.C.). Achaia became part of the province of Macedonia; Corinth itself, though not entirely abandoned, was reduced
to insignificance for the next hundred years. In 44 B.C. it was
re-established as a colony by Julius Caesar and named by him
Colonia Laus Julia Corinthiensis, "Corinth the praise of Julius"
(see note on 16:12). In 27 B.C. Augustus separated Achaia from
Macedonia and made Corinth its capital. The new province was
placed under the control of the senate and was given to the Senate again in A.D. 44 when another period of amalgamation with
its neighbors was ended (see disc. on 16:12 and 17:16). As a senatorial province it was ruled by a proconsul (see note on 13:7).

Prosperity returned to the revived city and with it its reputation for evil, though it must be questioned whether is was really
any worse than any other port city of the eastern Mediterranean.
There is a suspicion that Athenian propaganda had something
to do with the name Corinth had for licentiousness: the fruits
of commerce are often envied by those dedicated to culture.
Nevertheless, Corinth was undeniably a rip-roaring town where
"none but the tough could survive" (Horace, *Epistles* 1.17.36), and
this character is amply reflected in Paul's letters (e.g., 1 Cor. 5:1–
23; 6:9–20; 7:2, 5, 9; 10:8; 15:33f.). No wonder he also wrote: "I
came to you in weakness and fear, and with much trembling"
(1 Cor. 2:3). And yet he was determined even here to proclaim
"Jesus Christ and him crucified" (1 Cor. 2:2). If that message could
succeed here, it could succeed anywhere!

18:2 / Paul met up with a Jewish couple, Aquila and
Priscilla—both Latin names, Priscilla being the diminutive of
Prisca, the name used by Paul in his letters (see disc. on 9:6 and,
for the names, note on 12:12). Aquila was a native of Pontus, that
is, the province of Pontus-Bithynia or possibly the more easterly
client kingdom of Pontus, but more recently the couple had come
from Rome. They were victims of an edict of Claudius that had
ordered all Jews to leave Rome. The edict is probably to be dated
A.D. 49, and the disturbance that had prompted it was very likely
due to friction between Jews and Christians (see notes). From this
it would appear that there was a church in Rome by the late 40s
(cf. 2:10) to which Aquila and Priscilla may have belonged, since
they appear here to be Christians. They were to play an impor-

tant part in Paul's life and on at least one occasion "risked their lives" for him (Rom. 16:3f.; cf. 1 Cor. 16:19; 2 Tim. 4:19). In most of the references Priscilla is named before her husband, perhaps because she was more prominent in the church.

18:3–4 / Arrangements in the synagogue at Corinth may have been like those at Alexandria, where the various trades sat together (b. *Sukkah* 51b), and in this way Paul may have met with Aquila and Priscilla and found both lodging and work with them, **because he was a tentmaker as they were** (v. 3; they might be better described as leatherworkers; R. Hock, *The Social Context of Paul's Ministry: Tent Making and Apostleship* [Philadelphia: Fortress Press, 1980], p. 21). Rabbis were expected to learn and practice a trade, and Paul must have been glad of this in later life as he worked to support his ministry (cf. 20:34; 1 Cor. 4:12; 9:3–19; 2 Cor. 11:7ff.; 1 Thess. 2:9; 2 Thess. 3:8). Perhaps the shop became the center of evangelism during the week and the synagogue the same on the Sabbath, where **he reasoned, . . . trying to persuade Jews and Greeks** (v. 4; for the audience, see note on 13:14b, for the method, see disc. on 17:2).

18:5 / A change in this pattern of ministry appears to be indicated in this verse. It is not completely clear from the Greek whether Silas and Timothy, on their arrival from Macedonia, found Paul devoting **himself exclusively to preaching**, or whether this was something he was able to do only after they had rejoined him. If the latter—and this seems the more likely, taking the imperfect tense to be inceptive: "he began to devote his whole time . . . "—it may mean that they had brought gifts for the support of his work (cf. 2 Cor. 11:9; Phil. 4:15). Luke's description of this new phase is a striking one. NIV gives the sense of it, but the actual expression is that Paul "was seized by the message," as though it had overpowered him and he was no longer master of when he would preach but the servant of a message that would be preached "in season and out" (2 Tim. 4:2). So he was **testifying to the Jews**. Does this mark a change of method from discussion to a more dogmatic approach? (See disc. on 2:40; cf. 1 Cor. 2:4.) Silas is mentioned in this verse for the last time in Acts.

18:6–8 / The work in Corinth met with early success. There were a number of converts, including Titius Justus, possibly a Roman citizen and a *colonus*, **a worshiper of God** (v. 7) and **Crispus** [a Jew despite his Latin name] **the synagogue ruler** (v. 8). It would appear from the use of the definite article, "the ruler," that at Corinth only one person at a time held that office (see disc. on 13:15) and that Sosthenes, who is mentioned later in verse 17, succeeded to Crispus' office on the latter's conversion. The order of the verses implies that Crispus did not become a Christian until after Paul's break with the synagogue, but Haenchen may be right in supposing that he and his family came to faith while Paul was still in good standing with the Jewish community (p. 540). Among others were Gaius, whom Paul mentions with Crispus in 1 Corinthians 1:14, and "the household of Stephanas," who were "the first converts in Achaia" (i.e., Corinth? 1 Cor. 16:15).

But Paul's success aroused the hostility of the greater number of the Jews **who opposed Paul and became abusive** (v. 6). No objects are expressed in the Greek. We may agree with NIV, however, that Paul was the object of the first verb, and though the same object would naturally be assumed for the second, it is not impossible that a change was intended and that it was of Christ they said evil things (see disc. on 13:45). Under these circumstances Paul was forced to withdraw from the synagogue, and he established himself next door in the house of Titius Justus. This need not mean that he had left his lodging with Aquila and Priscilla, only that he made this the meeting place of the Christians (see disc. on 14:27 and notes). To have the Christians meeting so near must have rankled the Jews, the more so since Paul had marked his withdrawal by the symbolic act of shaking their dust from his clothes, in effect declaring them to be no better than the Gentiles (see disc. on 13:51). He told the Jews that he no longer held himself responsible for them. If they were doomed, it was their own fault. His words were, **Your blood be on your own heads!** (v. 6), where **blood** is a figure of destruction and **heads** simply means "themselves." He uses much the same expression in 20:26, and in both cases the allusion is to Ezekiel 33:6. **From now on,** he said, **I will go to the Gentiles** (v. 6). As in 13:46, the reference is simply to the local situation, for in verse 19 and again in 19:8 we find him back in a synagogue preaching to Jews.

As usual, the best response to Paul's preaching was from the Gentiles (initially the God-fearers). Thus **many of the Corinthians who heard him believed and were baptized** (v. 8; the tense in the Greek points to continuous growth). Most of the converts were from the lower classes. "Think of what you were," he later wrote. "Not many of you were wise by human standards; not many were influential; not many were of noble birth" (1 Cor. 1:26) There were exceptions, however, and most notably "Erastus, who [was] the city's director of public works" (Rom. 16:23, written from Corinth). It is interesting that at Corinth a pavement, apparently of the first century A.D., has been found bearing the inscription "*Erastus Pro Aed. S.P. Stravit*" (*Erastus pro aedilitate sua pecunia stravit*), which means that in return for his aedileship Erastus had laid out this pavement at his own expense. We cannot be certain that this was the same man as the one named in the letter, but since the office of aedile was that of public works, the coincidence is certainly striking. Such a man would have been both "influential" and of high social standing, if not exactly of "noble birth."

18:9-10 / Despite these encouragements and due to a number of factors, including the opposition of the Jews and the oppressive nature of the city itself, Paul seems to have given way to the fears that had haunted him since he had first come to Corinth (see disc. on v. 1). But in the depths of his depression, the Lord spoke to him in a vision (see disc. on 23:11). The message was couched in the language of the Old Testament (cf., e.g., Exod. 3:12; Deut. 31:6; Josh. 1:5, 9; Isa. 43:5; Jer. 1:8) and contains a twofold command: first, "stop being afraid" (the force of the Greek) and then, **keep on speaking** [as he had been doing] and **do not be silent** (v. 9). This idiom of affirmation and negation—"keep on . . . do not give up . . ."—adds a certain solemnity to the utterance. It was backed by a threefold promise: that the Lord would be with him (cf. Matt. 28:19f.); that none would harm him—not that the attempt would not be made, but that he would survive it (cf. vv. 12–17; cf. also Ps. 23:4; Isa. 41:10); and that in this city the Lord had many **people** (v. 10; cf. 1 Kings 19:18; Hos. 2:23). Significantly, this word (Gk. *laos*) is that used consistently for the people of God (in the first instance, Israel; see disc. on 15:14), though the people in question here were Gentiles and still pagan. But the Lord knew those whom he had "appointed for eternal life" (13:48; cf. John 10:16).

18:11 / With this encouragement, **Paul stayed for a year and a half, teaching them the word of God. Paul stayed** is literally "he took his seat," and though the verb itself is common enough in the New Testament, nowhere else is it used in this sense (though regularly so in the LXX). Luke may have chosen it, therefore, to draw attention to the more settled frame of mind to which Paul had come. He seems not to have visited Corinth with any definite intention of making it a great center of his work. On the contrary, Macedonia had still filled his mind, and he had been eager to return, especially to Thessalonica (cf. 1 Thess. 2:17f.). But the vision may have given him a new perspective. He saw himself, perhaps, as released from the call to preach the Good News in Macedonia (16:10) and under a new imperative to preach it now in Achaia. As in 4:31 and 15:35, this paragraph ends with the phrase **the word of God** and, like those other verses, may be intended to mark the completion of a subsection, in this case, the account of the founding of the churches of Macedonia and Achaia.

18:12 / The divine promise that none would harm him had a notable fulfillment **while Gallio was proconsul of Achaia.** Marcus Annaeus Novatus, as he was first called, was the son of Seneca the rhetorician and the brother of Mela (father of Lucan the poet) and of Seneca the Stoic philosopher and sometime tutor of Nero. Born in Spain, he came to Rome during the reign of Tiberius, was adopted into the family of his father's friend Lucius Junius Gallio, and took the name of his adoptive father (he was now Lucius Junius Gallio Annaeus). Proconsular governors normally took office on 1 July and held it for one year only. The year in which Gallio ruled in Achaia has been fixed with some certainty as July A.D. 51 to June A.D. 52 (this gives us a rare fixed point for Pauline chronology). All who knew Gallio spoke of him in the highest terms (Seneca, *Epistles* 104.1; Pliny, *Natural History* 21.33; Tacitus, *Annals* 15.73; Dio Cassius, *Roman History* 61.35).

Perhaps the Jews expected this man to be a "soft touch," or they may have been banking on his inexperience. Gallio had come to Achaia having only been a praetor and not yet a consul, the senior Roman magistracy, and in any case, he may have only recently arrived and would for that reason be the more ready to please his petitioners. At all events **the Jews made a united attack on Paul and brought him into court** for Gallio to hear their charge against him. The traditional site of this hearing is the agora, where a raised platform may have been used by the magistrates to dis-

pense summary justice. But it is doubtful whether Gallio would
have held court in such a public place, and we know from similar cases that Roman provincial courts were usually held in a basilica or in the praetorium. If this was so now, then the so-called
north basilica beside the Lecheum road suggests itself as a possible location.

18:13 / The indictment was that Paul was **persuading the
people to worship God in ways contrary to the law.** The question is, To what law were they referring? If the Jewish, then they
were asking the governor to enforce their own law, perhaps with
the hope of having him exclude the Christians who did not submit to it from the protection that the Jews enjoyed as a *religio licita*
(a permitted religion). But there is no reason to think that the
Jews had any grounds for expecting such an enforcement of their
law upon their own adherents. Perhaps, then, the charge related
to Roman law. Sherwin-White points out that the best charge for
the Jews to bring "was that Paul was preaching to Romans, not
to Jews, contrary to the Roman law, not the Jewish law, just as
at Philippi" (p. 101; see disc. on 16:20f.), that is, that he was attempting to proselytize Roman citizens.

18:14–16 / Paul was about "to open his mouth" in his own
defense (see disc. on 10:34) when Gallio cut him short. The governor was under no compulsion to enforce the law prohibiting
citizens from practicing foreign cults, and since he saw no threat
to the state or to public morals, he had no intention of doing so
now. His final words, **I will not be a judge of such things** (v. 15),
are "the precise answer," says Sherwin-White, "of a Roman magistrate refusing to exercise his *arbitrium iudicantis* within a matter
extra ordinem" (p. 102). To Gallio it was a purely Jewish dispute
about words and names (is this a reference to Jesus' name of
"Messiah"?) and their own law, and they could settle the matter
among themselves (v. 15; cf. 23:29; 25:19). With all his Roman
disdain of the Jews, he had his lictors drive the petitioners from
his court.

18:17 / What happened then is not clear except that **they
all turned on Sosthenes the synagogue ruler and beat him** (cf.
v. 8). Some manuscripts give an explanation of who **they** were,
but the best reading (adopted by NIV) leaves them unnamed. One
suggestion is that, despite Luke's failure to mark the change of

subject, it was the crowd who set upon Sosthenes. Encouraged by Gallio's attitude, they were quick to show their own contempt for the Jews. Alternatively, it may have been the Jews themselves who beat him up, as the context would suggest. On this understanding, having failed so ignominiously to make their charges stick, they vented their rage on their own leader, who had presented their case. Or if this was the Sosthenes of 1 Corinthians 1:1 (the coincidence is certainly striking), though still the leader of the synagogue, he may have shown some leanings toward the Christians, like his predecessor Crispus, and on that account suffered the rage of the Jews. In any case Gallio refused to intervene, allowing either an injustice against the Jews or by the Jews against one of themselves (as he would have seen it even if Sosthenes was by now a Christian). How little the Romans cared for Jewish life and limb is evident in their literature (e.g., Cicero, *Pro Flacco* 28; *De Provinciis Consularibus* 5; Horace, *Satires* 1.143; 5.100; 9.69; *Tacitus, Annals* 2.85). But for all that, something positive may have come out of this for Paul. He may have realized for the first time the full potential of the Roman state for protection. And if it offered that protection here, why not in Rome itself? Thus may the Spirit have sown the seed of an idea that gradually became Paul's great objective (see disc. on 19:21).

Additional Notes §48

18:2 / **Claudius had ordered all the Jews to leave Rome:** Luke's statement is corroborated by Suetonius (*Claudius* 25). But Dio Cassius (third century A.D.), in referring to what was probably the same edict, states that the Jews were not expelled, because of the difficulty of implementing such an order (*Roman History* 60.6). Another passage may throw some light on this seeming contradiction. Suetonius instances an earlier expulsion that was contemplated but not carried out (*Tiberius* 36), yet he describes it in terms similar to the Claudian edict. If indeed the expulsion under Claudius did not take place, this would explain the lack of reference to it in either Tacitus or Josephus. But what of the statements of Luke and Suetonius (concerning the Claudian edict)? Dio Cassius explains that though the Jews were not expelled, they were ordered not to hold meetings. As a result of this, many of them would have undoubtedly left Rome, so the two earlier writers have correctly described the results of the edict, if not the edict itself.

On the information of the fifth-century historian Orosius (*History* 7.6.15f.), the edict was issued in the ninth year of Claudius (25 January A.D. 49 to 24 January 50). He cites Josephus as his authority, but no mention of the decree is found in any of Josephus' extant works. On the other hand, it is thought by some that the reference in Dio Cassius is better ascribed to the first year of Claudius' reign, i.e., A.D. 41 (see, e.g., F. Millar, *A Study of Dio Cassius* [London: Oxford University Press, 1964], p. 40). But this earlier date is not without problems—apart, that is, from its calling into question the clear implication of Luke's text that the edict had been issued not long before Paul came to Corinth (at the earliest, in the late 40s). The whole question is fraught with uncertainties, and there is certainly no compelling reason to doubt Luke's accuracy on this point. (For a different opinion, see J. Murphy-O'Connor, *St. Paul's Corinth*, pp. 129ff.) As for the circumstances that gave rise to the edict, Suetonius describes them as follows: "because the Jews of Rome caused continuous disturbances at the instigation of Chrestus, he expelled them from the city." It is commonly supposed that Suetonius was referring to some commotion in the Jewish community over the preaching of Christ, but that he has confused Christus with Chrestus and assumed that this Chrestus was an actual leader in Rome. The two names are easily confused. Tacitus, for example, calls the Christians *Chrestiani*. On this supposition, there was already a Christian presence in Rome in the 40s.

18:7 / Titius Justus: The manuscripts variously render his name Titius or Titus or omit it altogether. There is no reason to think that he was the Titus of Paul's letter. We have assumed in the discussion that he and the Gaius of 1 Cor. 1:14 were different people. But following the hint of Rom. 16:23, E. J. Goodspeed ("Gaius Titius Justus," *JBL* 69 [1950], pp. 328ff.) suggests that they are one and the same person.

18:12 / While Gallio was proconsul of Achaia: The year in which Gallio was governor of Achaia has been determined by an inscription found at Delphi that was made after the twenty-sixth acclamation of Claudius as *Imperator*. These acclamations occurred at frequent but irregular intervals and by themselves do not establish a precise date. But other inscriptions have been preserved elsewhere that enable us to set fairly narrow limits for the Gallio inscription. There are two (*Corpus Inscriptionus Latinarum* 3.476.1977) that show that the twenty-second and twenty-fourth acclamations belong to the eleventh year of Claudius' reign (25 January A.D. 51 to 24 January 52). There is another on a monumental arch of an aqueduct in Rome, dedicated on 1 August A.D. 52, that shows that by that date Claudius had celebrated his twenty-seventh acclamation. Given this date, it seems most likely that Gallio's term of office extended from July A.D. 51 to June 52.

§49 Priscilla, Aquila, and Apollos (Acts 18:18–28)

The end of the "second" and the start of the "third missionary journey" are narrated here with almost breathless haste, as though Luke were anxious to have Paul start on his work at Ephesus. The brevity of the narrative leaves us guessing at a number of points as to where and why he went, but for the most part we can plot his course with reasonable confidence and make good sense of all that he did. Because of the broad similarity between this journey and that in 20:3–21:26—the common elements being a journey from Corinth to Jerusalem via Ephesus and Paul's taking a vow—it has been proposed that this section is simply a Lukan construction based on the other and intended to keep Paul in touch with Jerusalem and in receipt of that church's blessing, with the further motive of attributing to Paul a larger share in the establishment of the church in Ephesus. But if these verses were really written with those objectives in mind, surely Luke would have made a better fist of them than this. They give no result of Paul's preaching in Ephesus, and they only hint at his going up to Jerusalem. On the other hand, there is no reason why he should not have made this journey at this time, and good reasons can be given for why he did.

18:18 / During Paul's eighteen months or more at Corinth, we may suppose that the church in Cenchrea (the eastern harbor) was also established (Rom. 16:1), and perhaps other churches, for in 2 Corinthians 1:1 we read of "the saints throughout Achaia." But the day came when Paul felt that he must draw his work here to a close and return, if only briefly, to **Syria** (it is not certain whether this term is used here to include Judea or whether it simply indicates his final destination, with no reference to his visit to Judea). Before he left, Paul cut his hair in fulfillment of a vow that he had made, perhaps early in his stay at Corinth when he had been depressed and afraid (v. 9). These vows, based on the

Nazirite vow of Numbers 6:1–21, appear to have been a common feature of Jewish piety (cf. 23:21–26; m. *Nazir*). Their conclusion was marked by the shaving of one's head and the offering of sacrifice in the temple. Both acts were normally done in Jerusalem, but if the devotee was far from the city, he seems to have been allowed to trim his hair and to bring the trimmings to Jerusalem to be offered with the rest of his hair when his head was shaved (cf. Josephus, *War*, 2.309–314). This appears to have been what Paul did at Cenchrea, no doubt in a spirit of thanksgiving for all that God had done with him in Corinth. Luke's mention of this trivial matter may have been intended to show how unwarranted were the Jewish and even Jewish-Christian attacks upon Paul for his supposed antipathy to their traditions (see further the disc. on 21:23f.).

Paul took ship at Cenchrea, whose harbor had been rebuilt shortly after 44 B.C. Lucius Apuleius (second century A.D.) describes it as "the most famous town of all the Corinthians, bordering upon the seas called Aegean and Saronic. There is a great and mighty haven," he said, "frequented with ships of many and sundry nations" (*Metamorphoses* 10.35). He exaggerated. The harbor was nowhere near the size of Lecheum's (the western port of Corinth). Nevertheless, it must have been a sizable town in Paul's day. Priscilla and Aquila went with him. Presumably, Silas and Timothy stayed behind to superintend the work that Paul was leaving (see disc. on v. 23).

18:19–21 / The ship's first port of call was Ephesus. Here an impressive sight would have unfolded before the travelers' eyes as they entered the wide mouth of the Cayster on which Ephesus was built. In ancient times ships could come right up to the city, which lay between the sea and Mount Coressus (in time the harbor silted up, and the ruins of Ephesus now lie in a swampy plain some four or five miles from the sea). From the harbor the main thoroughfare led to the heart of the city, and from this road Paul and his companions must have had their first introduction to the metropolis of the province of Asia. During this brief visit Paul **went into the synagogue** where he **reasoned with the Jews** (v. 19; see disc. on 9:20 and 17:2). The prohibition on his preaching in Asia was now apparently lifted (16:6), as indicated by his warm reception (v. 20). The Ephesian Jews must have already heard much about "the Way" and no doubt would like to have heard more. But Paul would not stay, promising instead that if God willed he would return (cf. 21:14; James 4:15). Considering their eagerness, there must have been some pressing reason for his not remaining in Ephesus and making the most of this opportunity. He had his vow to complete, of course, but he may also have wished to be in Jerusalem for one of the festivals, perhaps the Passover (cf. 20:16), for which he would have to hurry since it came early in the traveling season (see disc. on 27:9 and 28:11). But over and above these things, if he had indeed begun to glimpse a wider prospect for his missionary enterprise (see disc. on v. 17), he may have wished to see Antioch again, for that church could no longer be an effective center for his work, and to take his leave of them. Meanwhile, Priscilla and Aquila remained in Ephesus, so that by the time Paul returned a church had already been formed. They had not yet separated from the synagogue, but were an identifiable group within it, in touch with their brothers in Corinth (vv. 26f.) and probably holding additional meetings of their own in Aquila and Priscilla's home (cf. 2:12; 1 Cor. 16:19, and for house churches, see disc. on 14:27 and notes).

18:22 / While these developments were taking place in Ephesus, Paul went on to Caesarea and, presumably, to Jerusalem, where he **greeted the church** (cf. 21:18). The uncertainty about his precise movements lies in the fact that the Greek text does not name Jerusalem, but unless we make the assumption that this was his destination, we are left with Paul "going up" (from the harbor?) to the church in Caesarea and "going down" from that city to Antioch. In neither case is the verb appropriate if that sense was intended, whereas the idiom was frequently "to go up to Jerusalem" (cf. 11:2; 15:2; 25:1, 9) and "down" when leaving (cf. 24:1; 25:6, 7). We take it, then, that this was Luke's meaning. The impression given is that Paul's stay in Jerusalem was a short one (perhaps a week, to complete his vow), but it would have been long enough to observe the economic plight of the church and to determine to do something about it (see disc. on 19:21). Thence he returned to Syrian Antioch.

18:23 / Here he made a stay of an indefinite period, perhaps until the following spring (A.D. 53?), after which he took to the road again on his "third missionary journey." Retracing his earlier steps (see disc. on 15:40f.), he passed through **the region of Galatia and Phrygia**, that is, the region of southern Galatia, which lay more or less in a direct line with Ephesus (see disc. on 16:6). The verb "to go through" may mean that he preached as he went (see disc. on 8:4), thus **strengthening all the disciples**. In this way he would have visited the cities of his former journeys: Derbe, Lystra, Iconium, and Antioch. From here, the main road would have taken him through Colossae and Laodicea in the Lycus Valley to the Maeander and along the river to the coast. But he appears not to have gone that way (cf. Col. 2:1), but by another, shorter route through the valley of the Cayster. As far as we know, he had no companion for the journey to Ephesus, but he probably hoped to rendezvous with Timothy, who is next heard of in that city (1 Cor. 4:17; 16:10f.).

18:24 / While Paul was making the journey described in the previous verses, Apollos arrived at Ephesus. He was a sufficiently important figure in the early church to warrant this notice of his coming to the metropolis. It serves also to show something of what was going on there before Paul's return. By that time, Apollos had gone, but later Paul and Apollos were together in Ephesus, and it is clear from a number of references in Paul's own writings that he regarded Apollos as a friend and a valued colleague (1 Cor. 3:5–9; 16:12; Titus 3:13). Apollos was a Jew, a native of Alexandria, and endowed with considerable gifts consistent with his city of origin (see note on 6:9). **He was a learned man**, where the Greek can mean "learned" or "eloquent," and in this case probably both—he had a learning that he effectively communicated. More specifically, he had **a thorough knowledge of the Scriptures**. This was the basis of his preaching in both Ephesus and Corinth.

18:25 / Apollos was already a Christian of sorts when he arrived at Ephesus and, to the extent that he understood it, was a great enthusiast for the faith. An expression is used that means literally "to boil in the spirit," that is, his own human spirit, and so perhaps "to bubble over with enthusiasm." This led him to speak and to teach (imperfects, indicating his habit) all that he knew about Jesus, though what he knew turned out to be incomplete. **He had been instructed in the Way of the Lord** (this implies that there was some kind of gospel preaching in Egypt by about A.D. 50). However, **he knew only the baptism of John**.

What, then, was lacking that he had not received Christian baptism and that Priscilla and Aquila should find it necessary to explain "to him the way of God more adequately" (v. 26)? If the "disciples" of 19:1-7 are any guide, then we must suppose that he did not yet know of the Pentecostal event—the gift of the Spirit in token that the age of salvation had come (see notes on 2:17ff.)— and the significance that it gave to baptism. For unlike John's, which merely anticipated the age of salvation, Christian baptism belonged to the new age, marking (among other things) the believer's entry into the gift of the Spirit (see notes on 2:2ff. and disc. on 2:38; 19:4). Apollos may have accepted that Jesus was the Messiah without knowing the full extent of his messianic achievement. One wonders whether he even knew of the resurrection of Jesus.

18:26 / Whatever his deficiencies, Apollos at least had the courage of his convictions. He first came to Aquila and Priscilla's notice when he spoke **boldly** (about Jesus) **in the synagogue** at Ephesus. Afterwards they took him home and made good what was lacking in his instruction. The way of God that they explained to him is a convenient summary of the theme that runs through all the early speeches of Acts, namely, that God "had foretold through all the prophets" the things concerning the Messiah (3:18, 21; etc.) and that those things have now been fulfilled in the life, death, resurrection, and ascension of Jesus and in the gift of the Spirit. Luke does not say whether Apollos received Christian baptism (but cf. 19:5). If he did, it was probably at the hands of his instructors.

18:27-28 / Later Apollos transferred to Achaia—these references seem always to indicate Corinth (cf. 19:1). The believers in Ephesus (see disc. on vv. 19-21) encouraged the move (or the Greek could mean that they encouraged the Corinthians to receive him) and wrote accordingly to the church in Achaia (v. 27). The idea of his going may have come from Priscilla and Aquila, thinking that Apollos' training and learning would attract the attention of a Corinthian audience. Certainly he proved to be **a great help to those who by grace had believed** (v. 27). Or perhaps it was that he was able to help "by his (gift of) grace," that is, by the knowledge and eloquence given to him by God. Either meaning is possible from the Greek. At all events, the Corinthians found in him a champion who was able to match the Jews in **pub-**

lic debate in the synagogue (v. 28). The verb means that he "argued them down," not necessarily convincing them, but, by bringing them to the test of Scripture, at least showing that their objections to Jesus as the Messiah were unwarranted. And not only was Apollos a help to believers, he was also used to bring some pagans into the fold (1 Cor. 3:5).

These verses give the impression that the church in Corinth had been under some pressure from the Jews since Paul's departure and that it was by his grasp of the Scriptures especially that Apollos was best able to help. But it was not long before he was back in Ephesus, and we find him in 1 Corinthians 16:12 refusing Paul's pressing request that he should revisit Corinth. The reason is not hard to find. In Corinth the people had begun to compare him with Paul, often to Paul's disadvantage. Apollos' eloquence and Alexandrian culture may have seemed superior to the simplicity of Paul's preaching. Partisan feeling was aroused, and the two men who only wanted to be fellow workers (1 Cor. 3:3–10) were represented as rivals (1 Cor. 1:12f.; 3:4, 22; 4:6). Evidently this was as painful for Apollos as it was for Paul.

Additional Notes §49

18:18 / He had his hair cut off at Cenchrea because of a vow he had taken: If the Greek grammar alone were heeded, these words would naturally be referred to Aquila. But it is difficult to see what point there would be in such a statement.

18:19 / Paul left Priscilla and Aquila: The Greek reads very awkwardly here. It appears that at first Luke had simply written that Paul that "left Priscilla and Aquila . . . (and) sailed from Ephesus," but that he later expanded the sentence by adding the intervening words.

18:23 / After spending some time in Antioch, Paul set out from there: It is usual to take this as the beginning of the "third missionary journey." But so little is made of it by Luke that there is some justification in the view that he himself did not see this as a third journey, but simply another phase of the second, which did not end until Paul reached Jerusalem in 21:17.

18:25 / With great fervor: The literal sense of this phrase has been given in the discussion, but instead of his own spirit (as we have taken it) the reference could be to the Spirit of God. On this understanding, it is conceivable that Apollos' faith had already brought him the gift of the Spirit before he received Christian baptism, or even that he did not receive the Christian rite, his earlier baptism being deemed sufficient in view of his charismata (see G. W. H. Lampe, *The Seal of the Spirit* [London: Longmans, Green, 1951], p. 66; see also disc. on 8:14ff. and 10:44). That Apollos had received the Spirit may have been assumed by Luke in his reference to his preaching "boldly" (v. 26; cf. 4:13; see disc. on 4:8).

§50 Paul in Ephesus (Acts 19:1–22)

This section and the one before it are a pair. They are both concerned with the relationship of Christianity to an imperfect form of the faith—"the baptism of John." In this case Paul deals with the situation himself. These verses include also a brief description of his ministry in Ephesus, aspects of which are illustrated in the following section. But again we must turn to Paul's letters to fill out our knowledge of these years. They show that his achievement in Ephesus was at the cost of much suffering (1 Cor. 15:32; 2 Cor. 1:8; 4:9ff.; 6:4ff.), including, perhaps, an imprisonment (cf. 2 Cor. 11:23) and a "flying visit" to Corinth in an attempt to bring order into that church's troubled affairs (cf. 2 Cor. 12:14; 13:1; also 2 Cor. 2:1; see disc. on 21:21).

19:1a / Paul appears to have made the journey to Ephesus by the shorter, though less frequented, route through Cayster Valley (see disc. on 18:23). At least this seems to be the meaning of the phrase "the upper country" (NIV **the interior**), since this road did lead over higher ground than the main road through Colossae and Laodicea. He was now in proconsular Asia. By the second century B.C. this region was under the rule of the Seleucids, but with the defeat by the Romans of the Seleucid king, Antiochus III (190 B.C. at Magnesia), much of it passed to Eumenes II of Pergamum, an ally of Rome. Subsequently, on the death of the last king of Pergamum, Attalus III (133 B.C.), it was bequeathed back to the Romans. The new province thus acquired was called Asia because the Attalids were known to the Romans as the kings of Asia. It took in Mysia (see disc. on 16:7f.); Lydia and Caria; the coastal areas of Aeolia, Ionia, and the Troad; and many of the islands of the Aegean. The province was enlarged in 116 B.C. by the addition of greater Phrygia. Its first capital was Pergamum, the former capital of the Attalids, but by the time of Augustus, Ephesus had assumed that position. The city governed its own affairs through its citizen assembly (*dēmos*) and elected magistrates.

The peace that Augustus had brought to the Roman world was especially welcomed by the people of Asia, whose own history had been turbulent. They developed a strong sense of loyalty to the emperor, which was expressed in the establishment of the cult of "Rome and the Emperor" in 29 B.C. The cult was administered on behalf of the participating cities (the Asian League) by their representatives, the asiarchs, appointed each year for that purpose. As a member city of the League, Ephesus had been a center of this worship from the outset, and coins and inscriptions show how much the city prided itself on being *neōkoros*, "Temple Warden," both of the imperial cult and of Artemis, its own patron goddess. Most of the evidence in this regard relates to the imperial cult, but the title "guardian of the temple of the great Artemis" (v. 35) is attested (though later than the New Testament), and there is no question that Ephesus was famous for the worship of the goddess. Her latest temple—that seen by Paul—was regarded as one of the wonders of the world.

19:1b-2 / Soon after his arrival in Ephesus, or so it seems, Paul came across a number of men ("about twelve," v. 7) whom Luke appears to have regarded as (in some sense) Christians, for he calls them **disciples** (v. 1) and they are said to have believed (v. 2), yet they only knew "the baptism of John" (v. 3). In these early days of the church there were probably any number of cases like this, where a clear distinction could not be drawn between the disciples of John and the disciples of Jesus. But something must have prompted Paul to investigate the faith of these men. He asked, therefore, **Did you receive the Holy Spirit when you believed?** (v. 2). His criterion for what distinguished the Christian is significant. So, too, is the way in which his question is framed. It implies that the Holy Spirit is received at a definite point in time and that that time is the moment of initial belief (the aorist participle, *pisteusantes*, being construed here as coincidental with the verb, *elabete*). The same thought is expressed, for example, in Ephesians 1:13: "Having believed, you were marked in him with a seal, the promised Holy Spirit" (cf. Acts 11:17). No space of time is envisaged between the two events; nor is the possibility entertained of believing without also receiving the "seal of the Spirit," of which Christian baptism is the outward and visible sign (see notes on 2:2ff. and disc. on 2:38).

These disciples were probably in much the same case as Apollos had been, having been "instructed in the way of the Lord" up to a point (18:25), but unaware of what had happened on the Great Pentecost some twenty years earlier (and perhaps of other things). This suggestion rests on an interpretation of verse 2. They had answered Paul's question by declaring: **We have not even heard that there is a Holy Spirit.** Now these men were almost certainly Jews, but even if they were Gentiles, being influenced by the teaching of John the Baptist and of Jesus, they must have at least heard of the Spirit. It is better, then, to understand their answer to mean that they did not know that the Holy Spirit had been given (cf. John 7:39, where the same expression in the Greek is found). Thus, whatever else they knew of Jesus, they were unaware of the one event that more than any other confirmed that the age of salvation had dawned. In short, they were essentially no further forward than where John the Baptist had left his followers.

19:3–4 / Further probing showed that in fact John's was the only baptism they had known. Paul explained that that baptism had only been a preparatory rite by which people had pledged themselves to amendment of life in anticipation of the coming Messiah in (lit. "into") whom they should believe (see disc. on 10:43). But the Messiah had now come, offering forgiveness where there was repentance, and blessing where there was belief. No doubt Paul set this out for them in full with proofs from Scripture, but Luke has summed it all up in the two words at the end of verse 4. All that John and the prophets had looked forward to had been accomplished **in Jesus** (see also the disc. on 18:25).

19:5–7 / These "disciples" had regarded themselves as Christians and yet were shown not to have a full understanding of the Christian faith. Perhaps for this reason **Paul placed his hands on them** (v. 6) to assure them that they were now in "the apostolic succession." Perhaps for this reason, too, the outward signs of the Spirit's presence were added in their speaking **in tongues** and prophesying. On their being baptized "into the name of the Lord Jesus" (v. 5), see note on 2:38 and disc. on 8:16. The tense of the verbs in the second half of verse 6 (imperfect) means either that they "began to speak and to prophesy" or that they "kept on speaking and prophesying." These two gifts are fully discussed in 1 Corinthians 12 and 14, which were written from this city. The indefiniteness of Luke's expression, **there were about twelve men in all** (v. 7), makes it unlikely that he attached any significance to the number.

19:8 / Paul's ministry in Ephesus followed his usual pattern. He returned to the synagogue (or so we suppose) in which he had preached during his brief visit of 18:19, and here, over a period of three months, he **spoke boldly** (see disc. on 4:13). His theme was **the kingdom of God**, that is, that God's rule could now be experienced in the Messiah, on the basis of the Messiah's death for our sins and through faith in him, with the idea also of future judgment by the Messiah (see disc. on 1:3 and note the disc. on 8:12). This was no different from his preaching elsewhere (e.g., 17:31; 18:5), for his message was concerned with both Jesus and the kingdom (28:31) and could be referred to in terms of either. Nevertheless, from the references here, in 20:25, and in 1 Corinthians (no less than five times), "the kingdom of God," for some reason, may have especially characterized Paul's preaching and teaching in Ephesus. He appears to have used again the technique of **arguing** as his usual means of presenting his message (see disc. on 17:2).

19:9 / As the weeks went by, Paul met with persistent opposition from **some of them** who **became obstinate** [lit. "hardened"; cf. Exod. 7:3] and **refused to believe** [the Greek expresses, not merely unbelief, but its display in disobedience] **and publicly maligned the Way** (for **the Way** see disc. on 9:2). This was probably the majority in the synagogue, so that in the end Paul had no option but to withdraw, taking with him **the disciples**. The Christians were probably already holding separate meetings (see disc. on 18:19ff., also 14:27 and note), but Paul had now to find a new base for his evangelistic preaching. His solution was to use **the lecture hall of Tyrannus**, where he continued his **discussions**—the same technique as before—but now with a much wider audience. The Western text has the very credible addition that Paul held his meetings between the fifth and the tenth hour each day (eleven in the morning until four in the afternoon). This would have been the time when most people were resting from work (cf. Martial, *Epigrams* 4.8), including Paul himself, for we know that he supported himself while at Ephesus (20:34; 1 Cor. 4:12) and, like other tradesmen, would have begun work before sunrise. He defines these hours himself in 1 Thessalonians 2:9 (where "night" is the hours before daybreak). If indeed it was between the fifth and the tenth hour that he had the hall, it may have been because Tyrannus had offered him "off-peak" rates. We know nothing of Tyrannus. His appearance here unannounced is one of those pieces of otherwise pointless information that inspire confidence in Luke's sources.

19:10 / Thus, for two years Paul labored in Ephesus, and from Ephesus the new faith radiated out into the province (cf. **all the Jews and Greeks** with the "large numbers" of v. 26; see disc. on 9:35). Ephesus was a great place of concourse for the peoples of Asia Minor. They were drawn to the city to trade, to see the great Roman festivals and shows, and to worship the goddess; so it was they were brought within the ambit of Paul's preaching. But Paul and his helpers may also have gone out on mission to some of the towns of the province. By one means or another (direct missionary preaching or the return home of converts from Ephesus), the churches in Colossae, Laodicea, and Hierapolis in the Lycus Valley were probably established and perhaps others of the churches in Asia (Rev. 2–3; cf. 1 Cor. 16:19).

19:11–12 / Luke tells us little of Paul's years at Ephesus, but the little he does tell shows how great an impact Paul had on the city; at the same time, it portrays accurately the religious and moral atmosphere of the place. "At Ephesus," writes Rackham, "Hellenistic culture and philosophy had made a disastrous union with oriental superstition" (p. 339). The result was a city preoccupied with magic. Paul must have deplored their superstition, and yet the very interest of the Ephesians in magic gave the gospel an entry. As elsewhere, Paul's preaching in Ephesus was accompanied "by the power of signs and miracles, through the power of the Spirit" (Rom. 15:19; cf. Acts 13:11; 14:3, 10; 16:18; 2 Cor. 12:12; Heb. 2:4), only here the miracles may have been unusually frequent (note the imperfect, "was doing") and appear to have been **extraordinary** in character (v. 11). It was God, of course, who was doing them; Paul was simply the agent (lit., "through the hands of Paul," v. 11; see note on 5:12). But the ordinary people were not concerned with these theological niceties. As far as they were concerned, it was Paul who worked the miracles, and so he became a center of interest. They would take his work clothes—sweat rags and aprons from the workshop—in the hope that by these means their sick would be healed.

It would be easy to dismiss this practice as simply reflecting the Ephesians' superstitious outlook and to explain the healings of verse 12 as due to some other, more proper means (not mentioned) of appropriating God's grace. But in fairness to Luke's text, the implication is that it was by contact with the clothes that **their illnesses were cured and the evil spirits left them** (v. 12). He does say that the miracles were **extraordinary**. It may have been a case of God meeting the needs of these people at their own level of understanding. The Ephesians set great store by amulets and charms (see vv. 18f.), and now, by these very means, they were being taught that in Paul's God there was a greater power than they had ever known before. In itself this was not enough. But it was a first step toward "believing without seeing" (John 20:29; see disc. on 5:15f.). There is no suggestion that Paul ever encouraged or condoned what they were doing.

19:13–14 / Among the many who were drawn to the metropolis were **some Jews who went around driving out evil spirits** (v. 13; cf. Luke 11:19), the seven sons of one Sceva. This Sceva is described as a "Jewish High Priest" (v. 14, GNB), but no person of that name was ever a high priest in Jerusalem. Of course, it may have been an entirely pretentious claim, but if the title is to be taken seriously and if it was a Jewish title, he may have been the head of one of the "courses" of priests or a member of one of the high priestly families (see disc. on 4:6). Or he may have been an apostate and a high priest of the imperial or some other cult. Luke tells us nothing about him except that his sons, and possibly Sceva himself, were professional exorcists—a practice for which the Jews especially seem to have had a predilection (see Josephus, *Antiquities* 8.42–49).

Exorcism usually involved the incantation of the name of some power, often many names, to be sure of including the one effective in the particular case. The sons of Sceva, therefore, or rather two of them as the Greek of verse 16 seems to suggest, having seen the power that Paul wielded by his appeal to "the name of the Lord Jesus," thought to include that name in their repertoire. There is a notable passage in Justin Martyr in which he complains that as a class the Jewish exorcists had adopted the same superstitions and magical aids as the heathen (*Dialogue* 85).

It need not surprise us, then, that these men were willing to try any formula that seemed to work, though they owed no allegiance to Jesus (for the use of Jesus' name by Jewish exorcists, cf. Mark 9:38ff.; later, the rabbis condemned such).

19:15–16 / In the end, the result was far from what the sons of Sceva had hoped for. The man (or the spirits that possessed him) declared: **Jesus I know, and I know about Paul, but who are you?** (v. 15); that is, he challenged their right to use the name. He then turned on them and drove them from the house **naked and bleeding** (v. 16). What was lacking here was Christian faith and prayer (cf. Matt. 17:19f.; Mark 9:28f.). In its rendering of the man's reply, NIV has attempted to show that the Greek has two different words for "knowing." The distinction between them is a fine one, but it would appear that the spirits had a more intimate knowledge of Jesus than they had of Paul, reminding us of the supernatural insight into the person of Jesus shown by the demoniacs of the Gospels (cf. Luke 4:34, 41; 8:28; see disc. on 16:17). The incident as a whole also reminds us of the warning of Jesus in Matthew 7:22f.

19:17 / News of what had happened soon got about, with two results: first, **the Jews and Greeks living in Ephesus . . . were all seized with fear** (cf. 5:11). This reaction is only to be expected of people gripped by superstition. The **all** of this verse again is equivalent to "many" (see disc. on 9:35). And second **the name of the Lord Jesus was held in high honor.** It is characteristic of Luke that he should note both reactions. Both were entirely natural under the circumstances and should not be dismissed as due merely to the "form" of such stories. The second reaction would not have been as widespread as the first, but was apparently the more enduring, as shown by the change from the aorist tense to the imperfect—they "continued to honor his name." Evidence in support of this statement is furnished by the following narrative.

19:18 / This verse is closely linked by the syntax with the one before it as a further result of the incident involving the sons of Sceva. It had helped the Christians to break the hold that superstition had had even on them. This, too, was an ongoing result, which saw them coming from time to time (imperfect) openly confessing **their evil deeds.** Luke has no doubt that their faith prior to this had been genuine (for the perfect tense of the participle

those who believed, see disc. on 14:23). But they were still "infants in Christ" (1 Cor. 3:1) learning to live their new life— profession was only slowly followed by practice (cf. Eph. 4:22– 24; 5:11).

19:19–20 / The final test of repentance is amendment, and one notable instance is now mentioned of the Ephesians' determination to bring their practice into line with their faith. **A number who had practiced sorcery** made a public burning of their **scrolls** containing the magical formulae for which Ephesus was famous (see Plutarch, *Symposiaca* 7.5; Clement of Alexandria, *Stromateis* 5.8.46). Here the tense (again imperfect) depicts them as throwing scroll after scroll into the flames. The value of the documents thus destroyed was reckoned as **fifty thousand drachmas** (probably Attic drachma). It is not easy to express this in a modern equivalent, but it was a very large sum indeed, though not out of proportion to the immense trade and rich commerce of this city. Luke's final note sums up this section as it prepares us for the next. **The word of the Lord spread widely**, that is, more and more people were hearing the lordship of Jesus proclaimed and, as many gave their lives to Jesus as Lord, so the message **grew in power**, in the sense that its effects were being increasingly felt both in Ephesus itself and in the province.

19:21 / The solemn formula, **After all this had happened**, marks what Luke probably saw as a new phase of the history, namely, the journey that would ultimately bring Paul to Rome. Like the one on which Jesus set out in Luke 9:51, this journey was one that brought Paul to his destiny, was marked by predictions of suffering, and ended in his arrest and trial before the Sanhedrin, a Roman procurator, and a Jewish king. In each case, the cry of the Jews was, "Away with him," and in each the victim was declared innocent by the Romans. Clearly Luke was struck by this similarity, and by introducing his account of Paul's journey in much the same way as he had the other, he tried to ensure that his readers saw the similarity also (see disc. on 5:17–42; 7:54–8:1a; 13:13–51; 21:17–26; and 27:1–12).

The idea of going to Rome may have been sown in Paul's mind at Corinth (see disc. on 18:17), but it was only while he was at Ephesus that he began to publicly air it. Clearly, he believed that it was God's will that he should go (see disc. on 1:16 for **I must**; cf. also 20:22), and Luke may have intended to show this

by his expression "Paul determined in the Spirit to travel," though
it could mean that he settled on it in his own spirit (NIV **Paul decided**). But before Rome there was something else that he had
to do. His reason for wanting to return to Greece and then to Jerusalem was twofold: to strengthen and encourage the churches
(implied in the verb "to go through," see disc. on 8:4) and to
gather up the proceeds of a collection that he had been organiz-
ing (cf. 24:17; Rom. 15:25–31; 1 Cor. 16:1–4; 2 Cor. 8–9). These
funds were for the relief of the Christian poor of Jerusalem, where
general unrest was exacerbating the effects on the church of earlier persecution and famine. The desperate plight of the church
must have been borne in upon Paul on his last visit to Jerusalem
(see disc. on 18:22), and he determined to do something about
it. After all, his own persecuting activity was partly responsible
(see disc. on 11:29) and now such a collection might serve to draw
Gentile and Jewish Christians together. He set great store by this
undertaking. Luke, on the other hand, mentions it only once and
then as Paul's statement, not his own (24:17). From his perspective it was not the collection but its sequel that proved to be of
greatest importance.

19:22 / In preparing for the journey, Paul sent Timothy
and Erastus ahead to Macedonia, probably to ensure that the
funds would be in hand by the time that he got there himself.
Timothy, last mentioned at Corinth in 18:5, had subsequently
made another visit to Corinth in an attempt to bring that church
into line on certain matters (1 Cor. 4:17; 16:10f.) but had returned
to Ephesus unsuccessful. Paul did not use him again as an emis-
sary to the Corinthians, choosing Titus instead (2 Cor. 2:13;
7:13ff.). But Timothy seems to have fared better in Macedonia,
and Paul had no qualms in sending him now to those churches.
This may be the visit of Philippians 2:19 (cf. also 2:24). As for
Erastus, it is unlikely that he was the man named in Romans 16:23
(see disc. on 18:6ff.). It would be surprising indeed had an itinerant companion of Paul risen in such short time to be treasurer
of the city of Corinth. However, he may have been another Erastus of Corinth with whom Paul later stayed (2 Tim. 4:20). The
name was a common one. Meanwhile, as these two traveled
northward, Paul himself **stayed in the province of Asia a little
longer**. This reference implies that his work was not confined to
the metropolis (cf. vv. 10, 26), whereas the earlier part of the verse

makes it clear that his eventual departure was not precipitated (though it may have been hastened) by what was to follow. It had already been planned in advance.

Additional Notes §50

19:1 / **He found some disciples**: It is sometimes assumed that these men were disciples of Apollos, raising the question why he did nothing to help them as he had been helped by Priscilla and Aquila. But there is no need to look for this kind of connection between them and Apollos. Indeed, Luke's words allow that they did not come to Ephesus until after Apollos had left for Corinth.

19:10 / **Two years**, exclusive of the three months of verse 8: In 20:31 Paul speaks of three years' residence in Ephesus, expressing in the usual manner of the ancients an intermediate period by the superior round number.

19:14–16 / **Seven sons of Sceva, a Jewish chief priest**: The reading **seven** has been questioned, since the word translated "all" in v. 16 (Gk. *amphoteroi*) usually means "both," though in late Greek the meaning "all" is attested. If indeed there were only two, the **seven** may have come in as a marginal note, or the name **Sceva** may have brought to mind the Hebrew word *šeba'*, "seven." But a simpler explanation may be that we are again the victims of Luke's brevity. He probably meant that of the seven sons only two were involved in this incident. We are not told that Sceva himself was at Ephesus.

19:21 / **I must visit Rome also**: He says nothing about establishing a church, for Paul knew that there was a church already in Rome. He only wanted to "impart . . . some spiritual gift" to them (Rom. 1:11f.; cf. 15:14) and saw his visit to Rome as only a temporary stop on his way to Spain (Rom. 15:24, 28).

§51 The Riot in Ephesus (Acts 19:23–41)

Before Luke could launch his travel narrative, he had one more story to tell of Paul's time in Ephesus. That the silversmiths' riot was simply a good story may almost have been reason enough to include it. But it had the added attraction of reinforcing Luke's earlier point that the Christian faith and the Roman state were compatible, as borne out by the attitude of the asiarchs and the city clerk (see disc. on 18:1–17). Incidentally, this story reveals an accurate knowledge of the municipal institutions of Ephesus (see Sherwin-White, pp. 83ff.).

19:23–24 / The last weeks of Paul's stay in Ephesus were marked by one of those "dangers in the city" of which he writes (2 Cor. 11:26). A certain Demetrius instigated a riot because of **the Way** (v. 23; see disc. on 9:2). He was a silversmith whose workshop produced **silver shrines of Artemis** (v. 24), competing in the very lucrative trade that Ephesus had in such things (cf. Dio Cassius, *Roman History* 39.20; Ammianus Marcellinus, *History* 22.13). Examples of model temples in terra-cotta and marble abound, but not surprisingly, none have been found in silver. Demetrius was probably in this business in a big way, but his taking the lead now may not have been for that reason alone, but because he was master of the guild of silversmiths for that year.

19:25–27 / His purpose was to involve all the related trades in a protest demonstration against the Christians. The time may have been the Artemisia, when the city was thronged with visitors and religious and national feeling was running high. A meeting was called, and it is clear from the outset that as far as Demetrius and his colleagues were concerned, economic considerations were uppermost (see disc. on 16:19). The silversmith put his finger on what was to them the salient point of Paul's preaching, namely, that **man-made gods are no gods at all** (v. 26; cf. 17:29). In a place like Ephesus, Paul must have often returned to this theme and with good effect, for he had succeeded, the meeting was told, in convincing **large numbers of people**, both in Ephesus and elsewhere in the province (v. 26). In fact, he had probably made little inroad on the worship of Artemis or, for that matter, on Demetrius' trade. The silversmith was concerned only with the **danger** that he might and that their business would **lose its good name** (i.e., for promoting idolatry). His appeal to the religious feelings of the Ephesians was specious, but he knew that though they may not have cared much about his business, they did care about Artemis.

19:28–29 / Demetrius was a demagogue who knew well how to work up an audience. On hearing him **they were furious and began** [or "kept on"] **shouting: "Great is Artemis of the Ephesians!"** They may have been meeting in a hall belonging to one of the guilds, but now we must picture them as spilling out into the street (as the Western text has it) and making off through the city, still shouting and gathering more people as they went. The theater was their objective—the usual place for public meetings in most towns (cf. Josephus, *War* 7.43–53; Tacitus, *History* 2.80) and in this instance well-placed to incite them still further, for the theater was in full view of the temple of Artemis. On their way, **the people seized Gaius and Aristarchus, Paul's traveling companions from Macedonia** (v. 29). The latter was from Thessalonica and was later to travel with Paul to Jerusalem (20:4). Gaius has sometimes been identified with the Gaius who was also a member of that party, but as the text of 20:4 stands, that man was a Galatian, not a Macedonian. We are not told whether the mob met these two by chance and seized them as well-known Christians, or whether they deliberately searched for the missionary team and took these two when they could not find Paul.

19:30–31 / When Paul learned what had happened, he wanted to face "the demos" himself (so the Greek), though they were less like a citizens' assembly than like a wild mob (cf. 1 Cor. 15:32). But **the disciples would not let him** (v. 30), and **some of the officials of the province, friends of Paul**, added their voice to the others, **begging him not to venture into the theater** (v. 31). These **officials** were the asiarchs (see disc. on v. 1). They were not strictly **officials of the province**, but in a broader sense were very much part of the establishment, and it is noteworthy that these men were to be found among Paul's friends. An asiarch's term of office was one year (reappointment was possible), but a retiring asiarch was evidently permitted to retain the title. Thus a city like Ephesus might have had a number of asiarchs.

19:32 / Luke uses here the technical term for a meeting of the demos (Gk. *ekklēsia*), but their behavior belied the name, and in the following verses he reverts to "the crowd" (so the Greek of vv. 33, 35). Most of them did not even know why they were there, but in any case "kept on shouting" (imperfect) one thing or another.

19:33–34 / One interested party did try to make its view heard, though how exactly Alexander fits into the picture is not clear. (Is he Alexander the metalworker of 2 Tim. 4:14f. and the heretical teacher of 1 Tim. 1:19f. ?) There are uncertainties as to both text and translation, but we should probably regard him as acting on instructions from the Jews (see notes) and attempting to speak on their behalf to dissociate them from the Christians. But when Alexander made as though to speak by motioning with his hand (see disc. on 13:16), the crowd recognized him as a Jew (by his dress?) and shouted him down—bearing out the wisdom of Paul's friends in keeping him from the theater—and for about two hours kept up the cry that someone had started in the earlier meeting: **Great is Artemis of the Ephesians!** (v. 34; cf. v. 28). They may have regarded this chanting as itself an act of worship. Ramsay contends that no verb should be introduced here (there is none in the original) and that the expression is not a statement of fact but an apostrophe, a cry of adoration—"Great Artemis of the Ephesians" (*Church*, pp. 135ff.). The noise must have been deafening. The acoustics of the theater are excellent even today and at that time were even better because of bronze and clay sounding vessels placed throughout the auditorium (cf. 1 Cor. 13:1).

19:35–37 / At last **the city clerk** succeeded in gaining control. This translation of his title (which Luke has used correctly) is deceptive, since he was actually the highest civic official in Ephesus. His standing is attested by coins and inscriptions. He was the chief magistrate of the city, and his speech has just that hint of contempt for the crowd and consciousness of his own authority that one would expect in such a man. He began by noting the close ties between the city and the temple—a sop to their ruffled vanity. Ephesus, he declared, was universally acclaimed as **the guardian of the temple of the great Artemis and of her image, which fell from heaven** (v. 35; see disc. on v. 1). The latter reference is, perhaps, to a meteorite, which had been taken to be the image of the goddess (perhaps long before the Greeks had settled the city). Similar cases are attested elsewhere, most notably in the temple of Cybele at Pessinus. Admittedly, we have no evidence that a stone was preserved at Ephesus, but it is difficult to know what other meaning to give to *diopetēs*, "fallen from heaven." This word may have been the city clerk's answer to the Christian attack on "man-made gods" (v. 26). The image, he implied, was not made with hands; it fell from the sky. But having uttered this gentle rebuke (if such it was), he saw that there was nothing more to be done with the Christians. No specific charges had been laid against Gaius and Aristarchus and, as far as the clerk knew, no reason to think that there should be. They had not **robbed temples**, which in the ancient world served as safe deposits, nor had they **blasphemed** the goddess. It is ironic that an inscription of this period reveals how the vast wealth deposited in the temple of Artemis found its way by bribery and corruption into the hands of the city officials. Hanson comments: "The town clerk might not relish the thought that this disorderly meeting in the theater on the subject of the temple of Artemis might lead to a close scrutiny of temple affairs (p. 197).

19:38 / The proper course, he said, was for Demetrius and the others to take any complaint they had to the appropriate authorities on the days appointed for such things (lit., "market days"). The clerk's reference was to the courts presided over by the provincial governor or his deputies, who traveled around the principal cities of the province for that purpose. Again Luke has used the correct title (in Greek) for the governor of a senatorial province (see note on 13:7), but he has used it in the plural. This has excited a good deal of comment. It may be nothing more than a generalizing plural: "There are such people as proconsuls." But it may describe what was actually the case. In the autumn of A.D. 54, two emissaries of Nero, Celer and Aelius, poisoned the proconsul of Asia, M. Junius Silvanus, at the instigation of the empress, Agrippina, and governed the province together until their replacement arrived in the summer of A.D. 55. Celer and Aelius may have been the "proconsuls" of this verse and their term of office such a time of unrest that the silversmiths' protest could take the form that it did.

19:39–41 / Failing the courts, Demetrius could bring his case, if he had one, to the public assembly. But the clerk was careful to stress that it should be a "legal meeting of the citizens." Under the best of circumstances, the Romans did not view these assemblies with any favor, and if they were found to be in blatant disregard of law and order, the Romans were just as likely to withdraw completely the right to hold them. As it was, these meetings were strictly controlled as to when they could be held, so that this present gathering was highly irregular. If the Romans should make inquiry about it, the Ephesians themselves were in danger of prosecution. These words had a sobering effect on the crowd, and the clerk was able to disperse them without further ado. As far as we know Demetrius took the matter no further.

Additional Notes §51

19:24 / **Demetrius, who made silver shrines of Artemis**: There is a title, *ho neopoios* ("temple repairer"), that is known to have been borne by an official who was responsible for the fabric of the temple of Artemis. On this basis, the suggestion has been made that Demetrius was a *neopoios*, but that Luke has mistaken his title for a description of his trade, a *naopoios* "temple maker." Some weight is added to this suggestion by an Ephesian inscription, possibly of the first century A.D., that actually gives the name Demetrius to a *neopoios*. On the other hand, A. Deissmann refers to another inscription found in the theater at Ephesus, according to which a distinguished Roman official, C. Vibius Salutaris, had presented a silver image of Diana (Artemis) and other statues "that they might be set up in every public assembly (*ekklēsia*) in the theatre upon pedestals" (*Light from the Ancient East*, p. 113). Although this is not exactly what Luke describes, it does give some support to his text. It should be noted, moreover, that he does not employ the term *naopoios* of Demetrius, but *poion naous*, "maker of shrines."

19:33 / **Some of the crowd shouted instructions**: The Greek does not make clear who the subject of the verb is. NIV takes it to be members of the crowd, since in the Greek this clause follows next after verse 32 and Luke gives no indication of a change of subject. We have chosen, however, to assume that the Jews, who are mentioned as having put Alexander forward, are also the subject of this verb, i.e., that some Jews in the crowd instructed him. Some texts have the crowd "concluding" that Alexander was responsible for the gathering, while others have them "throwing Alexander out" or "leading him on." These latter, however, are not well supported and are probably due to scribal bewilderment.

19:37 / **They have neither robbed temples**: The adjective used here in the sense of "robbers of temples" is found elsewhere with special reference to Ephesus (Strabo, *Geography* 14.1.22; Pseudo-Heraclitus, *Letter* 7; cf. Rom. 2:22). The cognate noun occurs in an inscription at Ephesus describing a crime involving the heaviest of penalties.

§52 Through Macedonia and Greece (Acts 20:1–6)

20:1a / It would appear that soon after the silversmiths' riot Paul departed Ephesus for Macedonia. The words of encouragement that he addressed to the believers before going may have been along the same lines as those he spoke to their leaders a few months later (vv. 17–35). He had already "decided to go to Jerusalem, passing through Macedonia and Achaia" (19:21), but he may have set out sooner than intended, partly because of the riot, partly because of his anxiety over the situation in Corinth. These had been stormy years in Paul's dealings with the Corinthians. They had repudiated his authority, and neither his letters nor his own or Timothy's visits had seemed to help. In desperation, therefore, he had sent Titus to Corinth with another letter (now lost) in the hope that either the message or the messenger might bring the church back to loyalty to him. And he could not wait any longer for Titus' return. Thus, full of anxiety and perhaps also physically ill (2 Cor. 1:8ff.), Paul went to Troas hoping to meet Titus there. Here he preached "the gospel of Christ and found that the Lord had opened a door" to him there (2 Cor. 2:12; see disc. on 14:27). But his heart was not in it. He could not rest until he had heard from Titus. When Titus failed to rendezvous at Troas, Paul resolved to go on to Macedonia (2 Cor. 2:13).

20:1b–3a / Luke takes up the story again at this point with a brief notice of what may have been quite a prolonged "missionary progress" through the province of Macedonia (see disc. on 8:4 for the verb "to go through"). It must have been a joy for Paul to renew old friendships. But this journey had its problems (2 Cor. 7:5), and always there was his nagging concern for the church in Corinth. His relief knew no bounds, therefore, when Titus met him with good news of that church (2 Cor. 7:6f.). From Macedonia Paul may have gone to Illyricum (cf. Rom. 15:19, but it is not clear from this reference whether he actually preached in Illyricum or simply named it as marking the western limit of the eastern world that had hitherto been his sphere; see disc. on

17:10). At all events, he came eventually **to Greece** (v. 2; meaning probably the province of Achaia, but Luke actually uses the word **Greece** [*Hellas*], its only occurrence in Acts), making Corinth his base for the winter.

20:3b / As Paul was preparing for the journey to Syria (see disc. on 18:18) a plot against his life was discovered. It may have been planned to attack him on board ship, especially if the vessel was crowded with Jewish pilgrims for Passover or Pentecost, or even in the crowded harbor of Cenchrea before the ship sailed. The reason is not given. It may have been a continuation of his earlier troubles with the Jews (cf. 18:12ff.), or simply because he was carrying money for the church in Jerusalem. So instead of going by ship, Paul set out by road through Macedonia, the way he had come three months earlier.

20:4 / The names of Paul's traveling companions are carefully noted, probably because they were official delegates appointed by their respective churches to make the journey with Paul and to present the collection. Sopater is probably the Sosipater of Romans 16:21 who was with Paul at Corinth when he wrote that letter. He was the delegate from the church in Berea. The reference to his father may mean that he was known to Luke's readers. Aristarchus was mentioned earlier in 19:29 as one of the victims of the riot. He and Secundus represented the church in Thessalonica. Gaius and Timothy were Galatians, unless we accept the Western text's description of Gaius as "the Doberian" instead of "the Derbean," in which case Gaius was another Macedonian and presumably a fellow victim, with Aristarchus, of the riot (19:29). Doberus was a Macedonian town near Philippi. Tychicus is well known from the later epistles as Paul's courier to Asia (Eph. 6:21; Col. 4:7; cf. 2 Tim. 4:12; Titus 3:12). He and Trophimus represented the Asian churches. Probably both were Ephesians. Trophimus certainly was and because of this became the unwitting cause of Paul's arrest in Jerusalem (21:29; see also 2 Tim. 4:20). Paul himself may have taken responsibility for the money raised by the Achaean churches, though this had not been his original intention (1 Cor. 16:3).

It is odd that the church in Philippi is not mentioned, but Luke, who apparently joined the company in Philippi, may have been their representative. The difficulty that the company only went to Philippi at the last minute is overcome if we allow that there was much more movement and discussion than Acts has recorded and that Luke may have been the brother "who is praised by all the churches" whom Paul had sent with Titus from Macedonia (2 Cor. 8:18). Titus was to carry Paul's latest letter (2 Corinthians) to Corinth and then to help the Corinthians to get ready for the collection. Luke may have taken the Philippian contribution with him but then returned to Macedonia to make arrangements for his own departure for Jerusalem as the Philippian delegate. He may have planned to meet up with the others somewhere along their route and so have been more or less ready to travel when they unexpectedly turned up at Philippi.

20:5–6 / It would appear that the whole group set out and traveled together through Macedonia, though it is not out of the question that the rest of them went by ship directly to Troas, while Paul made the journey alone by land. In any case, the party divided at some point (probably Philippi, if they were traveling together), with the others going on to Troas and Paul remaining to celebrate **the Feast of Unleavened Bread** at Philippi (i.e., the Passover, v. 6; see disc. on 12:3). He still observed the old ritual, but from 1 Corinthians 5:7f. we can see something of the new content he gave it—the Jewish Passover was becoming the Christian Easter. The resumption of the "we passages" in verse 5 can be taken to mean that Luke had rejoined Paul and that together they made the crossing from Neapolis to Troas (cf. 16:11). Why Paul spent a week in Troas when he was "in a hurry to reach Jerusalem, if possible, by the day of Pentecost" is not explained (v. 16), but there may simply have been no ship for the southward journey. The time spent in Troas gave him the opportunity to minister to these people again.

Additional Notes §52

20:2 / **Speaking many words of encouragement**: As far as Paul knew, he would not see these churches again and in the absence of his physical presence, his word, which would still remain, would be most important. This journey is the record of Paul's "last words" (vv. 1, 7, 11, 17–35).

§53 Eutychus Raised from the Dead at Troas (Acts 20:7–12)

There is a marked contrast between the meager information of the previous section and the detail that characterizes the remainder of the journey now that the "we passages" have resumed. It includes in this section a description of a "church service" in Troas.

20:7 / On the eve of the delegates' departure from Troas, they met with the local Christians for a "service." Luke allows us a glimpse of what was probably a typical meeting of Christians in these early days of the church. First, their purpose was **to break bread**. We should probably interpret this in the light of verse 11, where the best manuscripts read the definite article in the phrase, "having broken the bread." The reference, then, is almost certainly to the bread of the Lord's Supper (see disc. on 2:42) and the full sense of what they were doing expressed in 1 Corinthians 10:16. Second, they met on **the first day of the week**. This is a Jewish expression, but it must still be asked whether Luke was thinking in Jewish or Roman terms in marking the days. By Jewish reckoning this would have been a "Saturday" night (as we would call it), since the new day started for them at sunset, making Saturday night the beginning of the first day of the week. But because Luke speaks of "sunrise" as "the next day" (cf. vv. 11 and 7) he appears to be using Roman reckoning, according to which midnight, and effectively sunrise, marked the beginning of the new day. In this event, it would appear that the church had already made "Sunday" its day of meeting. Of course, it was still an ordinary working day, hence the meeting at night (Sunday night). Third, during the evening Paul preached a sermon. He used "discussion" as the most convenient means of dealing with any difficulties they had (see disc. on 17:2).

20:8–10 / The upstairs room where they were meeting was probably crowded (see note on 14:27), and what with the warmth of the crowd, the fumes of the lamps, and length of Paul's sermon, a boy named Eutychus (the term rendered **young man** suggests that he was between eight and fourteen years old) got sleepier and sleepier, until he finally went **sound asleep** and **fell to the ground from the third story** (v. 9). The meeting was probably being held in a tenement building of the kind common in Roman towns, providing housing for the poor. In Rome itself these buildings sometimes rose to nine and ten stories. The boy was apparently killed by the fall. The treatment that Paul immediately gave suggests artificial respiration (cf. 1 Kings 17:21; 2 Kings 4:34). His words, literally, "his life is in him" (v. 10), should probably be understood in the sense that the boy's life would be restored, though they are sometimes taken to mean that he was only concussed and unconscious. But that is not how Luke saw it. He spoke of the boy as **dead** (v. 9, not "as if dead") and **alive** (v. 12), and the vivid detail of the narrative suggests that it has come from a careful observer (e.g., **there were many lamps**, v. 8). On this basis, Paul is placed in the front rank of miracle workers with Peter and Jesus himself (cf. 9:36–41; Luke 7:11–15; 8:49–56). It was, of course, Jesus working through Paul who gave life to the boy.

20:11–12 / Verse 11 may indicate yet another feature of these early meetings, namely, the eating of a common meal (the Agape or "Love Feast") in the context of which the Lord's Supper was held, for Paul is said to have "eaten" ("tasted") as well as having "broken the bread." Luke uses the same word here as elsewhere for ordinary meals (10:10; 23:14; Luke 14:24). The only difficulty here is that the meal would have followed rather than preceded the Lord's Supper as was the case at Corinth (1 Cor. 11:17–34), assuming that that was the norm. In any case, Paul remained **talking** with them long after this part of the meeting was finished (v. 11). Meanwhile, Eutychus was left in the care of some of the members until the meeting had ended. He was then taken home. "Thus Paul left," says Luke, with particular reference to Eutychus' restoration: that is, Paul left them as the victor (through Jesus) over death.

Additional Notes §53

20:7 / **We came together**: The word is a general one for any gathering, but as the Christians gathered chiefly for worship, the "gathering together" or *synaxis* became the technical word for a "service" (cf. 4:31; 11:26; 15:6, 30; 1 Cor. 5:4).

§54 Paul's Farewell to the Ephesian Elders (Acts 20:13–38)

In this section is found the only example in Acts of an address given by Paul to Christians (cf. 14:22; 18:23). In it we see him as the pastor and friend of the Ephesians, and no other passage in this book shows greater feeling than this. There is a remarkable vividness about the speech, the reason for which is obvious: it is the only speech in Acts about which we can be reasonably sure that the author himself heard what was said. Even so, he has imposed his own style upon it. But in this speech more than in any other, we catch the Lukan accent; but behind it, clearly, sounds the voice of the speaker himself. As to content, it is thoroughly Pauline. As to form, it is of a type commonly found in farewell addresses, in which the speaker warns his audience of difficulties that lie ahead, holding himself up as a model for their own conduct (cf., e.g., Gen. 47:29–50:14; Deut. 1–3; Josh. 23:1–24:32; 1 Sam. 12; Tobit 14:3–11; John 13–16; 1 Tim. 4:1ff.; 2 Tim. 3:1ff.). Once this is recognized, any doubts about the authenticity of the speech on the grounds that Paul would not have paraded himself in this way are laid to rest (cf. also 1 Cor. 1:11). But some still contend that the speech is too apologetic to be original and that Luke must have composed it himself in defense of Paul against his later detractors—those of Luke's day, not the apostle's. But Paul had no lack of critics in his own day (cf., e.g., 2 Cor. 10–13; 1 Thess. 1–2). Even if they had not yet appeared in Ephesus, past experience would have taught him that they soon would, and this speech is (in part) his attempt to prepare his hearers for just that eventuality.

20:13 / On the next day, the others took ship for Assos, but Paul himself made the journey by land, intending to join the ship there. Assos lay south of Troas and some miles east of Cape Lectum on the Gulf of Adramyttium. Some forty miles farther east lay Adramyttium itself (cf. 27:2). A Roman road connected

Troas with Assos and provided a much shorter and quicker route for Paul (about twenty miles) than had he gone with the others by ship. He may have taken this option in order to spend a little more time with the Christians of Troas.

20:14–16 / As planned, Paul met the ship at Assos, though the imperfect tense raises the possibility that he sighted the ship while he was still on the way ("as he came to meet us," v. 14), and was taken on board at once. At all events, from Assos they sailed to Mitylene (about thirty miles from Assos), the chief town on the island of Lesbos, where a capacious harbor made it a natural stopping place for the ship overnight, especially if, as seems likely, it was a small coastal vessel. The next day they came opposite the island of Kios. A strait some five miles wide dotted with smaller islands separates Kios from the end of a long peninsula that juts out from the coast of Asia, with Smyrna (Izmia) to its north and Ephesus to its south. The ship spent the night in this picturesque channel, either anchored off shore or actually at a point on the mainland, and the next day **crossed over to Samos** (v. 15) and anchored there overnight or, perhaps, as the Western text implies, only "came near to" the island to spend the night at Trogyllium, a town on the mainland opposite Samos. They had already bypassed Ephesus, and the following day they reached its southern neighbor, Miletus.

Miletus was the farthest south of the great Ionian (Greek) cities of the coast of Asia Minor. It belonged to the region of Caria, now part of the Roman province of Asia. The city stood on a promontory projecting from the southern shore of the Latmian Gulf, which formed the estuary of the Maeander River. In Roman times Miletus was still a city of some importance, though Ephesus had long since eclipsed it both commercially and politically. Miletus is known to have been the home of a Jewish community, but whether Paul had ever preached there or whether a church had been established there during his years in Asia, we do not know.

20:17 / Miletus was a natural stopping place for a coastal vessel en route for the south and near enough to Ephesus for Paul to summon the elders. The verb gives a sense of both earnestness and authority. Evidently Paul could reckon on a stay of some days, for if we take into account the time spent in landing, the dispatch of the messenger, and the journey of the elders to Miletus, it could not have been until at least the third day that he addressed them.

20:18 / On their arrival, Paul spoke to them, first, of his own past ministry. This would have been well known to them, though he had in mind the work not only in Ephesus but that in the whole of the province. But the greater part of his time had been spent in Ephesus, so they especially had reason to be grateful for his ministry. Hence the emphasis of the Greek on "you" in the phrase **you know how I lived the whole time**. This appeal to their memory is a familiar Pauline idiom (cf. Phil. 1:5; 4:15; Col. 1:6; 1 Thess. 2:1f., 5, 10f.), though the verb "to know" is distinctively Lukan.

20:19 / His ministry had been marked by self-sacrifice. The **tears** were not for his own hard times (lit., "trials" or "temptations"), which were, on the contrary, a source of joy, but for the suffering of others—for those "in Christ" who faced trials (cf. v. 31; Rom. 9:2; 2 Cor. 2:4; Phil. 3:18) and for those without Christ who lived in a world "without hope and without God" (Eph. 2:12). We may take his reference to tears literally; Paul was no Stoic for whom impassivity was a virtue (see note on 17:18). He had served "with all humility" in a world in which humility was deemed to be a fault, not a virtue—the character befitting only a slave (both "all" and "humility" are typical of Paul; cf. Eph. 4:2; Phil. 2:3; Col. 2:18, 23; 3:12). But Paul saw himself as "the slave of the Lord" (NIV's **served the Lord** misses the force of his language; for the verb "to be a slave" cf. Rom. 12:11; 14:18; 16:18; Eph. 6:7; Phil. 2:22; Col. 3:24; 1 Thess. 1:9f.; for the noun, Rom. 1:1; Gal. 1:10; Phil. 1:1; Titus 1:1). His reference to **the plots of the Jews** reminds us that there is much in this history that Luke has not told us. Paul himself fills some of these gaps (1 Cor. 15:32; 2 Cor. 1:8–10; 11:23ff.; cf. Acts 9:23; 20:3; 23:12; 25:3; 1 Thess. 2:14–16 for other plots).

20:20–21 / His ministry had been all-embracing—**to both Jews and Greeks** (v. 21)—another Pauline expression (cf. Rom. 1:16; 2:9, 10; 3:9; 1 Cor. 1:24). It had involved both public preaching (in the synagogue and the hall of Tyrannus, 19:8, 9) and private (e.g., to the church that met in the house of Aquila and Priscilla, 1 Cor. 16:19). His preaching had included "hard sayings" as well as "comfortable words," warning his hearers that they should **turn to God in repentance and have faith in** (the) **Lord Jesus** (v. 21; see disc. on 2:38 for a similar appeal and disc. on 2:40 for the verb "to warn," or better, "to testify"). Some commentators see a chiasmus in verse 21, the preaching of repentance being addressed to the Greeks (cf. Gal. 4:8f.; 1 Thess. 1:9) and that of faith to the Jews. His emphasis would of course have varied as he spoke to these different groups, and it may be right to characterize these different emphases in this way. But all, whether Gentile or Jew, need to repent and believe (cf. Rom. 1:16; 10:9–13), and it is better to see in this verse a summary of Paul's preaching to all (cf. 14:15; 17:30; 26:20). In short, he "held nothing back" that would be of help to their salvation (v. 20; cf. 1 Cor. 10:33; 2 Cor. 4:2; Gal. 4:16). The verb (found again in v. 27 and Gal. 2:12 and nowhere else in the New Testament except a quotation in Heb. 10:38) has the sense "to draw or shrink back out of fear or regard for another," but Paul's preaching owed nothing to either the fear or the favor of other people. He was concerned only to express "the whole will of God" (v. 27).

20:22–24 / As far as Paul could see, his work in Ephesus was at an end and his thoughts were now turned to his second theme, his future ministry. He was on his way to Jerusalem "bound in spirit" (v. 22, so the Greek). Some take this as a reference to the Holy Spirit (so NIV); others understand it of his own human spirit. Perhaps the fact that the Holy Spirit is mentioned in the next verse (23) tells in favor of the latter, and so we have taken it, though in the long run it amounts to much the same thing. The point is that he felt himself (divinely) compelled to go. The tense suggests that he had felt this for some time, whereas the verb itself ("to bind") may give some hint of his forebodings about it. The Spirit had warned him that **prison** (lit., "bonds") **and hardships** awaited him in Jerusalem (v. 23; the same two nouns are found together in 2 Cor. 1:8 and Phil. 1:17), and he may have felt that, in effect, he was a prisoner already. Compared with 19:21, this passage represents an advance in Paul's perception of what lay before him, though he still had no idea in detail what would befall him or where. He only knew that in every city the Spirit had warned him of danger (cf. 21:4, 11). Not that he held his life dear. The uncertainty may have troubled him, but his chief concern was that he should **finish the race** (v. 24;

cf. Rom. 15:30ff.)—the familiar Pauline metaphor of the athlete competing in the games (see also the disc. on 24:16; cf. 1 Cor. 9:24; Gal. 2:2; Phil. 3:12; 2 Tim. 4:7)—by declaring to Gentiles and kings and to the people of Israel **the gospel of God's grace** (v. 24; cf. 9:15; Gal. 1:15f.). This was most characteristically **the work** (Gk. *diakonia*, "service") of an apostle (cf. 1:17, 25; 6:4; 21:19; Rom. 11:13; 2 Cor. 4:1; for grace, see disc. on 13:43).

20:25 / Paul was sure that the Ephesians would not see him again (cf. v. 38). It should be understood, however, that this was no more than an opinion based on human probabilities, for the Spirit had only warned of "prison and hardships" (v. 23). As it happened, they probably did see him again (2 Tim. 4:20). But in any case, the care of the church in Ephesus was no longer chiefly his, but the elders', and so, as his third theme, he spoke to them of their ministry. And now exhortation is added to the example of his own conduct among them—exhortation mainly in verses 26–30, the example here, and in verses 31–35. For **the kingdom**, see the discussion and notes on 1:3 and the discussion on 8:12.

20:26–27 / The allusion is to the watchman of Ezekiel 33:1–6, and is used as a figure of spiritual responsibility. Paul believed that he had discharged his duty to the Ephesians, so that if anyone now fell away he was not to blame. Literally, he was "clean of the blood of them all" (v. 26; see disc. on 18:6). The adjective "clean" is found seven times in Paul's epistles and only here and in 18:6 (each purporting to be Paul's own words) in the writings of Luke. The phrase "this very day" (v. 26, GNB) can also be claimed as Pauline (2 Cor. 3:14; cf. also Rom. 11:8). He was "clean" because he had held nothing back in proclaiming to them **the whole will of God** (v. 27; cf. Eph. 1:11; 3:4; see disc. on 2:23). His had been an "all round" ministry.

20:28–29 / In the same sense the elders, too, should take care to be "clean." **Keep watch over yourselves**, Paul urged, for only as leaders remain faithful to God can they expect faithfulness in their congregation. The elders' position vis à vis the congregation is an interesting one. Clearly, they were part of the people of God, and yet, in a sense, they stood apart, for they were to "watch over" the others (v. 28). This task had been given to them by none other than the Spirit himself. It is noteworthy that the verb, **made** (v. 28), is in the middle voice, as is the comparable verb in the account of Paul's own commissioning for missionary service in 13:2, the sense being that the Spirit had appointed them for himself and for his own purpose, not theirs. No mention is made either here or in chapter 19 of the ordination of these men to their office, but on the basis of 6:3ff. and 14:23 we may suppose that they had been formally appointed by the laying on of hands with prayer. Rather than remind them of that (cf. 2 Tim. 1:6), however, Paul called to mind the divine call that their ordination presupposed. His purpose was to urge upon them the seriousness of their task. To underline it still further, he recalled how God had made the church his own **with his own blood** (v. 28). The phrase **the church of God** (v. 28) is unique to Paul (cf., e.g., 1 Cor. 1:2), but the thought behind this part of the verse goes back to the Old Testament notion of God redeeming his people (Ps. 74:2; Isa. 43:21). The cognate noun of the verb "to make one's own" is found in Ephesians 1:14 ("those who are his") associated, like the verb in this verse, with the thought of redemption. This redemption was at the cost of "his own blood" (v. 28). On the face of it, the reference would appear to be to the blood of God himself, a unique expression in the New Testament. But there are many who interpret the Greek as God's "own son" (the Greek will allow this, cf. Rom. 8:32). On this view, it is worth noticing that verse 28 includes a reference to the three persons of the Trinity in their several relationships to the church. Moreover, this verse is one of the clearest assertions in the New Testament of the doctrine of the atonement (see notes on 8:32f. and disc. on 13:39).

As those to whom God has given the responsibility of watching over the church, Paul calls the elders **overseers** (v. 28), a term that is also found in his letters (Phil. 1:1; 1 Tim. 3:1f.; Titus 1:7; the same word is used of Jesus in 1 Pet. 2:25). The nature of their task is drawn out by a pastoral metaphor. The church is the **flock** (v. 28), a familiar figure for the people of God in both the Old Testament and the New; the elders are the **shepherds** (v. 28); and the danger threatening the flock is **savage wolves**, which will not spare them (v. 29). The thought was of heretical teachers, especially of hard-line Jewish Christians coming in after Paul had gone and leading the people astray (see disc. on 21:21). This had happened in Galatia and Corinth, with the preaching of "another gospel" (2 Cor. 11:4; Gal. 1:6ff.), and was threatening elsewhere (cf. Rom. 14:1–15:13; Phil. 3:2ff.). The verb "to spare" is found six times in Paul's epistles and beyond them only in 2 Peter 2:4, 5.

20:30 / In the previous verse the danger was from without. Here, Paul speaks of a danger from within—of teachers who would arise from among the Ephesians themselves to seduce the congregation. Experience had taught him to fear for this flock, and history has shown that his fears were justified (cf. 1 Tim. 1:3, 20; 2 Tim. 1:15; 2:17; 3:8, 13; 1 John 2:18f.; 2 and 3 John). The desire of these teachers would be **to draw away disciples after** themselves—an implied contrast with the call of the disciple to follow Christ. The verb means "to tear away from that to which one is attached."

20:31 / The pastoral metaphor is maintained as Paul urged the elders **to be on** (their) **guard**. For encouragement, they had his example. For three years (a round number; see note on 19:10), he had taught them **night and day with tears** (cf. v. 19). The order of the words **night and day** may be intended, as some think, to emphasize the tirelessness of his labor, but more likely expresses the normal pattern of work, starting before daybreak (= **night**) and extending to about midday when most people took a siesta, but Paul preached in the hall of Tyrannus (see disc. on 19:9).

20:32 / Finally, he commended them **to God and to the word of his grace** (see disc. on 13:43). Here the genitive is objective. It is "the message about grace." This message is able to **build . . . up** the believer, that is, to bring the believer to maturity in Christ (cf. 1 Cor. 3:9–15; Eph. 4:12) and to give him or her **an inheritance among all those who are sanctified** (cf. Rom. 8:17). The language is that of the Old Testament, which spoke of Israel's inheritance, first, in the land of Canaan, but beyond that, in God himself (cf., e.g., Ps. 16:5). But the themes are characteristically Paul's (for "building up," cf. Eph. 2:20f.; 4:12, 16, 29; for "inheritance," cf. Eph. 1:14, 18; 5:5). Notice that the leaders, no less than the rest of the congregation, are subject to the authority of God's message (the Scriptures).

20:33–34 / As the speech drew to a close, Paul once more set before the elders the example of his own conduct among them. Far from taking a reward, he had not even **coveted anyone's silver or gold or clothing** (v. 33; cf. 1 Cor. 9:15–18). These were traditional forms of wealth in the ancient world and symbols of status (cf. 1 Macc. 11:24; James 5:2f.). Paul's ministry had been entirely disinterested. Rather than rely on the Ephesians for his support, he had worked to support himself and his companions. With **these hands of mine**, he said, I **have supplied my own needs and the needs of my companions** (v. 34), and one can see him holding up his hands as he said this (the words are placed in an emphatic position in the Greek) in demonstration of something that they knew very well. It seems likely from this that he had pursued his trade again with Aquila and Priscilla (cf. 18:3; see also Rom. 12:13; Eph. 4:28; Titus 3:14). But though he had accepted nothing from the Ephesians, he may have received an occasional gift from another church (cf. Phil. 2:25; 4:16).

20:35 / To back up this point, he added some words of Jesus not found in the Gospels and yet familiar to the Ephesians ("remember . . ."): **It is more blessed to give than to receive**. Paul himself puts it more strongly. We are under a divine necessity to work hard in the interest of helping others—or so the word **must** seems to imply (see disc. on 1:16).

20:36–38 / When Paul had finished, they all prayed together. The solemnity of the occasion is marked by their kneeling (see disc. on 7:60 for kneeling and disc. on 9:11 for prayer). After a moving scene described in a manner reminiscent of the Old Testament (cf. Gen. 33:4; 45:14; 46:29), in which they made their protracted farewells (note the imperfect, "kept on kissing," v. 37), the Ephesians saw Paul and the others back to the ship (see disc. on 15:3). These verses provide us with "a picture drawn with Luke's inimitable command of pathos, which reveals the apostle's wonderful power in attracting personal affection and devotion" (A. J. Mattill, *Perspectives*, p. 81).

Additional Notes §54

An interesting comparison with the voyage described in this chapter and the next may be made with Herod's voyage by way of Rhodes, Cos, Kios, and Mitylene to the Black Sea (Josephus, *Antiquities* 16.16–26).

20:16 / **Paul had decided to sail past Ephesus**: It may seem odd that Paul should apparently dictate where the ship went. But he may have actually chartered the vessel. On the other hand, this comment may only mean that he had made a choice at Troas of a vessel that would not call at Ephesus but would put in at Miletus. A number of scholars take the line that not only had Paul latterly made things too uncomfortable for a return visit to Ephesus, but had never really succeeded either in the city or in the province (see, e.g., W. Bauer, *Orthodoxy and Heresy in Earliest Christianity*). This is too harsh a judgment, though at a later date he does appear to have lost the support of the Asian Christians (2 Tim. 1:15). Martin sees the letter to the Ephesians as "a last ditch stand by a well-known representative of Paul in his final attempt to regain Asia for the Pauline gospel by publishing an assemblage of Pauline teaching" (p. 233).

20:28 / **Has made you overseers** (Gk. *episkopos*): In secular use the title was given to "local officials or the officers of societies" who were involved in finance and general administration but there is no reason to think that the title as used by the church was ever restricted to finance. Rather, it seems to have been employed in the much broader sense illustrated by the LXX (e.g., 2 Kings 11:18; 2 Chron. 34:12, 17; Neh. 11:9, 14; Isa. 60:17; 1 Macc. 1:15) and enriched by its association with the idea of tending the flock (cf. 1 Pet. 2:25; 5:2; perhaps also Num. 27:16). The task of the Christian *episkopos*, therefore, "consists in a watchful and solicitous (both ideas are contained in the verb *episkopein*) direction of the congregation on the basis of the redeeming work of Christ to which alone the community owes its existence" (H. W. Beyer, "*episkopos*," *TDNT*, vol. 2, p. 616).

His own blood: The manuscript evidence is heavily in favor of the reading, "through the blood, his own" (Gk. *tou haimatos tou idiou*), which can be rendered either "his (i.e., God's) blood" or "the blood of his own (Son)." The second (see disc.) is to be preferred. There is no exact parallel to Christ's being called God's "own," but compare Rom. 8:31f. and the use in Eph. 1:6 and early Christian literature of the title "the Beloved."

20:35 / **The Lord Jesus himself said, 'It is more blessed to give than to receive'**: The use of the emphatic pronoun, the Lord Jesus **himself** said . . . rules out the view that the apostle was simply giving the sense of some of our Lord's sayings and not directly quoting. It also tells against the view that this was a Greek proverb taken over by the church and attributed falsely to Jesus, though parallels have been found in Greek literature (e.g., Thucydides, *History of the Peloponnesian War* 2.97.4). The form "Blessed is . . ." (as here in the Greek text) is, of course, distinctively Jewish.

§55   On to Jerusalem (Acts 21:1–16)

As the travelers resume their journey, the narrative shows the same detail as before (see disc. on 20:7–12). The most striking feature of this part of the story is the repeated warning of danger to Paul.

21:1 / The opening words of this chapter recreate the closing scene of the last, with the travelers having to "tear themselves away" from their friends (the same verb as in 20:30). From Miletus they sailed due south to Cos (about forty miles). Probably the city is meant on the island of the same name. Here they spent the night. Cos, besides being famous for its medical school, was a center of Jewish life in the Aegean (cf. 1 Macc. 15:23; Josephus, *Antiquities* 14.110–118; *War* 1.422–425). It is most unlikely, however, that Paul made any contact with the Jews. The following day they rounded the peninsula of Cnidus and came to Rhodes. Again the city is probably meant on the island of that name, and again (contrary to tradition) it is unlikely that Paul preached on the island. According to the best texts, the travelers terminated this part of their voyage at Patara on the Lycian coast (see disc. on 13:13f.). The Western text, possibly under the influence of 27:5, adds "and Myra," making the latter, fifty miles farther east, the port at which they transshipped to a larger vessel for the crossing to Syria. But there is reason to think that the prevailing winds made Patara the most suitable port of embarkation for the journey eastward and Myra the regular terminal on the westward run. We stick, then, with the accepted text. Patara was to the city of Xanthus what the Piraeus was to Athens.

21:2–3 / Here they **found a ship crossing over to Phoenicia** (v. 2), a journey of some four hundred miles by a course that took them south of Cyprus to Tyre, the chief city of Phoenicia, where the ship was to unload. From the time the unloading took, it would appear this was a vessel of some size (cf. v. 4). The main harbor of Tyre lay on the southern side of the "island" on which the city was built. This island, however, was now joined to the mainland by a mole (built by Alexander the Great) and the subsequent accumulation of sand on either side of it. In verse 5 Luke mentions one of these sandy beaches. The former glory of Tyre was somewhat diminished, but it remained an important center of trade and industry. In honor of its past greatness, the Romans had declared it a free city within the province of Syria.

21:4 / Paul used the time spent in unloading the ship to meet with the **disciples**. His week in Tyre probably included a meeting, as at Troas, for the celebration of the Lord's Supper (cf. 20:7–12). We need not take his seeming lack of haste to mean that he had given up all hope of reaching Jerusalem in time for Pentecost (cf. 20:16; also 21:15). His earlier urgency had probably taken into account the contingencies of sea travel in those days (cf. 2 Cor. 11:25), but having made a successful crossing to Tyre, he may have found that he now had time to spare. Paul would have visited this church before (cf. 11:30; 12:25; 15:3), and the use of the definite article in the Greek, "the disciples," bears this out— these were the Christians whom Paul knew to be there. Their presence went back to the events of 11:19. While he was with them, a warning came (perhaps through a Christian prophet) that he should not go to Jerusalem. But Paul was sure that he should go and would not be deterred (cf. 19:21; 20:22). This was probably similar to the incident a few days later in Caesarea, in which the Spirit made it known that Paul's future was fraught with danger. Others saw this as a reason for urging him to turn back, whereas Paul himself seems to have viewed the warning as God's way of preparing him for what lay ahead.

21:5–6 / When the ship was ready to sail (the definite article indicates that it was the same ship as before), the entire church accompanied Paul and the others to the beach (see disc. on 15:3), where they knelt together in prayer before parting (cf. 20:36; see disc. on 7:60 and 9:11). It does not appear to have been a large church.

21:7 / The RSV has the travelers leaving the ship at Ptolemais, about thirty miles south of Tyre. GNB and NIV imply that they continued their voyage to Caesarea. The difficulty is with the Greek verb, which can be understood either way, though in a nautical context it appears to be used consistently of continuing rather than of completing a voyage. Moreover, it makes better sense that they were prepared to wait in Tyre for a week in order to go as far as possible by ship than that they should wait so long to save themselves a walk of only thirty miles when they still would have forty more to walk from Ptolemais to Caesarea. Ptolemais was the ancient Accho, the name that it resumed after the Roman period (the Acre of the Crusaders). It was given its New Testament name in the late third or early second century B.C. when Palestine was ruled by the Ptolemies of Egypt. In Paul's day it was a *colonia*. But there were Jews there and a Christian church that probably dated from the same time as the church in Tyre (11:19). Doubtless, Paul had visited these Christians before, since Ptolemais lay on a road that he had traveled a number of times (11:30; 12:25; 15:3). He now spent a day with **the brothers.**

21:8–9 / The next day they continued to Caesarea. On two occasions at least (9:30; 18:22), and probably more, Paul had passed through Caesarea. Almost certainly he knew Philip and on this occasion stayed with him for a number of days. Philip was last heard of in 8:40 as having come to Caesarea some twenty years earlier. He had apparently made the city his home ever since (see *Didache* 13 for the "settling" of an itinerant minister). His title, **the evangelist,** may have been given to distinguish him from the apostle (though they still tended to be confused; see Eusebius, *Ecclesiastical History* 3.31.3 and 5.17.3). But it was no empty title. Philip could just as well have been known as "one of the Seven" (see disc. on 6:3ff.), but he had earned the right to be called by this name (8:4–40). He now had **four unmarried daughters who prophesied** (v. 9; see note on 11:27), their presence and their service to the church characteristically noted by Luke (see disc. on 1:14). Though they were prophets, they made no prediction concerning Paul, as far as we know. That role fell to another.

21:10–11 / The travelers had been in Caesarea for several days when the prophet Agabus **came down from Judea** (v. 10). Politically, Caesarea was part of Judea. It was in fact the administrative capital. But as a predominantly Gentile city, it was deemed by many Jews to be no part of their land, and Luke's reference reflects that attitude (see note on 1:8 and disc. on 10:1). Agabus is undoubtedly the same man as in 11:28, though Luke introduces him here as though for the first time. This may be because he was drawing on his travel diary and, at the time of this entry, had not before heard of Agabus. The prophet repeated the earlier warnings of danger to Paul (20:23; 21:4), using a symbolic action reminiscent of the prophets of old (cf., e.g., 1 Kings 11:29–39). **He took Paul's belt, tied his own hands and feet with it**, and declared that the owner of this belt would be treated thus by the Jews, who would hand him over, bound, to the Gentiles (v. 11). These words are not unlike Jesus' predictions concerning himself (Luke 9:44; 18:32; 24:7; cf. also his prediction concerning Peter, John 21:18) and may have been deliberately chosen (probably by Luke) to show the similarity between Jesus and Paul (see disc. on 19:21–41). Actually, though, the Jews did not hand Paul over as predicted, but were forced to relinquish him when the Romans intervened. There is no question, however, that the Jews were ultimately responsible for Paul's Roman imprisonment, so that the intention if not the detail of the prophecy was fulfilled (cf. 28:17). Agabus' introductory formula, **the Holy Spirit says**, corresponds to the "thus says the Lord" of the Old Testament.

21:12–13 / When Paul's friends heard this they **pleaded with** (him) **not to go up to Jerusalem**, but he would not heed their pleas (v. 12; cf. v. 4). Their grief was a grief to him, though we should probably take the expression **breaking my heart** (v. 13) to mean, rather, "breaking my spirit," that is, "weakening my resolve," for he was determined to go to Jerusalem. The Greek is emphatic: "I, for my part, am ready" (cf. Luke 9:51). See note on 2:38 for **the name** of the Lord Jesus.

21:14 / In the face of this determination, the others could only accept Paul's decision and leave the matter with God. In this context, **the Lord's will be done** seems to echo Jesus' prayer in Gethsemane (Luke 22:42; cf. also 18:21).

21:15–16 / Eventually they **got ready and went up to Jerusalem** (v. 15). It is possible that these preparations included the hire and harnessing of horses (the Greek will bear that meaning), for they still had about sixty-four miles ahead of them. If we accept the reading of the Western text, there is no question but that they were mounted, for it has them completing the journey in two days. Some of the Caesarean Christians accompanied them as far as the house of Mnason (v. 16; see disc. on 9:6ff. and 15:3). This man was a Cypriot with a name common among Greeks, though we cannot doubt that he was a Jew, for he is described as **one of the early disciples** (v. 16)—the phrase almost has the sense of "a charter member"—which may take his conversion back to the Pentecost of chapter 2. The same expression is used by Peter in 11:15 with reference to that event (cf. also 15:7). Mnason appears to have been a man of property, with a house in Jerusalem large enough to accommodate the visitors—an important consideration if this was indeed the season of Pentecost (see disc. on 2:1). There is, however, the possibility raised by the Western text that Mnason's house was not in Jerusalem, but in a village on the way in which they stayed overnight. But would Luke have troubled to mention his name if he was their host for only one night? At all events, Paul and his companions came at last to their destination.

Additional Notes §55

21:5 / **When our time was up**, i.e., "completed": The verb is a most unusual one in this context. It is used elsewhere of completing a building or some other piece of work. Here it may suggest that the ship was on a tight schedule, so that the travelers had an exact number of days ashore that they might not exceed. When this time was completed, they returned to the ship.

21:8 / **The evangelist**: The word occurs only twice elsewhere in the New Testament (Eph. 4:11; 2 Tim. 4:5). To be an evangelist was seen as a distinct gift, so that though all Christians were called to exercise this ministry, some were especially endowed to do so and so still today. In the second of the two passages cited, Timothy is exhorted to do the work of an evangelist, i.e., to make known the facts of the gospel. This was addressed to him when his work was largely local and pastoral. Similarly Philip was called "the evangelist" when he had settled in one place. Perhaps, then, this was the distinction (or one of them) between evangelists and apostles. One was itinerant, the other local.

§56   Paul's Arrival at Jerusalem (Acts 21:17–26)

The remaining chapters of Acts describe the "bonds and hardships" that Paul had to endure. That so much of the book is given to this may be due to a desire on Luke's part to simulate the passion narrative of the Gospel, in which the events of a few days are told at a length that seems disproportionate to the whole (see disc. on 19:21–41). But it must also be remembered that Luke himself was probably involved in these events, so that they would have loomed large in his mind and he would have had a wealth of firsthand experience on which to draw.

21:17 / Luke does not say whether they reached Jerusalem in time for the festival (20:16), but their leisurely progress as their journey drew to an end and the presence of many visitors in the city (cf. v. 20), including a number of Jews from Asia, suggests that they did. On their arrival, they were welcomed by some of **the brothers**—perhaps those most in sympathy with Paul's work.

21:18 / The next day a more formal meeting was held with James, now clearly at the head of the church in Jerusalem, which he governed with the support of the elders (see note on 11:30 and 12:17). Paul had been worried that the gifts of the Gentile churches might not be accepted (Rom. 15:31; see disc. on 19:21), but James and the other leaders (unlike some of their people) seem to have been well disposed toward Paul, and we may assume that they received the collection in the same spirit in which it was offered (cf. 24:17). The presence of the other delegates at this meeting (**Paul and the rest of us**—the last indication of Luke's presence until 27:1) would appear to bear this out.

21:19 / Paul **reported in detail** on his work (the Greek has the sense of recounting every single thing)—a long narration indeed! But since the reader already knows much of the story, Luke is spared the necessity of giving anything more than the one thread that ran through it all, namely, that God himself had done the work, but had been pleased to use Paul (cf. 14:27; 15:4; Rom. 15:18f.). It was important for Paul to make much of this theme, for there were those in this church who still questioned the legitimacy of the Gentile mission.

21:20 / The leaders readily praised God when they heard Paul's report. But they had to point out that his presence now in the city was likely to cause ructions among the **many thousands** of Christian Jews who remained **zealous for the law** (see note on 1:13). On the continuing adherence of large numbers of Jewish Christians to the law, see the introductory remarks to 15:1–21. James' reference to "thousands" of such believers has been looked at askance by some scholars, since the entire population of Jerusalem was not large (see note on 4:4). But the figure may have included many visiting Christians who were in Jerusalem for the festival.

21:21 / The trouble was that these people had been informed that Paul was preaching against the law. This was not something they had merely picked up as hearsay. The verb implies that they had been explicitly instructed along these lines, which can only mean that this was the doing of those intransigent "men of the circumcision" who went out of their way to hound Paul and to hinder his work (see disc. on 11:2; 15:1–5). It was very likely they who had been the cause of much of the trouble at Corinth, since they had been in Galatia and were threatening to be both in Philippi and in Rome (see Paul's respective letters). Everywhere he was misrepresented by these men because he was misunderstood. The more he enunciated the doctrine of salvation by grace, the more he was falsely accused of telling the Jews of the Diaspora **to turn away from Moses**, that is, to throw off all moral constraint (cf. Rom. 6:1ff.; Gal. 5:13). As for circumcision in particular, no doubt many Christian Jews were influenced by teaching such as Romans 2:25–30 and Galatians 4:9 and 5:6 and concluded that there was no more reason for them to maintain the rite than for the Gentiles to adopt it. Hence the accusation that Paul had been **telling them not to circumcise their children or live according to** (the Jewish) **customs**. But though Paul was certainly no advocate of circumcision (cf. Gal. 5:11), neither was he opposed to its practice by Jewish believers and, as far as we know, never gave them instruction against it (cf. Rom. 2:25; 3:1ff.; 7:12).

21:22 / No doubt Paul was able to reassure the elders and James on this matter. Indeed, they effectively endorsed his position by referring to the decision of the council of chapter 15 (v. 25). But there was still the problem of Paul's public image with those who were "zealous for the law."

21:23–24 / It was resolved, therefore, that he should demonstrate his respect for the law by publicly associating himself with four men who had recently taken a vow. He was to **join in their purification rites** (v. 24). These men appear to have been members of the church and, from the description that follows, to have taken a temporary Nazirite vow of the same type as Paul had taken some years before (18:18). The duration of such vows was optional, but thirty days seems to have been the minimum time (cf. Josephus, *War* 2.309–314). This being so, it is difficult to believe that Paul would have committed himself to such a length of time. But in the regulations governing these vows in Numbers 6:1–21 there is a provision covering accidental defilement (vv. 9–12). This called for a period of purification lasting seven days, at the end of which, on the seventh day, that man shaved his head and on the next day offered the appropriate sacrifice in the temple. He could then proceed with the original vow to its completion (vv. 13–21). From the references here to "purification" (vv. 24, 26) and to "seven days" (v. 27), it would seem that Paul was being asked to join with the four men in rites connected with accidental defilement and to **pay their expenses** as well as his own (v. 24; cf. Josephus, *Antiquities* 19.292–296). It is a question with many scholars, however, whether the historical Paul would ever have agreed to such a proposal. But we have seen that he appears to have remained a practicing Jew (see disc. on 15:1–21), and though he would not have admitted the efficacy of this rite (cf., e.g., 1 Cor. 1:30), it would not seem to have been such a difficult thing for him to have undertaken it in accordance with his own rule of 1 Corinthians 9:20f.

21:25 / However, it was clearly understood that what Paul was being asked to do had no implications for the Gentile believers. The decision of the Jerusalem council still stood, according to which no legal requirement was to be laid upon the Gentiles as necessary for salvation. They would only be asked, as Christians, to conform to certain standards of conduct and diet (cf. 15:19–21, 23–29). It is odd that the decrees are repeated verbatim, but it may have been for the sake of those who had not heard them before, unless Luke has simply filled out for his readers (as we might in a footnote) what was in fact only a passing reference to the decrees. Alternatively, Marshall suggests that this was the first mention of the decrees in the we-source and that Luke failed to edit the source in the light of the earlier reference (p. 356; cf. v. 10).

21:26 / Out of deference to the church leaders, Paul complied with their proposal and set about meeting the legal requirements. The next day he took the four men to the temple and underwent with them the rite of purification. At the same time he made provision for the sacrifice that would mark the completion of the rite.

Additional Notes §56

21:24–26 / The difficulty of these verses arises from their condensed nature and the distinct possibility that Luke himself was unclear as to what the church leaders wanted Paul to do. However, the advice that he should **join in their purification rites** (v. 24) must mean more than that he simply met their expenses, as some have suggested. He actually participated in some ceremony, and we have offered in the exposition what seems to be the most satisfactory explanation of what that ceremony was.

Pay their expenses (v. 24): It has sometimes been supposed that Paul met their expenses out of the collection. But there is some evidence that, despite his working to support himself and others on his missionary journeys, Paul had money of his own: he was able to maintain himself for two years in Caesarea and for two more in Rome, and Felix had hopes that Paul would offer him bribes.

We have written to them our decision (v. 25): The same authoritative tone as before (see disc. on 15:19f.), only here in the plural.

§57 Paul Arrested (Acts 21:27–36)

Though 21:18 sees the last of the "we passages" for the time being, the remainder of this chapter down to verse 29 may well be drawn from that source. But in verses 30 and following, Ehrhardt believes that he can discern a different style and, therefore, a different source. He thinks it unlikely that it came from any Jerusalem Christian. Probably, then, Luke "drew on notes of another member of the Pauline circle, mentioned in Acts 20:4, who was present in the temple at the time of the catastrophe [here to be described]. . . . Now the only one who was qualified to be there among those mentioned in Acts 20:4 was Timothy, and thus we conclude that Acts 21:30–40 may have come from his pen" (*Acts*, p. 109). However, the accuracy of Luke's topographical knowledge has suggested to Hengel that Luke "was not just working over an outside source," but was augmenting it by "drawing on his own memories" (p. 106).

21:27–29 / Paul's purpose was to mollify the Jewish Christians by being seen to practice the law. But his being seen by others—**some Jews from the province of Asia** (v. 27)—provoked the very situation that the Christian leaders had hoped to avoid. Near the end of the seven days of his purification (see note on 24:11) they saw Paul in the temple. Earlier they had seen him in the city with Trophimus and, knowing Trophimus (an Ephesian) to be a Gentile, concluded that Paul had now brought him and possibly the whole Gentile delegation (note the plural, **Greeks**, v. 28) **into the temple**, that is into the inner courts where no Gentile was permitted to go (v. 29; see notes on 3:2). (This was one offense for which the Sanhedrin was allowed by the Romans to execute the death sentence. See Josephus, *War* 6.124–128) Therefore, they apprehended Paul, shouting this charge to the crowd and adding another, that he was teaching **all men everywhere against our people and our law and this place** (v. 28; cf. 6:13). Emotions were running high. The Asian Jews were not inclined to make careful inquiry. In fact, as far as we know, Trophimus was not in the temple, much less in the inner courts. But Paul was their enemy. That was enough. And in any case the second charge was the real heart of the matter (cf. 24:17f. for Paul's own account of the incident).

21:30 / Their shouting excited the crowd. Confusion reigned. Luke's reference to **the whole city** is probably an exaggeration (see disc. on 9:35), but the outer court of the temple was in effect the city center and it was certainly in a turmoil. Paul was seized and dragged from the inner courts (as we suppose) to the Court of the Gentiles. The intention seems to have been to kill him then and there. As soon as the crowd was clear of the inner courts, their doors were closed (by the police), perhaps to prevent Paul from claiming sanctuary or perhaps to prevent further pollution, for the crowd was about to add murder to the alleged defilement by Gentiles (cf. 2 Kings 11:4-16; 2 Chron. 24:21).

21:31-32 / But a disturbance of this type could not break out without Roman intervention. The reference to a report being "sent up" (so the Greek) to the Roman commander (a prefect, since these were auxiliaries; see note on 10:1) vividly (and accurately) describes the scene (v. 31), for it would reach him in the Tower of Antonia, which overlooked the temple at its northwestern corner. Two flights of steps gave direct access from the Antonia to the Court of the Gentiles. There was also an underground passage to the Court of the Israelites (Josephus, *Antiquities* 15.403-409; 18.90-95 and esp. *War* 5.238-247). Some have suggested that the report was sent by the Christians. Luke's expression, however, suggests an official report, either from the temple authorities or from the guards patrolling the roofs. At all events, the prefect acted at once and with force, if the reference to **officers**, that is, "centurions " means that each had with him his full platoon (v. 32; see note on 10:1). The garrison at Jerusalem comprised an auxiliary cohort (five hundred or more infantry) with a detachment of horses. As always during the festivals, it would have been at the ready in case of riot (Josephus, *Antiquities* 20.105-112; *War* 5.238-247). Notice again the accuracy of Luke's description, with the troops rushing **down** to the crowd by the steps that led into the temple. This timely intervention saved Paul's life, though it cost him his freedom for some years to come (cf. 24:27; 28:30).

21:33–34 / It was clear to the commander that Paul was the cause of the trouble, so it was he whom he arrested and not his attackers. The **two chains** means that he was handcuffed to a soldier on either side (v. 33), to that extent fulfilling the prophecy of Agabus (v. 11; cf. 12:6). The commander naturally assumed that Paul was a criminal (cf. v. 38). He then attempted to find out what crime he had done. It is not clear whom he was questioning. It may have been Paul himself (but v. 37 may tell against this) or the crowd. In any case, Paul could not have made himself understood, for the people in the crowd were shouting, some one thing, some another (cf. 19:32). The prefect's only recourse was to take the prisoner into the Tower and question him there.

21:35–36 / As the troops withdrew to the steps, the crowd became increasingly violent, angry at seeing Paul snatched from their grasp. So violent were they that the soldiers had to carry Paul to safety with the crowd pressing after them, **shouting** all the while (present participle with the verb in the imperfect), **"Away with him!"** (to execution), as they had of Jesus in this very place some thirty years earlier (cf. Luke 23:18 and John 19:15, where the same verb is used; cf. also Acts 22:22).

Additional Notes §57

21:28 / **And besides, he has brought Greeks . . . :** The Greek conjunctions closely connect Paul's alleged act of introducing Gentiles into the temple with what precedes, as though to illustrate that he did not confine himself to teaching against the temple, but expressed that teaching in action.

§58 Paul Speaks to the Crowd (Acts 21:37–22:21)

There begins in this section the first of three speeches by
Paul in his own defense (22:1–21; 24:10–21; 26:2–23). To a certain
extent, these speeches are complementary with respect to both
the details they give of Paul's life and their theological thrust. The
latter is most evident in the two accounts of Paul's conversion
(22:6–16; 26:12–23). Acts 22:6–16 makes the point that Paul, alone
of all the disciples, had seen the Christ exalted in glory (vv. 11,
14) and that the glorified Christ had spoken in a way that only
he had understood (v. 9). The setting of Acts 26:12–23 is, on the
other hand, "that of an inaugural vision, such as the prophets
and seers received. . . . There may be intentional links with Acts
1 and 2 in terms of the prophetic witness now realized (2:17 =
Joel 2:28–32), which put Paul's experience on a par with that of
the original eye-witnesses of Pentecost" (Martin, p. 99). These emphases are Luke's. But there are others, giving rise to variations
of detail, that are undoubtedly Paul's. Insofar as the speeches are
autobiographical, they are in broad agreement with the statements of Paul's letters, and most notably with Galatians 1–2. Any
number of people could have recalled for Luke the general thrust
of this speech in the temple (see disc. on 21:27–36), but it now
comes to us largely in Luke's words. (The circumstances in which
it was made were hardly conducive to polished speech.) Paul's
aim was to show that as a Christian he was no less a Jew. This
speech is entirely autobiographical.

21:37 / As Paul was about to be carried into the Antonia,
he spoke to the prefect, who was somewhat taken aback to be
addressed in Greek, though it was the lingua franca of the ancient
world. He had assumed that Paul was a Palestinian of no education.

21:38 / This verse expresses a second conjecture and not
(as NIV) surprise that his first had proved wrong. The Greek is
not a negative question, but one that expects a positive answer:

"Are you, then, that Egyptian fellow . . . ?" This was the Egyptian of whom Josephus also wrote on two occasions, a "false prophet," who in about A.D. 54 had led thirty thousand men to the Mount of Olives to make an assault on Jerusalem. The procurator Felix had ordered an attack on the Mount, and the Egyptian had fled, leaving the "majority" of his followers to be either captured or killed (*War* 2.261–263; see disc. on 23:34 for the procurator Felix). In Josephus' second account of the incident, written some fifteen years later, he states that only four hundred were killed and two hundred wounded (*Antiquities* 20.167–172). This is likely to be nearer the mark. Josephus has a propensity to exaggerate numbers, which explains the difference between his thirty thousand and the prefect's estimate of the Egyptian's following as about four thousand men. He calls them "the four thousand," as though the number was well known. He also describes them as *sicarii* ("dagger men," from the Latin *sica*), the term applied to groups of militant Jewish nationalists who were active at this time. Josephus appears to distinguish between the *sicarii* and the followers of the Egyptian, but to the Roman commander they would have all seemed the same. And now he thought that the Egyptian had returned and been set upon as an imposter (see Hanson, p. 9, for Luke's "remarkable accuracy in relating his narrative to contemporary history").

21:39–40 / Thus it came as a further surprise when Paul identified himself as **a Jew from Tarsus** (v. 39)—a Jew, lest the commander should think him a Gentile and guilty of profaning the temple; a Tarsian, to distinguish himself from the Egyptian. Being a Tarsian carried no implication that he was also a Roman citizen (cf. 22:25). At the moment he was simply trying to say that he was not the man he had been taken for. He then asked to be able to speak to the people. Permission was granted, and when the people were quiet, he spoke to them in "Hebrew," that is (probably), **Aramaic**, from the steps of the Antonia (v. 40; see disc. on 13:16 for the motion with the hand). His choice of language was aimed at gaining the people's attention and, if possible, winning their hearts (cf. Rom. 9:1–3; 10:1). The whole episode has been questioned on two grounds: first, whether Paul would have been physically capable of speaking and, second, whether permission for him to speak would have been granted. There is no evidence, however, that he was actually hurt in the fracas, and though it seems odd that he was allowed to address the crowd, mere oddity is no reason to deny that it happened.

22:1 / Paul's aim was to conciliate, and this is evident at once in his address, "men, brothers and fathers" (see note on 1:16). Stephen had used the same form of address to the council (7:2), and it may have been that some members of the council were now present to see what was going on—hence the "fathers" (but in 23:1 Paul addressed the Sanhedrin simply as "brothers"). Paul felt that he was in a sense on trial, so he spoke of his **defense** (this term keeps recurring, 24:10; 25:8, 16; 26:1f., 24). In Acts the word means more than simply answering charges; it includes the thought of witnessing to the Lord. Defense becomes, as it were, attack, and the gospel is preached to the accusers.

22:2 / His opening gambit in Aramaic had at least one of the results he was aiming at: he gained their attention. Few Jews of the Diaspora could speak the language of Palestine (see disc. on 6:1), and one who could deserved to be heard. So they grow very quiet. He may have begun to win some hearts as well.

22:3 / The speech falls into three parts. First is his early conduct. In much the same way as in Galatians 1:13 17, Philippians 3:4–11, and 1 Timothy 1:12–16 (cf. also Acts 26:4f.), he recalled for them his past life. He tells the story as though seeing himself through the eyes of two different groups. To the Jews, he had appeared as a devotee of the law. Though born in Tarsus, he had been brought up in Jerusalem (see notes). This point needs to be noticed in view of the general assumption that Paul had become acquainted with Greek language and thought in his early years in Cilicia. This verse and 26:4f. have him in Jerusalem already as a young child, though he must have retained some links with Tarsus (cf. 9:30; 11:25; Gal. 1:21). He had been educated in Jerusalem at the feet of Gamaliel (see disc. on 5:34 and notes). His training had consisted of strict instruction **in the law of our fathers** (both the written law and the oral tradition; cf. Josephus, *Antiquities* 13.408–415 and 293–298). Josephus uses the same term, "strict instruction," of the Pharisees' training (*Antiquities* 18.39–52; *Life* 189–194; *War* 1.110–112; 2.143–144), and Paul's use of it now recalls his own former pride as a Pharisee in keeping the law (Phil. 3:6). In Galatians 1:14 he describes himself as once a "zealot" for the traditions; here, with exactly the same meaning, he says that he had been a "zealot" for God (see note on 1:13)—as indeed his hearers still were. But note the qualification of Romans 10:2. Zeal needs to be tempered with knowledge.

22:4 / To the Christians he had appeared as a persecutor of the church—the point is made to show his audience just how zealous he had once been. He had hounded **the followers of this Way to their death** (see disc. on 9:2), using the Jewish term for the church, not wishing to irritate these Jews by the introduction of Christian terminology. Some commentators take the phrase "to the death" as expressing only Paul's intention, for otherwise his reference to arresting believers and throwing them into prisons (plural in the Greek) is anticlimactic. But verses 22:20 and 26:10 are sufficient warrant to accept these words at face value. Clearly the persecution was more extensive than 8:3 and 9:1 would suggest (cf. 26:11). For the inclusion of women in the pogrom, see the discussion on 8:3, and for their role in the church the discussion on 1:14.

22:5 / But events at Damascus had changed his life. He had obtained letters of introduction to the **brothers** in Damascus (this use of this term stressing his kinship with the Jews) from **the high priest and all the Council.** This was not the current high priest (Ananias, 23:2), but (probably) Caiaphas. Either he was still alive for Paul to make the appeal of this verse (lit., "he is bearing witness . . .") or the appeal was to the collective memory of the Sanhedrin (or their records) as to what had been done in the past. The Greek of this verse could be construed to mean that he had gone to Damascus to arrest only those Christians who had fled there from Judea and not those already resident in the city. But the point cannot be pressed.

22:6 / The second part of his speech is about his conversion. The story, now told in Paul's words, is essentially the same as in 9:3-19. Where it adds to the earlier narrative, it does so with details that either reflect the personal nature of the recollection or are most likely to appeal to his Jewish audience. Thus he mentions here that it was at **noon** that he saw the light (cf. 26:13). This emphasizes its brightness, since it outshone the sun, and therefore its supernatural origin (cf. Ezek. 1:4, 28). Only under such a constraint would he have changed the course of his life.

22:7–8 / He fell to the ground (cf. 26:14, where they all fell) and heard the voice, as in 9:4, except that here Jesus is given the title **of Nazareth** (but cf. 26:15).

22:9 / Paul explained that the men who were with him **saw the light, but did not understand the voice of him who was speaking**. As in 9:4 and 7, so here in verses 7 and 9, the Greek text varies the case of the noun dependent on the verb "to hear" (though the cases are used in the reverse order in the two passages) to show that the hearing was different in each case. Paul heard intelligible words; his companions heard only a sound—to them it was not speech.

22:10 / The question **What shall I do, Lord?** is an addition to the earlier account (cf. 9:5f.). The address "Lord" would not at first have had the significance that it later had for the apostle, but he now dropped into the Christian use of the title in his narration: **the Lord said . . .** Jesus was not, of course, Lord to this Jewish crowd. Jesus' reply is essentially the same as in 9:6. Compare the more condensed account in 26.16ff.

22:11 / That the light was divine in origin is confirmed by the phrase "the glory of the light" (NIV **the brilliance of the light**). The reference is to the Shekinah—the glory of God manifested to human beings (see disc. on 7:2). This verse explicitly attributes Paul's blindness to this cause, as from his own reminiscence, whereas in 9:8 it is simply stated that he is blind. His companions, on the other hand, seem not to have been affected. They led him by the hand into Damascus.

22:12 / The third part of the speech is about his commission. With Paul, conversion brought an immediate call to service, however much it remained to be clarified in the years ahead (see disc. on 9:15f.). The instrument of his calling was Ananias (9:13f.), to whose earlier description Paul now added that he was **a devout observer of the law and highly respected by all the Jews living** in Damascus. This was undoubtedly true of Ananias, but it was to Paul's purpose to show that such a man played a key role in his conversion—no law-breaker, but a man highly regarded for his piety. He did not mention that Ananias was also a Christian.

22:13–15 / Because the story was being told from Paul's point of view, we hear nothing of Ananias' vision and of the struggle he had had in bringing himself to go to Paul (9:10–16). As far as Paul was concerned, Ananias had simply appeared at the house in Straight Street with two things to say: first, a word of healing—**Brother Saul, receive your sight!** (v. 13; cf. 9:17), second, an announcement concerning his future work. Paul, much more than Luke in the earlier narrative, retained the Jewish idioms of Ananias' speech: **the God of our fathers** and "the voice of his mouth" (v. 14; see disc. on 15:7b), to which may be added the archaic description of Jesus as God's **Righteous One** (cf. 3:14; 7:52; see note on 11:20). By recalling Ananias' phrase "the God of our fathers," Paul may have been hoping once again to show his oneness with his audience. The verb he **has chosen** (v. 14) is found again in Acts only in 3:20 and 26:16. It seems always to indicate a most pressing duty (cf. LXX Exod. 4:13; Josh 3:12; 2 Macc. 3:7; 8:9) and may be intended by Luke to express here what he knew to be Paul's own consciousness of his high calling (cf. 9:15). It indicates a choice and a calling made long before his own response to it (cf. Jer. 1:4). Out of consideration for his audience, Paul did not yet employ the word "Gentile" in stating to what precisely he had been called. He put it only in general terms—to be a **witness to all men of what** he had **seen and heard** (v. 15; cf. v. 21; 9:15; 26:17; Gal. 1:16). The verb "to see" (as in 1 Cor. 9:1) is in the perfect tense, expressing the abiding result of having seen Jesus. The image would remain in the mind's eye. The verb "to hear" is in the aorist with reference to the initial event. To have seen the risen Lord was an essential qualification of an apostle (cf. 1:22; 2:32; 3:15; 4:33; etc.).

22:16 / According to 9:17, Ananias had already announced the gift of the Holy Spirit to Paul. So the question of this verse runs parallel with that of Peter in 10:47, following the gift of the Spirit to Cornelius and his friends. The question is an abrupt one, sounding almost like a reproach. It demanded a clear response. The faith that is the prerequisite of forgiveness and the presupposition of baptism is implied in the phrase **calling on his name** (see note on 2:38 and disc. on 9:14).

22:17–18 / The commission that Paul had received through Ananias was subsequently confirmed by a vision ("an ecstasy"; cf. 10:10; see disc. on 23:11) as he was praying in the temple (see disc. on 9:11). This was not mentioned earlier but it was important to mention it now in proof that for Christian Paul the temple remained a place of prayer and worship. A man who had prayed in the temple was not likely to have profaned it (cf. 21:28). Almost certainly these verses belong to the period of 9:26–31. However, the different reasons given here and in 9:29f. for his leaving the city have troubled some people. The two passages are not irreconcilable. In the earlier account, Luke was describing the circumstances as they would have appeared to an objective observer—a Jewish plot against Paul (which he was hardly likely to have mentioned now) that had led the disciples to take the action they did. Paul, on the other hand, speaks here of his own inner experience as he wrestled in prayer with the knowledge of that plot, wondering what he should do. In the end it had seemed that the Lord was endorsing the action proposed by the disciples, bidding him to **leave Jerusalem immediately,** because the people would not accept his witness. The word *Lord* does not actually occur in these verses. The Greek of verse 18 has simply, "I saw him," but we understand from verse 19 that the Lord is intended. He is not further identified, for obvious reasons, but Luke's Christian readers would have known who was meant.

22:19–21 / Paul's prayer in the temple is recounted as though he had debated with the Lord the question of whether or not he should go. His argument was that if the people were going to listen to anyone it would be to him, for he had been a persecutor of the Way, going **from one synagogue to another,** arresting and beating the believers (see note on 26:11; for the construction "to believe toward . . . ," see disc. on 9:42). But then he had become a believer himself. Before that, he had even taken part in the murder of Stephen (notice how the word "witness," *martys*, applied here to Stephen, was acquiring its sense of "martyr"). Paul's intention in all this was to show that his life's work among the Gentiles had not been his own, but the Lord's, choice. He would have stayed in Jerusalem, but the Lord had been unmoved by his arguments and had sent him **far away to the Gentiles** (v. 21; cf. Eph. 2:13).

Additional Notes §58

21:39 / **A citizen of no ordinary city**: Originally it had been illegal to hold Roman citizenship along with the citizenship of one's own or another city, but by the time of Claudius at the latest (A.D. 41–54), this prohibition no longer applied. The pride that Paul exhibited in his native city "was still at this point a noticeable feature of city life in the Roman Empire" (Hanson, p. 213).

22:3 / **Born . . . brought up . . . trained** ("educated"): W. C. van Unnik has shown that these three verbs are found frequently in ancient writers and in the same order (*Tarsus or Jerusalem: The City of Paul's Youth*, pp. 17–45; cf. Acts 7:20–22 for the same three). The second indicates up-bringing at home. It is not clear how this relates to Paul's claim in 21:39 to be a citizen of Tarsus. His birth and later years of residence may have been sufficient to establish the claim.

Under Gamaliel I was thoroughly trained, lit., "educated at the feet of Gamaliel": Apparently the teacher sat on an elevated seat and his pupils on the ground at his feet, hence, perhaps, the metaphorical use of the phrase in 4:35, 37, and 5:2. There has been hesitation on the part of some scholars to accept the statement that Paul studied under Gamaliel, since his "statement of the Jewish doctrine of the law is so gross a caricature of anything which he could have learnt from Gamaliel" (*BC*, vol. 4, p. 279). But Paul's conversion and subsequent experience was such that he came to see that the Jewish reliance on the "works of the law" had no part in the doctrine of salvation by grace through faith. His revulsion from the Jewish position is entirely understandable. But for all that—and in confirmation of the claim made in this verse—his method of exegesis and argument retain the hallmarks of his rabbinic training and, indeed, of his training in the school of Hillel of which Gamaliel had been the head (see C. K. Barrett, *A Commentary on the Epistle to the Romans* [London: Adam and Charles Black, 1962], p. 89). Moreover, the Hillel family had always had an interest in the Diaspora, so that a child from Tarsus might naturally have gone to them for training. It is note-worthy that this family also had an interest in Greek language and cul-ture (b. *Sotah* 49b). Paul's Greek education may have been gained in Jerusalem.

22:13 / **I was able to see him**: The Greek verb (*anablepein*) can mean either "to recover sight" (cf. 9:18) or "to look up" (cf. Luke 19:5), but is used frequently as if combining both meanings. Ananias was "standing over" Paul (so the Greek), so naturally he would look up.

22:14–15 / **To hear words from his mouth. You will be . . .** : Be-tween these two clauses stands the Greek word *hoti* (not represented in NIV). GNB renders it as a causal conjunction, introducing the reason for God's choice of Paul. It is better understood, however, as signaling (like our quotation marks) the content of the message. Paul would hear God saying, "You will be my witness . . . "

22:16 / **Be baptized and wash your sins away:** Both verbs are in the middle voice in the Greek (so also perhaps in 1 Cor. 10:2 of baptism and certainly in 1 Cor. 6:11 of washing; cf. Eph. 5:26; Titus 3:5). As a rule, the verb "to baptize" is used in the passive when referring to the subjects of Christian baptism (cf., e.g., 9:18, "he was baptized"). But here the subject is presented as doing something for himself and not merely as receiving: "Get yourself baptized." The seeking of the outward sign and the claiming for oneself of what it signifies is the response of faith to God's grace.

22:22–23 / Until now the crowd had remained quiet (cf. v. 2) and prepared to hear what Paul had to say. But at the word "Gentiles" the riot was in danger of erupting again. No doubt what offended them was his claim to a divine commission to offer salvation to all peoples (this could have been read into his words from what they knew of him) without their submitting first to the "yoke" of the law (cf. 15:10). They would hear no more of this (cf. 7:57), and the opportunity was gone for Paul to defend himself, had that been his desire, against the specific charge that he had "brought Greeks into the temple area" (21:28b). But in any case, that charge was only incidental. The Jews' real objection, that he had taught "against our people and our law and this place" (21:28a), had been sufficiently borne out by what they had heard. So they took up again their cry, "Away with him," reinforced now by the phrase "from the earth" (NIV **Rid the earth of him**). **He's not fit to live**, they declared (v. 22)—the imperfect tense implies that this had been so in their opinion for a very long time. Their rage was given expression by their **throwing off their cloaks and flinging dust into the air** (cf. 2 Sam. 16:13; Job 2:12; Rev. 18:19) and **shouting** (v. 23). In the latter word we have another reminder of the story of Jesus. The expression is found in Acts only here, but six times in John and four times in the Johannine passion narrative of the cries of the Jewish people against Jesus (John 18:40; 19:6, 12, 15). Their rage against Paul is historically credible. In the years between A.D. 56 and 66 the intensity of Jewish hatred against all things foreign was white-hot.

22:24 / Meanwhile, the Roman commander could make little sense of what was happening. He may not have understood the language of Paul's speech, or if he did, why it should have produced such a reaction. He decided that the only way to get at the truth of the matter was to interrogate the prisoner under the scourge, and to that end he gave orders that Paul should be taken into the Tower.

22:25 / The Tower of Antonia served as both a residence for the governor and a barracks (Josephus, *Antiquities* 15.403–409; 18.90–95; *War* 5.238–247). Its central courtyard probably survives in the pavement found under the Convent of Our Lady of Zion and the Convent of Flagellation and may be identified with "the place called Gabbatha"—the stone pavement where Jesus was tried. The barracks, therefore, to which Paul was taken may also have been the scene of Jesus' scourging. As on that occasion, so now a centurion was in charge of the detail assigned to "interrogate" Paul. Roman practice in scourging varied with the status of the victim. Under some circumstances, a Roman citizen might be beaten with a rod, but in the case of slaves and non-Romans a whip of knotted cords or leather was used, often weighted with pieces of metal or bone (Josephus, *Antiquities* 15.284–291; 16.229–234 and 244–253). At times this torture proved fatal. Paul's "interrogation" was to have been by this means. He was stretched . . . out to be flogged (or "with thongs," referring to the straps by which the prisoner was held rather than to the scourge by which he would be whipped). But before the scourge was laid to his back, he asked the question that asserted his Roman citizenship and so brought an immediate halt to the proceedings. Not only was the method of beating illegal, but so was any beating of a citizen without trial. Hence the second half of Paul's question (see disc. on 16:36f.).

22:26–28 / The centurion reported this new development to the prefect, who then questioned Paul himself. He was clearly put out by Paul's claim. His remark about paying a big price for his own citizenship does not reflect doubt about Paul's, but only his bitterness that the status of citizen had seemingly been devalued. Under the early emperors citizenship was in process of being widely extended. Theoretically it was not a thing to be bought, but money often did exchange hands. This was especially so in the time of Claudius (Dio Cassius, *Roman History* 60.17), when the prefect, judging by his name, Claudius Lysias (23:26), was granted this status. Evidently, he was a Greek, but following custom, he had adopted the praenomen and nomen (Claudius) of his benefactor, retaining his own name, Lysias, as his cognomen (see note on 13:9). His sarcastic comment about the prisoner "debasing the currency" produced something of a put-down in reply. Whereas the prefect had purchased the privilege, Paul had been born to it. We know nothing of the circumstances in which Paul's father (or earlier) had come by his status, but as early as the first century B.C. there were many thousands of Roman citizens to be found in Asia Minor.

22:29 / No sooner were they convinced of Paul's claim than his would-be interrogators **withdrew**. The commander himself was fearful lest his unlawful action should have repercussions (cf. 16:38). Nevertheless, he kept Paul in custody, perhaps even in chains, for he still supposed that his prisoner had committed some crime.

Additional Notes §59

22:25 / **A Roman citizen**: Paul was a citizen of both Tarsus (21:39) and Rome. His enjoyment of this dual status was a mark of the imperial period and his evident pride in both a feature of the early part of that period in particular (see note on 21:39). Sherwin-White points out that, at this time, when citizens were still relatively few in the eastern empire, the privilege was valued for the political rights it conferred. After the end of the reign of Claudius (A.D. 54), Roman citizenship became a much more common phenomenon, and it was the social advantages of citizenship that came to the fore. But Acts "breathes the climate of the earlier phase" (pp. 172f.). This is further borne out by the circumstances in which the commander obtained his citizenship. As noted, under Claudius, the privilege was often won by means of bribery, but under Nero this scandal was brought to an end and, as far as we know, did not recur. So "the historical atmosphere of the Lysias incident is exactly right for the time of Claudius" (Sherwin-White, p. 156; see also Hanson, pp. 10f., who finds evidence in this detail that the author of Acts lived near to the events he was relating, or was using sources that derived from that time).

§60   Before the Sanhedrin (Acts 22:30–23:11)

The Roman commander treated Paul's case as a routine matter. It belonged to the jurisdiction of the local authority, the Sanhedrin, and so to that authority he referred it. But then we have the extraordinary spectacle of such violence erupting in the Sanhedrin that Paul's life was again in jeopardy and he had to be rescued. This was in some measure due to Paul himself, who showed neither tact nor any desire, as he had on the previous day, to conciliate his audience. A curious feature of the incident as Luke has reported it is that no mention is made of the charge that Paul had "brought Greeks into the temple area" (21:28b). But then we have already suggested that the real issue was his alleged teaching against "our people and our law and this place" (21:28a). The other was probably raised, but Luke has contented himself with giving us only the crux of the matter.

22:30 / The prefect was clearly mystified by his prisoner. Here was a man who knew and enjoyed his rights as a Roman citizen, yet had all the appearances of a troublemaker. In an attempt **to find out exactly why Paul was being accused by the Jews,** he summoned the Sanhedrin for a special meeting the next day. This meeting is not represented as a trial either here or in the letter that Lysias later wrote reporting it to the governor. It is only in Paul's words that the council is said to "judge" him (23:3, 6). Rather it appears to have been merely an inquiry, though the prefect might have expected formal charges to be laid as a result of it. It is a question with some whether the commander had the authority to summon a meeting of the Sanhedrin. But the council members were probably only too glad to oblige, in order to shift the blame for the riot of the previous day onto Paul and to see that the one whom they regarded as a dangerous enemy of the temple was not allowed to escape. "The charge of causing a riot was a very serious one, and could have very grave consequences if it came to the procurator's ears" (Hanson, p. 220). So Paul "was released"—whether from his chains or simply from his confinement in the Antonia—and taken to stand before the Sanhedrin (cf. 4:5–22; 5:27–40; 6:12–7:58; Luke 22:66–71; for its place of meeting, see disc. on 4:5). It is not clear whether the commander was present. Verse 10 implies that he was. Luke's narrative is compressed; he may have been called by someone only when the meeting got out of hand. There is no reason why he should not have been present. The desire of the council members to avoid contact with Gentiles in John 18:28 was under the special circumstances of the festival. Ordinarily they must often have had contact with Roman officials, and at this special inquiry, called for the prefect's convenience, there would have been nothing untoward in his auditing the proceedings.

23:1 / Luke seems to begin with the meeting well under way, but we may assume that the inquiry was formally opened and Paul accused of defiling the temple. For his part (addressing them as equals, "men, brothers"; see note on 1:16), Paul declared that he had a good **conscience** before God (a characteristically Pauline word; cf. 24:16 and twenty times in his epistles). The statement, **I have fulfilled my duty to God . . . to this day** should not be understood of his whole life (there were some things about which Paul had a bad conscience; cf. 22:20), but only of the recent past and the matters with which he was charged. The verb "to fulfil one's duty" (Paul's or Luke's?) is strictly "to be a citizen" or "to live as a citizen" and may represent Paul's claim, as a Christian, to belong to the commonwealth of God, whose laws he respected and observed (cf. Eph. 2:12, 19; Phil. 3:20). The idea of citizenship is prominent in these chapters (21:39; 22:28). For Paul's "straight look" compare 13:9; 14:9, and see the discussion on 3:4.

23:2 / The president of the council at this time was the high priest Ananias, not to be confused with the Annas of 4:6, but the son of Nebedeus, appointed to this office by Herod Agrippa II in A.D. 47 and dismissed in A.D. 58 or 59. His Roman sympathies kept him in office longer than most but made him an object of hatred to the Jewish nationalists. At the outbreak of the Jewish war against Rome in A.D. 66, he was murdered by the *sicarii*. By all accounts Ananias was a violent and unscrupulous man (he had not hesitated to use the *sicarii* himself; see Josephus, *Antiquities* 20.204–207; *War* 2.241–244 and 441–448), and it was in keeping with this reputation that he now ordered **those standing near Paul to strike him on the mouth.** He may have thought

that Paul was lying or he may have taken exception to his claim
to be a citizen of the heavenly commonwealth. Either way, it was
an unwarranted act. The parallel with Jesus is unmistakable (John
18:22), though this detail is not found in Luke's Gospel.

23:3 / It was both offensive and an offense for one Jew
to order another to be struck in this way. Paul's "knee-jerk" response was to declare that God would strike the high priest (lit.,
"God is about to strike you"). He called him a **whitewashed wall**,
a proverbial saying meaning that he was a hypocrite, like the
prophets of Ezekiel 13:10f. who covered a wall of loose stones with
whitewash so that it appeared to be other than it was (cf. Isa.
30:13; Matt. 23:27; Luke 11:44). Ananias bore the semblance of
a minister of justice, but he was not what he seemed (cf. Lev.
19:15), for in Jewish law the rights of the defendant were carefully safeguarded.

23:4-5 / Paul had right on his side, but his angry rejoinder only aroused the indignation of the council. Some of its
members reminded him that it was improper to speak to God's
high priest in this way (v. 4). To which Paul replied that he **did
not realize that he was the high priest** (v. 5). This has sometimes
been taken to mean that Paul had literally failed to recognize
Ananias, either through weakness of sight (but see v. 1) or because he did not know him by sight. But more likely he had
resorted to irony, as much as to say, "I did not recognize the high
priest in the behavior and speech of this man. His conduct belies
that he is God's representative" (for so the phrase **God's high
priest** means). But the moment of anger passed, and Paul's quotation of Exodus 22:28 was half apologetic (and also another tacit
assertion of his respect for the law).

23:6 / Events now took a fresh turn, with Paul aligning
himself with the Pharisees. It seems unlikely that he did this on
a sudden impulse, as would appear from our text. And it is even
less likely that he only now became aware of the presence of Sadducees and Pharisees in the council. Rather, something must have
happened to bring these divisions to his attention. In this connection we should keep in mind that the narrative is probably
highly condensed and that Paul may have been speaking for some
time. Verse 9 gives the impression that he had again recounted
the events of his conversion in which his encounter with the risen

Jesus (is "spirit" equivalent to "ghost" in v. 9?) brought to the fore the whole question of resurrection. At this the Sadducees may have grown restive (notice the verb, **he called out**, as though to make himself heard), and so he brought the speech to the sudden conclusion described here—not dishonestly, as claiming to be what he no longer was, but as still one with the Pharisees with respect to the hope of **the resurrection of the dead**. He made practically the same assertion before Agrippa in 26:5 (cf. Phil. 3:5).

23:7-8 / Paul may have acted from the best of motives. He may have genuinely hoped to point the Pharisees to a surer base for their own doctrine of resurrection by pointing them to Jesus. But one suspects that there was at least an element of gamesmanship in what he did. No love was lost between the Pharisees and the Sadducees, as he well knew, and an appeal to the Pharisees on these grounds could well have won them to his side, for the Sadducees repudiated the doctrine of resurrection, with its kindred belief in spiritual beings inhabiting a spiritual world.

23:9 / The effect of Paul's outcry was dramatic. Immediately there was a sharp division within the council, though he did not carry all of the Pharisees with him, for only **some of the teachers of the law** who belonged to their party defended the possibility that **a spirit or an angel** had spoken to Paul, and even then they were far from accepting his own account of what had happened on the road to Damascus (supposing that to be the reference; see disc. on v. 6.) For the general acceptance of Christians by the Pharisees, as long as they kept the law, see the discussion on 5:34f. The Sadducees, however, remained fixed in their opposition (see disc. on 4:1) and for the remainder of this book are Paul's chief opponents (cf. 23:14).

23:10 / With the members of the Sanhedrin now taking sides and perhaps even coming to blows, nothing more was to be gained from the inquiry, and Paul was in danger of being **torn to pieces** (as by a beast at its prey; cf. LXX Hos. 13:8). The commander therefore ordered in his troops, and Paul was once more taken into custody in the Antonia.

23:11 / Paul must have wondered what the issue of all this would be. His life seemed to hang by a thread, with three attempts on it in the space of two days (21:31; 22:22; 23:10; cf.

2 Cor. 11:23). If ever he had needed reassurance, it must have been now, and the Lord (Jesus) met that need. With the same word as he had spoken to the disciples in their storm-driven boat (Mark 6:50)—a word unique to Jesus in the New Testament—he spoke to Paul that night in the Antonia, bidding him to **take courage**. As he had witnessed in Jerusalem, so he would also in Rome. Notice that his task was not to defend himself but "to testify." This verb is found in each half of this sentence, but in the first half in an intensive form as though to acknowledge the thoroughness with which he had done it (see disc. on 2:40). For similar visions at decisive moments, see 11:5ff.; 18:9f.; 22:17ff.; 27:23f. This vision brought confirmation of Paul's own conviction (and desire) that he should see Rome (cf. 19:21; Rom. 1:10f.; also Ps. 34:4f.). Some commentators have seen the comparative statement of this verse as extending beyond the thought of witnessing to the circumstances in which he would do it—as he had been a witness in chains in Jerusalem, so he would be also in Rome.

Additional Notes §60

23:6 / **Because of my hope in the resurrection of the dead**, lit. "concerning [the] hope and [the] resurrection of the dead": This is generally taken to mean "[the] hope of [the] resurrection of the dead" (so NIV), but in 26:6 "hope" is used of the whole messianic salvation, of which the resurrection is but a facet. This is possibly the meaning here, but 24:15 and 21 support the rendering of NIV.

§61   The Plot to Kill Paul (Acts 23:12–22)

The Lord had assured Paul that he would witness in Rome, and that promise came a step nearer fulfillment with Paul's transfer to Caesarea. The story has all the marks of an eyewitness account, such that only the most skeptical would question Luke's veracity. Martin describes these verses as "a drama of suspense and mystery, with hurried exchanges of information, quick decisions, and sworn secrecy." The name of God does not appear once, yet "the undertone of divine providence runs throughout; and God is there, if unseen and unrecognized, in the plans and counter-plans of enemies and friends" (pp. 129f.).

23:12–13 / The next day, following the fiasco of the council inquiry, a group of more than forty Jews bound themselves by an oath to assassinate Paul. The identify of this group is not indicated. One suggestion is that they were a Pharisaic fraternity (an *haburah*), which might explain how Paul's family came to know of their plans. On the other hand, the conspirators seem to have had more rapport with the Sadducees than with the Pharisees, for it was only to "the chief priests and elders" that they went with their plan (v. 14). It is even possible that they were a band of *sicarii* employed by the high priest himself (see disc. on 23:2). The fanaticism evidenced by these men was becoming more and more a feature of life in Jerusalem.

23:14–15 / Their plan was to have Paul appear before the council again and, as he was being brought from the Tower, to kill him. It was a desperate plan with little chance of success, conceived perhaps in the knowledge that the Sanhedrin lacked the power in most cases to inflict capital punishment and as much a symptom of their frustration with Roman rule as of their desire to be rid of Paul. It is far from certain, however, that the prefect would have agreed to a new inquiry.

23:16 / As it happened, the matter was never put to the test. Somehow Paul's family got wind of the plot, and his nephew came to him with the story. It was customary for a prisoner's family and friends to have access to him in prison and, in this case, if his family, why not his friends? The story of what went on in the Tower is so vivid and circumstantial that it is almost certain that Luke was there. The reference to Paul's nephew is one of the few glimpses we have of his family connections.

23:17–19 / Paul immediately summoned a centurion and had him take the boy to the prefect. A prisoner would not normally have a centurion to do his bidding, but it must have been plain that the matter was urgent. The prefect took the boy aside, since the matter appeared to be secret, and asked what it was that he had to tell. The word used of the boy (the diminutive of **young man**, v. 17) suggests that he was only a youth. Probably in our terms a young "teenager," since the commander led him by the hand (an eyewitness touch). The phrase **Paul, the prisoner**, used here for the first time in Acts, is employed by Paul five times of himself in his epistles (Eph. 3:1; 4:1; Phil. 1:13; Philem. 1, 9).

23:20–21 / Paul's nephew repeated his story, and we now learn that the attempt on Paul's life was planned for the next day. The prefect may have already received the council's request that the prisoner be brought to them again, for the boy spoke of them as waiting even then for the prefect's decision (v. 21). He urged the prefect not to fall in with their plan.

23:22 / Even as the boy was speaking, the commander seems to have made up his mind what he would do. He may have already decided to send Paul to the governor, for he himself "lacked the necessary *imperium* to deal judicially with prisoners of provincial status, once he had restored public order" (Sherwin-White, p. 54), but now he determined to send him that night.

Additional Notes §61

23:12 / **The Jews ... bound themselves with an oath**, lit., "they placed themselves under an anathema," i.e., they declared themselves liable to the direst punishment of God if they failed to carry it through (cf. Josephus, *Life* 271–275; *Antiquities* 15.280f.). In the event of failure, however, rabbinic custom would grant them a dispensation (see m. *Nedarim* 3.3; cf. Matt. 5:34ff.).

23:23–24 / No sooner had his nephew departed than preparations were made to remove Paul to Caesarea under armed guard. They were to leave that night about the "third hour" (nine o'clock), and the guard would comprise **two hundred soldiers** [with their centurions], **seventy horsemen and two hundred spearmen** (v. 23). This would represent about half the garrison and is regarded by some as a far larger force than was warranted. Luke is accused of exaggeration. All of this gives added interest to the interpretation of the word rendered "spearmen." It is found only twice elsewhere in all of ancient Greek literature—and then in writings much later than Acts (the seventh and tenth centuries)— and it is by no means certain that it means "spearmen." The derivation suggests that has to do with taking hold with the right hand, and a number of other suggestions have been made, including "led horses." If we accept this, it eliminates the two hundred spearmen and replaces them with the right number of horses to carry the other foot soldiers to Antipatris on the first stage of their journey. If that stage was accomplished in one night (see disc. on v. 32), a distance of nearly forty miles, this possible interpretation becomes probable.

But even if the word does mean "spearmen," an escort of 470 men may not have been unreasonable in view of the troubled times and the fanaticism of the Jewish nationalists. And of course the commander had no idea of the extent of the plot. The boy had spoken of "more than forty men" (v. 21), but how many more he did not know. In any case, the foot soldiers were only to accompany Paul on the first and most dangerous part of the journey and would then return while Paul went on with the horsemen to Caesarea (cf. v. 32). Paul himself was mounted, but the plural, **mounts for Paul** (v. 24), raises a number of possibilities. The additional horses may have been for relays or for baggage or, if he was chained to a soldier, for that man as well. But it could equally mean that Paul had his friends riding with him (cf.

24:23)—Luke, perhaps, and Aristarchus, who were certainly with him in Caesarea at a later date (27:1f.). For **Felix**, see the discussion on 24:1.

23:25 / As the law demanded of a subordinate officer in this situation, a written statement explaining the case (the *elogium*) was sent with the escort. This is the only example in the New Testament of a secular letter. Its realistic style makes it possible that Luke had seen it or at least heard it read, perhaps in open court before Felix. Or a copy may have been given to Paul as part of the documentation for his appeal to Caesar. It bears the impress of what a Roman officer might have said, including a better presentation of his own conduct than a strict adherence to the truth might have suggested and a rather contemptuous reference to Jewish "questions about their law" (v. 29). However, we probably do not have the letter verbatim. Luke introduces it with the comment that it went "something like this." The original would have been in Latin.

23:26 / The letter began in the usual way, with the writer named first, then the person to whom it was addressed, and thirdly a word of greeting (cf. 15:23). Here, for the first time the prefect is named (see disc. on 22:28). The title **Excellency** was that appropriate to a man of equestrian rank (see note on 1:1), and though Felix was not of that rank, most procurators were and its use here was only natural (and diplomatic).

23:27 / Lysias outlined the circumstances that had brought Paul into his custody. His account conforms broadly with what we already know, except that he claims to have rescued Paul knowing that he was a Roman citizen, whereas, of course, it was only later that he made that discovery (for another version, see 24.5f.).

23:28 / In the Greek text, the statements of verses 27 and 28 are closely linked, as though the commander was anxious to move quickly from his rescue of Paul to the inquiry by the Sanhedrin, drawing a veil over his own conduct in the interim that was open to censure.

23:29 / As far as the commander was concerned, Paul had done nothing worthy of prison, much less of death, and this remained the Roman attitude throughout the affair (cf. 26:31; also

18:14f.). The charge that he had "brought Greeks into the temple area" (21:28b) had been shelved for lack of evidence (cf. 24:13). The Asian Jews on whose word alone it had rested had evidently returned home. The more general charge that he was teaching "all men everywhere against our people," and so on (21:28a; cf. 24:5) was now all that was left to the Sanhedrin, which had taken up the Asians' cause against Paul. But this was a theological, not a criminal, matter, and as such held no interest for the Romans.

23:30 / Lysias was probably glad to be rid of Paul, and in any case the governor was the proper authority to deal with the matter. He had told the Jews that if they wished to lay charges they should do so before the governor. The usual "farewell" at the end of a letter is omitted here by the best manuscripts.

23:31–32 / Antipatris had been rebuilt by Herod the Great and named in honor of his father, Antipater. It was not a fortress, but it was strategically placed and did serve as a military station (*mutatio*). The town marked the border between Judea and Samaria. From Jerusalem to Antipatris, by a descending and winding road, was a journey of thirty-seven miles, and Luke implies that Paul and his escort reached the town that same night. This distance might have been just possible in the time for well-trained foot soldiers (see R. Jewett, p. 139), but it is possible (contrary to the impression given by Luke) that the foot soldiers did not go that far, but only as far as was necessary to see the party out of the immediate danger, leaving the others to go on to Antipatris and the next day to Caesarea. But of course the possibility still remains that the whole party was mounted (see disc. on v. 23).

23:33–35 / The second leg of the journey, from Antipatris to Caesarea, was a distance of about twenty-five miles through open, mainly Gentile, country (the Plain of Sharon; see disc. on 8:40 and 9:35). Once in Caesarea, the escort delivered both the letter and their prisoner to the governor. When Felix had read the letter, he followed standard bureaucratic procedure by asking Paul what province he came from. Having discovered that it was Cilicia, he agreed nevertheless to hear the case. This little interchange reflects criminal law of the time. The practice had been to try criminals in the province in which their crime was committed, but by the beginning of the second century A.D., and almost certainly earlier, the possibility existed of sending the accused for trial in his own province. "The point," then, "of the question put to Paul, in mid-first century, was not to protect the rights of the accused . . . , but to enable the procurator . . . to avoid a tiresome affair altogether, if he felt inclined, either by expelling an accused person from a province to which he did not belong, or by a refusal of jurisdiction" (Sherwin-White, p. 31). Why then did Felix not take up this option? Patently, it would be a "tiresome affair." The answer may lie in the status of Cilicia, which was at that time was still apparently part of Syria (see note on 15:23) and "the legate of Syria was not to be bothered with minor cases." In any case, "the status of Cilicia did not require that its natives should be sent back to it for trial" (Sherwin-White, p. 56). So Paul was retained in Caesarea, **kept under guard in Herod's palace** (v. 35), now the headquarters of the Roman administration (see disc. on 10:1). This was his real "handing over to the Gentiles" that Agabus had foretold (21:11).

§63 The Trial Before Felix (Acts 24:1-27)

Paul's removal to Caesarea began a two-year imprisonment in that city. During these years he stated his case (and therefore the case for the gospel) before two governors and a king, thus further fulfilling the ministry to which he had been called (9:15). These were days of high drama as well as of tedious confinement, but through it all Paul maintained his unswerving purpose to serve Christ and the gospel.

24:1 / The first of the two governors to hear Paul's case was Antonius Felix, the brother of Pallas, the freedman and favorite of the emperor Claudius. It was through the influence of Pallas that Felix had been appointed to Judea. Josephus and Tacitus disagree as to the time and circumstances of his arrival in the province. Tacitus supposes that he was procurator of Samaria and Judea while Cumanus was procurator of Galilee (*Annals* 12.54). Josephus, on the other hand, says that Felix succeeded Cumanus as procurator of Judea (*Antiquities* 20.134-140; *War* 2.247-249). Most scholars prefer Josephus on this point, though it remains possible that Felix held some sort of office in Palestine during Cumanus' term of office (is the "many years" of v. 10 some corroboration of this?). At all events, he was procurator of Judea from A.D. 52 to about 58 (see disc. on v. 27 and notes). Like his brother, he had been a slave, and with reference to this Tacitus remarked that "with savagery and lust he exercised the power of a king with the disposition of a slave" (*History* 5.9). The picture drawn by Tacitus of Felix's public and private life is not a pretty one. Trading on the influence of his infamous brother, he indulged in every license and excess, thinking "that he could do any evil act with impunity" (Tacitus, *Annals* 12.54). Luke gives a rather better picture of him, though he was certainly not blind to the governor's faults.

Within five days of Paul's arrival in Caesarea, the Jews were ready to present their case against him (see note on v. 11). This suggests some haste on their part. Perhaps the Sanhedrin were afraid that unless they acted quickly he might be released for want of a reason for holding him. The delegation included Ananias, the high priest, a number of elders, and **a lawyer** (lit., "orator") **named Tertullus**, who was their spokesman. He may have been their regular legal consultant. Though the name Tertullus is Latin, it does not follow necessarily that he was a Roman (see note on 12:12), and if the words "according to our law" are retained in verse 6, he may well have been a Jew. On the other hand, he may simply have been identifying with his clients, for he seems to dissociate himself from the Jews in verse 2 when he calls them "this nation." (There is no equivalent in the Greek to NIV's "we" in this verse.) At all events, Tertullus appears to have been one of a class of hired pleaders who were often engaged in the provinces by those who were themselves ignorant of Roman law. The Sanhedrin was taking no chances! Latin was normally used in these courts, though Greek might be allowed by grace of the judge. Rackham thinks that this trial was conducted in Latin, or at least that Tertullus' speech reads like a translation from Latin (p. 442).

24:2–3 / The procedure would have been as follows: On the morning of the procurator's court, the Jewish embassy would have formally indicted Paul before Felix (cf. 25:6f.). Paul would then have been **called in** by the court crier (v. 2), and when he responded to his name, the counsel for the Jews would have opened the case for the prosecution. As it stands, Tertullus' speech is largely taken up with flattery, the charges against Paul are baldly stated without argument or proof, and his very expression leaves much to be desired, as though he found it difficult to string one word after another. Luke has probably done this professional advocate less than justice in his report of the speech, either because of the contingencies of translation or compression or, as Marshall suggests, deliberately, to make the point that the Jewish case against Paul was a poor one (p. 374). In fact, Tertullus probably knew every trick of the trade and could turn a good speech out of nothing. He was, after all, an orator (v. 1).

He began in the style of the orators of the day with a compliment to the governor (the *captatio benevolentiae;* cf. Cicero, *De Oratore* 2.78f.), though he must have been sorely pressed to find anything complimentary to say. The one thing in his opening remarks that had any foundation of truth was that Felix had brought

a kind of **peace** to the land by suppressing the robber bands that
had infested it (v. 2; cf. Josephus, *Antiquities* 20.160–166; *War* 2.252–
253). What Tertullus did not mention was the ruthlessness with
which he had done it, which in the long term only added fuel
to the fire of sedition (Josephus, *War* 2.264–265). Felix's governor-
ship is generally regarded as the turning point in the events that
led to the final conflagration of the Jewish War (A.D. 66–70). Before
his term, uprisings had been isolated and occasional; under him,
they became epidemic. The **reforms** with which Tertullus cred-
ited him are difficult to identify. Roman coins sometimes made
the same boast of emperors, often with as little substance. As for
Felix acting for the good of the country, this statement shows only
how far Tertullus was ready to go with his flattery. His actual expression is that the governor's reforms came about "through his
foresight." The Latin equivalent of this expression, *providentia*, is
also found on coins with reference to emperors. Elsewhere it was
used especially of gods!

24:4 / It was a conventional feature of these legal speeches
that they should claim brevity, but the little he could say to the
governor's credit made a necessity of convention. Nevertheless,
Tertullus turned this to his advantage. He implied that Felix must
have been so busy with his reforms that he did not like to keep
him any longer than needs be from his work. An appeal to the
judge's clemency was another convention that Tertullus duly employed. **I would request**, he said, **that you be kind**. This word
(*epieikia*) has a range of meanings, including "fairness," "mod-
eration," "gentleness"—a strange word to address to such a man.

24:5–7 / With this, the advocate turned to the charges
against Paul. There were three: First, he was **a troublemaker** (v.
5). The word is, literally, "a plague" (as in Luke 21:11), with the
implication perhaps that this pestilence was contagious. He was
trying to make out that Paul was one of the rash of messianic revo-
lutionaries who were appearing at that time (Josephus, *War*
2.228ff.). The accusation referred chiefly to Paul's activities elsewhere, but was designed to raise the ire of Felix, who prided himself on keeping order. Tertullus' ploy was the familiar one of
accusing Christians of treason in the hope of involving Rome in
what was essentially a religious dispute (cf. 17:7; 18:12ff.; 19:37ff.).
Meanwhile, all "questions about their law" (23:29) were kept out
of sight. The Greek syntax shows a close connection between the

first and second charge, as though Paul's alleged treason was carried out in his capacity as, second, **a ringleader** (lit., "one who stands in the front rank") **of the Nazarene sect** (v. 5). This is the only instance in the New Testament of the plural "Nazarenes" (so the Greek) being used of Christians. Clearly, it was used as an expression of contempt, as the singular had been of Jesus (cf. esp. 6:14), for Jesus' reputed origin in Nazareth had stamped him in Jewish eyes as a false Messiah (John 1:46; 7:41f.). The word **sect** (Gk. *hairesis*) meant "a choice" or "that which is chosen," particularly a philosophical principle, and from this, "those who made such a choice"—a school of thought, a sect (e.g., 5:17; 15:5; 26:5). It did not yet mean "a heresy," but in this verse and perhaps in 28:22, it had come close to this meaning. And from that charge, Tertullus moved to the next, that of sacrilege, for Paul, he said, had **tried to desecrate the temple** (v. 6). Notice that the original accusation has been modified to an "attempt" to defile it, with no reference now to the Gentiles, as though to insinuate that it was Paul who was punishable under the law that upheld the sanctity of the temple (see disc. on 21:27ff.). Trophimus, of course, was the one who should have been liable had the offense been committed. As a result of Paul's attempted desecration, they had arrested him—the advocate made it sound as though this had been an official action, legally carried out, not the wild scene of mob violence that Luke has described in 21:30f. Tertullus implied that the Jews had fully intended to try Paul themselves. Some texts indeed make this explicit, adding a complaint of the Jews against the Roman commander, as though he had interrupted the due process of the law (vv. 6b–8a). But this reading is poorly supported and is rightly relegated to the margin by NIV.

24:8–9 / The speech ends abruptly with an appeal to Felix to question Paul himself on these matters—a curious suggestion, unless Tertullus was clutching at straws and hoping that Paul would incriminate himself under cross-examination. The other members of the delegation expressed their agreement with the case presented by their advocate, but no other witnesses were called and one wonders how they expected to press these charges in the absence of anything but wild accusations.

24:10 / Felix did not take up the suggestion that he should question the prisoner. Instead, he indicated that Paul should speak for himself. The apostle began as Tertullus had done, with the *captatio benevolentiae*, but in this case nothing was said that was not true (2 Cor. 13:8). The "many years" (so the Greek) might have been rhetorical, or they might have referred to Felix's earlier years in the country before he was appointed to his present office (see disc. on v. 1), for it was to Felix as judge, not as governor, that Paul appealed.

24:11–13 / Paul began by answering the charge of treason. He had not been in Jerusalem long enough to stir up insurrection, even if he had wanted to. The **twelve days** (v. 11) appears to be intended as an actual figure. The shortness of the time would enable Felix to investigate the truth of this claim if he wished to do so. Various schemes have been proposed to fit the events of 21:17–24:1 into the twelve days, and there is no difficulty in doing so, though some uncertainty remains as to details (see notes). His coming to Jerusalem, he said, was **to worship** (v. 11). Indeed, this may be seen as his answer to all three charges—"reverence, not insurrection; conformity, not heresy; worship, not profanity." There were other reasons for his coming besides this, as he himself stated in verse 17, but naturally he mentioned first the one that represented his best defense. In verse 12 he took up Tertullus' charge of verse 5 that they had found him "a troublemaker" and flatly denied it: **My accusers did not find me arguing with anyone at the temple**. Even if they had, there was no crime in that, but in fact he had not engaged in any public debate. Indeed, the denial went further than that, for the expression means that he did not so much as cause a crowd to assemble (at least voluntarily), much less stir it up. This was true also with reference to the synagogues of the city (see note on 6:9) and, for that matter, to anywhere else (v. 12). As for causing sedition "among the Jews all over the world" (v. 5), where were their witnesses? The verb "to give proof" (v. 13) implies a formal setting forth of evidence that in this case was conspicuous by its absence.

24:14–16 / Next, he dealt with the charge of heresy. It was true that he was **a follower of the Way, which they call a sect** (v. 14; see disc. on v. 5). There had been a time when Paul had shared his accusers' estimate of the Way, but he regarded it now, not as a deviation from the Jewish religion, but as its fulfillment (cf. 13:32). Being a Christian, he claimed, did not make him an apostate. He was still a loyal Jew. He still worshiped **the God of**

our fathers (v. 14; cf. 22:3)—a biblical phrase (cf. Exod. 3:13), but perhaps chosen deliberately for this occasion, for the Romans paid great respect to their own ancestral religion and Felix might be expected therefore to warm to this statement. Paul still believed **everything that agrees with the Law and that is written in the Prophets** (v. 14; cf. 26:22; 28:23)—a familiar description of the Scriptures, but again, perhaps, chosen deliberately for the sake of his argument, to make the point that the Scriptures included prophecy and must look beyond themselves for fulfillment. Thus he came to speak of God's promise of **a resurrection of both the righteous and the wicked** (v. 15). Only here, whether in Acts or the Epistles, does Paul expressly declare his belief that all will rise, though it is implied in much of his teaching (e.g., 17:31). God's promise of a general resurrection is not prominent in the Old Testament, but may be found there nevertheless. Daniel 12.2f. is perhaps its clearest expression (see disc. on 10:42).

Paul shared this hope with the Pharisees (cf. 23:6), though it must be questioned whether they subscribed to his precise expectation that all would be raised (cf. Ps. Sol. 3:13; 1 Enoch 41:1f.; 51:1f; 54:1–6; Josephus, *Antiquities* 18.12–15). But he could not say this of the Sadducees. We can only suppose, then, that when he declared that his Sadducean accusers held this doctrine also, he spoke of them as representing the nation at large, unless of course he had turned to others who may have been present and was indicating them, not his accusers. At all events, there was sufficient support for the belief among the Jews to bear out his claim that he was not out of step with his people in embracing this hope himself. Moreover, this belief (and the judgment that the resurrection implied) was an incentive to good conduct (the Greek *en touto* by which verse 16 is introduced is ambiguous, but appears to express the reason for what follows), therefore he strove (the verb means "to exercise" and so "to take pains") **always to keep [his] conscience clear before God and man** (cf. 23:1). This statement expresses the familiar idea of duty to God and neighbor that became the theme of Paul's later conversation with Felix (v. 25).

24:17 / Last, he answered the charge of having profaned the temple. He explained that he had only recently returned to Jerusalem (the reference is probably to 15:4ff., 18:22 hardly counting). His purpose had been **to bring . . . gifts** to his own people—

Christians, to be sure, but Jewish Christians—**and to present offerings**. No mention has been made previously of these offerings as part of his reason for returning, but we do know that he had wanted to be in Jerusalem for Pentecost. And even if he had not intended to sacrifice in connection with the feast, he may still have wished to do so on his own account (cf. 18:18) or to make a thank offering in connection with the collection. At least it is difficult to suppose that the reference here is to the sacrifices of 21:23ff., since they could hardly have been given as his reason for coming back. Nor will the order of the Greek words allow us to suppose (though this has been argued) that the "alms and offerings" (as the Greek has it) both refer to the collection.

24:18 / It was while he was making these offerings, and in particular after he had undergone the rites of purification (21:26), that they had found him in the temple. Did his accusers really think that under these circumstances he would also have been bent on desecrating the place? **There was no crowd . . . nor . . . any disturbance**, none, that is, of his own making. He had simply been going about his legitimate business.

24:19 / **But some Jews from the province of Asia**—NIV supplies the verb **are** to complete the sentence; Paul breaks off with the sentence unfinished (a characteristic of his writing). There was no need for him to make direct reference to the events of 21:27ff. He only commented that his original accusers ought to have been present to make their own accusations, if in fact they had anything to say against him. This point was well made, for "Roman law was very strong against accusers who abandoned their charges" (Sherwin-White, p. 52). The point, however, was not decisive, for though the Asian Jews had dropped out of sight, the original accusation (in a modified form) had been taken up by the council. The Sanhedrin was now Paul's accuser, and its representatives were present. To them, therefore, he threw down his final challenge.

24:20-21 / He demanded of the court, **These who are here should state what crime they found in me when I stood before the Sanhedrin** (v. 20). Again the point was well made, for that meeting had been an official inquiry into his case, and all that it had established was Paul's belief in the resurrection. The question has been asked of verse 21 whether Paul was showing some compunction for having **shouted as** [he] **stood in their presence** and for having provoked such rancor among the council members (23:6ff.). But his reference to his "one crime" is surely ironical, the point being that the only issue between him and his accusers was a theological one that should never have come to this court.

24:22 / The governor may well have taken his point, but the case had come to court and for various reasons he was not disposed to give an early verdict. Instead, he simply adjourned the case. In reporting this, Luke has used a technical term, found only here in the New Testament, in which the Greek verb *anaballein* is equivalent to the Latin phrase *ampliavit eos*. Roman judges were wont to say *amplius* in cases where it was not possible to pass judgment without further inquiry (cf. Cicero, *In Verrem* 1.29). One reason for delaying the verdict appears later in verse 26, but here Luke mentions that Felix was **well acquainted with the Way**. The Greek participle behind this phrase is not adjectival as NIV has it (**Felix who was . . .**), but adverbial, "because he was . . . " This statement gives the impression that he was sympathetic toward the Christians—or at least had no desire to see them treated unjustly by the Jews—without wanting, on the other hand, to offend the Jews by setting Paul free.

An important question relating to this phrase is how best to translate the Greek adverb (NIV **well**). As the comparative of a word meaning "exactly," it could be rendered, "more exactly" (i.e., than might otherwise have been expected), or it could be an instance of the so-called elative use of the comparative, best expressed by "very." K. Lake and H. J. Cadbury make it even stronger: "He had complete knowledge of the facts about the Way" (*BC*, vol. 4, p. 304). At all events it shows that this Roman, with a good grasp of the facts, found himself unable to condemn the apostle. This was the real reason for the adjournment; the reason alleged was that he needed the evidence of the prefect in person. But we never hear of Lysias' coming, and we can only suppose that he was never summoned. How Felix had acquired his knowledge of the Way, we are not told. It may have been by meeting Christians in the ordinary course of his duties or by hearing about them in Caesarea or from his wife, Drusilla, who was a Jew.

24:23 / Meanwhile, Paul had no redress and no choice but to wait and hope for discharge. He remained a prisoner, though he was granted the privilege of what the Romans called "free custody" (*custodia libera*) as befitting his status. This meant that his friends could visit him and attend to his needs.

24:24 / Since this little incident adds nothing to the history and to Luke's portrait of Paul in particular, the suggestion that he invented it in the interests of magnifying his hero is needlessly skeptical. There was simply no point in introducing Drusilla into the story unless this meeting actually took place. Nor will it do to argue that Luke introduced her in order to draw a parallel with Herodias, Paul being cast in the role of John the Baptist, for Luke does not mention Herodias in his Gospel.

During the long months of imprisonment that ensued, Felix **sent for** Paul frequently and talked with him (v. 26). One such occasion is singled out for our interest on which Drusilla, Felix's wife, was also present. She was born about A.D. 38, the youngest of the three daughters of Herod Agrippa I. She had formerly been married to Azizus, king of Emesa, but Felix had enticed her to leave her husband and become his third wife. It was probably no more than superficial curiosity that drew the couple to hear what Paul had to say. "We have to remember the loneliness and the boredom of these Roman courtiers abroad, to appreciate the historical situation" (Ehrhardt, p. 116). The apostle's theme on this, as on most occasions, was **faith in Christ Jesus**. The addition of **Jesus** to this statement is important. He was not merely urging belief in the Christ, but belief that Jesus was the Christ to whom they should entrust themselves for salvation (for the expression, "to believe into," see disc. on 10:43).

24:25 / This led to a discussion of **righteousness**, no doubt along the lines of Romans 1–4, as the divine standard by which human conduct is tested and the attribute of God that led him to put humanity right with himself (see esp. Rom. 3:21ff.). History would show how far short Felix came of that standard, and the presence of Drusilla at his side was evidence that they both lacked the **self-control** of which Paul also spoke. Evidently what they heard brought conviction, for when Paul went on to speak of **the judgment to come** (see disc. on 1:10f.; cf. Rom. 1:18; Eph. 5:3), Felix became afraid and brought the interview to a close.

24:26 / One reason for these repeated meetings was Felix's hope of receiving a bribe. He could either keep Paul in prison indefinitely or, if he chose, could speed up the process of justice and have him acquitted (there was no way that Paul could justly be condemned). But before he would set him free, he wanted it made worth his while. The taking of bribes was forbidden by Roman law (the *Lex Julia de repetundis*), but provincial governors honored the law more in the breach than in the observance (cf. Josephus, *War* 2.271-276). Paul's mention, in his defense, of the money that he had brought to Jerusalem (v. 17) may have suggested to Felix that his prisoner was not without means, and the fact that he had the support of loyal friends may only have encouraged the governor in the hope that Paul would purchase his freedom. However, his hope was never fulfilled, and Paul remained a prisoner in Caesarea.

24:27 / As with many Mediterranean communities in New Testament times, not least the cities and towns of the Palestinian coast, Caesarea had a mixed population, in which the Jews were an important minority (see disc. on 8:40 and 10:1). In their present mood of inflamed nationalism, clashes were bound to happen between them and the other elements of the population, and happen they did. Thus during Paul's imprisonment a disturbance broke out that led to street fighting between the Jews and the Greeks. In the end Felix lost patience and suppressed it with such violence that the outraged Jews (who had suffered most at the hands of his soldiers) were able to force his recall (Josephus, *War* 2.266-270). This is best dated about A.D. 58, with Felix's successor taking office in the summer of A.D. 59 (see notes). Luke's statement that Felix had hoped to curry favor with the Jews by leaving Paul in prison accords well with the circumstances of his removal from office. Of his later history nothing is known. Meanwhile, Paul was left for the new governor, Porcius Festus, to deal with. These years of Paul's imprisonment may have been put to good use by Luke in collecting information for the books he would later write. But some scholars feel that he shows too little detailed knowledge of the country—especially of Galilee and Samaria—to have been there for long. In any case, it would have been far too dangerous for a Gentile companion of Paul to have hung about (see, e.g., Hengel, *Jesus*, p. 127). However, he was with Paul again in 27:1ff.

Additional Notes §63

24:1 / Five days later: This probably means "on the fifth day," on the analogy of Mark 8:31, where "after three days" clearly means "on the third day," as Luke 9:22 shows. Most commentators accept that the five days are from Paul's arrival in Caesarea, but Rackham dates it from the riot in the temple, in which case the Jewish delegation must have set out as soon as they received Lysias' summons (23:30).

24:5 / Stirring up riots among the Jews: Sherwin-White points out that the letter of Claudius to the Alexandrians is strikingly similar to the charge laid against Paul. In the letter, the emperor summed up his objection to certain political actions of the Jews as "stirring up a universal plague throughout the world" (cf. 17:6). "It is evident," says Sherwin-White, "that the narrative of Acts is using contemporary language. The charge was precisely the one to bring against a Jew during the Principate of Claudius or the early years of Nero. The accusers of Paul were putting themselves on the side of the government" (pp. 51f.).

The Nazarene sect: This Jewish designation of the Christians is maintained in the few references to them in the Talmud, where they are called the *nosrim*. The name is found also in Arabic. "It appears, therefore, that just as Antioch gave the Church the nickname of 'Christians,' Jerusalem gave it the name of 'Nazarenes,' which became as common a title in the East as 'Christians' in the West" (Ehrhardt, p. 114; cf. Jerome, *De Viris Illustribus* 2–3; *Epistles* 20.2 for evidence of Christian groups who still called themselves "Nazarenes").

24:11 / No more than twelve days ago I went up to Jerusalem: Broadly speaking, there are two interpretations of this statement: first, that the twelve days ran from Paul's arrival in Jerusalem to his arrest and, second, that they ran to the time of speaking. On either interpretation, there are uncertainties as to whether parts of days are included, such as the day of Paul's arrival in Jerusalem and the day on which he was speaking; at what point in the seven days of his purification he was apprehended; how long his journey from Jerusalem to Caesarea took; and from what point we must date the five days of 24:1. Since the whole point of the reference is to indicate the shortness of the period, we may assume that the figure does not include parts of days. On this basis, we suggest the following scheme: the first day would be his meeting with James; the second, his commencement of the vow; the sixth, his apprehension; the seventh, the day before the Sanhedrin; the eighth, departure for Caesarea; the ninth, arrival in Caesarea; and reckoning five days inclusively from the ninth, the day of Paul's trial would be the thirteenth, i.e., twelve full days.

24:27 / When two years had passed, lit., "had been fulfilled" (see note on 2:1): By this expression Luke may have intended to indicate that he was not reckoning as was usual among Jews, that is, counting parts of a year as a whole, but that Paul was in prison for two whole years.

Felix was succeeded by Porcius Festus: Josephus tells us that Felix was recalled by Nero and that he was only saved from further proceedings against him by the Jews through the influence of his brother, Pallas (*Antiquities* 20.182–184). This note has an important bearing on the dates of Felix's term, for Pallas was dismissed from office within a very short time after Nero's succession (A.D. 54), and it is argued that he could hardly have exercised this influence on behalf of his brother later than his own dismissal. Felix's recall, therefore, is dated by some to the early weeks of Nero's reign, while Pallas was still able to help him. Eusebius appears to support this view by having Felix's successor, Festus, take office in the second year of Nero's reign (A.D. 56). But Eusebius is clearly confused in his dates. The one certain reference he appears to have had from his sources is that Festus arrived in Judea in the tenth year of Herod Agrippa II. But he has wrongly calculated that year from the death of Agrippa I in A.D. 44, whereas Agrippa II's reign is reckoned from Nisan 1, A.D. 50, so that his tenth year began on Nisan 1, A.D. 59 (see Josephus, *War* 2.284). In any case, it is plain that Nero disliked Pallas and intended to dismiss him from the moment he became emperor. It is questionable, then, whether Pallas would have had any more influence before his dismissal than after it. Moreover, he was not disgraced by his dismissal and continued to enjoy a number of privileges, so that he may well have been able to help his brother at a later date. Further, Josephus appears to suppose only a short term for Festus, whereas the date of his successor, Albinus, is fixed at A.D. 62. We therefore accept the date of A.D. 58 for Felix's removal and A.D. 59 for Festus' arrival.

§64   The Trial Before Festus (Acts 25:1–12)

25:1a / Very little is known of Porcius Festus. Josephus contrasts him favorably with both his predecessor, Felix, and his successor, Albinus, stating that he acted promptly to rid the country of robbers and *sicarii* (*Antiquities* 20.182f.; *War* 2.271–276). He seems to have been disposed to govern the country well, but found himself unable to remedy the ill effects of Felix's rule. Ehrhardt calls him "the one honourable governor Rome ever sent to Judea" (p. 117). As far as Paul was concerned, though Festus bore him no malice, he was overeager to give way to Jewish demands, perhaps even against his own better judgment.

25:1b–5 / Within three days of his arrival in Caesarea (lit., "after three days," but see note on 24:1) he paid a courtesy visit to the Jewish capital. It was always important for the procurator to establish some sort of working arrangement with the high priest and the Sanhedrin as soon as possible. This was especially so at this time in view of the recent unpleasantness between the Jews and the procurator Felix. The high priest with whom Festus would have had to work may no longer have been Ananias (see disc. on 23:2), but Ishmael ben Phiabi, who held office until A.D. 61. However, the change of high priest meant no change of Jewish policy with regard to Paul. So, while Festus was in Jerusalem, the Jewish leaders told him about Paul and **urgently requested** him to grant a retrial in Jerusalem—both the word itself and the tense (imperfect) underline their importunity: "They kept on requesting" (v. 3). There may also have been a public demonstration (organized by the leaders?) in support of their plea (cf. v. 24; Luke 23:13ff.). It is not clear whether they were asking for Paul to be retried by the Sanhedrin or in a Roman court, but in any case their intention, according to Luke, was to assassinate him as he was being transferred back to Jerusalem. Indeed, Luke implies by the tenses he uses that even as they begged Festus to do them a favor, the Jewish leaders were formulating this plan to abuse it. From the Western text comes the suggestion that the original forty conspirators were to make the attempt, but there were many others like them on whom the leaders could call. Notice there is now no question (in Luke's mind at least) whose plan this was. To his credit, Festus did not accede at once to their request, though later he would attempt to do so (v. 9). Instead, he announced that he would conduct a new hearing in Caesarea and invited the Jewish leaders to return with him for that purpose (cf. vv. 14–16).

25:6–7 / Having concluded his visit of not more than eight or ten days, Festus returned to his capital; Paul's case was reopened the next day. No sooner had Paul entered the courtroom than his adversaries gathered around, **bringing many serious** ("weighty") **charges against him** (v. 7). But in terms of hard evidence their case was no better now than when Felix had heard it two years before. Luke does not record the speech for the prosecution, but it probably followed the lines of the earlier speech (24:2–8).

25:8 / Again, Paul's defense was denial. He had neither violated the Jewish law nor desecrated the temple, nor committed treason **against Caesar.** This specific mention of the emperor prepares the way for what follows, by showing Paul to have had as clear a conscience before him as before God or anyone else. He could appeal to the emperor with confidence.

25:9 / Festus may have been no more impressed with the Jewish case than Felix had been (cf. v. 18), but he was anxious to start out on good terms with the Jews, so he proposed to Paul, in response to the Jews' earlier request (v. 3), that he should go to Jerusalem for another hearing. This proposal was tantamount to acquitting Paul of any charge under Roman law. It had reference only to his alleged offenses against the law of Moses and the temple, which would be heard by the Sanhedrin. The phrase **before me** cannot mean that Festus would be the judge; otherwise, where was the favor to the Jews (in v. 20 this phrase is omitted)? It indicated, rather, his role as the final arbiter, who must either ratify or reject the council's decision.

25:10–11 / The governor's question brought Paul to the crossroads. If he agreed to another hearing, he would, on the one hand, play into the hands of his accusers by appearing to admit that there was a case to answer and that they were competent to hear it. Moreover, he could hardly have doubted that by fair means or foul they would bring down a verdict of guilty. Besides, he must have realized that his chances of even reaching Jerusalem were not good. On the other hand, if he left the matter with Festus, what could he expect? He had already seen enough to know that the political consideration of appeasing the Jews would very likely enter into any judgment the procurator made. Perhaps, then, a court at a distance from Palestine, in which his accusers would find greater difficulty in pressing their charges, would be in his best interests. So Paul came to a momentous decision.

In a carefully worded statement, which nonetheless could hardly have endeared him to Festus, since it called into question his impartiality as a judge, Paul pointed out that, having been held in Roman custody, he ought to be tried in a Roman court. He denied that he had done any wrong. If he had (under Roman law), he would expect to be punished, but he had not and the governor had no right to hand him over to a Jewish court as a favor to his accusers. He appealed, therefore, to the emperor. The procedure that he had invoked had originally been an appeal to the Roman people, in the person of their tribunes, but since the time of Augustus, the emperor had stepped into their place. There were certain restrictions on the right of appeal, details of which are not now fully known. Sherwin-White is satisfied, however, that the process of appeal as reflected in Acts is as it was until about the end of the first century A.D., according to which the accused made his appeal before the verdict was given or the sentence pronounced. Once an appeal was allowed, all further proceedings in the matter were stayed, and the magistrate had no choice but to transfer the case to Rome (see Sherwin-White, pp. 68–70, for a full discussion).

25:12 / Thus, as soon as Paul had made his appeal, Festus went into conference with his advisers, probably high officials in the Roman administration. The formality of consultation was probably followed in all cases, but in this instance there may have been a question whether the appeal was permissible. It was, however, allowed. There may have been something of a sneer in the way Festus announced his decision, or at least a hint that Paul little knew what he was letting himself in for. The case was to be transferred to the court of Nero, whose early years had given no hint of the cruelties that were to follow (cf. Suetonius, *Nero* 9f.). Thus God's purpose that Paul should go to Rome was set forward.

Additional Notes   §64

25:2 / **The Jewish leaders**, lit., "the first or chief men" (Gk. *prōtoi*), sometimes taken as "the elders" (Gk. *presbyteroi*) in v. 15 (cf. Luke 19:47, where we have "the chief priests, the teachers of the law, and the leaders [Gk. *prōtoi*] of the people." But Luke may have used the different word precisely because they were not identical with the elders, though perhaps including them or their chief representative. At all events, we assume that Paul's accusers were chiefly the Sadducees.

25:5 / **Your leaders**: A different word to that in v. 2. This is lit. "the powers" (Gk. *dynatoi*). Josephus uses the same word in connection with the chief priests to indicate members of the Sanhedrin, and this is probably its meaning here, though he also uses it in a more general way of the "influential" (cf. 1 Cor. 1:26).

25:8 / **Caesar** (cf. also vv. 11, 12): In each of these verses, and later in 26:32, the word used is **Caesar**, the name of the branch of the family of Julii that ruled as the first emperors—Octavian (Augustus), Tiberius, Gaius (Caligula), Claudius, and Nero. The name was adopted by later rulers as a title, but even with the Julian emperors themselves, it had something of the nature of a title (see also note on v. 21).

25:10 / **As you yourself know very well**: To express the comparative adverb, the rendering "as you are getting to know better" has been suggested. This, it is said, saves us from the ungracious and unjust retort that a number of versions, including NIV, ascribe to Paul. But v. 18 seems to indicate that Festus did know better than the question of v. 9 would suggest. The note of reproach is properly retained by NIV.

A state visit to Caesarea by Herod Agrippa II enabled Festus to canvass his opinion of Paul's case. Agrippa expressed an interest in hearing Paul, and so it was that Paul made yet another defense. That the story has a historical basis we need not doubt— "The picture of the puzzled Roman official, bewildered by a doctrine of the Resurrection, and seeking advice from a Palestinian princelet, is so naive that it must be true" (Williams, p. 261). Moreover, from the detailed description of the day's proceedings in 25:23–26:32, it is evident that if Luke was not himself present, then at least he was given the story by someone who was. There is, however, a historical problem with the narrative in 25:13–22. It purports to be a conversation between Festus and Agrippa, and it is hard (but not impossible) to imagine that any of Luke's informants were privy to it. We must allow, then, that these verses may be the author's own reconstruction of what led up to Paul's appearing before Agrippa. But though we may question these verses in respect to their setting, their content does not present any problem. For they are simply an outline of events that were well known to Luke, with a portrayal of Festus' bewilderment, which was evident to all.

25:13 / Not long after Festus had taken office, **King Agrippa** [Herod Agrippa II] **and Bernice arrived at Caesarea**—the verb has the sense of "came to stay" (see disc. on 16:1)—to pay their respects to the new governor. As a Roman vassal, involved to some extent in Jewish affairs, it was only proper that the king should do so. The aorist participle that is found in the best texts may mean that the king and Bernice had already "greeted" Festus, probably in Jerusalem, where Agrippa maintained a palace, but had now come on a formal visit to the governor's official residence. The king (born ca. A.D. 27) was the son of Herod Agrippa I (see disc. on 12:1). After his father's death, he was retained by the emperor in Rome (Agrippa had grown up in his court), who would not entrust Judea to a boy of seventeen. In A.D. 50, however, he was given the rule of Chalcis, with territory north and northeast of Galilee, which had formerly been ruled by his uncle (died A.D. 48). At the same time, the emperor transferred to him from the procurators of Judea the right of appointing the high priest and the custody of the sacred vestments. Agrippa was therefore a man to whom Festus would naturally look for an expert opinion on matters relating to the Jewish religion. In A.D. 56 Agrippa received from Nero, in exchange for Chalcis, the territories once ruled by Philip and Lysanias (see disc. on 12:1) and with this larger domain the title of king. Agrippa did his best to prevent the outbreak of the Jewish War against Rome. When his efforts failed, he remained loyal to Rome and was rewarded with a further increase in his kingdom. He died childless about A.D. 100.

His sister Bernice (properly Berenice), born A.D. 28, was the oldest of the three daughters of Agrippa I (cf. 24:24). She was married at the age of thirteen to her uncle Herod of Chalcis. Following his death, she lived with her brother—which gave rise to rumors of an incestuous relationship between them. To allay these rumors, she prevailed on Polemon, king of Cilicia, to marry her, but soon left him to return to her brother. Like Agrippa, she took the part of Rome in the Jewish War and became in turn the mistress of Vespasian and of Titus. She had expected to marry Titus, but the antipathy of the Roman people toward the Jews would not allow it (see Josephus, *Antiquities* 20.145–147; *War* 2.425–429; Juvenal, *Satires* 6.156ff.; Tacitus, *History* 2.81; Suetonius, *Titus* 7).

25:14–16 / The royal couple had been with Festus several days when he broached the matter of Paul with Agrippa. Naturally, he recounted the story from his own point of view. The case had come to his attention when **the chief priests and elders of the Jews** had asked him to condemn Paul. He had refused to do so. This is told in greater detail than in verse 4 and with all the hauteur of the Roman. He had pointed out that it was not Roman practice to condemn a man before he had faced his accusers. Felix, of course, had already seen to this, but Festus had had to satisfy himself in the matter.

25:17–19 / He had arranged to hear the case in Caesarea, and when Paul had been called up before him he had been surprised to hear that the charges were not of **crimes** as he had expected (v. 18)—accusations of political disturbance and sedition—but had to do with **some points of dispute** [the plural is used contemptuously, 23:29] **about their own religion** (v. 19). The word "religion" can also mean "superstition," and it is a question whether Festus meant it in that sense (see disc. on 17:22). The whole discussion had seemed to Festus to turn on the question of whether **a dead man named Jesus** had risen from the dead as Paul had claimed (v. 19). The imperfect tense suggests that Paul had made this claim repeatedly, but the verb itself (Gk. *phaskein*) reflects Festus' own opinion that it had been made without any grounds. The proposition had seemed to him to be quite absurd, yet he had put his finger on the real point at issue. There was more to the Jewish position than this, but the dispute revolved around Paul's claims concerning Jesus, which were of little interest to Festus.

25:20–21 / Festus then told how he had suggested to Paul that his case should be tried in Jerusalem. Notice the change of motive. The reason given here is that he had sought in this way to find out what the case was really about. There may have been an element of truth in this, but Luke's analysis in verse 9 reveals what was almost certainly the more pressing reason, namely, that he had wanted "to do the Jews a favor." In any case, Paul had not fallen in with the suggestion, but had appealed, asking **to be held over for the Emperor's decision** (v. 21). This wording throws a new light on the affair. Not only was Paul looking for Roman justice, he was appealing for Roman protection.

25:22 / Now that Paul had appealed, it had become incumbent on the governor that he should "investigate the matter" to get what information he could for the dossier that would accompany the prisoner (v. 20; cf. v. 26). Agrippa's visit was therefore a timely one, for he at least should be able to throw some light on the case. It was arranged that he should hear Paul the next day.

Additional Notes §65

25:21 / **Held over for the Emperor's decision**, lit., Paul asked to be kept for the decision of "Augustus" (Gk. *Sebastos*), here and in v. 25 rendered **Emperor**, since the title "Augustus" might lead to confusion (the second reference to the emperor in v. 21 is to Caesar). The Caesar

Augustus in Luke 2:1 was Octavian, upon whom the title was first conferred in 27 B.C. (Suetonius, *Augustus* 7). But the appellation was inherited by his successors and is ascribed in these verses to Nero. The divine sanctity that the name Augustus seemed to confer (cf. Dio Cassius, *Roman History* 53.16.18) excited the scruples of Tiberius, but succeeding emperors appear to have adopted it without hesitation. It may be significant, however, that the title was not apparently used by Paul himself, who preferred the word "Caesar" (vv. 11, 12), but by Festus in reporting Paul.

25:22 / **I would like to hear this man myself**: The imperfect may express a wish entertained for some time (cf. Luke 9:9; 23:8). On the other hand, the tense may be an instance of the "desiderative imperfect" intended "to soften a remark, and make it more vague or more diffident or polite" (C. F. D. Moule, *An Idiom Book of New Testament Greek* [Cambridge: Cambridge University Press, 1959], p. 9), with no suggestion of having previously wanted to hear him. The phrase "this man" (Gk. *anthrōpos*) is a somewhat contemptuous expression when compared with the more polite word for "man," *anēr*, used by Festus in verses 5 and 14.

§66 Paul Before Agrippa (Acts 25:23–26:32)

25:23 / On the morrow, Paul was brought in before a large and distinguished audience (cf. 9:15; Luke 21:12). Besides the governor and his guests of honor, there were **the high ranking officers**, that is, the tribunes or prefects of the cohorts stationed at Caesarea (see note on 10:1) **and the leading men of the city**. These may have included Jews, but the majority at least would have been Gentiles. The occasion was one of great **pomp**. This translates the word *phantasia* (cf. our "fantasy"), which points to the transitory nature of this "show of dress and ceremonial, of decoration and grand titles" (Rackham, p. 461). In contrast, Paul stood before them chained and in humble garb.

25:24–27 / In introducing Paul to his guests, Festus described him as the man concerning whom **the whole Jewish community** had petitioned him both **in Jerusalem and here in Caesarea** (v. 24). By "the whole Jewish community" he may only have meant the Sanhedrin, as representing the nation (cf. vv. 2, 7, 15). But it was not unheard of that a crowd in Jerusalem should add their voice to the demands of their leaders (cf. Mark 15:11), whereas in Caesarea, the great bitterness between Jews and Gentiles may well have found expression in a Jewish demonstration against the "apostle to Gentiles." Festus himself had found no crime in Paul **deserving death** (v. 25). It was **unreasonable**, however, that he should send him to Rome without an explanation of the charges against him (v. 27), and he hoped that as a result of this meeting Agrippa could help him to find something to say. It might seem from this that the procurator was not bound to write. But of course he was. A statement of the charges would have had to be sent to the emperor with the appellant. But Festus was hoping to do more and explain what the charges meant. Sherwin-White describes his dilemma: "The complication and prolongation of the trial of Paul arose from the fact that the charge was political—hence the procurators were reluctant to dismiss it out of hand—and yet the evidence was theological, hence the procurators were quite unable to understand it" (p. 51). The present occasion was not a trial. In that regard, the most that can be said of it is that it was an informal hearing. But above all, perhaps, it was an entertainment—"a gala performance of Roman justice" (Ehrhardt, p. 120).

26:1–3 / With regard to both its form and its content we have here the high point of the speeches of Acts. It is the most polished of all the speeches, adorned with rare words and marked by an elaborate, even grandiose, style. The credit for this must go largely to Luke, and yet Paul still makes himself heard. As for content—at Antioch we had his gospel for Jews (13:16–41), at Miletus his message for Christians (20:18–35), but here we have his Good News for all the world, proclaimed out of his own experience of God's grace. This is now the third and most important of Paul's statements in his own defense and the third account in this book of his conversion (see disc. on 21:37–22:5).

As guest of honor, it fell to Agrippa to invite Paul to speak, and it was to him especially that Paul addressed his remarks (cf. vv. 2, 13, 19, 27). Though chained, Paul does not appear to have been hampered in his movements and was able to adopt his customary pose (v. 1; see disc. on 13:16). Luke describes him as "defending" himself, though he was not formally on trial. Indeed, Paul uses this same terminology himself (see disc. on 22:1), declaring that he was glad to **make** [his] **defense** before the king, who was well acquainted with **Jewish customs and controversies** (vv. 2, 3, the *captatio benevolentiae;* see disc. on 24:2f.).

26:4–6 / He spoke first of his early life. This could be summed up as "sincere but mistaken," with verse 9 epitomizing his error. Paul assumed that his past was known to the Jews, but for the sake of his present audience, he touched briefly on its salient points. He had been brought up in his own **country,** literally, among his own "nation" (v. 4). This might have been a reference to Tarsus, but in view of 22:3, is more likely to have meant Judea, with **in Jerusalem** added by way of more precise definition. **For a long time** he had lived as a Pharisee, **the strictest sect** of the Jewish religion (v. 5). His purpose in stating this was to establish his credentials as a Jew (which were clearly impeccable) and then to suggest that there was no discontinuity between his Jewish upbringing and his present belief. The hope instilled by the one had been fulfilled by the other. It was a strange irony, therefore, that he should now be on trial—the reference was to the whole legal process in which he was embroiled—for the very hope that he shared with the Jews (v. 6).

26:7 / The hope of which Paul spoke was not merely that of resurrection (cf. 23:6; 24:15), but the broader hope of the Messiah and the kingdom of God, of which the resurrection of the dead was a part (cf. 28:20). This, at least, appears to be the implication of the reference to the **twelve tribes**, which conjures up thoughts of the eschatological in-gathering of the tribes and the restoration of the kingdom to Israel—conceived of by most Jews in terms of this world and by most Christians in spiritual terms (see disc. on 1:6 and 3:21 and notes). The longing of the Jews for the eschaton is expressed in the words, **as they earnestly serve God day and night** (see disc. on 12:5 for similar language and Luke 2:36–38 for the same earnest prayer for the Messiah).

26:8 / But the Messiah had already come. Paul's distress at the Jews' blindness to this lies behind the question of this verse (cf. v. 18; 28:26f.). The point of the question has been variously understood. Some see it as a reference to the general resurrection and therefore as an appeal to the Sadducees, some of whom may have been present. Others find here a reference to the instances in the Old Testament in which life was restored (e.g., 1 Kings 17:17–23; 2 Kings 4:18–37), seeing this as the first step in the argument that "there will be a resurrection of both the righteous and the wicked" (24:15). It seems best, however, to understand the question as an appeal to the great truth to which Paul was leading, namely, that Jesus, though crucified, had become "the first to rise from the dead" (v. 23) and so had been shown to be the Messiah and the one who had fulfilled all of Israel's hopes (cf. Rom. 1:4).

26:9–10 / Verse 8 was something of an aside, and Paul now returned to the narrative of his early life. His purpose was still to establish his credentials (see disc. on vv. 4ff.) and perhaps to make the point also that it had taken the most compelling of reasons to make him other than the zealous Jew he had been, bent on persecuting the church. Here a note of shame creeps into the narrative. By the emphasis of the opening words of verse 9 (in the Greek), Paul showed that he now regarded his opposition to Jesus as an act of utter self-delusion. The emphatic **I** of verse

10 (in the Greek) maintains that theme, as does the description of his victims as **the saints** (see disc. on 9:13). And not only had he put many of **the saints in prison** (the Greek has "prisons"), but had exacerbated his guilt by acquiescing in the execution of some of them.

It is difficult to know how literally to take Paul's statement in verse 10. It purports to give an account of what he had done **in Jerusalem**, and from that we must suppose that his reference was to decisions taken by the Sanhedrin, not some lesser synagogal court. But would Paul have been a member of that august body to have actually "voted against" Christians who had been brought before it? It is doubtful, not only on account of his probable age at the time, but also because of his apparently obscure origins. The Sanhedrin was an assembly of aristocrats, composed of men of mature years and influence. It is just possible, of course, that he had won a place in their ranks on sheer ability, but it is safer to assume that "voted against" means simply that he "approved," the expression used in 22:20. As for Christians being **put to death**, Paul may have been using a generalizing plural for dramatic effect, but the circumstances in Judea that had made possible Stephen's death may well have made others possible also (see note on 7:58).

26:11 / From Jerusalem he had extended his persecuting activities even **to foreign cities**. The imperfect tense of the verb "to persecute" may simply mark the beginning of his proposed foreign campaign, which, in fact, never got any farther than the outskirts of Damascus (the inceptive imperfect). Or (and this is preferable in view of the "prisons" of v. 10), it may be understood of repeated acts of persecution elsewhere before he set out for that city. He had worked from the synagogues, which functioned as local courts with powers of discipline over their members, that is, over the local Jewish communities. And by having those members **punished** who believed that Jesus was the Messiah, he had **tried to force them to blaspheme** (the name of Jesus) (cf. 13:45; 18:6). Again the tense of the Greek verb (imperfect) may indicate repeated attempts, but the real significance of the expression is that it leaves open the question whether he ever succeeded. In contrast to the abhorrence that he now felt for his own part in this, there is an undisguised note of admiration in Paul's words for the fortitude of those who suffered at his hands.

26:12-13 / Next Paul spoke of the critical moment of his life. His encounter with the risen Lord was a crisis both in the Greek sense of judgment and in the modern sense of a turning point. As he had traveled to Damascus armed with **the authority and commission of the chief priests** (v. 12; in 9:1 the high priest, but cf. 9:14, 21), who were now, of course, his chief accusers, a divine light had shone about him. If anything, the Greek expression rendered **about noon** (v. 13) is more emphatic than that similarly translated in 22:6. Paul wanted it clearly understood that what had happened had happened in the bright light of midday and that even then the light had outshone the sun (here expressly stated, though certainly implied in 9:3 and 22:6) to penetrate the darkness of his own mind. In the Greek, the sentence reaches its climax in the word **light**: "At midday, on the road, I saw, O King, from heaven, much brighter than the sun, shining around me, a light." This light had also enveloped his traveling companions. This is made clearer than in the earlier accounts (9:7; 22:6, 9). It was an important point, for it underlined the objectivity of the experience.

26:14-15 / At this, they all **fell to the ground**. In 9:4 and 22:7 Paul alone is said to have fallen, and in 9:7 Luke remarks that the men with Paul had "stood speechless," but they may have fallen and then stood up. Nothing is said here of Paul's being blinded by the light or, for that matter, of his entering Damascus and being visited by Ananias. The story is left incomplete when compared with 9:7 and 22:11ff. Instead, the focus here is on the voice. Paul alone had understood it (see disc. on 9:7 and 22:9), and it had spoken to him in Hebrew (Aramaic; cf. 21:40). This had been intimated in 9:4 and 22:7 by the use of the Semitic form of his name, **Saul**; however Paul added this explanation here because he was now speaking in Greek but, in citing the actual words, wished to retain the form in which they were indelibly imprinted on his memory.

The same question is found in all three accounts, **Why do you persecute me?** (v. 14), but here alone is added what was in fact a familiar proverb of the ancient world, **It is hard for you to kick against the goads** (cf. esp. Euripides, *Bacchae* 794f.; also Aeschylus *Agamemnon* 1624; Terence *Phormio* 1.2.27; Ps. Sol. 16:4). Some have seen in this a witness to Paul's uneasy conscience, which he had tried to quieten by ever more frantic activity, but it is not wise to press a proverbial saying too closely with regard to his state of mind (see disc. on 9:1–19). He may simply have added it now to stress (with the wisdom of hindsight) the foolhardiness of what he had been attempting to do (cf. 5:39; Ps. 2:3, 4). The general sense of the proverb is that it is foolish to struggle against one's destiny. Paul's question in verse 15 and Jesus' response are much as in the earlier accounts. As in 22:10, Paul fell back into the Christian habit of calling Jesus **the Lord**.

26:16 / Next he told of his commission. If this is indeed what Jesus said to him on the road, it is by far the most detailed account that we have of that part of the story. But in fact it is probably a conflation of what was later communicated by Ananias and later still was shown to Paul in the vision that he had in the temple (9:15; 22:14). These details were omitted here as of no consequence to his present audience. As Paul now told the story, he was ordered to **get up and stand on** (his) **feet**, for the Lord had work for him to do (cf. Ezek. 2:1). He had been appointed (for this verb, see disc. on 22:14) "as a servant and as a witness" (for "witness," cf. 1:8, 22; etc.; the word "servant" is used of John Mark in 13:5), that he should tell others what he had seen (the risen, ascended Son in the glory of the Father) and what he would be shown in time to come, literally (with Jesus speaking), "the things in which I will appear to you." The reference is to visions (cf. esp. 22:17–21; but also 18:9f.; 23:11).

26:17–18 / These verses detail Paul's calling and at the same time provide an outline of his life from his conversion to the establishing of churches among the Gentiles. He was promised protection **from your own people and from the Gentiles** (v. 17), but only in the sense that he would be enabled to fulfill his calling, not that he would be spared any suffering in the process (cf. 2 Tim. 2:9). He was given a commission to open the people's eyes (v. 18). There may have been some play intended on the idea of his spiritual blindness before and his physical blindness after his conversion. But more significantly, the language is that in which Isaiah had prophesied future salvation (Isa. 35:5; 42:6f.; cf. Matt. 9:30). That salvation was now a present reality, and Paul was to take news of it to Jews and to Gentiles. The **to them** of verse 17 includes both (cf. 9:15). His commission was to preach for conversion, to **turn them from darkness to light** (a frequent metaphor in the Pauline epistles, e.g., Rom. 2:19; 13:12; 2 Cor. 4:6; 6:14; Eph. 5:8; Col. 1:12; 1 Thess. 5:5), that is, **from the power of Satan** to God, that their sins might be forgiven and they might have a place among the people of God (lit., "an inheritance in those who have been sanctified," v. 18; see disc. on 9:13; 20:32). This statement bears a remarkable likeness to Colossians 1:12–14 and assures us that this résumé of Paul's speech is based on reliable information. (Note: Luke does not appear to have had access to Paul's letters.) But not any preaching will lead to conversion. Effective preaching to that end must center on Christ, for only in him is this salvation found (Jesus is the **me** of verse 18, for he is the speaker; cf. 4:12). Here the operative phrase is **faith in me,** placed for emphasis in the Greek text at the end of the sentence. The thought is of entrusting oneself entirely to Christ (it is the faith that is "into him"; see disc. on 10:43). Verse 18 is the epitome of the (Pauline) gospel.

26:19–20 / Finally, Paul told his audience what the outcome was of his calling. The renewed address, **So then, King Agrippa** (v. 19), marks the beginning of Paul's real defense. He had been accused of teaching contrary to the Jewish law, and though he flatly denied the charge, he recognized that some explanation was needed of his years among the Gentiles. These verses provide it. He **was not disobedient to the vision from heaven** (the Damascus Road experience, v. 19), which is to say that he obeyed it enthusiastically, preaching **first to those in Damascus, then to those in Jerusalem and in all Judea** (see note on 1:8), **and to the Gentiles also** (v. 20). If we take this verse as simply covering the sequence of events in 9:20–30, there is clearly a contradiction with Paul's statement in Galatians 1:22 that he was "personally unknown to the churches of Judea." But this might be another instance of the kind of compression that we noticed in verses 16–18, so that the one reference to his preaching in Judea encompasses all his subsequent contacts with the province, where over the years he may well have preached extensively and certainly had the opportunity to do so (11:30; 12:25; 15:3; 18:22; 21:7–16). A further difficulty, however, has been found in the change of construction in the Greek at the point where he speaks of his preaching **in all Judea.** This has led to speculation whether the text is corrupt or whether these words are a scribal addition. But though the sentence is admittedly awkward, it is not ungrammatical, and indeed, the change of construction makes some sense as marking the difference between preaching "in" Damascus and Jerusalem and "among" the Gentiles (all datives) and preaching "throughout" Judea (an accusative of extent). His message had been essentially a call to repentance (cf. 2:38; 3:19; 17:30; 20:21), to conversion—they were to **turn to God** (v. 20; cf. 9:35; 11:21; 14:15; 15:19; 1 Thess. 1:9), and to the kind of conduct that exemplified both. This message had been preached to Jews and to Gentiles alike.

26:21–23 / It was his ministry to the Gentiles, and that he had treated the Gentiles as on the same footing as they were, however, that had provoked the ire of the Jews (how far in Jewish thought the Gentiles were from equality may be seen in texts such as Psalms of Solomon 17:32 and 2 Baruch 72; see disc. on 22:22f.). So they had seized him in the temple and had tried to kill him. Paul said nothing of his alleged profanation of the temple. That was not an issue. Nor did he say anything of the Roman intervention. That was well known. It was also providential—**I have had God's help**, he declared, **to this very day** (v. 22). Hence he was able to stand before them, a witness **to small and great alike** (v. 22), probably a reference to the various ranks within his audience (cf. Rev. 11:18; 13:16; 19:5), though it could be understood in terms of their ages, "to the young (Agrippa?) and the old (Festus?)."

Despite what they said, there was nothing anti-Jewish in his preaching. On the contrary, it was concerned with the fulfillment of the prophecy found in their Scriptures **that the Christ would suffer** and be **the first to rise from the dead** (v. 23). This is almost the language of 1 Corinthians 15:20, 23. But where in **the prophets and Moses** is it said that the Messiah must suffer? The immediate answer would have been in the Servant Songs of Isaiah (see disc. on 8:32ff. and notes). And where does it say that he must be the first to rise from the dead? Again the answer may have been found in Isaiah, for it was said that the Servant would see life (Isa. 53:10). But there were other passages, such as Psalms 2, 16, and 118 (see disc. on 2:25ff.; 4:11; 13:33ff.). And because Jesus had fulfilled these prophecies, he could be said to have fulfilled all prophecies that spoke of the **light** of salvation (v. 23; cf. Isa. 9:1f.; 49:6; Luke 2:29ff.; Acts 13:47), for his resurrection was not merely a demonstration of his own life, but the grounds of the proclamation of life to all, both **to his own people and to the Gentiles** (v. 23).

26:24 / The speech had reached its climax in verse 23, so that Paul had already said what was most important for him to say when Festus interrupted him. The governor had found nothing in the speech of interest to him. He was out of his depth and angry because of it. "Too much study," the Preacher had said, "will wear you out" (Eccles. 12:12); Festus announced in a loud voice (because he was interrupting) that in Paul's case too much study was a danger to sanity. He was not jesting. Not only this talk of a resurrection, but the suggestion that Jesus, whom Festus could only describe as "a dead man" (25:19), should bring light and life to others was, he thought, the product of a disturbed mind (cf. 17:32; 2 Cor. 5:11, 13).

26:25 / Paul answered that he was not mad. What he had said about Jesus was **true and reasonable**. No one doubted his sincerity, but against the assertion that he was living in a world of fantasy, he claimed that he was speaking objective truth and that his appreciation of the facts was based on the opposite of madness, namely, "sobriety"—the possession of a right mind. There is nothing irrational in Christianity in the sense of claims that are contrary to reason, though there is much that goes beyond human reason and can only be apprehended by faith. For the title **most excellent**, see note on 1:1, and for the verb "to speak," which implies that Paul spoke as a prophet, see the discussion on 2:4.

26:26–27 / It was evident from this little exchange that Paul was not getting through to the governor. With Agrippa, however, it might be different. So Paul addressed him "with boldness" (NIV **I can speak freely**, v. 26; see disc. on 4:13), appealing to what was common knowledge concerning Jesus, for the "Jesus event" was not something **done in a corner** (v. 26; cf. Plato, *Gorgias* 485). He then pressed home the appeal by asking Agrippa whether he believed the Scriptures. He was certain he did and that the king would agree, moreover, that there was nothing irrational in believing that their prophecies would be fulfilled. After that, he could only hope that Agrippa would take the next step and accept that they had found their fulfillment in Jesus.

26:28–29 / But Agrippa backed away from this direct approach. He parried Paul's question with a facetious retort: **Do you**

think that in such a short time [or with so little effort] **you can persuade me to be a Christian?** Paul replied that it was his prayer that they all might become as he was, except for his chains. He had spoken of faith (vv. 11, 18) and hope (v. 6f.) and, in these closing words, had revealed a love that was "not rude" or "self-seeking" or "easily angered" and that kept "no record of wrongs" (1 Cor. 13:5f.). But he did not take up Agrippa's word "Christian," either because he did not know it or because he only knew it as an expression of contempt (see disc. on 11:26b). The lightness of his last remark about the chains (the plural may have been rhetorical) may have eased the situation a little, but for all that, the conversation had become uncomfortably personal and was quickly brought to an end.

26:30–32 / Agrippa rose, and with him the governor, Bernice, and the other guests (the order of rank was carefully observed), and withdrew from the hall. Later they readily admitted to one another that Paul had done nothing deserving even imprisonment, much less death, and could have been acquitted had he not appealed to Caesar. Legally, he could still have been acquitted, but it was no longer simply a question of law, "but of the relations between the emperor and his subordinates, and of that element of non-constitutional power which the Romans called *auctoritas*, 'prestige,' on which the supremacy of the Princeps so largely depended. No sensible man with hopes of promotion would dream of short-circuiting the appeal to Caesar unless he had specific authority to do so. . . . To have acquitted him despite the appeal would have been to offend both the emperor and the province" (Sherwin-White, p. 65). However, Agrippa's opinion of the case must have been noted in the report sent to Rome and may in some part account for the treatment accorded Paul on his arrival (28:16).

Additional Notes §66

25:26 / **To His Majesty,** lit., "to the lord," a title refused by Augustus and Tiberius because it savored too much of the relationship between master and slave and perhaps because it seemed more fitting of God (cf. Suetonius, *Augustus* 53; *Tiberius* 21; Tacitus, *Annals* 2.87): It was accepted by Caligula and succeeding emperors, though Alexander

Severus forbade its applications to himself (see A. Deissmann, *Light from the Ancient East*, p. 354).

26:5 / **I lived as a Pharisee**: It may be better, with GNB, to translate "have lived" as a Pharisee, instead of by the simple past as in AV, RV, NEB, NIV. Not merely would there have been little point in stressing to King Agrippa what he had done if he no longer did it, but in any case, it hardly brings out the force of the "and now" that follows, which implies not a contradiction, but an intensification (see H. E. Ellison, *AHG*, p. 199).

26:11 / **Many a time I went from one synagogue to another to have them punished**: For the competence of Jewish authorities to deal with capital offenses, see note on 7:60. For lesser offenses, not only the Sanhedrin, but the synagogues functioning as local courts, had the power to sentence and execute punishment. An offender might suffer excommunication ranging from a week's exclusion to permanent expulsion (cf. Luke 6:22; John 9:22; 12:42; 16:2). More commonly, breaches of the law for which specific penalties were not laid down in Scripture were punished by lashes (cf. Matt. 10:17; 23:34), the greatest number being forty, or in practice, thirty-nine, for fear of inflicting one in excess. It was first ascertained, though, that the culprit was able to bear the sentence. The instrument used was a scourge of leather thongs, but not studded as the Roman scourge was. Later Jewish writers say that there were 207 cases for which lashes were inflicted, but to judge from the freedom with which lashing was dealt out, it appears to have served the Jewish authorities, as it did the Romans, as a general coercive measure. Paul had himself been the victim several times of synagogal discipline (2 Cor. 11:24).

26:19 / **The vision**: Only here does Paul describe the appearance of Christ to him on the Damascus road as a **vision**. But the meaning of the Greek word (*optasia*) is not confined to subjective experience, and in this instance must be explained in terms of the objectivity with which Paul invests the whole narrative.

26:23 / **That the Christ would suffer and, as the first to rise from the dead, would proclaim light**: In the Greek, this is expressed in the form of a condition, "Whether the Messiah must suffer, whether he should be the first," either as a softening of dogmatic abruptness or as the protasis of the preceding sentence, "I say nothing beyond what the prophets and Moses said would happen, if I say that the Messiah should suffer." Yet another suggestion is that the conditional form reflects the early Christian use of testimonies, which may have been headed with short titles along the lines of these clauses: "Whether he should be a light to the Gentiles," etc. The Greek word translated **would suffer** (*pathētos*) properly means "is able to suffer." But this should not be read in the light of later theology as raising the questions concerning the two natures of Christ or whether the divine was touched with the feeling of our infirmities, but as meeting the difficulty of the Jews whose concept of the Messiah had no place for suffering.

26:24 / **You are out of your mind, Paul! . . . Your great learning is driving you insane:** The second half of this outburst was probably intended to soften the first. It was not that Paul was mad, but that his learning (lit., his "many letters") was "turning him toward madness." The reference may have been to the learning that Paul had displayed in the speech and, more precisely, to his knowledge of the Scriptures. But Paul may have actually used the word "letters" of the Scriptures and Festus may have picked it up in that sense: "Your many Scriptures are driving you mad." Or Paul may have had numerous scrolls with him in prison (cf. 2 Tim. 4:13), and it may have been to these that Festus was alluding: "Your many writings are turning your mind."

26:28 / **Do you think that in such a short time you can persuade me to be a Christian?** We have taken this as a rather superficial comment made to hide the king's embarrassment. Others have found in the words a gentle irony, as if Agrippa would answer Paul's appeal to his belief in the prophets by pointing out that it was not so simple a matter to become a Christian even if one did believe the prophets. Others again regard Agrippa as expressing cold disdain, adopting the tone, not of Roman indifference, but of Jewish orthodoxy in response to this Christian enthusiast (cf. 1 Cor. 1:23).

§67   Paul Sails for Rome (Acts 27:1–12)

As a piece of descriptive writing, this story of Paul's voyage and shipwreck shows Luke at his best and is a classic of its kind in ancient literature. Luke has been accused of inventing the story or at least of adapting an existing tale to his own purpose. But James Smith has long since demonstrated that the accuracy of the narrative in terms of geography, weather conditions, and navigational practice is such that it cannot be other than the record of a real voyage (p. xxxii), whereas the use of the first person is a fair indication that the voyage was made in the company of the author himself.

The traveler's urge to recount adventures and the fact that stories of shipwreck were something of a fashion in Luke's day would alone account for the length of the narrative. But to these may be added the further suggestion that Luke had in mind the popular motif of the sea taking vengeance on the wicked (cf. 28:4) and took delight, therefore, in telling this tale of deliverance. Again, it is possible that he was maintaining his parallel with the Gospel (see disc. on 19:21–41) and that he told the story in detail as corresponding to that of the death and resurrection of Jesus (using the storm and the safety of Malta). But whatever Luke's motive, it remains that he has left us a wonderful story of "journeying mercies" apart from which Paul would never have made it to Rome.

27:1 / If Festus arrived in Judea in the early summer of the year in which he took office (say, A.D. 59), it was probably in the late summer or autumn of the same year that Paul was put on board ship. Notice the resumption of the "we passages" (last noticed in 21:18) and Luke's rather loose inclusion of himself in the decision of the Roman authorities to send the prisoners to Rome. Paul was not the only prisoner for whom this decision was taken, though Luke's Greek may distinguish him from the others (strictly speaking, his word means "others of a different kind"; were they already convicted?). The prisoners were put in the charge of an escort under the command of a centurion named Julius of **the Imperial Regiment** ("the Augustan cohort"). This has been identified as the Cohors I Augusta, a regiment of auxiliaries attested by inscriptions to have been in Syria after A.D. 6 and in Batanea (Bashan, east of Galilee) in the time of Herod Agrippa II (ca. A.D. 50–100). A detachment of the cohort may have been stationed at Caesarea. The duty assigned to Julius normally fell to centurions.

27:2 / The more usual route to Rome was by way of Alexandria, but on this occasion Julius secured a passage for his charges on **a ship from Adramyttium about to sail for ports along the coast of the province of Asia**. At one of these, they would be sure to find a ship for Rome or, failing that, to find the means at Adramyttium of reaching Greece and so of crossing to Italy. Adramyttium was the metropolis of the region of Mysia in the province of Asia, situated at the head of the gulf to which it gave its name (see disc. on 20.13). Luke adds that **Aristarchus, a Macedonian from Thessalonica**, was with them. He had been one of the delegates who had accompanied Paul to Jerusalem (20·4; cf 19:29) and may now have been returning to Macedonia, intending to part company with Paul and Luke at some point on the journey. On the other hand, he is named in Colossians 4:10 and Philemon 24 as being with Paul in Rome. He may therefore have completed the journey with the others, though he is not mentioned again in Acts. Ramsay thinks that Aristarchus and Luke must have signed on as Paul's "slaves" in order to remain with him (*Paul*, p. 316). But this ship was not a military transport, and there is no reason why the two should not have bought passage on it as ordinary travelers. Ehrhardt (p. 124) takes literally Paul's description of Aristarchus in Colossians 4:10 as his "fellow prisoner" and supposes that he was remanded with Paul to Rome for trial.

27:3 / Their first port of call was Sidon, about seventy sea miles from Caesarea and about twenty-five miles north of Tyre. Though it had seen better days, this ancient city was still flourishing under Roman rule. It now had a (small) Christian community (cf. 11:19), evidently known to Paul from earlier times (11:30; 12:25; 15:3), and the centurion allowed him the unusual liberty of visiting them ashore, unless we accept the suggestion that the Greek should be rendered, "allowed his friends to visit him" on board. At all events, the Sidonian Christians were able to **provide for his needs**—perhaps food and other gifts for the journey. If Paul had gone ashore, it would, of course, have been under escort.

27:4-5 / Putting to sea again, the ship kept to the east and then to the north of Cyprus, in order to gain some shelter from the prevailing westerly and northwesterly winds of summer and early autumn. Two years before, these winds had helped Paul to make a good crossing in the other direction (21:2f.). By keeping to the coast, they were able to take advantage of the offshore winds and the current that here runs to the west. Thus the ship crept slowly along the Cilician and Pamphylian coast until it came to **Myra in Lycia** (v. 5). According to the Western text, this part of the voyage took fifteen days, which would be about right (cf. Lucian, *Navigium* 7). Myra proper was situated on the river Andracus, about two and a half miles from the sea. Its port was Andriaca, but common usage included the port in Myra, as Luke has done here. Under the Romans, when Lycia was a separate province, Myra was its capital (see disc. on 13:13).

27:6 / Here the centurion found **an Alexandrian ship** bound for Italy and had the prisoners transferred to it. Luke does not mention what kind of a ship it was, but the fact that it was on its way from Egypt to Italy and that its cargo included wheat (v. 38, but cf. v. 18) indicates that it was one of the fleet of grain ships in the government service. There is nothing odd in such a ship being found at Myra. Because of the direction of the prevailing winds (see v. 4), the Egyptian grain ships regularly followed this route to gain sea room for working across the winds on a westerly course.

27:7-8 / It would appear that the prevailing wind was in fact blowing as the ship sailed from Myra. It was with difficulty, therefore, that they made their way slowly westward until they reached a point off Cnidus. In the fourth century B.C. this city, which had once been situated farther east on the Cnidian peninsula, had been reestablished on the western tip of the promontory (the most southwesterly point of Asia Minor). Beyond this point they would no longer enjoy the protection of the land or the help of the local winds and currents. They could have put into Cnidus to await better conditions, but chose to go on, still confident of reaching Italy before the close of the sailing season.

The wind effectively prevented them from running straight across to the island of Cythera, north of Crete, as they might have wished to have done. Their only course then was to head south before the northwesterly and to sail under the lee of Crete (v. 7). Thus the ship rounded Cape Salmone, a promontory at the eastern end of the island (Cape Sidero?), and then worked its way westward again **with difficulty,** until **a place called Fair Havens** was reached on the central south coast of Crete, two miles east of Cape Matala (v. 8). This anchorage (still known by that name) opens to the east and the southeast and is partially protected by a few small islands. Such a harbor would have afforded them shelter for a time, for west of Cape Matala the land tends northward, where they would again have been exposed to the northwesterly winds. But in the winter, **Fair Havens** belies its name. At best, it would have been inconvenient, at worst, possibly dangerous, for the easterly and northeasterly winds of that season blow into the bay. Luke adds that **Fair Havens** was near **the town of Lasea,** which has been identified with some ruins five miles to the east (this may have been the Lasos mentioned by Pliny, *Natural History* 4.59; otherwise neither Lasea nor Fair Havens is named elsewhere in ancient literature).

27:9 / Here they lay at anchor for a long time hoping for better weather, and the longer they waited the more dangerous it became to go on, for it was now late in the year. Among the ancients the dangerous season for sailing was defined as extending from September to no later than early November (cf. Vegetius, *De re Militari* 4.39; Hesiod, *Works and Days* 619), after which all but the most urgent navigation on the open sea came to an end until the following spring. But the Day of Atonement was already past, a fact that may have been pressed upon Luke by Paul's observing **the Fast** that marked that day for Jews (see disc. on 13:2–3). The Day of Atonement fell on the tenth day of Tishri, the seventh month of the Jewish year, corresponding to a part of September and October. Because the Jewish calendar was based on the moon, the position of the month varied from year to year, but in A.D. 59 the date of the fast would have been 5 October, and since it was now later than that, they were well into "October" with little time left for safe sailing.

27:10 / There was some discussion, therefore, about whether they should brave the winter in Fair Havens or attempt

to reach a better place in which to lay up. Paul made his contribution to this debate by advising them to stay where they were.
His words, **I can see that our voyage**, may be intended to express
a God-given insight (cf. vv. 21–26), but there is no need to read
into them anything more than the insight that comes from experience. Paul was a seasoned traveler (cf. 2 Cor. 11:25), and it
was no doubt for this reason that his opinion was invited or, if
not invited, at least considered when volunteered. It is not clear
whether he was actually a party to the discussion or simply made
his opinion known through the centurion. In any event his advice
should have been heeded. Though matters did not turn out as
badly as he had expected, there was no loss of life.

27:11 / Luke gives the impression that the final decision
rested with the centurion, and commentators have supposed that
this must have been because the ship was in the government service. But he may only have meant that the centurion deferred to
the opinion of the seamen with whom the decision finally rested.
Considerations other than simply the weather would have entered
into their thinking, such as the difficulty of providing for the ship's
complement in Safe Harbors, with the only town a small place
five miles away (see disc. on v. 8). What the relative positions were
of the two seamen mentioned in this verse is not clear. One of
them could have been the owner (as NIV), but the word does not
necessarily denote ownership, and he may be better seen as the
captain and the other as the steersman or navigator.

27:12 / In the end it was decided that they should attempt
to reach Phoenix. Information given by Strabo (*Geography* 10.4)
and Ptolemy (*Geography* 3.17) seems to indicate that Phoenix was
in the Cape Mouros area of southern Crete, where modern Lutro
is the only safe anchorage and fits well enough the description
given by these writers. Here a peninsula runs out southward with
an arm extending eastward to make a harbor fully protected on
the northern, western, and southern sides. Only one difficulty
stands in the way of identifying this harbor with Phoenix, and
this is Luke's description of the harbor as facing **southwest and
northwest**, which better fits the western-facing bay still known
as Phineka across the peninsula from the harbor of Lutro. Modern
commentators have found difficulty in accepting Phineka as the
Phoenix of this narrative because it is a much poorer harbor than
Lutro. But recent examination of the area suggests that there has

been a change in the coastline since Luke wrote Acts. The western bay was once better protected, but earthquake disturbance has altered the topography, covering an inlet that faced northwest in classical times. A southwesterly facing inlet still remains and, given that the winter winds are from the northeast and the east, either of these inlets would have offered reasonable shelter for the ship. However, the very wind from which they sought protection was to deprive them of it and to drive the ship to destruction.

Additional Notes §67

27:3 / **His friends**, lit., "the friends," which could have been a designation for the Christians as in 3 John 14. This term was used by other groups in the first century, but its use by Christians, if it is intended in this sense, may stem from Jesus' habit of calling the disciples his friends (cf. Luke 12:4; John 11:11; 15:13ff.). But the definite article in Greek is frequently used in a possessive sense, which seems the more natural interpretation here—"his friends."

27:9 / **The fast**: Attempts have been made to identify this fast with other events. There seems little doubt, however, that it was the Jewish fast associated with the Day of Atonement. Paul usually reckoned by the Jewish calendar (e.g., 1 Cor. 16:8), and we could expect Luke to have done so as well if he were writing (as we believe he was) at a time when the Christian ethos was still largely Jewish, i.e., in the second half of the first century.

§68   The Storm (Acts 27:13-26)

27:13 / With a light wind blowing from the south, they had high hopes of reaching the more desirable anchorage of Phoenix some forty miles to the west. At first all went well, though Luke gives the impression that rounding Cape Matala was achieved only after some anxious moments. The emphatic way in which he introduces the statement that they sailed "closer" (than was desirable) along the coast of Crete implies that their ability to weather the point was for a time in doubt.

27:14-15 / But then, as they were crossing the open waters of the gulf of Messara, between Cape Matala and Phoenix, the wind suddenly swung round. **A wind of hurricane force** (Gk. *typhonikos*, cf. our "typhoon")—called the "northeaster," **swept down** from the island—a graphic description of a common experience in Cretan waters (J. Smith, p. 102). Ancient ships were unable to face into heavy seas or even to sail close to the wind, as a modern yacht can. With this gale sweeping down upon them from the mountains of Crete, they had no option but to run before it, and so were driven southward.

27:16 / Thus they came under the lee of the island of Cauda (Clauda in some texts), modern Gavdos, some twenty-three miles from Cape Matala. Under the temporary protection of the island, the crew made what preparations they could for facing the storm. The ship's boat, which was being towed astern, was brought on board (cf. v. 17). By this time it must have been swamped and hard work to pull in. The use of the first person plural, **we were hardly able to make the lifeboat secure**, may mean that Luke himself was pressed into service and spoke with some feeling of the effort involved. That this was so is rendered the more likely by the reversion to the third person in the next verse when describing the technically more difficult operation of undergirding the ship, which only the crew could perform.

27:17 / The mainsail had probably been kept on until now, but the strain of this great sail in a high wind would have been more than the hull could have sustained. The timbers would have started and the ship foundered had they not gained the shelter of Cauda. Here they **passed ropes under the ship itself to hold it together.** The Greek has, "with the use of helps"—a reference no doubt to the equipment, such as blocks and tackle. The operation that they carried out was literally "to undergird" the ship, from which it would appear that ropes were fastened vertically around the ship in a process now known as "frapping." The only difficulty with this interpretation is to know how they managed it in these conditions. "Frapping" was normally carried out with the ship beached. A number of commentators have reached the conclusion that it simply could not have been done and have made other suggestions, all of which must assume, however, that the verb had taken on a much broader meaning. On the whole, it may be better to allow the verb its plain meaning and to assume, rather, that the seamen had the technology to "frap" the ship even at sea in a storm.

Two dangers faced them: first, that the high seas would overwhelm the ship or smash the ship's structure, hence the undergirding; second, that they would be driven onto the Syrtis, the Greek name for two shallow gulfs on the coast of Africa. The larger of the two, Syrtis Major (the Gulf of Sidra), west of Cyrenaica, is the one meant in this reference. Sailors feared its shallow waters full of treacherous rocks and sandbanks, and though the danger was still some four hundred miles distant, these sailors were taking no risks. Luke tells us that they "lowered the gear" (so the Greek), by which he probably meant the mainyard, which carried the mainsail, though a variety of other suggestions have been made, ranging from the lowering of a **sea anchor** (NIV) to the whole of the rigging. Some sail, of course, would have been necessary, otherwise the ship would have been entirely at the mercy of wind and wave. The aim of the sailors was not merely to delay their course, but to change it. But Roman ships often carried a smaller foresail, as indeed this ship appears to have done (see disc. on v. 40), and this would have sufficed to keep its head as far as possible to the west and the north, away from the dangers of the African shore. So they were **driven along**—not helplessly, but doing what they could in a desperate situation.

27:18–19 / The next day, now driven by the storm beyond the shelter of Cauda, they began to lighten the ship by throwing what was probably the deck cargo into the sea (cf. v. 38; Jonah 1:5). The following day, **they threw the ship's tackle overboard** (v. 19)—probably anything movable lying on the decks. Some have included here the passengers' luggage, but then we should have expected "our" not **the ship's** equipment. It may be right, however, to include the fittings provided for the passengers, such as beds, tables, eating utensils, and the like. The comment that the sailors jettisoned this gear **with their own hands** seems strange, since how else could they have done it unless a contrast was intended between their present plight and the normal harbor facilities for shifting cargo and gear. A variant of verse 19 has "we threw out" instead of **they**, which gives greater point to the comment if Luke himself had (again) been involved. The reading, however, is not well attested.

27:20 / Worst of all was the uncertainty about where they were. **Neither sun nor stars appeared for many days** and so they were deprived of all means of estimating their position or even of determining with any certainty their direction (for of course they had no compass). As one day stretched into another all hope of deliverance "was being stripped" from them (imperfect passive). Passengers and crew alike settled into a state of despondency.

27:21–22 / When matters were at their worst and they **had gone a long time without food** (v. 21)—a not uncommon result in those days of storm at sea, through the spoiling of the food or their inability to cook it—Paul addressed the ship's company. Not for the first time was he facing the perils of storm (2 Cor. 11:25), and out of his past experience and present faith he had some words of encouragement for them—but not before he allowed himself the remark that they **should have taken** [his] **advice** and not have sailed from Crete (v. 1). "This trait of human nature, always so quick to prove itself in the right, is a sign of Luke's faithfulness: he does not forget the man in the apostle" (Rackham, p. 497). There is a certain irony in Paul's expression. The Greek speaks of them as "gaining" this "loss." Nevertheless, he assured them that they would not lose their lives (contrary to his earlier prediction, v. 10); only the ship would be lost.

27:23–24 / To this he added some words of explanation. During the night **an angel of the God** whose he was and whom he worshiped had given him this assurance (cf. Jon. 1:9). In the light of the promise of 23:11, Paul might have expected to somehow survive the storm, though depression often brings doubts and we have no reason to exclude Paul from the despondency that had overtaken them all (v. 20). At all events, as far as he was concerned, the angelic vision had brought confirmation of the promise that he would witness in Rome. But he was also told that God "had already granted him as a favor" (the sense of the Greek verb in the perfect tense) the lives of those who were with him. (Was this in response to his prayers on their behalf? See disc. on 1:14 and 9:11.)

27:25–26 / His last words were a testimony. He urged the ship's company to **keep up** [their] **courage**, because God could be trusted (v. 25). They would not be lost at sea, but **must run aground on some island** (v. 26). This detail may have been part of the divine revelation, and Paul could have been speaking prophetically, but it could equally have been his own deduction from the assurance that they would survive though the ship would be lost.

Additional Notes §68

27:14 / **Northeaster**: In the Greek the word is *Eurakylōn*, which appears to be a hybrid formation of the Greek *Euros*, the east wind, and the Latin *Aquilo*, the north wind, and presumably means "the northeast wind." The Greeks had their own name for this wind, *Kaikias*, but Latin had no equivalent and thus Roman seamen, for want of a specific word, apparently coined this one. It is attested in a Latin inscription. See C. J. Hemer, "Euraquilo and Melita," *JTS* 26 (1975), pp. 101–11.

27:15 / **The ship was caught by the storm and could not head into the wind**: Luke uses graphic language to describe this disaster. First, he speaks of the ship as "seized in the grasp of the wind," and thus carried away; second, of the ship being unable "to look the wind in the face, eye to eye." It was the custom to paint eyes on the prows of the vessels, and the expression may derive from that, though it was also in common use in ordinary life.

27:17 / **They passed ropes under the ship itself to hold it together**: As indicated above, the Greek, with its "undergirding," would suggest that the process was that known as "frapping." Other suggestions are that the ropes were tied longitudinally around the outside of the hull or across the ship inside the hull or longitudinally over the ship from stem to stern to prevent "hogging"—the breaking of the ship's back (i.e., its keel). "Undergirders" are known to have been part of the equipment of Greek warships, but it is not known how they were used.

§69   The Shipwreck   (Acts 27:27–44)

27:27 / **About midnight** on the fourteenth night of their leaving Fair Havens (or some say from Cauda) the seamen detected signs of approaching land. Perhaps they heard breakers on the beach, a suggestion that has the support of Codex Vaticanus, which instead of "a certain land approaching" (as most texts) has it "resounding." As a rule in seeking to identify a biblical location, tradition is an uncertain guide. In this case, however, there is every reason to think that they had come as tradition asserts, to Saint Paul's Bay on the island of Malta. If this was so, the ship would have passed within a quarter of a mile of Point Koura to the east of the Bay, and though the land here is too low to be seen when the night is dark and stormy, the breakers can be heard at some distance. Both the place and the time taken to reach it (a distance of about 475 nautical miles from Fair Havens) appear to be confirmed by Smith's calculations. Assuming the wind direction (ENE) and the average rate of drift of a large ship on the starboard tack (approximately one and a half miles per hour), he concluded that "a ship, starting late in the evening . . . would, by midnight on the 14th, be less than three miles from the entrance of Saint Paul's Bay" (pp. 120–24).

27:28 / The suspicions of the sailors were confirmed when they took soundings—the measurements of 120 and 90 feet (20 and 15 fathoms) correspond well with soundings taken off Point Koura at the approach to Saint Paul's Bay. The man casting the lead would have shouted the readings, so that Luke as well as the helmsman would have heard them.

27:29 / The proximity of land called for safety measures, **so they dropped four anchors** from the stern, lest they should run onto rocks, and waited for the day. These anchors were relatively light by modern standards, and so this number was needed. Anchorage from the stern was unusual, but to have anchored from the bow would have caused the ship to swing around into the wind, and without knowing how far from shore they were, the seamen may have doubted whether they could turn the ship from this position in order to beach it in the morning.

27:30 / But the crew, or some of them at least—we do not know how large a crew the ship carried or how big the ship's boat might have been—had no heart to wait until morning. With them it was "every man for himself," and pretending that more anchors from the bow would help steady the ship and that they must lay them out at cable's length rather than drop them out, they had the boat in the water ready to make their escape. What they were intending in the dark of night on an unknown shore seems to have been the height of folly, and perhaps that is all that can be said of it. One would think that they would have seen the larger vessel as offering the greater safety, at least until the morning. On the other hand, they may have genuinely wanted to lay out more anchors, their intention being misunderstood by the passengers.

27:31–32 / At all events, Paul appealed to the soldiers' own sense of self-preservation (**you cannot be saved**, v. 31) and urged that the seamen be kept on board. The centurion acted at once—perhaps overreacted—and had his soldiers cut away the ship's boat. As it happened, the boat might have been useful when they finally came to abandon ship, but the important thing was that the sailors were retained (supposing that they had planned to escape) to work the ship further inshore, otherwise the passengers may have been doomed. Throughout this narrative a nice balance is maintained between God's assurance of their safety and the efforts of the people involved to ensure it. Notice the authority with which Paul acted in this situation, as also in the next verses.

27:33–34 / As it was beginning to dawn, **Paul urged them all to eat** (v. 33). In all the time they had been wind-blown and wave-tossed from Crete to this place (cf. Eph. 4:14), they had **gone without food** (v. 33). The Greek is literally "had taken nothing." In ships of that day there were no tables spread or waiters to carry the food. Anyone who wanted to eat had to fetch the food from the galley himself. Thus Paul may have meant that they had not gone for their regular rations—either having lost the heart or the stomach for eating or because the galley could not function during the storm. People may have had some food by them on which to subsist, or they may simply have had to do without. In any case, Paul now urged them to eat. They would need all their strength if they were to make it ashore. The apostle was a man of practical faith (see disc. on vv. 31f.). Once more he assured them that they would be safe, using now what seems to have been a proverbial saying, **Not one of you will lose a single hair from his head** (v. 34; cf. 1 Sam. 14:45; 2 Sam. 14:11, RSV; 1 Kings 1:52; Matt. 10:30; Luke 21:18).

27:35–36 / To this exhortation Paul added an example by taking some bread, giving thanks, breaking a piece off, and eating it. That he **gave thanks to God** (v. 35) may indicate nothing more than the usual Jewish and Christian practice of saying "grace" before meals, and nothing more than an ordinary meal may be meant. But the description is so like that of a number of meals at which Jesus presided, and not least like that of the Last Supper (cf. Lk. 9:16; 22:19; 24:30), that it is sometimes supposed that this had become a "communion service" for the two or three Christians on board. This may be questioned, but Paul's action had the desired effect: **They were all encouraged and ate some food themselves** (v. 36).

27:37 / The number of people on board is given at two hundred seventy-six. This has sometimes surprised modern readers and inclined them to accept the lesser figure of seventy-six found in some texts. But the larger number presents no difficulty. Many Alexandrian grain ships were very large indeed. Josephus, who was also shipwrecked in these waters (the Sea of Adria; see note on v. 27), was one of about six hundred people on board that ship (*Life* 3). Luke may have mentioned the number at this juncture because the distribution of rations had brought it to his attention. But it also underlines the marvel that they were all saved. In Josephus' case only eighty of the six hundred survived.

27:38 / Afterwards **they** (perhaps only the crew) **lightened the ship by throwing the grain into the sea**. The other cargo had already been jettisoned (v. 18), but this had been kept until now, partly as ballast, partly, perhaps, in the hope that it might be saved. Wheat was always at a premium in Rome. Their purpose now was to make the vessel ride higher (loaded, it may have drawn eighteen feet) and so be able to come closer in shore.

27:39 / When at last there was sufficient light to look about them, still the sailors did not recognize where they were, but what mattered immediately was that they did see **a bay with a sandy beach**. They may often have touched at Malta (cf. 28:1), but Saint Paul's Bay is remote from the main harbor and not distinguished by any particular features. The imperfect tense gives the sense "they tried to recognize . . . but could not." In 28:1 we have the same verb, but in the aorist tense, indicating that recognition came immediately as they landed.

27:40 / Hoping to ground the ship on the beach (the objective being to save the people, not the ship), the sailors let go the stern anchors and **untied the ropes that held the rudders—**two oars, one on each quarter. These rudders had been lifted from the water and lashed up while the ship rode at anchor. At the same time, the foresail (the meaning of the Greek word is doubtful, but this gives the best sense; see disc. on v. 17), which had been furled overnight, was raised to give the ship steerage, and so they headed for the shore.

27:41 / But the ship ran aground on a shoal (lit., "a place of two seas"), where the bow stuck fast. With the wind behind them, there was no chance of getting off, especially since Saint Paul's Bay has a "bottom of mud, graduating into tenacious clay, into which the forepart would fix itself, and be held fast, while the stern was exposed to the force of the waves" (Ramsay, *Paul*, p. 341). Smith suggests that this happened in the channel, not more than a hundred yards across, between the small island of Salmonetta and the mainland. This might properly be called "a place where two seas met," as it joins the sea within the bay with the sea without. A more commonly accepted site, however, is Saint Paul's Bank, which lies at the entry to the bay and in ancient times was higher than it is today. The shock of the impact as much as the pounding of the waves would have caused the stern to break up. Some texts, indeed, omit the reference to the waves and so give this sense to the verse. The imperfect tense could be rendered "began to break up."

27:42–44 / With the ship doomed, the soldiers were all for killing the prisoners lest any should escape and they be held to account (cf. 12:19; 16:27). But for Paul's sake, the centurion **kept them from carrying out their plan.** He **wanted to spare Paul's life** (v. 43)—the word means to bring safely through danger. He therefore ordered everyone to get ashore as best he could—those who could swim, to do so at once. This may have included Paul, since he had three times been shipwrecked and had passed a day and a night in the sea (2 Cor. 11:25). Those who could not swim were to follow on **planks** or on broken **pieces of the ship** (v. 44). The latter phrase, however, could be rendered "on the backs of members of the crew." So by one means or another **everyone reached land in safety** (v. 44; cf. vv. 22, 34).

Additional Notes §69

27:27 / **We were being driven:** The translation of this verb (*diapherein*) differs widely, since it is supposed that they "were driven to and fro" (RV, cf. AV), as though out of control, or maintained a steady course. In favor of the latter is that in Acts the usual force of *dia-* in composition is to express continuous movement onward over an intervening space.

In the Mediterranean, lit., "in the Adria": "The Adriatic" is the modern name for the sea between Italy and the Balkans, but in ancient usage it covered the much larger area between Malta, Italy, Greece, and Crete (cf. Ptolemy, *Geography* 3.4 and 14ff.; Josephus, *Life* 13–16).

§70   Ashore on Malta (Acts 28:1–10)

28:1 / The island of Malta on which the travelers now found themselves is about sixty miles south of Sicily. The island itself is about eighteen miles long and eight wide. On the southwestern side, the cliffs descend abruptly to the sea, but on the northeastern coast, there are many inlets and bays. The largest harbor is the site of the present city of Valetta. Saint Paul's Bay is about eight miles northwest of the city. The Phoenicians had occupied the island soon after the beginning of the first millennium B.C. Their influence remained strong in the mix of cultures that followed and was still evident in the first century A.D. in the Punic dialect of the Maltese. This is attested in coins and inscriptions and is noticed by Luke in his description of the Maltese as "barbarians" (vv. 2, 4; NIV "islanders")—not in the modern sense, but as the Greeks used the word of those who did not speak their language (the foreign tongue sounded like "bar-bar" in their ears). This may indicate, incidentally, that Luke was a Greek. The name Malta (or Melita) is Phoenician, meaning "refuge." Luke may have known this when he wrote this verse, which might be paraphrased: "We recognized that the island deserved its name." The island had passed from the Sicilian Greeks to the Carthaginians and from them to the Romans. It was now ruled by a procurator, who may have been the Publius whom Luke mentions in verse 7.

28:2 / Strangers landing among rustic folk such as these often met with a hostile reception. On this occasion, however, the survivors found themselves treated with **unusual kindness**. Rain and cold had added to their miseries, and the fire that the locals had lit for them was a most welcome sight. It is difficult to imagine all two hundred seventy-six of the ship's company crowded around the one blaze, but Luke may be describing only what concerned the group that included the Christians. There may have been other fires with other groups huddled around them.

28:3-4 / Paul was under no great restriction, though he had probably been handcuffed again with a light chain. In any case, he was hardly likely to escape—or to succeed if he made the attempt. Thus he was able to make himself useful by tending the fire. As he did so, a viper came out of the brushwood he was holding and fastened onto his hand. The first reaction of the islanders was to see this as a judgment visited on the prisoner. In their words as Luke has recorded them we may see, perhaps, a reference to Dike, the Greek goddess of justice, the daughter of Zeus and Themis (according to Hesiod), or to one of their own gods whose name Luke has represented in this way. At all events, they thought that Nemesis had caught up with Paul and that he was as good as dead (**Justice has not allowed him to live,** v. 4). Bruce cites a Greek poem that tells of "a murderer who escaped from a storm at sea and was shipwrecked on the Libyan coast, only to be killed by a viper" (*Book,* p. 522, n. 11). With stories like this going around, it is little wonder that the Maltese reacted as they did. They could see that Paul was a prisoner, and they supposed from the incident itself that he was a murderer, for one death demanded another.

28:5-6 / But Paul simply **shook the snake off into the fire** (v. 5). He may not even have known that it was a viper, but was apparently unconcerned, knowing himself to be under God's care (cf. 23:11). Thus the promise of Mark 16:18 was shown to be true (unless that saying is based on this very incident; but cf. Luke 10:19, also Ps. 91:13). Paul suffered no ill effects. The locals, however, **expected him to swell up or suddenly fall dead** (v. 6). When he failed to do so, they changed their tune and hailed him as a god (cf. 14:11f.). Such is the fickleness of human opinion! Apparently they never stopped to question how a god could have permitted himself to fall into Roman custody. Luke's attitude to this incident has been much disputed. Some have accused him of virtually sharing the islanders' latest estimate of the apostle. But though Luke certainly believed that Paul, in common with all the apostles, possessed miraculous powers, he never set him apart, as the islanders did, from ordinary men (see disc. on 27:21). Indeed, far from endorsing their opinion of Paul, Luke seems more intent in this passage on poking fun at them. There are now no vipers on the island of Malta, but it is carping criticism at its worst to suggest (as some have) that for that reason the story is not true. Nineteen centuries of human habitation will account for their disappearance (as also for the lack of firewood in the vicinity of Saint Paul's Bay).

28:7 / As it happened, they had come to land near the estate of one **Publius, the chief official of the island**. It is not certain whether Luke means by this that he was the Roman procurator or merely a local dignitary, but the use on Malta of the title "chief" or "first man" (Gk. *prōtos*) is attested by inscriptions. It is curious that Luke does not give his full name, but only his praenomen (see note on 13:9). This may reflect the familiar usage of the locals. If, however, he was not the procurator, he may not have been a citizen, and Publius (Gk. *Poplios*) may have been his only name. Whether Publius welcomed all of the two hundred seventy-six or only a smaller group, which included Paul and his companions, is uncertain. Since it was only **for three days** and he probably had a large establishment with many slaves, he may well have been able to provide for the whole number. But it was done **hospitably** and there was nothing grudging in his hospitality. And his kindness was justly rewarded (cf. Matt. 10:40ff.).

28:8–10 / Publius' father was **sick in bed, suffering from** [gastric] **fever and dysentery**, which are said to be endemic as "Malta fever." Luke uses the plural "fevers" of recurring bouts. But now Publius had the happiness of seeing his father cured through Paul's prayers and the laying on of hands (see disc. on 1:14 and 9:11 for prayer and note on 5:12 for the laying on of hands). News of this cure soon spread, and sick people throughout the island came to Paul to find healing. This story bears some resemblance to Jesus' healing of Peter's mother-in-law, who was sick with fever, and subsequent healing of many who later came to the house (Luke 4:38ff.). Luke's use of **us** in verse 10 raises the question whether his own medical skill had been brought into play, so that he too was **honored** in return for his services. But Paul is the center of attention throughout, and Luke may only have included himself as the indirect beneficiary of the gifts given to the apostle. The expression in the Greek, many "honors" (NIV **in many ways**) is sometimes used in the sense of fees charged for services, but we cannot believe that Paul or Luke would have charged for any services they rendered (cf. Matt. 10:8). Rather, we should see in these gifts a spontaneous expression of gratitude, which provided the travelers with all that they needed (having lost all that they had) for the rest of the journey.

Luke does not comment on any deeper spiritual significance of these incidents. In the narrative of the storm and the shipwreck, he has shown Paul as a prophet; in its sequel, as a worker of miracles. For him that is enough. He leaves unanswered the questions that arise for modern readers: "Did Paul preach the gospel as he exercised a ministry of prayer and healing? Were any Maltese won for Christ? Did the apostolic party leave behind a Christian community? The record is silent; but we may surely believe that here was an evangelistic opportunity too good to be missed" (Martin, pp. 136f.).

Additional Notes §70

28:1 / **The island was called Malta**: The view is sometimes expressed that they had come, not to Malta (Sicula Melita), but to Melita Illyrica (Mljet) in the Adriatic Gulf (see A. Acworth, "Where was St. Paul Shipwrecked?" *JTS* 24 [1973], pp. 190–93; but see also C. J. Hemer, "Euraquilo and Melita," *JTS* 26 [1975], pp. 101–11). The theory rests on too narrow a definition of the Sea of Adria, which by the tenth century A.D., when the theory was first aired, was limited, as now, to the sea between Italy and the Balkans. In any case, it is too far from the probable route of the ship (see note on 27:27).

§71   Arrival at Rome (Acts 28:11–16)

28:11 / According to the elder Pliny, the winter season when the seas were closed to navigation ended on 7 or 8 February. We may suppose, then, that the travelers' three-month stay on Malta ended about then. The ship in which they resumed their journey was another Alexandrian vessel, very likely a grain ship, perhaps driven to the island by the same storm that had brought Paul and the others to its shores. Its "sign" was **the twin gods**. It may be right to say with GNB that the ship was called by that name, but the expression probably refers to the figurehead (as NIV). Cyril of Alexandria tells us that it was his countrymen's custom to ornament each side of the prow with figures of deities. In this case, it was with the twin sons of Zeus and Leda, Castor and Pollux, the "patron saints" of navigators in the ancient world. The mention of this irrelevant detail is a sure sign that we have an eyewitness account.

28:12 / The ship carried them first to Syracuse, the Roman capital of Sicily, a distance of about ninety miles from Malta. Here they stayed for three days, waiting, perhaps, for a wind from the south.

28:13 / There is an uncertainty in the Greek text of this verse. One well-supported reading has them "making a circuit" to Rhegium, which is strange, since Rhegium stood in a straight line with Syracuse. The phrase may be a nautical term. Ramsay suggests that they had failed to get the wind that they had been waiting for, but (and this is how he renders the phrase) "were able by good seamanship to work up to Rhegium" (*Paul*, p. 345). The alternative reading, supplied by the Alexandrian manuscripts, simply has them "casting off." So they came to Rhegium, a distance of about seventy miles from Syracuse, on the Italian shore of the Strait of Messina. Rhegium owed its importance to the difficulty of navigating the Strait, what with the Whirlpool of Charybdis and the Rock of Scylla, so that ships would wait in its harbor for the most favorable wind from the south. Things now went well for the travelers, for **the next day the south wind came up**, and they made the voyage of 180 miles to Puteoli in just two days.

28:14 / Puteoli (the modern Pozzuoli), on the Bay of Naples, was at this time the most important harbor in Italy. It was the main terminal for the Alexandrian grain ships and also for travelers from both the East and the West en route for Rome. Here, complained Juvenal, "the Syrian Orontes first disgorged its crowds on the way to the Roman Tiber" (*Satires* 3.62; see disc. on 11:19). And here a group of Christians was found. They are simply described as **brothers**, but it may be assumed that they were Christians and therefore to be distinguished from the Jews of verse 17 whom Paul also addressed as "brothers." The church in Puteoli probably had its roots in Alexandria, since the commerce between these two cities was so considerable. The absence of the definite article in the Greek, "we found brothers," indicates that the writer had known nothing of their presence beforehand. Paul may have found them through the synagogue, and he was again shown unusual kindness by the officer Julius in being allowed **to spend a week with them**. This week in Puteoli is best explained by Julius having to report his arrival and receive his orders from his superiors in Rome.

The simple statement at the end of verse 14, and **so we came to Rome**, not only marks the conclusion of the travel narrative, but is effectively the climax of the whole book. As Bengel long ago remarked, "The victory of the word of God: Paul at Rome, the climax of the Gospel, the conclusion of Acts." Verse 15 is little more than an addendum, mentioning some details of the short journey by land to the capital. Indeed, all the remaining verses of the book may be regarded in this light, as simply rounding off the statement of verse 14 by showing how the gospel was preached in Rome as it had been at first "in Jerusalem," then "in all Judea and Samaria" and in all of the places by which it had come to the "ends of the earth" (1:8). Their route for the last part of the journey probably took them by the Via Campana to Capua, some twenty miles from Puteoli. Here they would have joined the Via Appia, that "worn and well-known track, queen of the long roads" (Statius, *Silvae* 2.2.12), and by this road completed the remaining 120 miles to Rome.

28:15 / The Christians of the capital had received news of Paul's coming—either he had sent word himself or the Christians of Puteoli had—and a number of them came out to meet the party (cf. Rom. 16:24). There were two groups. One met them in advance at the **Forum of Appius** (Forum Appii) and the other nearer Rome at **Three Taverns** (Tres Tabernae). The former of these two staging places lay about forty-three miles from Rome. Horace claimed that travelers covered the distance from the capital to Forum Appii in one day, though he himself preferred to take two. He had no high opinion of the town, describing it as "crammed with boatmen and stingy tavern keepers" (*Satires* 1.5.3–6). The town formed the northern terminus of a canal that ran through the Pontine Marshes to Feronia, and the boatmen of whom Horace complained were employed in conveying passengers in boats towed by mules along the canal. The Appian Way ran parallel with the canal, so that the centurion and his charges might have traveled by either. The uncertainty as to which way they would come no doubt made the Christians wait where they did. The other town, Tres Tabernae, was also a frequent halting place, about thirty-three miles from Rome. It may well have been that the three *tabernae* of its name were inns, but not necessarily. A *taberna* in Latin is any shop at all. Here the party met up with the second group of Christians, and this proof that there were people in Rome who were ashamed neither of the gospel nor of Paul, a prisoner for the gospel's sake, was cause for his thanks to God and for great encouragement.

28:16 / As the text stands, we simply have a brief notice of Paul's arrival in Rome and of his being allowed to live privately, though with a soldier guarding him. The Western text, however, adds the interesting detail that the centurion handed the prisoners over as a group to "the commander" (Gk. *stratopedarch*). Even if this addition was no part of Luke's original narrative, it may well reflect a genuine tradition. It is not unlikely that Julius would at first have reported to the Castra Praetoria, the camp of the Praetorians. In that case, the commander in question may have been Afranius Burrus, who died A.D. 62. It is striking that both before and after him there were two prefects (Tacitus, *Annals* 12.42; 14.51), whereas the singular of this text may reflect that Burrus held office alone. Of course, the reference may only be to the prefect in charge of prisoners whether he had a colleague or not (but see Sherwin-White, p. 110).

If indeed the prisoners were taken to the Castra Praetoria, which lay beyond the walls to the northwest of the city, they must have had to cross the city, having entered it by the Porta Capena in the south. Thus they would have had opportunity to observe what the elder Pliny described (about this time) as a city that exceeded in size any in the world (*Natural History* 3.66f.) and to experience, in Horace's words, "the smoke and the wealth and the roar of Rome," the capital and hub of the Empire (*Odes* 3.29.12).

§72 Paul Preaches at Rome Under Guard (Acts 28:17–31)

The final scene depicts what was of greatest interest to Luke, namely, Paul's proclamation of the gospel in Rome. The pattern of Paul's ministry, which Luke has faithfully traced elsewhere, is repeated for the last time. As soon as the apostle was settled, he was in touch with the Jewish leaders, both to explain his own position and to tell them of Christ. As usual, a few were interested; some may even have believed, but the majority remained unconvinced. Paul declared, therefore, that the message would henceforth go to the Gentiles. With this the book ends, as though leaving the reader with what was now to be the program of the church. As for Paul's relationship with the church in Rome and the outcome of his appeal, of these things Luke says nothing. The suggestion, however, that he was silent concerning the church in order to present Paul as the pioneer of missionary work in the city is to do him an injustice. He has already acknowledged the presence of Christians in Rome (v. 15; cf. 18:2), and his purpose now is only to have Paul arrive there in (symbolic) demonstration of his theme that the Lord's witnesses had gone out from Jerusalem to the ends of the earth (cf. 1:8).

28:17 / It is apparent that arrangements were soon made for Paul to lodge somewhere in the city, for when he met with the Jewish leaders three days after his arrival, it could hardly have been in the Castra Praetoria or any other military or government establishment. He was housed at his own expense (see note on v. 30). This may have been possible either through the generosity of friends (cf. Phil. 4:10, 14, 18) or because he had resources of his own (see note on 21:24 and disc. on 24:26). He may even have plied his trade. According to Ulpian, an eminent Roman jurist of the third century A.D., prisoners awaiting trial were allowed to work and to live in hired lodgings. Paul's condition can be best described as "house arrest." He was still bound to a soldier by a light chain (v. 20), so that he could not go in and out as he pleased, but other than that he enjoyed considerable freedom, not least the freedom to receive into his lodgings whom he would (cf. Josephus, *Antiquities* 18.168–178).

His first task, once he was established in his own rooms, was to call together **the leaders of the Jews** in order to explain his position to them—his final defense to the Jews. At least thirteen synagogues are known to have existed in ancient Rome, though not all may have existed at this time (see notes on 2:9–11), and not all may have sent representatives now. Those who came would have been drawn from among the elders and rulers. Paul's attempt to put himself in the clear was not altogether successful, but at least he was able to make plain why he was a prisoner in Rome. It was the result, he explained, of Jewish agitation against him. The criticism has been leveled at Paul (or at his reporter) that he went beyond the facts in ascribing to the Jews the chief responsibility for his imprisonment, when in fact they were only its incidental cause (cf. 21:33). But this is merely a summary, not a detailed account, and what he said was essentially true, for undoubtedly Paul would have been free had not the Jews persisted with their persecution. And yet he had done nothing, he said, against his people or their customs (cf. 25:8).

28:18 / The reference in this verse is to the judicial inquiries conducted by Felix and Festus, which had failed to substantiate the charges against Paul. But nowhere has it been said until now that the governors had **wanted to release** him. But when Agrippa expressed the opinion that Paul "could have been set free" (26:32), Festus might have agreed, as he might at least be assumed to have done, whether he actually said so or not.

28:19 / It is not recorded that the Jews had expressly opposed the governor's desire to release Paul, but their opposition is clearly implied in their persisting with the charges against him even after the lapse of two years (25:2, 7). It is presupposed also in Festus' proposal of 25:9. Believing, then, that he would sooner or later fall victim to their plots, Paul had had no option but to appeal to Caesar. But he wanted to assure the Roman Jews that he bore his people no ill will. He still counted himself as one of them. Notice the conciliatory language: "my brothers," "our ancestors" (v. 17), **my own people**.

28:20 / For this reason, namely, that they were his people, he had asked to see the Roman Jews to tell them what had happened. What was really at stake was "the hope of Israel" in the Messiah and the kingdom (see disc. on 26:6f.) and his belief that both the kingdom and the Messiah had come. In short, he was wearing a Roman chain, not for any disloyalty to his people, but for his loyalty to the hope that they all shared.

28:21 / The Jewish leaders responded that they had heard nothing from Judea about the case either by letter or by messenger. This was only to be expected. If Paul had been dispatched to Rome soon after his appeal, the Sanhedrin may have been unable to get any word to them before Paul himself arrived in their city, for he must have come by one of the first ships to reach Italy in the new season. Nevertheless, it is far from certain that the Sanhedrin had any intention of proceeding with the matter. They had been singularly unsuccessful in prosecuting Paul before Felix and Festus, and Festus and Agrippa had actually pronounced him innocent of any crime. The prospect of gaining a conviction in Rome was not good, and the Roman authorities sometimes dealt harshly with accusers who failed to substantiate their case. Nor could the Sanhedrin have reasonably expected the Jews of Rome to take up their cause, since their own position was a precarious one and they would hardly have wished to draw attention to themselves by prosecuting Paul. In all likelihood, then, no message had been sent from Judea and none was likely to be.

28:22 / But though the Roman Jews had heard nothing about this particular matter, they must have heard something of Paul other than this, and they certainly knew something—though nothing good, they said—of the **sect** to which he belonged. They were interested, therefore, to hear his ideas. Evidently there was little contact now between the Christians and Jews of Rome (see disc. on 18:2 and notes), that they should have asked to hear Paul expound his beliefs, unless, of course, they asked only out of politeness.

28:23 / A date was set for Paul to address them, and when the day came a much larger number than before presented themselves at his lodging. Paul spent the whole day in demonstrating **from the Law of Moses and from the Prophets** that Jesus was the fulfillment of the Scriptures and the Messiah who would establish the kingdom of God (see disc. on 1:3 and notes and the disc. on 8:12). This summary of his preaching to the Roman Jews corresponds with the earlier summaries in 17:2f. and 18:5. In greater detail it probably followed the pattern of preaching in 13:16–41.

28:24–27 / Like the preaching, the outcome ran true to form. Paul's message divided his hearers into two camps. **Some were convinced by what he said, but others would not believe** (v. 24; cf. 14:4; 17:32). Even this might seem to have been a good result, but what does it mean that **some were convinced?** Perhaps it was no more than that they were interested and prepared to listen to what he had to say. But the fact that Paul appears to have addressed his final remarks to them all suggests that none of them had as yet been persuaded to the point of believing that Jesus was the Messiah. However, the tenses are imperfect, so the possibility remains that the process of persuasion went on until some were converted. Meanwhile, the others "were continuing in their unbelief."

Before the Jews took their leave, though they still **disagreed among themselves** (v. 25)—the Greek word is *asymphonoi*, a lack of harmony—Paul had one last thing to say. More in sorrow than in anger, he cited the words of Isaiah 6:9, 10, attributing them to the Holy Spirit himself (see disc. on 1:16). They are reproduced here in full from the LXX. Paul recognized that these words had first been addressed to an earlier generation, but their final fulfillment had come in the present generation of Jews who would not "understand" and "see," for **they hardly hear with their ears, and they have closed their eyes**, not wanting to hear the truth about sin and their need of salvation (vv. 26, 27). They were resisting the Holy Spirit (cf. 7:51), and as long as they did Paul would not own them. It is now **your forefathers** (v. 25), where earlier it had been "our" (v. 17). Jesus himself had cited these words from Isaiah (Matt. 13:14f.) as John would in writing his Gospel (John 12:40). Paul had already used them in writing to the Romans (Rom. 11:8). The frequency of their use suggests that they had passed into a list of Old Testament testimonies to provide the church with an explanation of Israel's hardness (see C. H. Dodd, *Scriptures*, pp. 38f.).

28:28 / But Paul ended on a note of triumph: **God's salvation has been sent to the Gentiles, and they will listen!** (cf.

13:48). It must be remembered, however, that this was spoken against the background of what Paul had already written in Romans 9–11, that God had not permanently cast his ancient people away. Their unbelief for the present meant that the Gentiles would be called, but that very inclusion of the Gentiles in the kingdom would in time so rouse the Jews to "jealousy" that they would turn and "all Israel would be saved" (Rom. 11:11, 26). We cannot doubt that Paul now spoke as he did, not merely to condemn, but in the hope that these Roman Jews would repent. In any case, the gospel would not fail, but would gather in "the full number of Gentiles" (Rom. 11:25; cf. Isa. 55:11). **They will listen** is the final word of the Pauline testimony. Nothing can stop the onward march of God's truth "to the ends of the earth" (1:8).

28:30–31 / By way of illustration of this theme, Luke leaves us with a picture—not unlike the series of cameos in the earlier chapters that depicted the steady growth of the church (see disc. on 2:42–47)—of Paul doing the work of an evangelist among **all who came to see him** in his rented rooms (v. 30). For two years he continued thus—himself a prisoner, but the word of God unfettered (cf. 2 Tim. 2:9). The closing words of the book: **Boldly and without hindrance he preached** (see disc. on 4:13), underline both Paul's personal confidence (cf. Phil. 1:20) and the scope he enjoyed in preaching **the kingdom of God and . . . about the Lord Jesus Christ** (v. 31; see disc. on 1:3 and notes and the disc. on 8:12). These two things—the preacher's boldness and the proclamation to all—are among the lasting impressions of this book. They stand, perhaps as a reproach, certainly as a challenge and a charter to all who now read it. Luke bids us follow Paul and the others in mission and devotion in the work of establishing "one body of Christ" in all the world.

Additional Notes §72

28:23 / **To the place where he was staying**: Behind this translation lies a Greek word that means primarily "hospitality," so that the phrase could be rendered they came "for hospitality." This cannot mean, however, that he provided meals for them, only that they were his guests because he could not go to them.

28:30 / **Paul stayed there in his own rented house**, lit., "Paul lived at his own expense," and nowhere do we find the sense of "a place rented" for *misthōma*: Nevertheless this meaning expresses what was no doubt the result of Paul's having an income (see disc. on v. 17) and is almost demanded by the context.

For Further Reading

Commentaries

Alford, H. *An Exegetical and Critical Commentary.* Vol. 2. 1895; Grand Rapids: Guardian Press, 1976.

Barker, C. J. *The Acts of the Apostles.* London: Epworth Press, 1969.

Blaiklock, E. M. *The Acts of the Apostles.* London: Tyndale Press, 1959.

Bruce, F. F. *The Acts of the Apostles.* London: Tyndale Press, 1951. (Bruce, *Acts*).

_____. *The Book of the Acts.* London: Marshall, Morgan & Scott, 1954. (Bruce, *Book*).

Foakes Jackson, F. J. *The Acts of the Apostles.* London: Hodder & Stoughton, 1931.

_____. F. J. & Lake, K., eds. *The Beginning of Christianity.* Vol. 5. London: Macmillan, 1920–1933.

Haenchen, E. *The Acts of the Apostles.* Translated by B. Noble and G. Shinn. Oxford: Basil Blackwell, 1971 (Haenchen).

Hanson, R. P. C. *The Acts.* Oxford: Clarendon Press, 1967 (Hanson).

Harrison, E. F. *Acts: The Expanding Church.* Chicago: Moody Press, 1975.

Knowling, R. J. "The Acts of the Apostles" in *The Expositor's Greek Testament.* Edited by W. R. Nicoll. Vol. 2. London: Hodder & Stoughton, 1900.

Knox, W. L. *The Acts of the Apostles.* Cambridge: Cambridge University Press, 1948.

Krodel, G. *Acts.* Philadelphia: Fortress Press, 1981 (Krodel).

Marshall, I. H. *The Acts of the Apostles.* Leicester: Inter-Varsity Press, 1980 (Marshall).

Munck, J. *The Acts of the Apostles.* New York: Doubleday, 1967.

Neil, W. *The Acts of the Apostles.* London: Marshall, Morgan & Scott, 1973 (Neil).

Rackham, R. B. *The Acts of the Apostles.* London: Methuen, 1901 (Rackham).

Williams, C. S. C. *A Commentary on the Acts of the Apostles.* London: Adam & Charles Black, 1964 (Williams).

Other Studies

Banks, R. *Paul's Idea of Community.* Grand Rapids: Eerdmans, 1979.

Barrett, C. K. *Luke the Historian in Recent Study.* London: Epworth Press, 1961.

_____. "Stephen and the Son of Man." In *Apophoreta. Festschrift Ernst Haenchen.* Edited by W. Eltester. Berlin: Töpelmann Verlag, 1964.

Bauer, W. *Orthodoxy and Heresy in Earliest Christianity.* London: S.C.M. Press, 1972.

Black, M. *An Aramaic Approach to the Gospels and Acts.* Oxford: Clarendon Press, 1967.

_____. *The Scrolls and Christian Origins.* London: Thomas Nelson & Sons, 1961.

Brown, S. *Apostasy and Perseverance in the Theology of Luke.* Rome: Pontifical Biblical Institute, 1961.

Bruce, F. F. *Paul: Apostle of the Heart Set Free.* Grand Rapids: Eerdmans, 1977.

Cadbury, H. J. *The Book of Acts in History.* New York: Harper Brothers, 1955.

_____. *The Making of Luke-Acts.* New York: Macmillan, 1927.

_____. *The Style and Literary Method of Luke.* Cambridge: Harvard University Press, 1919.

Caird, G. B. *The Apostolic Age.* London: Gerald Duckworth, 1955.

Cassidy, R. J., and Scharper, P. J., eds. *Political Issues in Luke-Acts.* Maryknoll, N.Y.: Orbis Books, 1983.

Conybeare, W. J., and Howson, J. S. *The Life and Epistles of St. Paul.* London: Longmans, Green & Co., 1889.

Conzelmann, H. *The Theology of St. Luke.* New York: Harper, 1960.

Cullmann, O. *The Early Church.* London: S.C.M. Press, 1956.

Dibelius, M. *Studies in the Acts of the Apostles.* New York: Scribner's, 1956.

Dix, G. *Jew and Greek. A Study in the Primitive Church.* London: Dacre Press, 1953.

Dodd, C. H. *According to the Scriptures.* New York: Scribner's, 1953 (Dodd, *Scriptures*).

_____. *The Apostolic Preaching and Its Development.* London: Hodder & Stoughton, 1944 (Dodd, *Preaching*).

_____. *History and the Gospel.* London: Hodder & Stoughton, 1938 (Dodd, *History*).

Duncan, G. S. *St. Paul's Ephesian Ministry.* London: Hodder & Stoughton, 1929.

Dunn, J. D. G. *Baptism in the Holy Spirit.* London: S.C.M. Press, 1975 (Dunn, *Baptism*).

_____. *Jesus and the Spirit.* London: S.C.M. Press, 1975 (Dunn, *Jesus*).

_____. *Unity and Diversity in the New Testament.* London: S.C.M. Press, 1977 (Dunn, *Unity*).

Dupont, J. *The Salvation of the Gentiles: Studies in the Acts of the Apostles.* New York: Paulist Press, 1979.

_____. *The Sources of Acts.* New York: Herder & Herder, 1964.

Ehrhardt, A. *The Acts of the Apostles.* Manchester: Manchester University Press, 1969 (Ehrhardt).

Ellis, E. E. *Prophecy and Hermeneutic in Earliest Christianity.* Grand Rapids: Eerdmans, 1978.

Foakes Jackson, F. J. *The Rise of Gentile Christianity.* London: Hodder & Stoughton, 1927.

Franklin, E. *Christ the Lord: Study in the Purpose and Theology of Luke–Acts.* Philadelphia: Westminster Press, 1975.

Gasque, W. W. *History of the Criticism of the Acts of the Apostles.* Grand Rapids: Eerdmans, 1975.

Gasque, W. W., and Martin, R. P., eds. *Apostolic History and the Gospel.* Exeter: Paternoster Press, 1970.

Hengel, M. *Acts and the History of Earliest Christianity.* London: S.C.M. Press, 1979 (Hengel, *Acts*).

_____. *Between Jesus and Paul.* London: S.C.M. Press, 1983 (Hengel, *Jesus*).

Hock, R. F. *The Social Context of Paul's Ministry. Tent Making and Apostleship.* Philadelphia: Fortress Press, 1980 (Hock).

Hull, J. H. E. *The Holy Spirit in the Acts of the Apostles.* London: Lutterworth Press, 1967.

Jervell, J. *Luke and the People of God: A New Look at Luke–Acts.* Minneapolis: Augsburg, 1972.

Jewett, R. *Dating Paul's Life.* London: S.C.M. Press, 1979.

Johnson, L. T. *The Literary Function of Possessions in Luke–Acts.* Missoula, Mont.: Scholars Press, 1977.

Keck, L. E., and Martyn, J. L., eds. *Studies in Luke–Acts.* London: S.P.C.K., 1968.

Knox, W. L. *St. Paul and the Church of Jerusalem.* Cambridge: Cambridge University Press, 1925.

Lindars, B. *New Testament Apologetic.* London: S.C.M. Press, 1961.

Maddox, R. *The Purpose of Luke–Acts.* Edinburgh: T. & T. Clark, 1982 (Maddox).

Manson, T. W. *On Paul and John.* London. S.C.M. Press, 1963.

Martin, R. P. *New Testament Foundations.* Vol. 2. Exeter: Paternoster Press, 1978 (Martin).

Metzger, B. M. *A Textual Commentary on the Greek New Testament.* New York: United Bible Societies, 1971.

Moule, C. F. D. *Worship in the New Testament.* London: Lutterworth Press, 1961.

O'Neill, J. C. *The Theology of Acts in its Historical Setting.* London: S.P.C.K., 1970.

O'Toole, R. F. *Acts 26: The Christological Climax of Paul's Defence.* Rome: Biblical Institute Press, 1978.

Richard, E. *Acts 6:1–8:4. The Author's Method of Composition.* Missoula, Mont.: Scholars Press, 1978.

Ridderbos, H. N. *The Speeches of Peter in the Acts of the Apostles.* London: The Tyndale Press, 1962.

Robinson, J. A. T. *Redating the New Testament.* London: S.C.M. Press, 1976.

Scharlemann, M. H. *A Stephen: Singular Saint.* Rome: Pontifical Biblical Institute, 1968.

Schmithals, W. *Paul and James.* London: S.C.M. Press, 1965.

Simon, M. *St. Stephen and the Hellenists.* London: Longmans, Green, 1958.

Stonehouse, N. B. *The Areopagus Address.* London: Tyndale Press, 1949.

Talbert, C. H. *Literary Patterns, Theological Themes, and the Genre of Luke–Acts.* Missoula, Mont.: Scholars Press, 1974.

_____. *Perspectives on Luke–Acts.* Edinburgh: T. & T. Clark, 1978.

Torrey, C. C. *The Composition and Date of Acts.* Cambridge: Harvard University Press, 1916.

Van Unnik, W. C. *Tarsus or Jerusalem. The City of Paul's Youth.* London: Epworth Press, 1962.

Weiss, J. *Earliest Christianity.* 2 vols. New York: Harper Brothers, 1959.

Wilcox, M. *The Semitisms of Acts.* Oxford: The Clarendon Press, 1965.

Wilson, S. G. *The Gentiles and the Gentile Mission in Luke–Acts.* Cambridge: Cambridge University Press, 1973.

Zehnle, R. F. *Peter's Pentecost Discourse. Tradition and Lukan Reinterpretation in Peter's Speeches of Acts 2 and 3.* New York: Abingdon Press, 1971.

General Background

Aharoni, Y. and Avi-Yonah, M. *Bible Atlas.* New York: Macmillan, 1968.

Austin, M. M. *The Hellenistic World from Alexander to the Roman Conquest.* Cambridge: Cambridge University Press, 1981

Barrett, C. K. *The New Testament Background: Selected Documents.* London: S.P.C.K., 1961

Barrow, R. H. *The Romans.* Harmondsworth: Penguin Books, 1969.

Brown, R. E., and Meier, J. P. *Antioch and Rome.* Ramsey, N.J.: Paulist Press, 1983.

Bruce, F. F. *New Testament History.* New York: Doubleday, 1971.

Buckler, W. H. and Calder, W. M., eds. *Anatolian Studies Presented to Sir William Mitchell Ramsay.* Manchester: Manchester University Press, 1923.

Carcopino, J. *Daily Life in Ancient Rome.* Harmondsworth: Penguin Books, 1981.

Chevallier, R. *Roman Roads.* London: D. T Batsford, 1976.

Cunliffe, B. *Rome and Her Empire.* London: The Bodley Head, 1978.

Daube, D. *The New Testament and Rabbinic Judaism.* London: Athlone Press, 1956.

Davies, W. D. *Paul and Rabbinic Judaism.* London: S.P.C.K., 1948.

Deissmann, A. *Light from the Ancient East.* London: Hodder & Stoughton, 1922.

Finegan, J. *The Archaeology of the New Testament.* Princeton: Princeton University Press, 1969.

Gowan, D. E. *Bridge Between the Testaments.* Pittsburgh: Pickwick Press, 1976.

Hengel, M. *Jews, Greeks and Barbarians.* London: S.C.M. Press, 1980.

Jeremias, J. *Jerusalem in the Time of Jesus.* Philadelphia: Fortress Press, 1969 (Jeremias, *Jerusalem*).

Jones, A. H. M. *The Greek City.* Oxford: Clarendon Press, 1940.

Larsen, J. A. O. *Greek Federal States.* Oxford: Clarendon Press, 1968.

Liversidge, J. *Everyday Life in the Roman Empire.* London: B. T. Batsford, 1976.

MacDonald, J. *The Theology of the Samaritans*. London: S.C.M. Press, 1964.

Malina, B. J. *The New Testament World*. Atlanta: John Knox Press, 1981.

Meeks, W. A. *The First Urban Christians*. New Haven: Yale University Press, 1983.

Metzger, H. *St. Paul's Journeys in the Greek Orient*. London: S.C.M. Press, 1955.

Meyers, E. M., and Strange, J. F. *Archaeology, the Rabbis and Early Christianity*. London: S.C.M. Press, 1981.

Moore, G. F. *Judaism*. 3 vols. Cambridge: Harvard University Press, 1927.

Murphy-O'Connor, J. *St. Paul's Church*. Wilmington, Del.: Michael Glazier, 1983.

Nickelsburg, G. W. E. *Jewish Literature Between the Bible and the Mishnah*. London: S.C.M. Press, 1981.

Nock, A. D. *Essays on Religion and the Ancient World*. 2 vols. London: Oxford University Press, 1972.

O'Sullivan, F. *The Egnatian Way*. Newton Abbot: David & Charles, 1972.

Ramsay, W. M. *The Bearing of Recent Discovery on the Trustworthiness of the New Testament*. London: Hodder & Stoughton, 1915.

_____. *The Church in the Roman Empire*. London: Hodder & Stoughton, 1897.

_____. *St. Paul the Traveller and the Roman Citizen*. London: Hodder & Stoughton, 1895 (Ramsay, *Paul*).

Reicke, B. *The New Testament Era*. London: Adam & Charles Black, 1968.

Sanders, E. P. *Paul and Palestinian Judaism*. London: S.C.M. Press, 1977.

Schürer, E. *The History of the Jewish People in the Age of Jesus Christ*. Revised and edited by G. Vermes, F. Millar, and M. Black. Edinburgh: T. & T. Clark, 1979.

Sherwin-White, A. N. *Roman Society and Roman Law in the New Testament*. Oxford: Clarendon Press, 1969 (Sherwin-White).

Smith, J. S. *The Voyage and Shipwreck of St. Paul*. London: Longmans, Green, 1880.

Stendahl, K., ed. *The Scrolls and the New Testament*. London: S.C.M. Press, 1958.

Tarn, W. W., and Griffith, G. T. *Hellenistic Civilization*. London: Edward Arnold, 1952.

Vickers, M. *The Roman World*. Oxford: Phaidon Press, 1977.

Wright, W. B. *Cities of Paul*. London: Archibald Constable, 1906.

Yamauchi, E. *The Archaeology of New Testament Cities in Western Asia Minor*. Glasgow: Pickering & Inglis, 1980.

Subject Index

Scripture Index

239, 254, 309, 331, 354, 453, 454; **1:4**, 21–22, 25, 27, 29, 194; **1:4f.**, 200; **1:5**, 20, 21, 22, 29, 40; **1:6**, 22–23, 24, 37, 39, 76, 262, 416; **1:6–8**, 21; **1:7**, 27, 71; **1:7–8**, 23–24; **1:8**, 14, 20, 22, 23, 24, 25, 27, 46, 57, 60, 69, 74, 93, 116, 145, 152, 153, 194, 215, 220, 239, 361, 419, 420, 447, 450, 454; **1:9**, 24–25, 110; **1:9–11**, 22; **1:10**, 25, 64, 188, 274, 309; **1:10–11**, 25; **1:10f.**, 56, 71, 107, 146, 161, 162, 194, 212, 213, 402; **1:11**, 25, 28, 36, 146; **1:12**, 24, 35, 37; **1:12–14**, 29–30; **1:12–26**, 29–38; **1:13**, 14, 35, 39, 365, 374; **1:14**, 29, 30, 36, 60, 87, 103, 118, 152, 155, 167, 170, 181, 212, 215, 282, 295, 299, 361, 374, 435, 444; **1:14f.**, 39; **1:15**, 30–31, 36, 39, 55, 62, 79, 222, 264; **1:15ff.**, 123; **1:16**, 20, 31, 32, 36, 49, 50, 52, 68, 71, 83, 88, 131, 232, 234, 253, 262, 263, 294, 304, 335, 357, 373, 384, 453; **1:16–17**, 31; **1:16–20**, 31; **1:16–22**, 48; **1:17**, 32, 36, 354; **1:18**, 32; **1:18** 19, 31–32; **1:18f.**, 135; **1:19**, 31; **1:20**, 32, 265; **1:21**, 20, 32, 33, 37, 208; **1:21– 22**, 31, 32–33; **1:21f.**, 14, 194, 269; **1:22**, 20, 33, 36–37, 69, 93, 193, 233, 376, 419; **1:23**, 33–34, 215, 269; **1:23ff.**, 255; **1:24**, 32, 33, 34, 36, 50, 99, 192, 208, 263; **1:24–25**, 34; **1:24– 26**, 30; **1:25**, 34, 354; **1:26**, 20, 34– 35, 36, 37–38, 60, 102; **1–12**, 6; **2**, 7, 41, 363, 371; **2:1**, 20, 35, 39–40, 42, 43–44, 62, 363, 404; **2:1–13**, 39–47; **2:1ff.**, 195; **2:2**, 40; **2:2–3**, 40–41; **2:2f.**, 200; **2:2–4**, 44–45; **2:2ff.**, 54, 61, 118, 325, 329; **2:3**, 40, 59; **2:4**, 22, 24, 41–42, 49, 54, 59, 81, 90, 101, 111, 146, 156, 196, 290, 422; **2.5**, 42, 45, 121, 151; **2:5–11a**, 42–43; **2:6**, 39, 41, 44, 45, 121; **2:8**, 41, 45; **2:9f.**, 241; **2:9–11**, 45–47, 451; **2:9ff.**, 24, 28, 127, 175; **2:10**, 122, 230, 313; **2:11**, 45; **2:11b–13**, 43; **2:12**, 43, 52, 108, 188; **2:13**, 47, 87; **2:14**, 36, 41, 49, 106; **2:14–39**, 11, 191; **2:14–41**, 48–58; **2:14–42**, 11, 229; **2:15**, 55–56; **2:15–21**, 49–50; **2:16**, 31; **2:17**, 22, 40, 53, 56, 71, 239, 278, 371; **2:17f.**, 50; **2:17–20**, 56; **2:17ff.**, 25, 26, 110, 309, 325; **2:18**, 49, 208; **2:19**, 49, 56; **2:20**, 50, 56; **2:20f.**, 208; **2:21**, 9, 55,

57, 62, 110, 171; **2:22**, 36, 50, 56–57, 60, 85, 90, 95, 102, 124, 138, 139, 155, 245; **2:23**, 50–51, 70, 89, 194, 234, 354; **2:23f.**, 109, 134; **2:24**, 51, 86, 235, 297; **2:25**, 208; **2:25–28**, 51–52; **2:25ff.**, 421; **2:27**, 52; **2:28**, 52, 251; **2:29**, 36, 234; **2:29–31**, 52, 236; **2:30**, 52, 208, 233; **2:31**, 52, 208; **2:32**, 52, 86, 194, 235, 297, 376; **2:32–33**, 52– 53; **2:33**, 21, 53, 110; **2:33f.**, 22; **2:34**, 53, 146; **2:34–35**, 57; **2:34f.**, 57; **2:34– 36**, 53; **2:36**, 33, 50, 53, 86, 93, 177, 192, 195, 208; **2:37**, 36, 53; **2:37–38**, 53–54; **2:38**, 44, 54, 57–58, 59, 65, 71, 82, 83, 90, 156, 162, 163, 172, 196, 200, 236, 264, 270, 283, 286, 290, 325, 329, 330, 353, 362, 376, 421; **2:39**, 21, 50, 54–55, 74, 76, 110, 192; **2:40**, 48, 55, 158, 194, 237, 314, 353, 387; **2:41**, 55, 79, 86, 103, 120, 162; **2:42**, 29, 33, 59–60, 61, 118, 155, 182, 205, 323, 347; **2:42–47**, 59–62, 92, 113, 218, 454; **2:43**, 37, 57, 60, 65, 93, 98, 100, 102, 139; **2:43–47**, 177; **2:44**, 60, 62, 92, 94, 207; **2:44–45**, 60–61; **2:44f.**, 55, 92, 116; **2:45**, 60, 62, 92; **2:46**, 29, 30, 61, 67, 290; **2:47**, 55, 60, 61– 62, 86, 93, 103, 105, 125, 205, 208, 275, 283, 295; **3:1**, 29, 56, 60, 61, 64, 66, 99, 107, 109, 118, 184, 189; **3:1– 10**, 63–66, 102, 247, 279; **3:1–11**, 105, 210; **3:1ff.**, 154; **3:2**, 64, 66, 67, 180, 240, 368; **3:2–3**, 64; **3:4**, 64–65, 67, 126, 146, 200, 226, 248, 384; **3:5–6**, 65; **3:6**, 14, 50, 57, 65, 66, 70, 94, 180, 248, 286; **3:7**, 104, 275; **3:7–8**, 65; **3:7f.**, 188, 191, 215; **3:8**, 61, 65, 66, 85, 154, 163, 204, 240, 262, 290; **3:9– 10**, 65–66; **3:9f.**, 248; **3:10**, 60, 66; **3:11**, 40, 66, 67, 102; **3:11–26**, 63, 67– 76; **3:12**, 36, 50, 64, 67, 68; **3:12–13**, 67–68; **3:12–26**, 78, 191; **3:13**, 67, 68, 69, 75, 84, 86, 88, 90, 138, 143, 164, 208, 238; **3:14**, 68–69, 75, 88, 208, 376; **3:14f.**, 109; **3:15**, 51, 69, 86, 106, 110, 194, 208, 235, 297, 376; **3:15f.**, 134; **3:16**, 11, 14, 57, 64, 65, 68, 69– 70, 75–76, 263, 275; **3:17**, 70, 73, 234, 250; **3:18**, 31, 51, 70, 72, 73, 76, 89, 195, 263, 325; **3:19**, 54, 74, 169, 236, 421; **3:19–20**, 70–71; **3:19–21**, 27; **3:19ff.**, 56; **3:20**, 71, 74, 208, 376;

1 John **1:1**, 85, 307; **2:1**, 69; **2:18f.**, 356; **2:20**, 68; **3:24**, 44

2 John, 356

3 John, 356; **6**, 191; **14**, 431

Jude **4**, 87; **11**, 100

Revelation **1:13**, 146; **2**, 215; **2:14**, 268; **2:22**, 268; **2–3**, 332; **3**, 215; **3:7**, 68; **5:6**, 22; **6:10**, 87; **11:18**, 421; **13:16**, 421; **18:19**, 380; **19:5**, 421; **19:10**, 190; **22:8f.**, 190; **22:20**, 207

Judith **5:6–18**, 130; **14:16f.**, 249

1 Maccabees **1:15**, 358; **3:9**, 28; **11:24**, 357; **12:6**, 114; **15:15**, 45; **15:23**, 95, 359

2 Maccabees **1:10**, 114; **3:3**, 77; **3:7**, 376; **4**, 202; **4:44**, 114; **6:18ff.**, 188; **7:23**, 305; **8:9**, 376; **9:5–12**, 218; **9:7–18**, 32; **11:27**, 114; **14:35**, 305

Sirach **3:14**, 184; **3:30**, 184; **16:14**, 184; **29:12**, 184; **36:8**, 43; **40:24**, 184; **50:26**, 134; **51:26**, 263

Tobit **4:15**, 268; **5:4**, 215; **14:3–11**, 350; **14:10f.**, 184

Wisdom of Solomon **1:7**, 306; **1:14**, 306; **6:7**, 88; **9:9**, 305; **11:17**, 305

PSEUDEPIGRAPHA

2 Baruch **72**, 421

1 Enoch **38:2**, 69; **41:1f.**, 399; **46:3**, 69; **51:1f.**, 399; **53.6**, 69; **54:1–6**, 399; **105:2**, 174

4 Ezra **7:28**, 174; **7:29**, 174; **13:32**, 174; **13:37**, 174; **13:52**, 174; **14:9**, 174

Jubilees **1:27ff.**, 143; **6:17–22**, 43

3 Maccabees **2:9**, 305

Psalms of Solomon **3:13**, 399; **7:8**, 263; **8:16**, 28; **16.4**, 418; **17:24ff.**, 88; **17:32**, 263, 421; **17:33–35**, 54

Sibylline Oracles **3.650f.**, 142; **3.702–28**, 54; **3.772–76**, 54; **8–12**, 142

Testament of Joseph, **8:4**, 279

RABBINIC LITERATURE

Babylonian Talmud, *Makkoth* **3.14**, 113; *Megillah* **26a**, 128; *Sanhedrin* **113a**, 110; *Shabbath* **10a**, 187; **31a**, 268; *Sotah* **49b**, 378; *Sukkah* **51b**, 314

Jerusalem Talmud, *Yebamoth* **2.6**, 275

Midrash Rabbah, 197, 215

Mishnah, *Ketuboth* **7.10**, 182; *Megillah* **4.3**, 242; *Middoth* **5.4**, 80; *Nedarim* **3.3**, 389; *Sanhedrin* **4.1**, 85; **4.3**, 81; **6:6**, 151; **7:1ff.**, 215 *Sotah* **9.15**, 114

QUMRAN

CD **1.13**, 167; **13.7**, 121; **14.7**, 121; **14.12**, 121; **15.8**, 121

1QS **6**, 62; **6.1**, 121; **6.7–9**, 121; **6.11–18**, 121; **6.19–20**, 62; **6.21**, 121; **6.25**, 121; **7.16**, 121; **8.1**, 37; **8.19**, 121; **8.26**, 121; **9.10f.**, 72; **9.17f.**, 167

4QFlor. **1.10–13**, 88

4QT Levi **5–7**, 72

JOSEPHUS

Against Apion **1.161–212**, 85; **2.1–7**, 19; **2.184–187**, 79; **2.262–275**, 303

Antiquities **1.154–157**, 131; **2.176–183**, 134; **2.198–200**, 134; **2.205–216**, 137; **2.232–237**, 136; **2.238–242**, 136; **2.254–257**, 137; **3.13–21**, 136; **3.79–**